SPUDASMATA 184.1

SPUDASMATA

Studien zur Klassischen Philologie und ihren Grenzgebieten
Begründet von Hildebrecht Hommel und Ernst Zinn

Herausgeberinnen
Irmgard Männlein-Robert und Anja Wolkenhauer

Wissenschaftlicher Beirat
Robert Kirstein (Tübingen), Jürgen Leonhardt (Tübingen),
Marilena Maniaci (Rom/Cassino), Mischa Meier (Tübingen)
und Karla Pollmann (Bristol)

Band 184.1

AUGUSTAN PAPERS
NEW APPROACHES TO THE AGE OF AUGUSTUS ON THE
BIMILLENNIUM OF HIS DEATH

2020

GEORG OLMS VERLAG HILDESHEIM · ZÜRICH · NEW YORK

Errata

SPUDASMATA, Band 184.1:
AUGUSTAN PAPERS
New Approaches to the Age of Augustus on the Bimillennium of his Death

As a result of an unfortunate technical oversight, the publisher points out the following corrections:

p. 201, 1st line:
„È significativo [...]"

p. 201 below / p. 202 above:
„Sui motivi del declino del ruolo in precedenza tenuto da Mecenate si possono formulare solo ipotesi prive della necessaria verifica:[6] la spiegazione più semplice è che Augusto, consolidatisi ormai i suoi poteri, non abbia più ritenuto necessaria una politica di attivo intervento e di vigile organizzazione del settore culturale, anche perché i letterati ormai avevano assunto di buon grado il ruolo di panegiristi del regime."

AUGUSTAN PAPERS
NEW APPROACHES TO THE AGE OF AUGUSTUS ON THE BIMILLENNIUM OF HIS DEATH

Volume 1

Edited by Maria Cristina Pimentel, Ana Maria Lóio,
Nuno Simões Rodrigues and Rodrigo Furtado

2020

GEORG OLMS VERLAG HILDESHEIM · ZÜRICH · NEW YORK

This work is financed with national funds through FCT (Foundation for Science and Technology), through the project UIDB/00019/2020.

This work and all articles and pictures involved are protected by copyright.
Application outside the strict limits of copyright law without consent
having been obtained from the publishing firm is inadmissible.
These regulations are meant especially for copies, translations and micropublishings
as well as for storing and editing in electronic systems.

Das Werk ist urheberrechtlich geschützt. Jede Verwertung außerhalb der engen Grenzen
des Urheberrechtsgesetzes ist ohne Zustimmung des Verlages unzulässig.
Das gilt insbesondere für Vervielfältigungen, Übersetzungen, Mikroverfilmungen und
die Einspeicherung und Verarbeitung in elektronischen Systemen.

The Deutsche Nationalbibliothek lists this publication in the
Deutsche Nationalbibliografie; detailed bibliographic data are available
on the Internet at http://dnb.d-nb.de.

Die Deutsche Nationalbibliothek verzeichnet diese Publikation
in der Deutschen Nationalbibliografie; detaillierte bibliografische Daten
sind im Internet über http://dnb.d-nb.de abrufbar.

Gedruckt auf säurefreiem und alterungsbeständigem Papier
Herstellung: KM Druck 2.0, Groß-Umstadt
Umschlagentwurf: Inga Günther, Hildesheim
Alle Rechte vorbehalten
Printed in Germany
© Georg Olms Verlag AG, Hildesheim 2020
www.olms.de
ISBN 978-3-487-15816-7
ISSN 0548-9705

Table of Contents

Volume I

Introduction
Festina lente, or *quo pro merito meo Augustus appellatus sum* 9

Abstracts 21

I. *Appellatus sum uiciens semel imperator* (*Mon. Anc.* 4)

Timothy Peter Wiseman
Augustus and the Roman People 35

Andrew Wallace-Hadrill
Augustus and the Transformation of Roman Citizenship 57

Leonardo Gregoratti
Augustus and the Parthians 79

Cristina Santos Pinheiro
Augustus and the Children: Family and Childhood in Augustus' Policies and in Augustan Literature 95

Paola Pinotti
La preghiera di Augusto 111

Darja Šterbenc Erker
Narrations on Epiphany and Deification: Romulus' Deification 133

Pedro Braga Falcão
Horace's Religion: a True Experience or an Augustan Artifice?
The Ritual Dimension 163

Carlo Santini
Le tre immagini del funerale di Augusto 185

II. *Poetica summatim attigit* (Suet. *Aug.* 85.2)

Paolo Fedeli
Augusto nel IV libro delle *Odi* d'Orazio 201

Irma Ciccarelli
Merses profundo, pulchrior evenit: l'elogio della Roma augustea nelle parole di Annibale (Hor. *Carm.* 4.4.50-72) 219

Joy Littlewood
Significant Conjunctions of Civil War and Roman Cult from Ovid's *Fasti* to a Flavian Metamorphosis of Horace's 16th Epode 237

Francis Cairns
Ovidian 'Learning' in *Heroides* 20 and 21 (Acontius and Cydippe) 255

Kristopher Fletcher
Ovid and the Evolution of the *sphragis* over the Course of the Augustan Principate 277

Cristiano Castelletti
Virgil's *sulcus primigenius* of Augustan Rome 301

Silvio Curtis
Stories on Temples: Monumental Art, Characterization, and Hospitality in the *Aeneid* 329

Robson Tadeu Cesila
'Desacralization' and the Lowering of Vergilian Epic in Three Epigrams of Martial 347

Pamina Fernández Camacho
A Gadibus ad ostium Albis fluminis.
Considerations on the Symbolic Image of Gades in the *Res gestae* 361

Victoria Emma Pagán
The Obituary of Augustus in Tacitus, *Annals* 1.9-10 377

Susan Jacobs
Plutarch's Augustus 395

Rafael Gallé Cejudo
Hellenistic Poetry in the Augustan Age:
the Metapoetic Prose of Parthenius of Nicaea 415

Nereida Villagra
Conon's Account of Caunus and Byblis (Cono 2): Structure and Innovation 427

Volume II

III. Vt iure sit gloriatus marmoream se relinquere (Suet. *Aug.* 28.3)

Louis Callebat
Le Prince et l'architecte 457

Victor Martínez
Image Matters: Augustan Renovation Before Actium 471

Robert Kebric
Identifying Augustus' Deceased Nephew and Heir Marcellus on the *Ara Pacis Augustae* 495

Lídia Fernandes
The Augustan Architectural Decoration in Western *Lusitania*:
between Archaism and the *Consuetudo Italica* 535

Maria de Fátima Abraços
The High Imperial Mosaics of the Oldest Roman House of *Bracara Augusta* ... 571

Licínia Nunes Correia Wrench
Analysis of a Mosaic Found in the 'Casa da Roda' in Braga 585

IV. Imperium sine fine dedi (Verg. *Aen.* 1.279)

Rosalba Dimundo
I tormenti d'amore di una regina, da Virgilio all'opera musicale barocca 607

Jonathan Perry
'Augusto non è morto': Celebrating the *Saeculum Augustum* in 1937 627

Fabio Stok
Augustus and Virgil in Contemporary Literature: Wishart, Nadaud, Vassalli 639

Maria José Ferreira Lopes
Interpreting the Revolution: Augustus, between Ronald Syme's *Roman Revolution* and Agustina Bessa-Luís' *Crónica do Cruzado Osb.* 657

Index Nominum 681

Abbreviations

Ancient authors and works are abbreviated according to the norm of the OCD.

CA   Powell, J.U. (1925), *Collectanea Alexandrina*, Oxford.

CIL   *Corpus Inscriptionum Latinarum* (1863-), Berlin.

CLE   Bücheler, F., Lommatzsch, E., edd. (1895-1926), *Carmina Latina Epigraphica*, Leipzig.

DEL   Ernout, A., Meillet, A., edd., (1932), *Dictionnaire étymologique de la langue latine*, Paris.

EO   Mariotti, S., ed. (1996-1998), *Orazio: Enciclopedia Oraziana*, Roma.

EV   della Corte, F. (1984-1991), *Enciclopedia Virgiliana*, Roma.

FGrH   Jacoby, F., ed. (1923-), *Fragmente der griechischen Historiker*, Leiden.

ILLRP   Degrassi, A. (1965[2]), *Inscriptiones Latinae Liberae Rei Publicae*, Firenze.

ILS   Dessau, H. (1892-1916), *Inscriptiones Latinae Selectae*, Berlin.

LIMC   *Lexicon Iconographicum Mythologiae Classicae* (1981-), Zurich.

OCD   Hornblower, S., Spawforth, A., Eidinow, E., edd. (2012[4]), *The Oxford Classical Dictionary*, Oxford.

OLD   Glare, P.G.W., ed. (1968-1982), *Oxford Latin Dictionary*, Oxford.

RE   Pauly, A., Wissowa, G., Kroll, W. (1894-1980), *Realencyclopädie der classischen Altertumswissenschaft*, Stuttgart / München.

SLG   Page, D.L. (1974), *Supplementum Lyricis Graecis*, Oxford.

ThlL   *Thesaurus Linguae Latinae* (1900-), Leipzig.

Festina lente,
or
quo pro merito meo Augustus appellatus sum

MARIA CRISTINA PIMENTEL
Centre for Classical Studies, School of Arts and Humanities, University of Lisbon

ANA MARIA LÓIO
Centre for Classical Studies, School of Arts and Humanities, University of Lisbon

NUNO SIMÕES RODRIGUES
Centre for History, School of Arts and Humanities, University of Lisbon
Centre for Classical Studies, School of Arts and Humanities, University of Lisbon

RODRIGO FURTADO
Centre for Classical Studies, School of Arts and Humanities, University of Lisbon

On the verge of celebrating his 77th year, the emperor Caesar Augustus died in Nola on the 19th of August, AD 14. Therefore August 2014 marked the bimillennium of the emperor's passing.

Aim

With the present volume we mark the bimillennium of the *princeps'* death with a set of essays that offer some new approaches to the emperor Augustus and the period of his reign. We acknowledge the difficulty of achieving results that are entirely original given that there is a host of studies on Augustus and his era, including those by Benario (1975), Bleicken (1998, 2016), Bowersock (1965), Canfora (2015), Earl (1968), Eck (2014⁶), Fraschetti (2013), Galinsky (1996, 2007), Gurval (1995), Jones (1970), Kienast (1999), Néraudau (1996),

Raaflaub and Toher (1990), Shotter (1991), Southern (1998), Syme (1939), and Zanker (1987).[1] Nevertheless, we propose to revisit Augustus and his reign in the chapters that comprise the first section. Some of the essays are innovative, while others revisit ancient Augustan themes.

We believe it is fitting to celebrate the anniversary that marks two thousand years since the death of a man who contributed so much to defining the destiny of our world. The essays we have gathered and published in this volume address a variety of themes that have as common denominators the figure and era of Augustus. In addition, the essays cover a variety of subjects tangential to Augustan scholarship from a twenty-first century perspective. Our title, *Augustan Papers*, is intended to commemorate the eightieth anniversary of the publication of Ronald Syme's *Roman Papers* (1939).

Background

The Augustan Age is a longstanding and well-known scholarly topic, which means it has been subjected to countless examinations and interpretations over a long period of time. With the production of this volume, we wish to join in the important discussion of this topic by presenting new subjects of investigation and readings by considering, for example, archaeological material from places like Roman Hispania and classical themes in contemporary Portuguese literature.

The collection of studies brought together here in *Augustan Papers* is the result of a selection of papers delivered and discussed by archaeologists, philologists, and historians of ancient Rome at the conference on 'XIV A.D. SAECVLVM AVGVSTVM. The Age of Augustus' held in Lisbon (the Roman Olisipo) in September 2014; these presentations were organized into sections titled 'History and Religion', 'Literature', 'Archaeology and Art', and 'Reception'. In the end, it is evident that everything is 'history', but we have decided to use this label in a more specific sense as referring to political, economic and social questions. On the other hand, it can also be argued that

---

[1] It would be unfair not to mention the recent biography written by Goldsworthy, which, however, despite the explanation that precedes the final bibliography at the end, does not explicitly cite books and articles not written in English.

the remaining topics are essentially expressions of cultural history and the history of mentalities. Given the specificities of the various topics of discussion, however, as well as the academic training of the contributors to this volume, it seemed appropriate to present the essays in the sections indicated here.

Part I: History and Religion

In the first part of *Augustan Papers*, we have included eight chapters, the majority of which is on political history. We have decided to include religion in Part I since its difference from politics in antiquity is not clearly defined, as is well known. This section endeavours to offer a fresh look into some of the political events of the time of Augustus. T. P. Wiseman discusses 'Augustus and the Roman People', which problematizes an old idea that the Roman republic ended in civil war and was then replaced by the institution that was the imperial regime. Wiseman challenges this perspective, which he considers to be too schematic, and proposes another theory to explain the political transition. In 'Augustus and the Transformation of Roman Citizenship', Andrew Wallace-Hadrill challenges the idea put forward by Claude Nicolet that Augustus put an end to the essence of republican citizenship in Rome. Wallace-Hadrill proposes that a more complex hierarchy transformed Roman society that was designed to meet the requirements of the principate. Leonardo Gregoratti re-examines the theme of 'Augustus and the Parthians' and argues, contrary to the *communis opinio* and the conclusions based upon what was written in the *Res gestae*, that the *princeps* had not definitively resolved the internal problems of the Arsacid government, which leads us to deduce that the words featured in the Augustan *Res gestae* should be interpreted as propaganda. Cristina Pinheiro studies the role of children in Augustan ideology by setting it within the *princeps*' concerns of family and social politics in 'Augustus and the Kids: Family and Childhood in Augustus' Policies and in Augustan Literature'.

In a chapter titled 'La preghiera di Augusto', Paola Pinotti examines the literary and epigraphic remains related to Augustus' prayer rituals by setting them within the context of the Secular Games of 17 B.C. Pinotti concludes that there must have been an intention to maintain ancient rituals, with the aim being to foster the idea of Roman traditionalism that was naturally associated with the idea of *mos maiorum*, which at that time manifested itself through the revival and restoration of ancient religious practices. Darja Šterbenc Erker is the author of 'Narrations on Epiphany and Deification: Romulus' Deification', which revisits the theme of the use of the founding figure of Romulus as an element of regime propaganda. In 'Horace's Religion: a True Experience or an Augustan Artifice? The Ritual Dimension', Pedro Braga Falcão analyses religious topics in Horatian poetry from an essentially ritualistic perspective rather than a merely literary one. The last chapter in the first section, 'Le tre immagini del funerale di Augusto' by Carlo Santini, offers a comparative analysis of reports of the Augustus' funeral ceremonies by drawing attention to the symbolism and ideological functions that can be deduced from the sources.

Part II: Literature

The second part of *Augustan Papers* is dedicated to Augustan literature with a special focus on the analysis of the character of the statesman. Within this context, we include essays about Horace by Paolo Fedeli, who analyses 'Augusto nel IV libro delle *Odi* d'Orazio', and Irma Ciccarelli, who in '*Merses profundo, pulchrior euenit:* l'elogio della Roma augustea nelle parole di Annibale (Hor. *Carm.* 4.4.50-72)' studies the poetic encomium of the Augustan *Vrbs*, which was a well-known and common *topos* in poetic texts of the period, through a historic projection of Drusus' successes into the past.

Part II features contributions on Ovid by Joy Littlewood titled 'Significant Conjunctions of Civil War and Roman Cult from Ovid's *Fasti* to a Flavian Metamorphosis of Horace's 16th *Epode*', an innovative study in which the author explores the textual juxtaposition and intersection of topics from civil war and Roman cult as symbols, allegories and metaphors in Roman poetry from the Augustan and Flavian periods; by Francis Cairns on 'Ovidian "Learning" in *Heroides* 20 and 21 (Acontius and Cydippe)', in which the author explores the poet's erudition, which manifests itself through Hellenistic influences, mainly Callimachus' poetry, and draws upon technical and specialized concepts related to various areas of knowledge ranging from geography to law; and by Kristopher Fletcher on 'Ovid and the Evolution of the *sphragis* over the Course of the Augustan Principate', which discusses how Ovid uses poetic *sphragides* as a way of demonstrating the political evolution of his time.

Three chapters in Part II discuss the poet Vergil. In 'Virgil's *sulcus primigenius* of Augustan Rome', Cristiano Castelletti considers the *Aeneid* in its original form to be a particularly significant poetic *sphragis*. Castelletti argues that the epic expresses a literalness that combines arithmetic and algebra with the geometry of the text in line with the idea inherent in the founding concept of *Roma quadrata*. Silvio Curtis examines the Augustan epics in 'Stories on Temples: Monumental Art, Characterization, and Hospitality in the *Aeneid*', which analyses the *ekphraseis* in the *Aeneid* and how these descriptions are put at the service of Augustan ideology. Finally, in '"Desacralization" and the Lowering of Vergilian Epic in Three Epigrams of Martial', Robson Tadeu Cesila undertakes an intertextual analysis of the *Aeneid* with the epigrams of the Hispanic poet Martial of the Flavian period. A well-known document from the Augustan era is *Res gestae diui Augusti*, which is the focus of Pamina Fernández Camacho's chapter titled '*A Gadibus ad ostium Albis fluminis*: Considerations on the Symbolic Image of Gades in the *Res gestae*'. Fernández Camacho examines the use of toponymy in the *Res gestae* by devoting special attention to the reference to Gades and the corresponding absence of any mention of Britain.

Augustus himself is the focus of two chapters in Part II. In 'The Obituary of Augustus in Tacitus, *Annals* 1.9-10', Victoria Emma Pagán discusses the figure of Augustus and his era in Graeco-Roman literature composed during his lifetime. Pagán shows how Augustus carefully defined and fostered his public image. According to Pagán, the *princeps*' aim was to ensure that the actions of his government and the dynasty that he had partly founded would be extolled not only while he was alive but also among future generations of Romans. The representation of Augustus in the biographies of Plutarch is the subject of Susan Jacob's study 'Plutarch's Augustus'. Although the frequently mentioned *Augoustou Bios* has not survived to our time, the image that Plutarch presents of the first emperor of Rome is significant even in his role as a secondary figure in texts devoted to Julius Caesar and Mark Antony.

Rafael Gallé Cejudo's chapter, 'Hellenistic Poetry in the Augustan Age: the Metapoetic Prose of Parthenius of Nicaea', examines Hellenistic poetry from the Augustan Age and various issues associated with it such as influences upon it and its cultural functions. Gallé Cejudo presents a case study of this Hellenistic poetry through the work of Parthenius of Nicaea, who is considered by some scholars to have brought narrative elegy and poetry in the style of Callimachus to Rome through his *Erotika Pathemata*. Finally, Nereida Villagra presents a study on 'Conon's Account of Caunus and Byblis (Cono 2): Structure and Innovation', which analyses the ancient Greek myth referred to in the title from the perspective of the foundation of Caunus, which was a myth dear to Romans of the Augustan period.

Part III: Archaeology and Art

The third part of *Augustan Papers* deals with art and material culture, with a special emphasis on architectural studies. Since the time of the studies of Galinsky and Zanker, we have learned that art was one of the main achievements of the Augustan era and that it was used to achieve various goals. In fact, art has been revealed to be an excellent way of viewing politics and culture in general. With this in mind, we have dedicated a section of this volume to the subject. In 'Le prince et l'architecte', Louis Callebat highlights the relationships we can establish between architecture and political ideology by using as basis Vitruvius' treatise *On Architecture*. Victor Martínez offers an iconographic analysis in 'Image Matters: Augustan Renovation Before Actium' by examining artistic productions before Antony and Cleopatra's defeat at Actium and by considering how they can be understood as the starting point of a political-ideological programme that continued after Octavius' victory. In 'Identifying Augustus' Deceased Nephew and Heir Marcellus on the *Ara Pacis Augustae*', Robert Kebric undertakes to identify Marcellus by means of an iconographic analysis of the famous monument.

The contributions of Lídia Fernandes ('The Augustan Architectural Decoration in Western Lusitania: between Archaism and the *Consue-*

tudo Italica'), Maria de Fátima Abraços ('The High Imperial Mosaics of the Oldest Roman House of *Bracara Augusta*'), and Licínia Wrench ('Analysis of a Mosaic Found in the "Casa da Roda" in Braga') are based upon information from material remains in local and provincial areas such as Lusitania and the Tarraconensis. These chapters reveal how Augustan politics and ideology achieved their most ambitious objectives by manifesting themselves in the empire's outermost territories.

Part IV: Reception

One of the most relevant topics for Classicists today is classical reception. Antiquity has left its traces down through history in various forms. In the modern and contemporary periods classical reception has proven to be a fertile field of investigation for researchers. The fourth and final part of *Augustan Papers* addresses the reception of Augustus and his age in subsequent periods and cultures. In 'I tormenti d'amore di una regina, da Vergilio all'opera musicale barocca', Rosalba Dimundo analyses the reception of the theme of Dido, particularly her depiction in *Aeneid* 4, in representations of the heroine in seventeenth- and eighteenth-century opera. Dimundo demonstrates how relevant Augustus' era has been for modern and contemporary European culture. Jonathan Perry devotes his attention to the theme of revivalism and the programmatic reuse of the figure of the *princeps* within the context of Italian fascism in his chapter titled '"Augusto non è morto": Celebrating the *Saeculum Augustum* in 1937'. In a comparative study, Fabio Stok discusses 'Augustus and Vergil in Contemporary Literature: Wishart, Nadaud, Vassalli'. Stok's study constitutes yet another demonstration of the continuity of the theme of Augustus in the contemporary world.

Augustan Papers concludes with a chapter by Maria José Ferreira Lopes on 'Interpreting the Revolution: Augustus, between Ronald Syme's *Roman Revolution* and Agustina Bessa-Luís' *Crónica do Cruzado Osb.*' Lopes outlines the grounds for Syme's historically marked readings and interpretations regarding Augustus and his ideology of power by comparing them with a literary work of Bessa-Luís, who is one of the most important contemporary Portuguese writers, and her perspective on the 'Carnation Revolution' that took place in April 1974.

Postscript

Ovid begins his *Tristia* ('Sad Things') with the verse *Sine me, liber, ibis* (1.1). To this celebrated verse of the Augustan poet we add: *A Lusitania in orbem*.

Note

We have respected the contributors' preference for either *u* or *v* in Latin quotations and for the spelling 'Vergil' or 'Virgil'. We would like to express our gratitude to the following colleagues who helped us in the editing of this volume, particularly those who helped to improve the expression in the chapters of non-native English speakers: Orla Mulholland, Jonathan Perry, Christopher Dawson, Eftychia Bathrellou, Barry Taylor, and William Dominik.

Bibliography

Benario, H.W. (1975), '*Augustus Princeps*', *Aufstieg und Niedergang der Römischen Welt* II.2, 75-85.
Bleicken, J. (1998), *Augustus. Eine Biographie*, Berlin.
Bleicken, J. (2016), *Augustus. The Biography*, London.
Bowersock, G.W. (1965), *Augustus and the Greek World*, Oxford.
Canfora, L. (2015), *Augusto, figlio di Dio*, Rome.
Earl, D.C. (1968), *The Age of Augustus*, London.
Eck, W. (2014[6]), *Augustus und seine Zeit*, Munich.
Fraschetti, A. (2013), *Augusto*, Rome.
Galinsky, K. (1996), *Augustan Culture. An Interpretive Introduction*, Princeton.
Galinsky, K., ed. (2007), *The Cambridge Companion to the Age of Augustus*, Cambridge.

Gurval, R.A. (1995), *Actium and Augustus. The Politics and Emotions of Civil War*, Ann Arbor.

Jones, A.H.M. (1970), *Augustus*, New York/ London.

Kienast, D. (1999), *Augustus: Prinzeps und Monarch*, Darmstadt, 78-99.

Néraudau, J.-P. (1996). *Auguste: La brique et le marbre*, Paris.

Raaflaub, K.A. and Toher, M., edd. (1990), *Between Republic and Empire. Interpretations of Augustus and his Principate*, Berkeley/ London.

Shotter, D. (1991), *Augustus Caesar*, London/ New York.

Southern, P. (1998), *Augustus*, London/ New York.

Syme, R. (1939), *The Roman Revolution*, Oxford.

Syme, R. (1986), *The Augustan Aristocracy*, Oxford.

Zanker, P. (1987), *Augustus und die Macht der Bilder*, Munich.

ABSTRACTS

Volume I

I. *Appellatus sum uiciens semel imperator* (*Mon. Anc.* 4)

TIMOTHY PETER WISEMAN, Augustus and the Roman People

It is generally assumed that the Roman republic ended in civil war and was replaced by the rule of emperors, of whom Augustus was the first. Close reading of contemporary sources reveals the inadequacy of this schematic view. The young Caesar, like his adoptive father, was empowered by the Roman People to seize back the republic from the dominant oligarchy that had usurped it. Once proper attention is paid to the politics of the populares and the willingness of their optimate opponents to resort to murder, the role of Augustus as the People's champion becomes clear, as does the failure of Tiberius to continue it. The development of the principate as a dynastic monarchy was a process that lasted three generations.

ANDREW WALLACE-HADRILL, Augustus and the Transformation of Roman Citizenship

It is too easily taken for granted that Augustus, whether or not he in any sense 'restored the Republic', continued to use the Roman citizenship as the essential structuring principle of Roman society. Despite Nicolet's suggestions that the essence of Roman citizenship ended with Augustus, it is more accurate to say that it was transformed. By his reforms, not only of the army and elections, but also of manumission, he ensured the place of citizenship in a more complex social hierarchy that served the purposes of empire.

LEONARDO GREGORATTI, Augustus and the Parthians

For what concerns the *res orientales*, the problematic relations with the Arsacid empire, Rome's rival in the East, the reign of Augustus is remembered in modern scholarship mainly for the diplomatic activity which led to an agreement between the two superpowers controlling western Asia. According to the *communis opinio*, Augustus settled the conflict with the Parthians and laid the foundations for the Roman expansionist policy which followed. This idea is based partly on the description of actual historical events, which the first princeps himself made on his *Res gestae*. Although the achievement of some important political and diplomatic goals is beyond doubt, this interpretation is still heavily influenced by the Roman propagandistic element. Taking into consideration the internal political situation of Parthia, it is possible to develop a more balanced point of view, which underlines the lights and the shadows of Augustus' policy in Parthia and Armenia showing that the strategy the first princeps conceived to deal with the Great King did not produce any long-lasting results.

CRISTINA SANTOS PINHEIRO, Augustus and the Children: Family and Childhood in Augustus' Policies and in Augustan Literature

The aim of this paper is to analyze the value attached to childhood in Augustan literature and how it is connected with images of fertility and public safety, but also with national identity. The Age of Augustus was crucial in the establishment of new ideas aiming at shaping families. Augustus' moral laws, implementing measures related to marriage, procreation and adultery, created a marked dichotomy between an ideal which aimed to restore and a reality that, by then, was far removed from the *exempla* of the past. The new appreciation of parenthood is a cornerstone in political discourse and helps in defining citizenship, leading as well to the new visibility assumed by children and childhood. The presence of children in official monuments like the *Ara Pacis* suggests a new view of dynastic questions, but more importantly, it asserts *Romanitas* as an ethnic, moral and political concept.

PAOLA PINOTTI, La preghiera di Augusto

The Saecular Games were celebrated in 17 BC with three days of ceremonies: Augustus alone offered nocturnal sacrifices to the Moerae, the *Ilithyiae* and *Terra Mater*, then, together with Agrippa, to the Olympian Gods. The text of his prayers is documented by epigraphic sources, and shows archaic language inspired by traditional rituals like those of Cato's *de agricultura*; this seems to disagree with Augustan classicism, as attested by Horace's *Carmen Saeculare*, sung at the same festival, as well as with the princeps' personal opposition to archaism in language. But this trend is in keeping with the Augustan religious restoration, which revives old rituals, transforming at the same time their meaning and aims.

DARJA ŠTERBENC ERKER, Narrations on Epiphany and Deification: Romulus' Deification

The paper explores epiphany narratives and their impact on the deification process in ancient Rome. It analyses narrations on Romulus' death and epiphany in the late Republican and Augustan literature to reveal how this narrative gained importance in the deification process. The narrations on crossing the boundary between mortals and immortals paved the way for the acceptance of deifications of Roman emperors. The paper also explores how the euhemeristic concept was reflected in the process of deification. According to Cicero's understanding of euhemerism, a political leader who provided benefactions to his people merits deification. The different views on deification of Romulus and his epiphany as a god range from credulous belief of the masses, scholarly scepticism or distance (Cicero, Livy,) to irony (Ovid).

PEDRO BRAGA FALCÃO, Horace's Religion: a True Experience or an Augustan Artifice? The Ritual Dimension

The religious element of Horace's work has been studied mainly from a perspective of literary scholarship. In this paper a different approach is taken, using the specific methodologies of religious studies and history of religions, which point to the potentially equivocal concept of 'religion' and allow for an exploration of its many dimensions. Here we survey the ritual dimension of Horace's lyrical work and interpret its numerous ritual references according to their sociological, historical and literary context. The conclusion is that the large majority of these rituals do not have a political or 'Augustan' motivation, but reflect a personal or civic ortopraxis.

CARLO SANTINI, Le tre immagini del funerale di Augusto

This essay aims to throw light on two rather peculiar, yet meaningful, aspects of Augustus' funeral. If the two images that must be assumed to be different from each other refer to his military and civil functions in the Roman state, the third one possibly refers to the *gens Iulia*'s domestic cult. This emphasizes the distance separating his quality as a public figure from him as a private individual – a distance which is also revealed in the habit which the imperial family adopted for a while of covering their heads. In this case an important role was also probably played by his personal character and his taste for the bon mot as a means of self-representation, which later historians tended to misinterpret.

II. *Poetica summatim attigit* (*Suet. Aug.* 85.2)

PAOLO FEDELI, Augusto nel IV libro delle *Odi* d'Orazio

Concerning the Augustan ideology, Horace and the poets of his time were not passive receivers but indeed active builders. In the fourth book of Odes, Augustus plays a central role that here is analyzed and evaluated.

IRMA CICCARELLI, *Merses profundo, pulchrior evenit*: l'elogio della Roma augustea nelle parole di Annibale (Hor. *Carm.* 4.4.50-72)

The purpose of this paper is to clarify how in Ode 4.4 Horace adapts the Pindaric epinician schema to a particular instance, that is to compose a celebratory poem in honor of Drusus' victory over the Alpine populations of Reti and Vindelici in 15 BC, and to a propagandistic aim, through the eulogy of Roman people, as Trojan offspring. Horace projects Drusus' success in the past: from the commemoration of Metaurus battle, he switches to the dramatisation of the final episode, through the speech pronounced by Hannibal after Hasdrubal's death. Horace creates a strong contrast between Hannibal's tone of resigned admiration towards the Roman ability of to strengthen in difficulties and the enthusiatic evaluation of strength of the *gens Claudia* at the time. In the final section of the ode the Pindaric schema is combined with the celebration of Roman history.

JOY LITTLEWOOD, Significant Conjunctions of Civil War and Roman Cult from Ovid's *Fasti* to a Flavian Metamorphosis of Horace's 16th Epode

This paper explores the juxtaposition and intersection in Roman poetry of the themes of Roman civil war and Roman religious cult. In a culture where fraternal devotion was highly valued, Rome's ktistic fratricide became, with suicide, a powerful literary symbol of civil conflict. If Rome's strength lay in *pietas*, absolute commitment to the Roman state manifested by devotion to Roman cult, her weakness was a propensity to civil war. At a decisive point in Virgil's epic narrative Aeneas shoulders a shield engraved with scenes of Roman cult alternating with Roman civil strife in a symbolic gesture that he accepts Rome's destiny: *famamque et fata nepotum*. In his *Fasti*, Ovid's references to Augustus' reconstruction of Roman cult are audaciously juxtaposed to the Battle of Philippi, while resonances of Horace's *Epode* 16, the spectre of Roman civil war and the dissolution of Roman values enriches a short-lived attempt at desertion in Silius' Cannae narrative with a rich and complex literary dimension.

FRANCIS CAIRNS, Ovidian 'Learning' in *Heroides* 20 and 21 (Acontius and Cydippe)

This paper treats various aspects of 'learning' as represented in Ovid's *Heroides* 20 and 21: his multiple exploitation of legal concepts (*pactum conuentum* in particular) and legalisms, his expertise in nautical and geographical matters, and his interactions with and corrections of his Callimachean original. Ovid's learning in the two elegies shows him drawing on his life experience as well as on his profound understanding of his Hellenistic predecessor.

KRISTOPHER FLETCHER, Ovid and the Evolution of the *sphragis* over the Course of the Augustan Principate

A comparison of two of Ovid's *sphragides*, or poetic 'seals', from earlier and later in his career suggests some of the ways that political discourse changed over the course of the Augustan principate. In *Amores* 3.15, Ovid identifies himself with his hometown of Sulmo and connects his poetic glory with that city; in *Metamorphoses* 15, however, he focuses on the connection between his poetic glory and the spread of Roman power. While the former passage reflects the tumultuous beginnings of the Augustan period by looking backwards to civil strife, the latter passage looks forward to the spread of Roman power facilitated by Augustus. Other Augustan *sphragides* show a similarless dramatic-change in focus, with earlier *sphragides* generally focusing on the poets' hometowns, and later sphragides focusing on Rome itself.

CRISTIANO CASTELLETTI, Virgil's *sulcus primigenius* of Augustan Rome

This paper provides a new reading of the incipit of the *Aeneid*, arguing that Virgil concealed a sophisticated *sphragis*, which can ultimately be considered as a (literary) act of foundation. In the wake of Aratus, the poet embedded in his text several *technopaignia*, the genuineness of which finds confirmation in Propertius' own sphragistic elegy (2.34). Exploiting numerology, Augustan imagery and the metaphor of ploughing as celestial and terrestrial writing, Virgil allusively reproduced in his text what Augustus was concretely building on the Palatine: the *Roma quadrata*.

SILVIO CURTIS, Stories on Temples: Monumental Art, Characterization, and Hospitality in the *Aeneid*

Three passages in the *Aeneid* describe historical narrative art displayed on temples in Carthage (1.466-493), Cumae (6.20-33), and Laurentum (7.177-191). Through their choices about what events to commemorate, the patrons of the art represent their social affiliations differently. Daedalus's temple at Cumae marks his isolation from the human realm and his affinity with the divine one. Dido's temple in Carthage and Latinus's in Laurentum contrast their attitudes to foreigners. Dido considers Carthage part of a wider zone of intercity cultural exchange, while Latinus emphasizes his local affiliations to Italy.

ROBSON TADEU CESILA, 'Desacralization' and the Lowering of Virgilian Epic in Three Epigrams of Martial

This paper aims to present an intertextual analysis of three epigrams of Martial (2.83, 3.78 and 3.85) that allude to passages in books 3, 5 and 6 of Virgil's *Aeneid*. By incorporating some elements of form and content brought from Virgilian passages in his epigrams, Martial creates interesting effects of meaning in the reading of all texts involved, mainly a sort of 'desacralization' and lowering of Virgil's epic poem when it is incorporated into a 'lower' genre of poetry as is the case of the epigram.

PAMINA FERNÁNDEZ CAMACHO, *A Gadibus ad ostium Albis fluminis*. Considerations on the Symbolic Image of Gades in the *Res gestae*

The use of geographical data in the *Res gestae diui Augusti* is revealing of the complex relationship between political power and the depiction of space. The toponyms mentioned in the text, the ways in which they are grouped, as well as the absence of other toponyms which could be expected in the same context, help to build an image of the Roman world which favours mythical connotations and mental associations over geographical and factual accuracy, blurring the edges of reality and showing the foreign policy of Augustus as a complete success without cracks. One of those toponyms is Gades in the expression *a Gadibus ad ostium Albis fluminis*, the object of this study. Located in the Southwest of Baetica, in the Ocean, this ancient island city was well established as a mythical and literary limit of the known world, even though scientific geography and a better knowledge of the West had already proved the inaccuracy of this notion. Its mention diverts attention from the non-mention of Great Britain, whose conquest had remained an abandoned project since Caesar.

VICTORIA EMMA PAGÁN, The Obituary of Augustus in Tacitus, *Annals* 1.9-10

In the obituary of Augustus (*Annals* 1.9-10) Tacitus shows how Augustus carefully crafted a public image and manipulated pre-existing institutions to his advantage. Yet Augustus also responded to the contingencies of specific circumstances, to which he might have reacted differently. Attention to the ironies of the passage reveals that the consolidation of power under the name of princeps was the product of a series of dynamic negotiations in response to the forces of contingency that beset Augustus at any given moment.

SUSAN JACOBS, Plutarch's Augustus

While Plutarch's Life of Augustus (listed as No. 26 in the Lamprias catalogue) has not survived, his judgment that 'Augustus became more kingly in his rule in later years than he was in his youth' (*An Seni* 784D) is illustrated in the portrait that emerges from the Lives and the Moralia. Augustus' appearance on the political stage as Octavian is recorded in Cicero and Brutus, while Antony portrays his conduct as co-imperator with Antony and then sole ruler after Actium. Additional aspects of Augustus' character as a mature leader emerge in anecdotes in both the Lives and Moralia. My paper explores the ways in which Plutarch's characterization of Augustus clarifies key precepts of statesmanship in the Moralia and provides lessons in moral character and effective leadership for readers to apply to their own political and military careers.

RAFAEL GALLÉ CEJUDO, Hellenistic Poetry in the Augustan Age: the Metapoetic Prose of Parthenius of Nicaea

Although it may seem a double *contradictio in terminis* to speak about Hellenistic Poetry in the Age of Augustus and about metapoetic values in a work written in prose, this chapter proposes an analysis of the Ἐρωτικὰ Παθήματα of Parthenius of Nicaea (one of the more illuminating examples of a work bridging the poetry of the Hellenistic period and the great Latin poetry of the Augustan Age) from a metapoetic perspective that sheds light on the Alexandrian poetic practice and its reception in the Roman world.

NEREIDA VILLAGRA, Conon's account of Caunus and Byblis (Cono 2): Structure and Innovation

The paper analyses the structure of Conon's narrative on Byblis and Caunus comparing it to other versions of the myth. It focuses on three elements, the erotic-incestuous theme, the aetiology of the water source called Byblis and the foundation of the city of Caunus, and how they are combined to build the plot. The divergence in the episode-order suggests that in this narrative Conon's interest was to emphasise the foundation of the city.

Volume II

III. *Vt iure sit gloriatus marmoream se relinquere* (*Suet. Aug.* 28.3)

LOUIS CALLEBAT, Le prince et l'architecte

In this paper the point studied is the nature and the forms of relationship established between the architectural and historical aims and concepts of an architect, Vitruvius

– writing and dedicating to Octavius a book on architecture declared by the author necessary for Rome – and the new ideological structures of the time. Concerning nevertheless a text written, for a large part, in the late Roman republic, the purpose of this paper is also to be more specific about the importance of this complex context for a more precise and enlarged interpretation of the Augustan ideology and of the related program of architectural renovation. In a wider perspective the problem of relationship between action and writing is stated and, particularly, the question of the essential value (*auctoritas*) attached by Vitruvius to the written work in a function of transmission and development of knowledge from generation to generation.

VICTOR MARTÍNEZ, Image Matters: Augustan Renovation Before Actium

The series of terracotta plaques discovered on the SE brow of the Palatine Hill in Rome in the late 1960's have come to be associated with Augustus' renovations of the city, including his house, that of Livia, and, most prominently, the construction of the Temple of Apollo. Accordingly, scholars have long agreed that the iconographies of these tiles referred to complex allegorical and historical narratives encompassing allusions to the young emperor's defeat of Antony and Cleopatra in 31 BC. Recent scholarship, however, indicates that all these terracotta tiles pre-date Actium. I argue that the terracotta tiles found in the area of the Temple of Apollo belong to a visual language linked to events before Actium and just after the defeat of Sextus Pompey in 36 BC. The iconography of the tiles may be better explained by Octavian's desire to rally support among his surrogates for the daunting task of urban renewal facing the young leader.

ROBERT KEBRIC, Identifying Augustus' Deceased Nephew and Heir Marcellus on the *Ara Pacis Augustae*

This paper uses history, sculpture, literature, and photographs to determine that a previously unidentified figure on the *Ara Pacis*, decreed in 13 BC and dedicated in 9 BC to commemorate Augustus' *Pax Romana*, is the emperor's deceased nephew and heir, Marcellus. The figure is part of the famous group of individuals about two-thirds down the south side of the Altar as it now stands, dominated by Agrippa. This view is supported by the widely accepted identification of Agrippa as the lead figure in the group; by the female figure to his left, who by comparisons with independent sculpture is closer in age and appearance to his wife and Augustus' daughter, Julia, than to Livia, with whom it is often identified; by the boy between Agrippa and Julia, who is, or is close to the age of their son and future heir, Gaius, when the *Ara Pacis* was voted; and, most revealing, by the figure behind Gaius with his right hand on the head of the boy (who might have been his own son) who displays an uncanny resemblance to the facial features, melancholy look, and tilted head depicted in other sculptures of Marcellus near the time of his death. This is Marcellus.

LÍDIA FERNANDES, The Augustan Architectural Decoration in Western *Lusitania*: between Archaism and the *Consuetudo Italica*

Analysis of the architectural decoration used in the city of *Felicitas Iulia Olisipo* (Lisbon), in particular in the theatre, built in the early years of the 1st century AD. The studied pieces are capitals of the building, which have a late-Republican decorative tradition. Comparisons with similar pieces from the northern region of *Lusitania* are established, seeking to enlighten the reasons for maintaining these decorative features, apparently archaic. Actually, there are profound reasons for this to occur, not only circumscribed for its distance from the most important urban centers or by the lack of knowledge of the stylistic currents in vogue. These are aspects that we seek to explain with this work.

MARIA DE FÁTIMA ABRAÇOS, The High Imperial Mosaics of the Oldest Roman House of *Bracara Augusta*

In 1976, the creation of the Archaeological Field in Braga enabled the making of dozens of archaeological interventions, which advanced understanding of the evolution of the Roman city of *Bracara Augusta* and provided for its preservation. Within this project, the site of the new building for the Museu Regional de Arqueologia D. Diogo de Sousa was the setting for an excavation, between 1990 and 1991. By then the structures of a house with two floors with mosaic were discovered, and due to its features, it was decided to keep it integrated in the crypt of the Museum building. We will present a brief study of the decorative motifs of these mosaics and make a characterization of the composition of their materials as well as the model of Vitruvius. These compositions, made with such different materials will be a local adaptation of classic imported compositions (since Augustus?).

LICÍNIA NUNES CORREIA WRENCH, Analysis of a Mosaic Found in the 'Casa da Roda' in Braga

It was in the Augustan century that Roman mosaics became an art which combined *firmitas*, *utilitas* and *uenustas*, the three principles of architecture recommended by Vitruvius. In fact, the *opus tessellatum*, integrating the structure of the pavement with its decoration, made it more resistant, easier to clean and more beautiful. It was also in the 1st century that new mosaic patterns and decorative motifs were created, enduring and expanding over the centuries and throughout the Roman Empire. The aim of our work is to analyse a floor mosaic from *Bracara Augusta* which can be dated to a phase a little after the city became the capital of *Galaecia*, being an example of the multiple decorative influences that the mosaic art experienced.

IV. *Imperium sine fine dedi* (Verg. *Aen.* 1.279)

ROSALBA DIMUNDO, I tormenti d'amore di una regina, da Virgilio all'opera musicale barocca

Dido's tragic vicissitudes, told by Virgil in the *Aeneid* (book 4), can be read in many versions in various artistic forms, especially in 17th-century opera. In Virgil, the Queen's love of the Trojan hero leads to the woman's tragedy of desolation, as well as her suicide. As a matter of fact, she is forced to accept the sacrifice of herself on behalf of the reason of State, of the gods' will and of Pietas leading Aeneas to ignore his feelings. The whole passage about suicide turns out to be dramatic. Mostly it focuses on the description of the sensorial sphere involved in the extreme gesture. The episode was successful in 17th and 18th-century melodrama, subject to alterations through which the myth is newly interpreted in a very unusual way. Busenello's Dido, set to music by Cavalli, is a Baroque work where music renders the same pathos as words. In this work Iarba becomes the protagonist who decides to kill himself together with her; eventually she desists from his purpose and accepts his love. In Tate's *Dido and Aeneas*, set to music by Purcell, situations and characters are different. Dido has a leading role both in a dramatic and musical sense. Thus the last scene is left vague, making the music responsible for framing the woman's tragic gesture.

JONATHAN PERRY, 'Augusto non è morto': Celebrating the *Saeculum Augustum* in 1937

As part of the commemoration of Augustus' 2000th birthday in 1938, a series of papers was delivered to the Accademia dei Lincei by Italy's most prominent Roman historians. This volume, composed of 12 papers, was published under the title *Augustus: Studi in occasione del Bimillenario Augusteo*, and its contents reveal the scope, depth, and strength of the connections the Fascist government hoped to make, in personal and direct terms, between *Augustus* and Mussolini. This paper offers a detailed analysis of several of the collected essays, written by Aldo Ferrabino, Vincenzo Arangio-Ruiz, and even by Arnaldo Momigliano, on military institutions and the disbursement of forces under Augustus. However, the bulk of the paper is devoted to the essays by Pietro De Francisci and by Roberto Paribeni, weighing them against their more in-depth analyses from the same period and against their public roles in service to the regime.

FABIO STOK, Augustus and Virgil in Contemporary Literature: Wishart, Nadaud, Vassalli

The relation between Augustus and Virgil and the story of the edition of the *Aeneid* are topics varioulsly treated by the exegetical and literary tradition. A tragic version of the story is proposed by three contemporary novelists (Wishart, Nadaud, and Vassalli), who were influenced by the pessimistic interpretation of the *Aeneid* proposed by the Harvard School.

MARIA JOSÉ FERREIRA LOPES, Interpreting the Revolution: Augustus, between Ronald Syme's *Roman Revolution* and Agustina Bessa Luís' *Crónica do Cruzado Osb.*

75 years ago, in a European context of warmongering totalitarianism and egocentric leaders, R. Syme published *The Roman Revolution*, creating an inescapable interpretation of Augustus as a ruthless revolutionary leader who won absolute power through civil war, and a cold and a cunning politician, true to his traditional roots. Proving his efficient manipulation of his own posterity, few have noted, under the *aurea aetas Augusti*, the revolutionary source of his power and the relentlessly artful mechanism of his rule. This path was followed by Agustina Bessa-Luís when, in the context of her almost 'live' analysis, based on historical diachrony, of the Carnation Revolution (*Crónica do Cruzado Osb.*, 1976), she defines the Princeps by his 'art of mediocrity', 'disdain for the aristocracy', control over the people through his 'popular image', and the 'inquisitive function' of the 'censorial power' – thus apparently evoking Syme's view and allowing a comparison, *mutatis mutandis*, between the two revolutions.

I.
APPELLATVS SVM VICIENS SEMEL IMPERATOR
(*Mon. Anc.* 4)

Augustus and the Roman People

TIMOTHY PETER WISEMAN
University of Exeter

To understand Augustus, we need to understand the late republic. To understand the late republic, we need to take seriously what our sources say about it. Those sources are uniquely authoritative and well informed, consisting as they do of the writings of contemporary participants whose understanding of the political culture of their time is, I think, beyond challenge. So in the following argument I shall concentrate entirely on primary evidence, and present a picture of Augustus' life and times through the words of contemporaries – including, of course, Augustus himself.

I

My first witness is Cicero, in the famous description of republican politics that he stitched into the text of his speech in defence of Sestius in 56 BC:

> 1. Cicero *Pro Sestio* 96
> duo genera semper in hac ciuitate fuerunt eorum qui uersari in re publica atque in ea se excellentius gerere studuerunt; quibus ex generibus alteri se populares, alteri optimates et haberi et esse uoluerunt. qui ea quae faciebant quaeque dicebant multitudini iucunda uolebant esse, populares, qui autem ita se gerebant ut sua consilia optimo cuique probarent, optimates habebantur.
>
> In this state there have always been two sorts of people who have been ambitious to engage in politics and distinguish themselves there. They have chosen to be, respectively, by name and by nature either *populares* or *optimates*. Those who wanted their words and deeds to be welcome to the multitude were considered *populares*, and those who acted so as to justify their policies to all the best people were considered *optimates*.

Of course Cicero was not going to say in a public speech that the term *optimates* was a euphemism for oligarchy, but he was perfectly well aware of the fact, and in a philosophical dialogue a couple of years later he was even prepared to admit it:

> 2. Cicero *De republica* 3.23
> cum autem certi propter diuitias aut genus aut aliquas opes rem publicam tenent, est factio, sed uocantur illi optimates.
>
> But when certain people control the republic by reason of their wealth or noble birth or resources, that is a faction, but they are called *optimates*.

But what these abstract definitions conceal is the violence with which, on the one hand, 'all the best people' defended their oligarchic privilege, and on the other, 'the multitude' supported their elected champions in trying to abolish it. The most effective of those champions were Gaius Caesar, as consul in 59 BC, and Publius Clodius, as tribune in 58.

The climax came in 52, with the cold-blooded murder of Clodius on the Via Appia, and the symbolic burning of the Senate-house by the Roman People at his funeral.[1] Caesar, the People's chosen commander, was away in Gaul, and the *optimates* were determined to prevent him from coming straight back to another consulship. My next witness is Aulus Hirtius, narrating Caesar's support in 50 BC for Antony's election as augur:

> 3. Hirtius *De bello Gallico* 8.50.2
> contendebat enim gratia cum libenter pro homine sibi coniunctissimo, quem paulo ante praemiserat ad petitionem, tum acriter contra factionem et potentiam paucorum, qui M. Antoni repulsa Caesaris decedentis gratiam conuellere cupiebant.
>
> He was glad to make the effort, both readily to help a close friend whom he had earlier sent on ahead to begin canvassing, and keenly to oppose the powerful faction of a few men who were eager to see Antony defeated and thus undermine the influence of Caesar on his return.

This 'faction of a powerful few' were the *optimates*, as described by their opponents. A similar phrase appears in a text of great historical

---

[1] Asc. 31-33C; Cass. Dio 40.48.1-49.3.

importance, Caesar's own self-reported speech at Corfinium in February of 49 BC:

> 4. Caesar *De bello ciuili* 1.22.5
> se non malefici causa ex prouincia egressum sed uti se a contumeliis inimicorum defenderet, ut tribunos plebis in ea re ex ciuitate expulsos in suam dignitatem restitueret, ut se et populum Romanum factione paucorum oppressum in libertatem uindicaret.
>
> I left my province not for any criminal purpose, but to defend myself against the slanders of my enemies, to restore to their proper place the tribunes of the *plebs* who had been expelled from the city for that reason, and to bring about the freedom of myself and the Roman People from oppression by the faction of a few men.

The Roman People, in a special law sponsored by all of the ten tribunes, had given Caesar the right to stand for his second consulship in absence,[2] but the oligarchs frustrated that by getting the Senate to declare him a public enemy, and driving out the two tribunes who tried to veto it.[3] So there is no reason at all to reject Caesar's presentation of the crossing of the Rubicon as an episode in the ongoing ideological struggle. Certainly he had the enthusiastic support of the People, as even Cicero privately conceded at the time.[4]

My next witness is Gaius Sallustius Crispus, who had been tribune at the time of the riots after Clodius' murder in 52.[5] Writing his historical works ten to fifteen years later, and insisting on the claims of truth over partisanship,[6] Sallust too saw the politics of the late republic as a struggle between the many and the few. The Roman People and a powerful aristocratic oligarchy had been at odds ever since the murderous events of 133 BC:

---

[2] Caes. *BCiv.* 1.32.3; Cic. *Att.* 7.3.4, 8.3.3. 'Populi Romani beneficium': Caes. *BCiv.* 1.9.2; Cic. *Att.* 9.11A.2 (to Caesar).
[3] Caes. *BCiv.* 1.1-5; Cass. Dio 41.1-3.
[4] Cic. *Att.* 7.3.5 (*illa urbana ac perdita plebs*), 7.7.6 (*plebes urbana*), 8.3.4 (*multitudo et infimus quisque*), 10.4.8 (*populi studium*).
[5] Asc. 37C, 49C.
[6] Sall. *Cat.* 4.2, *Hist.* 1.6M.

> 5. Sallust *Bellum Iugurthinum* 42.1
> postquam Ti. et C. Gracchus, quorum maiores Punico atque aliis bellis multum rei publicae addiderant, uindicare plebem in libertatem et paucorum scelerapate facere coepere, nobilitas noxia atque eo perculsa ... Gracchorum actionibus obuiam ierat.
>
> After Tiberius and Gaius Gracchus, whose ancestors had contributed much to the republic in the Punic and other wars, began to bring about the freedom of the *plebs* and expose the crimes of the few, the aristocracy, guilty and therefore on the defensive, ... opposed the actions of the Gracchi.

The same phraseology is used of the events of seventy years later:

> 6. Sallust *Bellum Catilinae* 39.1
> postquam Cn. Pompeius ad bellum maritumum atque Mithridaticum missus est, plebis opes imminutae, paucorum potentia creuit.
>
> After Gnaeus Pompeius was sent to the wars against the pirates and Mithridates, the resources of the *plebs* were diminished, and the power of the few increased.

Note that both these passages are in the author's own voice; many more such statements could be added from the speeches Sallust put into the mouths of the People's champions, Gaius Memmius in 111, Gaius Marius in 108, Licinius Macer in 73, Catiline in 63.[7] Moreover, at the start of his monograph on the Jugurthine war Sallust made it explicit that this ideological struggle had led seamlessly into the civil wars of his own time:

> 7. Sallust *Bellum Iugurthinum* 5.1
> bellum scripturus sum quod populus Romanus cum Iugurtha rege Numidarum gessit,... quia tunc primum superbiae nobilitatis obuiam itum est; quae contentio diuina et humana cuncta permiscuit eoque uecordiae processit ut studiis ciuilibus bellum atque uastitas Italiae finem faceret.
>
> I propose to write the history of the war the Roman People waged with Jugurtha, king of the Numidians ... because that was the first time a challenge was offered to the arrogance of the aristocracy. The conflict threw everything human and divine into confusion, and reached such a level of madness that the hostility between citizens ended in war and the devastation of Italy.

---

[7] Respectively Sall. *Iug.* 31, 85, *Hist.* 3.48M, *Cat.* 20.

That was evidently written in 41 BC, during the civil war that saw the destruction of Perusia and the sacking of other Italian cities.[8]

When Sallust wrote of 'the crimes of the few', and the 'guilty' aristocracy, he was no doubt referring to the murder of Tiberius Gracchus and his supporters by a group of senators led by Scipio Nasica, whom the *optimates* regarded as a national hero.[9] But we can be sure that his readers would think also of more recent murders, equally celebrated by the *optimates* – those of Clodius and of Caesar himself.

Similarly, Sallust's identification of arrogance as the defining characteristic of the aristocracy will have made perfect sense to anyone who had been in Rome in the months after the Ides of March 44 BC. The key witness here is Gaius Matius, replying to a letter in which Cicero had expressed the opinion that Caesar had been a tyrant (*rex*):

> 8. [Cicero] *Ad familiares* 11.28.2-3
> nota enim mihi sunt quae in me post Caesaris mortem contulerint. uitio mihi dant quod mortem hominis necessari grauiter fero atque eum quem dilexi perisse indignor; aiunt enim patriam amicitiae praeponendam esse, proinde ac si iam uicerint obitum eius rei publicae fuisse utilem ... 'plecteris ergo' inquiunt 'quoniam factum nostrum improbare audes.' o superbiam inauditam!
>
> I'm well aware of what they've said against me since Caesar's death. They consider it an offence that I find it hard to bear the death of a friend, and that I'm angry that someone I loved has died. They say patriotism should be put before friendship – as if they've already proved that his death was of benefit to the republic. ... 'You'll suffer for it, then,' they say, 'for daring to disapprove of what we did.' What unheard-of arrogance!

Not unheard-of, in fact, but familiar: it was the arrogance of men who claimed the right to decide who should or should not be allowed to live, without reference to the laws that bound the rest of the Roman People.

At this point I recall my first witness, Cicero, and this time not as a theorist of the republic but as a suspect for the crime of helping to destroy it. Here he is as praetor in 66 BC, explaining to a jury the nature of the rule of law:

---

[8] Prop. 1.22.3-4, Vell. Pat. 2.74.4, App. *BCiv.* 5.49 (Perusia); Cass. Dio 48.13.6 (Sentinum, Nursia).
[9] E.g. Cic. *Planc.* 88, *Tusc.* 4.51, *Off.* 1.109, *Phil.* 8.13; Val. Max. 3.2.17.

9. Cicero *Pro Cluentio* 146
hoc enim uinculum est huius dignitatis qua fruimur in re publica, hoc fundamentum libertatis, hic fons aequitatis: mens et animus et consilium et ententia ciuitatis posita est in legibus. ut corpora nostra sine mente, sic ciuitas sine lege suis partibus, ut neruis et sanguine et membris, uti non potest. legum ministri magistratus, legum interpretes iudices, legum denique idcirco omnes serui sumus ut liberi esse possimus.

This is the constraint of the status I enjoy in public life, this is the foundation of liberty, this is the fountain-head of justice: the mind and heart and judgement and verdict of the citizen body is placed in the laws. As our bodies cannot employ their parts – their sinews, blood and limbs – without a mind, so the citizen body cannot do so without law. The magistrates administer the laws, the jurors interpret the laws, all of us in fact for that reason are slaves of the laws so that we can be free men.

By contrast, here he is in 44 BC, writing to one of the assassins, Decimus Brutus:

10. Cicero *Ad familiares* 11.5.1, 11.7.2
qua re hortatione tu quidem non eges, si ne in illa quidem re quae a te gesta est post hominum memoriam maxima hortatorem desiderasti. ... nullo enim publico consilio rem publicam liberauisti, quo etiam est res illa maior et clarior.

So you of all people don't need encouragement, if you didn't require it for that deed you carried out, the greatest in human history. ... You liberated the republic without any public authority, which makes the deed even greater and more glorious.

For both men, and for all *optimates*, it was self-evident that Caesar had been a 'tyrant',[10] and his murder therefore both legitimate and heroic. But what criterion of 'tyranny' were they applying?

All Caesar's powers and honours had been voted to him by the Roman People, usually in his absence, and despite what Cicero later claimed,[11] the People were not coerced by military force. Caesar's rule was not tyrannical: on the contrary, it was conspicuously humane, as Cicero himself knew better than anyone. He had made the point

---

[10] E.g. Cic. *Att.* 7.11.1, *Off.* 3.82 (quoting Eur. *Phoen.* 506 and 524-525 respectively); *Phil.* 2.117 (*gloriosum* [*est*] *tyrannum occidere*).
[11] Cic. *Off.* 3.84: *qui exercitu populi Romani populum ipsum Romanum oppressisset.*

explicitly in a letter to his fellow-optimate Aulus Caecina in the autumn of 46:

> 11. Cicero *Ad familiares* 6.6.10
> admirari soleo grauitatem et iustitiam et sapientiam Caesaris. numquam nisi honorificentissime Pompeium appellat. at in eius persona multa fecit asperius. armorum ista et uictoriae sunt facta, non Caesaris. at nos quem ad modum est complexus! Cassium sibi legauit, Brutum Galliae praefecit, Sulpicium Graeciae; Marcellum, cui maxime suscensebat, cum summa illius dignitate restituit.
>
> I'm constantly surprised by Caesar's seriousness, fairness and wisdom. He never refers to Pompey except in the most honorific terms. You'll say he did him a lot of harm – but those were the acts of warfare and victory, not of Caesar himself. And how he has embraced us! He's made Cassius his legate; he's put Brutus in charge of Gaul, and Sulpicius of Greece; he's recalled Marcellus, who especially angered him, with all possible respect.

But clemency and generosity were soon forgotten. The only thing that mattered to the *optimates* was that Caesar's authority was something they didn't like. As with Tiberius Gracchus, it was enough to say 'He wants to be king', and the murder of an unarmed man, in defiance of religion as well as law (for both Gracchus and Caesar were protected by *sacrosanctitas*),[12] could be defined as the liberation of the republic.

That was not how the Roman People saw it. When the assassins eventually held a public *contio* on the Ides of March, they needed an armed escort of professional gladiators. But if the many were angry, the arrogant few were exultant.[13] Six months later Cicero could casually refer to Caesar's victory in the civil war as 'fouler than Sulla's', and feel no need to justify the judgement.[14]

II

Why does all this matter for Augustus? It matters because it was happening while he was growing up.

---

[12] In each case the murder was a pollution (μύσος, ἄγος): App. *B Ciu.* 1.2.5, 1.17.71 (Gracchus); 2.118.494, 2.124.520 (Caesar).
[13] Cic. *Att.* 14.9.2 (*laetamur*); 14.12.1, 14.13.2, 14.14.4 (*laetitia*); 14.22.2 (*laetati sumus*).
[14] Cic. *Off.* 2.27 (*uictoria etiam foediore*).

Young Gaius Octavius lost his father when he was four years old, and thereafter he was brought up by his mother Atia, who was Caesar's niece.[15] He was ten years old when the Roman People burned down the Senate house for Clodius' funeral pyre. He was thirteen years old when his great-uncle crossed the Rubicon to reinstate the People's tribunes. He was sixteen years old when Caesar put him in charge of the Greek theatre at the great triumphal games of 46 BC.[16] And he was eighteen years old, studying the arts of war and oratory in Epirus,[17] when the news came that Caesar had been murdered, and that he himself had been adopted as Caesar's son.

Six months later, not long after his nineteenth birthday, the young Caesar addressed the Roman People from the temple of Castor, next to the place where the People had burned Caesar's body and demanded vengeance on his murderers.[18] Cicero was at Arpinum, but heard all about it:

> 12. Cicero *Ad Atticum* 16.15.3
> quamquam enim in praesentia belle iste puer retundit Antonium, tamen exitum exspectare debemus. at quae contio! nam est missa mihi. iurat 'ita sibi parentis honores consequi liceat' et simul dextram intendit ad statuam. μηδὲ σωθείην ὑπό γε τοιούτου.
>
> Although for the moment that boy's doing a fine job of blocking Antony, still, we ought to wait and see what happens. But what a speech! (A copy was sent to me.) He swears 'So may I be allowed to attain my father's honours' as he holds out his right hand to the statue! I'd rather not have the help of *that* sort of person.

Six months later again, after Cicero had indeed used the boy's help to get Antony defeated at Mutina, he got a warning letter from Decimus Brutus:

> 13. [Cicero] *Ad familiares* 11.20.1
> saepe enim mihi cum esset dictum neque a me contemptum, nouissime Labeo Segulius, homo sui simillimus, narrat mihi apud Caesarem se fuisse multumque sermonem de te habitum esse; ipsum Caesarem nihil sane de te questum nisi dictum, quod diceret te dixisse laudandum adulescentem ornandum tollendum; se non esse commissurum ut tolli posset.

---

[15] Nic. Dam. *FGrH* 90 F127.5-7, 128.34; Suet. *Aug.* 4.1, 8.1.
[16] Nic. Dam. *FGrH* 90 F127.19.
[17] Nic. Dam. *FGrH* 90 F130.37-45; Suet. *Aug.* 8.2, 89.1.
[18] App. *B Ciu.* 3.41; Cass. Dio 45.12.4-5.

> Here's something I've often been told, and I think it's worth taking seriously. Just now Segulius Labeo, a very reliable person, tells me he's been with Caesar and talked much with him about you. Caesar himself didn't actually complain about you – except for something he says you said, that the young man ought to be praised, honoured, and got rid of. He said he didn't intend to make it possible to get rid of him.

Given the long-standing optimate tradition of killing politicians they disapproved of, no-one could have been in any doubt what Cicero had meant.

Decimus Brutus wrote that letter on 24 May, 43 BC. On 19 August the young Caesar was elected consul. On 27 November, along with Antony and Lepidus, he was elected *triumuir rei publicae constituendae*. On 7 December, Cicero was killed at their order. However much we admire Cicero, and however brutal we know the proscriptions were, it is still hard to disagree with the verdict of Augustus' friend the historian Titus Livius:

> 14. Livy fr. 50 (Seneca *Suasoriae* 6.22)
> ... mortem, quae uere aestimanti minus indigna uideri potuit, quod a uictore inimico nihil crudelius passus erat quam quod eiusdem fortunae compos ipse fecisset.
>
> On an honest estimate his death might seem less undeserved, in that he had suffered at the hands of his victorious enemy nothing more cruel than he himself would have inflicted if he had had the same chance.

And it is important, if uncomfortable, to remember that Cicero was killed legally.

The Roman People set up the triumvirate, by a tribunician law.[19] The Roman People elected the triumvirs, and their remit was to re-establish the *res publica*. Only the People were competent to legislate and empower. They had empowered Caesar and the *optimates* had killed him, on the arrogant claim that *they* had the right to determine what was good for the republic. Now the young Caesar and his colleagues were

---

[19] App. *B Ciu.* 4.7.27; Cass. Dio 47.2.1-2.

the People's agents in restoring the People's authority, and they acted with a ruthlessness that reflected the People's anger.

As always, proper understanding requires contemporary evidence, and here our witnesses are the triumvirs themselves:

> 15. Edict translated in Appian *Bella ciuilia* 4.8.31-32
>
> Μᾶρκος Λέπιδος, Μᾶρκος Ἀντώνιος, Ὀκτάουιος Καῖσαρ οἱ χειροτονηθέντες ἁρμόσαι καὶ διορθῶσαι τὰ κοινὰ οὕτως λέγουσιν· εἰ μὴ δι' ἀπιστίαν οἱ πονηροὶ δεόμενοι μὲν ἦσαν ἐλεεινοί, τυχόντες δὲ ἐγίγνοντο τῶν εὐεργετῶν ἐχθροί, εἶτα ἐπίβουλοι, οὔτ' ἂν Γάιον Καίσαρα ἀνῃρήκεσαν, οὓς ἐκεῖνος δορὶ λαβὼν ἐλέῳ καὶ φίλους θέμενος ἐπὶ ἀρχὰς καὶ τιμὰς καὶ δωρεὰς προήγαγεν ἀθρόως ...
>
> Edict of Marcus Lepidus, Marcus Antonius and Octavius Caesar, elected to regulate the republic and set it right: if evil men had not, by treachery, begged for mercy when they needed it and when they obtained it became enemies of their benefactors, and then conspirators, Gaius Caesar would not have been killed by those to whom he showed compassion when they were his prisoners of war, whom he made his friends, and whom he favoured collectively with magistracies, honours and personal gifts.

The *optimates* had had their chance. Caesar's clemency and generosity had been abused, and would not be repeated.

The People's vengeance was carried out at Philippi, and completed by the war in Sicily. To describe the triumvirs' opponents in those campaigns as 'the republicans', as some modern historians do, seems to me a gross distortion of the truth. Brutus and Cassius and the men who fled to Sextus Pompey were fighting not for the republic, a body of equal citizens under the rule of law,[20] but for the continued power of the *optimates* and the right of the few to dictate to the many.

Appian was surely right to end his history of the civil wars in 36 BC. The war against Cleopatra and Antony was much more like a traditional *bellum externum*, supposedly defensive and leading to conquest; Antony was regarded not as the leader of a political faction but as a renegade in alliance with a foreign ruler. Since the triumvirs' powers lapsed at the end of 33, Imperator Caesar needed the *ad hoc*

---

[20] Cic. *Rep.* 1.49: *cum lex sit ciuilis societatis uinculum, ius autem legis aequale, quo iure societas ciuium teneri potest cum par non sit condicio ciuium?* Equality: e.g. Dion. Hal. *Ant. Rom.* 2.7.4, 2.28.3, Ov. *Met.* 14.805-806 (Romulus); Flor. 2.1.3-4 (Gracchi); Cic. *Rep.* 1.43 (optimate objection, *ipsa aequalitas est iniqua*).

'oath of all Italy' to justify his command of the People's forces,[21] but the outcome shows clearly enough that his ideological position was what it had always been.

It was the Roman People who established by a law that conquered Egypt was to be governed by an equestrian Prefect;[22] that must be the origin of the remarkable rule that got Germanicus into trouble fifty years later,[23] prohibiting any senator from setting foot in Egypt without permission. A similar point was made by the *cistophoroi* minted in Asia after the victorious Imperator Caesar had completed his reorganisation of the eastern provinces in 28 BC:

> 16. C.H.V. Sutherland, *The Roman Imperial Coinage* (1984²), Aug. 476
> [obv.] IMP. CAESAR DIVI F. COS VI LIBERTATIS P. R. VINDEX [rev.] PAX.
>
> Imperator Caesar Diui filius, consul for the sixth time [28 BC], champion of the liberty of the Roman People. Peace.

The terminology is precisely what Sallust had used of Tiberius Gracchus and Caesar had used of himself: *populum Romanum uindicare in libertatem* (items 5 and 4 above). Also in 28 BC, an issue of 'aurei' reminded the users of gold coins that now the Roman People had got their republic back:

> 17. British Museum CM 1995-4-1-1
> [obv.] IMP. CAESAR DIVI F. COS VI [rev.] LEGES ET IVRA P. R. RESTITVIT.
>
> Imperator Caesar Diui filius, consul for the sixth time, has restored laws and justice to the Roman People.

On 13 January the following year the restoration of their powers to the sovereign People was formally completed, and Imperator Caesar was honoured with a new name:

> 18. *Fasti Praenestini* 13 Jan. (*Inscriptiones Italiae* 13.2.113)
> corona querc[ea, uti super ianuam domus imp. Caesaris] Augusti poner[etur senatus decreuit quod rem publicam] p. R. rest[it]u[it].

---

[21] *Mon. Anc.* 25.2: *iurauit in mea uerba tota Italia sponte sua et me belli quo uici ad Actium ducem depoposcit.*
[22] Ulp. *Dig.* 1.17.1 (*lege*).
[23] Tac. *Ann.* 2.59.3.

> Oak Crown: the Senate decreed that it be placed above the door of Imp. Caesar Augustus because he restored the republic to the Roman People.

The sovereign People entrusted their champion with military command over a large but limited *prouincia*, for a long but limited period.[24] He then left, as Julius Caesar would have left if he had lived, to fight their wars and secure their empire, and in his absence the proper business of the republic resumed.

One example of that was the conduct of elections in the traditional way, as we know from Horace's observations at the time:

> 19. Horace *Carmina* 3.1.10-14, *Epistulae* 1.6.49-54
>
> ... hic generosior
> descendat in Campum petitor,
> moribus hic meliorque fama
> contendat, illi turba clientium
> sit maior.
>
> si fortunatum species et gratia praestat,
> mercemur seruum qui dictet nomina, laeuum
> qui fodicet latus et cogat trans pondera dextram
> porrigere: hic multum in Fabia ualet, ille Velina;
> cui libet hic fasces dabit eripietque curule
> cui uolet importunus ebur.
>
> Of the candidates coming down to compete in the Campus, A is more aristocratic, B has a better character and reputation, C's crowd of clients is more numerous.
>
> If appearance and influence make a man fortunate, then let's buy a slave as a name-prompter – his dig in the ribs will get us crossing the cobbles with hand outstretched. 'This chap's big in the Fabia tribe, that one in the Velina. This one will give the *fasces* and curule chair to whoever he likes, and deny them to whoever he likes if he wants to be awkward.'

The elections were working as usual – and if Caesar Augustus and his trusted allies were regularly elected as consuls, that was by the will of the People, as we can infer from their riotous indignation when Augustus refused to stand for the consulship after 23.[25] In the Roman

---

[24] Cass. Dio 53.12.1-2 and 13.1.
[25] Cass. Dio 54.6.1-3, 54.10.1-2.

republic, as Polybius observed (6.14.9), 'the People bestow office on the deserving,' and that is what was now happening again.

A more unexpected indication of the way things now were comes from a neglected fragment of Livy, which happens to be preserved in a fifth-century commentary on the *Song of Songs*:

> 20. Livy fr. 55 (Apponius *In Canticum canticorum* 12.53, CCL 19.291-292)
> Caesar Augustus in spectaculis, sicut Liuius narrat, Romano populo nuntiat regressus a Britannia insula totum orbem terrarum tam bello quam amicitiis Romano imperio pacis abundantia subditum.
>
> Caesar Augustus, as Livy relates, on his return from the island of Britain, reported to the Roman People at the spectacles that the whole world had been subdued to the Roman empire in the abundance of peace, either by war or by treaties.

The reference to Britain is garbled (Augustus never went there in person), but otherwise this is a recognisable description of something Livy must have witnessed himself, Augustus' return in 24 from his Cantabrian campaigns. He had also settled affairs in Gaul and re-established the tribute from Britain,[26] so 'peace either by war or by treaties' was a precisely accurate phrase. What matters for our enquiry is *in spectaculis*: Caesar Augustus was in the theatre, or perhaps the Circus Maximus, addressing the Roman People *en masse*. He had received his command from them, and it was to them that he chose to report.

In the light of all this, it is not surprising that after Augustus refused to accept election to the consulship he used the tribunician power, granted in 23 BC by a law of the People[27] and conspicuously numbered year by year. Its purpose, as always, was 'to protect the *plebs*,'[28] and once again Horace provides contemporary confirmation:

> 21. Horace *Carmina* 4.15.17-20
>   custode rerum Caesare non furor
>   ciuilis aut uis exiget otium,
>   non ira quae procudit enses
>   et miseras inimicat urbes.

---

[26] Cass. Dio 53.22.5; Strabo 4.5.3 (C200).
[27] *Mon. Anc.* 10.1 (*lege*).
[28] Tac. *Ann.* 1.2.1 (*ad tuendam plebem*).

> While Caesar is the guardian of our affairs, no civil madness or violence will drive out peace, nor anger that forges swords and brings wretched cities to enmity.

Because Augustus, in the People's name, had tamed the arrogant aristocrats, there would be no more of the faction-fighting that had led to armed conflict and the sacking of cities. It was the *optimates* who had corrupted the republic, but now that their arbitrary power was held in check by tribunician authority, the conditions that had developed into civil war no longer applied.

III

Horace wrote those lines a few years after the celebration of the new *saeculum*, and he called the new age the age of Caesar.[29] I think it makes historical sense to use the 'Secular Games' of 17 BC as a convenient chronological marker. From now on, this restored republic, with Caesar Augustus empowered by the People as its guardian, may be regarded as no longer provisional but an established fact.

For this more stable period too, we must look for contemporary evidence. The best evidence of all is provided by Augustus' own words, and we are fortunate that our sources quote surprisingly often from his speeches, letters and edicts. Suetonius, for instance, gives us a wonderful extract from the proceedings in 2 BC when Messalla Corvinus spoke on behalf of the whole Senate:

> 22. Suetonius *Diuus Augustus* 58.2
>
> 'senatus te consentiens cum populo Romano consalutat patriae patrem.' cui lacrimans respondit Augustus his uerbis (ipsa enim, sicut Messallae, posui): 'compos factus uotorum meorum, patres conscripti, quid habeo aliud deos immortales precari quam ut hunc consensum uestrum ad ultimum finem uitae mihi perferre liceat?'
>
> 'The Senate, in consensus with the Roman People, joins in saluting you as *pater patriae*.' Augustus had tears in his eyes as he replied in these words (and I give them verbatim, like Messalla's): 'Now that I have achieved all I have prayed for, members of the Senate, I have only this to ask of the

---

[29] Hor. *Carm.* 4.15.4 (*tua, Caesar, aetas*).

immortal gods, that I may be permitted to extend this consensus of yours to the very end of my life.'

Consensus between Senate and People would mark the end of the enmity that Cicero and Sallust had taken for granted as inherent in the republic (items 1, 5 and 6 above). That was what Augustus hoped he had achieved.

Later that same year, at the dedication of the Forum Augustum, he carefully explained why it featured statues of the great commanders of the past, 'who had changed the *imperium* of the Roman People from very small to very great':

> 23. Suetonius *Diuus Augustus* 31.5
>
> ... statuas omnium triumphali effigie in utraque fori sui porticu dedicauit, professus et edicto commentum id se ut ad illorum <normam> uelut ad exemplar et ipse, dum uiuueret, et insequentium aetatium principes exigerentur a ciuibus.
>
> He dedicated statues of all of them in triumphal costume in the two porticos of his forum, declaring also in an edict that he had designed this so that he himself, while he lived, and the *principes* of later ages, might be held by the citizens to the standard of those men, as an example to imitate.

Note that the initiative lay with the citizens. Augustus evidently thought of the Roman People not as passively obeying their rulers, but as actively demanding the highest standards from the leaders they had empowered.

Where was the Senate in all this? Fifty years before, Cicero had put into the mouth of his own 'example to imitate', the orator Marcus Antonius (consul in 99 BC), an eloquent statement of the Senate's right to rule. Antonius was objecting to a phrase in a famous speech by his great contemporary Lucius Crassus (consul in 95):

> 24. Cicero *De oratore* 1.226
>
> quae uero addidisti, non modo senatum seruire posse populo sed etiam debere, quis hoc philosophus tam mollis, tam languidus, tam eneruatus, tam omnia ad uoluptatem corporis doloremque referens, probare posset senatum seruire populo, cui populus ipse moderandi et regendi sui potestatem quasi quasdam habenas tradidisset?
>
> As for your further statement, that the Senate not only can but should serve the People – what philosopher could be so soft, so languid, so feeble, so

ready to refer everything to the criterion of pleasure and pain, as to approve the idea of the Senate serving the People, which itself has handed over to the Senate the power – the reins, as it were – to guide and regulate it?

Even at the time, that was a partisan view. The phrase *senator populi Romani* was used by Cicero himself when he was a young outsider attacking the corrupt aristocracy,[30] and it alone is enough to show that Crassus was right: the Senate answered to the sovereign People.

The formal description of the Senate as *senatus populi Romani* is attested not only in Varro and Sallust but also in the proceedings of the decurions of Pisa after the death of Lucius Caesar in AD 2:

> 25. Varro fr. 58 Funaioli (Aulus Gellius 17.21.48)
> isdemque temporibus Diogenes Stoicus et Carneades Academicus et Critolaus Peripateticus ab Atheniensibus ad senatum populi Romani negotii publici gratia legati sunt.
>
> In the same period [155 BC] the Stoic Diogenes, the Academic Carneades and the Peripatetic Critolaus were sent by the Athenians as ambassadors on public business to the Senate of the Roman People.
>
> 26. Sallust *Bellum Catilinae* 34.1
> ad haec Q. Marcius respondit ... ea mansuetudine atque misericordia senatum populi Romani semper fuisse ut nemo umquam ab eo frustra auxilium petiuerit.
>
> To this Quintus Marcius replied ... that the Senate of the Roman People had always been of such forbearance and compassion that no-one ever sought help from it in vain.
>
> 27. *CIL* 11.1420.9-12 = *ILS* 139.9-12
> cum senatus populi Romani inter ceteros plurimos ac maximos honores L. Caesari Augusti Caesaris patris patriae pontificis maximi tribuniciae potestatis XXV filio auguri consuli designato per consensum omnium ordinum studio ...
>
> Inasmuch as the Senate of the Roman People, among the very many and very great other honours to Lucius Caesar, augur and consul designate, son of Augustus Caesar *pater patriae*, *pontifex maximus*, in the 25th year of his tribunician power, by the consensus of all classes and with enthusiasm [has decreed...]

---

[30] Cic. *Verr.* 2.1.156-157, 3.93, 4.25, 4.42.

Note again the emphasis on consensus. As for the Senate, the decurions' phraseology shows how the constitutional proprieties of the republic were observed; the only thing that had become obsolete was the *optimates*' own tendentious assertion of senatorial supremacy.

Even in the last decade of his life, when everything seemed to be going wrong, it seems that the ageing Augustus still kept faith with his vision of the republic as literally 'the People's thing'. Suetonius quotes two extracts from his letters to Tiberius, now his adopted son, who was fighting difficult campaigns in Illyricum and then Germany:

> 28. Suetonius *Tiberius* 21.7
> teque oro ut parcas tibi, ne si te languere audierimus, et ego et mater tua exspiremus et summa imperi sui populus Romanus periclitetur. ... deos obsecro ut te nobis conseruent et ualere nunc et semper patiantur, si non p. R. perosi sunt.
>
> 'Please look after yourself. If we heard you were ill it would be the death of your mother and me, and the Roman People would be risking the whole of their empire.' ... 'I pray the gods, if they don't simply hate the Roman People, to preserve you for us and allow you good health, now and always.'

It may be doubted whether Tiberius saw it in quite the same way. He was a patrician, and his father had voted in 44 BC that the assassins should be honoured by the Senate for their deed.[31] It seems clear that the Roman People didn't like Tiberius, despite Augustus' best efforts to persuade them:

> 29. Suetonius *Tiberius* 21.3, 68.3
> ... uitiis Tiberi uirtutibusque perpensis potiores duxisse uirtutes, praesertim cum et rei p. causa adoptare se eum pro contione iurauerit. ... quae omnia ingrata atque arrogantiae plena et animaduertit Augustus in eo et excusare temptauit saepe apud senatum ac populum professus naturae uitia esse non animi.
>
> [I believe that Augustus] weighed up Tiberius' faults and virtues and decided the virtues were more important, especially as he testified on oath at a public meeting that he was adopting him for the sake of the republic. ... Augustus noted these unpleasant and arrogant characteristics in him and often attempted to excuse them to the Senate and the People, claiming they were faults of his nature, not his attitude.

---

[31] Suet. *Tib.* 4.1.

Strictly speaking this is not contemporary evidence, since Suetonius does not give verbatim extracts from those speeches; but there is no reason to doubt that he had read them and reported their meaning correctly. The brute fact was that the successor to Augustus' position – his *statio*, as he put it[32] – had to be a Caesar, but in AD 4 the only person he could safely adopt seemed to have the characteristics of an old-fashioned optimate.

At this point we must listen to Augustus' final assessment, composed in AD 14 (or possibly late 13), of the achievements 'by which he subjected the world to the *imperium* of the Roman People.' This is how he began it:

> 30. *Monumentum Ancyranum* 1.1-4
> annos undeuiginti natus exercitum priuato consilio et priuata impensa comparaui, per quam rem publicam a dominatione factionis oppressam in libertatem uindicaui. eo [nomi]ne senatus decretis honorif[i]cis in ordinem suum m[e adlegit C. Pansa et A. Hirti]o consulibus con[sula]rem locum s[ententiae dicendae simu]l [dans et i]mperium mihi dedit. res publica n[e quid detrimenti caperet] me pro praetore simul cum consulibus pro[uidere iussit. p]opulus autem eodem anno me consulem, cum [consul uterqu]e in bel[lo ceci]disset, et triumuirum rei publicae constituend[ae creauit.]

> At the age of nineteen, on my own initiative and at my own expense, I raised an army with which I brought about the freedom of the republic from oppression by a dominant faction. On that account the Senate adlected me into the order with honorific decrees in the consulship of Gaius Pansa and Aulus Hirtius, giving me at the same time consular precedence in stating my opinion, and granted me *imperium*. It instructed me as pro-praetor, together with the consuls, to see to it that the republic suffered no harm. In the same year, when both consuls had fallen in war, the People elected me consul, and triumvir for the establishment of the republic.

The first sentence repeated Caesar's declaration of 49 BC (item 4 above), except that Augustus claimed to have freed not just the *populus Romanus* but the whole *res publica* from the domination of a faction. The Senate is the subject of the second and third sentences, the People of the fourth, and the phrase *res publica* is conspicuously repeated in the terminology of the Senate's decree and the title of the triumvirate.

---

[32] In a letter to his adopted son Gaius (Gell. 15.7.3).

Throughout the text the idea of consensus constantly recurs,[33] culminating in the grant of the title *pater patriae* by the Senate, the equestrian order and the *populus Romanus uniuersus* (*Mon. Anc.* 35.1).

Nevertheless, the ideology of Augustus' republic is clear from the start. The first two sentences do not encourage readers to remember the *real* details of November 44 BC, when the young Caesar was challenging Antony (item 12 above), or of January 43 BC, when the Senate's decrees were to cement an alliance of convenience between the young Caesar and the *optimates* for the war of Mutina. On the contrary, the message of the first sentence is explicitly *popularis*: the many were freed from the domination of the few. In the Greek version, *factio* is translated as 'the conspirators', and that is surely how the Latin version too was meant to be read. The assassins' power was illegal, and as the fourth sentence specifies, the Roman People, by election, gave the young Caesar constitutional authority against them.

IV

'Poor Roman People!,' the dying Augustus is supposed to have said after his final conversation with Tiberius in August AD 14.[34] Of course the story is apocryphal, but one can see why it was told in those terms.

One can also see why Tiberius was so contemptuous of the Senate's refusal to take responsibility. 'These men deserve to be slaves,' he is supposed to have said.[35] The reason is that they were accustomed to a republic of consensus, where Caesar Augustus and his body of advisers would convey to them what the Roman People wanted.[36] Tiberius abandoned that system; he took everything to the Senate, and expected them to make the decisions.[37] It looks as if he shared the view of Cicero's Marcus Antonius (item 24 above), that the Senate's job was not just to advise but to make policy, without any input, mediated or otherwise, from the Roman People.

---

[33] E.g. *Mon. Anc.* 5.1-2, 6.1, 25.2, 34.1.
[34] Suet. *Tib.* 21.2 (*miserum populum Romanum*).
[35] Tac. *Ann.* 3.65.3 (*o homines ad seruitutem paratos*).
[36] Advisers: Cass. Dio 53.21.4.
[37] Tac. *Ann.* 4.6.2 (*publica negotia et priuatorum maxima apud patres tractabantur*).

The result was a return to late-republican conditions – angry crowds shouting round the Senate house, and in AD 31 an orgy of violence on the streets after the fall of Sejanus.[38] But by then Tiberius had done what aristocrats like him normally did at his age, and retired to the peace and quiet of his palatial country estate. When he died, the Roman People were jubilant.[39]

What they got was Gaius 'Caligula' – a true Caesar, the Dictator's great-great-grandson. Like him, and for much better reason, he was assassinated, and by great good fortune we have a contemporary eye-witness account of the event and its aftermath, transmitted in the nineteenth book of Josephus' *Jewish Antiquities*. It contains a very revealing analysis:

> 31. Josephus *Antiquitates* 19.227-228
>
> οἱ μὲν ἀξιώματος τε τοῦ προτέρου ὀρεγόμενοι καὶ δουλείαν ἔπακτον αὐτοῖς ὕβρει τῶν τυράννων γενομένην φιλοτιμούμενοι διαδιδράσκειν χρόνῳ παρασχόν, ὁ δὲ δῆμος φθόνῳ τε πρὸς ἐκείνην καθιστάμενος καὶ τῶν πλεονεξιῶν αὐτῆς ἐπιστόμισμα τοὺς αὐτοκράτορας εἰδὼς καὶ αὐτοῦ καταφυγὴν ἔχαιρεν Κλαυδίου τῇ ἁρπαγῇ στάσιν τε ἔμφυλον, ὁποία καὶ ἐπὶ Πομπηίου γένοιτο, ἀπαλλάξειν αὐτῶν ὑπελάμβανον τοῦτον αὐτοκράτορα καθισταμένου.
>
> A clear difference had emerged between the attitude of the senators and that of the People. The aim of the senators was to regain their former dignity; they owed it to their pride to free themselves, now that it was possible at last, from the slavery imposed on them by the tyrants' insolence. The People, on the other hand, resented the Senate; they saw the emperors as a curb on its arrogant behaviour and a protection for themselves. They were delighted at the seizure of Claudius, believing that if he became emperor he would save them from the sort of civil strife there had been in the days of Pompey.

What this well-informed observer reveals is how much ground the People's cause had lost since the death of Augustus twenty-seven years before. In AD 41, the senators were again thinking like Brutus and Cassius (and Cicero): for them, it was self-evident that all the Caesars from the Dictator onwards had been 'tyrants'. The People were again fearful of optimate arrogance, and anxious to be protected against it.

---

[38] Tac. *Ann.* 3.14.4 (AD 20), 5.4.2 (AD 29); Cass. Dio 58.12.1.
[39] Suet. *Tib.* 75.1 (*Tiberium in Tiberim*), *Calig.* 13.

The only thing different now was the role of the Praetorian Guard in finding them a new protector.

To understand Augustus properly, it is necessary to consider Roman history over a long period of time, from Tiberius Gracchus to Claudius Caesar. To assume, as so many do nowadays, that the republic simply came to an end and power passed to the first of the emperors, is to be content with a historical travesty that misses all the essentials. The *optimates* of the late second and first centuries BC were not 'the republic', but a murderous corruption of it. Augustus was not 'the emperor', but a commander empowered for limited periods of time, with renewal not automatically assumed.[40] The time of *emperors* began when the Praetorians chose the ruler, when his house on the Palatine was a purpose-built palace, and when 'Caesar' was no longer an inherited or adoptive name but a title bestowed on whoever succeeded.

If, broadly speaking, Augustus presided over a period of peace and stability, and Tiberius over one of strife and discontent, perhaps that is because Augustus thought and acted like a *popularis*, and Tiberius like an optimate. The terms themselves may have gone out of use, but there is no reason to suppose that the ideologies they described suddenly become obsolete in 49 or 42 or 27 BC.

Let's look back at Cicero's classic definition (item 1 above). What Augustus did, and Tiberius failed to do, was keep the interests of 'all the best people' subordinate to those of what Cicero disdainfully called 'the multitude'. Augustus was Julius Caesar's son, and for fifty years, with conquests, spectacles and grand public works, Caesar Augustus gave the Roman People the confidence to believe that the *res publica* really was their thing. It belonged not to the few, but to the many.

The article is deliberately written as a presentation of primary evidence, with no reference to secondary literature, and therefore no bibliography.

---

[40] Suet. *Tib.* 4.1.

Augustus and the Transformation of Roman Citizenship

ANDREW WALLACE-HADRILL
Cambridge University

> Clementiae ciuilitatisque eius multa et magna documenta sunt.
> Suet. *Aug.* 51.1

> Magni praeterea existimans sincerum atque ab omni colluuione peregrinae et seruilis sanguinis incorruptum seruare populum, et ciuitates Romanas parcissime dedit et manumittendi modum terminauit.
> Suet. *Aug.* 40.3

Suetonius' Augustus, of course, comes as close as possible to the perfect emperor.[1] Among his virtues, alongside *clementia*, was the *ciuilitas* of which he gave so many proofs. The same Augustus put the highest premium on the Roman citizenship, which he tried to keep uncontaminated by foreign or servile blood. The two points, I shall argue, are intimately related. And whatever the intentions of Augustus, which were surely not racist in the way that some of his fascist imitators interpreted them, the effect of his actions was a transformation of the nature of the Roman citizenship.[2]

It is now 40 years since I set out on my doctoral research, to study Suetonius' image of the Roman emperor.[3] At the time, Fergus Millar was revolutionizing our understanding of the Roman Emperor, first by a series of articles, and then by the book of that title which emerged as I was writing.[4] A leitmotif of Millar's Roman Emperor was that the Emperor is what the Emperor does. It was a fruitful research theme, but I wanted more. The Emperor is also what people want him to be, how

---

[1] See now Wardle (2014), esp. 28-39 on the portrayal of Augustus.
[2] Well discussed by Dench (2005) 257-259.
[3] Wallace-Hadrill (1979).
[4] Millar (1967) and (1977).

they perceive his actions, how he tries to persuade them he is, and how posterity judges him to have been. All of that, it seemed to me, was packed up in Suetonius' imperial lives. In his rather pedantic, I prefer to say 'scholarly' way, Suetonius tended to look for the same qualities and defects in each of his Caesars.[5] It seemed to me worth asking what lay behind his selection of vices and virtues, which included the Augustan *clementia* and *ciuilitas*.

There was a standard answer, that there existed a canon of imperial virtues, first articulated in Rome in the Augustan *clupeus uirtutis*, and then repeated on thousands of coin issues, a set of virtues ultimately going back to Plato and incorporated in the Hellenistic 'Mirror of Princes' literature.[6] But when I looked at it, I found this assertion to be significantly misleading. Suetonius' set of virtues only partially overlap with any of these other canons.[7] Above all, I was struck that *ciuilitas*, which for Suetonius is of crucial importance, was absent from the *clupeus uirtutis*.[8] Nor can you find it on a single imperial coin, though I looked far and wide, and counted a good 50 virtues. Nor is it in Plato, or any Hellenistic Mirror of Princes. Indeed, Greeks found it a struggle to translate it at all. For Cassius Dio, Augustus was *demokratikos*. But that is not the same thing, and to be honest, it requires a warped sense of democracy to see Augustus as a democrat.

On the other hand, the ideal of the *ciuilis princeps* is fully present in Pliny's panegyric of Trajan: it was one of the central tenets of the Trajanic and Hadrianic regime. Trajan was so *ciuilis* that he took part in the consular elections, though a long rigmarole, *longum illud carmen* (Plin. *Pan.* 63.2). The idea of the 'ciuilis princeps' was certainly not a new one under Trajan, and goes back to Augustus himself, though Suetonius has the distinction of being the first Latin author we know to use the abstract noun, *ciuilitas*.

Emperors from Augustus to Trajan wanted to project themselves as being *ciuiles*, that is behaving to their fellow citizen, *ciues*, as if they were *ciues*, fellow citizens, a deeply anti-monarchical ideal. Why (I asked myself then and ask myself now)? Again, a standard answer

---

[5] Wallace-Hadrill (1983).
[6] Charlesworth (1937).
[7] Wallace-Hadrill (1981ᵇ); see now Noreña (2011) 37-100.
[8] Wallace-Hadrill (1982).

was to hand. It was all part of the myth of *res publica restituta*, a myth that Ronald Syme, deeply influenced by fascist dictators, regarded as a sham, and which Fergus Millar, who regarded the principate as an overt monarchy, not a sham, thought was a myth of modern scholars.[9] For Syme, Augustus pretended to be *ciuilis* to conceal the realities of a monarchical, or more accurately oligarchic, regime. For Millar, Augustus never concealed his monarchical power, and his *ciuilitas* was a matter of etiquette, principally directed at the senate.

My suggestion was that *ciuilitas* went deeper to the nature of imperial power. Augustus paraded himself as a citizen because it was to his advantage to do so. He was not simply putting up a smoke screen. The Roman citizenship was at the heart of his system of benefactions, as exposed by Fergus Millar. Augustus could make citizens. Suetonius thought Augustus restrained, but on Augustus' own figures, the number of Roman citizens rose from just over 4 million to just under 5 million in the course of his reign. He may not have given the impression of shelling out the citizenship at random, as did Claudius and Messalina, but he increased the citizen body by nearly 22%.[10]

Today, I want to push this thought a little further. I want to argue that the Roman citizenship was crucial to the Augustan model of society and political power, but that in putting it at the heart of his reforms, he changed it profoundly. I doubt whether this claim is particularly controversial. But if it is true, it ought to feature in standard discussions of Augustus. I have looked at the recent accounts of Augustus, by Werner Eck,[11] Augusto Fraschetti,[12] Barbara Levick[13] and Karl Galinsky,[14] and in vain have I searched for any discussion of why citizenship mattered to Augustus and what he did with it. Maybe it is so obvious nobody thinks it is worth saying. Please bear with me, then, while I state the obvious for a while, and explore why it is in fact rather complicated and subtle.

Perhaps the best place to begin is with Claude Nicolet's fundamental account of 'le métier de citoyen' (the title is more precise than the 'world

---

[9] Millar (1973). For more recent discussion, see Rich, Williams (1999); Lobur (2008) 22.
[10] See Wardle (2014) 305. The increase in numbers recorded in the *Res gestae* is remarkable, whether or not we maintain that he included women and children in his count.
[11] Eck (2003), first published Eck (1998).
[12] Fraschetti (1998); compare the detailed studies of Fraschetti (1990).
[13] Levick (2010).
[14] Galinsky (2012). Brief mentions of citizenship at pp. 160, 167-168.

of the citizen' of the English translation, and anyway, 'citoyen', thanks to the French Revolution, is charged in a way not so true of the English 'citizen').[15] Republican Rome, for Nicolet, is no democracy, but it very much is a citizen state, and it is this engagement of the citizen that you have to grasp if Roman history is not to be reduced to an account of the ruling class. Citizenship is analysed as a bundle of obligations and rights, military, financial and political. There is *militia*, the obligation and right of the *ciuis Romanus* to serve in campaigns when called on; *tributum*, the obligation to pay taxes when called on; there are *comitia*, the various citizen assemblies at which the *ciuis* could vote to elect magistrates, pass laws and judge cases; and there is *libertas*, the freedom of the *ciuis* from the arbitrary power of magistrates which is partly dependent on the vote, but more specifically on *prouocatio*, the right to appeal to the *populus Romanus*, made effective by the powers of the *tribuni populi* of *auxilium* and *intercessio*.

By no coincidence, Nicolet limits his discussion to Republican Rome, for an underlying theme is that Augustus' victory spelled the end to this entire bundle of rights and obligations. In *militia*, the process that starts with Marius' recruitment of *proletarii* and professionalization of the citizen militia culminates with Augustus' separation of soldier and civilian.[16] In the relation of the citizen to the *aerarium*, the republican principle is that the citizen only pays *tributum* when absolutely necessary, and from 167 BC this was suspended. Civil wars brought back taxes in oppressive forms, and though Augustus initially suspended all direct taxes, in the end the inheritance tax, *vicesima hereditatum*, represented a permanent direct tax, against all republican principles.[17] The vote evidently stands at the centre of the freedoms and powers of the republican *ciuis*; this was killed by Augustus by a reform 'smuggled in' by the *lex Valeria Cornelia* of AD 5; despite all pretences that the elections were free, 'the Republic was dead and the Princeps was its master.'[18]

---

[15] Nicolet (1980), first published as *Le Métier de citoyen dans la Rome républicaine* (Nicolet [1976]).
[16] Nicolet (1980) 89-148, esp. 146-148. At p. 91 he rightly stresses that even after Augustus, service in the legions was limited to citizens.
[17] Nicolet (1980) 148-206, esp. 184-185.
[18] Nicolet (1980) 207-315, esp. 314-315.

Thus for Nicolet, Augustus brought the end of the bundle of rights and obligations that gave citizenship its substance. A crucial role is played by the censorship. It is the periodic census which defines who is a *ciuis Romanus*, what his property is worth and so what his precise voting rights and military obligations are. Augustus is seen as bringing the end (despite his tenure of the office) to the censorship as the mechanism for defining citizenship. It is replaced by the new obligation on citizens to register the birth of children, made law by the *lex Aelia Sentia* of AD 4.[19]

Nicolet's analysis is pretty gloomy. Despite Sherwin-White and his story of the imperial expansion of the citizenship,[20] Nicolet makes clear that he regards it as an empty shell. But then, we might ask why Augustus bothered to preserve it at all. After all, there was another way. If Augustus was the Hellenistic ruler he is sometimes made out to be, why not abolish the citizenship, or at least render it meaningless as did Caracalla by extending it to all free men?[21] Why not rely on a true professional army, abandoning the restriction to citizen recruitment and opening up the reservoir of all abled bodied males in the empire? If he wanted a separation between army and civilians, why not recruit the army from barbarians who would owe loyalty to the emperor alone? Why retain voting in Rome giving an undeserved importance to the *plebs urbana*, who were thus able to extort free grain rations from the imperial budget?

It is worth indulging this fantasy just for a moment to realize how unthinkable it would have been to Augustus and his contemporaries. As Peter Brunt often stressed, Augustus was by instinct profoundly conservative.[22] Think of the scene described by Suetonius, when Augustus laments the presence in the forum of *pullati*, men in the dark tunics of the working class, and cites Vergil's *Romanos rerum dominos*

---

[19] Nicolet (1980) 49-88, esp. 65-67.
[20] Sherwin-White (1973), a study which for all its importance does not address the issue of the changing significance of the citizenship.
[21] The impact of Caracalla's extension of citizenship in AD 212 requires reassessment. On the crucial question of what proportion were already enfranchised, Lavan (2016), arguing that it is unlikely that more than a third of provincials were citizens before 212.
[22] E.g. Brunt (1988) 56-58.
[23] See Wardle (2014) 308 ad loc.; Wallace-Hadrill (2008) 38-70 on citizenship, dress and Roman identity.

gentemque togatam, instructing the aediles henceforth to insist on the wearing of the toga (Suet. *Aug.* 41.5).[23] He would surely have been horrified by any suggestion that the master race should be defined other than as *ciues Romani* in their togas. But then, that leaves us asking what on earth he thought the citizenship should be if he was depriving it of its substance.

Perhaps the first point to make is that the suggestion, implicit in Nicolet, that Republican citizenship was one thing, and imperial citizenship another, is a false contrast, or rather a tendentious oversimplification. Roman citizenship never was one stable, definable thing. It was in constant development and change, throughout the Republic and throughout the Empire. Augustus' reign marks indeed a point of transition, perhaps the most important, but it is very gradual, and it both sums up preceding transitions and makes way for later ones.[24]

To take some of the most important changes in republican citizenship to which Nicolet draws attention. The abolition or suspension of *tributum* in 167 BC takes away a central element of the bundle of obligations on the citizen, and the progressive introduction of the *annona*, subsidised grain distributions, from 123 BC onwards, made the Roman citizen privileged in a way that went beyond any Greek democracy. Marius' recruitment of *proletarii* was seen by contem-poraries as a death-blow to the Republic, though it is evident that Rome could not sustain the sort of overseas campaigns on which it was engaged with a militia of farmers, and the restriction to *assidui* must seem by this stage pointless. The most profound change to the nature of the citizenship was by the *lex Julia* of 90 BC, extending it to Latin cities and (loyal) Italian *socii*. Henrik Mouritsen has argued that the citizenship cannot have been the true aim of the Italici fighting against Rome, on the grounds that what it was before the war was so different from what it became subsequently. He has a point, but the answer is that if you double or treble the number of citizens and break the tie with one specific city, the citizenship must inevitably change, and that is what the rebels wanted.[25]

The *ciuitas Romana* of the Republic was scarcely a stable, well-defined entity, and Augustus himself might have been very surprised by

---

[24] See Dench (2005) 93-151.
[25] Mouritsen (1998).

any suggestion it was. Particularly in the turmoil of the civil wars, when civil elections were abandoned, and troops recruited wherever dynasts could find them, the citizenship must indeed have lost semblance of any ideal. Augustus' claim is that he was trying to restore its old dignity to the citizenship. Was this just a cynical pretence, or indeed a bit of romantic nostalgia for a lost past, or was Augustus using it as part of a vision of a new order?

Comitia

The reason why this question is so hard to answer is that there is no one stable Augustan policy or intention, present throughout his reign, but a continuous experimentation and response to circumstances. Take the vote, a fine example of how contradictory and confused the evidence is of Augustus' intentions, if you imagine he always had one plan in mind. Suetonius firmly states, *comitiorum quoque pristinum ius reduxit* (*Aug.* 40.2). Tacitus equally firmly states that at the first elections after Augustus' death, *tum primum e campo comitia ad patres translata sunt* (*Ann.* 1.15). It is clear that the reign of Augustus in effect spelled the end of popular elections, but it took the entire reign to reach that point.[26] Augustus experimented. He allowed popular elections to happen, and sometimes intervened, sometimes did not, depending on whether he thought the situation was getting out of hand (cf. Cass. Dio 53.21.6-7). He toyed with new systems, exploring the idea of some sort of postal vote for the decurions of Roman colonies (Suet. *Aug.* 46). The lack of representation of the extra-urban citizen population was problematic, and a sign that the implications of the *lex Julia* of 90 BC had still not been fully realized, but this solution seems to have been abandoned.

For lack of an explanation of electoral reform in the sources, modern historians have invented one, in the shape of the *lex Valeria Cornelia* of AD 5, the occasion when Nicolet maintains reform was 'smuggled in'.[27] We know of this law only thanks to the progressive discovery of bronze inscriptions: from the Tabula Hebana, to the Tabula Siarensis.

---

[26] Wardle (2014) 303-304.
[27] For the debate, Brunt (1961); Levick (1967); Staveley (1972); Holladay (1978).

They reveal the posthumous honours voted by the senate to Gaius and Lucius Caesar in AD 5, then to Germanicus in AD 19, finally to Drusus in AD 23. Among the numerous honours is the introduction or extension of voting centuries composed of senators and *equites* to give the lead in the elections for consuls and praetors. This sort of 'predestination' made real popular elections otiose.

Brunt long ago argued that it was implausible to see an honorific degree as introducing a major electoral reform. In fact, it is clear that popular elections continued after AD 5, since Dio tells us Augustus felt impelled to intervene in the elections of AD 7 to put an end to disturbances, and thereafter offered annual guidance (Cass. Dio 54.10.2; 55.34.2).[28] But the fact that under Tiberius, when supposedly elections had been transferred to the senate, they continued to add to these honorific voting centuries, shows that the *comitia* did indeed continue in the Saepta Julia. Those formalities were still in place in AD 100, when Pliny claims that Trajan took part as candidate in his *comitia*, was seen by the *populus Romanus* in its ancient seat of power, and endured *longum illud carmen comitiorum*, showing himself to be one of us, *unus ex nobis*, the Roman people (Pliny *Pan.* 63). It was only the substance, not the form of election that passed to the senate. This is unlikely to be the result of an explicit reform: presumably the change is that candidates now made their speeches in the senate rather than the Campus, since those were seen as provoking disturbances.

In a word, Augustus did not deprive the Roman citizen of the vote, but in the end effectively ritualized it by not allowing candidates to stir real passions at the hustings. But there is little sign that Augustus *wanted* to deprive the citizen of the vote. It was what the logic of the situation demanded, the ultimate consequence of a process inescapably set in motion by the extension of citizenship to Italy in 90 BC. What Augustus consciously *wanted* was to make Roman citizens behave properly, in line with the fantasy of the consensual state, the *consensus omnium ordinum*, which Romans projected on their republican past.

---

[28] See Rich (1990) 155.
[29] Bispham (2007).
[30] Laurence, Esmonde Cleary, Sears (2011); Crawford (1996) n. 25 for the Urso charter.
[31] Franklin (1980), qualified by Mouritsen (1988).

And to this we must surely add that, whatever happened to popular elections by citizens in Rome, they continued in the cities of the empire.[29] As Roman emperors multiplied the number of cities, so they gave municipal charters that imposed the habit of elections.[30] Sceptics may claim that as at Rome, these were little more than a ritual performance, but surely the evidence of Pompeii confirms that elections to local magistracies were the occasion of lively exchange between citizens and elite.[31] It is undeniable that imperial Roman society was hierarchical and heavily tilted in favour of the rich; but the same is true of most societies. The Roman empire, unlike the British empire, made its citizens voters.

Militia

What about *militia*? Did Augustus break the tie between citizen and military service? It is true of course that the Augustan army looks very different from any republican predecessor. A fixed number of legions instead of constant fluctuation; fixed terms of service, with the traditional maximum liability of 16 campaigns converted into a fixed- term minimum of 16, soon increased to 20, and a retirement land assignation or grant guaranteed, in place of the controversial land bills of the previous century.[32] Soldier and civilian were separated in other ways too: the *lex Julia de spectaculis* assigned the soldiers separate seating (Suet. *Aug.* 44),[33] and the marriage legislation, while imposing the duty of marriage and procreation on civilians, made the same in theory illegal for soldiers.[34]

But none of these changes moved the army in the direction of a Hellenistic mercenary army recruited from outside the citizen body. To call Augustus' legions 'volunteers' is a bit optimistic: conscription was still in force.[35] The legions were still recruited from the citizen body. Doubtless it happened that some conscripts acquired citizenship in the process of recruitment, but that was not how it was supposed to happen. On the contrary, what marks out the imperial army is a strong sense of

---

[32] Davies (1989).
[33] Wardle (2014) 331-333; Rawson (1991) 525-527.
[34] Phang (2001).
[35] Brunt (1971) 414.

social hierarchy. Just as the republican legions fought alongside *socii*, before the Social War predominantly from Italy, so the imperial citizen legions fought alongside *auxilia*, recruited from non-citizens, though with the prospect of citizenship as a reward after a rather longer and less well paid term of service.[36] One of the principles of the republican army was that freedmen, though citizens, should not join the legions. Augustus respected this, but then treated the navy as a special case, recruiting from *liberti*. The seven cohorts of *uigiles* in Rome may not have been regarded as *milites*, though their officers moved between them and fully military formations: the *uigiles* were recruited from freedmen and other non-citizens like Junian Latins. One of the incentives to serve was that after six years service, later reduced to three, *uigiles* were rewarded with full citizenship and became entitled to draw the grain dole.[37]

So while it is true that the relationship between soldier and citizen was no longer what it had been under the Republic, it is not true that Augustus abandoned the linkage between citizenship and military service. What we see is a hierarchy in which citizenship is both a privilege and a reward. You have to be a freeborn citizen to serve in the legions; and you are rewarded with better pay and pension. But citizenship is also a reward for those who are not *ciues Romani ingenui*, an incentive to compensate for worse terms. From this perspective, maintaining a clear distinction between citizen and non-citizen was advantageous to Augustus: it is how he made the system work.

Census

Nicolet rightly pointed to the importance of the censorship in defining the citizen body. But Augustus can hardly be accused of abolishing the census. Notoriously, the office had broken down in 70 BC: it became simply impracticable to review the citizen body in Rome in the old fashion, and even if the *lex Julia Municipalis* preserved on the Heraclea tablet shows provision for census taking at local level in the cities of Italy, there was no completed census for a generation. If there

---

[36] Holder (1980).
[37] Baillie Reynolds (1926); Sablayrolles (1996); Virlouvet (2009).

is one thing Augustus was keen on, it was taking censuses of the citizen population. He did it in Rome, following Caesar's initiative to review lists *uicatim*, neighbourhood by neighbourhood. He needed accurate lists of citizens resident in Rome if he was to regularize distributions of grain, and on several occasions of money donatives, and as he reveals in the *Res gestae* (15), he kept a careful count, peaking in 5 BC at 320,000 persons. Without his counting, we would have no idea of the population of Rome; and it is significant that what he counted was the citizens, not the resident population, the figure we are after.[38]

Equally, he counted citizens empire-wide, and takes care to tell us in the *Res gestae* of the numbers of *capita ciuium* on the three occasions the census was completed: 4,063,000 in 28 BC, 4,233,000 in 8 BC, 4,937,000 in AD 14 (*RG* 8).[39] The dates entirely span his reign. These numbers are at the centre of the current demographic storm about the population of the Roman Empire.[40] Let us suspend judgement on whether he was counting adult male citizens (as the expected reading of the text would suggest), or citizens plus their wives and children, or some combination of these elements. The point that is relevant here is that he cared about the citizen count. It represented his reservoir of manpower. He is evidently deeply proud of overseeing an increase of nearly 22%, from just over 4 million to just under 5.

Increase of the citizen population could be achieved by various means. One was the foundation of colonies and the enfranchisement of entire communities.[41] Another was the promotion of the birth rate of free citizens; and whatever the underlying agenda may have been of the laws on adultery and *de maritandis ordinibus*, he certainly claimed that his purpose was to increase the numbers of freeborn citizens.[42] The third mechanism was the enfranchisement of slaves, and it is here that his interventions were particularly subtle, and demand detailed discussion.[43]

---

[38] Wallace-Hadrill (2008) 292-294.
[39] Brunt (1971) 113-120.
[40] Lo Cascio (1994); Scheidel (2007) 45-49; Launaro (2011); de Ligt (2012) 79-134; Hin (2013).
[41] Brunt (1971) 234-265.
[42] On which, see Treggiari (1991) 60-80; Gardner (1998) 47-55; and my observations in Wallace-Hadrill (1981ᵃ).
[43] Buckland (1908) 533-551 for the basics; Gardner (1993) 39-41.

In Suetonius' account, Augustus' concern was not to increase numbers of enfranchisements, but to limit the infusion of foreign and servile blood. Since their implications were crucial to Roman lawyers, we hear rather a lot about the three crucial pieces of legislation, the *lex Fufia Caninia* of 2 BC, the *lex Aelia Sentia* of AD 4, and the *lex Junia*, possibly *Junia Norbana*, of a much disputed date. The *lex Fufia Caninia* is the least controversial: it limited the number of slaves you could free by your will, and set a sliding scale setting the maximum in proportion to the total number of slaves owned. The point is that everybody who had several slaves had to be selective in giving them freedom, and with it citizenship: you gave it as a prize to the deserving, not a blanket act of generosity and demonstration of wealth.

Logically, the *lex Junia* has to precede the *lex Aelia Sentia* of AD 4, since several features of the *lex Aelia Sentia* presupposed the *lex Junia*. This law created a new status group, the Junian Latins, one which in my view is the most revealing about Augustus' transformation of the citizenship. It was traditional for non-Roman communities of free men to be given Latin status, on analogy with the old Latin colonies in which Romans forfeited full citizenship. The innovation of the *lex Junia* was to extend the same analogy to freedmen, creating a hierarchy between freedmen with full *ius Quiritium*, Roman citizenship, and those with *ius Latinum*. It had always been the case that those who were not formally and correctly manumitted could not be citizens, but their freedom was protected by the praetorian edict. But the status of these freed-but-not-citizens was ill-defined. The *lex Junia* created a new status category with rights and limits the lawyers could define in detail.

The importance of the category of Junian Latins can be said to have been neglected by all except specialists in Roman law until Paul Weaver published his article, 'Where have the all Junian Latins gone?' He pointed out that since Junian Latins were also entitled to use the *tria nomina* form supposed to be distinctive of citizens, it was likely that thousands of the *incerti* in Roman funerary inscriptions who mention neither fathers nor patrons are likely to have been Junian Latins.[44]

The importance of this status group became critical only after the passage of the *lex Aelia Sentia* in AD 4. Ostensibly, its aim like that

---

[44] Weaver (1990) and (1997).

of the *lex Fufia Caninia* was to limit the flood of *liberti*. What it did was to divide them more sharply into two status groups, Romans and Latins. By regulating a high minimum age for manumission at 30, and a minimum age for the patron of 20, it provided that any manumission outside these limits, unless justified by special circumstances, resulted in the creation of Junian Latins. In fact it also created a significant third status group, the *dediticii*. Any slave who had been formally subjected to physical punishment was banned from ever achieving citizen or Latin status, and was to be given rights on analogy with a surrendered enemy.

The law thus distinguished carefully three status groups, placing them in a hierarchical relationship of civil rights. But in placing a fence of propriety around the Roman citizenship, it also provided a ladder for climbing over the fence. A Junian Latin who entered into a formal marriage, therefore someone of similar status, and who produced a formally registered child which reached the age of one could by declaration before the magistrates be granted full *ius Quiritium*, citizen rights. It made a big difference, because a citizen could receive legacies from Roman citizens; and on his death, his property could pass at least in part to his children, though unless there were three, the patron could claim a share. A Junian Latin on death, let alone a *dediticius*, reverted to the status of a slave, and his entire property passed to the patron and his heirs.

These provisions for the promotion of a Junian Latin to full citizenship through what the lawyers called *anniculi probatio*, proof of a one-year-old child (Gaius *Institut.* 1.9-17), would have remained one of those obscure legal details safely neglected by historians if it were not for the dossiers of waxed wooden tablets excavated in Herculaneum just before WW2. Over the last few decades, many of these *tabulae Herculanenses* have been illuminatingly republished by Giuseppe Camodeca. One of the most fascinating case studies is that of Venidius Ennychus, among whose dossier are 3 documents, dating from AD 60 to 62, showing him passing through the process of *anniculi probatio*.[45]

The first is the registration of the birth of a daughter by his wife Livia Acte. It seems to have been the same *lex Aelia Sentia* that made

---

[45] Camodeca (2002), (2006), (2008). See now Camodeca (2017) 57-84.

compulsory registration of births of citizens. But non-citizens could not be registered. Therefore Venidius' document is not properly speaking a registration, but a witnessed declaration before magistrates. There are several examples from Egypt of similar informal declarations. Non-citizens too now wanted to register births, because the document could prove useful in legal cases. How much the daughter of Petronia Vitalis must have wished her mother had made such a witnessed declaration in order to prove in court that she was the freeborn Petronia Spuri filia Iusta, as she claimed.

Venidius, however, had it all planned, and the second document, just one year after his daughter's birth, shows him declaring his one-year-old child before the local meeting of decurions in the Basilica Noniana. The third document shows the completion of the legal process, as his case is referred to the praetor in Rome. This reveals that promotion under the law was not automatic, but required a formal act before a Roman magistrate with *imperium*, as did manumission. It reveals a procedure more elaborate than we had suspected, and the emphasis on formal legal documentation.

What is impossible to tell is how common was the sort of procedure through which Venidius went. One might have imagined that any Junian Latin would have got married and produced children as soon as possible in order to get promotion; yet in our one documented case, Venidius Ennychus seems to have waited about 20 years after manumission before settling down and having a child. There seems to be no way of estimating what proportion of the citizen population were freedmen, let alone promoted Junian Latins, though Augustus himself must have had good statistics thanks to his census taking. Probably the truth was too dangerous to publicize.

It is for this reason that recently I have been studying another extraordinary inscription from Herculaneum, the fragments of the great Album, which in its surviving form names over 500 men, all citizens unless they include Junian Latins, but which in the original must have named at least 2000 persons.[46] They are listed in three categories, *ingenui*, freeborn citizen with father's names, *liberti* with patron's names, and what we can call *incerti*, with neither fathers nor

---

[46] Wallace-Hadrill (2015) 135-143.

patrons given. The implication of the surviving fragments is that the *ingenui* were very much in a minority, the *liberti* in a majority. As for the *incerti*, Paul Weaver and I originally suggested that these were promoted Junian Latins, but a number of scholars have disagreed.

What has struck me as I have dug deeper into this question, turning to Gaius' *Institutes* for guidance, is just how complex and varied the Roman citizenship was.[47] You took your status from your mother: her status at the time of birth (rather than conception) determined yours. But given the range of different statuses, the combinations between marriage of a Roman citizen (male or female) and someone of inappropriate status for having a citizen child were enormous. Above all, you might marry in honest error someone of the wrong status (Gai. *Inst.* 1.67-73). So a Roman citizen man might marry a Latin woman or a *peregrina*, mistaking her for a citizen, and the result would be a Latin or peregrine child, unless you could demonstrate honest error, in which case both mother and child became citizens. On the other hand, if you married a *dediticia* in error, the child could become a citizen, but not the mother, since *dediticii* were permanently banned from becoming citizens. Conversely, a Roman citizen woman might in error marry a peregrine thinking him a citizen, and the child's citizen status could be rescued; or she might marry a peregrine thinking him a Latin and expecting promotion under the *lex Aelia Sentia*, and a *senatus consultum* specifically specified that the child could become a citizen if the error was genuine. Similarly, a Latin woman might marry a peregrine of a *dediticius* thinking him to be a Latin, and planning on promotion under the *lex Aelia Sentia*. Yet again, if the error was honest, the situation was rescued.

One may rub one's eyes in astonishment at the generosity of Roman law over honest error; one may feel dizzy at the spectacle of how all these different statuses, citizens, Latins, *dediticii* and peregrines might intermarry by mistake; and one may be amazed that even after the registration of birth introduced by the *lex Aelia Sentia*, there could be so much ignorance about the true status of a person. And lest we think these are eccentric exceptions who got into muddles over status, we should recall that the emperors Titus and Domitian would have

---

[47] Gai. *Inst.* 1.13-141 on questions of status, with Gardner (1993) 1-51.

been born Latins, if their mother Domitilla, who initially passed for a Latin, had not found a citizen to declare in court that she was a citizen after all.[48]

We tend to imagine Roman society as based on a simple divide between citizens, freeborn or freed, and slaves. Take the scrupulously careful calculations by Peter Brunt for the population of Rome.[49] Starting from the figures for the grain dole, available only to adult male citizens, he considers that one only need double the number for women and children. He states there is no evidence for a middle class, so that we only have to add a number for slaves, so arriving at three quarters of a million. But where, we hear Paul Weaver asking, have all the Latins gone? And where have the *peregrini*, the free non-citizen immigrants, gone? Think of Seneca's picture of the capital, with its population drawn from all corners of the globe, attracted by all the opportunities for display of virtue and indulgence of vice (Seneca *Cons. ad matrem Heluiam* 6.2-3). Over half, he thinks, were immigrants from outside Rome. His figure, which of course includes citizen immigrants like himself, as well as slaves and freedmen, is probably a cautious one. No great city has ever grown without massive immigration.

And it is in this world of early imperial Rome, of many statuses jostling alongside each other, and even marrying each other by mistake, that legal precision over status and rights mattered so much, and in which Augustus' 'defence' of the status of citizen could work to his advantage, in delivering what he conceived as an ordered society.

Conclusion

Pulling the threads together, we may concede to Nicolet that the reign of Augustus spelt the end of certain features of the Roman citizenship that had been definitive under much of the Republic, and which were recognisably part of the typology of the city-state as analysed by Aristotle. The link between citizenship and military service on the one

---

[48] Suet. *Vesp.* 3: *inter haec Flauiam Domitillam duxit uxorem, Statili Capellae equitis R. Sabratensis ex Africa delicatam olim Latinaeque condicionis, sed mox ingenuam et ciuem Rom. reciperatorio iudicio pronuntiatam, patre asserente Flauio Liberali Ferenti genito nec quicquam amplius quam quaestorio scriba.*

[49] Brunt (1971) 376-388, esp. 383.

hand, and the vote on the other, was effectively broken, though in both cases we are looking at the result of long-term changes that followed from the logic of a Mediterranean empire. But if these relationships changed, it does not mean that the Roman citizenship was left an empty shell, or that Augustus regarded it as being of little importance. On the contrary, it was central to his strategy of a new Roman order.

One can debate endlessly what were the precise advantages of citizenship under the Empire. One key element was the imperial transformation of the right of *prouocatio*.[50] By making the *tribunicia potestas* the highest title of his power, *summi fastigi uocabulum*, Augustus absorbed the power of tribunes to intervene in support of the citizen. The appeal to Caesar was an instrument of great power on both sides of the deal: how important it was to the citizen in a far flung province is made clear by the Apostle Paul, who got a far better deal than Verres' victim Sthenius.[51] But it was also important to Augustus, making himself the champion of the Roman citizen, and a sort of Supreme Court of Appeal.

The Roman citizen, as Nicolet emphasises, valued *libertas*. Liberty is hard to define because it is, as Arena has recently argued, a metaphor: liberty is defined by its opposite, slavery.[52] To be free is not to be a slave. This, as I have tried to show, is an issue in which Augustus through legislation intervened decisively. His legislation determined that freedom has many shades. A *dediticius* was free, but only the sense that a prisoner on parole is free, and quite without citizen rights or the prospect of their acquisition. The Junian Latin was free, and had the conditional prospect of the greater freedom of citizenship, but also the prospect of reversion to the status of slave on death, giving the patron total rights of succession to property. The *libertus iure Quiritium* was free, though it remains unclear whether he was free to collect a grain ration in Rome,[53] and still owed *obsequium* to his patron, and was not

---

[50] Garnsey (1966).
[51] Sherwin-White (1963) 57; Garnsey (1970) 75. As Garnsey shows, citizen status alone was insufficient protection, and the further distinction of rank of the *honestiores* became more important.
[52] Arena (2012).
[53] Virlouvet (2009) 43 and 56 supports van Berchem's argument that *liberti* were only exceptional granted the right of *frumentum publicum*.

free to marry into the senatorial order, neither in the first or even fourth generation.

Augustan freedom was then far from an absolute. The citizen was free, and free to vote, but not free to riot and cause disturbance. The creation of the office of *praefectus Vrbi* must have done much to limit the freedom of the citizen resident in Rome. There is nothing radical about Augustus' concept of citizenship or *libertas*. It is deeply hierarchical, a status within a spectrum of statuses. But as such, it was part of his *arcana imperii*. Thus I suggest that the reason that he made a virtue of *ciuilitas* was that it was in his interest to make *civitas Romana* the underpinning of his social order.

Bibliography

Arena, V. (2012), *Libertas and the Practice of Politics in the Late Roman Republic*, Cambridge.

Baillie Reynolds, P.K. (1926), *The Vigiles of Imperial Rome*, Oxford.

Bispham, E. (2007), *From Asculum to Actium. The Municipalization of Italy from the Social War to Augustus*, Oxford.

Brunt, P.A. (1961), 'The *Lex Valeria Cornelia*', *Journal of Roman Studies* 51, 71-83.

Brunt, P.A. (1971), *Italian Manpower 225 BC-AD14*, Oxford.

Brunt, P.A. (1988), *The Fall of the Roman Republic and Related Essays*, Oxford.

Buckland, W.W. (1908), *The Roman Law of Slavery*, Cambridge.

Camodeca, G. (2002), 'Per una riedizione dell'archivio ercolanese di L. Venidius Ennychus I', *Cronache Ercolanesi* 32, 257-280.

Camodeca, G. (2006), 'Per una riedizione dell'archivio ercolanese di L. Venidius Ennychus II', *Cronache Ercolanesi* 36, 189-211.

Camodeca, G. (2008), 'Le tabulae Herculanenses: il dossier sulla concessione della *civitas romana* all'ercolanese *L. Venidius Ennychus, Latinus Iunianus*', in M. P. Guidobaldi (ed.), *Ercolano. Tre secoli di scoperte*, Milan, 99-102.

Camodeca, G. (2017), *Tabulae Herculanenses. Edizionie e commento* I, Rome.

Charlesworth, M.P. (1937), 'The virtues of a Roman emperor: propaganda and the creation of belief', *Proceedings of the British Academy* 23, 105-136.
Crawford, M.H. (1996), *Roman Statutes*, London.
Davies, R.W. (1989), *Service in the Roman Army*, Edinburgh.
de Ligt, L. (2012), *Peasants, Citizens and Soldiers. Studies in the Demographic History of Roman Italy 225 BC-AD 100*, Cambridge/ New York.
Dench, E. (2005), *Romulus' Asylum. Roman Identities from the Age of Alexander to the Age of Hadrian*, Oxford.
Eck, W. (1998), *Augustus und seine Zeit*, Munich.
Eck, W. (2003), *The Age of Augustus*, transl. D. L. Schneider, new material by S. A. Takács, Oxford.
Franklin, J.L. (1980), *Pompeii. The Electoral Programmata, Campaigns and Politics, AD 71-79*, Rome.
Fraschetti, A. (1990), *Roma e il principe*, Rome. Fraschetti, A. (1998), *Augusto*, Rome/ Bari.
Galinsky, K. (2012), *Augustus. Introduction to the Life of an Emperor*, Cambridge.
Gardner, J.F. (1993), *Being a Roman Citizen*, London.
Gardner, J.F. (1998), *Family and* Familia *in Roman Law and Life*, Oxford.
Garnsey, P. (1966), 'The *lex Iulia* and appeal under the empire', *Journal of Roman Studies* 56, 167-189.
Garnsey, P. (1970), *Social Status and Legal Privilege in the Roman Empire*, Oxford.
Hin, S. (2013), *The Demography of Roman Italy. Population Dynamics in an Ancient Conquest society 201 BCE-14 CE*, Cambridge.
Holder, P.A. (1980), *Studies in the Auxilia of the Roman Army from Augustus to Trajan*, Oxford.
Holladay, A.J. (1978), 'The election of magistrates in the early Principate', *Latomus* 37, 874-893.
Launaro, A. (2011), *Peasants and slaves: the rural population of Roman Italy (200 BC to AD 100)*, Cambridge.
Laurence, R., Esmonde Cleary, S., Sears, G. (2011), *The City in the Roman West*, Cambridge.

Lavan, M.P. (2016), 'The spread of Roman citizenship 14-212 CE: quantification in the face of high uncertainty', *Past & Present* 230, 3-46, Oxford.

Levick, B. (1967), 'Imperial control of the elections under the early Principate: *commendatio, suffragatio*, and *nominatio*', *Historia* 16, 207-230.

Levick, B. (2010), *Augustus. Image and Substance*, Harlow.

Lo Cascio, E. (1994), 'The Size of the Roman Population: Beloch and the Meaning of the Augustan Census Figures', *Journal of Roman Studies* 84, 23-40.

Lobur, J.A. (2008), *Consensus, Concordia, and the Formation of Roman Imperial Ideology*, New York/ London.

Millar, F. (1967), 'Emperors at work', *Journal of Roman Studies* 57, 9-19.

Millar, F. (1973), 'Triumvirate and principate', *Journal of Roman Studies* 63, 50-67.

Millar, F. (1977), *The Emperor in the Roman World (31 BC-AD 337)*, London.

Mouritsen, H. (1988), *Elections, Magistrates and Municipal Elite. Studies in Pompeian Epigraphy*, Rome.

Mouritsen, H. (1998), *Italian Unification. A Study in Ancient and Modern Historiography*, London.

Nicolet, C. (1976), *Le Métier de citoyen dans la Rome républicaine*, Paris.

Nicolet, C. (1980), *The World of the Citizen in Republican Rome*, transl. P. S. Falla, London.

Noreña, C.F. (2011), *Imperial Ideals in the Roman West: Representation, Circulation, Power*, Cambridge.

Phang, S.E. (2001), *The Marriage of Roman Soldiers (13 BC-AD 235). Law and Family in the Imperial Army*, Leiden/ Boston.

Rawson, E.D. (1991), *Roman Society and Culture. Collected Papers*, Oxford.

Rich J.W., Williams, J.W.H. (1999), 'Leges et iura P.R. restituit: a new aureus of Octavian and the settlement of 28-27 BC', *Numismatic Chronicle* 159, 169-213.

Rich, J.W. (1990), *Cassius Dio: the Augustan Settlement*, Warminster.

Sablayrolles, R. (1996), Libertinus miles. *Les cohortes vigiles*, Rome.

Scheidel, W. (2007), 'Demography', in W. Scheidel, I. Morris, R. Saller (edd.), *The Cambridge Economic History of the Greco-Roman World*, Cambridge, 45-49.
Sherwin-White, A.N. (1963), *Roman Society and Roman Law in the New Testament*, Oxford.
Sherwin-White, A.N. (1973), *The Roman Citizenship* (2nd ed.), Oxford.
Staveley, E.S. (1972), *Greek and Roman Voting and Elections*, London.
Treggiari, S. (1991), *Roman Marriage. Iusti Coniuges from the Time of Cicero to the Time of Ulpian*, Oxford.
Virlouvet, C. (2009), *La plèbe frumentaire dans les témoignages épigraphiques: essai d'histoire sociale et administrative du peuple de Rome antique*, Rome.
Wallace-Hadrill, A.F. (1979), *Suetonius on the Emperor. Studies in the Representation of the Emperor in the Caesars*, D. Phil. thesis, Oxford.
Wallace-Hadrill, A. (1981[a]), 'Family and inheritance in the Augustan marriage laws', *Proceedings Cambridge Philological Society* 27, 58-80.
Wallace-Hadrill, A. (1981[b]), 'The emperor and his virtues', *Historia* 30, 298-323.
Wallace-Hadrill, A. (1982), '*Ciuilis princeps*: between citizen and king', *Journal of Roman Studies* 72, 32-48.
Wallace-Hadrill, A. (1983), *Suetonius: the Scholar and his Caesars*, London.
Wallace-Hadrill, A. (2008), *Rome's Cultural Revolution*, Cambridge.
Wallace-Hadrill, A. (2015), 'The album of Herculaneum: problems of status and identity', in A. B. Kuhn (ed.), *Social Status and Prestige in the Graeco-Roman World*, Stuttgart, 115-151.
Wardle, D. (2014), *Suetonius Life of Augustus. Translated with Introduction and Historical Commentary*, Oxford.
Weaver, P. (1990), 'Where have all the Junian Latins gone? Nomenclature and status in the Roman Empire', *Chiron* 20, 275-305.
Weaver, P. (1997), 'Children of Junian Latins', in B. Rawson, P. Weaver (edd.), *The Roman Family in Italy. Status, Sentiment, Space*, Oxford, 55-72.

Augustus and the Parthians

LEONARDO GREGORATTI
Durham University

No serious attempt to approach the gigantic personal and political figure of Octavianus Augustus Rome's first *princeps*, comprehensively or even partially can avoid taking into account one of the most important sources on Augustus' activity: the *Res gestae diui Augusti*.[1] Even this contribution, about a rather secondary aspect of his policy, the *res orientales*, the problematic relations with the Arsacid empire,[2] Rome's rival in the East, has to start from Augustus' political testament, that is to say from the record, in what are considered his own words, of what he wanted posterity to remember. This includes not only his deeds, but more importantly, how his actions must be interpreted and understood by his contemporaries and by his successors as Roman leaders. In sum the description of how he wanted to appear.

As is known there is still lively discussion concerning the function and purposes of Augustus' text. It is still not clear beyond doubt to which literary genre the text should belong: political testament, autobiography, memories/ *commentarii*, funerary inscription.[3] What is certain is that the *Res gestae* do not present a mere series of facts, of deeds, and they are of course far from being an historical account. Many facts are narrated summarily or with emphasised propagandistic tones, very few persons apart from Augustus himself are mentioned, his political adversaries remain anonymous. The *Res gestae* are primarily an epitaph, a funerary text, conceived and drawn up many

---

[1] The literature concerning the *Res gestae* is of course ample. Some of the most recent studies include Ramage (1987); Ridley (2003); and Cooley (2009) especially at 230-256.
[2] On the Parthian (1980) empire ruled by the Arsacid dynasty: Debevoise (1938); Ziegler (1964); Schippmann (1980); Bivar (1983); Dąbrowa (1983); Frye (1984); Wolski (1993); Wiesehöfer (1994); Wiesehöfer (1998) and the more recent Shayegan (2011); and Ellerbrock, Winkelmann (2012). For the sources concerning the history of the Parthian Kingdom, see the recent Hack, Jacobs and Weber (2010).
[3] Borsak (1998).

years before his death, which surely went through different versions and modifications. In this respect the *Res gestae* are similar to all those hundreds of funerary inscriptions conceived and written by more or less anonymous men, found all over the empire and used every day in our researches. All those men, or those in charge of writing down their last words to the world, put on the stone only the things they wanted to be remembered for, reporting their deeds in the most favourable way.

Considering the *Res gestae* only a funerary inscription would be reductive. They are the political testament of the most important ruler of the Roman empire, a man whose political action reformed and influenced all aspects of Roman state and culture, a man who was able to emerge triumphant from the bitter fight for power of the late Republic and restore a Roman state authority. The *Res gestae* are thus a dazzling masterpiece of scintillating success, a shining example of the right and good rule. There is no room for shadows: these are left to the work of the historians ancient and modern.

Among the various luminous robes Octavianus chooses to wear in his text, the politician, the leader, the builder, the pious man, one is particularly significant for the Near East: the conqueror, the leader who massively expanded the Roman state and made its power much bigger. Some decades before Rome had established with Pompey a firm control on the Near East through the founding of the Roman province of Syria and the submission of the many local kings and dynasts who ruled between the Mediterranean Sea and the Syrian desert.[4] The whole sector fell into the hands of Antony, who ruled over the petty kings like a sort of oriental sovereign.[5] After Actium the Near Eastern cities and potentates again came under the central Roman authority in Rome, that is to say under Augustus; most of the dynasts were pardoned for their allegiance to Antony and allowed to remain on their thrones.[6]

Surprisingly almost no reference to Antony's and Rome's former possessions is contained in the text. The *princeps*' attention is focused on something else. Augustus states explicitly 'I extended the boundaries of all the provinces which were bordered by races not yet subject to our

---

[4] Downey (1951); Sartre (2001) 444-451; Butcher (2003) 19-35.
[5] Butcher (2003) 35-38.
[6] Braund (1988); Millar (1993) 27-43; Sartre (2001) passim.

empire.'[7] With regards to the Near East this role of Augustus seems to assume peculiar characteristics. The attention of the reader is directed to the people and kingdoms which lay outside the area of Rome's direct influence,[8] Armenia, Media, Parthia, that is to say east of the Euphrates river, which by this time was felt to be a sort natural boundary for the imperial expansion.[9] In AD 2 an important meeting between Augustus' grandson and adopted son Gaius Caesar, representing Rome's authority, and the Parthian Great King Phraates V took place on an island in the middle of the river Euphrates. Velleius Paterculus, at that time a young military tribune, eye witness of those events, described the royal meeting with these words: 'this spectacle of the Roman army arrayed on one side, the Parthian on the other, while these two eminent leaders not only of the empires they represented but also of mankind thus met in conference (...) it was my fortunate lot to see.'[10] It seems clear that in the eyes of the enthusiastic officer, the delegates of the two rival powers divided the whole known world. They met at the Euphrates river, as the limit of their respective spheres of political influence.[11]

Velleius' words prove that the river was not only commonly felt to be the natural boundary of the Roman empire in the east, but also that the choice of meeting place was symbolic and meant the explicit acknowledgement of that frontier. The meeting itself was undoubtedly the masterpiece of Augustus' policy in the east, the climax of a long-lasting political activity aimed at bringing the two rival superpowers closer, thanks to the open attitude showed by Phraates IV and his son Phraataces. In the end Augustus decided to consider the Great King as equal and to establish a peaceful dialogue with the Roman-friendly monarch of the largest most powerful empire in Western Asia. This achievement did not prevent of course Augustus and his successors

---

[7] *Mon. Anc.* 26: *Omnium prou[inciarum populi Romani], quibus finitimae fuerunt gentes quae non p[arerent imperio nos]tro, fines auxi.*

[8] Kingdoms and people that in Augustus' narration, but of course not in the historical reality, are forced to acknowledge Rome's supremacy.

[9] Edwell (2010) passim; Edwell (2013).

[10] Vell. Pat. 2.101.2-3: *Quod spectaculum stantis ex diuerso hinc Romani, illinc Parthorum exercitus, cum duo inter se eminentissima imperiorum et hominum coirent capita (...) mihi uisere contigit.*

[11] Cass. Dio 55.10.18-19; Suet. *Tib.* 12.2; Oros. 7.3.4; Zetzel (1970) 259-266; Romer (1974) 171-173; Campbell (1993) 224-225; Greatrex (2007) 151-153; and Luther (2010) 103-127.

from attempting to influence and control Parthian leadership by supporting Roman-friendly candidates to the throne. The Euphrates was the official limit of Rome's direct and indirect control area, but not of Rome's political action.[12]

Since 247 BC the Arsacids in fact were able to gain the best advantages from the weakening of the Seleucid kingdom by spreading their control over large territories of Western Asia. From the remotest borders of that empire, after consolidating their control over Hyrcania, Parthyene and other regions north of the Elburz range, the Parthian monarch began expanding their domains south of the Caspian Gates, over the Iranian plateau and Mesopotamia. By the period during which the struggle with Rome took place, the Arsacid rule stretched from the Euphrates to North-Western India, including Mesopotamia, Iran and all the territories lying between the Persian Gulf and the Indian Ocean to the South and the Caspian Sea and the Caucasus to the North.

Despite the importance of this achievement, that is to say the establishing of peace between the two superpowers marked by the meeting at the Euphrates, in the *Res gestae* there is no mention of such success of Octavianus' *Realpolitik*. In Augustus' narration the Parthians are never treated as equal political interlocutors: instead, they are 'compelled to restore the spoils and standards' and 'to seek as suppliants the friendship of the Roman people.'[13] They are always portrayed as an inferior power hardly distinguishable from the other minor kings in the region, dependent on Augustus' political decisions.

In the same way almost no attention is paid to the restoration of the Near Eastern province or to the Kings already subjected to Rome, like Herod the Great, to cite only the most important, despite their role being vital for the consolidation of Roman rule west of the river. All attention is driven to the lands and kings beyond the Roman borders, that is to say beyond the Euphrates.

---

[12] Augustus learnt by Crassus' and Antony's defeats that the Parthian empire was not a minor political subject. Rome's power in the east after the civil wars needed a rigorous reorganization. A formal agreement with the 'Eastern barbarians' had to be found to set the things west of the river and to continue the confrontation with other means east of it.

[13] *Mon. Anc.* 29: *Parthos trium exercitum Romanorum spolia et signa re[ddere] mihi supplicesque amicitiam populi Romani petere coegi*; 32: *Ad me rex Parthorum Phrates, Orod[i]s filius, filios suos nepot[esque omnes] misit in Italiam, non bello superatus, sed amicitiam nostram per [libe] ror[um] suorum pignora petens*. Wiesehöfer (2010) 187-188.

The image of the Roman empire that Augustus wants to provide, by focusing on the territories outside the Roman borders and by representing the Parthians as a 'client state', is that of a dynamic state, an empire expanding in every direction, whose political influence stretches well beyond its actual limits in the East. The power of Augustus' Rome in the *princeps*' narration keeps on extending eastwards, following Alexander's footsteps to include all the inhabited lands. Augustus wishes to show that he was able to take imperial influence beyond the supposed natural limits of the Roman world and what is more, without leading invading armies into distant lands like the unsuccessful Crassus and Antony, but only through politica means.

Dealing with Armenia he states 'In the case of Greater Armenia, though I might have made it a province after the assassination of its King Artaxes, I preferred, following the precedent of our fathers, to hand that kingdom over to Tigranes.'[14] Following the example of his predecessors' policies in the region, especially those of Pompey the Great, victor over the Armenian superpower and conqueror of the East,[15] Augustus decided to maintain the pre-existing political structures, exerting his control by appointing or removing kings as the circumstances required. To Armenia, a strategic kingdom with strong cultural bounds with Parthia, he tried to apply the same policy which had worked among the kings west of the Euphrates, but with completely opposite results. In the passage in which the frequently revolting Armenians appear to be forced into submission by having to accept kings appointed by Rome,[16] Octavianus depicts himself as a sort of 'Kingsmaker', endowed with the superior power of placing kings on thrones even beyond the Euphrates. But the extraordinarily long list presented by Augustus of monarchs appointed in Armenia conceals a rather different reality.

---

[14] *Mon. Anc.* 27: *Armeniam maiorum, interfecto rege eius Artaxe, c[u]m possem facere prouinciam, malui maiorum nostrorum exemplo regn[u]m id Tigrani, regis Artauasdis filio, nepoti autem Tigranis regis.*

[15] Gregoratti (2012a).

[16] *Mon. Anc.* 27: *Et eandem gentem postea d[e]sciscentem et rebellantem domit[a]m per Gaium filium meum regi Ariobarzani, regis Medorum Artaba[zi] filio, regendam tradidi et post eius mortem filio eius Artauasdi. Quo interfecto, Tig[ra]ne qui erat ex regio genere Armeniorum oriundus, in id regnum misi.*

The murder of Artaxias rendered the throne of Armenia, a kingdom were the influence of the Arsacids was very strong, vacant in 20 BC. A candidate was chosen from among the members of the Armenian ruling dynasty living at Rome and proposed by Augustus: Tigranes III.[17] Tigranes died in 6 BC and the Armenian aristocracy placed his son Tigranes IV and the sister Erato on the throne without Roman agreement.[18] To Rome, this constituted an open rebellion. Another exiled brother, Artavasdes II, became Augustus' new candidate; despite being supported by imperial troops, he managed to contest the throne for only a few years.[19] The instability generated by Armenian situation therefore risked spreading war throughout the East. Augustus then sent his young grandson and heir G. Caesar, with full authority to resolve the crisis. But the young prince fell in the following Armenian civil war, mortally wounded during an attack on a mountain stronghold defended by a local lord named Addon, in the attempt to consolidate the position of another Roman candidate: Ariobarzanes, Prince of Media Atropatene (3 AD).[20] Augustus' policy of attempting constantly to place new kings on the Armenian throne, proved to be a failure, leaving the country in a state of continuous anarchy, more and more permeable to the influence of the Arsacids.

The emperor's mistake, perhaps caused by an inadequate understanding of the peculiarities of the Armenian situation and of the strong dynastic and cultural ties connecting its society's leaders to the Arsacids, was to underestimate the determination of the feudal groups at the local level. They were the masters of inaccessible valleys or, as in the case of *Addon*, of the strongholds perched between the mountains. They were absolutely sovereign in their lands, controlling the mountain passes and communication routes from their virtually impregnable strongholds, and in the final analysis they decided whether or not a

---

[17] Cass. Dio 51.16.2, 54.9.4-5; Suet. *Tib.* 9.1; Strab. 17.1.54; Vell. Pat. 2.94.4, 26; Pani (1972) 33-38; Chaumont (1976) 76; Schippmann (1980) 46; Dąbrowa (1983) 43.

[18] Cass. Dio 55.9.4-8 and 10.18-21, where Tigranes seems to have been a acceptable candidate for Augustus as well; Suet. *Tib.* 9.1; Vell. Pat. 2.100.1; Debevoise (1938) 146; Pani (1972) 17, 24-25, 36-44; Chaumont (1976) 76-77, 80-81; Bertinelli (1979) 51-52; Frye (1984) 235-236; Frézouls (1995) 488-493; Wolski (1993) 149.

[19] Tac. *Ann.* 2.3-4; Asdourian (1911) 69-70; Pani (1972) 43; Bedoukian (1978) 35-36, 75.

[20] Asdourian (1911) 76-78; Pani (1972) 52-61; Romer (1974) 173-174; Chaumont (1976) 81-82; Bedoukian (1978) 37-40, 76-77.

foreign king had the right to govern Armenia, pledging their agreement or rising up in great numbers. The Armenian internal political situation was simply too complex for Rome to be able to choose which of the princes living at the imperial court would rule Armenia.[21]

A very similar policy followed regarding the kingdom of Parthia, ruled by the Arsacid dynasty, a real continental superpower that had already proved its strength in 53 BC by inflicting a disastrous defeat on Crassus' legions at Carrhae, in northern Mesopotamia.[22]

The implementation of Augustus' policy towards the Parthians went through a number of strictly connected phases, some of which are mentioned and elaborated in the *Res gestae*. It is difficult however to establish whether or not these connected events, which are reported by various sources, were part of a carefully planned strategy. What is certain is that at the end of a long process Augustus was in the position to impose his 'kingsmaker' strategy on the Parthian throne too and was able to exploit the political crisis in which the Arsacid kingdom was then embroiled in the most advantageous way for Rome.

In the year 20 BC the negotiations between Rome and Phraates the great King of Parthia reached a satisfactory conclusion which made possible the much desired restitution of the ensigns and prisoners captured during of the victories over Crassus and Mark Antony.[23] The special importance of this event was that imperial propaganda presented it to the Roman people as proof of the Parthians' submission and their willingness to make peace with the Rome.[24] Shortly after Augustus presented Phraates IV with an Italic slave girl named Musa, intended to add to the company of royal concubines. The enterprising Musa, reluctant to assume the role of a simple concubine among the many in the gynaeceum, actively did her best to increase her power and influence within the royal palace and upon the Great King himself. Soon afterwards, with the birth of his son Phraates, she was elevated to the rank of Queen. Having apparently earned the King's favour, the

---

[21] Gregoratti (2012a).
[22] See the recent Traina (2010).
[23] Oltramare (1938) 131-132; Ziegler (1964) 46-47, 50; Timpe (1975); Chaumont (1976) 74; Bertinelli (1979) 52; Vin (1981), 117-139; Dąbrowa (1983) 41; Barzanò (1985) 211; Wolski (1993) 147-148; Lerouge (2007) 99-104.
[24] *Mon. Anc.* 29. See note 11.

major obstacle to her winning power for her own line of descent was the presence of the other, older princes, born of the other royal consorts.[25]

A few years later Phraates IV decided to send his own sons, Seraspadane, Phraates, Rodaspes and Vonones, together with two of their wives and four grandchildren, to Rome.[26] Such events were often considered by a large number of contemporary critics to be the fruit of the strong influence that Queen Musa, could exert on the great King.[27] According to this view, Phraates IV, unable to oppose the desires of his spouse, accepted the exclusion of his older sons from the Parthian political scene, leaving the field open to the succession of the young Phraates, her child. This was Musa's political triumph.

Recent historiography tends to depict the Phraates IV of those years as a weak King, at the mercy of his wife and victim of the fear of a conspiracy by his sons. It is undisputed that his preference for the Prince born of Musa and the memory of how he himself had obtained access to the throne at the expense of his father are key elements for understanding the motivations of such a gesture. We cannot exclude the possibility that at the time of the handover of his sons to M. Titius, governor of Syria between 10 and 9 BC, Phraates IV had already a precise plan in mind. The throne would go to his favourite son Phraates, born of the Roman Musa. To prevent a dynastic crisis and a subsequent civil war, it was therefore necessary to eliminate completely the risk that one of his other sons would exploit the indignation that such a choice would undoubtedly have provoked in the eastern parts of the kingdom, were the opposition to the King was stronger, and rise up in arms against the young heir.[28] The unfortunate nature of Phraates' decision would only reveal itself as such in later years, when Rome found in the exiled members of the royal family in Rome a useful instrument for advantageously filling the power vacuum arising in Parthia after the extinction of the direct Arsacid lineage. The death of the old Great king was conveniently arranged

---

[25] Joseph. *AJ* 18.39-41; Täubler (1904) 24-25; Debevoise (1938) 143; Krämer (1973) 247; Frye (1984) 236; Karras-Klapproth (1988) 95-96.
[26] *Mon. Anc.* 32; Joseph. *AJ* 18.42; Tac. *Ann.* 2.1-2; Vell. Pat. 2.94.4; Just. 42.5.12; Strab. 6.4.2, 16.1.28; Suet. *Aug.* 21.3, 43.4; Eutr. 7.9; Oros. 6.21.29; Nedergaard (1988).
[27] Strugnell (2008) 275-298.
[28] Ziegler (1964) 51-52; Krämer (1973) 247; Romer (1979) 200; Schippmann (1980) 47-48; Dąbrowa (1983) 65 n. 213; Frye (1984) 230; Dąbrowa (1987) 64-65; Wolski (1993) 148.

by a lethal poison, but the reign of Musa and her son lasted only a few years; they were overthrown in 4 AD due to their policy, too explicitly oriented towards a compromise with Rome. Nonetheless according to Flavius Josephus, their rule ended due to the indignation stirred among the aristocratic groups by their scandalous behaviour.[29]

With the end of Musa and her son's rule Augustus lost the chance to strongly influence Parthian policy towards an alliance and a probable submission to Rome.

The leaders of the aristocracy, now the only ones with political power, given the absence of direct descendants of the Arsacid dynasty, now either dead or exiled, offered the crown to Orodes, a prince belonging to a junior branch of the royal family. Just two years later, Orodes himself was the victim of a conspiracy (6 AD). Due to his cruelty, or more likely his attempts to liberate himself from aristocratic control, he fell victim to hired killers during a hunting trip.[30]

At the beginning of the first century AD until 50 AD the Arsacids found in a condition of deep social and institutional instability. The king's leadership had been in fact overruled. Arsacid monarchs were maintained on the throne by the aristocratic groups and royal family members, were induced to rebel against the ruling king with the sole intent of providing a formal legitimacy to the power gained and wielded by one or the other groups of the aristocracy. Parthia was torn apart by competition between the main noble factions embodying the different political orientations coexisting inside the kingdom. They had a common interest in weakening the crown to enlarge their power, thus enhancing their independence from the king.

Having lost the advantages gained during Phraates IV and Phraataces' rule, Augustus realized that as several members of the Arsacid family, the only household entitled to rule Parthia, lived in Rome, he had the opportunity of proposing a Roman candidate for the throne and still playing an important role in intestine struggle for the Arsacid throne.[31] Between 6 and 8 AD in fact a diplomatic delegation headed to Rome to ask Augustus for the return of one of the sons

---

[29] Gregoratti (2012^b).
[30] Joseph. *AJ* 18 45; Wolski (1993) 149.
[31] For the Parthians living in the Roman empire see Gregoratti (2015).

of Phraates IV.[32] The oldest was chosen, Vonones against whom the rival nobility quickly pitted Artabanus, a native Media Atropatene nobleman with strong ties to the eastern nomadic tribe of the *Dahae*. The two pretenders simultaneously minted coins between 9 and 12 AD. Artabanus, initially defeated, was later able to rally a powerful army from the eastern satrapies forcing Vonones to take refuge initially in Seleucia on the Tigris, than in Armenia (12 AD).[33]

For about 50 years almost every emperor of the Julio-Claudian dynasty followed Augustus' policy example of sending to Parthia a prince chosen from the growing community settled in Central Italy, though with no better results.

This series of complicated events appears in the *Res gestae* as a short enumeration of Parthian kings 'who took refuge with me as suppliants'[34] (Tiridates,[35] the usurper and the young Phraates IV), who sought his friendship 'by means of his own children as pledges' (Phraates IV) or were received by the Parthians who asked Augustus for them[36] (Vonones).

Despite the triumphalist tones adopted in the *Res gestae* Augustus' 'kingsmaker' policy failed in Parthia just as it had in Armenia. The kings he claims in the *Res gestae* to have given to the Parthians and the Armenians never managed to secure their throne for more than few years or even months. Augustus' strategy was successful in finding agreement with the Arsacids and selling it as a diplomatic victory and as an act of submission. It was successful in creating the conditions for a robust Roman intervention in Parthian internal affairs. But it failed to realize the audacious ambition of creating a Parthian vassal kingdom, the ambition which had probably induced Crassus to cross the Euphrates half a century before.

---

[32] Joseph. *AJ* 18.46; Suet. *Tib.* 16.1; Tac. *Ann.* 2.1-3, 6.36, 42; Cass. Dio 40.15.3-4; Debevoise (1938) 151; Kahrstedt (1950) 17-18; Ziegler (1964) 56; Pani (1972) 125; Bertinelli (1979) 53; Schippmann (1980) 49; Dąbrowa (1983) 44-45; Wolski (1993) 150.

[33] Joseph. *AJ* 18.48-50; Wiesehöfer (2010) 190-191.

[34] *Mon. Anc.* 32: *Ad me supplices confugerunt reges Parthorum Tirida[te]s et post[ea] Phrates regis Phratis filius.*

[35] Just. 42.5.4-6; Cass. Dio 51.18; Hor. *Epist.* 1.12; *Carm.* 1.26.5; Debevoise (1938) 136-138; Ziegler (1964) 45-46; Timpe (1975) 155-158; Bertinelli (1979) 51; Schippmann (1980) 20, 105-106 and n. 13; Dąbrowa (1983) 40; Frye (1984) 235; Dąbrowa (1989) 312-313; Wolski (1993) 146.

[36] *Mon. Anc.* 33.

The Parthian kingdom was too large, too complex and too torn by civil strife between too many and too diverse aristocratic groups and political subjects. The Romans simply ignored most of the kingdom's delicate internal dynamics and were probably not interested in understanding the changes underway in its ruling structure. Augustus probably underestimated the resources of one of the largest and most powerful states the Romans faced in Asia. This was fatally undermined his plans.

Independently of this reality, the *Res gestae* represent a more simplified, centralized and stereotyped reality, a vision of the world that contained all the information a Roman citizen needed according to Augustus' propaganda. In this propagandistic fiction the Parthians were viewed and treated similarly to the other Near Eastern client kingdoms.

Augustus does not mention the famous meeting at the Euphrates in his political testament because he was well aware of its ideological and political meaning. Acknowledging the existence of a frontier on the Euphrates and meeting Phraataces as an equal ruler, Rome was de facto forced to admit that a limit existed to its expansion in the east. This contrasted openly with the universal aspirations of Augustus' to rule over all the civilized lands. Rome was forced to accept the existence of something else beyond itself, the Parthian state, an insuperable obstacle to the dominion of the world in general and to Alexander's Hellenized East in particular.

In Augustus' fictitious reconstruction of the *res orientales*, the list of kings beyond the river, eager to pay homage to him, wants to prove that despite the military setbacks and the presence of the Parthians, Rome' policy and area of influence had no real boundary in the east and that Augustus' authority was acknowledged beyond the Euphrates like in the west. In other words Rome's propagandistic dream has remained intact.

Of course the reality was very different. All Augustus' attempts to appoint a ruler in Parthia and Armenia were ill-fated. The Euphrates river, although never mentioned in the inscription, stopped Rome's expansion in the east and continued to mark the eastern border of the area under Roman firm control for a long time after Augustus' death. Indeed, until the warlike Trajan attempted to pass this limit with the most formidable invasion army seen since Alexander's time.

Bibliography

Asdourian, P. (1911), *Die politischen Beziehungen zwischen Armenien und Rom von 190 v. Chr. bis 428 n. Chr.*, Freiburg i. d. Schweiz.

Barzanò, A. (1985), 'Roma e i Parti tra pace e guerra fredda nel I secolo dell'impero', in M. Sordi (ed.), *La pace nel mondo antico*, Milano, 211-222.

Bedoukian, P.Z. (1978), *Coinage of the Artaxiads of Armenia*, London.

Bertinelli, M. G. Angeli (1979), *Roma e l'Oriente. Strategia, economia, società e cultura nelle relazioni politiche fra Roma, la Giudea e l'Iran*, Roma.

Bigwood, J.M. (2004), 'Queen Mousa, Mother and Wife (?) of King Phraatakes of Parthia: A Re-evaluation of the Evidence', *Mouseion* 4, 35-70.

Bivar, D.A. (1983), 'The Political History of Iran under the Arsacids', in E. Yarshater (ed.), *The Cambridge History of Iran. The Seleucid, Parthian and Sasanian Periods*, Cambridge, 3.1, 21-99.

Borsak, I. (1998), 'Zum Monumentum Ancyranum', *Acta antiqua Academiae Scientiarum* 38, 41-50.

Braund, D. (1988), 'Client kings', in D. Braund (ed.), *The Administration of the Roman Empire (241 BC-AD 193)*, Exeter, 69-96.

Butcher, K. (2003), *Roman Syria and the Near East*, London.

Campbell, B. (1993), 'War and Diplomacy: Rome and Parthia, 31 BC-AD 235', in J. Rich, A. Shipley (edd.), *War and Society in the Roman World*, London/ New York, 213-240.

Chaumont, M.-L. (1976), 'L'Arménie entre Rome et l'Iran I. De l'avènement d'Auguste à l'avènement de Dioclétien', in H. Temporini, W. Haase (edd.), *Aufstieg und Niedergang der römischen Welt* II.9.1, Berlin/ New York, 71-194.

Cooley, A. (2009), *Res gestae diui Augusti. Text, Translation and Commentary*, Cambridge.

Dąbrowa, E. (1983), *La politique de l'état parthe à l'égard de Rome – d'Artaban II à Vologèse I (ca 11 – ca 79 de n. è.) et les facteurs qui la conditionnaient*, Kraków.

Dąbrowa, E. (1987), 'Les premiers 'otages' parthes à Rome', *Folia Orientalia* 24, 63-71.

Dąbrowa, E. (1989), 'Les héros de luttes politiques dans l'état parthe dans la première moitié du Ier siècle de notre ère', *Iranica Antiqua* 24, 311-322.
Debevoise, N.C. (1938), *A Political History of Parthia*, Chicago.
Downey, G. (1951), 'The Occupation of Syria by the Romans', *Transactions and Proceedings of the American Philological Association* 82, 149-163.
Edwell P. (2010), *Between Rome and Persia. The Middle Euphrates, Mesopotamia and Palmyra under Roman Control*, New York/ London.
Edwell P. (2013), 'The Euphrates as a Boundary between Rome and Parthia in the Late Republic and Early Empire', *Antichton* 47, 191-206.
Ellerbrock, U., Winkelmann, S. (2012), *Die Parther, Die vergessene Grossmacht*, Darmstadt/ Mainz.
Frézouls, Ed. (1995), 'Les relations romano-parthes avant l'époque flavienne', in Ed. Frézouls, A. Jacquemin (edd.), *Les relations internationales. Actes du Colloque de Strasbourg (15-17 juin 1993)*, Paris, 479-498.
Frye, R.N. (1984), *The History of Ancient Iran*, München.
Greatrex, G. (2007), 'Roman frontiers and foreign policy in the East', in R. Alston, S. Lieu (edd.), *Aspects of the Roman Near East, Papers in Honour of Professor Fergus Millar FBA*, Turnhout, 103-173.
Gregoratti, L. (2012[a]), 'Between Rome and Ctesiphon: the problem of ruling Armenia', in Армения – Иран: История. Культура. Современные перспективы развития: Сборник статей [научный редактор Иванов В. Б., научный редактор, составитель Зулумян Б. С.]. Институт стран Азии и Африки МГУ, *Proceedings of the Conference Armenia – Iran: History. Culture. The Modern Perspectives of Progress, June 28, 2010*, Moscow.
Gregoratti, L. (2012[b]), 'Parthian Women in Flavius Josephus', in M. Hirschberger (ed.), *Jüdisch-hellenistische Literatur in ihrem interkulturellen Kontext. Akten der Tagung*, Düsseldorf, 10-11 Februar 2011, Frankfurt, 183-192.
Gregoratti, L. (2015), 'In the Land West of the Euphrates: The Parthians in the Roman Empire', in P. Militello, H. Oniz (edd.), *Proceedings of the 15th Symposium on Mediterranean Archaeology, held at the University of Catania, March 3-5th, 2011 = B.A.R., British Archaeological Reports* 2695, 2, 731-735.

Hackl, U., Jacobs, B., Weber, D., edd. (2010), *Quellen zur Geschichte des Partherreiches*, Göttingen.

Kahrstedt, U. (1950), *Artabanos III. und seine Erben* Dissertationes Bernenses I 2, Bern.

Karras-Klapproth, M. (1988), *Prosopographische Studien zur Geschichte des Partherreiches auf der Grundlage antiker literarischer Überlieferung*, Bonn.

Krämer K. (1973), 'Zum Freundschaftsvertrag zwischen Rom und Parthien unter Augustus', *Klio* 55, 247-248.

Lerouge, Ch. (2007), *L'image des Parthes dans le monde greco-romain. Du début du Ier siècle av. J.-C. jusqu'à la fin du Haut-Empire romain*, Stuttgart.

Luther, A. (2010), 'Zum Orientfeldzug des Gaius Caesar', *Gymnasium* 117, 103-127.

Millar, F. (1993), *The Roman Near East (31 BC – AD 337)*, Cambridge (MA)/ London.

Nedergaard, E. (1988), 'The four sons of Phraates IV in Rome', *Acta Hyperborea* 1, 102-115.

Oltramare, A. (1938), 'Auguste et les Parthes', *Revue des études latines* 16, 121-138.

Pani, M. (1972), *Roma e i re d'Oriente da Augusto a Tiberio (Cappadocia, Armenia, Media Atropatene)*, Bari.

Ramage, E.S. (1987), *The Nature and Purpose of Augustus'* Res gestae, Wiesbaden.

Ridley, R. (2003), *The Emperor's Retrospect: Augustus'* Res gestae *in Epigraphy, Historiography and Commentary*, Dudley.

Romer, F.E. (1974), *G. and L. Caesar in the East*, (Ph.D.thesis), Stanford.

Romer, F.E. (1979), 'Gaius Caesar's Military Diplomacy in the East', *Transactions and Proceedings of the American Philological Association* 109, 199-214.

Sartre, M. (2001), *D'Alexandre à Zénobie: le Levant antique, IVe siècle av. J.-C.-IIIe siècle apr. J.-C.*, Paris.

Schippmann, K. (1980), *Grundzüge der parthischen Geschichte*, Darmstadt.

Shayegan, M.R. (2011), *Arsacids and Sasanians. Political Ideology in Post-Hellenistic and Late Antique Persia*, Cambridge.

Strugnell E. (2008), 'Thea Musa, Roman Queen of Parthia', *Iranica Antiqua* 43, 275-298.
Täubler, E. (1904), *Die Parthernachrichten bei Josephus*, Berlin.
Timpe, D. (1975), 'Zur augusteischen Partherpolitik zwischen 30 und 20 v. Chr.', *Würzburger Jahrbücher für die Altertumswissenschaft* 1, 155-169.
Traina, G. (2010), *La resa di Roma. Battaglia a Carre, 9 giugno 53 a.C.*, Roma/ Bari.
van der Vin, J.P.A. (1981), 'The Return of Roman Ensigns from Parthia', *Bulletin antieke beschaving* 56, 117-139.
Wheeler, E.L. (2002), 'Roman treaties with Parthia: Völkerrecht or power politics?', in P. Freeman, J. Bennett, Z. T. Fiema, B. Hoffmann (edd.), *Limes 18. Proceedings of the 18th International Congress of Roman Frontier Studies held in Amman, Jordan (September 2000)*, Oxford, 281-286.
Wiesehöfer, J. (1994), *Das antike Persien. Von 550 v. Chr. bis 650 n. Chr.*, München/ Zürich.
Wiesehöfer, J. (1998), *Das Partherreich und seine Zeugnisse, Beiträge des internationalen Colloquiums. Eutin (27.-30. Juni 1996)*, Stuttgart.
Wiesehöfer, J. (2010), 'Augustus und die Parther', in R. Aßkamp, T. Esch (edd.), *Imperium. Varus und seine Zeit*, Münster, 187-195.
Wolski, J. (1993), 'L'Empire des Arsacides', *Acta Iranica* 32, Leuven.
Zetzel, J.E.G. (1970), 'New Light on Gaius Caesar's Eastern Campaign', *Greek, Roman and Byzantine Studies* 11, 259-266.
Ziegler, K.-H. (1964), *Die Beziehungen zwischen Rom und dem Partherreich. Ein Beitrag zur Geschichte des Völkerrechts*, Wiesbaden.

Augustus and the Children: Family and Childhood in Augustus' Policies and in Augustan Literature

CRISTINA SANTOS PINHEIRO
Universidade da Madeira
Centro de Estudos Clássicos da Faculdade de Letras da Universidade de Lisboa

The aim of this volume is to celebrate the completion of the second millennium after Augustus' death, but according to Tacitus (*Ann.* 1.53), Julia, Augustus' only daughter, whom he exiled for adultery in 2 BC, died in that same year of AD 14. United in death, the stern father and the adulterous daughter represent two central and opposing facets of the *Saeculum Augustum*: the *Princeps'* striving for morality and Julia's supposedly dissolute way of life.

The Augustan era was characterized by this and many other contradictions. Combining an omnipresent evocation of the past with conspicuous innovations, the *Princeps* refashioned the ancestral virtues in order to make them the chief tenet of his political and social agenda. Augustus' unprecedented moral laws, implementing measures related to marriage, procreation and adultery, introduced in Roman society an obvious opposition between the ideals they attempt to restore and a reality that, by then, was far removed from the *exempla* of the past. Families had changed. Marriage patterns had changed. Marriage with *manus* was by then obsolete, so that married women remained legally a member of their birth families. Divorce and remarriage were increasingly recurrent practices as was the refusal to marry and to enter *iustae nuptiae*.[1]

The elegiac love poets created a literary genre supported by these new features and related to what has been classified as a 'new woman' or an 'emancipated woman', expressions that describe a woman in a

---

[1] On the date of the disappearance of *manus* marriage, cf. Treggiari (1991) 21, 30-31; Dixon (1992) 73-74; Grubbs (2002) 21.

high social position, 'who nevertheless claims for herself the indulgence in sexuality of a woman of pleasure,' as Fantham[2] states. But an ideal featuring a chaste and loving wife endures even in love elegy. These two different types of women create an ironic tension in elegiac poetry that is sometimes difficult to resolve. Tibullus may dream in his bucolic idylls with an humble Delia, as he does in 1.5.19-36, living in the country like the virtuous matrons of the past. But this is just a dream, for Delia is enslaved to a procuress and must look for a wealthier lover.

The elegiac mistress can be imagined in a harmonious relationship, but motives like the *seruitium* and the *militia amoris* are contrary to conventional social values. In elegy 2.7, about a law that was withdrawn and that would have coerced Propertius to marry another woman, he declares with disgust:

> Vnde mihi patriis natos praebere triumphis?
> nullus de nostro sanguine miles erit.
>
> vv. 13-14

In spite of the obscurity involving this elegy and the law mentioned, and leaving aside the complexity of its being classified as Augustan or anti-Augustan, it is clear that for the poetic persona war, marriage and parenthood were not his aims.[3] He concludes:

> Tu mihi sola places: placeam tibi, Cynthia, solus:
> hic erit et patrio nomine pluris amor.
>
> vv. 19-20

We do not know why Propertius could not have married Cynthia – was she a *femina probrosa*,[4] a woman not eligible for marriage? – but this kind of relationship is typically described as self-sufficient and

---

[2] Fantham (1994) 280.
[3] As Propertius Book 2 was probably published c. 26 or 25 BC, this poem has led scholars like Galinsky (1981) 127 and Bauman (1992) 107-108 to suggest that Augustus had tried to introduce some measures related to marriage in the early 20s. Cf. Badian (1985), defending that there was no law, but a tax, the *aes uxorious*, implemented by the triumvirs and abolished by Augustus. For an analysis of the poem, cf. Gale (1997). Hallett (1973) is still a good study about women in elegy.
[4] Astolfi (1986) 54 ff. According to Thomas (2007) 247, *femina probrosa* 'est une expression juridique mettant l'accent sur la dégradation morale et sociale, alors que *meretrix* réfère à l'immoralité sexuelle.'

hildren take no part in it.[5] The conflict between the demands of love and of society and the complex equation of giving oneself to *nequitia amoris* or to public obligations are certainly elegiac conventions, but nevertheless, and even if they are not to be taken at face value, they are important elements of Augustan poetry. Wallace-Hadrill[6] rightly asserts that:

> The benefit and the danger of the poets to Augustus was not that they could support or oppose any particular measure of his, but that they could (intentionally or not) articulate acceptance or rejection of the social order he was struggling to restore and of his own role in doing so.

In fact, a rise in individualism was perceived as a threat to family life, especially when associated with the feeling that Roman society was experiencing religious and moral degeneration. Decades of disruption caused by civil struggle and political insecurity were viewed as the consequence of moral and familial decay. The exploitation of pessimistic topics like a decline in piety, sexual immorality, indulgence in pleasure, excessive ambition or civic upheaval is omnipresent in Augustan literature. I will merely cite here Horace's characterizing his age as *impia... deuoti sanguinis aeta*s (*Ep.* 16.9) and *fecunda culpae saecula* (*Carm.* 3.6.17) or rebuking his contemporaries for having destroyed the virtuous austerity of the Romans' ancestors.[7]

Nevertheless, ideals related to family relationships, intermingled with these pessimistic traits, assume a new prominence. Dixon[8] claims that an affectionate ideal of family life was under development by the late Republic. Augustus shrewdly exploited it and the poets in his entourage, especially Horace, evoke the *Princeps*' responsibility for restoring the ancestors' virtuous way of life. Linking Augustus and an idea of a new golden age emerging as a result of his policies is a

---

[5] In Ovid *Amores* 2.13 and 2.14 – two poems about Corinna's abortion – the worries expressed are not related to the loss of the *foetus*, but to Corinna's possible death. About these poems, cf. Cahoon (1988), Gamel (1989), and Pinheiro (2010).
[6] Wallace-Hadrill (1985) 184.
[7] An important piece of evidence for this is, of course, Livy's preface, with its bleakness and misgiving. The decay of *disciplina* and *mores* led to a time with no hope of recovery: *donec ad haec tempora quibus nec uitia nostra nec remedia pati possumus peruentum est.* (*praef.* 9).
[8] Dixon (1996) 111.

commonplace to be found in texts such as Vergil's *Aeneid* or Horace's *Carmina*.[9] Advertising his and his family's links with the *summi uiri* of the Roman past, as he does in his Forum, Augustus constructs his own public image and legitimizes his newly acquired political position. He shrewdly assumes his identity as *Diui filius*, thus justifying his right to vindicate Caesar's death. Some decades later, though, he becomes the *Pater Patriae*. The point was that he was not a newcomer: he was a member of the *Julii*, but, more importantly, he was a descendant of Aeneas through a long line of the most important and praiseworthy heroes of the Roman past.[10]

The *leges Iuliae* on marriage were issued in 18 BC – the *lex Iulia de maritandis ordinibus* and the *lex Iulia de adulteriis coercendis* – and were revised by *the lex Papia Poppaea* in AD 9. We do not know for sure which provisions belong to the former or to the latter because later jurists usually talk about them without making a clear distinction, referring to them generally as 'laws about marriage' or *leges Iulia et Papia*. They were designed to penalize those citizens who refused to marry (or remarry after divorce or the death of the spouse) and those who were childless, men between the ages of 25 and 60, and women between 20 and 50 years old. The penalties were mainly constraints in receiving and bequeathing inheritances. The laws also imposed some restrictions upon the choice of a spouse, especially among the upper classes: senators and their descendants were prohibited from marrying freedmen or freedwomen. Free citizens should not marry *infames*. By the *ius trium liberorum*, granted to free citizens with three or more children and to freedmen and freedwomen with four or more, women could attain freedom from guardianship and men had priority in receiving government appointments.[11]

The adultery law established heavy penalties for those who were involved in extramarital liaisons. A permanent court was established and hence the jurisdiction was removed from the familial sphere, where these failings had been treated in the past. By transforming adultery and *stuprum* into civil crimes, the laws curtailed the power of

---

[9] Cf. Galinsky (1996) 90 ff. and Verg. *Aen.* 1.291-296, 6.791-795; Hor. *Carm.* 4.5.21-24, 4.15.9-11.
[10] About Augustus' connection with the symbols of the Roman past, cf. e.g. Alberto (2004).
[11] About the laws, cf., for instance, Raditsa (1980), Astolfi (1986), Cohen (1991), and McGinn (1998).

the *paterfamilias* to cope with this kind of situation, as was expected previously. These regulations blurred the lines between public and private and family life came under state inspection. The policing of sexual behaviour was part of the aforementioned attempt to reinforce the *exempla* of the past. Family, sexuality and reproduction were now opened to public scrutiny.

Reaction to Augustus' legislation seems to have been fierce, and it was revised in AD 9. It is hard to believe that when he read Quintus Metellus' speech in the Senate, he voiced every Roman man's opinion about marriage, but the choice of this particular speech was not irrelevant. In this, a Metellus, probably the Metellus Macedonicus who had been censor in 131 BC or, according to Aulus Gellius, Metellus Numidicus, censor in 102 BC, urged Romans to marry and to have children, subjugating thereby their personal wishes to the public well-being. In Aulus Gellius' version, the speech, entitled *De ducendis uxoribus*, reads as follows:

> Si sine uxore possemus, Quirites, omnes ea molestia careremus; set quoniam ita natura tradidit, ut nec cum illis satis commode, nec sine illis ullo modo uiui possit, saluti perpetuae potius quam breui uoluptati consulendum est.

Livy asserts that the speech seemed to have been written with his and Augustus' own times in mind (*oratio... uelut in haec tempora scriptam*).[12]

Suetonius mentions an event, maybe the same described by Cassius Dio in AD 9. When the knights attending a public show persistently called for the repeal of the law about marriage, Augustus sent for the children of Germanicus and exhibited them, some in his own lap and some in their father's, suggesting by his gestures and his expression that the *equites* should not refuse to follow Germanicus' example (Suet. *Aug.* 34).

The claim that marriage and children are civic duties springs from a deep-rooted patriotic sense and re-emerges with special strength in the Augustan age. We can identify this same topic in two speeches Cassius

---

[12] *Q. Metellus censor censuit, ut cogerentur omnes ducere uxores liberorum creandorum causa. extat oratio eius, quam Augustus Caesar, <cum> de maritandis ordinibus ageret, uelut in haec tempora scriptam in senatu recitauit.* (Livy *Per.* 59).

Dio assigns to Augustus (56.1-5). In AD 9, the *equites* were seeking the repeal of the *lex Papia-Poppaea*, which revised some of the measures of the *leges Iuliae* of 18 BC. In one part of the Forum, Augustus assembled the married *equites*, in the other the single and childless. With grief he realised that the former, the married, were much fewer in number than the latter. First he addressed the married *equites*, whom he highly praised, because, as he supposedly said, they aggrandize the fatherland and, bringing children into the world, they achieve a kind of immortality. In fact, the generations succeeding like torch-bearers in a race ensure the existence of Rome, not only its physical existence, but also and more importantly, its cultural legacy, the deeds and virtues of the Roman past.[13] Then he added:

> πῶς μὲν γὰρ οὐκ ἄριστον γυνὴ σώφρων οἰκουρὸς οἰκονόμος παιδοτρόφος ὑγιαίνοντά τε εὐφρᾶναι καὶ ἀσθενοῦντα θεραπεῦσαι, εὐτυχοῦντί τε συγγενέσθαι καὶ δυστυχοῦντα παραμυθήσασθαι, τοῦ τε νέου τὴν ἐμμανῆ φύσιν καθεῖρξαι καὶ τοῦ πρεσβυτέρου τὴν ἔξωρον αὐστηρότητα κεράσαι; πῶς δ' οὐχ ἡδὺ ἀνελέσθαι τέκνον ἐξ ἀμφοῖν συμπεφυκὸς καὶ θρέψαι καὶ παιδεῦσαι, εἰκόνα μὲν τοῦ σώματος εἰκόνα δὲ καὶ τῆς ψυχῆς, ὥστε ἐν ἐκείνῳ αὐξηθέντι ἕτερον αὐτὸν γενέσθαι; (Cass. Dio 56.3.3-4)

> (...) is there anything better than a wife who is chaste, domestic, a good house-keeper, a rearer of children; one to gladden you in health, to tend you in sickness; to be your partner in good fortune, to console you in misfortune; to restrain the mad passion of youth and to temper the unseasonable harshness of old age? And is it not a delight to acknowledge a child who shows the endowments of both parents, to nurture and educate it, at once the physical and the spiritual image of yourself, so that in its growth another self lives again?
>
> transl. Cary (1924) 8-9

The description of the wife must be stressed. This wife is not the *molestia* referred to by Metellus. She gladdens, she tends, she consoles... She is the ideal woman. And the experience of raising and educating children is delightful and extremely rewarding. These married equestrians embraced parenthood as their duty and, as Dio's Augustus asserts, they alone are rightfully called 'Romans, citizens and fathers'. The speech he addresses to the unmarried exploits the same topic, but

---

[13] About life as a torch-bearers race, cf. Luc. 2.77-79: *augescunt aliae gentes, aliae minuuntur,/ inque breui spatio mutantur saecla animantum/ et quasi cursores uitai lampada tradunt.*

in the reverse mode. They are not to be called men, nor citizens, nor Romans, because they refuse to act like true citizens, ensuring Rome's safety through parenting.[14] Instead, they are destroying their families and betraying their country:

> καὶ γὰρ μιαιφονεῖτε, μηδὲ τεκνοῦντες ἀρχὴν τοὺς ἐξ ὑμῶν γεννηθῆναι ὀφείλοντας, καὶ ἀνοσιουργεῖτε, τά τε ὀνόματα καὶ τὰς τιμὰς τῶν προγόνων παύοντες, καὶ ἀσεβεῖτε, τά τε γένη ὑμῶν τὰ καταδειχθέντα ὑπὸ τῶν θεῶν ἀφανίζοντες, καὶ τὸ μέγιστον τῶν ἀναθημάτων αὐτῶν, τὴν ἀνθρωπίνην φύσιν, ἀπολλύντες, τά τε ἱερὰ διὰ τούτου καὶ τοὺς ναοὺς αὐτῶν ἀνατρέποντες. καὶ μέντοι καὶ τὴν πολιτείαν καταλύετε, μὴ πειθόμενοι τοῖς νόμοις, καὶ τὴν πατρίδα προδίδοτε, στερίφην τε αὐτὴν καὶ ἄγονον ἀπεργαζόμενοι. (Cass. Dio 56.5.1-3)

> For you are committing murder in not begetting in the first place those who ought to be your descendants; you are committing sacrilege in putting an end to the names and honours of your ancestors; and you are guilty of impiety in that you are abolishing your families, which were instituted by the gods, and destroying the greatest of offerings to them, – human life, – thus overthrowing their rites and their temples. Moreover, you are destroying the State by disobeying its laws, and you are betraying your country by rendering her barren.
>
> transl. Cary (1924) 13

The vocabulary of crime, sacrilege and subversion (μιαιφονεῖτε; ἀνοσιουργεῖτε; ἀσεβεῖτε; μὴ πειθόμενοι; προδίδοτε) is firmly stressed. What they are doing endangers the social order and the legacy of their ancestors, he says.

The speeches are obviously Dio's invention. Nevertheless, they show us how, even centuries later, Augustus' public image was still so strongly connected with the ideal of marriage and family as civic duties. The main topics explored by Dio are consistent both with Augustan propaganda and with Dio's perspective of Augustus' 'immense institutional achievement as founder of a stable monarchy,' as Kemezis[15] states, analysing the complex image of the first *princeps* conveyed in Dio's text. In fact, the composition of the speeches shows

---

[14] Cass. Dio 56.4.2: ἄνδρας; ἀλλ' οὐδὲν ἀνδρῶν ἔργον παρέχεσθε. πολίτας; ἀλλ' ὅσον ἐφ' ὑμῖν, ἡ πόλις ἀπόλλυται. Ῥωμαίους; ἀλλ' ἐπιχειρεῖτε τὸ ὄνομα τοῦτο καταλῦσαι. 'Men? But you are not performing any of the offices of men. Citizens? But for all that you are doing, the city is perishing. Romans? But you are undertaking to blot out this name altogether,' transl. Cary (1924) 11.
[15] Kemezis (2007) 273.

how Augustus came to be identified with the moralizing purposes of the laws, even if these purposes stand in contrast with the actual behaviour of the *princeps* and of many of the members of the imperial *domus*, creating thus what Kemezis identifies as an 'ironic paradigm'.

This sentimental and affectionate ideal of the family as a network of relationships that makes life complete is not an invention of the Augustan age,[16] but Augustus and the Augustan poets – and even Livy – thoroughly exploited a set of ideas about family that included (among many others) female chastity, procreation as civic duty, compliance to the *exempla* of the Roman past, etc. We can identify this feeling in the early 40's BC. Regardless of how we decide to interpret Vergil's *Eclogue* 4, the so-called 'Messianic eclogue', the same picture is there. The unknown *puer* associated with fertility and peace and a symbol of the new golden age is a Vergilian innovation. But if we set aside the religious, political and metaphorical overtones, we still have a tender description of the birth of a child as a blessed event, with all expectation and hope for the future it involves. Whether this is a real boy or not – maybe the much hoped-for child of Antonius and Octavia after Brundisium – he is urged to smile at his mother, because if he refuses to do so, 'no god will invite him to table, no goddess to bed' (*Ecl.* 4.62-63).[17]

In Vergil's epic masterpiece, although some scholars point to the loss of Creusa and the abandonment of Dido as proof that Aeneas' succession proceeded through males only, I would suggest that, in spite of the dismissal of these two characters, there is a strong presence of the loving family ideal.[18] Lavinia stands for this, and there is a conspicuous feeling that in the future there will be peace for the Trojans. This peace will come from the marriage to Lavinia. Because, almost as the *puer* of *Eclogue* 4, Lavinia is the symbol of a new age for Aeneas and for the Trojan refugees. She represents Aeneas' duty to carry on, in a way that was not possible for Creusa or Dido. Destiny, family and duty are

---

[16] We can see it for example in Lucretius, *De rerum natura*. When describing the losses caused by death, he writes: *Iam iam non domus accipiet te laeta neque uxor/ optima, nec dulces occurrent oscula nati/ praeripere et tacita pectus dulcedine tangent*. (3.894-396).

[17] *qui non risere parenti,/ nec deus hunc mensa, dea nec dignata cubili est.*

[18] But it was Dido who in the first place voiced this ideal, when, revolted at Aeneas' decision to leave her, she regretted not having a *paruulus Aeneas*, a little Aeneas, playing in her palace.

so strongly connected in Aeneas' mind that Mercury can confidently remind the Trojan of Ascanius' future and expect the father immediately to leave Carthage, despite Dido's accusations.[19]

This brings me to Ascanius' importance in the epic. Although it has been variously interpreted, Ascanius is, in my opinion, not a peripheral but a chief character. This is not primarily because of his prominence as an agent, but especially for the reason that he symbolizes the future. In addition, he seems at times to have the capability of embodying every woman's child. Masquerading as *dulcis Ascanius*, Cupid can infect Dido with passion. Fascinating her with the presence of Aeneas' son, whom Dido embraces, Venus and Cupid are able to guarantee that the Trojans are safe in Carthage. The queen seems to be enchanted, in fact, with the tender image of the child, possibly because he is a symbol of the family she longs for.[20] For Andromache, in Book 3, Ascanius can also be a substitute for Astyanax (3.485); in Book 9, he assures Euryalus that Euryalus' mother will be like his own (9.297-298); in Book 5, to stop the Trojan women from burning the ships, he shouts at them: 'I'm your Ascanius,' throwing his helmet to the floor so that the women can recognize his face (5.672-673).[21] In the much debated farewell of father and son in Book 12, the fact that Aeneas does not remove the weapons, before issuing the words *disce, puer, uirtutem ex me uerumque laborem/ fortunam ex aliis*, contrary to what Hector had done in *Iliad* 6, proves that here Ascanius is not just the tender and much beloved son, but his father's heir, the inheritance being precisely *uirtus* and *labor*.

Ascanius is one of Aeneas' motives – maybe the stronger motive – to move towards the future. Aeneas is, in more than one sense, a torch bearer. He must pass it on to his descendants. The prominence of the Anchises-Aeneas-Ascanius group at this time demonstrates how

---

[19] Verg. *Aen.* 4.272-276: *Si te nulla mouet tantarum gloria rerum/ [nec super ipse tua moliris laude laborem,]/ Ascanium surgentem et spes heredis Iuli/ respice, cui regnum Italiae Romanaque tellus/ debetur.*

[20] Cf. *Aen.* 4.32, 4.84-85, 4.373-430.

[21] Merriam (2002) 853, analysing Ascanius' presence in the *Aeneid*, concludes that he '(...) does not mature into a replica of his father through the course of the epic, showing more and more concern for the welfare of others, but instead remains a heedless child, concerned only with its own interests, passions and enthusiasms?' I think that his lack of maturity is linked precisely with the importance of his characterization as a substitute child. Cf. Pinheiro (2012) 226 ff. and Golden (2013) 253 ff.

important familial values like *pietas* were. Aeneas must carry on, in order to save the Trojan legacy and pass it on to his Roman descendants. *Pietas*, the central moral value in the *Aeneid*, blends exactly the three central dimensions of the Augustan age: gods, fatherland, and family.

That is, I think, a key feature in Augustus' social policies: private aspects of life, like marriage, parenthood and sexuality are combined – not always easily – with public life, being in the process introduced into a political discourse that defines Roman civic identity. Being a Roman was, like never before, being a husband or a wife, a father or a mother. Not complying with this is a religious, a moral and a social fraud that endangers the existence of the *Res publica*.

According to Pliny the Elder, Augustus had a statue of Cornelia, mother of the Gracchi, previously displayed in the *Porticus Metelli*, moved to the *Porticus Octauiae*, built in his sister's name.[22] Talking about the number of children a woman can conceive, Aulus Gellius wrote that one of Augustus' slaves had given birth to quintuplets, but all, mother and children, were dead within a few days. By Augustus' order, a statue was built to her memory on the Via Laurentina (Gell. 10.2.2).[23] Statues of women displayed in public places were very rare under the Republic. According to Flory,[24] the references to women being honoured with public monuments usually concern mythical, legendary or divine women. Real women seem not to have been granted this kind of tribute until Augustan times. Cornelia, in particular, is a case in point. The statue, whose base reads *Cornelia mater Gracchorum*, was, according to Plutarch, voted by the people of Rome in the last decades of the Republic. The connection between Cornelia and the slave seems straightforward and extremely productive in terms of Augustan propaganda. They were both symbols of femininity and motherhood and they were important and active – or as active as they could have

---

[22] Plin. *HN* 34.31: *Exstant Catonis in censura uociferationes mulieribus statuas Romanis in prouinciis poni; nec tamen potuit inhibere, quo minus Romae quoque ponerentur, sicuti Corneliae Gracchorum matri, quae fuit Africani prioris filia. sedens huic posita soleisque sine ammento insignis in Metelli publica porticu, quae statua nunc est in Octauiae operibus.* About the dedication of the statue, cf. Plut. *Vit. C. Gracch*, 4.4.

[23] *Sed et diuo Augusto imperante, qui temporum eius historiam scripserunt, ancillam Caesaris Augusti in agro Laurente peperisse quinque pueros dicunt eosque pauculos dies uixisse; matrem quoque eorum non multo, postquam peperit, mortuam, monumentumque ei factum iussu Augusti in uia Laurentina, inque eo scriptum esse numerum puerperii eius, de quo diximus.*

[24] Flory (1993).

been – in politics. Virtuous wives and fertile mothers, they strove for the *Res publica*, offering their services as *genetrices* to the state. The three marriages of Julia were certainly in line with her father's clear intention to make her assume a familial role. Augustus was at pains to show his daughter as a model Roman matrona.[25] *Romanitas* for women, even more than for men, meant being married and having children. So Treggiari asserts that: 'Being a mother was a particular service. The sudden appearance of portraits of women in public spaces in the city as role models as well as objects of veneration showed that all citizen women had a role to play.'[26]

For their fertility, these women had become a symbol of social well-being and safety and, as such, they seem to have deserved an honour that was awarded to men who had distinguished themselves in politics or war. In 35 BC, extraordinary honours were granted to Octavia and Livia: *sacrosanctitas*, the tribunician safeguard against physical violence, freedom from guardianship, and statues.[27] These seem to have been the first statues of real women in the imperial family to have been displayed in public spaces. Many more were yet to come. Notwithstanding the established practice of erecting monuments representing women and even entire families in the East, the western part of the empire seems to have been more reluctant to accept the commemoration of women and children, at least in official art. In this respect, Augustus seems to have led the way.

Some children appeared in republican public art, but their presence was not frequent and usually it was idealized. They were often represented as generic figures. If we consider, even briefly, the *Ara Pacis*, women and children – both real women and children, and idealized or mythological characters – are conspicuous. For my argument, it is not important *to play the 'Who was who?' game* imposed by the frieze. However, the representation of children in various ways, some as little Romans, with togas and *bullae*, others in barbarian costumes, with *torques*, poses some interesting questions. According to Uzzi, 'the Ara Pacis is the earliest imperial monument on which children appear.'[28]

---

[25] Cf. Severy (2003) 67.
[26] Treggiari (2005) 142.
[27] According to Cass. Dio 49.38.
[28] Uzzi (2005) 142.

Their presence among the adults, both members of the imperial family and magistrates, must therefore be of importance. The basis for the recognized dynastic nature of the frieze lies in the representation of the different generations composing the family of Augustus. Children stand for the future.

I shall agree with authors like Pollini,[29] Rose,[30] Uzzi[31] or Kleiner, Buxton[32] here and consider the little barbarians as foreign princes and not as Gaius Caesar and Lucius Caesar dressed as Trojans. With their non-Roman costumes and hairstyles, these two boys show how the empire had grown to encompass foreign countries, not only through conquest but also and, more importantly, through diplomacy. Suetonius reports that Augustus treated these children as his own, educating them and encouraging intermarriages, as was for instance the case of Juba, king of Mauretania, and Cleopatra Selene, Cleopatra's and Antonius' daughter, raised in Octavia's household.[33] This was a strategy to expand Augustus' power that demonstrates the external acknowledgment of Roman hegemony. In the *Ara Pacis* frieze, these children represent the global nature of the *pax augusta*. So, the altar is not just a commemoration of family and empire; it also shows how children – both Roman and foreign – are important to the establishment of peace.

According to McGinn,[34] the Augustan marriage laws reinforced a previous trend in Roman law towards the favoring of children. As time went by, children and women became frequent presences both in private and in public art, showing thus a new appreciation of the family unit. Ex-slave families advertised their newly acquired citizen status in family memorials where children were given a special place. Dressed in togas and wearing *bullae*, these children are tokens for citizenship. That was exactly what Augustus had wished.

---

[29] Pollini (1986).
[30] Rose (1990).
[31] Uzzi (2005) 147-148.
[32] Kleiner, Buxton (2008).
[33] Suet. *Aug.* 48: *Regnorum quibus belli iure potitus est, praeter pauca, aut iisdem quibus ademerat reddidit aut alienigenis contribuit. Reges socios etiam inter semet ipsos necessitudinibus mutuis iunxit, promptissimus affinitatis cuiusque atque amicitiae conciliator et fautor; nec aliter uniuersos quam membra partisque imperii curae habuit, rectorem quoque solitus apponere aetate paruis aut mente lapsis, donec adolescerent aut resipiscerent; ac plurimorum liberos et educauit simul cum suis et instituit.*
[34] McGinn (2013) 357.

Bibliography

Alberto, P.F. (2004), 'O simbólico na construção da imagem e do programa ideológico de Augusto: os mitos da fundação da Cidade', *Ágora* 6, 27-50.
Astolfi, R. (1986²), *La Lex Iulia e Papia*, Padua.
Badian, E. (1985), 'A phantom Roman marriage law', *Philologus* 129, 82-98.
Bauman, R. (1992), *Women and Politics in Ancient Rome*, London.
Cahoon, L. (1988), 'The bed as battlefield: erotic conquest and military metaphor in Ovid's *Amores*', *Transactions and Proceedings of the American Philological Association* 118, 293-307.
Cary, E. (1924), *Dio Cassius. Roman History*, vol. 7, books 56-60, London/ Cambridge (MA).
Cohen, D. (1991), 'The Augustan law on adultery: the social and cultural context', in D.I. Kertzer, R.P. Saller (edd.), *The Family in Italy from Antiquity to the Present*, New Haven, 109-126.
Dixon, S. (1992), *The Roman Family*, Baltimore.
Dixon, S. (1996), 'The sentimental idea of the Roman family', in B. Rawson (ed.), *Marriage, Divorce, and Children in Ancient Rome*, Canberra/ Oxford/ New York, 99-113.
Fantham, E. (1994), 'Women, family, and sexuality in the Age of Augustus and the Julio-Claudians', in E. Fantham, H.P. Foley, N.B. Kampen, S.B. Pomeroy, A. Shapiro (edd.), *Women in the Classical World. Image and Text*, New York/ Oxford, 294-329.
Flory, M.B. (1993), 'Livia and the History of Public Honorific Statues for Women in Rome', *Transactions and Proceedings of the American Philological Association* 123, 287-308.
Gale, M.R. (1997), 'Propertius 2.7: *Militia Amoris* and the ironies of elegy', *Journal of Roman Studies* 87, 77-91.
Galinsky, K. (1981), 'Augustus' legislation on morals and marriage', *Philologus* 125, 126-144.
Galinsky, K. (1996), *Augustan Culture. An Interpretive Introduction*, Princeton.
Gamel, M.-K. (1989), 'Non sine caede: abortion politics and poetics in Ovid's *Amores*', *Helios* 16, 183-206.

Golden, M. (2013), 'Children in Latin Epic', in J. Evans Grubbs, T. Parkin, R. Bell (edd.), *Childhood and Education in the Classical World*, Oxford, 249-263.

Grubbs, J.E. (2002), *Women and the Law in the Roman Empire*, London/ New York.

Hallett, J.P. (1973), 'The role of women in Roman elegy: counter-cultural feminism', *Arethusa* 6, 104-124.

Kemezis, A.M. (2007), 'Augustus and the ironic paradigm: Cassius Dio's portrayal of the *Lex Julia* and *Lex Papia Poppaea*', *Phoenix* 61, 270-284.

Kleiner, D.E.E., Buxton, B. (2008), 'Pledges of Empire: The *Ara Pacis* and the Donations of Rome', *American Journal of Archaeology* 112, 57-89.

Lee, G. (1994), *Propertius. The Poems*, Oxford.

McGinn, Th.A.J. (1998), *Prostitution, Sexuality, and the Law in Ancient Rome*, New York.

McGinn, Th.A.J. (2013), 'Roman children and the law', in J. Evans Grubbs, T. Parkin, R. Bell (edd.), *Childhood and Education in the Classical World*, Oxford, 341-362.

Merriam, C.U. (2002), 'Storm warning: Ascanius' appearances in the *Aeneid*', *Latomus* 61, 852-860.

Pinheiro, C.S. (2010), '*Suos utero quae necat* (*Am.* 2.14.38): aborto, sexualidade e medicina no tempo de Ovídio', in C. Pimentel, N.S. Rodrigues (coords.), *Sociedade, Poder e Cultura no Tempo de Ovídio*, Lisboa/ Coimbra, 173-186.

Pinheiro, C.S. (2012), *Orbae Matres: A dor da mãe pela perda de um filho na Literatura Latina*, Lisboa.

Pollini, J. (1986), 'Ahenobarbi, Appuleii and some others on the Ara Pacis', *American Journal of Archaeology* 90, 453-460.

Raditsa, L.F. (1980), 'Augustus' legislation concerning marriage, procreation, love affairs and adultery', *Aufstieg und Niedergang der römischen Welt* II.13, 278-339.

Rose, C.B. (1990), 'Princes and barbarians on the *Ara Pacis*', *American Journal of Archaeology* 94, 453-467.

Severy, B. (2003), *Augustus and the Family at the Birth of the Roman Empire*, London/ New York.

Teixeira, C.A. (2009), 'Casamento, adultério e sexualidade no Direito Romano: o caso particular da *lex Iulia de maritandis ordinibus* e da *lex Iulia de adulteriis coercendis*' in M. Ramos, M.C. Fialho, N.S. Rodrigues (coords.), *A Sexualidade no Mundo Antigo*, Porto/ Coimbra/ Lisboa, 361-366.

Thomas, J.-F. (2007), *Déshonneur et honte en Latin: étude sémantique*, Leuven.

Treggiari, S. (1991), *Roman Marriage. 'Iusti Coniuges' from the Time of Cicero to the Time of Ulpian*, Oxford, Clarendon Press.

Treggiari, S. (2005), 'Women in the time of Augustus', in K. Galinsky (ed.), *The Cambridge Companion to the Age of Augustus*, Cambridge, 130-147.

Uzzi, J.D. (2005), *Children in the Visual Arts of Imperial Rome*, Cambridge.

Wallace-Hadrill, A. (1985), 'Propaganda and dissent? Augustan moral legislation and the Love-Poets', *Klio* 67, 180-184.

La preghiera di Augusto

PAOLA PINOTTI
Università di Bologna

Suetonio informa dettagliatamente, nella *Vita di Augusto*, sulle preferenze del *princeps* in campo linguistico:

> genus eloquendi secutus est elegans et temperatum, uitatis sententiarum ineptiis atque concinnitate et reconditorum uerborum, ut ipse dicit, foetoribus (...). Cacozelos et antiquarios, ut diuerso genere uitiosos, pari fastidio spreuit (...)...nec Tiberio parcit et exoletas interdum et reconditas uoces aucupanti(...);[1]

rimproverando poi M. Antonio per le sue scelte *in eligendo genere dicendi*, scriveva:

> tuque dubitas, Cimberne Annius an Veranius Flaccus imitandi sint tibi, ita ut uerbis, quae Crispus Sallustius excerpsit ex Originibus Catonis, utaris? an potius Asiaticorum oratorum inanis sententiis uerborum uolubilitas in nostrum sermonem transferenda?[2]

Dunque emerge dalla testimonianza dello storico una insofferenza di Augusto sia per la vacua leziosità degli oratori asiani, sia soprattutto per lo stile arcaizzante e l'uso di vocaboli disusati.[3]

D'altra parte, nella sua azione volta a ripristinare gli antichi *mores* e i valori religiosi caduti in disuso nell'ultimo periodo della repubblica, il *princeps* dovette di necessità impegnarsi non solo a restaurare a livello architettonico gli edifici sacri fatiscenti,[4] ma a rivitalizzare collegi sacerdotali come i *fratres Aruales* o i *sodales Titii*, dei quali entrava a far parte in qualità di *magister*, partecipando personalmente a cerimonie decisamente connotate dall'arcaismo così nel rituale come

---

[1] Suet. *Aug.* 86.1-2.
[2] Suet. *Aug.* 86.3.
[3] Cf. Vannini (2013) 210.
[4] *Mon. Anc.* 20 vanta gli 82 templi restaurati: cf. Cook, Adcock, Charlesworth (1968) 10.2, 693 ss.

nel linguaggio precatorio.⁵ Si configura così nell'azione di Augusto quella 'combinazione di conservatorismo e innovazione'⁶ che sarà una caratteristica del suo operato non solo in ambito religioso ma anche politico, e che costituirà uno dei punti di forza del nuovo principato.

Quanto ai culti degli dei stranieri, ci testimonia ancora Suetonio (*Aug.* 93): *peregrinarum caerimoniarum sicut ueteres ac praeceptas reuerentissime coluit, ita ceteras contemptui habuit*; dunque un rispetto ostentato della tradizione consolidata, e il rifiuto di innovazioni.

Uno dei momenti culminanti dell'età augustea, forse il più rappresentativo e il più ambizioso progetto del *princeps* nel campo della creazione d'immagine e dell'autopromozione ideologica del proprio operato, è costituito dalla celebrazione indetta nel 17 a. C.: in un periodo finalmente caratterizzato dalla *pax Augusta* nei domini di Roma,⁷ il *princeps* celebra i *Ludi Saeculares*, nella sua qualità di primo fra i cinque *magistri*⁸ dei *quindecimuiri sacris faciundis*, collegio sacerdotale preposto ai culti stranieri e a custodire ed interpretare i *Libri Sibyllini*: questi oracoli in esametri greci, attribuiti alla sacerdotessa ispirata dal dio Apollo, furono trasferiti da Augusto nel 12 (almeno a quanto ci dice Suetonio)⁹ nel tempio di Apollo sul Palatino, da quello di Giove Capitolino, ma sembra ingenuo pensare che il *princeps* non avesse sotto controllo già prima del 17 questi importantissimi testi profetici.¹⁰

---

⁵ Cf. per es. gli *Acta Fratrum Arualium* editi, fra gli altri, da Pasoli (1950) e più recentemente da Scheid (1998).
⁶ Nock in Cook, Adcock, Charlesworth (1968) 10.2, 693.
⁷ Nel 20 Roma ottiene la restituzione delle insegne catturate dai Parti alle legioni sconfitte. Augusto nel 19 torna a Roma festeggiato dal Senato (v. Scheid [2005] 190); si erige un' ara a *Fortuna Redux* (*Mon. Anc.* 11).
⁸ Moretti (1985) 371: la lista dei 5 *magistri* si ricava da *CIL* 6.4.2, 3244, e comprende pure Agrippa: cf. anche Zanker (1989) 180. Ridley (2005) 275-300, esamina il problema della carica di Pontefice Massimo, che nel 17 era ancora appannaggio dell'emarginato Lepido, il quale di proposito non viene coinvolto nel rituale: solo alla sua morte, nel 12 a.C., Augusto assumerà il sacerdozio (*Mon. Anc.*10).
⁹ Secondo Davis (2001)113 ss. non si può prestare fede a Suet.*Aug*.31, che data al 12, all'assunzione del Pontificato Massimo, la revisione e lo spostamento dei Libri nel tempio di Apollo. Per Putnam (2000) 58 è probabile che i Libri fossero collocati nel tempio sul Palatino già dal 28. Tac. *Ann.* 6.12.3 registra una procedura ancora in uso ai tempi di Tiberio, dall'epoca di Augusto, in base alla quale i Libri non potevano essere in mano a privati, e i sacerdoti dovevano verificarne l' autenticità.
¹⁰ Si veda la notizia data da Cass. Dio 54.17.2: nel 18 Augusto fece trascrivere dai sacerdoti di loro pugno i Libri Sibillini, in modo che nessun altro li potesse leggere. Davis (2001) 113 ritiene che

Ora l'oracolo della Sibilla, conservato da Phlegon di Tralles e da Zosimo,[11] fissa la periodizzazione del *saeculum* a 110 anni,[12] in contrasto con la scansione temporale che aveva determinato la celebrazione dei precedenti *Ludi saeculares* a intervalli (in teoria) di 100 anni, ma in sospetta consonanza con il progetto augusteo che sceglie la data del 17, sufficientemente lontana dagli strascichi delle guerre civili e delle proscrizioni, e coincidente con il decennale della grande riforma costituzionale del 27 che aveva sancito i nuovi poteri dell'*Augustus*, il suo stesso titolo e la sua eccezionale *auctoritas*.[13]

Il testo dell'oracolo mostra una corrispondenza quasi perfetta con i riti effettivamente celebrati nel 17 e registrati negli *Acta* epigrafici, tanto da far supporre un intervento di Augusto, attraverso la compiacente trascrizione dei Quindecemviri, per pilotare il cerimoniale della festa nella direzione più consona al programma della sua restaurazione religiosa e politica: trattandosi del *princeps* che non lasciava nulla al caso per legittimare il proprio potere,[14] è probabile che le cose siano andate proprio in questo modo.

---

l'oracolo dei Ludi sia stato fabbricato da Augusto (e a 125 n. 23 considera falsa la data del 12 fornita da Suetonio); Gagé (1955) 626 ss. ammette che la ricopiatura dei Libri Sibillini avvenuta fra il 20 e il 18 aveva potuto permettere inserzioni e rimaneggiamenti; anche Romano (1991) 950 è convinta che Augusto abbia manipolato l'oracolo. La consultazione doveva comunque essere autorizzata dal Senato o da un magistrato *cum imperio*: cf. Latte (1960) 160-161; Scheid (1995) 25. V. anche Cook, Adcock, Charlesworth (1968) 10.1, 195; 10.2, 694.

[11] Phlegon von Tralles n. 257 in Jacoby (1962) 1189-1191; Zosimo 2.6, Paschoud (2000) 75-77.

[12] Sul problema della durata del *saeculum*, passata da 100 a 110 anni, cf. p. es. Radke (1986) 300; Hall (1986) 2567-2568 (con eccessiva accentuazione dell'influsso etrusco); Davis (2001) 113 ss. Nelle *Res gestae* (*Mon. Anc.* 22), ma significativamente solo nella redazione in greco, compare l'indicazione di 100 anni, mentre nella redaziona latina si tace prudentemente sulla questione. Censorinus *DN* 17.7-14 testimonia la confusione nella periodizzazione. August. *De ciu. D.* 3.18 parla di un periodo di 100 anni. Sulle date contraddittorie tramandate per i Ludi precedenti al 17, v. Nilsson (1920) 1696-1720. La più recente (e ricca di informazioni) edizione degli *Acta* dei Ludi augustei, di Schnegg-Köhler (2002), tratta il problema alle pp. 156 ss., con tabelle della cronologia e delle fonti: da Mommsen in poi è diffusa la convinzione che la lista dei Ludi precedenti al 17 sia in buona parte fabbricata da Augusto e dai compiacenti XV *uiri*; in particolare desta sospetti la data del 126 a.C. che sembra inventata per situare una celebrazione circa 110 anni prima del 17/16: cf. anche Gagé (1955) 626 ss.; Beard, North, Price (1998) 1.201 ss.

[13] Fra il 13 e il 16 gennaio del 27 il *princeps* ottiene l'*imperium proconsulare* per 10 anni e, fra l'altro, il diritto a portare il titolo di *Augustus*: cf. Gagé (1977) e Scheid (2007) ad *Mon. Anc.* 6 e 34.

[14] Si ricordi il prodigio degli avvoltoi riferito da Suet. *Aug.* 29 e da Cass. Dio 40.6.46: Scheid (2005) 185 ss. sostiene che fu pianificato da Augusto. Davis (2001) 113 è convinto del ruolo attivo di Augusto nella redazione dell'oracolo; così anche Romano (1991) 950; Polara (1995) 73 è persuaso del contrario; Schnegg-Köhler (2002) 221 ss. è certa di una riformulazione dell'oracolo al servizio degli scopi del *princeps*. Del resto nelle linee iniziali degli *Acta* (*CIL*

Il rituale prescritto dalla Sibilla elencava sacrifici notturni nel *Tarentum* (o *Terentum*), nel campo di Marte vicino al Tevere, offerti dapprima alle Μοῖραι, poi alle Εἰλείθυιαι,[15] dee delle nascite, infine a Γαῖα;[16] durante i tre giorni, dopo ciascuno dei sacrifici notturni, immolazione di tori bianchi a Giove, una giovenca a Giunone, e 'sacrifici analoghi' ad Apollo;[17] dovevano seguire canti di peana in latino da parte di due cori separati di fanciulli e fanciulle con i genitori viventi, e una supplica delle matrone all'altare di Giunone. Poi purificazioni e altre offerte propiziatorie non meglio specificate agli dei infernali e olimpici.

Fin qui l'oracolo sibillino, che appunto abbiamo la fortuna di poter confrontare con gli *Acta* ufficiali, incisi su una colonna di marmo i cui frammenti sono stati ritrovati nel Campo di Marte a partire dal 1890 (editi nel *CIL* e commentati per primo da Mommsen).[18] Nel testo epigrafico si registra questo rituale: la prima notte (31 maggio) nel

---

3239, ll.26) si dichiara espressamente *ut scripsit ad nos imperator Caesar Augustus*. Si parla comunque (cf. Gagé (1955) 627), anche in base a Zos. 2.4.2, di un intervento di Ateio Capitone, grande esperto di diritto canonico, nell'organizzazione del rituale, se non nella formulazione dell'oracolo; ma, dato che Tac. *Ann.* 3.70 e 3.75 non risparmia pesanti giudizi sulla tendenza di Ateio all'*obsequium dominantibus*, è facile immaginare quanto egli potesse essere influenzabile dal volere di Augusto.

[15] Sono le dee greche che presiedono alle nascite: v. *LIMC* 3.1 s.v. e Roscher 1.1 s.v., coll. 1219-1221, e sono nominate qui per la prima volta con il nome latino di *Ilithyiae*; v. Davis (2001) 120 e n. 74; secondo Schnegg-Köhler (2002) 229 ss. le dee erano ignote a Roma, in quanto la loro azione era svolta da Giunone Lucina; tuttavia Hall (1986) 2572-2573 segnala un precedente (peraltro isolato) del loro culto in ambito italico.

[16] L'oracolo parla della divinità greca (da Hes. *Theog.* 45). *Tellus* era la dea venerata a Roma nel tempio *in Carinis* e invocata dai *pontifices* (Varro ap. August. *De ciu. D.* 7.23: cf. Wissowa [1912] 192 ss.) e viene ricordata da Orazio al v. 29 del *Carmen saeculare*. *Terra Mater* (attestato in Varro, *Rust.* 1.1.5 e in Lucr. 1.251; 2.993; 5.1402: *ThlL* 8.442, 71 ss., s.v. 'mater') è nelle formule precatorie di Augusto (v. Latte [1960] 69, 299). Secondo Ridley (2005) 279 la connessione rituale del *Pontifex Maximus* con *Tellus* testimoniata da Varrone sarebbe il motivo dell'assenza della dea e del suo teonimo nei riti dei Ludi, al fine di non evocare l'assente Lepido.

[17] Cf. l.17-18 dell'oracolo (in Phlegon e Zosimo), che non specifica il tipo di vittime, ma allude chiaramente ad un sacrificio cruento. Dato che invece il rituale augusteo offre ad Apollo solo focacce di vario tipo, già Wilamowitz (seguito da Mommsen) aveva cercato di emendare il testo di Zosimo: una sintesi del problema è in Gagé (1955) 630 ss., che crede al sacrificio incruento (benché unico tra i sacrifici offerti al dio in precedenza, nel tempio arcaico *extra pomerium*, poi restaurato da C. Sosio). Cf. anche Feeney (1998) 54; Schnegg-Köhler (2002) 145; v. infra n. 73.

[18] *CIL* 6.4.2, 32323 (= *ILS* 5050); 3238-43 (32326-32336 per i Ludi di Settimio Severo). I frammenti epigrafici furono editi da Mommsen (1891) 617-672 (= [1913] 567-672). Fondamentale lo studio di Pighi (1941 = 1965). Moretti (1985) 362 ss. rettifica in parte l'interpretazione di Mommsen in base ai nuovi ritrovamenti degli anni '80 del secolo scorso, contenenti due *senatusconsulta* relativi alla preparazione e al finanziamento dei Ludi. La già citata edizione Schnegg-Köhler si occupa solo degli *Acta* augustei.

Tarentum Augusto sacrifica, da solo, *Achiuo ritu*, nove agnelle e nove capre alle *Moerae*.

1 giugno: Augusto e Agrippa sacrificano due tori a Giove Ottimo Massimo sul Campidoglio; la notte del primo giugno Augusto sacrifica alle *Ilithyiae* con tre volte nove focacce.[19]

2 giugno: Augusto e Agrippa sacrificano ciascuno una giovenca a Giunone Regina sul Campidoglio; segue una preghiera di centodieci matrone (il cui numero coincide con gli anni del *saeculum*); notte del 2 giugno: Augusto sacrifica a *Terra Mater* una scrofa gravida.

3 giugno: Augusto e Agrippa, sul Palatino, sacrificano ad Apollo e Diana con focacce di vario tipo; finito il sacrificio, 27 *pueri* e 27 *puellae patrimi et matrimi carmen cecinerunt*; si specifica subito dopo che ne era autore *Q. Horatius Flaccus*, e il carme viene ripetuto sul Campidoglio.[20]

Seguono *Ludi scaenici* (come nei giorni precedenti) e *sellisternia* delle matrone agli dei.[21]

Appare innegabile il valore ideologico e spettacolare dei *Ludi Saeculares quinti* nel rafforzare ed innalzare agli occhi dei cittadini di Roma la figura di Augusto,[22] il quale officia da solo i sacrifici del *trinoctium*: si tratta di cerimonie espiatorie rivolte alle dee ctonie che sostituiscono *Dis Pater* e Proserpina, gli antichi destinatari dei

---

[19] Riguardo ai vocaboli usati, *libum* è termine tecnico-sacrale, già in Catone *agr.* 75; *popanum* un raro sinonimo (per *focaccia*) attestato in Varrone (apud Lyd. *mens.* 4.2), qui e in Iuv. 6.541, forse collegato con *popa* ('sacerdote'): *ThlL* 10.1.2691, 4 ss.; *pthois* translittera un termine tecnico greco ed è attestato solo all'ablativo plurale, unicamente qui e negli *Acta* severiani: *ThlL* 10.2.2428, 1 ss.

[20] Si è discusso sul carattere processionale o meno del *Carmen saeculare*, che era sostenuto da Mommsen, ma viene escluso dalla maggior parte degli studiosi, per es. da Kiessling-Heinze nell'introduzione al *Carmen saeculare*, da Gagé (1955) 634 ss.; da Fraenkel (1993) 516; un riassunto della questione si trova in La Bua (1999) 162. Il canto dell'inno si ricollega al rituale celebrato nel 207 a.C., con fini di lustrazione per presagi infausti, per mezzo di un *carmen* composto da Livio Andronico e cantato da 27 fanciulle in processione attraverso la città (Liv. 27.37.7): cf. Gagé (1955) 634 ss.; Schnegg-Köhler (2002) 235 ss.; sulle differenze tra le due cerimonie e la novità del secondo coro v. infra n. 66.

[21] Gli *Acta* epigrafici non sono del tutto chiari riguardo alla ripetizione di *ludi scaenici* e *sellisternia*, ma lo schema delle cerimonie nei tre giorni è chiaramente ripetitivo: cf. Schnegg-Köhler (2002) 234 ss.

[22] Tuttavia La Penna (1969) 157 sottolinea con ragione che il ruolo del *princeps* come salvatore, connesso con le attese messianiche del nuovo *saeculum*, è tenuto deliberatamente in ombra nel rituale dei Ludi; analogamente Schnegg-Köhler (2002) 242 ss. rileva come la menzione dell'età dell'oro sia assente sia nelle formule precatorie del Ludi, sia nel *Carmen saeculare* oraziano.

precedenti Ludi, e Latte suggerisce che il *princeps* voglia riservare a se stesso ciò che era in rapporto con il passato, mentre nella liturgia diurna indirizzata agli dei olimpici si farebbe affiancare dal suo presunto successore Agrippa per preparare il futuro dell'impero;[23] egli tende comunque, sia attraverso i cerimoniali sia per mezzo dell'iconografia visibile sui monumenti coevi, a rendere sempre più autorevole la propria voce in materia religiosa.[24]

Zanker[25] sottolinea giustamente l'impatto emotivo dei riti notturni alla luce delle fiaccole, e dei solenni sacrifici davanti ai due templi più rappresentativi della religione di stato, quello di Giove sul Campidoglio e quello più recente sul Palatino,[26] dedicato al dio protettore del *princeps*, a quell'Apollo che era presentato come l'artefice della vittoria di Azio. Ma non meno coinvolgente, anzi quasi ipnotico dovette essere sui presenti l'effetto uditivo delle formule di preghiera fortemente allitteranti, scandite nel *silentium* rituale, specialmente di quelle riservate alla voce del solo Augusto e ossessivamete ripetute[27] durante i sacrifici notturni (celebrati *Achiuo ritu*, quindi a capo scoperto, dando ancora maggiore visibilità all'orante).[28] Notiamo che pochi anni più tardi l'iconografia dell'*Ara Pacis* (dedicata nel 9 a.C.), che ritrae con assoluto rilievo il *princeps* nel suo aspetto di sacrificatore, lo rappresenta *capite velato*, secondo l'uso romano, come del resto avviene nella famosa statua in veste pontificale (ora a Palazzo Massimo) e in altre raffigurazioni.[29]

L'estrema visibilità conferita alla figura di Augusto dal suo agire a capo scoperto secondo l'*Achiuus ritus* evidenzia l'eccezionalità del

---

[23] Latte (1960) 299.
[24] Green (2008) 40 ss.
[25] Zanker (1989) 180 ss.; belle pagine anche in Fraenkel (1993) 515 ss., specialmente sulla performance del *Carmen saeculare*.
[26] Il Tempio di Apollo Palatino fu dedicato il 9 ottobre del 28; Prop. 2.31 descrive le meraviglie artistiche dell'edificio appena inaugurato: cf. Fedeli (2005) 870 ss.
[27] Per es. nel sacrificio alle Moire di nove agnelle e di nove capre nere, come fa notare Schnegg-Köhler (2002) 127 ss., la formula che accompagnava l'*immolatio* dei singoli animali veniva ripetuta da Augusto per 18 volte!!! E tutto il rituale poi compiuto dai sacerdoti che uccidevano le vittime, e dagli aruspici che ne esaminavano le interiora, poteva durare buona parte della notte...
[28] Sulla natura del *ritus Graecus*, cf. Scheid (1995) 13-31: le cerimonie celebrate *Graeco/ Achiuo ritu* erano considerate parte del *patrius mos* romano, da cui spesso si differenziano solo per il fatto che l'officiante agisce a capo scoperto; viceversa la presenza di riti di *haruspicina* rimanda all'influsso etrusco. Cf. anche Barchiesi (2002) 119.
[29] Green (2008) 43, Zanker (1989) 126-129, Bianchi Bandinelli (1969) 199-200 e fig. 216.

cerimoniale dei Ludi secolari; e d'altra parte anche il protagonismo dell'officiante che ripete a memoria per diciotto volte la *precatio* ad ogni sacrificio notturno appare una forzatura imposta dal *princeps* a se stesso in omaggio alla centralità del suo ruolo, se si ricorda che, secondo la testimonianza di Suet. *Aug.* 84.1, egli *ne periculum memoriae adiret aut in ediscendo tempus absumeret, instituit recitare omnia*, al punto che persino con Livia parlava di argomenti importanti solo dopo aver preparato annotazioni.

Gli *Acta* epigrafici conservano, benché in forma mutila, le invocazioni di Augusto, che peraltro possono facilmente essere integrate, nelle parti lacunose, grazie alla ripetitività formulare che accomuna le tre preghiere, dopo l'*epiklesis* iniziale alle diverse divinità; fra l'altro possediamo anche estesi frammenti degli *Acta* relativi ai *Ludi* celebrati nel 204 d.C. da Settimio Severo,[30] che riproducono fedelmente il cerimoniale augusteo, e almeno in un caso permettono di integrare correttamente una lacuna comune al testo delle preghiere del 17, correggendo la proposta di Mommsen.[31]

Per brevità ci concentriamo sul testo della preghiera alle *Moerae*, la prima, che appunto viene poi ricalcata dalle successive.

> 90 Nocte insequenti in campo ad Tib[erim deis Moeris imp(erator) Caesar Augustus immolauit agnas feminas ix]
> 91 prodigiuas Achiuo ritu eodem[que modo capras feminas ix prodigiuas; precatus est hoc modo:]
> 92 Moerae uti uobis in illeis libr[eis scriptum est quarum rerum ergo quodque melius siet p(opulo) R(omano) Quiritibus uobis ix]
> 93 agnis feminis et ix capris fem[inis propriis sacrum fiat; uos quaeso precorque uti uos imperium maiestatemque p(opuli) R(omani)]
> 94 Quiritium duelli domique au[xitis utique semper Latinus obtemperassit, sempiter-
> 95 nam uictoriam ualetudine[m p(opulo) R(omano) Quiritibus duitis, faueatisque p(opulo) R(omano) Quiritibus legionibusque p(opuli) R(omani)]
> 96 Quiritium, rem p(ublicam) p(opuli) R(omani) [Quiritium saluam seruetis maioremque faxitis, uti sitis] uolentes pr[opitiae p(opulo) R(omano)]

---

[30] Per gli *Acta* dei Ludi severiani del 204 d.C., v. *CIL* 6.4.2, 32326-32335 e Hülsen (1932) 366-394, Pighi (1941) 137-194.
[31] Alla linea 94 Mommsen integrava *utique semper Latinum nomen tueare*, che in base alle formule dei Ludi severiani va sostituito con *utique semper Latinus obtemperassit*. V. infra per la bibliografia relativa e il significato da dare alla formula, pp. 121 e nn. 61-62.

97 Quiritibus xv uir(or)um collegi[o mihi domo familiaeque, uti huius]
sacrifici acceptrices sitis viiii agnarum
98 feminarum et viiii capraru[m feminarum propri]arum immolandarum;
harum rerum ergo macte hac agna femina
99 immolanda estote fitote [uolentes] propitiae p(opulo) R(omano)
Quiritibus xv uir(or)um collegio mihi domo familiae. (ed. Schnegg-Köhler)

Innanzitutto le dee che sovrintendono al destino umano, le Μοῖραι greche,[32] sono apostrofate da Augusto con la traslitterazione del teonimo greco (Orazio nella settima strofa – v. 25 – del *Carmen saeculare* le chiamerà *Parcae*, con il termine latino che secondo l'etimologia varroniana[33] era collegato con il verbo *pario*). Il *princeps* prosegue facendo uso di forme arcaiche, a partire da *uti*,[34] e dalla desinenza dell'ablativo plurale *in illeis libris* in cui compare il dittongo *ei* non ancora chiuso (nella forma intermedia *-eis*, dall'originario *-ois*).[35] Rileviamo anche la menzione della fonte sacra, i Libri Sibillini, che prescrive e legittima con la sua *auctoritas* tutto il cerimoniale.

L'arcaicità della preghiera si accentua con il ricorso a *ergo* posposto, in funzione di preposizione con il genitivo, un uso analogo agli ablativi *causa, gratia* col significato di 'in conseguenza di': questa particolarità sintattica è prediletta da Catone nelle formule precatorie del suo *de agricultura*[36] proprio in unione con *res,* ma era già attestata nelle XII Tavole (per. es. 10.4 *funeris ergo*) e sarà ripresa in contesti solenni dalla

---

[32] L'etimologia riconduce il nome a μείρομαι. Le dee costituiscono una triade già in Esiodo *Theog.* 211 ss., e hanno un originario carattere ctonio, anche se vengono poi accolte nel pantheon olimpico come figlie di Zeus e Themis: v. *RE* 15.2, coll. 2449 ss.; Roscher 2.2, coll. 3084 ss.; *LIMC* 6.1, 636 ss.; Schnegg-Köhler (2002) 116 ss. La traslitterazione con il dittongo *oe* è consueta nei grecismi accolti in latino: cf. *moechus*, *Adelphoe*: v. Tronskij (1993[4]) 146; Niedermann (1953[4]) 61 ss.

[33] L'etimologia di Varrone è riportata da Gell. 3.6.10 *Parca a partu nominata* ... cf. Van der Horst (1943) 212-227, criticato da Latte (1960) 53 per il tentativo di vedere nelle *Parcae* la semplice traduzione delle Moire greche, mentre è attestato dai cippi di Tor Tignosa (Lavinio) un culto latino arcaico ad esse dedicato (Guarducci [1946-48] 1-10); cf. anche Dumézil (1977) 431 n. 5; Hall (1986) 2571 ss. Più tardi ovviamente, e sicuramente in età augustea, opererà il sincretismo religioso romano che le identificherà con le Moire, pur differenziandole a livello iconografico, perché le *Parcae* romane sono rappresentate nell'atto di scrivere il destino su un *uolumen*, e non in quello di filare, tipico della tradizione greca: *LIMC* 6.1.638; 647.

[34] V. Cato *Agr.* 134.1-2 *uti sies*…, nella preghiera a Giove e Giano; 141 2, a Marte: Traina, Bernardi Perini (1992[4]) 184 e *DEL* s.v. *ut, uti*.

[35] Cf. Ernout (1974) 33: la desinenza *-eis* è attestata in iscrizioni di età repubblicana ma ormai generalmente normalizzata in età augustea.

[36] Cato *Agr.* 139; 141.2 e 3 (con *ergo* posposto): cf. De Meo (1983) 150 ss. Pighi (2009 = 1967) 23 ss. analizza la faticosa sintassi delle preghiere di Catone e di quelle dei Ludi saeculares.

prosa ciceroniana e liviana e dalla poesia di Lucrezio (per es. 3.78) e in Verg. *Aen.* 6.670 *illius ergo*.[37]

La morfologia arcaica è ancora presente nel congiuntivo *siet* al posto del classico *sit*,[38] inserito nel formulare *quodque melius siet*, parallelo a espressioni come *quodque bene eueniat* di Cato 141.1, con un congiuntivo dal valore ottativo e una funzione parentetica nella sintassi del periodo ('e ciò vada a buon fine per il popolo etc').[39]

Notiamo anche la tipica formulazione binaria del linguaggio sacrale, con i sinonimi[40] a contatto *quaeso precorque*, in cui si conserva l'originario desiderativo di *quaero* (da * *quais-so*, che sfugge al rotacismo per la presenza della doppia sibilante),[41] poi cristallizzato nella formula di cortesia;[42] poco dopo, il nesso allitterante *duelli domique* sostituisce al locativo *belli*, ormai acquisito da secoli, la forma originaria (attestata, dopo il periodo arcaico, solo in contesti poetici o elevati).[43]

Il congiuntivo *auxitis*, introdotto da *uti* nella sostantiva volitiva, è un ulteriore relitto (come *siet*) dell'antico ottativo in *-im/-sim* dei verbi tematici, conservato in forme come *ausim, faxim* anche nelle commedie plautine, e sarà replicato poco dopo con *duitis* e *faxitis*.[44]

L'invocazione prosegue ricercando l'effetto fonico dei nessi allitteranti nella coppia asindetica *uictoriam ualetudinem*, come nel successivo *saluam seruetis*. Il formulare *uolentes propitiae* conserva la struttura asindetica del lessico religioso;[45] la successiva perifrasi

---

[37] Cf. Norden (1995⁹) ad loc.
[38] Per *siet* cf. Ernout (1974) 177: si tratta di un antico ottativo formato sul tema ridotto **s*.
[39] Pighi (2009) 59 traduce 'e in quanto meglio avvenga al popolo romano'; Schnegg-Köhler (2002) 37: 'und weil es wegen dieser Dinge noch besser für das römische Volk werde.'
[40] Sull'accumulo sinonimico nella lingua sacrale e giuridica cf. von Albrecht (1989) 7; De Meo (1983) 141 ss.
[41] Cf. Ernout (1974) 137; *DEL* s.v. *quaero*.
[42] In Cato *Agr.* 141.2, l'ordine è inverso: *precor quaesoque*.
[43] *DEL* s.v. *bellum*, da cui i composti *perduellio* e *perduellis* che, cristallizzati nel lessico conservativo del diritto, indicano l'alto tradimento e chi lo compie: *Dig.* 48.4.11; cf. Varro *Ling.* 7.49; *ThlL* 2.1822.33 ss., s.v. *bellum*; il nesso *domi duellique* è in Plaut. *Asin.* 559; *Capt.* 68, prima degli *Acta* dei Ludi in cui l'ordine è scambiato. Ricordiamo l'arcaismo forzato della cancelleria senatoria in *Duelonai* (per *Bellonae*) nel *Senatusconsultum de Bacchanalibus* del 186 a.C.: cf. Marchetta (1981) 97 ss.; per l'uso di *duellum* in Orazio cf. Fedeli, Ciccarelli (2008) ad 4.15.8.
[44] Ernout (1974) 165 ss.
[45] Ricordiamo *felix faustus, optimus maximus, bonum faustum felix* ...: cf. Appel (1909) 122, De Meo (1983) 151 ss. In Catone compaiono gli stessi termini al singolare nella preghiera a Giano e Giove per la *porca praecidanea* (134.2) e in quella per il *lucus* (139).

esortativa *acceptrices sitis* – al posto di un più comune congiuntivo presente oppure di un imperativo del verbo *accipio* – rientra in quella tendenza a preferire costrutti più espressivi (in origine tipica della lingua popolare)[46] che genera espressioni dello stile giuridico-burocratico come *scientes esetis* nel *Senatusconsultum de Bacchanalibus*, con lo scopo di conferire maggior solennità alla formulazione.

Quanto alla *iunctura* della linea 96, *rem publicam populi Romani Quiritium*, se ne può osservare la persistenza negli *Acta fratrum Arualium* dall'epoca di Tiberio (7a 2.20 Scheid) fino a M. Aurelio.

Nell'ambito della lingua religiosa rientrano poi a pieno diritto gli aggettivi *prodigiuus* e *proprius*, riferiti alle vittime da sacrificare, rispettivamente alla linea 91 nella descrizione iniziale dell'offerta alle Moire, e alle linee 93 e 98 nella preghiera di Augusto.[47]

Tecnicismi liturgici sono anche la definizione del sacrificio stesso come *immolatio,* con allusione allo spargimento della *mola salsa* sull'animale,[48] e il *macte* (*estote*) rivolto alle *Moerae*, caso limite di cristallizzazione lessicale, che nelle preghiere è usato spesso in forma non declinata, con valore avverbiale, pur essendo derivato dal participio passato del verbo *mactare* 'offrire un sacrificio, onorare un dio.'[49] In unione con un imperativo (*estote* qui, *macte esto* per es. in Cato 134.3 a Giano e a Giove) invita la divinità ad essere soddisfatta dell'offerta: Pighi traduceva, nelle preghiere catoniane, 'sii aggrandito', ricordando l'etimologia antica.

Certo è noto il conservatorismo della lingua sacrale romana e la persistenza di lessico e fraseologia, tanto è vero che le preghiere a noi rimaste dei *Ludi* severiani del 204 d.C. ripetono quasi alla lettera quelle del 17 a.C. È anche opinione condivisa che le invocazioni del

---

[46] De Meo (1983) 90 ss.
[47] *ThlL* 10.2.2093 ss.; 10.2.2106, 24 ss.: *proprius 'de hostia probata, deo accepta'*, cf. Plaut. *Capt.* 872: *agnum proprium pinguem*; dopo gli *Acta* solo in Tert. *Orat.* 28; cf. Pighi (1941) 310 ss. Schnegg-Köhler (2002) 124 ricorda a proposito di *capris feminis propriis* (l. 93, integrata da Pighi) e di *caprarum feminarum propriarum* (l. 98) che le bestie offerte alle dee ctonie dovevano essere, oltre che femmine, di colore nero; a pp. 118 ss., quanto a *prodigiuus*, che sembra un *hapax* attestato solo negli *Acta* augustei e severiani (cf. anche *ThlL* 10.2.1610.10 ss. e Gagé [1933] 175) cita Fest. 296-297 Lindsay: *prodigiuae hostiae uocantur... quae consumuntur*, cioè si tratterebbe di un olocausto.
[48] *DEL* s.v. *molo*, e per es. Fest. 97.22 Lindsay. L'azione era compiuta dal *princeps* in persona per 18 volte, come si è detto (v. supra n. 27).
[49] Per l'etimologia da 'magis'+'auctus' di Festo 112, 13 Lindsay, v. *DEL* s.v. *mactus*.

cerimoniale fossero in larga parte modellate sul formulario presente nei commentari dei pontefici e stratificato nei secoli; tuttavia il linguaggio ostentatamente arcaico che Augusto riserva alla propria voce di officiante, nell'occasione dei *Ludi saeculares quinti*, appare in assoluto contrasto con le testimonianze suetoniane, citate in precedenza, sulle sue preferenze linguistiche.

L'Augusto purista e contrario all'asianesimo e agli eccessi arcaizzanti si è dunque prestato a recitare con la massima enfasi preghiere che sembrano uscite dalla bocca di Catone, trasferendone per di più le formulazioni dall'ambito privato della *precatio patris familias* alla religione dello stato romano: tanta era la sua determinazione nel perseguire la restaurazione degli *antiqui mores*, non solo in tutta l'attività legislativa ma anche nella più solenne delle celebrazioni pubbliche.

Se però confrontiamo fonetica, lessico, morfologia e sintassi delle *precationes* augustee con un altro dei momenti più significativi della festa, il *Carmen Saeculare*, posto a suggello dei riti precedenti, e destinato alla performance davanti ai due templi del Palatino e del Campidoglio dove il *princeps* e Agrippa avevano sacrificato nelle cerimonie diurne, sarà evidente la differenza.

I commentatori dell'inno oraziano concordano nel rilevare il tono enfaticamente solenne[50] e la corrispondenza con molti caratteri dell'inno cletico:[51] apostrofe iniziale alle divinità, *Du Stil*, costrutti appositivi (*appositional style*), elencazione delle ἀρεταί e δυνάμεις, *Relativsätze*, *polyonymia*, uso del *si* nella *ratio precationis* (ai vv. 37 e 65), ma anche il fatto che, sotto l'aspetto formale, il *Carmen saeculare*[52] corrisponde in pieno ai canoni della lingua dell'età augustea.

Per esempio i tre più appariscenti arcaismi lessicali del *Carmen saeculare*, *sospes* del v. 40, *proles* e *suboles* dei vv. 17-19, sono fortemente motivati dall'ipotesto virgiliano: *sospes* è in *Aen.* 8.470, riferito ad Enea nelle parole di benvenuto di Latino; 11.56 nel contesto

---

[50] Per es. Fraenkel (1993) 511 ss.
[51] Il riferimento obbligato è a Norden (1913 = 1974), e a La Bua (1999) passim. Barchiesi (2002) 112 ss. esamina il rapporto del *Carmen saeculare* con il genere e la tradizione del peana greco.
[52] Maurach (2001) 396 ss. insiste sulla semplicità ('ganz einfacher Wortwahl in moderne syntaktische Verbindungen'). Plessis (cit. in Cremona [1982] 349) parlava di 'semplicità elegante'; La Penna (1969) 158 riconosce una 'eleganza semplice e solenne'.

patetico del compianto di Enea sul morto Pallante. *Proles* e *suboles* si trovano in passi dalla tonalità profetica: Norden ad *Aen.* 6.784 (Roma) *felix prole uirum* ricorda il carattere 'altertümlich-feierlich' del primo, mentre per il secondo, pure arcaico e poetico, il modello forte nella poesia virgiliana è l'ecloga dei *Saturnia regna* che tornano, 4.49, *cara deum suboles*.[53]

Per il resto, la lingua del *Carmen saeculare* appare caratterizzata non dagli arcaismi, ma semmai da una ricerca di originalità sul piano lessicale: segnaliamo il primo uso di *almus* per una divinità maschile,[54] di *Genitalis* e di *bicornis* come epiteti sacrali, di *maritus* nel senso di 'relativo alle nozze',[55] di *Albanus* con il significato di *Romanus*. Quanto alle innovazioni sul piano sintattico, nuova è la costruzione di *ueraces* con l'infinito *cecinisse* (v. 25), e analogamente di *lenis* con *aperire* (vv. 13-14), e anche l'uso di *super* con l'ablativo del gerundio (vv. 18-19 *iugandis feminis*);[56] infine sul piano morfologico e fonetico la lingua appare conforme al cosiddetto classicismo augusteo.

Si configura così una parte di quel complesso di opposizioni (secondo la definizione di Feeney)[57] o meglio di polarità che caratterizza i *Ludi saeculares*: notte/ giorno; greco/ romano, antico/ nuovo, divinità ctonie/ celesti etc.: in questo caso, a livello formale, all'ostentato arcaismo delle formule pronunciate da Augusto si contrappone la lingua normalizzata di Orazio, che inoltre invoca le dee del destino con il nome romano di *Parcae*, invece del grecizzante *Moerae* del sacrificio notturno;

---

[53] Per *ecl.* 4.49 cf. Traina (1980) 221; Fraenkel (1993) 511 su *suboles* e *proles*. Citiamo un'ulteriore consonanza con il poema virgiliano, non in Orazio ma nel testo dell'oracolo sibillino, che ai vv. 3-4 (Zos. 2.6) esorta i romani a ricordare il rituale prescritto con l'anaforico μεμνῆσθαι 'Ρωμαῖε. Norden *ad Aen.* 6.851 *tu regere imperio populos Romane memento* rileva la concordedanza come 'interessante' ma non si spinge oltre; cf. anche Feeney (1998) 60. Il rapporto intertestuale potrebbe essere una prova ulteriore del rimaneggiamento dei Libri Sibillini in età augustea.
[54] Cf. Putnam (2010) 242; a p. 249 si propone che *Genitalis* sia stato suggerito ad Orazio da Lucr. 1.111 *genitabilis aura Favoni*.
[55] Orazio allude alla *Lex Iulia de maritandis ordinibus* e a quella *de adulteriis*, probabilmente promulgate da Augusto solo l'anno precedente, nel 18; cf. Cook, Adcock, Charlesworth (1968) 10.1, 512-513; Schnegg-Köhler (2002) 258-260; questo uso di *maritus* è ripreso da Prop. 4.11.33: *faces maritas*.
[56] Putnam (2000) 146 ss. insiste sull'originalità della lingua del *Carmen saeculare*; Davis (2001) 121 e n. 77 segnala la presenza della costruzione *super* + gerundivo solo in Tacito, Ammiano e nel Digesto, a cui si può aggiungere Gell. 19.12.7: in queste espressioni il gerundivo assume il valore di un sostantivo astratto verbale, e forse nel *Carmen saeculare* costituisce un'eco del linguaggio giuridico.
[57] Feeney (1998) 52.

analogamente introduce *Tellus*, ai vv. 29-30, con l'appellativo cultuale della dea che possiede anche un tempio nell'Urbe, mentre *Terra Mater* nella formula del sacrificio di Augusto non era titolo sacrale; quanto alle *Ilithyiae*, nella quarta strofa il poeta le riduce a una singola divinità, dal plurale del secondo rito notturno, e sembra quasi riassorbirle nella *dynamis* romana di Diana/ Lucina (ricordiamo Catull. 34).[58]

Quanto all'ordine dei rituali, il *Carmen saeculare* si apre dando estremo risalto alla coppia Apollo/ Diana, onorata invece nelle cerimonie diurne di Augusto e Agrippa solo al terzo giorno; all'inverso, la coppia dei sommi déi capitolini, Giove e Giunone, destinatari dei solenni sacrifici cruenti del primo e del secondo giorno, appare in Orazio decisamente sbiadita, con Giove ricordato solo *in extremis* nella strofa finale; Giunone non è nominata, e viene anche obliterata nel suo ruolo di protettrice delle nascite, in quanto l'epiteto di *Lucina* (che a Roma condivide con Diana), come si è visto, viene ceduto ad *Ilithyia*.[59]

Alla fissità formulare delle preghiere recitate da Augusto e Agrippa, che si ripetono identiche per ciascuna divinità, si sostituiscono in Orazio invocazioni estremamente variate e dettagliate, che di volta in volta mettono in evidenza le *dynameis* dei vari dei: l'incremento delle nascite per *Ilithyia* (vv. 13 ss.), il ruolo profetico delle *Parcae* garanti del destino di Roma (vv. 25 ss.), la fertilità e l'abbondanza derivanti da *Tellus*, la poliedrica protezione assicurata ai Latini da Apollo che è insieme *Augur*, dio della poesia e *Medicus* (vv. 61 ss.). Anche sul piano fonostilistico i nessi allitteranti riservati alla voce di Augusto appaiono deliberatamente mimetici del *carmen* sacrale arcaico, mentre nel *Carmen saeculare* sono le *callidae iuncturae* a generare ricorsività

---

[58] Feeney (1998) 59 vede in questo riscrivere la nomenclatura greca dei riti notturni un intento oraziano di latinizzare la cerimonia; Schnegg-Köhler (2002) 232 ss. preferisce leggere i teonimi scelti dal poeta come sottolineature del tema della generazione e della discendenza, centrale nel *Carmen saeculare*. Günther (2013) 439 ritiene che qui *Ilithyia* sia identificata con Diana.

[59] Schnegg-Köhler (2002) 232 ss. registra puntualmente le coincidenze e le deviazioni del *Carmen saeculare* rispetto all' oracolo e agli *Acta*. Tra i molti studiosi che commentano la prevalenza di Apollo e Diana, Feeney (1998) 58 in particolare rileva una vera eclisse degli dei capitolini, anche se la ripetizione conclusiva del *Carmen saeculare* sul Campidoglio sembra essere una sorta di compenso finale. Radke (1986) 302 ricorda che sul Campidoglio aveva il primato Lepido che era ancora *Pontifex Maximus*: sarebbe perciò chiara la volontà di Augusto di tenere l'ex-triumviro fuori dal cerimoniale dei *Ludi saeculares*, come dice Scheid (2005) 188 ss.; su Lepido in generale, v. Ridley (2005). Per Fraenkel (1993) 515 la preghiera finale rispecchia la *generalis inuocatio* della normativa rituale, che non poteva traslaciare gli dei capitolini; cf. anche Cremona (1982) 342 ss.

fonica: vv. 2-3 *colendi...et culti*; 7-8 *dis...dicere*; 13-4 *maturos... matres*; 17-19 *producas...prosperes...prolisque*; 29 *fertilis frugum*; 38 *tenuere turmae*; 57-58 *Pudorque priscus*; 60 *copia cornu*; 61 *Augur... arcu*; 71-72 *amicas applicat aures*.[60]

E'lecito vedere la regia di Augusto nell'alternanza di elementi greci e romani e nella commistione di tradizione e innovazione che caratterizzano i Ludi? Abbiamo già ricordato come il *princeps* fosse contrario all'introduzione di nuovi riti stranieri: ora è vero che Moire e *Ilithyiae* non possono certo essere definite divinità latine, e tuttavia la loro presenza appare giustificabile sulla base della loro connessione con le nascite (v. infra n. 64).

Quanto alle formule precatorie dei riti notturni e diurni, pur celebrati *Achiuo ritu*, esse si rifanno, come si è visto, alla più romana delle tradizioni di lingua sacrale, testimoniata dalle preghiere catoniane del *de agri cultura*; nella sostanza liturgica, poi, le dee onorate dai primi sacrifici possiedono in parte il carattere ctonio delle originarie divinità dei *Ludi saeculares* precedenti, *Dis Pater* e Proserpina (v. n. 32 e infra), così come è conservata la sede delle cerimonie del *trinoctium* nel *Tarentum* sulle rive del Tevere, del tutto inusuale nel primo secolo.

Quanto alla formula *utique semper Latinus obtemperassit* (l. 94, restituita in base agli *Acta* severiani in sostituzione dell'integrazione di Mommsen *semper Latinum nomen tueare*: v. supra, n. 31), è sembrata poco appropriata in un'epoca in cui le guerre contro i popoli della penisola erano ormai un remoto ricordo';[61] ci domandiamo, tuttavia, se non possa essere letta, oltre che come citazione di antiche invocazioni, quasi come uno scongiuro per esorcizzare i recenti fatti della guerra

---

[60] Sembra isolata la consonanza di *Carmen saeculare* 66 *remque Romanam Latiumque felix/ alterum in lustrum meliusque semper/ prorogat aevum* (sogg. Apollo) con l. 96 della preghiera augustea, *remque publicam populi Romani Quiritium salvam servetis maioremque faxitis*, secondo alcuni unica eco oraziana delle formule rituali: La Bua (1999) 168 n. 107.

[61] Sarebbe una formula senza attualità secondo Davis (2001) 116 ss., secondo il quale viene inserita per dare un aspetto arcaico alla preghiera. Invece Gagé (1933) 179 ss. discute a lungo sul momento della storia di Roma a cui si potrebbe far risalire la frase, avanza varie ipotesi di guerre fra Roma e popoli italici, e sottolinea come la profezia della sottomissione dei Latini e dell'Italia sia presente negli ultimi versi dell'oracolo sibillino (Zos. 2.6.36-37). Schnegg-Köhler (2002) 125 ss., considera la formula sia come ripresa di preghiere antichissime, sia come allusione alla politica di integrazione degli Italici portata avanti da Augusto. Cf. anche Hall (1986) 2570 n. 33. D'altra parte Barchiesi (2002) 118 rileva nel *carmen* oraziano il silenzio completo sull'Italia, tema fondamentale nella letteratura augustea.

civile, specialmente quel *bellum Perusinum* che aveva opposto Ottaviano agli antoniani in Umbria, in uno scontro fra sudditi italici della *res publica*.[62]

Ma nello stesso tempo il *princeps* innova la finalità dei Ludi precedenti, indirizzati, come testimoniano le fonti,[63] agli dei inferi con scopo apotropaico o lustrale, in occasione di pestilenze, guerre e prodigi ominosi. Viceversa Augusto sceglie di sacrificare non solo a divinità di origine più o meno ctonia come le Moire,[64] le *Ilithyiae* e *Terra Mater*, ma a queste associa nei riti gli dei olimpici, Giove, Giunone, Apollo e Diana; e la liturgia non ha più la funzione di allontanare le sciagure da Roma, ma di perpetuare e garantire nei secoli la persistenza della *pax Augusta*, della prosperità, della rinascita morale e materiale dell'Urbe e dell'Italia: voti che la formularità arcaica, sulle labbra dell'officiante, esprime con *imperium maiestatemque... auxitis... sempiternam uictoriam ualetudinem... duitis... saluam seruetis maioremque faxitis...*

Ora i Ludi, prima celebrati nel *Tarentum* su altari semi-sotterranei e spesso eretti per l'occasione, si estendono, anche scenograficamente, a tutta l'Urbe e ai colli più sacri, Palatino e Campidoglio.

Quanto al rituale, due aspetti in particolare appaiono inediti e problematici: innanzitutto il coinvolgimento delle matrone in solenni *sellisternia*, che costituisce un'altra innovazione, modellata sulla tradizione greca, ma finalizzata a sottolineare l'apporto indispensabile della componente femminile della popolazione nel programma di incremento delle nascite che era caro al *princeps*, e destinata a ricollegarsi con il computo del *saeculum* grazie al numero di 110 celebranti;[65] sempre in quest'ottica è da leggere il raddoppiamento del coro tradizionale delle ventisette *puellae* con altrettanti *pueri*, come un'inclusione dell' elemento maschile dei *ciues* e futuri soldati di

---

[62] A questo proposito v. Fedeli (2013) 448 ss., per il ricordo traumatico del *bellum sociale*, non ancora svanito in età augustea, e rispecchiato, nell'*Eneide*, dalle difficili relazioni tra Latini e Troiani e dalla mancanza di un patto finale di alleanza fra i due popoli.

[63] Per le fonti sui Ludi precedenti v. Schnegg-Köhler (2002) 156 ss., con tabelle cronologiche. Su Augusto antiquario e innovatore cf. Barchiesi (2002) 120.

[64] Le Moire, peraltro mai onorate prima nell'Urbe, sono connesse alla generazione e alla fecondità come le altre entità invocate: erano infatti collegate originariamente alla nascita; cf. Latte (1960) 52 ss., 95 ss. (e si ricordi l'etimologia di *Parca* da *pario*, supra n. 33).

[65] Cf. Schnegg-Köhler (2002) 259.

[66] Cf. Schnegg-Köhler (2002) 257. Barchiesi (2002) 117 mette invece in luce la novità del coro femminile aggiunto rispetto alla tradizione greca del peana.

Roma.[66] Tuttavia, per chi considera il ruolo determinante di Livia come sposa di Augusto, *femina princeps* (Ov. *ex P.* 3.1.125), *principe digna uiro* (*cons. ad Liuiam* 344), protetta già dal 35, insieme con Ottavia, dalla *sacrosanctitas* tribunizia,[67] restauratrice di templi arcaici come quelli della Bona Dea e della Fortuna Muliebris,[68] raffigurata pochi anni dopo, a fianco del *princeps*, nella processione sacrificale dell' *Ara Pacis*, potrebbe apparire singolare la mancanza di visibilità della *first lady* come anche di altre donne della famiglia nei rituali dei Ludi: se fecero parte delle centodieci matrone che officiavano i *sellisternia*, gli *Acta* non lo registrano; d'altra parte può valere per i Ludi quanto osserva Scheid[69] a proposito dell'assenza di Livia dal testo delle *Res gestae*: 'le modèle ancestral de la pudeur matronale interdisait qu'on parle publiquement de Livie.'

Certamente il protagonismo del *princeps* (di cui Agrippa appare un *alter ego*, un doppio legittimato in quanto successore *in pectore*) avrà messo in secondo piano la presenza di un personaggio rappresentativo, non nuovo a ruoli pubblici e 'maschili', quale era la *uxor Caesaris*;[70] ma del resto nulla negli *Acta* sembra attestare una partecipazione di Augusto ai riti celebrati dalle centodieci matrone, nei quali semmai si ipotizza da parte di Wissowa un intervento di Agrippa;[71] il *princeps* riserva a sé solo i riti notturni, e concelebra con il genero e collega i sacrifici diurni agli dei capitolini, lasciando poi Agrippa a presiedere ai ludi *circenses*, almeno a quanto si ricava dagli *Acta* (3243.165) *M. Agrippa quadrigas [misit]*.

Un altro aspetto del rituale, l'innovazione augustea del sacrificio ad Apollo e Diana, ha dato molto da pensare agli storici della religione;

---

[67] Cass. Dio 49.38.1; cf. Cook, Adcock, Charlesworth (1968) 10.1, 90; Purcell (1986) 85; Scheid (2005) 179 ss.; Treggiari (2005) 141.
[68] Grimal (1953) 15 ss.; Purcell (1986) 87; Beard, North, Price (1998) 1.297; Treggiari (2005) 142.
[69] Scheid (2007), intr. 59. La sposa di Augusto è ricordata insieme ad Ottavia a proposito della *supplicatio* per il ritorno del *princeps* dalla Spagna nel 24, ma solo con una perifrasi, e comunque in uno dei *carmina* oraziani (3.14.5 ss.) non in un documento ufficiale. Diverso sarà il protagonismo di Iulia Domna, ricordata come *Augusta* nelle *supplicationes* a Giunone dei Ludi severiani, da lei officiate con altre centonove matrone, delle quali sono in parte conservati i nomi: Pighi (1941) 241 ss.
[70] Purcell (1986) 87 ss. Su Livia nel fregio dell'*Ara Pacis*, cf. Rossini (2006) 55; Kleiner (2005) 223-224 e fig. 22; Treggiari (2005)142 (ricordiamo che l'*Ara Pacis* fu dedicata da Augusto nel giorno del compleanno di Livia, il 30 gennaio del 9 a.C.).
[71] Cf. *CIL* 3241, 123 e la nota al testo lacunoso, in cui si opta per integrare il nome di Agrippa e non di Augusto come soggetto di *praeit*.

l'associazione della sorella al culto del dio, già di per sé inedita a Roma e non attestata nel tempio antico *in pratis Flaminiis*, è garantita dagli *Acta* dei Ludi e giustificata dalla presenza di un simulacro della dea a fianco del nume titolare nella cella sul Palatino.[72] Ma l'offerta incruenta delle focacce, menzionata negli *Acta* contro i vv. 17-18 dell'oracolo,[73] e unica nei sacrifici per il figlio di Latona, ha indotto Gagé[74] a ipotizzare influssi pitagorici, Feeney[75] ad attribuire ad Apollo un ruolo di mediatore tra rituali antichi e moderni, Schnegg-Köhler[76] a suggerire una posizione inferiore del dio rispetto alle divinità capitoline, ipotesi che sembra improbabile se si pensa all'importanza di Apollo nell'ideologia e nella stessa propaganda augustea fin dal tempo della contrapposizione con Antonio (discendente di Ercole e *Neos Dionysos*).[77] Si può essere tentati di mettere in relazione il sacrificio incruento con l'immagine del dio *condito mitis placidusque telo* di *Carmen saeculare* v. 33, simbolo della nuova era della *pax Augusta*, ma è bene ricordare che l'uccisione delle vittime sacrificali era offerta indistintamente a divinità bellicose o pacifiche nella religione romana; il problema resta dunque aperto.[78]

A livello formale, abbiamo sottolineato la fissità del linguaggio sacrale, che tuttavia si carica, sulle labbra di Augusto, di significati e contenuti nuovi: la preghiera che chiede benevolenza *mihi domo familiae* era in Catone un'invocazione del *pater familias* per sé e per chi viveva nella proprietà, ma ora appare una richiesta di protezione per quella *domus* già colpita dalla perdita di Marcello nel 23, e ora piena di speranze, in una prospettiva di successione dinastica, grazie alla prole di Giulia e Agrippa – Gaio bambino di tre anni e Lucio forse appena nato, adottati dal nonno già in quello stesso anno;[79] analogamente la

---

[72] Cf. Gagé (1955) 630 ss.; sulle tre statue (compresa Latona) collocate nel tempio palatino v. la testimonianza di Prop. 2.31.15-16 e il commento di Fedeli (2005) ad loc.
[73] Cf. supra n. 17: Schnegg-Köhler (2002) 224 attribuisce la notizia dell'oracolo a un errore di compilazione.
[74] Gagé (1955) 632.
[75] Feeney (1998) 53 ss.
[76] Schnegg-Köhler (2002) 224.
[77] Cf. Pinotti (2012) 239 ss.
[78] Cf. Green (2008) 39 ss. sulla presenza a Roma di un dibattito relativo al sacrificio cruento, contro il quale prendevano posizione i Pitagorici, ma che appare perfettamente legittimato in età augustea, anche grazie ai Ludi saeculares.
[79] Gagé (1955) 628 osserva che, non essendo noto il mese di nascita di Lucio, nel 17, non ci è possibile sapere se poté divenire un *signum* del nuovo *saeculum* che iniziava; la simbologia della monetazione imperiale infatti sfrutta spesso l'immagine di un neonato come allegoria di una nuova era.

formula inedita che implora il favore divino *populo Romano Quiritibus legionibusque* è una spia dei tempi nuovi della *res publica*,[80] in cui l'esercito non è più formato dai cittadini nel momento del bisogno, ma rappresenta una realtà professionale autonoma (a volte minacciosa) al servizio del capo militare di turno (ricordiamo *exercitum priuato consilio et priuata impensa comparaui* di *Mon. Anc.* 1).

Considerati tutti gli elementi di novità introdotti dal *princeps* nella liturgia dei Ludi, si potrebbe dare ragione a Hall,[81] quando respinge la diffusa valutazione secondo la quale il rituale del 17 sarebbe stato ellenizzato, e suggerisce piuttosto una 'Julianization': è infatti innegabile che l'impronta data da Augusto alla cerimonia non si può ricondurre all'esclusivo influsso greco (pure presente nella cooptazione di Moire e *Ilithyiae* ai sacrifici, nello spazio dato alle matrone, e soprattutto nella presenza del dio di Delfi). La personalità dell'erede di Cesare e la sua capacità di mediazione e di sincretismo (di greco e romano, di antico e moderno, di tradizione e innovazione) fanno dei *Ludi saeculares quinti* un *unicum*, che peraltro si costituisce come modello per i suoi successori fino a Settimio Severo.

Bibliografia

Appel, G. (1909), *De Romanorum precationibus*, Giessen.
Barchiesi, A. (2002), *The Uniqueness of the Carmen Saeculare and its Tradition*, in T. Woodman, D. Feeney (edd.), *Traditions and Contexts in the Poetry of Horace*, Cambridge, 107-123.
Barchiesi, A. (2005), 'Learned Eyes: Poets, Viewers, Image Makers', in K. Galinsky (ed.), *The Cambridge Companion to the Age of Augustus*, Cambridge, 281-305.
Beard M., North J., Price S. (1998), *Religions of Rome*, vol. 1, *A History*, Cambridge.

---

[80] Cf. già Mommsen (1891 = 1976) 356; Feeney (1998) 53; Schnegg-Köhler (2002) 126 collega la novità della preghiera all'*imperium proconsulare maius* che Augusto deteneva già dal 27, riconfermato ed esteso nel 23: cf. Cook, Adcock, Charlesworth (1968) 10.1, 183 ss.; Syme (1962) 337 ss.
[81] Hall (1986) 2586.

Bianchi Bandinelli, R. (1969), *Roma. L'arte romana nel centro del potere*, Milano.
Cook, S.A., Adcock, F.E., Charlesworth, M.P., edd. (1968), *L'impero di Augusto 44 a.C.-70 d. C., Cambridge Ancient History*, vols. 10.1, 10.2, trad. E. Lattanzi, Milano.
Cremona, V. (1982), *La poesia civile di Orazio*, Milano.
Davis, P.J. (2001), 'The Fabrication of Tradition: Horace, Augustus and the Secular Games', *Ramus* 30, 111-127.
De Meo, C. (1983), *Lingue tecniche del latino*, Bologna.
Dumézil, G. (1977), *La religione romana arcaica*, trad. F. Jesi, Milano.
Ernout, A. (1974), *Morphologie historique du latin*, Paris.
Fedeli P., Ciccarelli I. (2008), *Q.Horatii Flacci Carmina liber IV*, Firenze.
Fedeli, P. (2005), *Properzio. Elegie, libro 2*, Cambridge.
Fedeli, P. (2013), 'L'idea di Italia negli scrittori augustei', in *Da Italìa a Italia. Le radici di un'identità, Atti del LI Convegno di studi sulla Magna Grecia*, Taranto, 435-451.
Feeney, D. (1998), *Letteratura e religione nell'antica Roma. Culture, contesti e credenze*, Roma.
Fraenkel, E. (1993), *Orazio*, trad. S. Lilla, Roma.
Gagé, J. (1933), 'Recherches sur les Jeux Séculaires 7.2', *Revue des études latines* 11, 172-202.
Gagé, J. (1955), *Apollon Romain. Essai sur le culte d'Apollon et le développement du ritus Graecus à Rome des origines à Auguste*, Paris.
Gagé, J. (1977), *Res Gestae Divi Augusti*, Paris.
Green, S.J. (2008), 'Save our Cows? Augustan Discourse and animal Sacrifice in Ovid's *Fasti*', *Greece and Rome* 55, 39-54.
Grimal, P. (1953), *Les intentions de Properce et la composition du livre IV des Elegies*, Brussels.
Guarducci, M. (1946-1948), 'Tre cippi latini arcaici', *Bollettino della Commissione Archeologica del Governatorato di Roma* 72, 1-10.
Günther, H.C. (2013), 'The *Carmen Saeculare*', in H.-Ch. Günther (ed.), *Brill's Companion to Horace*, Leiden/ Boston, 431-443.
Hall, J.F. (1986), 'The *Saeculum Nouum* of Augustus and its Etruscan Antecedents', *Aufstieg und Niedergang der römischen Welt* II.16.3, Berlin/ New York, 2564-2589.

Hülsen, C. (1932), 'Neue Fragmente der Acta Ludorum Saecularium von 204 n. Chr.', *Rheinisches Museum* 81, 366-394.
Jacoby, F. (1962), *Die Fragmente der griechischen Historiker*, Berlin (2 B, 257, Phlegon von Tralles).
Kleiner, D.E.E. (2005), 'Semblance and Storytelling in Augustan Rome', in K. Galinsky (ed.), *The Cambridge Companion to the Age of Augustus*, Cambridge, 197-233.
La Bua, G. (1999), *L'inno nella letteratura poetica latina*, S. Severo.
La Penna, A. (1969), *Orazio e la morale mondana europea*, Firenze.
Latte, K. (1960), *Römische Religionsgeschichte*, München.
Marchetta, A. (1981), 'Contestazione e repressione religiosa nella Roma repubblicana', in *Latino e società*, Roma, 89-129.
Maurach, G. (2001), *Horaz. Werk und Leben*, Heidelberg.
Mazzarino, S. (1962), *Trattato di storia romana*, vol. 2: *L'impero romano*, Roma.
Mommsen, Th. (1891), 'Die Akten zu den Säkulargedicht des Horaz', *Reden und Aufsätze*, Hildesheim/ New York (= 1976), 351-359.
Mommsen, Th. (1913), 'Commentarium ludorum saecularium quintorum et septimorum', *Gesammelte Schriften* 8, Berlin, 567-672 (= *Ephemeris epigraphica* 8, 617-672).
Moretti, L. (1985), 'Frammenti vecchi e nuovi del commentario dei Ludi Secolari del 17 A.C.', *Atti della Pontificia Accademia Romana di Archeologia, Rendiconti* 55-56, 361-379.
Niedermann, M. (1953[4]), *Phonétique historique du latin*, Paris.
Nilsson, M.P. (1920), s.v. 'Saeculares Ludi', 'Säkularfeier', 'Säkulum', *Paulys Realencyclopädie der classischen Altertumswissenschaft* I A 2, Stuttgart, 1696-1720.
Norden, E. (1913), *Agnostos Theos. Untersuchungen zur Formengeschichte religiöser Rede*, Leipzig/ Stuttgart (= 1974).
Norden, E. (1995[9]), *Vergilius, Aeneis Buch 6*, Stuttgart-Leipzig.
Pasoli, E. (1950), *Acta Fratrum Arualium*, edidit... commentario instruxit Ae. P., Bologna.
Paschoud, F., ed. (2000), *Zosime, Histoire nouvelle*, Paris.
Pighi, G.B. (1941), *De Ludis Saecularibus Populi Romani Quiritium libri sex*, Milano (=Amsterdam 1965).
Pighi, G.B. (2009), *La preghiera romana*, Forlì (=1967).

Pinotti, P. (2012), 'Prop. 3,18. Marcello e il discorso del princeps', *Paideia* 67, 223-253.
Polara, G. (1995), 'Lettura del *Carmen Saeculare*', in M. Gigante, S. Cerasuolo (edd.), *Letture oraziane*, Napoli, 165-182.
Purcell, N. (1986), 'Livia and the Womanhood of Rome', *Proceedings of the Cambridge Philological Society* 212, 78-105.
Putnam, M.C.J. (2000), *Horace's Carmen Saeculare. Ritual Magic and the Poet's Art*, New Haven.
Putnam, M.C.J. (2010), 'The *Carmen Saeculare*', in G. Davis (ed.), *A Companion to Horace*, Oxford, 231-249.
Radke, G. (1986), s.v. 'Carmen Saeculare', *Enciclopedia Oraziana* 1, Roma, 300-303.
Ridley, R.T. (2005), 'The absent *Pontifex Maximus*', *Historia* 54, 275-300.
Romano, E. (1991), *Q.Orazio Flacco, Le Opere*, Roma.
Rossini, O. (2006), *Ara Pacis*, Milano.
Scheid, J. (1995), '*Graeco ritu*: a tipically Roman way of honoring the Gods', *Harvard Studies in Classical Philology* 97, 15-31.
Scheid, J. (1998), *Recherches archéologiques à La Magliana. Commentarii fratrum arualium qui supersunt: les copies épigraphiques des protocoles de la confrérie arvale*, par J.S. avec P. Tassini et G. Rupke, Rome.
Scheid, J. (2005), 'Augustus and Roman Religion: Continuity, Conservatism and Innovation', in K. Galinsky (ed.), *The Cambridge Companion to the Age of Augustus*, Cambridge, 175-193.
Scheid, J. (2007), *Res Gestae Divi Augusti, Hauts faits du divin Auguste*, texte établi et traduit par J.S., Paris.
Schnegg-Köhler, B. (2002), 'Die Augusteischen Säkularspiele', *Archiv für Religionsgeschichte* 4, München/ Leipzig.
Syme, R. (1962), *La rivoluzione romana*, trad. A. Momigliano, Milano.
Traina, A. (1980), '*Magnum Iovis incrementum* (*Ecl.* 4,49)', *Poeti latini (e neolatini)*, vol. 1, Bologna, 219-226.
Traina, A., Bernardi Perini, G. (1992[4]), *Propedeutica al latino universitario*, Bologna.
Treggiari, S. (2005), 'Women in the Time of Augustus', in K. Galinsky, *The Cambridge Companion to the Age of Augustus*, Cambridge, 130-147.

Tronskij, J.M. (1993[4]), 'La formazione della lingua letteraria latina', app. a F. Stolz, A. Debrunner, W.P. Schmid, *Storia della lingua latina*, Bologna, 129-172.

Van der Horst, P.C. (1943), '*Fatum, Tria Fata; Parca, Tres Parcae*', *Mnemosyne* 11, 217-227.

von Albrecht, M. (1989), *Masters of Roman Prose from Cato to Apuleius. Interpretative Studies*, trad. N. Ackin, Leeds.

Wissowa, G. (1912), *Religion und Kultus der Römer*, München.

Zanker, P. (1989), *Augusto e il potere delle immagini*, trad. F. Cuniberto, Torino.

Narrations on Epiphany and Deification: Romulus' Deification

DARJA ŠTERBENC ERKER
Humboldt-Universität zu Berlin

1. Ritual, orthopraxy and narrative

According to Émile Durkheim, religion is composed of beliefs and rituals.*[1] Durkheim interprets rituals as the means by which collective beliefs and ideas are generated, experienced and affirmed as real by the cultic community. Thus, ritual activity constitutes interaction between the collective representations of social life and individual experience and behaviour. Stanley Tambiah and Catherine Bell, who dismiss the dichotomy of belief and ritual action, have argued that cosmological and social ideas as well as the ideology of any society are embedded in its myths, rituals and laws.[2] Each performance of a ritual is a symbolic communication which revives the ideas expressed in myths, laws, and customs of a society. From the background of the performativity of rituals I will explore in this paper what kind of sense of a ritual a person in ancient Rome could experience during a ceremony of deification of an emperor. My main point of enquiry is about the relationship between narratives and the invention of new rituals in Augustan Rome.

Orthopraxy, i.e. the correct performance of rituals, was a characteristic feature of ancient religions.[3] This concept of orthopraxy was forged as a reaction against the presumptions of pietistic scholars (e.g. Friedrich Schleiermacher) of the 19th century who assumed that an individual's inner belief in a god, his inner feeling (*Gefühl*) and communication with the god was the only way a religion could func-

---
* I am very grateful to the participants of the conferences *Ancient Narratives in Lived Ancient Religion* in Weimar (organised by Jörg Rüpke) and *Saeculum Augustum* in Lisbon, and to my colleague Roland Baumgarten (= Müller 1993) for their suggestions. Equally, I want to express my thanks to Ulrike Stephan for correcting my English.
[1] Durkheim (1912).
[2] Tambiah (1979) 116-142; Bell (1992) 19-29.
[3] Linder, Scheid (1993), Scheid (2005ᵃ), Schlesier (2003) 1-20.

tion.[4] John Scheid shows that the idea of 'distressing emptiness of the mechanical gods of a religion already dead at the end of the third century BC' was promulgated by Georg W. F. Hegel and by Theodor Mommsen.[5] Roman rituals appeared to protestant scholars of the 19th century to be empty and meaningless, but they considered Greek religious devotion and Christian faith to be acceptable forms of a religion. Monica Linder and John Scheid rectify wrong expectations of modern scholars who wanted to detect counterparts of Christian faith and belief in ancient Roman religion and stress instead the immense importance of ritual practice.[6] Great emphasis on practice of Roman public religion has led to the contemporary unanimity of the last 15 years: 'To ensure the favor of the gods, the Romans relied on the correct performance of ritual (orthopraxis).'[7] Ittai Gradel even dismisses any pertinence of belief in Roman rituals the emperor cult as follows: '... but the relevance of "faith" and "belief" lay in philosophy, not in the workings of traditional ritual.'[8] However, such understanding of Roman ritualism does not take into account the dynamic relationship between a narrative and a ritual.[9] Immense importance of ritual does not mean that belief was excluded from ancient religious experience.[10]

---

[4] Already Georg Wissowa criticised this view which we now call 'ethnocentric' and doubted that 'Religiosität' was an anthropological constant which remains the same in all cultures and historical contexts, Wissowa (1912) viii. See also Bendlin (2006) 227-256, especially 229-230; Scheid (1987) 303-325.

[5] Mommsen in his History of Rome perceived the religion of Rome as a dry, prosaic religion, which rapidly lost its interiority and degenerated into an empty, laborious formalism in its evolution which headed to degeneration, Scheid (1987) 307.

[6] Linder, Scheid (1993), cf. Price (1984ᵃ) 10-15; Beard, Crawford (1985) 26-27; Feeney (1998) 18-46 presents the main problems of our modern understanding of religious belief in ancient Rome.

[7] Orlin (2007) 58. Cf. Williams (2007) 150; Scheid (1992) 122; Dupont (1986) 233: 'À Rome la religion consiste en pratiques, non en théories.' Nevertheless, Dupont (1986) 237 draws attention on 'idéologie implicite' of rituals: 'Les rituels à Rome, et c'est le cas ici, peuvent fonctionner comme discours collectif, être une façon d'expliciter par le spectacle une idéologie implicite.'

[8] Gradel (2002) 267 n. 9.

[9] For a critical approach to Gradel's rejection of narratives from interpretation of the emperor cult, Cole (2013) 10 n. 32.

[10] Linder and Scheid emphasise that two types of belief were implied by the ritual practice of the Romans, the rites were not empty '... but implicitly stated the facts concerning the gods and the order of things ... The Roman religion, as the ensemble of Roman mental attitudes, had at its base a real faith in the order of the city, guaranteeing liberty for all and justifying the effectiveness of cold ritualism,' Linder, Scheid (1993) 47, cf. 55-58. Sacrificial rituals stressed the supremacy of gods over humans, hierarchy among the human participants and their place in society, Linder, Scheid (1993) 53. Harrisson (2013) 4 does not take into account this implicit meaning stressed by both authors in her interesting discussion of belief.

Therefore, I will argue for a more complex understanding of a Roman ritual and its sophisticated relationship with narratives, philosophical discussions and social realities.

Narratives (legends, aetiologies, and myths) play an important role within rituals. The question of priority of myth or ritual has been debated by James Frazer and later by the 'Cambridge ritualists'. The 'myth and ritual school' argued in favour of primacy of a ritual from which the myths originated and interpreted the meaning of ritual primarily as enhancement of fertility in agricultural society.[11] Mary Beard has rejected the agricultural interpretation of Roman religion and has argued that rituals together with their aetiological narratives form Roman religious experience, construct religious meanings and define Roman identity.[12] The changes of aetiologies show, according to Beard, that the meaning of rituals was actively reinterpreted in the increasingly urban society of Rome.[13] Scheid has elucidated various strategies of Ovid's exegesis in his *Fasti* as an intellectual reflection on rituals.[14] Jörg Rüpke argues for the reciprocal influence of ritual performance and discursive reflection on ritual.[15] The meaning of a ritual performance could have been interpreted from the background of texts which were circulating, therefore Rüpke explores the role of narration in invention of Augustan rituals.[16] From this methodological background I will study epiphany narratives and their impact on the deification process at the end of the Republic and in Augustan times.

---

[11] Frazer (1907-1915); Ackermann (1991).
[12] Beard (1987) 1-2.
[13] Beard (1987) 11.
[14] Ovid as *poeta doctus* follows in his learned elaboration on festivals the Hellenistic aetiological tradition which does not describe festivals but discusses their various *causae*, Scheid (1992) 125, 29. Lindsay Driediger-Murphy explores how Dionysius of Halicarnassus used 'theology' in his *Antiquitates Romanae* to evaluate the veracity of the myths of the Roman historical tradition, Driediger-Murphy (2014).
[15] Rüpke (2004) 23-43.
[16] Rüpke (2004) 40. Wiedemann (1986) 478-490 draws attention to the fact that Livy 1.32.6-10, 12-14 describes a theatrical ritual of priests *fetiales* as a ritual performed in times of a mythical king Tullus Hostilius. He argues convincingly that Livy in fact comments on Octavian's ritual declaration of war against Antonius and Cleopatra in 32 BC which deflected from the fact of civil war. Livy's literary representation of the *fetiales* legitimises the ritual invented by Octavian as a revival of a forgotten ritual of Rome's ancestors, Rüpke (2004) 30-32.

2. Epiphany as a literary motif

Epiphanies (the manifestations of deities and heroes to mortals) were a well-known literary motif.[17] Literary representations of epiphanies were modelled on a similar narrative pattern: The gods manifesting their identity to the human beings appear to be larger than life; light and glowing and a divine sweet fragrance reveal their presence.[18] By epiphany gods provide support in battle or on travel, they can give advice and help mortals in many different ways.[19] Gods were supposed to appear in the semi-official possession cults (possession meaning here that a god enters the body of the possessed person).[20]

Individuals reported epiphanies which occurred in dream visions or by daytime. Sulla described his military successes as being due to the support of the goddesses Athena, Aphrodite/ Venus and Ma/ Bellona who manifested themselves to him and gave him advice.[21] In contrast to Sulla's presentation of his personal religious experience which led his political actions, Julius Caesar describes in his *Commentarii* divine signs and portents only before one event, his victory at Pharsalus.[22] Individual self-fashioning and interpretations of military achievements may vary, but the expectation that gods favoured charismatic generals was immanent to Roman tradition. Together with emphasising divine ancestry, the narrations on gods appearing to mortals in their dreams or by daylight and proclaiming that they would provide their support were considered to be necessary for obtaining political power in Roman literature.[23] Narratives on epiphanies legitimised political claims and justified political actions. Therefore, I am going to argue that the late

---

[17] For the definition see Platt (2011) 7, Graf (2004) 1122.
[18] Ov. *Fast.* 1.94, 6.252.
[19] Platt (2011) 14 stresses that the epiphanies in battle were described particularly often in the tumultuous decades of the third century BC in Hellenistic Greece.
[20] In private contexts, which differ slightly from the studied case of epiphany, religious specialists claimed that they were able to evoke an epiphany of a powerful deity to provide help to the individual seeking their assistance. Neoplatonic philosophers and theurgists also wanted to experience the epiphany of a deity in their own rituals, Plotinus, *Enn.* 5.8.2; Graf (2004).
[21] Plut. *Vit. Sull.* 9.7, 27.
[22] Caes. *BCiv.* 2.105.3-5; Feeney (1998) 19-20 stresses Caesar's emancipation from the traditional religious guarantees of success which was replaced by his self-presentation as a charismatic general to whom gods manifest their favour.
[23] Hekster (2010) 601-615.

Republican and Augustan narratives on epiphany were crucial for the invention of some elements in the ritual process of deification of the emperor in the city of Rome.[24]

3. Romulus' death and epiphany

I will start with a narration on Romulus' death and epiphany and focus on its literary representation in the late Republican and Augustan literature to reveal how this narrative gained importance in the practice of religion in the Augustan age and in the literature of the empire. The analysis will help to draw some conclusions about the relationship between narratives and the invention of a ritual of deification of a Roman emperor.

Ancient authors reflect in their depictions of the mythic-historical past on issues which were at stake in their own time.[25] When narrating a mythic-historic topic historiographers and poets reflected on laws, customs, morals, actions and rituals which were established in their own time.[26] By projecting newly established institutions into a mythical past they legitimised them as a revival of long-forgotten practices of the Roman ancestors. The tradition (*mos maiorum*) had to be observed; the emphasis on continuity of (forgotten) tradition was an important argument for the introduction of innovations in religious tradition.[27] Projecting the contemporary inventions into the past either ennobled them or called them into question. The attitude of authors towards the past is never neutral; it was 'a focus of a power struggle' as Andrew Wallace-Hadrill highlights.[28] Proclaiming with authority one version of the past reveals that the author has a powerful instrument of control over society's past and present.[29]

---

[24] Epiphany may lead to a foundation of a new cult, Graf (2004).
[25] Von Ungern-Sternberg argues that the Romulus narration explains contemporary concerns in an ideal way, von Ungern-Sternberg (1993) 96; cf. Cole (2013) 95.
[26] Dion. Hal. *Ant. Rom.* 2. 25.6-7; cf. Koortbojian (2013) 20. On *leges Iuliae* of 18 BC projected into the mythic past of Romulus and Remus, Šterbenc Erker (2008) 45-46.
[27] The self-understanding of the *nobiles* consisted in imitation and transmission of the *mos maiorum*, Sall. *Iug.* 5-6, e.g. at the funerals of family members, cf. Polyb. 6.53, Wallace-Hadrill (1997) 13. On Augustus' restoration of the religion of the Romans' ancestors, Scheid (2005ᵇ) 177-192.
[28] Wallace-Hadrill (1997) 13.
[29] Wallace-Hadrill (1997) 12-14.

Roman historiography was intention-driven from its beginnings; annalists presented moralistic *exempla* of the past, in which they attributed important roles to their patron's family.[30] In Augustan times, Dionysius of Halicarnassus wants to advise Roman politicians and statesmen how to act and how to persuade others to act. The author stresses that the aim of his history of Rome is to offer precedents for statesmen to use in various situations, thus he does not just present bare events but also their mental background, the ways in which things were done, the motives of the mythic-historical figures and the instances of divine intervention.[31] Whereas Livy, with a similar intention, depicts at length in his mythic historiography moral *exempla* of proper behaviour of Roman men and women,[32] Ovid in his elegiac poem *Fasti* prefers irony to moralising and describes the mythical *exempla* of Roman virtues, achievements and manners in an ironic way.[33] According to their literary genre and authorial intentions, the authors present a plurality of interpretations of Romulus' epiphany.[34]

4. Cicero on Romulus' death and epiphany and the question of divine qualities

Cicero, Livy, Dionysius of Halicarnassus, Ovid and Plutarch report at length Romulus' death and epiphany.[35] The Romulus narrative had already been treated by early historians of Rome – who had not mentioned his death – and by Ennius.[36] Ennius transmitted to the Romans the Hellenistic conception of the gods formulated by Euhemerus who rationalised the growing trend of deification by claiming that even Zeus himself was a great ruler deified for his merits.[37] In his *Annales*, Ennius stresses Romulus' divine ancestry when he speaks of his deification;

---

[30] Timpe (1996) 289; Hölkeskamp (1996) 323; Krasser (2005) 360-362.
[31] Dion. Hal. *Ant. Rom.* 5. 56.1.
[32] Livy *praef.* 8-12; Mehl (2003) 106; Forsythe (1999) 65-73; Davies (2004) 27.
[33] Cf. Scheid (1992) 118.
[34] Feeney (2007) highlights the importance of literary genre and authorial intentions in representations of Roman religion.
[35] For a detailed discussion of the differing narratives, see Robinson (2011) 297-304.
[36] For a careful reconstruction of the annalistic tradition on Romulus, see von Ungern-Sternberg (1993) 90-100, for the silence of the annalists about Romulus' death, ibid. 104.
[37] The extant fragments of Ennius' translation are found in Cic. *Rep.* and in Lactant. *Div. inst.*

his account is the first uncontested evidence of Romulus' divinisation.[38] Cicero in his *De re publica* and *De legibus* appeals to the Ennian precedent for a mortal attaining divinity, but he distances himself from the idea of a physical journey of a divinised mortal to heaven.[39] Cicero puts in the mouth of Scipio Africanus that Romulus' age rejected that which could not possibly have happened, but that in Romulus there was such a strength of talent and virtue that people believed Julius Proculus, the witness of his divinisation.[40] Nevertheless, Scipio expresses a sceptical view about Julius Proculus' vision and presumes that the senators who wanted to free themselves from all suspicion in regard to Romulus' death had the peasant Julius Proculus state before a public assembly that he had seen the deified Romulus.[41] This statement of Scipio's reveals a rationalisation of the narrative and stands in a tradition of euhemeristic interpretation.

Euhemerus of Messena reflected on the practices of self-deification of the Ptolemaic rulers and proposed in his *Sacred Record* an interpretation of the Olympic gods as deified men of power, personal charisma and merit.[42] Thus, Euhemerus rationalises cults of gods and diminishes their powerful status. Cicero, in his reception of Euhemerus in *De re publica*, highlights the personal charisma of deification candidates (*uis ingenii atque uirtutis*).[43] The men of old times, as Cicero quotes from Ennius' *Annales*, called righteous kings guardians of the fatherland (*patriae custodes*), fathers (*patres*) and gods (*deos*) for their merits for the *res publica*.[44] Cicero disregards Romulus' divine origin

---

[38] Cic. *Rep.* 1.64, cf. 1.25; Enn. *Ann.* 54f, 110; Skutsch (1985) 260-262; Robinson (2011) 303. Varro does not mention the deification of Romulus, Robinson supposes that the location of Romulus' grave (see Porph. *Epod.* 16.13; Ps.-Acro *Epod.* 16.13-14) was discussed already in Varro's time, a line of argumentation which would oppose Romulus' deification.
[39] Whitton (2013) 158-159.
[40] Cic. *Rep.* 2.17, 19-20; Cole (2013) 93-94.
[41] Cic. *Rep.* 2.20: *Sed profecto tanta fuit in eo (sc. Romulus) uis ingenii atque uirtutis, ut id de Romulo Proculo Iulio, homini agresti, crederetur, quod multis iam ante saeculis nullo alio de mortali homines credidissent; qui inpulsu patrum, quo illi a se inuidiam interitus Romuli pellerent, in contione dixisse fertur a se uisum esse in eo colle Romulum, qui nunc Quirinalis uocatur; eum sibi mandasse, ut populum rogaret, ut sibi eo in colle delubrum fieret; se deum esse et Quirinum uocari.* Cf. Lact. *Div. inst.* 1.15; Porte (1981) 334 stresses that Cicero presents Proculus in an ironic fashion.
[42] Diod. Sic. 6.1.8-6.2, Müller (1993) 280-282.
[43] Cic. *Rep.* 2.19-20; Cole (2013) 93.
[44] Cic. *Rep.* 1.64. In this treatise Cicero emphasises his own title *pater patriae*, cf. Cole (2013) 91 and n. 75; Skutsch (1985) 258-259.

from Mars and focuses on Romulus' merit-based achievement of divine status.[45] Unlike Ennius who mentions the god Mars as Romulus' father who took his son to the heavens, for Cicero only merits let a mortal approach the gods, not hereditary claims to divinity.[46] The author does not confirm Julius Caesar's claims to divinity traced back to Troy.[47] Not only the Romulus narrative but also the connection between merits for a *res publica* (foundation of a city, saving the city from ruin, victory over enemies), the title *pater patriae* and concepts of divinisation of a mortal belonged to a political rhetoric which emphasised a person's merits for the *res publica* and the possibility of her/ his divinisation.[48]

The identification of Romulus with Quirinus is made by Cicero in *De re publica* where he draws on the connection which has already been made by the *gens Julia*, but presents a hostile view on Proculus, stressing the person's naivety and superstitious credence in miracles and corporeal deification.[49] Thus, Cicero probably reacts to a strategy of religious self-presentation of Julius Caesar who encouraged a connection of his person and the deified first king of Rome.[50] The Senate erected a statue of Julius Caesar in the Quirinus temple in 45 BC

---

[45] Cic. *Rep.* 6.13; Cole (2013) 92, 101, 109 et passim.

[46] Cicero refers in his recitation of the laws of his ideal city, in which he transposes the existing sacral laws of Rome, to the cult due to those men who have been raised to the heavens on the account of merit, Cic. *Leg.* 2.19: *Diuos et eos qui caelestes semper habiti sunt colunto et ollos quos endo caelo merita <l>ocauerint, Herculem, Liberum, Aesculapium, Castorem, Pollucem, Quirinum, ast olla propter quae datur homini<bus> ascensus in caelum, Mentem, Virtutem, Pietatem, Fidem, earumque laudum delubra sunto nec ulla uitiorum sacra sollemnia obeunto*; Cole (2013) 109. Thus, he emphasises the difference between the souls of all men which are immortal and those of good and brave men that are divine, Cic. *Leg.* 2.27. Nevertheless, Cotta attacks Epicureanism and all 'those who teach that brave or famous or powerful men have been deified after their death,' *Nat. D.* 1.119. Koortbojian argues convincingly that Cicero criticises with this passage the exceptional honours granted to Julius Caesar, Koortbojian (2013) 1-4.

[47] Burkert (1962) 356-359; Cole (2013) 194. Nevertheless, Cicero uses the argument of divine qualities of a mortal in favour of his protégés and in his own favour. He underlines e.g. that divine spirit was acting in Marius (and in other saviours of the cities) when he won battles over enemies, therefore he should be called *pater patriae*, Cic. *Rab. Post.* 27, 30, 49; Weinstock (1971) 179; Cole (2013) 76-80. After Cicero as consul had suppressed the Catilinarian conspiracy, he wrote that Romulus' apotheosis was the reward for founding Rome and mentioned at the same time his own saving Rome from the peril of the Catilinarian conspiracy, Cic. *Sen.* 3.2; Weinstock (1971) 180.

[48] Cic. *Rep.* 1.12; Weinstock (1971) 180; Cole (2013) 50-56.

[49] Cic. *Rep.* 2.20; *Leg.* 1.3; *Off.* 3.41; Ogilvie (1965) 85; Porte (1981) 334-335 interprets the proliferation of the myth variants on Proculus in a context of fights of the Roman 'clans politiques'.

[50] Burkert (1962) 356-369. Skutsch argues that Proculus' speech in Livy 1.16 goes back to Ennius' *Annals* because of its poetic colouring. He supposes that Proculus owes his family name to

and decreed that Caesar's ivory statue should be carried together with Quirinus' statue in a *pompa circensis*.[51]

Cicero presents in his writings and speeches Greek and Hellenistic ideas on the possibility of crossing the boundary between mortals and immortals. Thus, he reflects on habits of politicians who presented themselves as divine-like in different media.[52] Theatrical self-staging of Pompey and Caesar by which they approximated themselves to the gods, tracing mythic genealogies to gods in speeches or by minting coins with allegedly ancestral divinities and receving divine honours granted by the senate contributed to the acceptance of statesmen as political leaders.[53] Michael Koortbojian connects Caesar's statue within the temple of Quirinus, which he argues must have been fashioned as Romulus, with Caesar's deification and highlights that Romulus played an important role not only in the Caesarian drama but also in the establishment of deification.[54]

5. Livy's account of Romulus' mysterious death and epiphany

Livy focuses on the circumstances of Romulus' death:

> his immortalibus editis operibus cum ad exercitum recensendum contionem in campo ad Caprae paludem haberet, subito coorta tempestas cum magno

---

Julian ambition which was attributed to him towards the end of the second century BC, Skutsch (1985) 260; but the first clear evidence for this self-fashioning of the *gens Iulia* is Cicero's, Robinson (2011) 314; cf. Porte (1981) 333-340.

[51] Cic. *Att.* 12.45.2, 13.28.3: *contubernalis Quirini*; Cass. Dio 43.45.2-4; Augustus restored the temple in 16 BC, *Mon. Anc.* 19.2; Cass. Dio 54.19.4; Burkert (1962) 357; Porte (1981) 336; Fishwick (1987) 58. Koortbojian argues referring to Caesar's statue in Quirinus' temple and his image on coins that they '... envisioned Caesar first as the "New Romulus", and then as the new *divus*, the equal of Quirinus,' Koortbojian (2013) 93. On Caesar's statue carried at games: Cic. *Att.* 13.28.3; Cass. Dio 43.42. 3; Weinstock (1971) 175.

[52] Spencer Cole argues that Cicero's philosophical and theological explorations of concepts of deification 'shaped the core architecture of related religious innovations,' Cole (2013) 198. In my opinion Cole overemphasises Cicero's merit, since he was not the only person who reflected on divinisation of a mortal in Rome, but he was the only Republican author whose texts present to us Roman ways of adaptation of the Greek and Hellenistic ideas at length. Varro's *Antiquitates rerum diuinarum* offer precedents for Caesar's divinisation according to Cole (2013) 194, but they are only fragmentarily transmitted.

[53] Pompey was granted a triumph for his victory in Africa in 79 BC. He tried to drive into Rome on a chariot drawn by elephants in Hercules' or Dionysos' style, but the door gate was too narrow so that he had to use a normal chariot, Plut. *Vit. Pomp.* 14.6; Weinstock (1971) 37; Cole (2013) 7 stresses that Cicero develops his concepts of deification by referring to the Greek tradition of self-presentation as a god and the Roman tradition of a divine general in a triumphal ritual.

[54] Koortbojian (2013) 84, cf. n. 51.

fragore tonitribusque tam denso regem operuit nimbo ut conspectum eius contioni abstulerit; nec deinde in terris Romulus fuit. Romana pubes sedato tandem pauore postquam ex tam turbido die serena et tranquilla lux rediit, ubi uacuam sedem regiam uidit, etsi satis credebat patribus qui proximi steterant sublimem raptum procella, tamen uelut orbitatis metu icta maestum aliquamdiu silentium obtinuit. deinde a paucis initio facto, deum deo natum, regem parentemque urbis Romanae saluere uniuersi Romulum iubent; pacem precibus exposcunt, uti uolens propitius suam semper sospitet progeniem.[55]

When these deeds, worthy of immortality, had been accomplished, one day he gathered the men together on the Campus Martius, near the marsh of Capra, to hold a review of the citizens under arms. Suddenly a storm blew up with great claps of thunder and covered the king in such a thick cloud that he became completely invisible to the gathering. From that moment on Romulus was no more on earth. The Roman troops eventually recovered from their panic, when a bright and peaceful sunny day returned after the confusion of the storm. But when they saw that the king's chair was empty, although they believed the senators who had been standing nearby and claimed that he had been swept up aloft in the blast, they nevertheless kept a sorrowful silence for some time as though overcome with the fear that they had been left as orphans. Then, when a few men gave the lead, they all decided that Romulus should be hailed a god, son of a god, king, and father of the Roman state. And in prayers they begged his grace, beseeching him to be favourable and propitious towards them and ever to protect his descendants.

transl. Beard, North, Price (1998[b])

Livy gives a fuller version of Romulus' disappearance than Cicero. With the mysterious vanishing of Romulus he alludes to divine kidnapping of heroes which usually occurs in a storm.[56] Here it can be implied that Jupiter kidnapped Romulus, because he is the master of thunderbolt which accompanied the tempest. Julius Caesar was closely connected with Jupiter; Dio, who wrote much later, mentions that he was called 'Jupiter Julius'.[57] Livy alludes here to Caesar's death by mentioning that Romulus became completely invisible to the gathering, Ovid and Plutarch express the same idea when they write that the people fled.[58]

---

[55] Livy 1.16.1-4.
[56] Ogilvie (1965) 84.
[57] Cass. Dio 44.6.4: Δία ...'Ιούλιον, cf. Koortbojian (2013) 7.
[58] Ov. *Fast.* 2.496: *fit fuga*; Plut. *Quest. Rom.* 27.7; Weinstock (1971) 347. The Romulus story may have been constructed on solar eclipses which occurred in the years when Rome was said to have been founded, Robinson (2011) 312.

Suetonius relates that self-fafter Caesar was stabbed on the Ides of March, everybody fled from the Curia and left the corpse alone, then three slaves took it home.[59] An even clearer identification of Romulus' death with Caesar's is contained in Livy's saying that some of the Roman citizens, astonished to see that Romulus had disappeared, started acclamations: *deum deo natum, regem parentemque urbis Romanae saluere uniuersi Romulum iubent...*[60] The way the disappeared Romulus was spontaneously hailed resembles very much the self-fashioning of Julius Caesar. Caesar presented his family, the Julii, as descendants of the goddess Venus, therefore the phrase 'god and god's son' (*deum deo natum*) could be read as a reference to his divine ancestry.[61]

The Senate granted Caesar an honorific title, *parens patriae*, to which a part of the phrase King and Father of the Roman City (*regem parentemque urbis Romae*) alludes.[62] As already shown, the connection between the title *parens patriae* and the divinity of its holder was present in late Republican discourses. Together with the title parens patriae Caesar was also granted the right of portraiture on coins. It is also possible that the formula refers to *uota* which were pronounced at the statue of the deified Julius Caesar in the Forum.[63]

Livy's text alludes only to some of the extraordinary honours conferred on Caesar which expressed his higher status. The Senate bestowed on Caesar numerous honours which implied his proximity to the ancient kings of Rome and triumph: triumphal and regal dress, a golden throne for the Curia, the right to drive in a chariot in Rome, a pediment at the *domus publica* (only temples of the gods had a

---

[59] Suet. *Caes.* 82: *diffugientibus cunctis.*
[60] Livy 1.16.3.
[61] This is another parallel between Romulus and Caesar. Ennius in his *Annales* 1.106-108 stresses the divine ancestry of Romulus. Caesar in his funeral oration for his aunt Julia in 69 or 68 BC claimed divine origin of his family from the goddess Venus through the Trojan Aeneas, Suet. *Caes.* 6; Fishwick (1987) 56. Barchiesi (1994) 107 interprets the emphasis on the spontaneous reaction and the emergence of the cult as a political manipulation.
[62] Suet. *Caes.* 85 (see below n. 67), Cass. Dio 44.4. Ennius addresses Romulus as father, because he was a founder of Rome, Cic. *Rep.* 1.64; Enn. *Ann.* 108: *o pater, o genitor, o sanguen dis oriundum!* cf. Cic. *Div.* 1.3, Skutsch (1985) 259; Weinstock (1971) 201-205; cf. Cole (2013) 90-91. Such an honour for a living person was without precedents in the Roman Republic but analogous to the practices in the Hellenistic kingdoms; in the later empire the honour was restricted to the emperor and his family.
[63] Weinstock (1971) 274-275.

pediment) which was his office in his function as pontifex maximus.[64] These honours reminded the Roman people of Greek ideas and Hellenistic practices about making exceptional men gods.[65] Suetonius relates that people took Caesar's bier to the Capitoline with the intention of cremating his corpse in the *cella* of Jupiter which would have meant that he was placed among the gods.[66] Unofficially, Caesar was honoured by his supporters as a god immediately after his death in March 44, an altar and a column with his statue with an inscription *parens patriae* were set up in the Forum on the site of his funeral pyre.[67] In the rivalry of Antonius and Octavian after Caesar's death, rhetorical claims for and against Caesar's divinity played an important role.[68]

---

[64] Weinstock (1971) 270-281. Some of Caesar's privileges of 45 BC were previously reserved only for gods in Rome, such as a golden throne in the theatre (in Caesar's absence his golden crown was put on it to signal his symbolic presence) and a special carriage (*tensa*) to drive his ivory statue in the *pompa circensis* to the Circus Maximus to be put on his 'pulvinar' (couch for a divine banquet, *lectisternium*), Cic. *Phil.* 2.110; Suet. *Caes.* 76.1. In 45 the Senate decreed that a temple of Clementia Caesaris was to be built for Caesar (but this never happened); Antonius was elected for their priest (*flamen*), Weinstock (1971) 309.

[65] Koortbojian (2013) 4. Ptolemaic and Seleucid kings encouraged the ruler cult, Platt (2011) 124f. Fishwick resumes the scholarly discussion on the problem of Caesar's deification in his life or posthumously, Fishwick (1987) 56-72. The author argues for a gradual agglomeration of Caesar's powers and not as a strategy planned in advance, Fishwick (1987) 71.

[66] Suet. *Caes.* 84.3: *quem cum pars in Capitolini Iouis cella cremare pars in curia Pompei destinaret.* Appian writes that people took the corpse to the Capitoline but were prevented by the priests from burning it there, Appian, *B Ciu.* 2.148; Cass. Dio 44.50.2; Weinstock (1971) 355. Antonius, who staged himself as a guarantor of Caesar's divinity to gain the support of Caesar's veterans, intoned at the end of his funeral oration a hymn on Caesar as a celestial god, raised his hands to the sky in a theatrical manner to testify to Caesar's divine birth, Appian, *B Ciu.* 2.146; Weinstock (1971) 352; Koortbojian (2013) 26.

[67] Suetonius writes that people performed sacrifices, made vows and ended quarrels at Caesar's column (with his statue) in the Forum for a long time, Suet. *Caes.* 85: *postea solidam columnam prope uiginti pedum lapidis Numidici in foro statuit <in>scripsitque PARENTI PATRIAE. apud eam longo tempore sacrificare, uota suscipere, controuersias quasdam interposito per Caesarem iure iurando distrahere perseuerauit.* Cf. Valerius Maximus 1.6.13. For the consecration of *Diuus Iulius:* Dessau, *ILS* 72: *Genio Deiui Iuli/ parentis patriae/, quem senatus/ populusque/ Romanus in/ deorum numerum/ rettulit*; Weinstock (1971) 214, 309, 366; Koortbojian (2013) 8, 27, 130-131.

[68] Cole (2013) 170-184; Koortbojian (2013) 7. The belief in Caesar's divinity, ascertained by the *sidus Iulium*, enforced the pertinence of the new cult of *Diuus Iulius*. Against the view of Ramsey, Licht (1997) 1-15 that Octavian himself interpreted the meaning of the comet: Pandey (2013) 406-407 et passim. An appearance of a comet at Octavian's *ludi Victoriae Caesaris* in August 44 BC confirmed the belief that Caesar had emerged as a new god, therefore Octavian placed a star over Caesar's statue in the Forum, Plin. *HN* 2.93-94; Suet. *Caes.* 88; Serv. *Ecl.* 9.46; Serv. Dan. *Ecl.* 9.46: *Cum Augustus Caesar ludos funebres patri celebraret, die medio stella apparuit. Ille eam esse confirmauit parentis sui... inscriptum in basi fuit: 'Caesari emitheo.'* Cf. Weinstock (1971) 370; Cole (2013) 171; Koortbojian (2013) 120-121. The belief

Only in 42 BC, when Octavian successfully succeeded Caesar, did he push for Caesar's consecration, which was then officially decreed by the Roman senate.[69]

Whereas Cicero's account of Romulus' death may be interpreted as a mythic precedent for the belief of the Roman people in the divinisation of a mortal, Livy's narration of Romulus' death provided a legitimisation of Caesar's deification and his official consecration as *Diuus Iulius*. The discussed part of the narrative dignified the already existing cult of *Diuus Iulius* by projecting similar actions (death of an almost divine person of merit for the *res publica*, their divinisation and divine worship) into the mythic past.

But, as Livy continues, the idea that Romulus became a god was not shared by everybody, since some men silently thought that the senators had killed king Romulus, and this rumour was persistent:

> fuisse credo tum quoque aliquos qui discerptum regem patrum manibus taciti arguerent; manauit enim haec quoque sed perobscura fama; illam alteram admiratio uiri et pauor praesens nobilitauit. et consilio etiam unius hominis addita rei dicitur fides. namque Proculus Iulius, sollicita ciuitate desiderio regis et infensa patribus, grauis, ut traditur, quamuis magnae rei auctor in contionem prodit. 'Romulus' inquit, 'Quirites, parens urbis huius, prima hodierna luce caelo repente delapsus se mihi obuium dedit. cum perfusus horrore uenerabundusque adstitissem petens precibus ut contra intueri fas esset, "abi, nuntia" inquit "Romanis, caelestes ita uelle ut mea Roma caput orbis terrarum sit; proinde rem militarem colant sciantque et ita posteris tradant nullas opes humanas armis Romanis resistere posse." haec' inquit 'locutus sublimis abiit.' Mirum quantum illi uiro nuntianti haec fidei fuerit, quamque desiderium Romuli apud plebem exercitumque facta fide immortalitatis lenitum sit.[70]

> I believe that there were some men, even then, who privately claimed that the king had been torn apart at the hands of the senators. For this story too,

---

in Caesar's immortality was shared by the Roman people, but also literary texts refer to it as a sign of the beginning of a new *saeculum*. Suetonius speaks of the belief of the crowd, *Caes.* 88: *persuasione uolgi*, Livy of plebs and soldiers. Cf. Hor. *Carm.* 1.12.46: *Iulium sidus* (here it could also be a reference to Augustus). Vergil and Properce mention the reappearance of the star in the battle of Actium, Verg. *Aen.* 8.681; Prop. 4.6.59; Koortbojian (2013) 132. The star reappeared in 17 BC, the year of Augustus' Saecular Games (see Šterbenc Erker [2018]) and was reinterpreted by Augustus as a sign of a *saeculum Augustum*; for the discussion: Weinstock (1971) 370-371.
[69] App. *B Ciu.* 2.148; Cass. Dio 47.18.3; Weinstock (1971) 386; Beard, North, Price (1998ª) 148-149; Koortbojian (2013) 130-131.
[70] Livy 1.16.5-8.

obscure as it is, has spread. But men's admiration for him, as well as the strength of their fear, has given the other version greater weight. And it is said that it received added credence by the device of one man. For, when the citizens were troubled by the loss of their king and in hostile mood towards the senate, Proculus Julius, a man of considerable authority, so it is said, even though reporting a strange occurrence, came forward to address the assembly. 'Quirites', he said, 'Romulus, the father of this city, suddenly descended from the heavens this morning at first light and made himself known to me. I was overcome with fear and awe, and stood in front of him beseeching him in prayer that it should be lawful for me to gaze upon him. And he said "Depart. Proclaim to the Romans that the gods so wish it that my Rome should be the capital of the whole world. So let them foster the art of war and let them convey to their descendants that no human strength can resist the arms of Rome."[71] He made this pronouncement,' he said, 'then departed on high.' It is extraordinary how much credence was granted to the man's story and how the grief felt by the people and army for the loss of Romulus was assuaged by belief in his immortality.

transl. Beard, North, Price (1998[b])

At this point the historicising of the Romulus narrative by reference to Julius Caesar's assassination is quite clearly a subversion of Caesar's divinity as it was promoted by the opponents of his divinisation.[72] Livy stresses that the admiration for Romulus and the extent of people's fear rendered the deification variant of the mythic narrative famous and ennobled it ('nobilitavit').[73] In order to explain why the divinisation variant gained more credence, the historiographer gives an account of Proculus who was said to have provided a decisive argument in favour of Romulus' deification.[74] Julius Proculus testifies at the assembly that Romulus descended suddenly from the sky (*caelo delapsus*) and departed on high after his speech (*locutus sublimis abiit*), thus he

---

[71] Cf. Anchises' speech at Verg. *Aen.* 6.847-853, esp. 851-852: *tu regere imperio populos, Romane, memento/ hae tibi erunt artes, pacique imponere morem...*
[72] Weinstock (1971) 372; Beard, North, Price (1998[a]) 149; Beard, North, Price (1998[b]) 50-51. The consul Dolabella destroyed Caesar's statue and altar in the Forum. Cic. *Att.* 14.15f; Lact. *Div. inst.* 1.15.30; Koortbojian (2013) 26-42. Caesar's veterans intended to re-erect the altar, Cic. *Fam.* 11.2.2; Weinstock (1971) 364-367; Koortbojian (2013) 5. Caesar's opponents expressed their polemic also in scientific discourse. The Epicurean Philodemus who objected in 44 BC to the Stoic doctrine on divinity of the stars and astral immortality of distinguished men opposed Caesar's divinisation on this ground, Weinstock (1971) 372; cf. Varro *Ant. rer. diu.*1, frg. 32 (Cardauns).
[73] Livy 1.16.5.
[74] Cic. *Rep.* 2.20.

describes an epiphany of the celestial god.[75] Livy stresses how much credence was granted to the man's story and how the Romans' grief for the loss of Romulus was assuaged by belief (*facta fide*) in his immortality.[76]

Although Livy himself is not partial to either side, he distances himself from the narrative variant of Romulus' dismemberment by qualifying the sceptic view on deification as an 'obscure rumour' (*perobscura fama*).[77] Livy's explanation of why the deification narrative gained more support rests on moral grounds: he presents the deification narrative as a version of greater weight because Julius Proculus was a *grauis uir*, a venerable man. As such a person he could have easily persuaded Romulus' men who already admired him (*admiratio uiri*). Thus, the charismatic quality of Romulus is for Livy, like for Cicero, one of the reasons for the people's belief in his divinisation.

6. Dionysius' Quirinus: an addressee of a hero cult

Dionysius of Halicarnassus in his *Antiquitates Romanae* offers even more discordant versions of the mythic narrative on Romulus' death. Dionysius presents the mythical deification as a product of authors who give rather fabulous accounts of Romulus' life (οἱ μὲν οὖν μυθωδέστερα τὰ περὶ αὐτοῦ ποιοῦντες) and believe that Romulus was taken to the

---

[75] Ogilvie (1965) 87 recognises here *katabasia, descensio*; cf. Verg. *Aen.* 8.423.

[76] Cicero writes in his letters to Atticus that he thinks about consecrating his dead daughter Tullia to assuage his own grief, Cic. *Att.* 12.18.1 (March 11th 45 BC); Cole (2013) 1-6. The disturbance of the citizens might allude to the tumult which Antonius' invitation to the people to mourn Caesar in his funeral oration has incited (see above, note 66), the people improvised a funeral pyre (they took benches from the Curia) and cremated Caesar's body in the Forum. Cic. *Phil.* 2.91; *Att.* 14.10.1; Suet. *Caes.* 84.3; App. *B. Ciu.* 2.146, 148; Weinstock (1971) 353-355.

[77] Weinstock (1971) 347 interprets the death of Romulus as a precedent for literary representations of Caesar's death. Ogilvie (1965) 85 remarks that after 44 BC the death of Caesar was a model for narrations on the death of Romulus. My interpretation of the Romulus-Quirinus narrative follows Stefan Weinstock. It differs from the previous attempts of scholars who dissociated the narratives on Romulus' death from their historical background in order to show ethnographic or structural parallels of Romulus as a founder of a city of Rome: Brelich (1960); Burkert (1962) 370-371; Bremmer (1987) 46-47; von Ungern-Sterberg (1993) 104. Von Ungern-Sternberg connects the disappearance of Romulus with a festival *Regifugium*, because the priest *rex sacrorum*, who offered sacrifices in the Comitium had to run away, so to say to 'disappear', von Ungern-Sternberg (1993) 105. All these interpretations do not take into account the historicising of the narrative and its political intention which focused on the question of divinisation of a mortal. On this issue see Koortbojian (2013) 84-93; Cole (2013).

heavens in a cloud by his father Mars (πεπιστεύκασιν ὑπὸ τοῦ πατρὸς Ἄρεος τὸν ἄνδρα ἀνηρπάσθαι).[78] The second variant of the narrative which Livy dismisses as 'very obscure rumour', Dionysius accords to those who write more plausible accounts (οἱ δὲ τὰ πιθανώτερα γράφοντες), who say that Romulus was killed by his own people. Patricians formed a conspiracy against Romulus to slay him because of his tyrannical behaviour.[79] Also according to this variant of the narrative, the conspirators murdered Romulus when rain and darkness occurred, the assembly of the people was dispersed and their chief left without his guard. This flight of the people Dionysius considers as an aition of the festival *Populifugia*.[80]

Dionysius emphasises that the narrative on Romulus' ascension gives great authority to people who make gods of mortal men. But Dionysius himself sticks to his own principles of antiquarian research which offers moralistic *exempla* from which Roman politicians should learn how to act appropriately. The antiquarian searches for the earliest variant of a narrative, and rationalises it by accommodating it to the norms of likelihood and contemporary plausibility.[81] Due to his rationalisation of myth, Dionysius often rejects mythological elements of narratives.[82] Therefore he qualifies in Romulus' case the narrative which does not take into account action of gods as a more plausible account. Nevertheless, Dionysius mentions the worship of Romulus as Quirinus when he describes religious innovations of Numa, the second legendary king:

> αὐτόν τε τὸν Ῥωμύλον ὡς κρείττονα γενόμενον ἢ κατὰ τὴν θνητὴν φύσιν ἱεροῦ κατασκευῇ καὶ θυσίαις διετησίοις ἔταξε Κυρῖνον ἐπονομαζόμενον γεραίρεσθαι.[83]
>
> He also ordered that Romulus himself, as one who had shown a greatness beyond mortal nature, should be honoured, under the name Quirinus, by the erection of a temple and by sacrifices throughout the year.

---

[78] *Ant. Rom.* 2.56.3; Enn. *Ann.* 110, Skutsch (1985) 260. Cf. Driediger-Murphy (2014) 335: 'Dionysius seems to accept the possibility of deification of mortals ... but nevertheless appears to reject the story of Romulus' apotheosis.'
[79] *Ant. Rom.* 2.56.3; cf. Cic. *Rep.* 2.20 (see above).
[80] *Ant. Rom.* 2.56.5-6; Plut. *Vit. Rom.* 29.8. A variant of the festival's name is *Populifugia*.
[81] Feeney (2007).
[82] Šterbenc Erker (2008) 34-35.
[83] *Ant. Rom.* 2.63.3.

Here Dionysius accepts that a mortal Romulus is to be honoured under the name Quirinus. Then he mentions Julius Proculus' who saw Romulus departing from the city fully armed and was told:

> Ἄγγελλε Ῥωμαίοις Ἰούλιε τὰ παρ' ἐμοῦ, ὅτι με ὁ λαχὼν ὅτ' ἐγενόμην δαίμων εἰς θεοὺς ἄγεται τὸν θνητὸν ἐκπληρώσαντα αἰῶνα· εἰμὶ δὲ Κυρῖνος.[84]

> Julius, announce to the Romans from me, that the genius to whom I was allotted at my birth is conducting me to the gods, now that I have finished my mortal life, and that I am Quirinus.

Dionysius continues with Numa's religious innovations which he categorises, according to his antiquarian rationalising method, into eight parts.[85] Dionysius' choice of the aetiology of the cult is based on two premises: firstly, that it was the great mythic king Numa who founded the Romulus-Quirinus cult, a fact that vouches for its legitimacy. Secondly, Dionysius' moralistic intention is apparent in his emphasis on the sincerity and integrity of Julius Proculus.[86] In his presentation of Romulus' laws, Dionysius limits his discussion to those of which he approves.[87] In Dionysius' eyes, who establishes his authority as a Greek historian of Rome reporting on beliefs of the Romans, it is the admirable Quirinus cult which revives for the Romans under Augustus the virtues of heroic age.[88] The Quirinus cult seems to be acceptable from Dionysius' Greek perspective as a hero cult. Like in Livy's text, the epiphany of the deified Romulus highlights the close relationship between the god and the Julii and implies the divine support for the family.

7. Ovid's ambivalent representation of Romulus in his *Fasti*

The Romulus-Quirinus narrative was not only connected with Julius Caesar, but also with Octavian, who contemplated seriously naming

---
[84] *Ant. Rom.* 2.63.4.
[85] *Ant. Rom.* 2.64-74.
[86] *Ant. Rom.* 2.63.3. On Dionysius' intentions see n. 31.
[87] *Ant. Rom.* 2.24.1
[88] Ibid. On Dionysius' construction of his authorial authority as a Greek historiographer of Rome, Luraghi (2003) 285; Feeney (2007) 190-191.

himself Romulus.[89] This correspondence was well known to Ovid, who narrates the story in a completely different way: he presents the narration as an *aition* of the foundation of Quirinus' temple and his festival Quirinalia on February 17th.[90] In his humorous didactic elegy *Fasti*, Ovid surprises his readership with his almost naïve credence: he does not use any subtle distancing devices like Livy and Dionysius to underline that he does not vouch for the belief in Julius Proculus' vision.[91] Ovid rejects the belief of some people that the senators have murdered Romulus as false; for him, there is no doubt that the king Romulus rode with Mars' horses straight to the heavens.[92] The poet even confirms the narrative by Mars' words urging Jupiter to fulfil his promise of a deification and give him back his son.[93] Unlike Livy and Dionysius of Halicarnassus who allude to tensions between Romulus and the senate before his death, Ovid presents Romulus as a sovereign lawgiver and does not mention any strains.[94] These verses present evidence for 'supportive readers' of this highly political poem who do not expect the poet to undermine his praise of Augustus.[95] Ovid

---

[89] Cf. Suet. *Aug.* 7; Herbert-Brown (1994) 60-61. The identification of Romulus with Quirinus was mentioned in an inscription underneath Romulus' statue in the Forum Augustum, *CIL* 1².189; Verg. *Aen.* 1.292; Ov. *Fast.* 2.475-476, 5.565-566; Barchiesi (1994) 103.

[90] 2.511-512. Romulus' transformation to Quirinus is supposed to take place on the Nones of July (*Nonae Capratinae*), Cic. *Rep.* 1.25. Plutarch beliefs wrongly that the *Nonae Capratinae* and the festival *Populifugia* fell on the same day, the 5th July, Plut. *Vit. Rom.* 27.4; for discussion see Robinson (2011) 300-301.

[91] Livy 1.16.5-8: *dicitur, ut traditur*. Cf. Barchiesi (1994) 105. On distancing devices, Feeney (2007) 185-186, Whitton (2013) 159.

[92] Ov. *Fast.* 2.497-8: *falsaeque patres in crimine caedis/ haesissetque animis forsitan illa fides*; for the dark side of Romulus in Augustan literature see Herbert-Brown (1994) 49-52. Ov. *Fast.* 2.496: *rex patriis astra petebat equis*; cf. 478: *uenit in astra deus*; *Met.* 14.820. This is a common literary representation of deification, as Robinson (2011) 313 argues.

[93] 2.482-3: *'Iuppiter', inquit, 'habet Romana potentia uires:/ sanguinis officio non eget illa mei/ redde patri natum'...* Mars quotes Jupiter's promise made in Enn. *Ann.* fr. 54f, cf. Varro, *Ling.* 7.5, Ov. *Met.* 14.806-807, Skutsch (1985) 20. Cf. Barchiesi (1994) 108, Robinson (2011) 314. Similarly, Ovid presents Julius Caesar's deification as a fact, mentioning his admission to Jupiter's palace and his temple in the Forum, Ov. *Fast.* 3.696-710.

[94] 2.492: *forte tuis illic, Romule, iura dabas*. The people liked Romulus more than the senate did, Livy 1.15.8; Dionysius and Plutarch enumerate several cases of Romulus' tyrannical behaviour, Dion. Hal. *Ant. Rom.* 2.56.3; Plut. *Vit. Rom.* 27.1-2; Robinson (2011) 310.

[95] On supportive and suspicious readers of Ovid's *Fasti*, see Robinson (2011) 9-10, on a more favourable view on Romulus in comparison with other authors, Robinson (2011) 310. The reference to Remus' fate may evoke Romulus as a murderer, Robinson (2011) 311.

emphasises the fabulous side of the narrative by taking the narrative too literally:[96]

> sed Proculus Longa ueniebat Iulius Alba,
>   lunaque fulgebat, nec facis usus erat,
> cum subito motu saepes tremuere sinistrae:
>   rettulit ille gradus, horrueruntque comae.
> pulcher et humano maior trabeaque decorus
>   Romulus in media uisus adesse uia
> et dixisse simul 'prohibe lugere Quirites,
>   nec uiolent lacrimis numina nostra suis:
> tura ferant placentque nouum pia turba Quirinum,
>   et patrias artes militiamque colant.'
> iussit et in tenues oculis euanuit auras;
>   conuocat hic populos iussaque uerba refert.
> templa deo fiunt: collis quoque dictus ab illo est,
>   et referunt certi sacra paterna dies.
> Lux quoque cur eadem Stultorum festa uocetur
>   accipe: parua quidem causa, sed apta, subest.
> non habuit doctos tellus antiqua colonos:
>   lassabant agiles aspera bella uiros.
> plus erat in gladio quam curuo laudis aratro:
>   neglectus domino pauca ferebat ager.
> farra tamen ueteres iaciebant, farra metebant,
>   primitias Cereri farra resecta dabant:
> usibus admoniti flammis torrenda dederunt,
>   multaque peccato damna tulere suo;
> nam modo uerrebant nigras pro farre fauillas,
>   nunc ipsas ignes corripuere casas.
> facta dea est Fornax: laeti Fornace coloni
>   orant ut fruges temperet illa suas.[97]

> But Julius Proculus was coming from Alba Longa;
> the moon was shining and he had no need of a torch,
> when the hedges suddenly shook and trembled to his left;
> he took a step back, and his hair stood on end.
> Handsome, larger than life, resplendent in his trabea,
> Romulus seemed to be there in the middle of the road,
> and to have spoken as well: 'Forbid the Quirites to mourn,

---

[96] Whitton (2013) 158: 'Recounting tales of apotheosis with wide-eyed innocence, Ovid constantly threatens to destabilize these Roman and Julian myths by taking them just too literally.'
[97] Ov. *Fast.* 2.499-525.

and let them not violate my divinity with their tears.
Let them bring incense, let the pious crowd appease the new Quirinus,
and let them cultivate my father's military arts.'
He gave his orders and vanished from sight into thin air.
Proculus calls the People together and reports the words that were ordered.
A temple is built for the god; the hill too has its name from him,
and fixed days bring back the paternal rites.

Learn too why the same day is called the fool's festival.
There's a reason for it – trivial, yes, but appropriate.
The land in ancient times did not have expert farmers.
Harsh wars used to wear out the able-bodied men;
there was more glory in the sword than in the curved plough.
The field, neglected, produced little for its master.
But the ancients did sow spelt, and spelt they reaped,
and harvested spelt they gave as first-fruits to Ceres.
Taught by experience, they exposed it to the flames to be roasted,
and many losses they suffered by their own mistake.
For sometimes they used to sweep up black ashes instead of spelt,
and sometimes the fire caught hold of the huts themselves.
Oven was made a goddess. Delighting in Oven,
the farmers prayed that she would control the heat to their crop.

transl. A. Wiseman and P. Wiseman

The overture of the epiphany of the deified Romulus is not very divine, and 'the hedges suddenly shook and trembled to his left' of Julius Proculus provide a rather limp fanfare for the epiphany of the newly deified Romulus.'[98] There is no glowing nor a divine sweet fragrance, which mark divine presence in other epiphanies in Ovid's *Fasti*.[99] Nevertheless, Julius Proculus himself believes that a god has become manifest to him. Ovid describes his fear as a usual reaction of mortals to epiphanies.[100] Romulus' dress, the royal *trabea*, points to his status as a king but not as a god.[101] After Romulus has demanded divine honours for the new god Quirinus, he vanishes into thin air (*in tenues*

---

[98] Robinson (2011) 316.
[99] Ov. *Fast.* 1.94, 101; see n. 18. In the *Metamorphoses* Ovid describes Romulus' and Hersilia's metamorphoses into gods as deifications of heroes, *Met.* 14.805-851.
[100] Ov. *Fast.* 3.331-332; 6.19.
[101] The words of Quirinus' epiphany are narrated by Ovid and not by Julius Proculus as in the accounts of Livy and Dionysius of Halicarnassus. Ovid himself adds credibility to the narration, Robinson (2011) 315.

auras),[102] which is not a description of a *Himmelfahrt* as in Livy's text (*sublimis abiit*).[103] The poet's ingenuous *persona* also explains why the same day is known as the *Feriae stultorum*. Robinson sees one possible effect of this swift shift as follows: '... In giving a prominent role to Proculus, often viewed with suspicion in other sources, the narrative becomes particularly vulnerable to associations with *stultitia*.'[104] Ovid's narration is very ironic about literal, physical divinisation and the epiphany as well as deliberately ambivalent and open to subversive reading. Ovid is far more pessimist about the witness than Livy and Dionysius of Halicarnassus; he joins Cicero in his scepticism.[105] Nevertheless, older editions of the *Fasti* do not allow this ambivalent reading as an option.[106] Bömer for instance separates the Quirinalia from the account of *Feriae stultorum* by a space as a passage to a new topic.[107] But Alessandro Barchiesi and Matthew Robinson suggest that Ovid presents the events of the narrative on the *Feriae stultorum* with an *aition* about deification of an oven by a prayer as if it followed on the first one, the Quirinalia narrative.[108]

As shown, the differing attitudes of Cicero, Livy, Dionysius and Ovid towards the epiphany of the deified Romulus are sceptical but they all stress the cognitive reliability of Julius Proculus' viewing the epiphany for his contemporaries (though in Ovid's *Fasti* it is only Proculus who believes it), thus emphasising the belief in Romulus'

---

[102] Cf. Verg. *Aen*. 4.278; Ov. *Fast*. 5.375 (Ceres): ... *tenues secessit in auras*.
[103] For a topical depiction of an ascension, Verg. *Aen*. 4.278, 9.658.
[104] Robinson (2011) 321; cf. Barchiesi (1994) 102.
[105] Similarly Cicero refers to mocking at and rejecting with scorn that which could not possibly have happened already in Romulus' time, Cic. *Rep*. 2.19.
[106] Carole Newlands reminds us that Ovid's sudden changes of subject incite the reader's reflection about the possible connection between two issues which do not have anything but calendaric structure in common, at least at first glance, Newlands (1995) 44-47; Pfaff-Reydellet (2009) 161, 167.
[107] Ov. *Fast*. 2.512, 513; Bömer (1957) 118; Wiseman, Wiseman (2013), 31 also separate both entries, cf. Porte (1981) 341.
[108] Barchiesi (1994) 102-109; Robinson (2011) 321-322. The narration culminates in Ovid's reference to different dates of the Feast of Ovens, the Fornicalia. Ovid underlines that the stupid among the citizens (*stulta pars populi*) did not know to which *curia* they belong, therefore they celebrated the Fornicalia on the last day, which coincided with the date of the Quirinalia, Ov. *Fast*. 2. 531-532. Scheid (2012) 165 highlights that most of the Roman citizens did not know which of the 30 Roman *curiae* they were a member of. Against this background, Ovid's allusion to the stupid citizens applied to most of the citizens (who accepted the narrations on the epiphany of the deified Romulus).

deification at least for some Romans. Mary Beard argues that the Roman élite had for centuries been used to arguing about epiphanies and discussing what counted as a sign from the gods.[109] The belief in deification was an important element in the contemporary discussions about the formation of a ruler cult in Rome.

8. Interference of the narrative with the elements of the deification process

The euhemeristic concept, according to which a political leader who provided benefactions to his people merits deification, was reflected in two elements of the ritual process of deification of Roman emperors. A necessary element to start the deification was a discussion in the senate whether the dead emperor had been a deserving ruler and merited this extraordinary honour or not.[110] This discussion on the merits reflects Euhemerism as transmitted to the Romans by Cicero's writing about Romulus' deification. Brian Bosworth suggests that Augustus' *Res gestae* could be interpreted as an account of his conquests and benefactions to demonstrate his merits for divinisation.[111]

Another element of the deification process results from narrations on Romulus' deification and his epiphany, the role of a witness who testified under oath in the senate that he had seen the deified emperor ascending to the sky.[112] Cassius Dio writes that Numerius Atticus, a senator and ex-praetor, swore that he had seen Augustus ascending to heaven in the manner reported by the tradition concerning Proculus and Romulus.[113] The widow of the deceased Augustus, Julia Augusta, bestowed a million sesterces upon Numerius Atticus for his oath. The historical oath of a witness could only had been deduced from the narrative.[114] Thus, the narrative which legitimised the cult of the *Diuus*

---

[109] Beard (2012) 39.
[110] Price (1984b) 83; Beard, North, Price (1998b) 51; Koortbojian (2013) 21. For a parody of the discussion of the Roman senate on deification of Claudius, Sen. *Apocol.* 8-11.
[111] Bosworth (1999).
[112] Suet. *Aug.* 100.4: *nec defuit uir praetorius, qui se effigiem cremati euntem in caleum uidisse iuraret*; Sen. *Apocol.* 1.2.
[113] Cass. Dio 56.46.2.
[114] Gradel mentions the 'obvious parallel' between the Romulus-Quirinus narrative and the witness' oath after the deification of Augustus, Gradel (2002) 273, cf. Porte (1981) 334. The witness testifying physical divinisation is ridiculed by Seneca, *Apocol.* 1.2, Whitton (2013) 158-159.

Julius offered an intellectual framework from which new elements of the ritual process of deification were invented.[115]

The narrative on the epiphany of the deified Romulus was an argument in political discourse and offered an important basis for paving a way for the emergence of a new ritual of divinisation. This bridge from narratives on divinisation of a mortal to invention of a deification ritual was created in Rome in a time of profound political, social and cultural changes. A change of the Republican political system, in which the nobility contended for public offices and power, to the factual rule of one person (principate) facilitated the emergence of new religious modes of representation and legitimisation of power.

9. Conclusion: Orthopraxy and narrative

Although the Romulus narrative offered a model for the invention of a deification ritual, the euhemeristic, sceptical attitude to deification which Cicero transmitted to Romans and other philosophical opinions on the nature of gods continued to be pronounced without harming the state cult of the *diui*.[116] Ancient texts do not reveal any discrepancy between performance of rituals of the public cult of the *diui* which continued to be accomplished for centuries on one side and critical discussions about divinisation or literary representations of 'bad' emperors on the other. The literary representations and the public cult of the *diui* were two different levels of perception of the gods.[117] A new status of a human who was consecrated after his death and joined the celestial gods as a minor divinity (*diuus*) was scrupulously respected. The *diui* received sacrifices according to the traditional

---

[115] Starting with Augustus, a kind of routine for imperial deification was developed, Herz (2007) 315. Nevertheless, Herz does not discuss the meaning of the fact that the releasing of an eagle from the funeral pyre is testified for the deification ritual which took place almost two centuries later. Cass. Dio 75.5.5 describes Pertinax' apotheosis in AD 193. Dupont (1986) 250 thinks that the witness of the deified emperor disappeared when the practice of releasing an eagle was enacted. In fact, we do not know exactly when the *iurator* disappeared, Gradel (2002) 295. This change in the deification ritual and the underlying mythic model about Jupiter as an eagle that carried away the Trojan prince Ganymede is another example of a narrative figuring as starting point of the ritual change.

[116] Feeney (1991) 45-48; Šterbenc Erker (2013ᵇ) 119-125.

[117] Varro categorises three different ways of speaking of gods and perceiving them, Varro, *Ant. rer. diu.* fr. 7 Cardauns; Rüpke (2005).

model of correct ritual performance; they were honoured after the Capitoline triad and other deities, since their status was not the same as the one of the major gods.[118]

Plurality of different views on gods and on deification of mortals did not undermine the public cult, nor was it a sign of hypocrisy of the Roman religion, but of continuous discussion and discursive fights over the identity and character of gods, over the political impact of narratives about divine ancestors and over the sense and meaning of the rituals. The fact that they were reflected by two elements of the ritual process of the deification in the Roman ruler cult, the discussion in the senate and the oath of a witness of the *diuus* ascending to heaven reveals a belief implied in this ritual act that the dead emperor was transformed into a *diuus*.

Bibliography

Ackermann, R. (1991), *The Myth and Ritual School: J. G. Frazer and the Cambridge Ritualists*, New York/ London.

Barchiesi, A. (1994), *Il poeta e il principe: Ovidio e il discorso Augusteo*, Rome/ Bari.

Beard, M. (1987), 'A Complex of Times: No more Sheep on Romulus' Birthday', *Proceedings of the Cambridge Philological Society* 33, 1-15.

Beard, M. (2012), 'Cicero's 'Response of the haruspices' and the Voice of the Gods', *Journal of Roman Studies* 102, 20-39.

Beard, M., Crawford, M. (1985), *Rome in The Late Republic. Problems and Interpretations*, London.

Beard, M., North, J., Price, S. (1998[a]), *Religions of Rome*, vol. 1: *A History,* Cambridge, New York/ Melbourne.

Beard, M., North, J., Price, S. (1998[b]), *Religions of Rome*, vol. 2: *A Sourcebook*, Cambridge/ New York/ Melbourne.

---

[118] The *diui* ranked last among all gods worshipped by the Arval Brothers. Cf. a sacrifice of fulfilment and pronouncement of the new vows performed by the Arval Brothers on January 3rd, 59 AD, *Commentarii Fratrum Arualium*, Scheid (1998) 27, 45: ... *diuo Claudio boues m(ares) (duos)*...; Šterbenc Erker (2013[b]) 123, cf. 120-124; Gradel (2002) 275-276. On rituals in honour of Augustus' birthday in AD 18, Koortbojian (2013) 175-178.

Bell, C. (1992), *Ritual Theory, Ritual Practice*, New York/ Oxford.

Bendlin, A. (2006), 'Eine wenig Sinn für Religiosität verratende Betrachtungsweise': Emotion und Orient in der römischen Religionsgeschichtsschreibung der Moderne', *Archiv für Religionsgeschichte* 8, 227-256.

Bömer, F. (1957), *P. Ovidius Naso. Die Fasten I*. Herausgegeben, übersetzt und kommentiert, Heidelberg.

Bosworth, B. (1999), 'Augustus, the *Res Gestae* and Hellenistic Theories of Apotheosis', *Journal of Roman Studies* 89, 1-18.

Brelich, A. (1960), 'Quirinus', *Studi e Materiali di Storia delle Religioni* 31, 63-119.

Bremmer, J. (1987), 'Romulus, Remus and the foundation of Rome', in J. N. Bremmer, N. M. Horsfall (edd.), *Roman Myth and Mythography*, London, 25-48.

Burkert, W. (1962), 'Caesar und Romulus-Quirinus', *Historia* 11, 356-376.

Cole, S. (2013), *Cicero and The Rise of Deification at Rome*, Cambridge/ New York.

Davies, J.P. (2004), *Rome's Religious History. Livy, Tacitus and Ammianus on their Gods*, Cambridge.

Driediger-Murphy, L. (2014), 'Theology as a Historiographic Tool in Dionysius of Halicarnassus', *Phoenix* 68, 330-349.

Dupont, F. (1986), 'L'autre corps de l'empereur-dieu', *Le temps de la réflexion* 7, 231-252.

Durkheim, É. (1912[1]), *Les formes élémentaires de la vie religieuse. Le système totémique en Australie*, Paris.

Feeney, D.C. (1991), *The Gods in Epic. Poets and Critics of the Classical Tradition*, Oxford.

Feeney, D.C. (1998), *Literature and Religion at Rome. Cultures, contexts, and beliefs*, Cambridge.

Feeney, D.C. (2007), 'On Not Forgetting the 'Literatur' in 'Literatur und Religion': Representing the Mythic and the Divine in Roman Historiography', in A. Bierl, R. Lämmle, K. Wesselmann (edd.), *Literatur und Religion*, vol. 2: *Wege zu einer mythisch-rituellen Poetik bei den Griechen*, Berlin/ New York, 173-202.

Fishwick, D. (1987), *The Imperial Cult in the Latin West: Studies in the Ruler Cult of the Western provinces of the Roman Empire*, vol. 1, Leiden/ New York.

Forsythe, G. (1999), *Livy and Early Rome: A Study in Historical Method and Judgement*, Stuttgart.

Frazer, J.G. (1907-1915), *The Golden Bough* 1-12, London, 3rd edition.

Gradel, I. (2002), *Emperor worship and Roman religion*, Oxford/ New York.

Graf, F. (2004), 'Epiphany', in H. Cancik, H. Schneider (edd.), *Brill's New Pauly* 4, Leiden/ New York, 1121-1123.

Harrisson, J. (2013), *Dreams and Dreaming in the Roman Empire. Cultural Memory and Imagination*, London u.a.

Hekster, O. (2010), 'Reversed Epiphanies: Roman Emperors Deserted by Gods', *Mnemosyne* 63, 601-615.

Herbert-Brown, G. (1994), *Ovid and the Fasti. An Historical Study*, Oxford.

Herz, P. (2007), 'Emperors: Caring for the Empire and Their Successors', in J. Rüpke (ed.), *A Companion to Roman Religion*, Malden/ Oxford, 304-316.

Hölkeskamp, K.-J. (1996), '*Exempla* und *mos maiorum*. Überlegungen zum kollektiven Gedächtniss der Nobilität', in H.-J. Gehrke, A. Möller (edd.), *Vergangenheit und Lebenswelt: Soziale Kommunikation, Traditionsbildung und historisches Bewußtsein*, Tübingen, 301-333.

Koortbojian, M. (2013), *The Divinization of Caesar and Augustus. Precedents, Consequences, Implications*, Cambridge/ New York.

Krasser, H. (2005), 'Universalisierung und Identitätskonstruktion: Formen und Funktionen der Wissenskodifikation im kaiser-zeitlichen Rom', in G. Oesterle (ed.), *Erinnerung, Gedächtnis, Wissen*, Göttingen, 357-375.

Linder, M., Scheid, J. (1993), 'Quand croire c'est faire. Le problème de la croyance dans la Rome ancienne', *Archives de sciences sociales des religions* 81, 47-62.

Luraghi, N. (2003), 'Dionysios von Halikarnassos zwischen Griechen und Römern', in U. Eigler et al. (edd.), *Formen römischer Geschichtsschreibung von den Anfängen bis Livius: Gattungen, Autoren, Kontexte*, Darmstadt, 268-286.

Mehl, A. (2003), 'Antike Geschichtsschreibung', in M. Maurer (ed.), *Aufriß der Historischen Wissenschaften*, vol. 5: *Mündliche Überlieferung und Geschichtsschreibung*, Stuttgart, 42-147.

Müller, R.J. (1993), 'Überlegungen zur ΙΕΡΑ ΑΝΑΓΡΑΦΗ des Euhemeros von Messene', *Hermes* 121, 276-300.
Newlands, C.E. (1995), *Playing with Time. Ovid and the Fasti*, Ithaca, London.
Ogilvie, R.M. (1965), *A Commentary on Livy Books 1 – 5*, Oxford.
Orlin, E. (2007), 'Urban Religion in the Middle and Late Republic', in J. Rüpke (ed.), *A Companion to Roman Religion*, Malden/ Oxford, 58-70.
Pandey, N.B. (2013), 'Caesar's Comet, the Julian Star, and the Invention of Augustus', *Transactions of the American Philological Association* 143, 405-449.
Pasco-Pranger, M. (2006), *Founding the Year. Ovid's Fasti and the Poetics of the Roman Calendar*, Leiden/ Boston.
Pfaff-Reydellet, M. (2009), 'Ovids *Fasti*. Der Kaiser tritt in den öffentlichen Kalender ein', in A. Bendlin, J. Rupke (edd.), *Römische Religion im historischen Wandel: Diskursentwicklung von Plautus bis Ovid*, Stuttgart, 157-170.
Platt, V.J. (2011), *Facing the gods. Epiphany and Representation in Graeco-Roman Art, Literature, and Religion*, Cambridge/ New York.
Porte, D. (1981), 'Romulus-Quirinus, prince et dieu, dieu des princes: Étude sur le personnage de Quirinus et sur son évolution, des origines à Auguste', *Aufstieg und Niedergang der römischen Welt* II.17.1, 300-342.
Price, S.R.F. (1984[a]), *Rituals and Power. The Roman Imperial Cult in Asia Minor*, Cambridge/ New York.
Price, S.R.F. (1984[b]), 'Gods and Emperors: The Greek Language of the Roman Imperial Cult', *Journal of Hellenic Studies* 104, 79-95.
Ramsey, J.T., Licht, A.L. (1997), *The Comet of 44 BC and Caesar's Funeral Games*, Atlanta.
Robinson, M. (2011), *A Commentary on Ovid's Fasti: Book 2*, Oxford/ New York.
Rüpke, J. (2004), '*Acta aut agenda*: Relations of Script and Performance', in A. Barchiesi et al. (edd.), *Rituals in Ink. A Conference on Religion and Literary Production in Ancient Rome, Held at Stanford University in February 2002*, Stuttgart, 23-43.

Rüpke, J. (2005), 'Varro's *Tria Genera Theologiae*: Religious Thinking in the Late Republic', *Ordia Prima* 4, 107-29.

Scheid, J. (1987) 'Polytheism Impossible; or, the Empty Gods: Reasons Behind a Void in the History of Roman Religion', *History and Anthropology* 3, 303-325.

Scheid, J. (1992), 'Myth, Cult and Reality in Ovid's *Fasti*', *Proceedings of the Cambridge Philological Society* 38, 118-131.

Scheid, J. (ed.) (1998), *Commentarii fratrum Arvalium qui supersunt. Les copies épigraphiques des protocoles annuels de la confrérie arvale (21 av.-304. ap. J.-C.)*, Rome.

Scheid, J. (2005ᵃ), *Quand faire, c'est croire: Les rites sacrificiels des Romains*, Paris.

Scheid, J. (2005ᵇ), 'Augustus and Roman Religion: Continuity, Conservatism, and Innovation', in K. Galinsky (ed.), *The Cambridge Companion to the Age of Augustus*, Cambridge, 175-193.

Scheid, J. (ed.) (2012), *Plutarch, Römische Fragen. Ein virtueller Spaziergang im Herzen des alten Rom*, Darmstadt.

Schlesier, R. (2003), 'Die Leiden des Dionysos', in A. Kneppe, D. Metzler (edd.), *Die emotionale Dimension antiker Religiosität*, Münster, 1-20.

Skutsch, O. (1985), *The Annals of Q. Ennius, edited with Introduction and Commentary*, Oxford.

Šterbenc Erker, D. (2008), 'Das antiquarische Wissen und das *exemplum* der *confarreatio*-Ehe (Ov. *fast.*, Dion. Hal. *ant. Rom.*)', in G. Schörner, D. Šterbenc Erker (edd.), *Medien religiöser Kommunikation im Imperium Romanum*, Stuttgart, 27-51.

Šterbenc Erker, D. (2013ᵃ), *Religiöse Rollen römischer Frauen in 'griechischen' Ritualen*, Stuttgart.

Šterbenc Erker, D. (2013ᵇ), 'Religion', in M. T. Dinter, E. Buckley (edd.), *A Companion to the Neronian Age*, Malden, Oxford, 119-125.

Šterbenc Erker, D. (2018), 'Augustus' "New" Festival: The Centrality of Married Women's Rituals at the Ludi Saeculares of 17 B.C.E.', *Numen. International Review for the History of religions* 65, 377-404.

Tambiah, S.J. (1979), 'A Performative Approach to Ritual', *Proceedings of the British Academy* 65, 116-142.

Timpe, D. (1996), '*Memoria* und Geschichtsschreibung bei den Römern', in H.-J. Gehrke, A. Möller (edd.), *Vergangenheit und*

Lebenswelt: Soziale Kommunikation, Traditionsbildung und historisches Bewußtsein, Tübingen, 277-299.
von Ungern-Sternberg, J. (1993), 'Romulus-Bilder: Die Begründung der Republik im Mythos', in F. Graf (ed.), *Mythos in mythenloser Gesellschaft: Das Paradigma Roms* Stuttgart/ Leipzig, 88-108.
Versnel, H.S. (2011), *Coping with the Gods. Wayward readings in Greek theology*, Leiden/ Boston.
Wallace-Hadrill, A. (1997), '*Mutatio morum*: the idea of a cultural revolution', in T. Habinek, A. Schiesaro (edd.), *The Roman Cultural Revolution*, Cambridge, 3-22.
Weinstock, S. (1971), *Divus Julius*, Oxford.
Whitton, C. (2013), 'Seneca, *Apocolocyntosis*', in M.T. Dinter, E. Buckley (edd.), *A Companion to the Neronian Age*, Malden/ Oxford, 151-169.
Wiedemann, T. (1986), 'The *Fetiales*: A Reconsideration', *Classical Quarterly* 36, 478-490.
Williams, J. (2007), 'Religion and Roman Coins', in J. Rüpke (ed.), *A Companion to Roman Religion*, Malden/ Oxford, 143-163.
Wiseman, A., Wiseman, P. (2013), *Ovid, Fasti. A New Translation*, Oxford.
Wissowa, G. (1912²), *Religion und Kultus der Römer*, München.

Horace's Religion:
a True Experience or an Augustan Artifice?
The Ritual Dimension

PEDRO BRAGA FALCÃO
Universidade Católica Portuguesa
Centro de Estudos Clássicos da Faculdade de Letras da Universidade de Lisboa

1. Defining 'religion' in the context of Horace's work: some preliminary remarks

The question that we first wish to ask is as seemingly simple as it is academically relevant: how can we interpret the numerous religious references present throughout the work of Horace? In the context of this volume, we are particularly interested in looking at the relationship between Augustan power (and its many religious undertones) and Horatian poetry. In this perspective, does the poet's literary work fulfil a clear agenda, finding in poetry a means to amplify Augustus' religious propaganda? Or is there more to this author's relationship to religion?

We know that in Augustus' principate religion played a very special role. Even a hasty reading of his *Res gestae* yields countless religious references: rituals scrupulously observed by the *princeps* (4.1, 11.1), the complete and comprehensive catalogue of the many religious offices he held, including a detailed account of how he was designated *pontifex maximus*, and the enormous popular demonstration that celebrated the nomination. Also significant is the massive and nearly endless list of temples that Augustus erected or restored. It would then be tremendously naïve or even anachronistic to think that religion does not have a political role in the Augustan principate; perhaps it is harder to pinpoint the actual role religion played in his agenda.[1] In the light of modern experience, we could assume a radical point of view, like the one heralded by Karl Marx, and consider religion 'the opiate of

---

[1] For a fairly recent survey on the subject cf. Scheid (2005) 175 ff. A good starting point is also Beard, North, Price (1998⁸) 182 ff.

the masses', underlining its power to subdue and to serve as a form of social and political legitimation of established power. However, as relevant as the institutional and social dimension may be, it represents just one of the many characteristics of religion, and does not define it exclusively. But we should not be too amazed if Augustus, a very perceptive politician, realized the enormous potential a *cultus deorum* could have on his political career. Especially when we consider that he permitted himself to be appointed *Augustus*, and deliberately oversaw the beginning of what was later called the 'imperial cult'.

If, very briefly, these are the premises that make us regard religion as a predominantly political experience when it comes to Augustus' principate – even though not exclusively political – that is not the main concern of this text. We are trying here to find clues to how Horace, or more precisely the *persona* of Horace presented through his work, saw religion. This task is not as straightforward as it seems. 'Religion' or 'religious' are not unequivocal terms whose meanings have remained stagnant throughout the ages. On the contrary, the question of Horace's religiosity should not be answered based on our modern sense of these terms, but rather on a wider understanding of their meaning in his time, what did it meant to be religious then. What were the main aspects of the religious experience and which of these, if any, were an integral part of Horace's life?

Jasper Griffin's excellent synthesis paper 'Gods and religion', in *The Cambridge Companion to Horace*,[2] gives us a fairly recent state of scholarship on the subject.[3] Towards the end there is one sentence that, while making sense to a learned reader of Horace, raises some very important questions: 'he [Horace] was hardly what we think of as a religious man' (194). It is not by chance that Griffin adds to his claim the expression 'what we think of as', admitting that one's perspective on the subject is inexorably drawn to one's own conception of religion. So, is Horace a 'religious man', or not? Can we even ask that question?

---

[2] Griffin (2007) 181-194.
[3] No systematic and exhaustive approach to the subject of Horace's theology or religiosity has been made. Mythology, for instance, has been well studied in the context of the *Carmina*: cf. Breuer (2008) or Labate (2013) 205-227. The relationship between mythology and religion, however, is both subtle and complex, and it was not the main goal of the many studies of the use of myths in Horace's lyrical work, or even the main perspective of the commentaries.

Our main purpose is not to establish if Horace was in fact a 'religious man', at least in the modern sense: that would be an unattainable goal, but Griffin's claim made us curious about the methodologies that have been used to address the religious issues that surrounded Horace. The subject has been approached through the literary, historical and even social perspectives. In one of the possible analyses the fact that the *Odes* are based on the Greek lyrical patrimony, where hymns and religious compositions were endemic, explained why so many of Horace's *Odes* were of this type: a sort of 'conventional literary forms', as Wilkinson[4] already defended. By another reading, assuming a Horatian metalanguage, the constant reference to the muses and to the Delphic inspiration has the sole purpose of endearing his literary career. In the article dedicated to religion, by Teivas Oksala in the *Enciclopedia Oraziana*,[5] the question is put in the following terms: 1) what was Horace's religiosity?; 2) how does Horace see religion? Although premises are clear and well concatenated, the truth is that all arguments advanced are from specific criteria of literary studies, and within the context of the Horatian exegesis.

For our part, we think the question of Horace's religion has never been raised in the field that seems to be the most appropriate: religious studies or the history of religion. In this broad field, let us put to examination Griffin's claim that: 'he was hardly what we think of as a religious man.' First of all, what exactly is a 'religious man'?

Maybe it is helpful, as a starting point and as a warning of the apparently insurmountable difficulties this question raises, to consider a passage from Horace's *Satires* (1.9.70-71). Taken out of its context, the sentence would be a clear answer to our questions: *nulla mihi (...) religio est*. If we literally translate *religio* to 'religion' – as in 'I have no religion' – we are perpetuating a misunderstanding that is not only common among classicists, but also in society in general: that 'religion' is an unequivocal concept. This is not true at all. In this passage, Horace tries desperately to get rid of an inopportune acquaintance. Much to his delight, he finds a friend, Aristius Fuscus, who could rescue him from such unpleasant company. Fuscus senses the poet's

---

[4] Wilkinson (1945) 27, apud Griffin (2007) 188. Cf. also Barchiesi (2000) 167-182.
[5] Oksala (1997) 2.285-288.

despair, but he decides to have some fun and makes up a flimsy excuse not to pay attention to his friend's needs. On that day some Jewish festivity is taking place,[6] and he does not want to hurt the feelings of his circumcised friends. It is in this moment that Horace desperately replies that he has no *religio* whatsoever.

The term *religio*, from where the word 'religion' takes its origin, has a great number of ambiguous meanings. For instance, according to the *OLD*, the word can refer not only to 'a supernatural feeling of constraint' but also to 'a consideration enforcing conformity to a religious or moral principle.' If we notice some of the *OLD*'s examples, we are bound to think how distant *religio* is from our modern 'religion'. In Rome, an historian of religion would risk hearing sentences such as 'it is unlawful (*religio*) for the priest of Jupiter to ride upon a horse,' *equo Dialem flaminem uehi religio est* (Gell. 10.15.3), 'C. Marius had no scruples (*religio*) about killing the praetor Caius Glaucius,' *religio C. Mario ... non fuerat, quo minus C. Glauciam praetorem occideret* (Cic. *Cat.* 3.15), 'one thinks that those unproductive trees are damned due to a religious non-observance (*religio*),' *infelices existimantur arbores damnataeque religione* (Plin. *HN* 16.108), 'favourable manifestation of the divine (*religio*) has shown me the way,' *cursum mihi prospera dixit religio* (Verg. *Aen.* 3.363), or even 'it is desire to love a wife when alive, religion when she is dead,' *uxorem enim uiuam amare uoluptas est, defunctam religio* (Stat. *Silu.* 5 pr.). That is why Horace says to his friend that he has no 'religion': no supernatural feeling of constraint can make him observe any ritual, much less a Jewish one, which to him sounds remendously obscure.

This is just one example, given within the context of Horace's work, of how hard it is to define a 'religious man', especially if we bear in mind the extreme difficulty of finding a consensual and satisfactory definition of what religion is. Nevertheless, from the example given above, we can surely try to find in Horace's texts references to religion and use them to investigate the relation that the author had with this particular aspect of his society. Of course we are well aware that we will probably never find out what Horace, the man, actually thought

---

[6] Maybe the *Sukkot* (Feast of Tabernacles), or more plausibly (Fedeli [1994] 505) a double reference to the Sabbath observance and to the celebration of the New Moon.

about religion; even if we could ask him, it would be very hard to ask the right question. We are neither trying to demonstrate or rebuke Jasper Griffin's claim that Horace is not 'a religious man'. Our aim is to study the religious elements present in Horace's work in order to draw a clearer picture of how the author of the *Odes* experienced his religion and interacted with it. In doing so we will try to take this subject from the exclusive realm of Horatian studies and open our discussion to other fields.

2. The ritual dimension according to Ninian Smart. Making Horace's work a case-study

Among the many attempts to define religion, maybe the one that most interests us is the one given, for example, by Ninian Smart, which wisely circumvents the question by describing the many dimensions that exist within almost all world religions. He thus avoids the pitfall of not embracing the spectacular variety of this complex sphere of human activity and provides us with a very helpful methodology to study it. Although other and more recent writers have adopted the same strategy, and his proposal has been considered somewhat old-fashioned, Ninian Smart's 1970s reasoning is still appealing not only because of its simplicity, but also because of its versatility. It is highly improbable to find a religion that does not have almost all of the dimensions the author presents in *The Religious Experience of Mankind* (1971), namely the ritual, mythological, doctrinal, ethical, social and experiential.[7]

The question, 'What is the place religion occupies in Horace's work?' must therefore be answered in the context of his own particular religious experience; by not assessing the context, we run the risk of judging him according to the same principles that would be used to ascertain whether Luís de Camões or William Shakespeare were truly religious men. That answer would be founded on a modern religious perspective, based on a Christian theological matrix.

---

[7] To these dimensions he added a last one, the 'material dimension' in the later *Dimensions of the Sacred. An Anatomy of the World's Beliefs* (1998).

If it is true that in both *Epistles* and *Satires* the religious question seems to be irrelevant,[8] *Epodes* and *Odes* offer us opposite examples. This may be or may not be an important clue, as we can interpret this fact in many possible ways. For instance, we can argue that Horace did not give much importance to religion, since it does not play any significant role in more 'personal' or 'intimate' texts (even though, as we know, the epistles are far from being 'letters' in the ordinary sense of the word). The same argument, however, can be used to demonstrate precisely the opposite: perhaps Horace is giving the gods their proper place, more befitting of their majesty, i.e., the lyric poetry. In whatever way we interpret this fact, it is undeniable that we must start our analysis from his lyric oeuvre.

To learn if Horace, or at least his literary *persona*, was just using religion to amplify Augustus' religious policy, we ought to understand first which role religion played in his lyric work. We cannot discuss here the presence in Horace's work of all of the dimensions presented by Ninian Smart; this is just the first from a series of studies exclusively dedicated to this theme and methodology. But let us begin precisely with the paramount dimension in defining classic religiosity: the ritual dimension. As Ninian Smart puts it, religion tends to express itself through ritual – cult, prayers, offerings, for example.[9] There are many passages in Horace's *Odes* in which precise rituals are referred to, performed either by the poet himself, or by someone else. If religion is opportunistically used by Horace to spread Augustan propaganda, then we would expect that in the ritual dimension some particular rituals directly connected to Augustus' principate ought to be put in evidence, as they are described in his *Res gestae*, or at least be the most common. But that is simply not true.

---

[8] As Griffin puts it, '[in Horace's *Satires*] Gods are remarkable for their absence. Moral standards come, not from religion, but either from a popular version of contemporary philosophical preaching, or from native common sense, while examples and illustrations are drawn from literature' (Griffin [2007] 186).

[9] Smart (1971) 15 ff.

3. The ritual dimension in Horace's *Carmina*

On the many instances Horace describes religious rituals performed by himself, there are some than can be given a metapoetical reading, especially in the context of Venus' cult. *Ode* 1.5 is an example; the final strophe refers to the ritual of affixing a table to a temple wall to commemorate an escape from danger[10] or a retirement from public life (cf. Hor. *Epist*. 1.1.5):

> (...) Me tabula sacer
> uotiua paries indicat uuida
> suspendisse potenti
> uestimenta maris deae.
>
> *Carm*. 1.5.13-16

In Venus' universe, the ritual implies that the poet survived love, and thanks the Goddess for it. Also in 1.19 we have the description of a ritual: fresh turf, green sprigs and incense with a cup of unmixed two-years old wine. The objective: to make the poet overcome is passion for Glycera:

> Hic uiuum mihi caespitem, hic
> uerbenas, pueri, ponite turaque
> bimi cum patera meri:
> mactata ueniet lenior hostia.
>
> *Carm*. 1.19.13-16

Obviously these kinds of rituals can have a metonymical reading. Nevertheless, the degree of reality used in their description implies they are not just a simple literary *mise-en-scène* as we will find in some Renaissance references to Venus' cult. They echo a common religious practice, observed and experienced *in loco*.[11] *Carm*. 3.27 (1-16) is a

---

[10] Nisbet, Hubbard (1970) 78.
[11] We should at least refer *Epist*. 5 and 17, a puzzling description of magic love rituals, although in this context is very hard to make them examples of religious rituals, since they seem to be largely symbolic (cf. Mankin [1995] 299-301), as we can read in this example: *effare: iussas cum fide poenas luam,/ paratus expiare, seu poposceris/ centum iuuencos, siue mendaci lyra/ uoles sonare* (*Epist*. 17.37-40). A hyperbolic expression, *centum iuuencos*, describes a hypothetical sacrifice designed to deliver Horace from the black magic of Canidia, the

clearer example. It reveals an informed knowledge of auguries, and many in a specifically Roman context: an owl, a pregnant bitch, a she-wolf, a gravid vixen, a serpent, a woodpecker or a wandering crow are reckoned amongst bad omens, as the poet, serving as an augur, casts them off, wishing a prosperous journey to Galatea. Though one can admit, with Nisbet and Rudd, that 'Horace of course is not taking augural lore seriously,'[12] it is still true that the poet uses ritual language – the augural one in particular, which was of great importance in the Romans' idiosyncratic religiosity – to wish a pleasant journey, and its usage has nothing to do with a more political agenda. This reflects in fact a ritual experience.

A more blatant example is *Carm.* 3.8, in which the poet describes a ritual presided over by himself, on the first day of March, a date when the *Matronalia* were celebrated:

> Martiis caelebs quid agam Kalendis,
> quid uelint flores et acerra turis
> plena miraris positusque carbo in
>   caespite uiuo,
>
> docte sermones utriusque linguae?
> Voueram dulcis epulas et album
> Libero caprum prope funeratus
>   arboris ictu.
> Hic dies anno redeunte festus
> corticem adstrictum pice dimouebit
> amphorae fumum bibere institutae
>   consule Tullo.
>
> *Carm.* 3.8.1-12

---

sorceress, in a ritual known as *expiatio*. In *Epist.* 5 the recipient of the magic seems not to be the poet, but 'a boy' whose identity is uncertain, which makes the ritual references different from those centred in Horace's poetical *persona*. The relationship between *superstitio* and *religio* in Rome is a matter of debate, and maybe it is more prudent only to refer to these two examples of rituals as 'magic love rituals' and stress that they have no obvious relation to politics. The importance of magic in religious ritual, though, as we shall see when dealing with *Carmen saeculare*, should not be neglected, but we are reluctant to make *Epist.* 5 and *Epist.* 17 examples of religious rituals. The same can be said about a reference to a sacrifice made in *Epist.* 10.21-24 (*opima quodsi praeda curuo litore/ porrecta mergos iuuerit,/ libidinosus immolabitur caper/ et agna Tempestatibus*), a 'rovesciamento parodico del sacrificio che si fa in onore dei venti per ottenere un viaggio tranquillo' in the words of Romano (1991) 987.

[12] Nisbet, Rudd (2004) 324.

Maecenas, the recipient of this composition, is supposedly surprised as he finds his friend making a sacrifice – on the *Matronalia* married men prayed for their wives, but confirmed bachelors such as Horace did not. The festival was actually a celebration of marriage. Horace clears up the misunderstanding: he celebrates having survived a falling tree on his Sabine estate. He made a vow to Bacchus on that occasion: every year we would sacrifice a white goat – a ritual that he scrupulously kept. The vow was not made to Apollo – perhaps a more 'Augustan' god – but to Liber, the god of poets and wine. We do not see why we should doubt his words – at least we should believe him as much as we would believe a Christian poet writing that he promised God to undertake a pilgrimage to Santiago, should he escape a particular disease. We have here a common religious practice in the ancient world: someone escapes danger and performs a thanksgiving ritual to the gods (a ritual known as *supplicatio*).[13] As tradition demanded, since the honoured god was male,[14] Liber is offered a he-goat, a *caper*, which after the sacrifice is used in a ritual banquet (*epulae*, v. 6).[15]

We can say the same about *Carm.* 3.13: a sacrifice of a kid in the spring of Bandusia, maybe on the *Neptunalia*:

> O fons Bandusiae splendidior uitro
> dulci digne mero non sine floribus,
>   cras donaberis haedo,
>   cui frons turgida cornibus
> primis et uenerem et proelia destinat;
> frustra: nam gelidos inficiet tibi
>   rubro sanguine riuos
>   lasciui suboles gregis.
>
> *Carm.* 3.13.1-8

The animal is vividly described, to the point of letting the listener imagine the carmine blood of the beast colouring the icy flow of the spring. We can read this ode merely as a literary exercise, or we can

---

[13] On the subject, cf. Freyburger (1977) 283-315. For an interpretation of the *supplicatio*, cf. Scheid (2011) 269-270.
[14] Cf. Scheid (2011) 264.
[15] We can find a ritual banquet also in *Epist.* 2. 59, *agna festis caesa Terminalibus*. The context is however too broad to make this an example of rituality in Horace's work.

face it, in the light of the history of religions, precisely as it is – an account of a ritual, described by a poet. And we can say even more: as Nisbet and Rudd underlined,[16] this ode is indeed representative of an ancient religious tradition that saw water springs as a hierophany, to use Mircea Eliade's categories. The depiction of a ritual sacrifice of a *haedus* poetically emphasises the importance of water and the religious significance of the aquatic element: *nullus enim fons non sacer* (Serv. *Aen.* 7.84). And exactly which political motivation would lead Horace, in his hymn to Faunus (3.18), to pray to the god for his protection over his cattle, describing the sacrifice of a tender kid? Why should we consider fiction his own words: *si tener pleno cadit haedus anno* (*Carm.* 3.18.5), 'if a tender kid is offered at year's end'? We are not short of examples in antiquity where a *uotum* is made to a god, in a public or a private context.[17] And why should we mistrust Horace when he claims that every year he offers Diana a young boar, if he says so in *Carm.* 3.22? In the same way should we doubt any Hindu poem where the author claims that he carefully followed every ritual due to Shiva. Of course we will never know whether Horace actually performed the rituals he says he did, but given the Roman religious and ritualistic context, one should assume he did, as it would be difficult to justify why he would be lying about it. In fact it would be very difficult to find a Roman that had never performed any kind of sacrifice, and Horace is probably no exception.

Carm. 1.31 is another example of rituality:

> Quid dedicatum poscit Apollinem
> uates? Quid orat de patera nouum
>   fundens liquorem?
>
> *Carm.* 1.31.1-3

The celebrated act is the consecration of the new Temple of Apollo on the Palatine on 28 BC. If the connection between Apollo and Augustus

---

[16] Nisbet, Rudd (2004) 172.
[17] Cf. Beard, Price (1998ª) 32 ff.

is indisputable,[18] we should focus our attention on the fact that in this poem, as Nisbet and Hubbard[19] pointed out, the purported occasion is in fact the festival of the *Meditrinalia*, when libations of new and old wine took place, as described by the poem. Once again, they echo a religious practice and a religious experience that we expect to be the author's own religious experience – let us not forget that the main goal of the *libatio* comes only at end of the ode:

> Frui paratis et ualido mihi,
> Latoe, dones, at, precor, integra
>   cum mente, nec turpem senectam
>   degere nec cithara carentem
>
> *Carm.* 1.31.17-20

The two ritual references to what was later called the 'imperial cult', not by coincidence present in the Venusian poet's last book of odes, must therefore be read within this broad context, and not considered in isolation:

> Condit quisque diem collibus in suis,
> et uitem uiduas ducit ad arbores;
> hinc ad uina redit laetus et alteris
>   te mensis adhibet deum;
> te multa prece, te prosequitur mero
> defuso pateris et Laribus tuum
> miscet numen, uti Graecia Castoris
>   et magni memor Herculis.
>
> 'Longas o utinam, dux bone, ferias
> praestes Hesperiae!' dicimus integro
> sicci mane die, dicimus uuidi,
>   cum sol Oceano subest.
>
> *Carm.* 4.5.29-40

A *paterfamilias* is pictured here pouring wine in honour of the divinity (*numen*) of his Lares in conjunction with Augustus, who is

---

[18] The reasons of this identification, motivated perhaps by the fact that Antony deliberately likened himself to Dionysus (Plut. *Vit. Ant.* 24.26.60), are extensively studied by authors such as Miller (2009) or Loupiac (1999).
[19] Nisbet, Hubbard (1970) 347.

literally considered *deus* (32), and compared with Castor and Hercules, in an unheard-of apotheosis, since the *princeps* was still alive. Also in 4.15 there is a prayer concluding the poem (25-32). Although Augustus is not named, he is embraced in a *progenies Veneris*, which included Aeneas or Julius Caesar:

> Nosque et profestis lucibus et sacris
> inter iocosi munera Liberi
>   cum prole matronisque nostris,
>   rite deos prius apprecati,
>
> uirtute functos more patrum duces
> Lydis remixto carmine tibiis
>   Troiamque et Anchisen et almae
>   progeniem Veneris canemus.
>
> *Carm.* 4.15.25-32

From the ritual point of view, however, one must underline the fact that the poet is mentioning a libation (4.5)[20] and a prayer (4.15).[21] As Beard and Price[22] underline 'animal sacrifice, the ritual killing of an animal and the offering to the gods of parts of its body, burnt on the altar, was a (perhaps the) central element of Roman ritual.' So it seems that the rituals directed to an Augustan divinity are not as explicit and widespread as one might have thought, and are in fact just a small part of the many rituals referred to in the *Odes* that include several cults and divinities that were not part of Augustus' 'political' agenda. Furthermore, we can read certain rites that translate personal experiences, not only in the poet's artistic and literary life, but also in his own quotidian existence.

Returning to our initial question and in the light of the above, we must conclude that the large majority of the many ritual references Horace makes do not have any political content, especially considering Augustus' religious propaganda. On the contrary: they reveal an author

---

[20] In the religious Roman sphere, Libation is a 'rather general formula for ritual action', as Moede (2011) 168 puts it.
[21] For an introduction to Roman *precatio*, cf. Hahn (2011) 239 ff.
[22] Beard, Price (1998ᵇ) 148.

who, well aware of his own ritualistic society,[23] performs the same rites and sacrifices, but with very different purposes, at least according to his account. By this references we can assume that the author of the *Odes* is a man of his age: a *homo ritualis*.[24] In Rome that is almost the same as saying that he was, in fact, a *homo religiosus*.

4. The *Carmen saeculare* and its own place in the discussion about the ritual dimension

Last but not least we must mention a lyric work that is peculiar in any way we view it: the *Carmen saeculare*. From the ritual point of view, there is an obvious and mandatory relationship with the eminently religious rite of the *Ludi Saeculares*. This occasion was unquestionably one of the most flagrant moments of the Augustan principate, appropriating the religious ritual to serve his ultimate political aspiration: the celebration of a new age. Zanker summarizes this idea best:[25] 'after ten years of religious and moral renewal, the festivals and sacrifices, buildings and images, now visible everywhere in Rome, began to take effect. Confidence in the ability of the restored Republic to stand firm and faith in its ruler grew apace. (...) The successes of the new regime had had an impact on every individual. It was now time to give permanent expression to his mood of optimism, to create a new imagery that would transcend reality and eternalize the happiness of the present moment. The state needed a myth and here again Augustus was able to latch onto something that was already in the air before he came along. (...) From May 30 to June 3 the great Secular Games took place, heralding the beginning of the new age.'

---

[23] We should not have a prejudiced view of 'ritualism' in Roman Religion; as Nicole Belayche puts it, 'ritualism does not go necessarily with a utilitarian, cynical relationship, as the comic author Plautus depicted that of some devotees in order to make the audience laugh. Nor does it imply a 'cold' or 'blasé' relationship, as dominant historiography portrayed it for long, because it was influenced by a spiritualistic experience. Ritualism is the relational procedure that goes coherently with the way Romans conceived the respective places of men and gods within the world' (Belayche [2011] 291).
[24] There are many disciplines that have focused on the *homo ritualis*: psychology, anthropology, religious studies, history, sociology, etc. For an introduction to the subject, see Bell (2009^a) 397-411, also the author of the influential *Ritual Theory, Ritual Practice* (2009^b).
[25] Zanker (1988) 167.

Horace was the chosen poet to compose the chant that concluded a ceremony central to Augustus' principate, a fact that by itself testifies the religious idoneity of the lyricist. The rituals that *Carmen saeculare* alludes to are a direct reflection of what happened in the *Ludi*, as documented in the Acts of the Games that were found at the end of the nineteenth century. The aspects that the *carmen* highlights or neglects, as we have had the opportunity to discuss in other circumstances,[26] are revealing of the way the poet interpreted his poem in the context of the ritual it was part of. For example, the darker and chthonic divinities, worshiped during the nights of the Games, acquire their own luminosity in the poem, through carefully selected adjectives. The opposition between Olympic and Chthonic gods, manifest in the Acts, is blurred as is the opposition between day and night. We do not wish to delve excessively into the textual coincidences between the *carmen* and the Acts of the *Ludi*, but we do wish to underline an aspect Michael Putnam already emphasized in his book *Horace's Carmen saeculare: ritual magic and the poet's art*:[27] Horace's poem is a ritual by itself, performed at a specific moment that was also central to the history of Roman Religion.

The fact that these games were fundamental to the Augustan ideology becomes, when we examine Horace's idiosyncratic religiosity, a difficult paradox. On the one hand, Horace, being the minstrel 'on duty', incarnates in his text the religious and political principles of the *princeps* – the devotion to Apollo and Diana, the moral legislation, the idea that Augustus had a divine filiation from Venus and Anchises – even though we cannot find traces in this poem of the so-called 'imperial cult'. On the other hand, the fact that the poem is by itself a chanted ritual makes us think that the poet thought of his verses as part of a public religious ceremony – a liturgy, in the etymological sense of the word. It is at least questionable to refuse Horace's religiosity, to consider him 'faintly religious' just because he decided the poem should be a faithful expression of what happened during those three days and nights. Yes, we can suppose it was his non-cloaked pride that led him to accept the invitation. Yes, we can even suppose his verses

---

[26] Falcão (2010) 187-205.
[27] Putnam (2000).

are subservient to and lean on Augustan propaganda. But how can we ascertain the 'degree of religiosity' of a poet that serves the *kairos* of his people? How can we guarantee that, for example, Henry Purcell was a very religious man when he put to music Psalm 122 ('I was glad when they said unto me'), on the occasion of King James II's coronation?

But as we already suggested, better than to speak according to ambiguous criteria such as 'very' or 'little' religious, a scheme of values that is scientifically irrelevant, we can opt for more precise terms, such as 'rituality' or 'religious experience', that are drawn from the methodologies of the history of religions. In this context, it is undeniable that *Carmen saeculare* represented a ritual and a religious experience, which is indeed well documented, perhaps better than any other in antiquity. This experience was lived not only in community, but also in the intimacy of its composer: Quintus Horatius Flaccus. From the ritual point of view, maybe it has not been properly stressed that the textual and numerological organization of the poem reveals a profound commitment by the poet to the religious moment he experiences. Special importance is given to the number three, a key element in the ceremony that is skillfully engrained in the structure of the text.

According to the Acts,[28] we know that the games were divided among three days and three nights. During these three days three sacrifices were made, in honor of Jupiter, Juno, and the twins Apollo and Diana and during the three nights three other sacrifices, in honor of the *Moirai*, the *Ilithyai* and *Terra Mater*. During the first night nine ewes and nine goats are sacrificed. Number three again present as $9 = 3 \times 3$ and as 18 (the total number of sacrifices) divided by three equals six, the number of moments the ceremony had, corresponding to three days and three nights. In the second night and in the third day, 27 $(9 + 9 + 9)$ sacred cakes are consecrated, another multiple of 3, and we must not forget that there were three types of cake. The rituals without blood sacrifices occur in identical positions based on cycles of three: respectively concluding every three ceremonies. As for the number of boys and girls in the chorus, $27 + 27$, they are the same number of sacred cakes, 54, equally a multiple of 3.

---

[28] *CIL* 6.3237 n. 32323.

This numerological restraint that can nowadays be easily discarded as 'superstition' and not taken seriously – despite the 'magical' essence present in many traditional religions (not to mention several 'civilized' religions)[29] – is very present in the Horatian text, but purposely in a covert way. In the *Carmen*'s division, each part is composed by three sets of three strophes each (triads), as we can observe in the following scheme:[30]

> **A(Prayer)**
> I (1-12) – Initial invocation of Apollo and Diana
> II (13-24) – Wishes for fertility and renewal
> III (25-36) – Summoning of the *Parchae* and *Tellus*, Apollo and Diana
> **B (Confirmation)**
> I (37-48) – Little *Aeneid*. Invocation of all the gods
> II (49-60) – Augustus arises. Expression of trust
> III (61-72) – Final invocation of Apollo e Diana
> **CODA(73-76)** – Epilogue.

Number three is also present in the metrical setting of the ode. The Sapphic stanza presents three hendecasyllables, and in the end of each triad we have three chanted Adonics. There are even subtler relations: 3 hendecasyllables x 19 strophes equals 57, and 57 divided by 3 equals 19, precisely the number of Adonic verses. We have 54 hendecasyllables, the exact number of boys (27 = 3 x 3 x 3) and girls (27 = 3 x 3 x 3) of the chorus. Number three actually appears in verse 23, and nine in verse 62. Each strophe summons three divinities (or divine epithets) or sets of three:

> **A**
> I – Phoebus, Diana, Sol;
> II – Ilithyia, Lucina, Genitalis;
> III – Parcae, Tellus, Ceres; Iuppiter, Apollo, Luna;

---

[29] For the importance of numerology in Augustine and its relation to his religious context, cf. Ackroyd, Evans (1970) 559 ff. It is also a main feature in Sefer Yetsirah, an ancient Hebrew treatise on cosmogony and cosmology (cf. Dan [1997] 618), the source of many kabbalistic commentaries. Cuomo (2001) 249 ff. offers a good introduction to the subject in late ancient mathematics.

[30] This is the division already proposed by Fränkel (1957) 370 ff. and Kiessling, Heinze (1958) 471.

B
I – (no gods are invoked)
II – Venus, Fides, Pax; Honos, Pudor, Copia;
III – Phoebus, Camenae, Diana;
CODA – Iuppiter, Phoebus, Diana.

Focusing on the ritual dimension of Roman religion, and in view of these considerations, we can believe that the composer of the *Carmen saeculare* had a clear religious intention in his hymn. He ingrained in the structure of the text a number linked to Rome's majesty and the inner organization of rituals. This was achieved on a mystical or even magical level, since no one, just by hearing the *carmen* in its original performance, could immediately perceive the number 3 in the actual structure and organization of the text. How can we say that the poet's intention was just to amplify the religious agenda of the *princeps*, due to personal interest or ambition? When *Carmen saeculare* is in fact a genuine compositional and ritual experience, with 'supernatural' intentions? A song that aims to imperceptibly give power to the chanted word, imploring for the eternity not of Rome's rulers, but of the *Vrbs* herself? As Habinek[31] puts it, 'much as the *Carmen Saliare* celebrates the role of music in modulating the Roman state to the rhythms of the cosmos, the *Carmen Saeculare* concerns itself with the role of song in securing the reproduction of the state over time.'

5. A possible conclusion

If we judge him according to Christian theology, from a Hindu or even a Buddhist viewpoint, obviously Horace is not a religious man. Thus, the main reason he talks about religion must be to amplify Augustus' own religious policy, or perhaps his attitude is simply a literary fiction, a blasé account of superfluous rituals. However, when we examine his work in the light of history of religion, we become more alert to the religion and religions with which Horace was imbued, in which the ritual dimension played a much more important than the doctrinal one. We are then bound to think of Horace as someone

---

[31] Habinek (2005) 151.

who lived and participated in the *cultus deorum*, so much so, or even more than any man of his age, and moreover as someone who had an active role in religion. If western theology (or even modern atheism) normally relies on a typical *credo*, that is simply not the case with many traditional and classical religions, like the Roman. Even so, Horace is one of the few classical writers that offers us a sort of 'testimony to the faith': *caelo tonantem credidimus Iouem regnare* (3.5) are his exact words. In this poem we may find ground for the future exploration of that other aspect of the religious phenomenon, the doctrinal dimension as Ninian Smart puts it, an idea to which we would like to come back on a later occasion. But it is important to clarify that in the Roman religious realm, there was no incoherence whatsoever in observing the ritual and at the same time scorning its utility, for instance, when it comes to death:

> non si trecenis quotquot eunt dies,
> amice, places illacrimabilem
>   Plutona tauris, qui ter amplum
>   Geryonen Tityonque tristi
>
> compescit unda, scilicet omnibus,
> quicumque terrae munere uescimur,
>   enauiganda, siue reges
>   siue inopes erimus coloni.
>
>   *Carm.* 2.14.5-12

Many religions based on an *orthopraxis* share this feature. The Jewish 'Trial of God', during the Holocaust, as witnessed by Eliezer Wiesel, is an excellent example of this: 'one evening, amid all the squalor and horror of the concentration camps, a group of pious Jews gathered together. They were going to put God on trial. How could an all-good, all-powerful and all-knowing God tolerate what was happening to His Chosen People? All night the debate raged back and forth. In the end there could be only one possible conclusion. There is no God. The Heavens are empty. The evil of the concentration camps could exist because there was no one to stop it. The Jewish religion was based on a fallacy. When the discussion was finished the dawn was breaking. Another day of brutal, hack-breaking work lay ahead. All the participants stood up and they all prayed the traditional morning service together.'³² Therefore, one ought not try to study Horace's religion based on the assumption that one *has to believe* to *be religious*. Even though our main discussion here is not to demonstrate that Horace, the author, was a 'religious man', we can argue in the light of the above that he was in fact 'religious' in the Roman sense, as he respected Roman *orthopraxis*, and performed the rituals demanded by the *mos maiorum*, even if their utility was open to discussion. In terms of Roman religion, the *augur* was not expected to 'believe' in his *auguria*: he only had to watch two things: the skies and tradition. Anything more was of no consequence.

More important to us, though, is to conclude that based on textual evidence one is inclined to think that the rituals depicted in Horace's work reflect, at least statistically speaking, more of a personal religious experience than a political or social one. Almost all of the rituals referred to in the *Odes* are of 'personal interest' – the author performs rituals for the sake of his own erotic happiness (1.5.13-16, 1.19.13-16, 3.27.1-16), health (3.8.1-12, perhaps 3.13.1-8,³³ 1.31.1-3) and wealth (3.18.6-8, 3.22.1-8). On the other hand, we have only two examples of 'political' rituals, even though these were not actual blood sacrifices (4.5, 4.15), the presence of which in the last book of *Odes* attests to the growing influence of Augustus in the Roman religious climate. But that is a matter for another kind of discussion. *Carmen saeculare* plays its own special role: a sense of communitarian religiosity that is felt within the intimacy of the composition and in the religious, mystical and numerological signature of its composer.

From this we may conclude that: a) it is important to look at Horace's references to religion through different perspectives, and not exclusively through philological studies. The fields of history of religion and religious studies, which categorize and treat separately the different aspects of what can many times vaguely be referred to as 'religion', allow for some degree of objectivity; b) in a Roman religion often depicted as socially, politically and institutionally motivated, we find an example of a *corpus* of texts in which almost all of the described rites have none of these intentions: they rather reflect a

---

³² Cohn-Sherbok (1997) 19-20.
³³ In a very loose and general sense, we must admit, but we definitely cannot see in this ode any political motivation.

personal experience or motivation. That can only make us more curious to investigate the other dimensions that we did not have the chance to explore here: mythological, doctrinal, ethical, social and experiential. This last category naturally involves a holistic reading of the other five, as Ninian Smart suggests, and will offer itself as a conclusion to these reflections.

Bibliography

Acroyd, P.R., Evans, C.F. (edd.) (1970), *The Cambridge History of The Bible*, vol. 1: *From the Beginnings to Jerome*, Cambridge.

Barchiesi, A. (2000), 'Rituals in Ink: Horace on the Greek Lyric Tradition', in M. Depew, D. Obbink (edd.), *Matrices of Genre. Authors, Canons, and Society*, Cambridge, 167-182.

Beard, M., North, J.A., Price, S.R.F. (1998[a]), *Religions of Rome: A History*, vol. 1, Cambridge.

Beard, M., North, J.A., Price, S.R.F. (1998[b]), *Religions of Rome: A Sourcebook*, vol. 2, Cambridge.

Belayche, N. (2011), 'Religious Actors in Daily Life', in J. Rüpke (ed.), *A Companion to Roman Religion*, Oxford, 275-291.

Bell, C. (2009[a]), 'Ritual', in R.A. Segal (ed.), *The Blackwell Companion to the Study of Religion*, Malden, 397-411.

Bell, C. (2009[b]), *Ritual Theory, Ritual Practice*, Oxford.

Breuer, J. (2008), *Der Mythos in den Oden des Horaz: Praetexte, Formen, Funktionen*, Göttingen.

Cohn-Sherbok, D., Cohn-Sherbok, L. (1997), *Judaism: A Short Introduction*, Oxford.

Cuomo, S. (2001), *Ancient Mathematics*, London.

Dan, J. (1997), 'Sefer Yetsirah', in R.J. Zwi Werblowsky, G. Wigoder, *The Oxford Dictionary of the Jewish Religion*, Oxford, 618.

Falcão, P.B. (2010), 'O Ofício Sagrado do Poeta: a Música de Horácio nos Jogos de Augusto', in M.C. Pimentel, N.S. Rodrigues (edd.), *Sociedade e Poder no Tempo de Ovídio*, Coimbra/ Lisboa, 187-205.

Fedeli, P. (1994), *Q. Orazio Flacco, Le Opere*, vol. 2: *Le Satire, Le Epistole, L'Arte Poetica. Tomo Secondo: Commento di Paolo Fedeli*, Roma.

Fraenkel, E. (1957), *Horace*, Oxford.
Freyburger, G. (1977), 'La supplication d'action de grâces dans la religion romaine archaïque', *Latomus* 36, 283-315.
Griffin, J. (2007), 'Gods and Religion', in S.J. Harrison (ed.), *The Cambridge Companion to Horace*, Cambridge.
Habinek, T. (2005), *The World of Song. From Ritualized Speech to Social Order*, Baltimore.
Hahn, F.H. (2011), 'Performing the Sacred: Prayers and Hymns', in J. Rüpke (ed.), *A Companion to Roman Religion*, Oxford, 275-291.
Kiessling, A., Heinze, R. (1959), *Q. Horatius Flaccus, Oden und Epoden*, Berlin.
Labate, M. (2013), 'Constructing the Roman myth: The History of the Republic in Horace's Lyric Poetry', in J. Farrell, D. Nelis (edd.), *Augustan Poetry and the Roman Republic*, Oxford.
Loupiac, A. (1999), *Virgile, Auguste et Apollon : Mythes et Politique à Rome : L'arc et La Lyre*, Paris/ Montréal.
Mankin, D.(1995), *Horace, Epodes*, Cambridge.
Miller, J.F. (2009), *Apollo, Augustus, and the Poets*, Cambridge/ New York.
Moede, K. (2011), 'Reliefs, Public and Private', in J. Rüpke (ed.), *A Companion to Roman Religion*, Oxford, 164-175.
Nisbet, R.G.M., Hubbard, M. (1970), *A Commentary on Horace. Odes, Book 1*, Oxford.
Nisbet, R.G.M., Rudd, N. (2004), *A Commentary on Horace. Odes, Book 3*, Oxford.
Oksala, T. (1997), 'Religione', in S. Mariotti (ed.), *Enciclopedia Oraziana*, 2, Roma, 285-288.
Putnam, M.C.J. (2000), *Horace's Carmen Saeculare. Ritual Magic and the Poet's Art*, New Haven.
Romano, E. (1991), *Q. Orazio Flacco, Le opere, 1: Le Odi; il Carme secolare; gli Epodi. Tomo Secondo: Commento di Elisa Romano*, Roma.
Scheid, J. (2005), 'Augustus and Roman Religion: Continuity, Conservatism, and Innovation', in K. Galinsky (ed.), *The Cambridge Companion to the Age of Augustus*, Cambridge.
Scheid, J. (2011), 'Sacrifices for Gods and Ancestors', in J. Rüpke (ed.), *A Companion to Roman Religion*, Oxford, 263-271.

Smart, N. (1971), *The Religious Experience of Mankind*, London.
Smart, N. (1998), *Dimensions of the Sacred. An Anatomy of the World's Beliefs*, Berkeley.
Wilkinson, L.P. (1945), *Horace and His Lyric Poetry*, Cambridge.
Zanker, P. (1988), *The Power of Images in the Age of Augustus*, transl. A. Shapiro, Ann Arbor.

Le tre immagini del funerale di Augusto

CARLO SANTINI
Università degli Studi di Perugia

Nessuna fonte letteraria coeva attesta cosa sia successo esattamente in quel periodo di tempo intercorso tra il 19 agosto, giorno della morte di Augusto, e il 17 settembre in cui venne proclamata in senato la sua apoteosi, ma i dettagli dei riti che ci sono trasmessi almeno ad un secolo di distanza (Tacito, Suetonio, Dione Cassio) ci rendono edotti sulle cerimonie che si succedettero in quel mese di lutto, a cui presero parte varie migliaia di persone in una sorta di performance collettiva.[1]

Una fonte contemporanea in realtà furono proprio i *mandata de funere suo*, le disposizioni sul suo funerale, che Augusto con la prudenza e la meticolosità che gli erano proprie, aveva scritto già da tempo, prendendo ad esempio il funerale del genero Vipsanio Agrippa. L'importanza di queste disposizioni coincise con la qualità della scelta del successore; svaniti da tempo i progetti di avere un successore del suo stesso sangue, Augusto con l'indicazione di un erede all'interno della famiglia giulio-claudia rendeva chiaro di perseguire un intento dinastico. Non era Tiberio il prediletto del principe tra i due figli maschi di Livia, ma la decisione di costringerlo ad adottare Germanico dovette risultare ai suoi occhi un provvedimento sufficientemente cautelativo. Poiché questo opuscolo, o codicillo che dir si voglia,[2] ora andato perduto, fu letto in pubblico unitamente al suo testamento da Druso minore, secondo quanto fu dichiarato da Suetonio e da Dione Cassio, sembra impossibile sostenere che le cose andarono troppo diversamente da come avrebbe stabilito, salvo specifici ritocchi dovuti alla contingenza del momento.

Non c'è dubbio, credo, che le precauzioni prese in occasione dal servizio pubblico di stato, con il dispiegamento dell'esercito, siano dipese dall'effetto, lontano nel tempo, ma sempre vivo, prodotto su Ottaviano, che appena uscito dall'adolescenza si trovava ad Apollonia

---

[1] Gnoli (2014) 193.
[2] De Blasi, Ferrero (2003) 554-555.

in attesa di ricongiunersi con il suo padre adottivo, dal ricordo di quanto era successo in occasione dell'attentato di cui era rimasto vittima Giulio Cesare.

Il corpo che, in un primo momento, doveva essere gettato nel Tevere, come volevano i Cesaricidi, poi, per interposizione della fazione di Calpurnio Pisone Cesonino,[3] suocero di Cesare e tuttavia mirante ad arginare quello che era ormai il partito antoniano – era in gioco per altro l'esecuzione degli *acta* del *dictator* alcuni dei quali erano in favore degli stessi congiurati – fu deciso fosse cremato con le onorificenze prescritte nel Campo Marzio, per essere poi deposto nel prossimo sepolcro della *gens Iulia*. La situazione tuttavia degenerò in seguito alla lettura del testamento e sfuggì di mano al potere costituito; subito dopo un tentativo di portare il morto sul Campidoglio quasi fosse ritenuto un dio da porre accanto alla triade capitolina, fallito per l'interdizione del ceto sacerdotale, il suo corpo venne cremato nel Foro stesso. Si trattava di un atto illegale e inusitato trattandosi di un luogo in cui vigeva in età delle XII tavole il divieto di seppellire i morti, sia per inumazione che per incinerazione, proprio perché incluso nel perimetro dell'*urbs*.

Le fonti ci informano che proprio lì sorse una sorta di culto popolare per Cesare, a cui si dedicò soprattutto Amazio, il presunto figlio (o piuttosto nipote) di Caio Mario, che aveva tentato senza riuscirvi di farsi iscrivere nel piè di lista della *gens Iulia* e che ora fungeva da capo popolo della fazione integralista dei cesariani. Prima che Amazio fosse fatto sopprimere dal console Dolabella con l'assenso dello stesso Marco Antonio, o immediatamente dopo,[4] tale forma di culto si rafforzerà mediane l'erezione di un altare (βωμός) secondo le fonti greche, ovvero di un *bustum* e di una *columna* secondo Suetonio, con l'iscrizione 'Parenti Patriae', che nonostante vennero poi distrutti costituirono il primo nucleo del tempio a Cesare, che sarà innalzato dai triumviri dopo Filippi con la conservazione di un'abside in corrispondenza di un originario altare rotondo.

La stessa logica del timore di un *tumultus* come quello già verificatosi ai tempi della morte di Silla e di altri leaders tardo-republicani aveva indotto Augusto, Livia, Tiberio a schierare l'esercito per controllare

---

[3] Cristofoli (2012) 70-71.
[4] Cristofoli (2002) 150.

e eventualmente intervenire nei luoghi dell'evento, anche se tali misure apparivano superflue dopo tanti anni di *pax Augusta*. Per noi, invece, questo continuato confronto con il funerale di Cesare appare di fondamentale importanza per riuscire a comprendere cosa nel corso degli anni il giovane Ottaviano pensasse di quell'evento e come avesse deciso, divenuto poi Augusto, di modellare il proprio.

La divinizzazione di Cesare costituì un punto determinante nella ascesa di Ottaviano, che era stato *inaspettatamente* prescelto dal defunto come suo figlio adottivo – in realtà era il pronipote in quanto la madre Azia era infatti la figlia della sorella Giulia – per una di quelle variabili che fanno mutare il loro corso agli eventi. Se nel riprendere in mano il testamento per aggiungere *in ima cera* l'adozione *in familiam nomenque* di Ottavio, Cesare compì una scelta che si dimostrò *a posteriori* la più rilevante dei suoi ultimi atti, sarà Ottaviano ad effettuare un gesto di personale 'audacia'[5] che, pur senza avere alcun contatto formale con le azioni di Amazio e dei suoi dell'aprile passato, rilanciò alla fine di luglio, in occasione dell'assemblea del *collegium* per i Ludi di Venere Genitrice, i cui adepti sappiamo appartenere esclusivamente[6] alla *gens Iulia*.

Forse in base a conoscenze acquisite o filtrate dal gruppo di astronomi alessandrini raccolti intorno a Sosigene, con cui Cesare aveva collaborato per la riforma del calendario, Ottaviano prese la decisione di fare un annuncio pubblico concernente la natura divina e cosmica di suo padre. La voce dell'apparizione di una 'stella vastissima coronata di raggi come nastri' ('stella amplissima, quasi lemniscis, radiis coronata'), visibile a tutti in data 23 settembre, che il popolo riteneva essere un atto di gloria per il giovane Ottaviano, venne da lui rettificata con la notizia che si trattava invece dell'attestazione visibile che suo padre stava salendo verso la volta celeste, in base alla posizione dei fiocchi che la facevano identificare come una cometa. La notizia si divulgò rapidamente, Virgilio la inserirà nella nona egloga[7] e lo stesso Augusto più di venti anni dopo la ricordò nel secondo

---

[5] Fraschetti (1990).
[6] Kornemann (1900) 384.
[7] Cf. *Serv. Dan. Ecl.* 9.46.

libro dei *Commentarii de uita sua*, da dove la assunse testualmente Plinio il Vecchio.[8]

La cometa assunse la forma di una stella che invariabilmente accompagnò la statuaria di Cesare e di Augusto come simbolo di identità e di partecipazione alla divinità almeno fino al 23, quando, dopo la vittoriosa eliminazione di tutti gli avversari, si procedette ad una rettifica della politica religiosa in modo da lasciare a sé il ruolo di *deus praesens*. Cesare era entrato dopo la battaglia di Filippi a pieno diritto tra gli dei del *pantheon* e dell'anno romano, ma risultò sostanzialmente inattivo, a parte le cerimonie che riguardavano il calendario, così come osserva Ovidio nel concludere con la sua menzione la sue *Metamorfosi*: 15.750-751: *Neque enim de Caesaris actis/ ullum maius opus quam quod pater exstitit huius*.

L'anno 23 segna per Augusto, trattenuto in Cantabria al fine di pacificare quelle regioni, la prima crisi della strategia dinastica che, contestualmente, rappresenta un periodo di grande precarietà della sua salute, durante il quale questa si aggravò tanto da costringerlo a confrontarsi con l'imminenza della morte. Pure essendo divenuto il suocero del nipote Marcello con le nozze della figlia Giulia, non si spinse mai al punto di dargli, come riferisce Dione, il sigillo, con il quale segnava tutti gli atti, cosa che invece fece con Agrippa, riferendosi al gesto di Alessandro, che lo aveva trasmesso a Perdicca. La memoria di tale gesto risultava tanto più incalzante in quanto era stato proprio lui ad impadronirsi dell'anello durante la campagna di Egitto.

Augusto tuttavia sopravvisse grazie ad una terapia di bagni e bevande fredde dispostegli dal medico Antonio Musa, sventò la congiura di Murena e ritornato in sede, allontanò con un mandato in Siria Agrippa per evitare frizioni con il nipote geloso; quest'ultimo tuttavia, già provato dalla malattia, in quello stesso anno morì. Furono approntate un'immagine aurea del defunto, una corona d'oro e una sella curule, che, collocate tra i magistrati nel teatro dove si tenevano i ludi, ne rammentavano a tutti la presenza. Questa data pare contrassegnare, come ho già accennato, un cambiamento nel culto di Cesare, che

---

[8] Cf. Plin. *HN* 2.93, che notando come la cometa generalmente ritenuta di cattivo augurio sia invece oggetto di venerazione nella sola Roma (*in uno totius orbis loco*) riporta le parole di Augusto alla quali aggiunge di suo la soddisfazione interiore nel constatare che quell'evento era nato per lui e che lui era nato in esso (*interiore gaudio sibi illum natum seque in eo nasci interpretatus*).

è stato notato da Fraschetti,[9] e un ulteriore favore verso Agrippa, a cui fa sposare la figlia Giulia e insieme al quale celebra nel 17 i *ludi saeculares*, che rappresentarono dal punto di vista della storia religiosa l'avvicendamento del prestigio e dell'importanza degli dei palatini (Apollo e Diana) rispetto alla triade capitolina.

Intanto cominciarono a diffondersi nelle province dell'impero atti di culto nei suoi riguardi provenienti da cittadini privati (*sacra priuata*), ma anche da istituzioni e confraternite pubbliche, come nell'Oriente greco, in Gallia e nei municipi italici, con la sola eccezione della capitale, Roma, dove tali forme di divinizzazione non sono state reperite, verosimilmente perché non era stato dato loro libero accesso.[10] La formula usata in queste epigrafi era quella di *numen Augusti*; è già attestata da Orazio nella prima epistola del libro secondo[11] con la quale si intendeva fare una sottile distinzione tra la natura umana e il potere divino, che la impersonava in vita per divenire assolutamente prevalente alla sua morte. Orazio si dimostra quindi il portatore di una spinta occulta verso la deificazione del principe, indossando al posto del ruolo di *uates* dei primi tre libri delle *Odi* quello globale di 'quiuis ex populo' del libro quarto, come osservato da Fraenkel, che sancisce la nascita della lirica civile a Roma.[12]

Un evento che riportò Augusto all'idea del suo funerale fu l'improvvisa e imprevista morte del genero Agrippa nel 12 a.C., che il principe sentì come la fine dell'esperimento di un possibile tentativo di diarchia improntato su lui stesso, discendente di una antica *gens*, e sul valoroso concorso di un *homo nouus*. Un papiro di Colonia, pubblicato negli anni settanta del secolo scorso, poi oggetto di successive revisioni per la scoperta di un secondo frammento,[13] ci trasmette alcune linee della *laudatio funebris* tenuta da Augusto sul corpo velato del collega ed amico, in cui ricorda le due massime attestazioni di autorità ricevute da costui, vale a dire la *tribunicia potestas*, ottenuta nel 18 e rinnovata

---

[9] Fraschetti (1990) 65 parla di una 'spersonalizzazione' di Cesare che coincide con lo 'stacco profondo tra la figura umana e l'entità divina del padre.'
[10] Koortbojian (2013) 165-179.
[11] Cf. 1.15-7: *Praesenti tibi maturos largimur honores/ iurandasque tuom per numen ponimus aras,/ nil oriturum alias, nil ortum tale fatentes.*
[12] Sulla questione cf. Fedeli (2008) 50-51.
[13] Si tratta del *P. Colon. 4701*, le cui due parti furono edite insieme da Gronewald (1987) 113-115. Si veda per gli aspetti giuridico-istituzionali del testo Hurlet (1997).

nel 13, e la possibilità di un comando, in qualsiasi provincia dell'impero si fosse recato, superiore a quello del personale amministrativo e politico lì inviato dal senato di Roma. Si trattava quindi di una forma di *proconsulare imperium* (forse non *maximum et infinitum* come nel caso di Augusto), tramite la quale Agrippa era divenuto la seconda autorità nell'impero e virtualmente il suo successore.

Si aggiunga poi che nello stesso anno[14] risultò visibile la cometa di Halley, alla quale fa riferimento Dione Cassio in questi termini a 54.29.8: 'un astro chiamato *la cometa* splendette in cielo per diversi giorni sulla città e si dissolse in fiaccole.' Suscita qualche interrogativo la ripetizione di quanto si sarebbe verificato nell'anno 44, anche se in questo secondo caso abbiamo la conferma delle fonti cinesi che parlano diffusamente del fenomeno. La cometa di Halley fu visibile nei mesi di settembre e ottobre dopo la morte di Agrippa e viene elencata dallo storico greco tra gli *omina* negativi e non, come il *sidus Iulium*, tra i segni capaci di produrre gioia nel popolo perché attestavano che un nuovo dio si era aggiunto agli altri.[15] Ignoriamo il perché il corpo di Agrippa sia stato coperto con un velo, così come capitò a lui stesso; poteva forse trattarsi del *caeruleum vexillum* che il principe gli aveva donato per la vittoria in Sicilia.[16] Onorare Agrippa negli anni successivi alla sua morte aveva il solo scopo di preparare il regno ai suoi figli; ciò troverebbe corrispondenza con la scena di uno dei bassorilievi dell'Altare del Belvedere che rappresenta il saluto della sposa Giulia e dei suoi due figli ad Agrippa che s'incammina alla volta delle regioni celesti.[17]

Quanto esposto fin qui può servire da testimonianza, quasi non ve ne fosse prova nel libretto di istruzioni funebri da lui composto, del costante confrontarsi di Augusto con la morte, a lungo attesa e quasi pregustata, che doveva sancire il significato ultimo e il sigillo di una esistenza spesa nel proclamare la sua congenita capacità di governo dello stato romano.

---

[14] Maffei (1984) 157-161.
[15] In realtà in entrambi i casi una notizia negativa entrava in conflitto con la positiva; nel 44, secondo Servio Danielino *Ecl.* 9.46 *Vulcanius haruspex in contione dixit cometen esse, qui significaret exitum noni saeculi et ingressum decimi,* ma Ottaviano avrebbe dichiarato abilmente che il messaggio riguardava solo il popolo degli Etruschi, come attestata dalla morte improvvisa dell'aruspice *quod invitis dis secreta rerum pronuntiaret,* cf. Wiseman (2009) 116-117.
[16] Suet. *Aug.* 25.
[17] Fraschetti (1990) 299-300.

Quella di Augusto era la visione di un vecchio e provetto statista, non esente dal compiacimento per i successi ottenuti; dinanzi al suo giudizio non servivano adulazioni o infingimenti, così come si ricava già parecchio tempo prima dalla risposta in Egitto, dopo Azio, quando a chi gli chiedeva se, oltre il sepolcro di Alessandro, desiderasse vedere le tombe dei Ptolomei, rispose che il suo intento era quello di visitare i re e non i morti.[18] Alla franchezza della dichiarazione imbastita sulla contrapposizione asimmetrica tra l'eternità del potere e la contingenza della morte, con la quale Ottaviano, non ancora Augusto, si liberava una volta per tutte dell'ossequio verso le monarchie dei Diadochi che considerava deboli ed inette, corrisponderà infatti, quarantaquattro anni dopo, l'invito rivolto agli amici più stretti ad applaudirlo se avesse giocato bene la commedia della sua vita.[19]

Le immagini fatte sfilare partendo da luoghi diversi identificano in essi con un mirato simbolismo ternario (3 = 1 + 2) la puntuale memoria dei traguardi raggiunti nel corso della sua esistenza; da un lato si vuole infatti affermare il significato dell'essere un esponente gentilizio, dall'altro i titoli perpetui di *princeps* e di *imperator* spettanti solo al *Diui filius* tanto che ci è dato assistere ad 'una vera e propria triplicazione di immagini' per un solo defunto. La discesa dal Palatino con la maschera cerea attesta la celebrazione della sua morte secondo il *mos* della antica tradizione repubblicana. Le immagini ceree degli antenati comprendevano quella dello stesso Enea, così come aveva voluto Giulio Cesare in occasione del funerale della zia Giulia, quella di Romolo e quella di Pompeo,[20] legata alla sua *gens* dall'infelice matrimonio con la figlia di Cesare Giulia, mentre era assente per ragioni di devozione quella dello stesso Cesare, che era un dio nel suo tempio.[21]

Le altre due immagini fanno riferimento alle mete che era impossibile ad un *ciuis* romano acquisire e conservare nel tempo. Si notifica in questo modo tramite due maschere non più funebri, ma già quasi divine il potere sovraumano dell'*Augustus*: quella crisoelefantina – i materiali sono quelli del potere vetusto di Roma – che sta a rappresentare ostensibilmente la *tribunicia potestas*, dalla curia senatoria raggiungeva

---

[18] Suet. *Aug.* 18.
[19] Suet. *Aug.* 99.
[20] Fraschetti (1990) 78.
[21] Fraschetti (1990) 79-80.

il Foro, mentre l'altra, che i senatori stabilirono salisse lungo la via trionfale, rappresenta il potere militare, riguardo al quale le scenografie dei popoli sottomessi e delle città vinte attestano la prova della *felicitas* di chi lo ha rivestito.

In occasione del suo funerale Augusto aveva voluto che il suo cadavere non fosse visibile; scrive infatti Dione Cassio 56.34.1 in questi termini: 'un feretro fatto d'avorio e di oro, adornato di coperte purpuree ed auree, conteneva nascosto il corpo, sotto, dentro una bara.' Lo stesso autore a proposito delle esequie di Agrippa ci dice che il suo corpo era coperto da un velo, ma non sa spiegarne il motivo (54.28.4 παραπέτασμά τι πρὸ τοῦ νεκροῦ παρατείνας. ὅπερ ἐγὼ μὲν οὐκ οἶδα διὰ τί ἐποίησεν), pur escludendo tuttavia che esso riguardi l'interdizione per il pontefice massimo di vedere un cadavere, come invece aveva sostenuto Seneca per il rito funebre di Druso Cesare nella *Cons. Marc.* 15.3: *interiecto tantummodo uelamento, quod pontificis oculos a funere arceret*. Siffatte spiegazioni rivelano in genere l'incertezza degli autori posteriori nei confronti di un uso che, per quanto ne sappiamo, riguardò i funerali di quattro membri della dinastia vale a dire, oltre Augusto, Agrippa, Druso Cesare e Ottavia (54.34.4 παραπετάσματι καὶ τότε ἐπὶ τοῦ νεκροῦ χρησάμενος), per poi sparire definitivamente senza lasciare traccia di sé.

Sulle cause di siffatto velo posto sul cadavere hanno discusso gli antichisti, tenendo conto solo della posizione di chi parla in occasione della *laudatio funebris*, come pensava Dione; Scheid e Lemosse sono giunti a conclusioni divergenti, il primo a favore della carica rivestita dal pontefice massimo[22] ed il secondo dal flamine diale,[23] che invece non troviamo tra quelle rivestite da Augusto. L'atto di coprire gli appartenenti della *gens Iulia* in occasione delle loro esequie fu una decisione presa da Augusto, come crede Gnoli,[24] e durò solo pochi anni dopo la sua morte. Se fu un'iniziativa individuale, come pensa lo storico, fu però rispettosa del suo status e del futuro della sua *gens*.

---

[22] Scheid (1981) 135.
[23] Cf. Lemosse (1968) 523: 'Dion Cassius remémore une réminiscence déformée d'une réalité archaïque lointaine et oubliée' almeno nel periodo tardo-repubblicano, tanto che Seneca non riusciva a capirla.
[24] Cf. Gnoli (2014) 209: "una mera invenzione da parte di Augusto ... particolarmente consona a quanto sappiamo dell'atteggiamento dell'imperatore nei confronti della morte."

La pratica di coprire o avvolgere il cadavere con panni era indubbiamente legata al rito indoeuropeo di bruciare il corpo eliminandone i liquidi che lo componevano e riducendolo ai soli *ossa*, che a Roma era usuale,[25] ma la scelta di Augusto mirava piuttosto a individuare un ambito speciale che garantisse a lui e alla sua *gens* un'immortalità cui non potevano aspirare i *manes* di un semplice individuo.

Occorre un mutamento di prospettiva con la quale leggiamo il racconto del suo funerale, commisurando quanto dicono gli storici, antropologi e filologi moderni al pensiero di Augusto, vale a dire che lui e la sua *gens* fossero convinti di essere *dis geniti deosque genituri*, una formula lealista che Seneca ripete prendendola da Virgilio, là dove Apollo saluta nell'*Eneide* a 9.642 il giovane Ascanio. Lo scetticismo dell'uomo privato coesiste in Augusto con una visione teleologica delle sue imprese, di Roma e dell'impero. Si tratta di un 'paradosso'[26] che non ammette di essere altrimenti specificato.

Due erano i pensieri che crediamo operanti nel *princeps*, il primo proveniva dalla forza ancestrale della tradizione gentilizia per la quale aveva deciso di prendere le armi per vendicare l'uccisione di suo padre ed aggiungere ai nomi il nuovo patronimico *Divi filius*. Abbiamo visto Ottaviano in tali determinate occasioni farsi interprete di una sorta di forza magnetica proveniente dalla *gens Iulia* che, pensiamo, lo attorniava e lo consigliava.[27] La sosta a Boville del suo feretro prima dell'arrivo a Roma implicava da parte degli *equites* e dei suoi familiari un atto di doveroso omaggio conseguente al culto della *gens Iulia*, come risulta da un'epigrafe degli inizi del I secolo a.C. che attesta esistere nel piccolo centro alle porte di Roma un'ara dei *GENTILES IVLIEI*, che identificavano Vediove con Iulo.[28]

Poi è evidente l'influenza di una tradizione culta, che, in base alla *kenning* del 'corpo chitone dell'animo' della sapienza greca e della dottrina platonica, si sarebbe indissolubilmente congiunta con l'idea romana che la *consecratio* non è altro che il transfert dallo spazio

---

[25] Onians (1998) 314-315.
[26] Koortbojian (2013) 179.
[27] Smith (2006) 44, dopo essersi soffermato sui caratteri della *gens* dal punto di vista giuridico, accenna alla sua preminenza nelle attività religiose, tra cui quella attestata appunto dagli *Iulii* e concernente l'ara di *CIL* I² 807 = *ILS* 2988.
[28] Weinstock (1971) 4-12.

profano a quello sacro.[29] Nel tramonto del II secolo dell'impero, ma probabilmente per effetto di circostanze contingenti, sarebbe invalso l'uso di tenere due riti funebri, rispettivamente con il cadavere e con un manichino di cera, in modo da distinguere gli *ossa* da collocarsi sotto terra e la cera che dissolvendosi integralmente nel rogo attestava la apoteosi (*consecratio*) dell'imperatore.[30] Si trattava però di simbologie al pari di quella dell'aquila che saliva in cielo, quando era dato fuoco alla pira, che pure anche essa è menzionata da Dione Cassio in occasione del funerale di Augusto.[31]

Tutto questo ha probabilmente poco a che fare con le disposizioni di Augusto, che aveva inteso stabilire nascondendo i corpi della sua *gens* il limite estremo oltre il quale non è consentito allo sguardo degli uomini di spingersi. Forse il corpo nudo richiamava il concetto di nudità divina[32] sul quale si erano esercitati intere generazioni di scultori greci fin dall'età arcaica. Le cere delle *imagines* erano invece le maschere che erano state tratte per impressione dal viso del morto; venivano usate di volta in volta nei funerali e conservate nell'*atrium* delle dimore gentilizie, ma non avevano nulla a che vedere con i manichini che rappresentavano il corpo nella sua interezza. È quindi possibile una confusione negli autori greci del II e III secolo d.C.

È singolare che Augusto non nomini mai nelle *Res gestae* i capolavori letterari della sua età; non una parola sul *carmen* composto da Orazio per i *ludi saeculares* o sull'*Eneide* rispetto ai dati precisi forniti sul numero di templi restaurati o eretti ex novo, sui teatri, sulle statue che adornavano la città. Probabilmente la raffinata cultura del testo scritto riusciva a penetrare nella classe che oggi chiameremmo media, ma non riceveva quel consenso collettivo che riguardava gli ambiti più ristretti di intenditori della aristocrazia senatoria e i letterati di professione. Sembrava che l'architetto-ingegnere Vitruvio avesse vinto con le sue concrete realizzazioni agli occhi di Augusto il confronto con i grandi poeti della sua età; questi del resto erano tutti morti quando scriveva a 76 anni gli atti del suo regno, ad eccezione di uno solo che aveva

---

[29] Dupont (1986) 234.
[30] Dupont (1986).
[31] Arce (1988) 131-140.
[32] Koortbojian (2013) 203.

relegato a Tomi, quasi a voler dimostrare lo scarso successo della politica culturale nell'ultima parte della sua vita.

E però, se si accredita la presenza di consiglieri della *gens Iulia* a fianco di Augusto, perché non pensare al ricordo del poeta che aveva dato vita immortale al mito di Iulo, aveva fabbricato con la *Heldenschau* un passato che si faceva futuro e la cui opera era stata tanto apprezzata dal principe da imporre a Vario e Tucca di conservarla, nonostante Virgilio ne avesse chiesto insistentemente la distruzione? La distinzione tra i due Augusti, quello individuale e quello politico con l'occhio sempre fisso alla collettività ed al *consensus uniuersorum* vacilla nell'immaginare tale ipotesi.

È noto dalla *Vita Vergiliana* di Donato che la lettura fatta dallo stesso Virgilio del libro sesto dell'*Eneide* procurasse il deliquio[33] per la madre Ottavia quando giunse al celebre emistichio *Tu Marcellus eris*, mentre i familiari le prestavano soccorso. Se leggiamo anche noi le parole con le quali Enea nella sfilata degli eroi di Roma chiede al padre Anchise chi sia mai quel giovane che l'oscurità avvolge in una atmosfera lugubre, nonostante abbia tutti i requisiti per compiere grandi imprese – *sed nox atra caput tristi circumvolat ore* – ci troviamo dinnanzi ad un verso di grande efficacia dove 'notte', metafora immediata per 'morte' che Virgilio frappone per procedimento analogico, pare lambire come un velo mosso dal vento il capo del giovane, che alla fine ne sarà completamente avvolto. L'atto del morire nel caso di Marcello è concepito come un'azione lentamente progressiva.

Questo verso, unico nel contesto della *Heldenschau*, ma formalmente connesso con il v. 272 dello stesso libro, dove la similitudine dello scolorirsi di ogni cosa per l'oscurità incipiente prelude all'ingresso nel Tartaro, dovette restare come un marchio nel pensiero di Augusto suggerendogli una via di uscita dall'ineluttabile necessità che lo aveva colpito e che, ripetendosi, sarebbe riuscito a mettere in crisi tutti i suoi progetti dinastici.

Se dinnanzi alla morte Augusto non trova altro che rifugiarsi nella scenografia di una fastosa e convenzionale[34] cerimonia condita di ironia per propiziare l'ascesa del defunto all'etere celeste, la diceria

---

[33] *Vitae Vergilianae Antiquae* 32.
[34] Fraschetti (1990) 70.

diffusasi intorno alla morte di Tiberio causata da un *puluinus* gettatogli sul viso per riuscire finalmente a soffocarlo, della quale si fece interprete Suetonio,[35] appare come una grottesca parodia che getta in controtendenza una luce sinistra sul futuro della dinastia.

Bibliografia

Arce J. (1988), *Funus Imperatorum. Los funerales de los emperadores romanos*, Madrid.
Brugnoli, G, Stok, F. (1997), *Vitae Vergilianae Antiquae recenserunt*, Roma.
Cristofoli R. (2002), *Dopo Cesare. La scena politica romana all'indomani del cesaricidio*, Napoli.
Cristofoli, R. (2012), 'Epicureo e politico. L. Calpurnio Pisone Cesonino', *Giornale Italiano di Filologia* 64, 63-81.
De Blasi, L., Ferrero, A.M. (2003), *Gli atti compiuti e i frammenti delle opere di Cesare Augusto Imperatore*, Torino.
Dupont, F. (1986), 'L'autre corps de l'empereur-dieu', *Le Corps des dieux: Le temps de la réflexion* 7, 231-252.
Fedeli, P. (2008), 'Introduzione', *Q. Horatii Flacci Carmina Liber 4*, Firenze, 9-58.
Fraschetti, A. (1990), *Roma e il principe*, Roma/ Bari.
Gnoli, T. (2014), 'L'apoteosi di Augusto', in T. Gnoli, F. Muccioli (edd.), *Divinizzazione, culto del sovrano e apoteosi tra Antichità e Medioevo*, Bologna, 193-210.
Gronewald, M. *et alii* (1987), *Kölner Papyri* VI (*Papyrologica Coloniensia* 7), Opladen.
Hurlet, F. (1997), *Les collèges du prince sous Auguste et Tibère. De la légalité républicaine à la légitimité dynastique*, Rome.
Koortbojian, M. (2013), *The Divinization of Caesar and Augustus. Precedents, Consequences, Implications*, Cambridge.
Kornemann, E. (1900), s.v. '*Collegium*', *Realencyclopädie der classischen Altertumswissenschaft*, 384.

---

[35] *Vita Tiberii* 73.

Lemosse, M. (1968), 'Mort et lustratio à propos de Dio Cass. 54,28,4', *Tijdschrift voor Rechtsgeschiedenis* 36, 519-524.
Maffei, P. (1984), *La cometa di Halley*, Milano.
Onians, R.B. (1998), *Le origini del pensiero europeo*, Milano.
Scheid, J. (1981), 'Le délit religieux dans la Rome tardo-républicaine', in *Le délit religieux dans la cité antique*, Rome, 117-171.
Smith, C.J. (2006), *The Roman Clan. The Gens from Ancient Ideology to Modern Anthropology*, Cambridge.
Wiseman, T.P. (2009), 'Augustus, Sulla and the supernatural', in Ch. Smith, A. Powell (edd.), *The Lost Memoirs of Augustus and the Development of Roman Autobiography*, Swansea.
Weinstock, S. (1971), *Diuus Iulius*, Oxford.

II.
POETICA SVMMATIM ATTIGIT
(Suet. *Aug.* 85.2)

Augusto nel IV libro delle *Odi* d'Orazio

PAOLO FEDELI
Università degli Studi di Bari Aldo Moro

È signifi cativo che nella produzione oraziana il sistema della dedica muti radicalmente dopo il I libro delle *Epistole*: sino ad allora, nel dedicare ogni sua fatica poetica a Mecenate,[1] Orazio si era premurato di metterlo in evidenza nei primi versi del carme iniziale di ogni raccolta;[2] in seguito è Augusto a divenire il destinatario del II libro delle *Epistole* e la sua figura domina nel IV libro delle odi: ciò è tanto più significativo in quanto in precedenza non mancavano nei primi tre libri delle odi carmi di elogio ad Augusto, ma rarissimo era il caso – come in *Carm.* 1.2.52 *te duce, Caesar* – di un'apostrofe a lui rivolta.[3] Nel IV libro, invece, di Mecenate ci si ricorda solo per il genetliaco: è probabile, però, che la sua assenza nella poesia di Orazio dopo il I libro delle *Epistole* debba essere messa in rapporto con un deterioramento della sua amicizia con Augusto.[4] Anche se in merito non abbiamo altre attestazioni, tutto lascia credere che dopo il 20 a.C. sia Augusto stesso a gestire direttamente i rapporti con gli esponenti della cultura.[5] Sui motivi del declino del ruolo in precedenza tenuto da Mecenate si possono formulare solo ipotesi Augusto, consolidatisi ormai i suoi poteri, non abbia più ritenuto necessaria una politica di attivo intervento e di vigile organizzazione del prive della necessaria

---

[1] Per non parlare del suo ruolo nel libro 1 e nel libro 2 delle odi – nel libro 3 a lui erano stati dedicati addirittura tre carmi (8, 16, 29) e nel suo nome si era aperta ogni opera oraziana, dagli *Epodi* alle *Satire*, dal I libro dei *Carmina* al I delle *Epistole*.
[2] Cf. *Epod.* 1.3-4, *Sat.* 1.1.1, *Carm.* 1.1.1, *Epist.* 1.1.3.
[3] Cf. Brink (1982) 536.
[4] Lo attesta Tacito, che negli *Annales* (3.30.3-4) – a proposito di C. Sallustio Crispo, nipote della sorella dello storico – sostiene che *aetate prouecta speciem magis in amicitia principis quam uim tenuit*, e aggiunge: *idque et Maecenati accidarat, fato potentiae raro sempiternae, an satias capit aut illos cum omnia tribuerunt, aut hos cum iam nihil reliquum est quod cupiant*.
[5] In merito cf. La Penna (1963) 115, che oltre all'atteggiamento di Orazio mette in rilievo la totale assenza di Mecenate nel IV libro delle elegie di Properzio, e più recentemente Lyne (1995) 136 ss., 189 ss.

verifica:[6] la spiegazione più semplice è che settore culturale, anche perché i letterati ormai avevano assunto di buon grado il ruolo di panegiristi del regime.

A convincere Orazio a fare ritorno alla poesia lirica sarà stato decisivo il grande onore a lui tributato nel 17 a.c., allorché fu scelto quale poeta ufficiale nella celebrazione dei *ludi saeculares*: il *Carmen saeculare* costituisce un'evidente ripresa della celebrazione del programma augusteo, che tanta parte aveva già occupato nell'ambito del III libro, e rappresenta un punto di passaggio significativo alla presenza delle stesse tematiche nei carmi del IV libro. A stare alla biografia oraziana nel *De poetis* di Svetonio, il ritorno alla poesia lirica non sarebbe stato il frutto della libera scelta del poeta, ma dell'imposizione di Augusto che, entusiasta dei versi di Orazio, dopo il *Carmen saeculare* lo avrebbe indotto a celebrare la vittoria di Tiberio e di Druso sui Vindelici.[7] Tuttavia da tempo la critica[8] ha messo in rilievo l'inattendibilità di una simile notizia: se, infatti, si accordasse fiducia alla testimonianza di Svetonio, se ne dovrebbe dedurre che cronologicamente i primi carmi della raccolta siano il IV e il XIV, scritti tra la fine del 15 e l'inizio del 14 a.C. per cantare la vittoria ottenuta da Druso e da Tiberio sui Vindelici e sui Reti nell'estate del 15 a.C.; sia pur nell'incertezza cronologica della maggior parte dei carmi del IV libro e ammettendo pure che il carme incipitario non sia necessariamente anteriore agli altri, ad un'epoca precedente appartengono sicuramente 4.2 e 4.3, e probabilmente 4.8 e 4.9. Ancor più improbabile appare che 4.4, e 4.14 siano stati scritti prima di 4.3, perché si tratta di un carme che andrà datato ad un'epoca molto vicina alle celebrazioni del 3 giugno del 17 a.C.:[9] lo stesso può

---

[6] Sulle possibili cause del raffreddamento dell'amicizia di Mecenate con Augusto cf. Brink (1982) 528-529. La notizia di Suet. *Aug.* 66.3, secondo cui Mecenate *secretum de comperta Murenae coniuratione uxori Terentiae prodidisset*, e le speculazioni costruite dagli storici su tale base sono state sottoposte a una dura critica da Williams (1990) 258-275, che non crede a un deterioramento dei rapporti di Augusto e Mecenate.

[7] Suet. *De poetis* p. 116, 38-43 Rostagni: *scripta quidem eius usque adeo probauit mansuraque perpetua opinatus est, ut non modo Saeculare carmen componendum iniunxerit sed et Vindelicam uictoriam Tiberii Drusique priuignorum suorum, eumque coegerit propter hoc tribus carminum libris ex longo interuallo quartum addere.*

[8] Almeno a partire da Fraenkel (1957) 364-365.

[9] È certo, infatti, che l'altisonante e superba proclamazione della certezza di una gloria poetica ormai accettata dai Romani vada messa in rapporto col successo del *Carmen saeculare* e con la popolarità che ad Orazio ne era derivata.

dirsi di 4.6, che insieme a 4.3 interpreta lo stato d'animo di Orazio al tempo dell'esecuzione del *Carmen saeculare* o nel periodo immediatamente successivo.[10] Il riferimento al *Carmen saeculare*, d'altronde, sembra esplicito sia in 4.3 (vv. 22-23) sia in 4.6 (vv. 29-44).[11] Se, poi, destinatario di 4.8 è L. Marcio Censorino, anziché il figlio G. Marcio Censorino, il carme a lui dedicato sarà del 17 o del 16 a.c., e dunque fra i più antichi della raccolta. Ce n'è abbastanza, dunque, per ritenere che la notizia di Svetonio sia imprecisa, almeno per quanto riguarda l'origine del libro: se, infatti, non c'è alcuna difficoltà nell'ammettere un vincolante invito di Augusto per la genesi di 4 e 14, è assurdo pensare che si tratti dei due carmi più antichi e che, di conseguenza, l'ultima esperienza lirica di Orazio si sia rapidamente consumata tra la fine del 15 (o l'inizio del 14) e il 13 a.C.

È certo che la pubblicazione del IV libro sarà stata solo la fase conclusiva di un processo che, grazie alle letture private e pubbliche, consentiva ai carmi una preliminare circolazione. Tuttavia anche nell'impianto definitivo si nota un'accorta cura nel privilegiare il ruolo sia dei carmi d'elogio al principe e ai suoi familiari sia di quelli rivolti a personaggi influenti del tempo. Sin dall'ode proemiale il libro faceva capire ai lettori che nei singoli carmi l'attenzione sarebbe stata rivolta a personaggi vicini al principe e a lui legati da vincoli d'amicizia o di parentela: tali erano allora, oltre a Paolo Massimo (carme 1), Iullo Antonio (carme 2), Druso (carme 4), Tiberio (carme 14), Torquato (carme 7), L. Marcio Censorino (carme 8), Marco Lollio (carme 9) e, naturalmente, Mecenate (carme 11), che tuttavia compare in modo piuttosto surrettizio, nell'invito a Fillide in occasione del genetliaco dell'illustre amico.

Convinto, dunque, della bontà del progetto augusteo e della gestione augustea del potere, orgoglioso dell'onore che gli era stato tributato nel 17 a.C., Orazio cedette, se si presta fede a Svetonio, alle pressioni del principe che, in assenza ormai del ruolo di mediatore sercitato con molto equilibrio da Mecenate, non si faceva scrupolo d'imporre con decisione le sue richieste; oppure, come sembra più probabile, decise di sua iniziativa di accordare nel nuovo libro di poesia lirica un ampio

---

[10] È questa la condivisibile opinione di Fraenkel (1957) 400.
[11] Cf. Du Quesnay (1995) 131 e, sui rapporti di 4.6 col *Carmen saeculare*, Hardie (1998) 285-291.

spazio all'elogio del principe e del suo 'entourage'. Il IV delle odi, però, è un libro composito, nel quale un ruolo tutt'altro che irrilevante continua ad essere occupato dalla poesia d'occasione e da quella d'amore: se, quindi, per forza di cose il mio discorso si soffermerà sui *carmina* che, più degli altri, esibiscono motivi augustei (4, 5, 14, 15), non va dimenticato che proprio i due che in tono encomiastico chiudono il libro sono preceduti dagli insulti a una *meretrix* che invecchiando ha perso il fascino di un tempo.

Per comprendere l'articolazione del discorso augusteo nell'ultimo libro dei carmi è necessario muovere dal ruolo di *tutela* e di *custodia* nei confronti dello Stato, che Orazio attribuisce al principe: un ruolo che Augusto si è conquistato di diritto, eliminando le lunghe discordie interne sfociate nelle sanguinose guerre civili e mettendo fine al pericolo esterno grazie ai successi suoi e dei suoi generali.

Nel XIV carme l'elogio delle vittorie di Druso sui Genauni e sui Breuni, con la conquista delle rocche alpine (4.14.10-13), precede quello di Tiberio, il *maior Neronum* (4.14.14) che ha messo in fuga i Reti con lo stesso impeto travolgente dell'Ofanto in piena (4.14.25-32).[12] È il principe, però, a venire considerato come il reale artefice dei successi di entrambi, in ossequio alla cosiddetta 'teologia della vittoria imperiale':[13] *milite ...tuo*, sottolinea Orazio rivolgendosi ad Augusto a proposito del successo di Druso (4.14.9), e più sotto ribadisce *te copias, te consilium et tuos/ praebente diuos* (4.14.33-34).[14] In tal modo, in un carme che dovrebbe celebrare i successi militari di Druso e di Tiberio, è l'elogio di Augusto a occupare l'ampia sezione conclusiva e ad assumere i toni degli inni sacri, scandito com'è dal 'Du-Stil'.[15] La *climax* raggiunge l'apice nella definizione del principe come *tutela praesens* dell'Italia e di Roma: che per l'Orazio del IV libro sia questa la funzione principale di Augusto lo si deduce dall'immagine dei

---

[12] Nel concedere un'attenzione maggiore al più giovane dei Neroni Orazio non fa altro che rendersi interprete di una sicura preferenza da parte di Augusto: tuttavia l'articolazione dell'elogio di Tiberio, con l'analogo ricorso a un periodo di tipo pindarico e a immagini dall'epica solennità, fa capire che il poeta non poté sottrarsi alla necessità di rivolgere un degno tributo di lodi anche al *maior Neronum*, tanto più che esso era funzionale alla celebrazione di Augusto stesso.

[13] In merito cf. La Penna (1963) 116-117.

[14] La stessa *uirtus* di Druso e di Tiberio era già stata presentata come frutto della saggia educazione impartita personalmente e con affetto paterno da Augusto, le cui virtù si riflettono sui due *Nerones* (Hor. *Carm.* 4.4.25-28).

[15] Hor. *Carm.* 4.14.33, 34, 41, 42, 45, 46, 47, 49, 51.

nemici che, pur sconfitti e sottomessi, non riescono a nascondere la loro ammirazione per il condottiero vittorioso (*Carm.* 4.14.41-44):

> Te Cantaber non ante domabilis
> Medusque et Indus, te profugus Scythes
>   miratur, o tutela praesens
>   Italiae dominaeque Romae.

Praesens, abitualmente detto di un dio che si manifesta sulla terra, è qui epiteto di *tutela*, che definisce la protezione assicurata da quel dio all'umanità. Il ruolo di *tutela* è una conseguenza diretta dei successi militari, che hanno consentito a Roma di estendere l'*imperium* sino ai limiti del mondo conosciuto e civilizzato. Nell'esordio dello stesso carme, che vede *patres* e *Quirites* incapaci di scegliere onori adeguati a tramandare nei secoli le *uirtutes* di Augusto, il poeta a lui si rivolge con un altisonante *o, qua sol habitabiles/ inlustrat oras, maxime principum* (vv. 5-6). In tal modo egli vuole dare l'idea di un dominio immenso, in perfetta linea col motivo dell'ecumenicità dell'impero che molto deve all'influsso delle monarchie orientali:[16] alla lista dei popoli sopra citati si aggiungono nei versi conclusivi, in serrata successione, le terre solcate dai grandi fiumi (il Nilo, il Danubio, il Tigri), l'Oceano e poi i Britanni, i Galli, gli Iberici e i Sigambri (vv. 45-52):

> Te fontium qui celat origines
> Nilusque et Hister, te rapidus Tigris,
>   te beluosus qui remotis
>   obstrepit Oceanus Britannis,
>
> te non pauentis funera Galliae
> duraeque tellus audit Hiberiae,
>   te caede gaudentes Sygambri
>   compositis uenerantur armis.

È chiaro l'intento di chiudere in *climax* la lista dei popoli vinti, in modo che l'entità del successo militare sia adeguata alla loro pericolosità: in tal senso l'immagine dei Sigambri, assetati di sangue, che non solo hanno deposto le armi ma addirittura venerano il condottiero vincitore, costituisce una degna chiusa ad effetto del carme. La realtà, però, era

---

[16] Cf. La Penna (1963) 116-117.

ben diversa: da Cassio Dione (54.20.4), infatti, sappiamo che nell'estate del 16 a.c. i Sigambri, attraversato il Reno, erano penetrati nella Gallia e avevano sconfitto un contingente romano. Ciò indusse Augusto a un'immediata partenza per la Gallia: alla notizia dell'imminente arrivo dell'esercito da lui guidato, i Sigambri decisero di fare ritorno nel loro territorio e conclusero con i Romani un trattato che prevedeva la restituzione degli ostaggi.[17]

Qui, dunque, come spesso nei poeti augustei, si è in presenza di un'iperbolica enfatizzazione di imprese che di bellico hanno ben poco. Emblematico, anche in Orazio, è il caso della restituzione delle insegne romane ad opera dei Parti, che viene invariabilmente presentata come conseguenza di un atto di forza: quando il poeta nei vv. 6-8 del XV carme parla in tono trionfalistico dei *signa .../ derepta Parthorum superbis/ postibus* ed elogia Augusto che tali insegne *nostro restituit Ioui*, egli presenta l'avvenimento come frutto di un intervento con la forza da parte di Augusto lo fa capire *derepta* (v. 7),[18] che invita il lettore a immaginarsi una violenta azione di rapina. D'altronde il Regolo di *Carm.* 3.5 nel parlare delle insegne strappate ai Romani dai Cartaginesi adopera lo stesso lessico, e sembra quasi che già preveda la disfatta di Carre (vv. 18-21 '*signa ego Punicis/ adfixa delubris et arma/ militibus sine caede' dixit/ derepta uidi'*). Meno drammaticamente, ma più obiettivamente, in *Epist.* 1.18.56 *sub duce, qui templis Parthorum signa refigit*, Orazio si era limitato a parlare di *signa refixa* ('tirati giù') da Augusto, perché in realtà la restituzione delle insegne era stata il frutto di un'abile trattativa diplomatica con Fraate IV.[19] Il comportamento di Orazio è chiaramente in linea con la propaganda augustea, come mostra l'analogo livello di enfatizzazione con cui Augusto parla dell'episodio nelle sue *Res gestae* (*Mon. Anc.* 29.2): *Parthos trium exercitu[u]m Romanorum spolia et signa re[ddere] mihi supplicesque amicitiam populi Romani petere coegi.*[20]

---

[17] Cf. Vell. Pat. 2.97.1, Tac. *Ann.* 1.10, Cass. Dio 54.20.4-6.

[18] Si tratta della giusta correzione ad opera dei recenziori di *direpta,* tràdito dai codici più autorevoli (cf. Nisbet, Rudd [2004] a *Carm.* 3.5.21).

[19] Sull'avvenimento cf. Nisbet (1996) 222 con l'annessa bibliografia e Nisbet, Rudd (2004) nell'introduzione a *Carm.* 3.5.

[20] In merito agli avvenimenti dell'anno 20 a.C. cf. anche Prop. 4.6.79, Ov. *Fast.* 5.579-580, *Trist.* 2.227-228.

Augusto, però, a dispetto degli ingigantiti successi militari è un principe di pace: non a caso il IV libro si chiude con tranquille immagini di pace e di prosperità, perché il futuro della Roma augustea, assicura Orazio, non prevede né guerre intestine né sollevazioni di popoli sottomessi: a condizione, beninteso, che Augusto continui a esercitare la sua vigile *custodia* (*Carm.* 4.15.17-24):

> custode rerum Caesare non furor
> ciuilis aut uis exiget otium,
> non ira, quae procudit enses
> et miseras inimicat urbes;
>
> non qui profundum Danuuium bibunt
> edicta rumpent Iulia, non Getae,
> non Seres infidique Persae,
> non Tanain prope flumen orti.

Nulla, dunque, potrà turbare la pace che regna sovrana sulla terra finché Augusto proteggerà Roma e il suo *imperium*. Che sia questa la condizione indispensabile è messo in chiaro dall'ablativo assoluto *custode rerum Caesare* (v. 17), opportunamente collocato all'inizio della strofa e ulteriormente enfatizzato dal legame allitterante: grazie ad esso Augusto diviene vigile protettore e garante della pace interna ed esterna. L'ablativo assoluto può essere inteso almeno in due modi, e probabilmente Orazio, giocando sulla sua ambivalenza, vuole che entrambi siano contemplati: in senso ipotetico ('se Augusto resterà *custos rerum*') o con valore temporale ('finché Augustò resterà *custos rerum*'); ma non si può escludere neppure un senso causale ('poiché Augusto è *custos rerum*'). Epiteto che indica la tutela degli dèi sugli uomini,[21] *custos* lo era divenuto anche dei più illustri tutori dello stato romano, primo fra tutti Romolo,[22] e frequente è la designazione di Augusto come *custos imperii*.[23]

---

[21] In tal senso Orazio lo riferisce a Giove (*Carm.* 1.12.49), a Nettuno (1.28.29), a Diana (3.22.1), a Sileno (*Ars* 239).

[22] Sin da Enn. *Ann.* 106-107 Sk. *o Romule, Romule die,/ qualem te patriae custodem di genuerunt!*, da cui dipende Hor. *Carm.* 4.5.1-2 *diuis orte bonis, optime Romulae/ custos gentis*, dove *custos* è ugualmente epiteto di Augusto (altri esempi di un tale uso in *ThlL* 4.1576.3 ss.).

[23] Oltre al già citato *Carm.* 4.5.1-2 *optime Romulae/ custos gentis* (al cui commento si rinvia), per Augusto *custos* i.e. *tutor* – come in greco φύλαξ designa il sovrano in quanto 'pastore di popoli' – cf. le attestazioni del *ThlL* 4.1576.3 ss. e Fraenkel (1957) 296 n. 2, La Penna (1963) 105-106; da Orazio la funzione di *tutor* era stata attribuita ad Augusto anche in *Epist.* 2.1.1-2: *cum .../ res Italas armis tuteris*.

Esclusa la possibilità, *custode rerum Caesare*, di guerre civili, ora si tratta di esorcizzare la minaccia di sollevazioni dei popoli irrequieti, stanziati nelle zone più lontane dell'impero: qui in ordinata serie si susseguono i Daci, i Vindelici, i Pannonii (v. 21), i Geti (v. 22),[24] i Cinesi, i Parti e gli Sciti (vv. 23-24) e da parte di tutti si dà per scontato il rispetto rigoroso degli editti di Augusto (v. 22). Nel v. 22 Orazio interrompe l'elenco per anticipare, subito dopo la prima serie di popoli, il verbo (*non ...rumpent*) e l'oggetto (*edicta Iulia*): in tal modo egli pone in grande evidenza l'impossibile rottura degli *edicta Iulia* da parte delle genti sottomesse. A lungo i commentatori, sin da Porfirione (*a nullis gentibus dicit leges Augusti contemni*), hanno visto negli *edicta Iulia* un rinvio diretto alle leggi emanate da Augusto.[25] È chiaro, tuttavia, che qui Orazio non vuole accordare ad *edicta* il senso tecnico di 'disposizioni emanate dal pretore al momento di entrare in carica,' ma lega piuttosto il termine al senso etimologico del verbo *edicere* ('ordinare'): gli *edicta Iulia* saranno, quindi, le condizioni di pace imposte da Augusto. Con una tale formulazione Orazio raggiunge due scopi: quello di proclamare in modo altisonante che tutto il mondo si piega alle condizioni fissate da Augusto e, grazie alla definizione degli *edicta* come *Iulia*,[26] quello di collegare il principe alla sua *gens*, con un gesto che ad Augusto sarebbe stato sommamente gradito.

Conseguenza logica di un tale modo di concepire il ruolo di Augusto è l'esistenza di un rapporto diretto tra la sua *incolumitas* e la *salus* dello

---

[24] I Daci (*Carm.* 3.6.13-14), i Vindelici (*Carm.* 4.4.18) e i Pannonii sono probabilmente 'coloro che bevono le acque del profondo Danubio': se così è, si tratta delle popolazioni che abitano lungo il bacino superiore del Danubio, perché poi sono menzionati a parte, in maniera esplicita, i Geti (*Carm.* 3.24.11), che vivono nel bacino inferiore dello stesso fiume; successivamente i Cinesi e i Parti stanno a rappresentare la parte estrema a oriente dell' *imperium*, mentre gli Sciti, 'nati uicino al Tanai' (v. 24) indicano i popoli del nord-est, lungo il corso dell'odierno Don. Dei Cinesi, in realtà, si avevano solo vaghe nozioni, ma la fantasia dei Romani doveva essere particolarmente stimolata da quei popoli tanto lontani: basta pensare a *Carm.* 1.12.55-56: *siue subiectos Orientis orae/ Seras et Indos*, 1.29.9-10: *doctus sagittas tendere Sericas/ arcu paterno*, 3.29.25-28: *tu ciuitatem quis deceat status/ curas et urbi sollicitus times,/ quid Seres et regnata Cyro/ Bactra parent Tanaisque discors.*
[25] Già il Lambino e il Torrenzio, ad esempio, rinviavano alla *lex Iulia de adulteriis* e a quella *de maritandis ordinibus*. Sulla buona strada, però, mette – come al solito – Dacier (1691), quando sostiene che 'sous les mots *edicta Iulia* Horace comprend icy tout ce qu'Auguste avoit ordonné aux peuples qu'il avoit assujetis.'
[26] Di una 'ganz ungewöhnliche Benennung mit dem Gentile' parlano Kiessling e Heinze nel loro commento ad loc.

Stato, che solo il principe è in grado di assicurare e di garantire: Orazio lo proclama nel V carme ricorrendo a una serrata serie di domande destinate a fugare il timore dei popoli tradizionalmente nemici (4.5.25-28):

> quis Parthum paueat, quis gelidum Scythen,
> quis Germania quos horrida parturit
> fetus, incolumi Caesare, quis ferae
>   bellum curet Hiberiae?

I nemici, come al solito, sono equamente individuati fra i popoli a Oriente e ad Occidente, ma nessuno di loro incute timore, beninteso *incolumi Caesare*. Con le stesse possibilità di significato del già discusso *custode rerum Caesare*, l'ablativo assoluto chiarisce che, se e finché Augusto sarà sano e salvo, non vi sarà motivo per i Romani di aver paura dei nemici esterni: la loro condizione di tranquillità, dunque, è strettamente legata all'incolumità fisica del principe.

Il V carme non si limita a esaltare l'apporto della *tutela* e della *custodia* di Augusto alla sicurezza dei Romani, ma mette in risalto gli effetti benefici del suo buon governo, con l'avvento di una nuova fase di prosperità dello Stato. Il carme, che sin dall'inizio manifesta una spiccata affinità con gli inni sacri, è un'appassionata invocazione ad Augusto perché si decida a tornare in patria dopo un'assenza troppo lunga (Hor. *Carm*. 4.5.2-4). Orazio si fa interprete dei desideri della patria tutta, che formula voti per il ritorno del *princeps* allo stesso modo di una madre che prega per il ritorno del figlio impegnato in lunghe campagne militari in terre lontane (4.5.9-16). Augusto è definito *optimus custos* dei discendenti di Romolo (4.5.1-2) e *dux bonus* (4.5.5 e poi, con una chiara ripresa ad anello nella chiusa del carme, v. 37); ma, soprattutto, di lui viene proclamata l'origine divina fin dalle parole di apertura (4.5.1 *diuis orte bonis*),[27] in cui l'invito a restituire la propria luce alla patria (4.5.5), rafforzato per di più dalla rappresentazione del suo volto radioso come la primavera, lo colloca allo stesso livello di un sovrano ellenistico (4.5.6-8). In tal modo viene preparata la strada all'implicita divinizzazione del principe in vita nella descrizione conclusiva della serena giornata dell'agricoltore, che fa ritorno a casa

---

[27] Non può essere casuale l'apertura dell'ode successiva col vocativo *diue*, riferito ad Apollo, divinità solare come qui è rappresentato Augusto.

dopo il lavoro nei campi (4.5.29-31) e nelle seconde mense invoca Augusto come dio (4.5.32 *te ...adhibet deum*). Il culto domestico del principe ancora in vita prevede libagioni in suo onore (4.5.33-35) e voti perché possa donare all'Italia lunghi giorni di festa (4.5.37-38). Il carme, però, non si limita a una divinizzazione del principe, che rischierebbe di collocarlo a un livello d'inattingibile superiorità nei confronti dei sudditi, ma sviluppa anche una descrizione delle condizioni di vita dei Romani sotto Augusto: sicurezza e prosperità nei campi (4.5.17-18), tranquillità nei mari (4.5.19), trionfo della *fides*, della castità, della pudicizia e dei sani costumi (4.5.20-23), rispetto della legge (4.5.22) e immediata repressione delle colpe (4.5.24) contraddistinguono un mondo che agli occhi del panegirista appare ideale. Negli anni in cui il principato di Augusto si è definitivamente consolidato, è ovvio che da parte di un suo convinto sostenitore non si sentano più le tirate moralistiche contro il lusso o la dissoluzione dei costumi: tutto ciò in passato faceva parte del bagaglio ideologico di Ottaviano; ora, invece, si tratta di esaltare l'avvenuto ritorno della *Fides*, del *Pudor*, degli antichi e incorrotti costumi. Allo stesso modo è logico che scompaiano i motivi di preoccupazione per l'incerta situazione interna e che in merito alla piuttosto languente politica di conquiste ci si riduca a vagheggiare e a profetizzare guerre con i popoli ai confini del mondo conosciuto o al di là del misterioso Oceano.

Se nei vv. 21-24 del carme 5 è evidente il richiamo alla recente legislazione augustea in materia matrimoniale e in favore della moralizzazione dei costumi, risulta ancor più significativo che nell'ultimo carme della raccolta prenda a delinearsi con precisi contorni l'idea di una vera e propria età di Augusto (v. 4: *tua, Caesar, aetas*), in cui sono state restituite ai campi le messi e ai templi le insegne sottratte dai Parti (Hor. *Carm.* 4.15.4-8). Ora, finalmente, regna la pace ed è stato chiuso il tempio di Giano (4.15.8-9); posto un freno alla licenza, sono stati eliminati i crimini e ripristinate le *artes* del buon tempo antico, che hanno reso grande Roma e diffuso in ogni dove la fama e la maestà dell'impero (4.15.10-16). Nei vv. 4-16 i meriti di Augusto sono elencati in una serrata successione polisindetica, in cui grazie alla presenza costante della particella coordinativa ogni merito va a sommarsi ai precedenti e ne vien fuori l'immagine di una serie impressionante e illimitata d'interventi risolutivi da parte del principe: non solo nel campo dell'agricoltura (v. 5), ma anche in quelli della guerra e della pace (vv. 6-9), del risanamento dei costumi corrotti (vv. 9-11), della restaurazione dei valori tradizionali (vv. 12-16).

È significativo che l'attività di Augusto sia scandita da alcuni composti col prefisso *re-*, perché ciò sta a significare che i suoi pur rivoluzionari interventi, lungi dal voler scardinare il sistema preesistente, si propongono di restaurare e di ripristinare i sani valori della tradizione repubblicana. Ciò verrà confermato da Augusto stesso, che nelle sue *Res gestae* affermerà con orgoglio (8.5): *legibus noui[s] m[e auctore l]atis m[ulta e]xempla maiorum exolescentia iam ex nostro [saecul]o red[uxi et ipse] multarum rer[um exe]mpla imitanda post[eris tradidi]*. Nel contesto oraziano è particolarmente accorta non solo la scelta del lessico, ma anche la collocazione dei termini: gli iniziali *rettulit* e *restituit*, infatti, sono ripresi a cornice dal conclusivo *reuocauit,* mentre al centro della serie vanno a collocarsi gli altri tre verbi (*clausit ...iniecit ...emouit*).

L'*aetas* di Augusto si configura con gli stessi tratti dell'età dell'oro, la cui menzione Orazio aveva inserito con grande accortezza nel carme 2: lì egli non l'aveva posta in rapporto diretto con Augusto, ma era ricorso all'espediente di ricordarla proprio nella strofa che contiene uno straordinario elogio del principe (*Carm.* 4.2.37-40),

> quo nihil maius meliusue terris
> fata donauere bonique diui
> nec dabunt, quamuis redeant in aurum
>   tempora priscum.

Nell'espressione conclusiva non è necessario ravvisare né una proclamazione di una nuova età dell'oro sotto Augusto né una risposta alle attese soteriologiche dell'epodo 16: se si conferisce alla frase l'intonazione concessiva che *quamuis* esige, Orazio vuol dire che, quand'anche il fato e gli dèi concedessero una nuova età dell'oro, non si tratterebbe mai di un dono più grande di quello che hanno fatto alla terra con Augusto. Ovviamente ciò non vuol dire, per quanto l'iperbolica proclamazione dell'impossibilità di trovare qualcuno degno di essere confrontato con Augusto trovi un parallelo nell'elogio di Pindaro a Ierone, che qui non si sia in presenza di un motivo propagandistico: infatti l'età dell'oro, anche se non è attualizzata, tuttavia viene messa in rapporto con Augusto.

Sul IV libro delle *Odi* continua a gravare il giudizio severo dei molti che, in epoche diverse, hanno decisamente accusato Orazio di servilismo. Una parte importante dell'accusa si fonda sulla divinizzazione di Augusto, che nei carmi è espressa in modo chiaro; in questo campo non c'è dubbio che Orazio già nei primi tre libri si sia spinto molto avanti nell'elogio della natura divina di Ottaviano-Augusto, presentato come un eroe, un semidio, un'incarnazione di Mercurio sulla terra (1.2.41-44), un oggetto di culto e di venerazione: in 3.3.11-12 egli è raffigurato mentre beve il nettare degli dèi e in 3.5.2 è *praesens diuus* (come verrà ribadito in *Epist.* 2.1.15), anche se questa condizione è vincolata alla vittoria sui Britanni e sui Parti. Ciò nonostante si può constatare che – fatta eccezione forse per *Carm.* 1.2, e 1.12.49-60 – nella prima raccolta mancano carmi spiccatamente celebrativi o esempi di poesia sfacciatamente panegiristica:[28] anche il ritorno trionfale del principe dopo una campagna vittoriosa assume in *Carm.* 3.14 toni ben più intimi a confronto delle celebrazioni in seguito concepite nell'ambito del motivo della 'teologia della vittoria imperiale'. Nel IV libro, invece, una volta che Augusto è divenuto destinatario e interlocutore principale del poeta, mutano sia il tono con cui a lui ci si rivolge sia le tematiche che lo riguardano: l'atteggiamento di Orazio s'inserisce in un'atmosfera ampiamente diffusa in quegli anni, in cui il culto imperiale fu principalmente espressione di una religiosità cittadina che, sia nelle province sia in Italia, si manifestava nei templi, nelle statue, nella celebrazione di feste e doveva attestare il consenso dei ceti dirigenti urbani a Roma e al principe.[29] D'altra parte Augusto in questo campo agì con accortezza, scegliendo d'inserire il proprio culto in una tradizione romana e preoccupandosi soprattutto di diffonderlo in ambito familiare e popolare:[30] è proprio questo l'aspetto che Orazio indi-

---

[28] Cf. le giuste osservazioni di Brink (1982) 547 e l'acuta analisi di Putnam (1986) 17, che mette in giusto rilievo le differenze nell'atteggiamento di Orazio verso Augusto nei libri 1-3 dei *Carmina*.

[29] Così Fraschetti (1998) 111, per il quale è significativo che tutto ciò sia avvenuto 'nel contesto di pratiche cultuali esse stesse, come era tipico nella città antica, eminentemente politiche e fondate in quanto tali sulla credenza che il 'buon sovrano' fosse assimilabile alla manifestazione terrena di un dio vero e proprio.'

[30] Cf. La Penna (1963) 119. Sulla politica religiosa di Augusto cf. Galinsky (1996) 280-331 (in particolare 312-322).

vidua e privilegia nella sezione conclusiva del V carme (vv. 31-40). In una tale atmosfera anche motivi panegiristici di antica tradizione e di grande solennità, come l'identificazione del principe col sole o con la primavera, finiscono per assumere un senso nuovo, perché Orazio non intende affatto collocare Augusto ad una inaccessibile altezza, ma vuole inserire il suo culto in una concezione popolare, che fa del principe un buon padre, pronto a dare tutto se stesso per il bene del popolo;[31] anche in questo caso, dunque, il suo atteggiamento coincide con quello che era l'atteggiamento del principe stesso.

Di fronte agli elogi rivolti da Orazio al principe si è parlato spesso di propaganda, da parte di un poeta cortigiano che ha messo il suo ingegno e la sua ispirazione al servizio del principe. Forse, però, prima di parlare di propaganda, con la connotazione deteriore che il termine ha finito per assumere ai giorni nostri, c'è da chiedersi in via preliminare se i fruitori di un libro di poesia dell'ultimo ventennio del I sec. a.C. siano assimilabili ai moderni lettori. E poi, negli anni intorno al 13 a.C. Augusto aveva realmente bisogno della 'propaganda' di Orazio? Chi mai avrebbe dovuto convincere una tale 'propaganda'? Forse quel limitato numero di lettori aristocratici dei suoi carmi, che da tempo avevano consegnato di buon grado nelle mani di Augusto il loro ruolo politico, oppure un'ancora inesistente opposizione senatoria o piuttosto gli irrequieti aspiranti alla successione imperiale?

Ben si capisce che dal nostro punto di vista possa risultare non troppo entusiasmante riconoscere che l'atteggiamento di Orazio, come d'altronde quello di Virgilio e di Properzio, va considerato alla luce di una progressiva e convinta adesione al nuovo regime: d'altra parte noi siamo giustamente diffidenti, perché avvezzi ai tanti totalitarismi spesso sanguinari che hanno contraddistinto la nostra storia recente, ma riusciamo anche ad essere molto ingenui quando assimiliamo Augusto e il suo regime di due millenni fa alle moderne dittature.[32] Ancora una volta dobbiamo sforzarci di fare nostro il punto di vista degli scrittori antichi, indipendentemente dai giudizi che sul loro atteggiamento è lecito esprimere. Se, dunque, si giudica assumendo il loro punto di vista, allora si può capire che per i poeti augustei il principe

---

[31] Cf. La Penna (1963) 120.
[32] Cf. i giusti rilievi di Doblhofer (1964) 325-326.

era degno di elogio perché da un lato con la vittoria aziaca aveva riportato la pace nell'Italia e a Roma dopoché le discordie interne, che per i Romani avevano avuto inizio all'epoca dell'assassinio di Tiberio Gracco, erano culminate nelle sanguinose guerre civili,[33] dall'altro si era dimostrato in grado di tenere a bada i nemici esterni. È su queste basi che viene costruita una trionfalistica mistica delle vittorie imperiali, che culminano nella pace apportatrice di sicurezza e di prosperità; si tratta, in sostanza, della identica visione trionfalistica delle raffigurazioni dell'*Ara Pacis*.[34] Si può addirittura sostenere che Orazio sia stato abile non solo nell'individuare e nel privilegiare gli aspetti fondamentali dell'ideologia augustea, ma addirittura nell'anticiparne alcuni che nel corso degli anni si sarebbero definiti in modo chiaro:[35] sicché non ci si stupisce nel trovare notevoli coincidenze fra la sua rappresentazione dei meriti del regime di Augusto e quella che nelle sue *Res gestae* fornirà il principe stesso. Muovendo dalla convinta certezza di una piena e sincera adesione di Orazio agli ideali augustei, Eduard Fraenkel individua con ottimistica fiducia la grandezza del IV libro nello slancio con cui il poeta esprime i sentimenti suoi e dei concittadini, senza cedere alle preghiere e alle sollecitazioni del principe.[36] La novità dell'Orazio del IV libro risiederebbe nel suo abbandono del ruolo di *uates* che si rivolge alla comunità: adesso Orazio intende apparire come *quiuis ex populo* e ama adottare un linguaggio che deve sembrare dettato dai suoi sentimenti di uomo comune per esprimere la gratitudine popolare nei confronti di Augusto.[37] Non c'è motivo per negare che Orazio nel IV libro assuma questo atteggiamento, ma è discutibile che la sua poesia abbia tratto giovamento dall'abbandono del ruolo di *uates* per rivolgersi direttamente al principe come *unus ex*

---

[33] Putnam (1986) 15 rinvia giustamente a questa continuità nelle guerre civili, che per i Romani del tempo di Augusto non erano solo quelle fra Cesare e Pompeo o fra Ottaviano e Antonio.

[34] In merito cf. soprattutto Benario (1960) 351. Sulle coincidenze fra il contenuto del carme 15 e le raffigurazioni dell'*Ara Pacis* cf. Putnam (1986) 327-339.

[35] Basta pensare all'anticipazione di motivi delle *Res gestae* di Augusto, come il *consensus uniuersorum*, la restituzione delle insegne sottratte dai Parti, la chiusura del tempio di Giano, la rinascita della gloria di un tempo e dell'antica saldezza morale, il ritorno della prosperità e della sicurezza; oltre a Nisbet, Hubbard (1970) xviii e a Nisbet, Rudd (2004) xxi, su tutti i motivi si sofferma McNeill (2001) 133, mentre La Penna (1963) 116-119 mette in risalto la teologia della vittoria imperiale e la collocazione del culto del principe in ambito familiare.

[36] Fraenkel (1957) 440.

[37] Fraenkel (1957) 439-440.

multis. D'altra parte si può intuire il significato politico di questo nuovo orientamento della lirica oraziana, che sembra dettato da un senso di modestia e di umiltà, ma non fa altro che enfatizzare il motivo ideologico del *consensus uniuersorum* tanto caro ad Augusto.

Non credo, comunque, che per giustificare Orazio e le sue scelte sia necessario forzare l'interpretazione della sua poesia e scorgervi, se non una palese insofferenza nei confronti delle pressioni del principe, almeno 'signs of a certain resentment'.[38] Per non parlare, poi, delle conclusioni a cui sono giunti quanti sono riusciti a fare di Orazio un subdolo sovversivo, che vorrebbe dare l'impressione di elogiare il principe, ma in realtà lo prenderebbe in giro e ironizzerebbe continuamente sui potenti e sulla loro politica: evidentemente si pensa che Augusto e i suoi uomini di fiducia siano stati talmente idioti da non accorgersi d'essere presi in giro.

A me sembra che l'interrogativo realmente importante sia stato formulato con grande lucidità da Nisbet e dalla Hubbard:[39] esponente di punta nel circolo di Mecenate, amico personale non solo del suo *patronus* ma anche di Augusto e da entrambi colmato a più riprese di doni importanti, cantore ufficiale dei *ludi saeculares*, Orazio negli anni fra il 17 e il 13 a.C. era realmente in grado di dire qualcosa di diverso o di assumere un atteggiamento critico nei confronti del regime? I rapporti fra *clientes* e *patroni*, che nel caso di Orazio e Virgilio erano fortemente attenuati dal forte legame di schietta amicizia che li univa ad Augusto e a Mecenate, non consentivano al *cliens* un comportamento diverso: tutt'al più si trattava di salvare la propria dignità.

Dobbiamo, dunque, concludere che Orazio è stato un poeta cortigiano, ignobilmente prono al servilismo e all'adulazione del principe? Sarebbe una conclusione superficiale e affrettata perché se tessere l'elogio di un potente può sembrare un'impresa facile e redditizia, tuttavia un poeta che vagheggia per sé una fama duratura si espone al pericolo di passare per un servile adulatore e le sue iperboliche lodi corrono il rischio di produrre comici effetti. Non credo che questo sia il caso di Orazio: da un poeta cortigiano e servile ci si sarebbe atteso un ciclo omogeneo di carmi in onore delle virtù e delle gesta del prin-

---

[38] Lyne (1995) 207.
[39] Nisbet, Hubbard (1970) xviii.

cipe; invece Orazio si è guardato bene dal farlo e addirittura non ha neppure dedicato ad Augusto un libro che veniva diffuso dieci anni dopo la precedente raccolta dei carmi lirici. Forse il *canemus* con cui il libro si conclude sottintende un progetto, che però non verrà mai realizzato; per di più il passaggio dagli elogi del principe – qui e nel II libro delle *Epistole* – all'*Ars poetica* fa pensare piuttosto a un disegno di tutt'altro tipo, alla prosecuzione cioè da parte di un *poeta senex* della riflessione sul far poesia e sull'essenza della poesia.

Nel suo ampio e articolato giudizio sulla poesia politica di Orazio, Brink giunge alla conclusione che, mentre alcune delle odi politiche del III libro sono un esempio di grande poesia, i 'panegirici' del IV libro, 'in spite of some powerful passages and masterly structures,'[40] non lo sono affatto. Per parte mia, dopo aver confessato che mi sento molto meno sicuro di saper distinguere fra poesia e non poesia, debbo riconoscere che se la mia preferenza va ai carmi privi di contenuti panegiristici, ciò dipende dalla sensazione di fastidio che in me suscita qualsiasi tipo di poesia al servizio del potere e dei potenti. Però, nonostante tutto, continuo a credere che quella del IV libro sia una poesia grande, alla cui definizione non possono concorrere solo i carmi di contenuto politico. Si fa torto a Orazio se si riduce il IV libro alla sua componente politico-propagandistica e si dimenticano le appassionate difese della funzione eternatrice della poesia, le polemiche nei confronti dello stile sublime e in difesa del *tenue*, i rinnovati slanci amorosi in aperto dissidio con l'ormai raggiunta *senectus*, il senso del trascorrere del tempo e delle stagioni della vita umana. Se, poi, si riflette sulle scelte lessicali e retoriche, sull'uso sapiente degli espedienti fonici, sulla cura strutturale e sugli aspetti formali, sull'accorto sistema di richiami e di riprese fra un carme e l'altro, sulla saggia combinazione dei modelli e sul ricorso all'allusività, sugli stessi 'tours de force' pindarici, si ricava la netta sensazione di essere in presenza, anche nei carmi che tessono l'elogio di Augusto, della vigorosa manifestazione di un ingegno straordinariamente maturo, grazie al quale la poesia augustea ha raggiunto le vette più alte.

---

[40] Brink (1982) 550.

Bibliografia

Benario, J.M. (1960), 'Book 4 of Horace's *Odes*: Augustan Propaganda', *Transactions of the American Philological Association* 91, 339-352.

Brink, C.O. (1982), *Horace on Poetry. Epistles, Book 2: the Letters to Augustus and Florus*, Cambridge.

Dacier, A. (1691), *Les oeuvres d'Horace, traduites en François, avec des notes et des remarques critiques sur tout l'ouvrage*, vol. 4, Paris.

Doblhofer, E. (1964), 'Zum Augustusbild des Horaz (c. III,14,1-4 und c. IV,2,46 f.)', *Rheinisches Museum für Philologie* 107, 325-339.

Du Quesnay, I.M.Le M. (1995), 'Horace, *Odes* 4.5: *Pro reditu imperatoris Caesaris Diui Filii Augusti*', in S. Harrison (ed.), *Homage to Horace. A Bimillenary Celebration*, Oxford, 128-187.

Fraenkel, E. (1957), *Horace*, Oxford.

Fraschetti, A. (1998), *Augusto*, Roma/ Bari.

Galinsky, K. (1996), *Augustan Culture. An Interpretative Introduction*, Princeton.

Hardie, A. (1998), 'Horace, the Paean and Roman *Choreia* (*Odes* 4.6)', *Papers of the Leeds International Latin Seminar* 10, 251-293.

Kiessling, A., Heinze, R. (1960), *Oden und Epoden*, Berlin.

La Penna, A. (1963), *Orazio e l'ideologia del principato*, Torino.

Lyne, R.O.A.M. (1995), *Horace Behind the Public Poetry*, New Haven/ London.

McNeill, R.L.B. (2001), *Horace. Image, Identity, and Audience*, Baltimore/ London.

Nisbet, R.G.M. (1996), 'La vita', *Enciclopedia Oraziana I*, Roma, 217-224.

Nisbet, R.G.M., Hubbard, M. (1970), *A Commentary on Horace. Odes. Book I*, Oxford.

Nisbet, R.G.M., Rudd, N. (2004), *Horace. Odes. Book III*, Oxford.

Putnam, M.C.J. (1986), *Artifices of Eternity. Horace's Fourth Book of Odes*, Ithaca/ London.

Williams, G. (1990), 'Did Maecenas 'Fall from Favor'? Augustan Literary Patronage', in K.A. Raaflaub, M. Tober (edd.), *Between Republic and Empire. Interpretations of Augustus and His Principate*, Berkeley/ Los Angeles/ Oxford, 258-275.

Merses profundo, pulchrior evenit: l'elogio della Roma augustea nelle parole di Annibale (Hor. *Carm*. 4.4.50-72)

IRMA CICCARELLI
Università degli Studi di Bari Aldo Moro

Nell'ode 4.4 Orazio adatta lo schema dell'epinicio pindarico ad una istanza vincolante, cioè l'invito a lui rivolto da Augusto a comporre due carmi (4.4 e 4.14) che celebrino la vittoria riportata dai suoi figliastri Druso e Tiberio sulle popolazioni alpine dei Reti e dei Vindelici nell'estate del 15 a.C.,[1] e ad un intento propagandistico, che si manifesta nell'elogio dei Romani in quanto discendenti dei Troiani. All'esaltazione dei successi militari dei figliastri di Augusto sono dedicati i primi ventotto versi del carme, che sono scanditi da due similitudini parallele (*qualem* v. 1/ *qualemue* v. 13)[2] e inequivocabilmente inscritti nel motivo della teologia della vittoria imperiale: lo rivela subito il primo verso dell'ode, con la solenne definizione dell'aquila, protagonista della prima similitudine, come *ministrum fulminis alitem*.[3] All'aquila,

---

[1] Secondo la biografia oraziana nel *De Poetis* di Svetonio (pp. 116, 38-43 Rostagni), sarebbe stato Augusto in persona a imporre a Orazio il ritorno alla poesia lirica con la celebrazione della vittoria di Tiberio e di Druso sui Vindelici: se da un lato tale notizia permette di collocare la composizione di 4.4 e 4.14 a ridosso degli eventi a cui i due carmi si riferiscono, quindi tra la fine del 15 e l'inizio del 14 a.C., dall'altro essa risulta inattendibile ai fini dell'individuazione della cronologia della raccolta e dell'origine del quarto libro; su tale questione cf. Fedeli (2008) 13-14.

[2] Analogamente contrassegnati dalla collocazione di una similitudine all'inizio del componimento, gli esordi della sesta *Istmica* e della settima *Olimpica* di Pindaro si caratterizzano per il procedere maestoso e per il frequente ricorso all'"enjambement'; cf. Caviglia (1995) 449-450. In ambito latino Fraenkel (1957) 427 individua altri esempi di similitudini doppie collegate da nessi paralleli in Verg. *Georg.* 3.89-94, *Aen.* 4.469-473, Prop. 1.3.1-7, che si caratterizza per l'analoga collocazione di *qualis* in incipit di elegia (cf. Fedeli, *ad loc.*); tuttavia la breve estensione di tali passi induce Thomas, nel commento ad loc., a suggerire il confronto con le più ampie similitudini parallele di Cat. 68.57-65, 119-134 (sulla cui struttura cf. Maggiali [2008] 141-143).

[3] L'espressione è resa particolarmente solenne sia dall'impiego di *minister*, che afferisce all'ambito sacrale e qui è detto in senso traslato di un animale in rapporto con gli dèi (esempi in *ThlL* 8.1002.18 ss.), legato ad *ales*, di tono più elevato rispetto ad *auis* del v. 2 (non a caso l'aquila è definita *ales* in contesti in cui si allude al suo rapporto con Giove: cf. *ThlL* 1.1527.51 ss.), sia dal ricorso all'assonanza creata dalla successione <u>ministrum</u>/ <u>fulminis</u>.

minister fulminis, Giove permise di regnare sugli uccelli (vv. 1-2): su tale concessione ha influito la fedeltà dimostrata dal rapace quando il sovrano degli dei gli affidò il compito di rapire Ganimede.[4] Il ricorso a termini come *minister* nel v. 1 e *permittere* nel v. 3 suggerisce l'idea di un potere che si esercita nei limiti di una delega;[5] il rapporto stabilito da Giove con l'aquila sembra rinviare ad una circostanza precisa, cioè alla concessione straordinaria accordata da Augusto a Druso di poter ricoprire le cariche pubbliche cinque anni prima dell'età prescritta,[6] e a un tema d'importanza primaria nell'evolversi del disegno ideologico augusteo,[7] che è espresso con piena consapevolezza da Orazio fin dal primo libro delle *Odi*, cioè il paragone tra il *princeps* e il re degli dei. Il riferimento alla *fidelitas* dell'aquila-Druso, come condizione indispensabile per la concessione del *regnum* da parte di Giove-Augusto, cela un'allusione al rapporto di delega instaurato dal principe con i generali, che venivano considerati suoi *legati*: l'adempimento di tale ruolo sostitutivo implicava che le vittorie riportate dai 'legati' fossero considerate vittorie del *princeps*, anche se egli non partecipava direttamente alle spedizioni militari.[8] Alla descrizione dell'evoluzione 'biologica' dell'aquila Orazio dedica ben due strofe (vv. 5-12); le qualità che inizialmente spingono l'aquila a uscire dal nido, la *iuventas* e il *vigor patrius*, sono funzionali all'assimilazione dell'uccello con Druso: l'una, infatti, allude alla giovane età del generale all'epoca della spedi-

---

[4] Orazio riprende la versione del mito narrata da Apollodoro (*Carm.* 3.12.2) e ripresa da Virgilio (*Aen.* 5.252-257).
[5] Simile è il valore *di permittere* in Liv. 34.7.2-3.
[6] Cf. Cass. Dio 54.10.4 e Thomas (2011) ad loc.
[7] Cf. Hor. *Carm.* 1.12.49-60 con il commento di Nisbet-Hubbard: il motivo è ripreso nel ciclo delle odi romane del terzo libro (cf. 3.4.42-80, 3.5.1-4 con il commento di Nisbet-Rudd) e nel primo libro delle *Epistole* (1.17.33-4, 1.19.43-44); cf. Fedeli (2008) e Putnam (1986) 86 n. 4.; A La Penna (1963) 96-97 spetta il merito di aver messo in rilievo il rapporto tra tale motivo propagandistico e una serie di concetti filosofici ereditati da platonismo, pitagorismo e stoicismo. Da tali correnti il principato augusteo mutua sia l'idea dell'universo come unità dominata da un dio supremo, a cui corrisponde la terra unita nell'impero e retta dall'imperatore, sia l'assimilazione del sovrano 'ecumenico' a Zeus, che è un *topos* ricorrente nella trattatistica politica stoica e pitagorica e nella letteratura encomiastica. Sul piano politico quest'ultimo aspetto concorre alla costruzione dell'immagine del sovrano come vicereggente di Zeus, responsabile del proprio operato solo dinanzi a lui.
[8] I risvolti ideologici e politici di tale rapporto, che Ovidio svilupperà in *Trist.* 2.173-174 *per quem bella geris, cuius nunc corpore pugnas,/ auspicium cui das grande deosque tuos*,' e 229-230 *nunc te prole tua iuvenem Germania sentit/ bellaque pro magno Caesare Caesar obit* (cf. Ciccarelli [2003], sono chiariti da La Penna [1963] 115-117 e da Zanker [1989] 239).

zione, mentre l'altra chiama in causa il motivo del carattere ereditario del *vigor*, che, espresso in forma sentenziosa nei vv. 29-32, trova una chiara dimostrazione nel debito contratto da Roma nei confronti dei Neroni (vv. 37 ss.). Indotto dalla giovane etá e dal vigore innato, lo slancio istintivo che spinge l'aquila ad abbandonare il nido è rafforzato dall'opera di 'ammaestramento pedagogico'[9] svolta dai *venti* (vv. 7-9), che al rapace ancora trepidante (*paventem* v. 9)[10] insegnano sforzi inconsueti in occasione dei suoi primi tentativi di volo dopo l'abbandono del nido. A tale fase subentrerà in breve tempo dapprima il *vividus impetus* che spinge l'aquila a calare sugli *ovilia* (vv. 9-10), quindi l'*amor dapis atque pugnae*[11] dal quale è condotta contro serpenti che cercano di divincolarsi dalla stretta degli artigli (vv. 11-12).[12] La descrizione dell'evoluzione del rapace, che si era aperta con il riferimento alla *iuventas* e al *patrius vigor* dell'aquila-Druso, si chiude, dunque, con l'allusione ad un epico scontro con nemici pericolosi e non disposti ad arrendersi.

Un evidente mutamento di prospettiva caratterizza la seconda similitudine, introdotta da *qualemve* (v. 13): si assiste, infatti, al rapido passaggio dal punto di vista del vincitore (l'aquila-Druso) a quello del vinto (il capriolo),[13] che è costretto ad assistere inerme all'arrivo

---

[9] Così Caviglia (1995) 451.
[10] Come chiarisce La Penna (1969) ad loc., *paventem* non indica viltà, ma solo la naturale trepidazione dovuta all'inesperienza'; tale accezione, del resto, trova un significativo riscontro nell'impiego di *pavor* nel senso di 'eccitazione neruosa', attestato in due contesti virgiliani (Verg. G. 1.330-331 ... *fugere ferae et mortalia corda/ per gentes humilis stravit pavor*, ripetuto in *Aen.* 5.137-138), nei quali si descrive rispettivamente lo stato di trepidazione che precede l'inizio di una gara e della regata al largo di Drepano.
[11] Il nesso *amor dapis*, di ascendenza omerica (cf. Hom. *Il.* 1.469 e Thomas [2011] ad loc.), contribuisce ad elevare il tono della descrizione, al pari di 'iuncturae' virgiliane affini, in cui *amor* è sinonimo di *cupiditas*, *desiderium* (cf. Fedeli, *Amor*, *EV* 1.144), che sono riprese da Ovidio nelle *Metamorfosi* (cf. e.g. 3.705 *amor pugnae* con Bömer, ad loc.). Solenne è l'impiego del singolare *daps*, termine arcaico afferente all'ambito sacrale (in Orazio, cf. *Carm.* 1.32.13-14, 2.7.17 con il commento di Nisbet-Hubbard; *Epod.* 5.33, 17.66; *Sat.* 2.6.89; *Epist.* 1.17.51); la sua presenza conferisce qui dignità al bisogno fisiologico di cibo, che trova il suo naturale completamento nell'*amor pugnae*.
[12] *Reluctari* esprime l'idea della resistenza e della ribellione ad un'azione di forza; l'ostilità tra l'aquila e il serpente è un tema attestato fin dall'epica omerica (cf. *Il.* 12.200-207), che diverrà proverbiale (cf. Plut. *Mor.* 537c) e sarà ripreso prima da Cicerone in una citazione poetica del *De divinatione* (1.47), poi da Virgilio in *Aen.* 11.751-756.
[13] È opinione di Putnam (1986) 86-87 che nell'elaborazione della seconda similitudine Orazio abbia tenuto presente una scena del decimo libro dell'Eneide (vv. 723-728), in cui l'attacco sferrato da Mezenzio contro i nemici è paragonato all'aggressione di un leone affamato ai danni

del leone e a subirne l'attacco mortale. A infrangere la serenitá dello scenario bucolico in cui è ambientata la seconda similitudine è l'avvistamento del leone, che è giovane e affamato, da parte del capriolo; l'accostamento di *vidit a peritura* (v. 16) ne preannuncia la fine imminente: il capriolo è destinato a morire ancor prima di vedere il leoncino, anche perché esso è pronto ad aggredire il capriolo *dente novo*.[14]

Collocate in successione, le due similitudini puntualizzano i rapporti di forza che hanno condotto Druso alla vittoria contro i Reti e i Vindelici: pienamente coerenti con tale discorso, i vv. 17-24 chiariscono che a tale risultato ha contribuito l'impeto bellico del figliastro di Augusto, reso più efficace dalla giovane etá e dalla conseguente capacità di sconfiggere nemici particolarmente pericolosi. Nell'immagine dei vv. 17-18, infatti, confluiscono sia la prospettiva del capriolo destinato alla morte per opera del leone, sia quella dell'aquila che affronta imprese sempre più difficili.[15]

Al termine della digressione eziologica dei vv. 18-22, nella quale Orazio affida ai moduli espressivi tipici della *praeteritio* (*quaerere distuli* v. 21 e *nec scire fas est* v. 22) il compito di alludere all'impossibilità di conoscere le origini del *mos* che stabilisce un legame tra i Vindelici e la scure usata dalle Amazzoni,[16] la vittoria conseguita da

---

di una capra o di un cervo; tuttavia Orazio inverte il punto di vista del passo virgiliano: lì, infatti, è il leone a scorgere le sue vittime, mentre nel contesto oraziano è il capriolo che, *intenta laetis pascuis*, vede il giovane leone, tanto più affamato perché è stato da poco allontanato dal seno materno; come nota Thomas (2011) ad loc. 'the stanza is replete with words for abundance and consumption: *laetis... pascuis, ubere, lacte/lactante, dente, peritura*.'

[14] *Novus* allude al fatto che i denti dell'animale sono spuntati da poco e, dunque, entrano per la prima volta a contatto con una preda (cf. il comm. di ps. Acrone ad loc.: *dente novo adhuc inconsueto ad praedam*).

[15] Lo sottolineano sia la ripresa di *videre* in apertura del v. 17, un esempio di ripetizione con funzione di transizione (per la ricorrenza di tale procedimento nelle similitudini, cf. Wills [1996] 348), che dà luogo a un perfetto parallelismo tra la condizione del capriolo, che vede arrivare il leoncino appena svezzato, e quella dei Reti e dei Vindelici, che assistono alle imprese belliche del giovane Druso, sia la collocazione dei nomi dei due popoli agli estremi della frase, che ne ribadisce il ruolo di spettatori dell'impresa di Druso, la cui importanza è messa in rilievo dall''enjambement'.

[16] Porfirione, ad loc., ci informa dell'esistenza di una tradizione secondo la quale i Vindelici, dopo essere stati cacciati dalla Tracia per opera delle Amazzoni, ne avevano adottato le armi; la vicenda è ripresa solo da Servio, il quale nel commento a Verg. *Aen.* 1.243 afferma che tale popolazione discende dalle Amazzoni e cita i versi oraziani; ad Amazzoni munite di scuri allude Arriano (*Anab.* 7.13.2; cf. *LIMC* s.v. *Amazones* 1.1.1-571). Sulle differenti opinioni circa l'opportunità di inserire una digressione del genere in un carme celebrativo si rinvia al commento di Fedeli-Ciccarelli (2008).

Druso sui Reti e sui Vindelici è presentata come l'esito dei *consilia* del figliastro di Augusto: la sua capacità di prendere decisioni adatte alle singole circostanze è tanto più degna di elogio in relazione alla giovane etá,[17] che rinvia alla *iuventas* dell'aquila (v. 5). Il possesso di capacità militari e strategiche ha permesso al giovane Druso di avere la meglio sulla forza delle orde nemiche, *revictae* benché esse fossero *diu lateque victrices*;[18] l'elogio della vittoria offre a Orazio lo spunto per affrontare il tema del rapporto tra *vis* e *doctrina* a partire dal caso specifico della formazione ricevuta dal figliastro di Augusto. A sperimentarne dolorosamente le conseguenze sono proprio i Reti e i Vindelici, come mette in rilievo *sensere* in apertura del v. 25, simmetrica a quella di *videre* nel v. 17: spettatori delle operazioni militari condotte da Druso, i nemici ne percepiscono anche la superiorità strategica. Nell'educazione di Druso, Augusto ha avuto un ruolo di primo piano con il suo *animus paternus*[19] verso i *pueri Nerones*; tale legame conferisce una giustificazione etica al concetto della teologia della vittoria imperiale: ciò che i Reti e i Vindelici hanno sperimentato non è tanto la gloria del generale, quanto l'influenza paterna esercitata su di lui dal *princeps*.[20]

All'elogio dell'educazione impartita da Augusto ai figliastri sembra opporsi quello del carattere innato della *virtus*, che è sviluppato in una sezione gnomica (vv. 29-32) di ispirazione pindarica;[21] messo in rilievo dal poliptoto, l'assunto secondo il quale *fortes creantur fortibus et bonis* allude al carattere congenito di specifiche qualità morali che afferiscono al codice etico dell'aristocratico romano, nel quale sia *fortis* sia *bonus* qualificano chi dà prova di *virtus*. Il contrasto tra qua-

---

[17] Tale prerogativa, infatti, caratterizza di solito personaggi dotati di una notevole esperienza (cf. Hellegouarc'h [1972] 254-256).
[18] Per il passaggio dal termine semplice al composto con prefisso intensivo (*victrices...revictae*), cf. Wills (1996) 443-445; la forza dei nemici è evidenziata sia dal riferimento all'*Amazonia securis* del v. 20, sia dall'impiego di *catervae* nel v. 23: il termine, infatti, indica le orde dei barbari in opposizione alle *legiones* o alle *cohortes* romane (cf. ThlL 3.609.65 ss.).
[19] Seguito da *in* e l'accusativo, *animus* ha qui l'accezione di *studium in aliquem* (cf. *Carm.* 2.2.6 *notus in fratres animi paterni* e Cic. *Rosc. Am.* 46 *qui animus patrius in liberos esset*), mentre *paternus* sottolinea che l'atteggiamento di Augusto verso i figliastri fu quello di un vero e proprio padre responsabile della loro educazione.
[20] Cf. Lowrie (1997) 329-330.
[21] In questi versi l'ispirazione pindarica si manifesta sia nell'inserimento di una *sentenzia* in un epinicio, sia nell'accostamento di frasi semplici nelle quali predomina l'uso di termini astratti (cf. e.g. Pind. *Ol.* 12.5-12) e il rinvio al mondo animale per esemplificare una concezione aristocratica della virtù: cf. Pind. *Ol.* 11.19-20 e Syndikus (2001) 305-306.

lità innate e acquisite grazie all'educazione si risolve nei vv. 33-36: come preannuncia *nutrita* nel v. 26, perché la *vis* congenita si rafforzi, è necessario il contributo della *doctrina*[22] e del *cultus recti*;[23] la decadenza dei *mores*, infatti, pregiudica anche i privilegi legati alla nascita. La vittoria di Druso sui Reti e sui Vindelici, dunque, è stata favorita dall'associazione di fattori congeniti e acquisiti, che trova un'opportuna giustificazione nella sintesi tra modelli etici differenti.

A partire dal v. 37 il recente successo di Druso nella campagna militare contro i Reti e i Vindelici è proiettato nel passato: dalla rievocazione della battaglia del Metauro a testimonianza del debito contratto da Roma verso gli avi di Druso (vv. 29-48), Orazio passa alla drammatizzazione dell'episodio conclusivo di tale evento, con il discorso pronunciato da Annibale dopo la morte di Asdrubale (vv. 49-78). Chiara è la rielaborazione dello schema pindarico, in cui la sezione gnomica è seguita da quella mitologica: al mito Orazio sostituisce la storia in funzione dello scopo celebrativo del carme e delle istanze ideologiche del principato. Topos ricorrente negli epinici pindarici, l'elogio degli antenati del *laudandus* permette a Orazio di saldare la lode della vittoria di Druso con il ricordo di una specifica vicenda storica che ne costituisce il degno precedente.

Collocata nella parte centrale del v. 37, la solenne apostrofe a Roma di enniana memoria[24] fa della città la vera destinataria del carme;[25]

---

[22] La dicotomia *nomos/ cultura* vs. *physis/ natura* è sviluppata da Verg. *G.* 2.9, 22-34, 47-82, 420-425, 458-540 (cf. Thomas [1988] ad loc.). *Doctrina* designa qui l'educazione in senso lato, in relazione ad un insegnamento che permette un perfezionamento etico, e con la nozione aggiuntiva di esortazione ad apprendere (cf. *Epist.* 1.18.100; Quint. *Inst.* 2.8.3, 6.3.12, 12.1.9-10); essa permette lo sviluppo della *vis insita*, nesso ambiguo che, grazie alla duplice accezione di *inserere*, evoca non solo l'idea di una *virtus* innata, ma anche di un intervento esterno finalizzato a promuoverla: cf. Thomas (2011) ad loc.

[23] Termine tecnico del linguaggio agricolo, *cultus* qui è sinonimo di *educatio* (come in Cic. *Part. or.* 91, Val. Fl. 5.357, Gell. *praef.* 23, Amm. 27.6.8), e *rectus* ne connota il carattere corretto e appropriato. Benché i commentatori antichi divergano sull'interpretazione di *recti* (Porfirione lo considera genitivo e intende il verso nel senso di *colendo rectum pectora conroborantur*, mentre lo ps.-Acrone lo interpreta come nominativo e conferisce al nesso *recti cultus* l'accezione di *bona institutio*), tra quelli moderni prevale la tendenza a ritenerlo un nominativo plurale. L'interpretazione di *recti* come genitivo, infatti, determinerebbe l'introduzione di un concetto di giustizia che appare fuori luogo in una sezione in cui Orazio mira a evidenziare il valore della buona educazione (sulla questione cf. Fedeli-Ciccarelli [2008] ad loc.).

[24] Cf. Enn. *Var.* 6 V.² *desine Roma tuos hostis*.

[25] Lo mettono in rilievo Kiessling-Heinze nel commento ad loc. alla luce della presenza dell'interiezione.

il ricorso a termini tecnici del lessico commerciale (il verbo *debere* nel v. 37 e *testis* in apertura del v. 38) e l'accostamento di *Roma* a *Neronibus* amplificano il debito di gratitudine che lega Roma ai *Nerones*. La collocazione simmetrica di coppie formate da un toponimo e da un nome proprio (*Roma Neronibus* nel v. 37, a cui nel v. 38 corrispondono *Metaurum flumen* e *Hasdrubal*) proietta il debito di Roma in uno spazio e in un tempo remoti, ma ben circoscritti. A offrire una solenne e viva testimonianza di tale vincolo sono il fiume Metauro,[26] Asdrubale *devictus* e il *pulcher dies* della vittoria, disposti in crescendo in un *tricolon abundans*. Che il fiume Metauro abbia avuto un ruolo di primo piano nella battaglia, tanto da ostacolare l'avanzata dell'esercito di Asdrubale grazie al corso tortuoso e alle rive scoscese, è testimoniato da Livio 27.47.10-11: furono proprio le difficoltá incontrate dai nemici nei ripetuti tentativi di guadare il fiume a favorire l'assalto finale dei Romani. All' 'enjambement' (*Hasdrubal/ devictus*) è affidato il compito di mettere in rilievo l'importanza della sottomissione totale[27] di un avversario quale Asdrubale, la cui presenza in Italia era fonte di crescente preoccupazione per i Romani.[28]

A conclusione dell'elenco dei testimoni del debito contratto da Roma nei confronti dei Neroni Orazio colloca un dato cronologico preciso (vv. 38-39 *pulcher.../ ille dies*), che trova ampio sviluppo nella strofa successiva; messo in rilievo dal contrasto metaforico luce/tenebre, il giorno della vittoria è quello *pulcher* per il Lazio,[29] cioè 'splendido', 'illustre' per eccellenza, in opposizione alle *tenebrae fugatae*.[30]

Al *dies pulcher*, collocato al culmine del crescendo che era iniziato con la menzione del fiume Metauro, è riservata una solenne celebrazione nel v. 41: ad essa concorrono sia la personificazione del *dies* con

---

[26] Sin da Ennio l'uso di *testis* in riferimento ad entità geografiche è prettamente poetico (cf. e.g. Enn. *Var.* 8 V.²; Catull. 64.357; Prop. 2.9.41, 4.8.17; Tib. 1.7.9; Hor. *Carm.* 3.4.69; Ov. *Pont.* 4.9.114); qui concorre all'innalzamento di tono della sezione storica.

[27] Per *Hasdrubal devictus*, in cui il participio passato con valore predicativo è legato ad un sostantivo in modo da formare un nesso nominale con funzione di soggetto, cf. Laughton (1964) 84.

[28] Cf. Liv. 27.36.1 *de Hasdrubalis adventu in Italiam cura in dies crescebat*.

[29] Benché la funzione di *Latio* sia controversa per la sua particolare collocazione (può trattarsi di un dativo in dipendenza da *pulcher* oppure di un ablativo di allontanamento in rapporto a *fugatis*), sembra preferibile considerare *Latio* come dativo dipendente da *pulcher* (cf. il commento di Fedeli-Ciccarelli [2008] ad loc.).

[30] Tale opposizione risale ad archetipi tragici greci, nei quali essa è funzionale ad esprimere la tranquillità dopo l'angoscia del pericolo (cf. Aesch. *Pers.* 300-301, Eur. *Or.* 243).

risit che evidenzia la gioia per la vittoria, sia l'allusione al carattere propizio della gloria con l'impiego del nesso allitterante *alma adorea*.[31] Il giorno splendido della vittoria non solo è testimone del debito di Roma verso i Neroni, ma costituisce anche il limite temporale tra l'invasione di Annibale in Italia e la riscossa romana. Lo sottolinea *primus*,[32] che da un lato introduce una successione temporale proiettata verso il futuro, scandita da *post hoc* nel v. 45 e da *tandem* nel v. 49, dall'altro sancisce la conclusione di eventi di segno negativo, ormai relegati nel passato.

La celebrazione del giorno della vittoria è immediatamente seguita dal ricordo del passato, su cui si impone l'immagine del *dirus Afer* che attraversa le città italiche; termine della lingua religiosa, *dirus*[33] nel v. 42 caratterizza l'impeto atroce con cui il condottier cartaginese si scaglia contro le città italiche. A nobilitare lo slancio bellico del nemico contribuiscono due similitudini naturalistiche di ascendenza epica: la velocità inarrestabile con cui si propagano il fuoco attraverso gli alberi e il vento sul mare[34] costituiscono opportuni termini di paragone per amplificare la furia di Annibale e per presentare a tinte fosche il nemico per eccellenza dei Romani prima che egli prenda direttamente la parola nel v. 50. Che l'avanzata del *dirus Afer* in Italia sia stata impetuosa e inarrestabile come quella del fuoco tra gli alberi e del vento sul mare è ribadito tanto dall'anafora di *per* nei vv. 43-44, quanto dal chiasmo *per urbis...Italas/ per Siculas...undas*.

---

[31] *Adorea*, che a livello etimologico deriva probabilmente da *ador* (*farro*), è termine arcaico e raro (prima di Orazio si trova solo in Plaut. *Amph.* 193 e poi sarà ripreso dagli arcaizzanti: cf. *ThlL* 1.814.5 ss.) per indicare la gloria militare, poiché anticamente ai soldati più valorosi si distribuiva farro (cf. Plin. *HN* 18.3.9) o perché il possesso di grandi quantità di farro era ritenuto un segno di distinzione (cf. Paul. Fest. 3.22 L.). Alla luce del senso originario di *adorea*, *almus* recupera qui il rapporto etimologico con *alere* e suggerisce l'idea del nutrimento, da cui deriva quella del carattere propizio della gloria che mette fine all'oscurità della situazione precedente (per l'uso dell'aggettivo in riferimento ad entità astratte cf. *ThlL* 1.1704.75 ss.).

[32] 'The *primus dies* formula is a marker of turning points, for good or ill,' cf. Thomas (2011) ad loc.

[33] Usato in riferimento ad Annibale come in *Carm.* 3.6.36, l'aggettivo diventerá negli autori successivi suo epiteto convenzionale (cf. Sil. *Pun.* 16.622, Quint. *Inst.* 8.2.9, Iuv. 7.161, Sid. Apoll. *Carm.* 7.129).

[34] Per il paragone tra l'impeto bellico e il divampare del fuoco attraverso le selve, cf. Hom. *Il.* 11.155 e Verg. *Aen.* 10.405-406, 12.521-522; anche la similitudine della furia di Annibale con i soffi dell'Euro sulle onde sicule rinvia alla tradizione epica, in particolare ad un passo del dodicesimo libro dell'*Eneide* (vv. 365-370).

La presenza minacciosa e contemporanea dei due generali cartaginesi in Italia amplifica la pericolosità della guerra[35] e rende tanto più degna di lode l'immediata reazione della gioventù romana dopo il *pulcher dies* della vittoria; il valore militare dimostrato in occasione della sconfitta di Asdrubale sul fiume Metauro non viene meno dopo tale evento, ma è costantemente alimentato da imprese sempre più prospere: a sollecitarlo, infatti, è la giovinezza che spinge gli uni e l'altra verso nuovi *labores*. Al progressivo e continuo incremento di imprese militari propizie si associa il ripristino dell'ordine in ambito religioso (vv. 47-48): la sconfitta di Asdrubale, infatti, pone fine alle disastrose conseguenze materiali e morali (*impio...tumultu/ vastata... fana*) provocate dalle manifestazioni di empietà ai danni dei templi romani,[36] che riprendono ad accogliere *deos...rectos*.[37]

Un tono di rassegnata ammirazione nei confronti dell'indiscutibile superiorità militare e strategica dei Romani costituisce lo sfondo delle parole che Orazio immagina pronunciate da Annibale dopo la sconfitta di Asdrubale sul Metauro (vv. 50-72).[38] I rapidi trapassi concettuali in stile pindarico delle strofe precedenti cedono il posto a una ben definita scansione delle singole strofe: introdotte nel v. 49 dal solenne *dixitque*,[39] le parole di Annibale si collocano – come sottolinea *tandem* – a conclusione del suo passaggio attraverso le città italiche e a ridosso del *dies primus* della vittoria romana sul Metauro. Il condottiero cartaginese, definito *perfidus* nel v. 49, secondo il tradizionale giudizio dei

---

[35] Cf. Liv. 27.44.5-6 *nunc duo bella Punica facta, duos ingentes exercitus, duos prope Hannibales in Italia esse*.
[35] Ne è un esempio la descrizione della devastazione del tempio di Feronia ad opera di Annibale in Liv. 26.11.8-10.
[37] La 'iunctura' *deos rectos* allude alla ricollocazione in posizione eretta delle statue degli dèi nei templi (per tale valore di *rectus*, cf. Thuc. 5.42.2) e mette in rilievo il ripristino dell'ordine dopo l'*impius tumultus Poenorum* grazie alla posizione in clausola di *rectos*; per *deus* nel senso di 'statua di un dio' cf. *OLD* s.v. *deus* [3] e il commento di Murgatroyd a Tib. 2.5.22.
[38] Una parte della critica, tra cui Pasquali (1964) 766 e Syndikus (2001) 306, ha evidenziato l'affinità strutturale che lega la collocazione del mito con funzione celebrativa alla fine di alcuni carmi pindarici (in particolare *Nem*. 1 e 10) e quella della 'storia' a conclusione dell'ode oraziana per esaltare le gesta della *gens Claudia*. A questo influsso, però, si associa la ripresa di una modalità caratteristica della lirica greca arcaica, evidenziata da Wilamowitz-Moellendorff (1913) 306 n. 1, e attestata anche in Pindaro (cf. *Ol*. 4.24-27), che consiste nel concludere il componimento con il discorso diretto di un personaggio inserito all'interno di un *exemplum* mitologico: Orazio 4 ricorre giá in *Epod*. 13.11-18 (su cui cf. il commento di Cavarzere) e poi in *Carm*. 1.7.25-32, 1.15.5-36, 3.11.37-52, 3.27.69-76.
[39] Cf. e.g. Verg. *Aen*. 4.650, 5.467, 6.231.

Romani sui Cartaginesi (cf. *Carm.* 3.5.33, Liv. 21.4.9 *perfidia plus quam Punica*; Auson. *Epist.* 29.54, p. 287 Peiper) esordisce nel v. 50 con una metafora tratta dal mondo animale che chiama in causa i rapporti di forza tra vincitori e vinti, in stretta relazione con le similitudini iniziali: cervi e lupi sono protagonisti di una scena paradossale in cui i primi, tradizionalmente non bellicosi e assimilati ai Cartaginesi, sono descritti mentre inseguono ostinatamente i lupi rapaci, identificati con i Romani (v. 51).[40] Il riconoscimento da parte di Annibale dell'inferiorità dei Cartaginesi rispetto ai lupi romani si scontra con un accanimento contro i nemici che non è certamente caratteristico degli inoffensivi cervi. Tale incongruenza potrebbe costituire un'allusione all'indole infida propria dei Cartaginesi, che apparentemente non sono più in grado di attaccare, ma in realtà si ostinano a dar la caccia ai Romani. Non è casuale, infatti, che nel v. 52 Annibale presenti non solo la fuga, ma anche l'inganno come mezzi adatti a conseguire un *opimus...triumphus sui Romanos*;[41] dal punto di vista del Cartaginese sconfitto conseguire un *opimus triumphus* sui Romani può equivalere solo a *fallere et effugere*:[42] i due termini, messi in rilievo dall'assonanza, associano l'idea della frode a quella della fuga e definiscono una tattica militare, che, se da un lato è l'unica possibile per i cervi cartaginesi contro i rapaci lupi romani, dall'altra appare in linea con la *perfidia* attribuita ad Annibale nel v. 49.

Dopo aver constatato la superiorità dei Romani sui Cartaginesi, Annibale rievoca le vicende mitiche che, a partire dall'incendio di Troia, segnarono l'origine di Roma e della sua forza. Grazie a una serie di reminiscenze virgiliane, il condottiero cartaginese riassume l'intera trama dell'*Eneide*;[43] l'allusione a Virgilio è evidente già nell'impiego di *gens* per definire il popolo romano, con un chiaro rinvio alle parole ostili pronunciate da Giunone in *Aen.* 1.67-68 (*gens inimica mihi*

---

[40] La definizione dei Romani come lupi rapaci potrebbe alludere al probabile impiego da parte di Druso della *Legio XXI Rapax* nella campagna militare del 15 a.C.: cf. Thomas (2011) ad loc.

[41] Cf. il commento di Porfirione, ad loc.: *Ultro, inquit, bello petimus Romanos, quorum manus si effugerimus, gaudere debemus, similesque in hoc sumus cervis, qui ultro lupos insectentur, quos alioqui fugere debeant.*

[42] A una tattica militare basata su *fallere* e *effugere* Annibale era ricorso dopo le sconfitte subite a Grumentum e a Venosa (cf. Liv. 27.42.5, 17).

[43] Un procedimento analogo si incontra oltreché in *Carm. saec.* 37-44, 49-52 anche in *Carm.* 4.6.21-24, 4.15.31-32.

Tyrrhenum navigat aequor,/ Ilium in Italiam portans victosque Penates); la collocazione di *fortis*, che ha funzione predicativa, tra *cremato* e *ab Ilio*, riconduce il coraggio e il valore dei Romani alla dolorosa vicenda della distruzione di Troia. Si delinea, dunque, quella che secondo Annibale è la caratteristica principale del popolo romano fin dalle origini, cioè la sua capacità di rafforzarsi nelle prove più impegnative. Le *Ausoniae urbes* (v. 56) costituiscono il punto di arrivo di un viaggio ricco di peripezie che, però, non ha impedito alla *gens Romana* di dare prova di quella *pietas* propria dello stesso Enea: essa, infatti, si manifesta sia verso i *sacra*, sia verso i genitori e i figli; quest'ultimo aspetto è sottolineato nel v. 55 dal nesso polisindetico, tipico della dizione epica, *natosque maturosque patres*, che estende all'intera *gens Romana* l'atteggiamento di Enea nei confronti del figlio e del padre.

Una nuova similitudine naturalistica, attinta questa volta dall'ambito vegetale, costituisce lo strumento di cui Annibale si serve per ribadire la capacità dei Romani di rafforzarsi attraverso le difficoltà. Il paragone con il leccio tagliato dalle scuri rinvia, all'immagine pindarica della quercia recisa, che, attraverso il suo legno, continua a offrire testimonianza di sé.[44] Pianta sempreverde dal legno particolarmente robusto, il leccio è in grado di resistere ai tagli inferti da solide scuri; la sua natura è in perfetta sintonia con il rigoglioso aspetto del monte Algido: legato a *frondis* dall'allitterazione, *ferax* amplifica, grazie al suffisso intensivo -*ax*, l'idea della fertilità del monte.[45] Come il leccio resiste ai colpi delle scuri, così i Romani si rafforzano p*er damna, per caedis* (v. 59); la *geminatio* di *per* e l'asindeto mettono in rilievo l'incalzare degli ostacoli esterni disposti in *gradatio*: *damnum* associa all'idea della perdita quella della sventura procurata dalla sorte, che *caedes* intensifica con il riferimento concreto alle stragi belliche. Alla coppia *damna/ caedes* si oppongono nel v. 60 *opes animumque*, cioè

---

[44] Lo mette in rilievo Fraenkel (1957) 430 in riferimento a Pind. *Pyth.* 4.468-479; all'allusione al passo di Pindaro si associa quella al paragone virgiliano, di ascendenza omerica (cf. *Il.* 13.389-391), tra l'orno, abbattuto dai boscaioli con frequenti colpi di scure, e la caduta di Troia (*Aen.* 2.626-631 su cui cf. Austin ad loc.).
[45] La 'iunctura' *nigrae...frondis* è posta da alcuni in relazione con *ferax* (come in Varr. *Rust.* 1.9.7, Columella, *Rust.* 3.2.24, 9.1.5, Hil. *In Psalm.* 51.22), mentre da altri è considerata come genitivo di qualità riferito a *ilex*: la *dispositio uerborum*, tuttavia, rende più probabile la prima ipotesi, anche perché *ferax* è legato a *frondis* dall'allitterazione.

le risorse militari e il coraggio che i Romani sono in grado di trarre *ab ipso... ferro*.

Nei vv. 61-64 sono alcuni celebri mostri mitologici a costituire il termine di paragone per descrivere la capacità dei Romani di rigenerarsi attraverso situazioni svantaggiose: dall'ambito della natura, dunque, il discorso di Annibale passa, con un'evidente *gradatio* tematica, a quello del soprannaturale; dal punto di vista del Cartaginese la forza dei Romani non puó che essere amplificata grazie all'associazione con figure prodigiose di ascendenza orientale.[46]

Dall'Idra di Lerna, alla cui uccisione è legata la seconda fatica di Ercole, che era capace diventare sempre più robusta e resistente nonostante i tagli inferti al suo corpo dall'eroe,[47] Annibale passa nei vv. 63-64 alla rievocazione degli esseri mostruosi che popolavano la Colchide e Tebe, luoghi tradizionalmente associati alla presenza di *monstra*:[48] ai comparativi *firmior* (v. 61) e *maius* (v. 64) è affidato il compito di amplificare la forza incomparabile propria del popolo romano.

A conclusione della rassegna di soggetti reali e soprannaturali dotati di resistenza e di forza straordinarie, Annibale non puó che ribadire

---

[46] Su tale aspetto cf. Thomas (2011) ad loc.

[47] Orazio allude ad una sconfitta del personaggio, secondo la versione del mito narrata da Apollodoro (2.5.2) in cui Ercole, dopo vani tentativi, riesce ad avere la meglio sul serpente a nove teste solo con l'aiuto di Iolao, tanto che Euristeo si rifiuta di includere tale prova tra le altre imposte all'eroe. Alla rappresentazione della sconfitta di Ercole, ad opera dell'Idra, alcuni, come Putnam (1986) 99 n. 34, hanno attribuito un significato ironico, ipotizzando persino che Orazio abbia voluto scherzare su una possibile identificazione tra Ercole e i Cartaginesi: in realtà il riferimento alla seconda fatica di Ercole non ha qui una funzione propagandistica in relazione ad Augusto, ma si inserisce in una serie di paragoni mitologici che mirano a conferire un carattere 'mostruoso' alla capacità dei Romani di rafforzarsi in circostanze negative. Tale finalità è dimostrata anche dal fatto che la tradizione attribuisce il confronto tra il popolo romano e l'Idra ad un altro celebre nemico, Pirro, o al suo ambasciatore Cinea (cf. Plut. *Vit. Pyrrh.* 19; Flor. 1.13.19); tuttavia Thomas (2011) ad loc. rovescia il senso di *vinci dolentem* poiché interpreta l'espressione nel senso di 'averse to/annoyed to defeat', i.e. *invictus*.

[48] Sia la Colchide sia Tebe sono connotate in qualità di procreatrici di *monstra*, come si evince da *submittere*, che va inteso qui nell'accezione di 'far nascere uno dopo l'altro' (cf. Lucr. 1.8 *tellus submittit flores* e Orelli-Baiter-Hirschfelder, ad loc.). Secondo Kiessling e Heinze ad loc., il *monstrum* del v. 63 si riferisce ai guerrieri armati fatti nascere in Colchide dalla semina dei denti del drago sacro ad Ares ad opera di Giasone, analogamente a quella fatta da Cadmo a Tebe, dalla quale aveva avuto origine Echione; in effetti, i due episodi (argonautico e tebano) sono collegati dalla tradizione (cf. *Pherecyd.* fr. 22 Jacoby) e riproducono il medesimo motivo fiabesco (in proposito cf. M. Cantilena, *Echione, EO* 2.359). È anche possibile, però, che l'allusione al 'monstrum' generato nella Colchide implichi un riferimento più ampio ai numerosi mostri che l'abitavano.

in forma sentenziosa e con tono perentorio la capacità dei Romani di rafforzarsi nelle difficoltà (vv. 65-68). A tale effetto concorre la sostituzione dell'ipotassi con la paratassi, tipica della lingua parlata, che, ponendo sullo stesso piano la condizione e la sua conseguenza, suscita l'impressione di una successione rapida e incalzante di azioni. Nel v. 65 una suggestiva metafora tratta dall'ambito marino mette in rilievo, grazie all'allitterazione chiastica, la capacità del popolo romano di riemergere più forte dopo ripetute immersioni.[49]

A *merses* del v. 65 corrisponde simmetricamente *luctere* del v. 66, seguito da un'ampia descrizione della risposta dei Romani, che giunge fino al termine della strofa. L'allitterazione chiastica sottolinea il contrasto semantico tra i due *kola* del verso; quella romana è la reazione rapida e immediata di un popolo valoroso.[50] Il discorso di Annibale ritorna all'ambito militare: la forza con cui la *gens Romana* reagisce all'aggressione nemica è enfatizzata dall'impiego di *proruere*, che va inteso nel senso di 'abbattere' e, grazie al prefisso, esprime un'idea di impeto violento; per di più esso è rivolto *cum multa...laude* contro *integrum...victorem*: i due nessi – sottolineano, grazie all'iperbato, la grande gloria militare conseguita dai Romani per aver abbattuto un avversario che non solo è vittorioso, ma è uscito anche incolume dallo scontro.[51] L'uso del futuro (*proruet* v. 66; *geret* v. 67) proietta in un tempo indefinito la superiorità bellica di Roma e rafforza il tono sentenzioso delle parole del cartaginese. Dei gloriosi *proelia* rimarrà

---

[49] Lo sottolinea l'uso del frequentativo *mersare*, che evoca l'idea di una ripetuta immersione nel mare, dalla quale, però, Roma *pulchrior evenit*.

[50] Lo evidenzia l'impiego del comparativo *pulchrior* accostato al presente *evenit*; per quanto riguarda l'impiego di *evenire* nel senso originario di 'venire fuori', 'emergere' (cf. *ThlL* 5.2.1012.8 ss.) e non in quello più comune di *accidere*, Orelli-Baiter-Hirschfelder, ad loc., osservano che esso risponde alla tendenza di Orazio a recuperare il valore etimologico dei termini: alla luce dei pochi esempi da loro citati, tuttavia, sembra più probabile che qui il poeta intenda nobilitare la forza dei Romani attraverso l'accostamento del solenne *pulchrior* ad un verbo come *evenire*, usato in un'accezione inconsueta.

[51] Il concetto espresso in questi versi richiama il riferimento dei vv. 23-24 alle *victrices catervae* che sono state *revictae* da Druso e la ripresa del motivo è funzionale a sottolineare come la *gens Romana* mantenga intatte nel tempo quelle capacità militari che le hanno permesso di ribaltare gli esiti delle guerre; la stessa tematica ritorna sia nelle parole pronunciate da Annibale in Liv. 27.14.1 (*cum eo nimirum...hoste res est, qui nec bonam nec malam ferre fortunam potest. Seu vicit, ferocier instat victis; seu victus est, instaurat cum victoribus certamen*), sia in una sezione del discorso, che è attribuito ad Annibale da Pompeo Trogo ed è rivolto ad Antioco III di Siria (cf. Iustin. 31.5 *cum Romano seu occupaveris prior aliqua seu viceris, tamen etiam cum victo et iacente luctandum esse*).

un vivido ricordo nei racconti narrati dai soldati romani alle legittime spose, secondo un topos che risale alla tradizione epica.[52] Il concetto espresso nel passo appare coerente con il riferimento alla grande gloria che i Romani conseguono trasformando in sconfitta la vittoria dei nemici: il nesso *proelia... loquenda*, infatti, enfatizza, attraverso l'iperbato a cornice e l'assonanza, l'importanza delle battaglie combattute dai soldati romani, il cui ricordo continua a riecheggiare nei loro racconti alle spose.

Dopo aver sottolineato la forza morale e la superiorità militare del popolo romano a partire dalle sue origini, Annibale riconosce con un tono rassegnato le nefaste conseguenze della sconfitta subita dai Cartaginesi sul Metauro; la collocazione del nome di Cartagine in apertura del v. 69 sancisce l'unione tra il destino negativo del condottiero e quello della sua città. Benché l'enfatico *ego* conferisca un tono apparentemente autoritario alla decisione di Annibale di non mandare più *nuntii...superbi* ai Cartaginesi, quella del condottiero suona, in realtà, come un'ammissione chiara e definitiva di inferiorità rispetto ai Romani, messa in rilievo dall'accostamento di *iam a non*. Il ricordo del tono orgoglioso e sprezzante dei messaggi riferiti dai *nunti* di Annibale a Cartagine, quando egli confidava ancora nella vittoria,[53] lascia il posto alla sconsolata ammissione della rovina: nel v. 70 la 'geminatio'

---

[52] Controversa nel v. 68 è l'interpretazione di *coniugibus*; gli scoliasti lo intendono sia come dativo di termine (Roma intraprenderà guerre degne di essere narrate alle mogli) sia come dativo di agente (allusione a *proelia* tali da essere raccontati dalle spose). Tra i commentatori, tanto Orelli-Baiter-Hirschfelder quanto Kiessling e Heinze considerano *coniugibus* come dativo d'agente sulla base di un'analoga espressione oraziana (*Carm.* 4.9.21 *dicenda Musis proelia*); Giangrande (1967) 329-30, però, fa notare che le affinità tra i due passi si limitano al livello formale, ma non riguardano quello stilistico, poiché *loqui* ha un tono più colloquiale rispetto al solenne *dicere*; egli, dunque, attribuisce a *coniugibus* il valore di dativo di termine e rinvia al *topos* epico, attestato in Virgilio (*Aen.* 4.79) e poi ripreso da Ovidio (*Her.* 1.30, 13.117-118), delle donne che ascoltano con attenzione i racconti di guerra dei loro uomini. L'intepretazione di Giangrande appare fondata: non ha senso, infatti, dare alle mogli dei soldati romani un ruolo attivo nella narrazione delle imprese dei mariti, dal momento che la tradizione epica tende a conferire alle donne il ruolo di ascoltatrici dei racconti di guerra. La ripresa del *topos* è in linea con l'impiego del tono epico che caratterizza il discorso di Annibale e, in particolare, la sua rievocazione delle origini della *gens Romana*. Alla luce di tali considerazioni, sembra ingiustificato considerare corrotto il brano in questione, come fa da ultimo Shackleton Bailey, che colloca *geretque proelia coniugibus loquenda* tra *cruces*.

[53] A tal proposito si può rinviare alla testimonianza di Livio (23.11.8 ss.), il quale afferma che Annibale aveva fatto annunciare al Senato cartaginese il successo di Canne da Magone, che aveva sottolineato con arroganza le gravi perdite dei Romani.

di *occidit*[54] esprime con una intensa tonalità patetica la morte di tutte le speranze e della *fortuna…nominis*, in cui al riferimento alla buona sorte del nome dei Barca si associa quello alla fortuna dell'intero popolo cartaginese. L'allusione di Annibale all'iperbolica morte di *omnis spes*, della *fortuna* della sua stirpe e della sua nazione si chiude con il riferimento alla fine violenta del fratello di Annibale,[55] che ha posto fine alla speranza[56] e ha pregiudicato inesorabilmente il destino di tutto il popolo cartaginese.

In forte contrasto con il tono disperato delle parole pronunciate da Annibale a conclusione del suo discorso, l'ultima strofa contiene una valutazione entusiastica da parte di Orazio della forza dimostrata dalla *gens Claudia* nella storia, a partire dalla vittoria ottenuta contro Asdrubale sul Metauro fino ai recenti successi militari di Druso contro i Reti e i Vindelici. Nel v. 73 *perficiunt*[57] sottolinea con vivacità la presa d'atto del poeta delle capacità dei Claudii, di cui la litote, strutturata sotto forma di doppia negazione, sottolinea iperbolicamente il carattere illimitato. In particolare, la collocazione enfatica di *nil* determina una forte contrapposizione tra la condizione della *gens Claudia*, a cui nulla è impossibile dopo la vittoria, e quella dei Cartaginesi, per i quali è venuta meno *spes omnis* (v. 71) con l'uccisione di Asdrubale.

La constatazione delle possibilità illimitate di cui la *gens Claudia* dispone è seguita dall'indicazione, scandita dalla correlazione *et…*

---

[54] Per l'impiego oraziano della 'geminatio' in funzione di una tonalitá patetica, cf. Tosi (2000) 87; la rarità della 'geminatio' di due forme verbali adiacenti è messa in rilievo da Wills (1996) 104-105.

[55] Orazio sembra riferirsi al momento in cui Claudio Nerone, reduce dalla vittoria sul Metauro, espose la testa di Asdrubale di fronte all'accampamento cartaginese (cf. Liv. 27.51.11) e *Hannibal tanto simul publico familiarique ictus luctu, agnoscere se fortunam Carthaginis fertur dixisse* (Liv. 27.51.12).

[56] Cf. Liv. 28.12.6 *post Hasdrubalis exercitum cum duce, in quibus spes omnis deposita victoriae fuerat, deletum…*

[57] Il riferimento carico di pathos di Annibale alla morte di Asdrubale come evento rovinoso che ha posto fine alla *spes* e alla *fortuna nominis* dà alle sue parole il carattere di una conclusione; il tono perentorio con cui al v. 73 si sottolinea la capacità delle *Claudiae…manus* di conseguire qualsiasi obiettivo, il riferimento del v. 74 alla benevola protezione di Giove e l'allusione del v. 75 alle *curae sagaces* messe in atto *per acuta belli* hanno una precisa funzione di segnali: essi, infatti, conferiscono all'ultima strofa il carattere di una valutazione entusiastica della forza dimostrata dalla *gens Claudia* nella storia, a partire dalla vittoria ottenuta contro Asdrubale sul Metauro fino ai recenti successi militari di Druso contro i Reti e i Vindelici, che può essere attribuita solo ad Orazio. Alla luce di tali considerazioni, nel v. 73 è preferibile accettare la lezione *perficiunt* del *Blandinianus*, come ha fatto da ultimo Shackleton Bailey, il quale attribuisce i versi finali ad Orazio.

et, delle cause che concorrono ai suoi successi: Orazio menziona in primo luogo il favore di Giove, mettendola in opportuno rilievo grazie alla collocazione del nome nella chiusa del v. 75; il dio protegge i Claudii *benigno numine*: la *iunctura* amplifica l'idea della protezione accordata da Giove attraverso l'allusione al carattere benevolo del suo – cenno –, che ne rappresenta il potere e la capacità di condizionare le vicende umane. Al favore di Giove si associano fattori prettamente umani: la posizione simmetrica ad inizio di verso di *defendit* al v. 75 e di *expediunt* al v. 76, enfatizzati entrambi dall'*enjambement*, sottolinea l'azione complementare dell'intervento divino e dei meriti dei Claudii nel conseguimento di tutti gli obiettivi possibili. Il nesso *curae sagaces*, in cui *cura* evoca l'unione di *labor* e di *diligentia*, allude a iniziative belliche di cui *sagax* enfatizza, grazie al suffisso intensivo, l'acuta sagacia: chiaro è il rinvio alle qualità razionali e alle capacità strategiche che hanno permesso a Druso di sconfiggere i Reti e i Vindelici. Alla rievocazione dei successi di Druso concorre nel verso conclusivo l'uso di *expedire*, che allude al favorevole superamento di difficoltà *per acuta belli*, cioè nelle fasi più pericolose della guerra.[58] Negli ultimi versi, dunque, il poeta ritorna al tema iniziale, cioè alla celebrazione della campagna militare condotta dal figliastro di Augusto e, alla luce delle vittorie conseguite dai suoi avi, ne amplifica la portata: non è un caso che la sezione storica dell'ode si apra nel nome dei Neroni (v. 37) e si chiuda con la menzione della *gens Claudia*. La storia passata e recente dimostra che tutto è possibile alla *gens Claudia*; in particolare il riferimento conclusivo alla capacità dei Claudii di superare con successo gli *acuta belli* richiama l'elogio della forza del popolo romano sviluppato da Annibale: nell'ultima strofa, quindi, le modalità dell'epinicio in stile pindarico si saldano con la celebrazione della storia di Roma e del suo popolo.

---

[58] Cf. Porph. *ad loc.*: '*acuta belli*' *absolute dicuntur ea, quae sunt in bello pericolosissima*.

Bibliografia

Caviglia, F. (1995), 'Hor. *Carm*. 4.4. Etologia del potere', in L. Belloni, G. Milanese, A. Porro (edd.), *Studia classica Iohanni Tarditi oblata*, Milano, vol. 1, 447-469.

Ciccarelli, I. (2003), *Commento al II libro dei Tristia di Ovidio*, Bari.

Fedeli, P. (1980), *Sesto Properzio. Il primo libro delle elegie*, Firenze.

Fedeli, P., Ciccarelli, I. (2008), *Q. Horatii Flacci Carmina liber IV*, Firenze.

Fraenkel, E. (1957), *Horace*, Oxford.

Giangrande, G. (1967), 'Two Horatian Problems', *Classical Quarterly* 17, 329-331.

Hellegouarc'h, J. (1972), *Le vocabulaire latin des relations et des partis politiques sous la République*, Paris.

La Penna, A. (1963), *Orazio e l'ideologia del principato*, Torino.

La Penna, A. (1969), *Orazio. Le opere. Antologia*, Firenze.

Laughton, E. (1964), *The Participle in Cicero*, Oxford.

Lowrie, M. (1997), *Horace's Narrative Odes*, Oxford.

Maggiali, G. (2008), *Il Carme 68 di Catullo*, Cesena.

Nisbet, R.G.M., Hubbard, M. (edd.) (1978), *A Commentary on Horace. Odes Book II*, Oxford.

Nisbet, R.G.M., Rudd, N. (edd.) (2004), *A Commentary on Horace. Odes Book III*, Oxford.

Pasquali, G. (1964), *Orazio lirico*, con introduzione, indici ed appendice di aggiornamento bibliografico a cura di A. La Penna, Firenze.

Putnam, M.C.J.(1986), *Artifices of Eternity. Horace's Fourth Book of Odes*, Ithaca/ London.

Syndikus, H.P. (2001^3), *Die Lyrik des Horaz. Eine Interpretation der Oden*, vol. 2, Darmstadt.

Thomas, R.F. (1988), *Virgil. Georgics*, Cambridge.

Thomas, R.F. (2011), *Horace. Odes Book 4 and Carmen Saeculare*, Cambridge.

Tosi, C. Facchini (2000), *'Euphonia'. Studi di fonostilistica (Virgilio, Orazio, Apuleio)*, Bologna.

Wilamovitz-Moellendorf, E. (1913), *Sappho und Simonides*, Berlin.

Wills, J. (1996), *Repetition in Latin Poetry*, Cambridge.

Zanker, P. (1989), *Augusto e il potere delle immagini*, trad. ital., Torino.

Significant Conjunctions of Civil War and Roman Cult from Ovid's *Fasti* to a Flavian Metamorphosis of Horace's 16th Epode

JOY LITTLEWOOD
Independent Scholar, Oxford

Rome's poetic identity has been influenced by two disjunctive strands, originating from each of her two founders, Aeneas and Romulus. In the language of folk tale the two founders bestow on the nascent city two ktistic gifts: one good, one bad. In Roman culture, history and literature they are mutually antagonistic. On the one hand the Romans claimed to surpass all races in devotion to their gods, who in turn rewarded them with empire: *imperium sine fine*.[1] In a religious context the national virtue derived from Aeneas, *pietas*, was fulsomely illustrated by the iconography of the Ara Pacis Augustae. On the other hand Rome's tendency to self-destruction through civil war,[2] defined by the Roman poets as *scelus*,[3] clearly had its origin in the ktistic fratricide.[4] The paradox and consequences of their mutual incompatibility invited varying responses from Rome's rulers and her poets. Roman cult and Roman civil war might, for instance, be regarded as symbiotic. Horace attributes recent civil strife to Rome's neglect of ancient cultic rituals which maintained the *pax deorum*, suggesting that renewed devotion to Roman cult may atone for the guilt of civil war.[5] According to this argument Augustus' frenetic restoration of 82 temples[6] and studiedly dynastic reorganisation of Roman cult could, in part, be construed as

---

[1] Verg. *Aen*. 1.279; Liv. 5.50.1: *inuenietis omnia prospera euenisse sequentibus deos, adversa spernentibus*.
[2] Hor. *Ep*. 16.2: *ipsa Roma uiribus ruit*.
[3] Hor. *Carm*. 1.2.29, 1.35.33; Virg. *Ecl*. 4.13; *G*. 1.506; Luc. 1.2.
[4] Hor. 7. 17; Verg. *G*. 2.510; Luc. 1. 95: *fraterno primi maduerunt sanguine muri*. See Jal (1963) 393 ff.
[5] Hor. *Carm*. 3.6.1-2, 3.24.45-50.
[6] *Mon. Anc*. 20.4.

atonement for the slaughter of Roman citizens required to achieve victory over his brother-in-law and Cleopatra at Actium.

This paper sets out to explore the significance of some literary juxtapositions of Civil War and Roman religion beginning in the Augustan period with Ovid's *Fasti*. Conventionally critics have defined Ovid as a poet of the Pax Augusta, distinctive from Virgil, Horace and Propertius who witnessed civil conflict on Italian soil. I should like to demonstrate that the spectre of civil war haunted the Roman poetic imagination through the early imperial period. Further, the new outbreak of civil war after the murder of Nero in 68 reactivated this topic as a literary theme in the Flavian epicists.

The ktistic fratricide has been cogently interpreted as a foundation sacrifice necessary for the strength and prosperity of the new city.[7] Alternatively it might be suggested that so grave a breach of family *pietas* committed by the first ruler must generate a lasting pollution within the Roman community. Such pollution might be reactivated in the future by immoderate personal ambition, causing civil war and extinction of social and civic order. The following discussion involves a conjunction of two themes which is not only significant but inevitable because we are dealing with a strong taboo. One point at issue is this: to what extent and in what manner was it appropriate for an Augustan poet such as Ovid to allude to Rome's civil wars in conjunction with Augustus' reformed dynastic religion? To adapt Ovid's own words in the Proem to *Fasti* Book 1: *quid licet? quid fas est?*

In Roman culture fraternal loyalty was highly rated. As an example of fraternal *pietas,* the Dioscuri, worshipped in Lavinium from the sixth century, provided a divine counterpart to the legend of Romulus and Remus.[8] When Ovid, in *Fasti* 2, summons 'beloved family members', *cognati ...cari*, to the *Caristia*, the Feast of the Ancestors which expressly celebrates familial *pietas* and *Concordia*,[9] he singles out, first and foremost, *impius frater* for exclusion from the feast.[10] Apart from sharing responsibility for family land and inheritance, brothers

---

[7] Propertius 3.9.50, *caeso muris firma Remo*; Ov. *Fast.* 4.840. Wiseman (1995) 117-125 for another sacrifice in the interest of the Roman community see Ov. *Fast.* 5.624. See Girard (1977) 49.
[8] Sixth century inscription honouring the Dioscuri in Lavinium, see Weinstock (1960) 112.
[9] Val. Max. 2.1.8 states that family quarrels must be put aside in favour of conviviality and affection. See also Robinson (2011) 393-394.
[10] Ovid *Fast.* 2.623-630.

from Rome's leading *gentes* often held high office together or supported each other as commanders in the field, as for example, the two elder Scipiones in the Second Punic War whose mutual harmony is poetically enhanced by Silius in in his narrative of their jointly-led Spanish campaign.[11] In planning his dynastic succession Augustus set a high value on brotherly concord. His two stepsons, Tiberius and Drusus, formed the first pair to take on civic duties together, followed by his grandsons Gaius and Lucius. The deaths of Drusus, Gaius and Lucius forced him to create artificial pairs of 'brothers', beginning with the improbable combination of Tiberius and Agrippa Postumus. Following Postumus' disgrace, new pairs were created by the adoption of cousins and other relatives. Temples built in the name of Concordia or Castor and Pollux, the supreme divine example of fraternal devotion,[12] advertised concord within the imperial family. This same architectural ideology would later mask the impression of antagonism between the Flavian brothers, Titus and Domitian.

While pairs of devoted brothers fighting or dying side by side represented an ideal of *pietas* in Roman poetry, conversely the theme of fraternal strife, *fraternas acies*, was a *locus communis* for civil war.[13] The *Anthologia Latina* contains two poems in which Maevius unwittingly kills his brother at Actium and, when he discovers what he has done, kills himself with his brother's sword.[14] On the eve of his narrative of Battle of Cannae Silius invents a similar episode as a literary symbol of the self-destruction of civil war as a comparison with the destructive animosity between Rome's two consular commanders. The theme of hostility between brothers intersects with religious ritual in the literary symbol of the divided flame on the pyre of Oedipus' sons, Eteocles and Polynices.[15] Lucan extends the idea by interweaving the portent of the divided flame with images drawn from Roman cult, describing the extinction of the Vestal flame at the approach of civil

---

[11] Sil. *Pun.* 13.650, *simulacra uirum concordia, patris unanimique simul patrui.* Their military disaster is shared, *geminae...ruinae* (694), as also their funeral rites, *tumulus...geminus* (659-660).

[12] On the harmony of the Dioscuri, Ovid *Fast.* 5.693-720. On the iconography of the statuary in Tiberius' temple of Concord, see Kellum (1990) 276-307.

[13] Luc. 2.149-151: *nati maduere paterno/ sanguine; certatum est cui ceruix caesa parentis/ cederet; in fratrum ceciderunt praemia fratres.*

[14] *Anth. Lat.* 462, 463. Sil. *Pun.* 9.66-177.

war in 49 BC, when the ceremonial bonfire at the Ludi Latini symbolically splits in two.[16] When Ovid, towards the end of his *Metamorphoses*, asks what is Thebes but a name (15.429), he describes that city with an adjective which answers his question: *Oedipodioniae quid sunt nisi nomina Thebae*. Defined as a symbol of civil war through the fratricide of Oedipus' sons, Thebes too began with a fratricide committed by the men sown from dragon's teeth. Lucan would later evoke this very scene as an image of Rome's civil war.[17]

Within five years of the Battle of Actium Augustus' circle of poets appears to have distanced themselves from poetic reflections on Rome's civil wars by tactful imagery. In Virgil's eloquent vision the ominous legacy of the fratricide is dispelled by a significant grouping of four noble dispensors of Justice: *Fides*, Vesta, and Romulus and Remus.[18] *Fides*, made venerable by her white hair, personifies absolute loyalty to the Roman state.[19] With *Fides* is Vesta, elevated by Augustus into Rome's most ancient cult figure. Completing the quartet is Romulus now reconciled with his brother Remus. Together they represent *pietas* towards the state, Roman cult and family. In direct contrast to their civic harmony is a monstrous personification of War chained up within the confines of the Temple of Janus by Augustus himself. Defined by Virgil as *Furor impius*, he will reappear in later poetry as the very spirit or personification of civil conflict.[20]

We see the same Augustan rescripting in Virgil's foundational narrative in *Aeneid* 8 which culminates in an interweaving of Roman cult and civil conflict on the Shield of Aeneas. Representing Roman religion, Virgil lists the dance of the Salian priests, the ritual of the Luperci,

---

[15] Ovid *Tr.* 5.5.33-36; Sen. *Oed.* 321-7; Stat. *Theb.* 12.431-432.

[16] Luc. 1.549-52: *Vestali raptus ab ara/ ignis, et ostendens confectas flamma Latinas/ scinditur in partes geminoque cacumine surgit Thebanos imitate rogos*. Roche (2009) n. 550, points out that, significantly, in 49 BC Caesar delayed his journey to Greece, and Pharsalus, in order to celebrate the *Feriae Latinae* when, according to Lucan, this portent occurred.

[17] In Ovid *Met.* 3.117, Cadmus is told by an earthborn warrior: *ne te ciuilibus insere bellis*.'Cf. Luc. 4.549-551. See also Hardie (1990); Feldherr (1997); Braund (2006).

[18] Verg. *Aen.* 1.292-293: *cana Fides et Vesta, Remo cum fratre Quirinus/ iura dabun*t.

[19] Ennius (Cic. *Off.* 3.104) defines *Fides* as scrupulous observance of the sacrosanctity of oath Numa's affinity with Fides (Verg. *Aen.* 6.809) derives from cultic *pietas* evident in his foundation of a temple to *Dius Fidius*, the god representing the sanctity of oaths (Liv. 1.21.4, Dion. Hal. *Ant. Rom.* 2.75.3, Plut. *Vit. Num.* 16.2).

[20] Verg. *Aen.* 1.295-297: *Furor impius intus,/ saeua sedens super arma, et uinctus aenis/ post tergum nodis*.

Numa's sacred *ancilia* and chaste Roman *matronae* in solemn procession to Roman temples. Breaking the contract of civic unity are the Alban traitor Mettius Fufetius and the Roman revolutionary Catiline who are depicted receiving grim punishments. At the shield's climactic scene, the Battle of Actium is represented by Virgil as a foreign war against Cleopatra's Egypt through a direct confrontation of national gods: the guardian gods of Rome facing down Egypt's bestial hybrids so that the ecphrasis ends where it began: with Roman cult. But fratricide shadows the two Roman commanders, unequivocally identified by name, Augustus Caesar and Antonius, facing each other at the head of their armies. If not brothers, these two men were violating the family bond as brothers in law, as an earlier civil conflict was made more shocking by Caesar making war on his father in law. It could be argued that Virgil offers a positive and optimistic outlook for Augustan ideology by interweaving the spectre of civil war with new and dynamic images of Roman cult, for among Augustus' divine supporters are *penatibus et magnis dis*,[21] the Romano-Trojan *penates* and the Great Gods of Samothrace, which were represented by a sacred artefact supposedly brought from Troy by Aeneas himself.[22] In Augustan ideology these deities linked Augustus as a priest figure with Aeneas, an analogy preserved in the marble sculpture of Aeneas sacrificing on the Ara Pacis Augustae.[23]

Let us move forward through 30 years of the *Pax Augusta* to a time when the now elderly victor of Actium might prefer to enumerate his peacetime achievements rather than to recollect the path to his Principate. Roman poetry is dominated by a new talent who had barely put on his *toga uirilis* when Octavian closed the doors of the temple of Janus and two years later accepted the name Augustus as an implicit promise to obliterate the pollution of civil war by restoring Rome's ancient cults. Like Augustus, Ovid too was engaged in cultivating a public *persona*. Self-assured in his literary ability and advantageous social connections, Ovid saw no reason why he should not present his love elegies as a witty foil to topical issues of the Augustan regime:

---

[21] Verg. *Aen.* 8.679.
[22] See Erskine (2001) 233 n. 39.
[23] On significance of Trojan *di penates* in Augustan religious ideology see Stöckinger (2013) 129-148.

an urbane guide to conducting erotic affairs in Rome at the time when Augustus' *Leges Iuliae* became law and the *Ludi Saeculares* set the seal on an unpopular programme of moral rearmament. A decade later the iconography of the newly constructed *Ara pacis Augustae* advertised Rome's peace and prosperity and a united Domus Augusta observing the rituals of state religion. Ovid, meanwhile, sharpened the wit of his *Ars Amatoria* by proposing amorous escapades around the new Augustan monuments and especially on dynastic occasions. Regrettably, the circulation of the *Ars amatoria* coincided with the elder Julia's banishment and Augustus receiving the title of *pater patriae*, for saving the Roman state from conspiracy. Ovid smoothly changed course, demonstrating his commitment to Augustan culture with a loyal celebration of Augustus' religious reforms in his *Fasti*. There were pitfalls for a poet so self-assured, intelligent and, thanks to Pollio's well-stocked libraries, so well informed in the cultic background to Augustan iconography. In a decade marred by dynastic tension and civil unrest, AD 4-8, Ovid explores, with unflinching audacity, the literary intersection of the latest tenets of Augustan dynastic ideology with an earlier civil war. We may suspect that his target audience was initially intrigued and entertained, but privately aghast at his audacious ambiguity.

Which brings us to the heightened profile which Augustus was currently giving to the goddess Vesta,[24] memorably linked with *Fides* in Virgil's vision of Rome's destiny. This was one of Augustus' most important dynastic adjustments to Roman cult: a closer union of the Trojan *penates* and the ancestor cult of Aeneas at Lavinium with the cult of Vesta in Rome. The temple of Vesta housed the *penates* together with other sacred objects tended by priestesses whose chastity was inextricably linked to the military power of the Roman state.[25] Augustus decreed that Roman magistrates about to enter office must make their

---

[24] On Augustus' dynastic cult of Vesta see Ovid *Fast.* 3.425-426: *ortus ab Aenea tangit cognata sacerdos/ numina cognatum, Vesta, tuere caput*; 3.699, 4.954, 5.573; *Met.* 15.864-865: *Vestaque Caesareos inter sacra penates/ et cum caesarea, tu, Phoebe domestice, Vesta*. See Fraschetti (1988); Herbert-Brown (1994) 65-80; Beard (1995) 166-177; Newlands (1995) 123-140; Parker (2004); Littlewood (2006) 79-83, 101-103.

[25] The *Iliacae pignora Vestae* included the Palladium, the *fascinum*, two terracotta pots one containing the ancient Samothracian gods of Dardanus (Dion. Hal. *Ant. Rom.* 2.66.5) and a second traditionally empty. These, it was believed, were entrusted to Aeneas fleeing Troy: *sacra suos tibi commendat Troia penates* (Verg. *Aen.* 2.293).

oath of civic loyalty and sacrifice to Vesta and the *penates* at Aeneas' original foundation at Lavinium.[26] The Princeps gave new prominence to Vesta's worship as the keystone of Roman cult in Rome, eventually in 12 BC establishing a Vestal shrine within his Palatine home, where, in the image of Rome's ancient King Numa, Augustus tended the Vestal flame.[27] Explaining the cult of Vesta in *Fasti* 6, Ovid attributes to King Numa the inauguration of the ancient cult, on the fortieth celebration of the rustic festival of the *Parilia* in April, which marked the anniversary of Rome's foundation and the murder of Remus. The duties of the Vestal Virgins included roasting a calf foetus and 'tail' of the October horse, and mixing together the two sets of ashes so that they could be scattered ceremonially on the Parilia as a fertility ritual to purify the fields of lingering evil before the crops grew. By describing this ash as *februa tosta*[28] purifying or expiatory ash, Ovid hints that the ritual to promote Rome's agricultural fertility might also be an expiation for the fratricide which he now relates euphemistically, in a manner which exculpates Romulus from open hostility towards his brother. The murder, or execution, is done by a henchman, Celer, whose name suggests rash haste. However, there is a sinister intertext in Romulus' pronouncement: *audentem talia dede neci*. In ordering that anyone who dares cross the nascent walls should be put to death, Romulus' last words *dede neci*, echo a Virgilian phrase alluding to the elimination of the inferior of two rival 'king' bees.[29]

Both these ideological tenets, the priesthood of Vesta and the divinity of Augustus, make their first appearance in *Fasti* 3 at the end of the rollicking festival of Anna Perenna, in conjunction with the most sensitive of all the Roman civil war battles, the Battle of Philippi. Philippi was sensitive because the victor now ruled Rome but also because, unlike at Actium, there could be no argument that a foreign

---

[26] Lavinium was reputedly founded by Aeneas to mark his landfall in Italy (Varro *Ling.* 5.144; cf. Verg. *Aen.* 1.2-3). He was worshipped as Indiges (Liv. 1.2.6; Ov. *Met.* 14.602-604) at the site of a seventh century heroon (Dion. Hal. *Ant. Rom.* 1.64.4-5). See Castagnoli (1972) 71-75; Holloway (1994) 128-141.
[27] Ovid *Fast.* 4.949-954.
[28] Ovid *Fast.* 4.726.
[29] Verg. *G.* 4.90; Ovid *Fast.* 4.838-840. For the intertextual force of *dede neci* see Barchiesi (1997) 160-162.

power was being defeated.³⁰ Ovid confronts the challenge unflinchingly. Introducing an artfully shocking allusion to *gladios in principe fixos* in the form of a *praeteritio*, the poet is immediately interrupted by Vesta herself. No mere pool of amorphous purple radiance, as she is in *Fasti* 6, this Vesta is a lucid authority on Augustan religious discourse. In acknowledging Julius Caesar as her priest, she discloses an ideological retrojection associated with Augustus' establishment of the Vestal flame in his Palatine house.³¹ To this the poet-narrator adds a dogma of equal importance, Caesar's apotheosis, which figured prominently in Augustan ideology because it made Augustus *diui filius*.³² To bear witness to the miracle the poet solemnly invokes the battlefield of Philippi, white with scattered bones, an uncomfortable reminder that the victors killed all prisoners, thus violating a religious scruple by refusing formal burial to Roman aristocrats. If a contemporary reader sensed ambiguous loyalty in this slick outpouring of Augustan ideology, his sense of unease would surely be increased by Ovid's unequivocal collusion with the Party Line as set forth in Augustus' *Res gestae*. Caesar's murder is *nefas*, the death of the *coniurati* well deserved, *morte merita*, and the duty imposed on the young Octavian to avenge his father heavily underlined with a Virgilian allusion, *hoc opus, haec pietas*, before the significant *patrem*, concludes both the line and the festival. If we believe Tacitus, many of Ovid's contemporaries at this time took Augustus 'filial loyalty' as a convenient pretext for deciding the power struggle at Philippi.³³

It may be relevant here to insert a brief digression on the subject of Caesar's apotheosis. Ancient tradition and iconography going back to Etruscan tomb painting associated apotheosis with the religious ritual of the Roman triumph. Elevated to his new status by valour in conquest, the apotheosed leader transcends mortality and becomes one of

---

³⁰ Barchiesi (1997) 128: 'It was Philippi, not Pharsalus, which was seen as ultimate Civil War.'
³¹ Ovid *Fast.* 3.701-702; cf. Venus in *Met.* 15.843ff. In *Fast.* 2.499-512 apotheosis rescues Romulus from political assassination, making him Quirinus. On the connection of this with Ovid's Ides of March, see Barchiesi (1997) 129; Herbert-Brown (1994) 70-73.
³² Ovid, *Fast.* 3.703: *ille quidem caelo positus Iouis atria uidit*. See also Plin. *HN* 2.94. Weinstock (1971) 370-384; Zanker (1988) 34-37.
³³ Tac. *Ann.* 1.10: *dicebatur contra: pietatem erga parentem et tempora rei publicae obtentui sumpta*. Cf. *Mon. Anc.* 2: *qui parentem meum trucidauerunt, eos in exilium expuli iudiciis legitimis ultus eorum facinus, et postea bellum inferentis rei publicae uici bis acie*. See Koortbojian (2013).

the guardian gods of Rome. To draw the artisan and merchant classes into Augustus' new dynastic Rome, the Lares Compitales had been rebranded as Lares Augusti with vicomagistri appointed to conduct their ritual. The Genius Augusti was regularly inscribed between the twin Lares on the compital altars which began to display scenes involving other members of the ruling family. One such altar from the vicus Sandalarius features Augustus as priest, flanked by Livia and Gaius, with a sacred chicken at his feet devouring corn as a portent of military success in Gaius' forthcoming Parthian campaign. Once politically volatile, the vici had become mouthpieces of the regime, spreading Augustan ideology, such as the apotheosis of Caesar, among the inhabitants of the Roman *uici*. As a piece of Augustan ideological propaganda Caesar's apotheosis was depicted on the front panel of one of the altars sacred to the Lares Compitales, the Belvedere Altar: Caesar is swept heavenward in a blazing chariot while his divine ancestress, Venus explains what is happening to his watching descendants, Gaius and Lucius Caesar, and also to the inhabitants of the *uici*.[34]

Ovid's aition for the origin of the Lares Compitales at the end of his *Feralia* begins, topically enough, with religious ritual neglected through Roman wars.[35] The birth of the Lares, which concludes the tale, is the consequence of the rape of a gossipy, but otherwise blameless, nymph Lara whom Jupiter has punished by cutting out her too loquacious tongue and banishing her to the Underworld.[36] It is hard to avoid interpreting rape as a take-over and this particular mutilation as a ban on free speech.

One might think that enough had been said in *Fasti* 3 concerning the Battle of Philippi. But Ovid returns to Philippi and Augustus' obligation to avenge the murder of Caesar more explicitly in *Fasti* 5. To give added weight to the victor's propaganda Mars Ultor himself, looking out from his temple, is the focalizer, who remembers clearly the occasion on which the temple was vowed to him. He visualizes the young

---

[34] On Augustus' reorganisation of the cult of the Lares Compitales, see Fraschetti (1990) 204-276, Lott (2004) 30-60.
[35] Ovid *Fast.* 2.547-556.
[36] Ovid *Fast.* 2.607-609: *Iuppiter intumuit.../ eripuit huic linguam, Mercuriumque uocat,/ Duc hanc ad manes; locus ille silentibus aptus.*'On the relevance of Ovid's aition of the Lares Compitales to freedom of speech, see Feeney (1992); Newlands (1995) 161; Robinson (2011) 370-376.

Octavian standing on the battlefield before battle is joined, gesturing to his own soldiers on one side and those of the *coniurati* on the other. He cites Octavian's pretext, that this battle was not a choice but a filial duty imposed on the victor by double *pietas,* filial and religious: *si mihi bellandi pater est Vestaeque sacerdos/ auctor.* Finally, for the avoidance of doubt, the god 'quotes' a colourful version of the exact wording of Octavian's vow: *Mars, ades, et satia scelerato sanguine ferrum* ('Be with us, Mars, and glut our swords with criminal blood'). As Barchiesi has pointed out, this line recalls Aeneas' last words to Turnus: *Pallas...poenam scelerato ex sanguine sumit (Aen.* 12.949), which, in turn, resonate with Ennius' version of the Roman fratricide and Romulus' words to Remus: *nam mi calido dabis sanguine poenas.*[37] In dramatizing with such a potent focalizer the exact nature of Augustus' filial piety, Ovid affects the ingenuous pose of a poet absolutely confident that his new *persona* as a clear-eyed expounder of Augustan discourse can survive challenge.

Civil War did not end in Rome with Actium. Following a new cycle of civil conflict in 69 Vespasian, establishing a new dynasty, made use of much of the ideology associated with Pax Augusta and Fortuna Redux, peace reestablished after civil war. We may observe some marked similarities with the Augustan settlement. Vespasian himself closed the doors of the temple of Janus and initiated a lavish building programme.[38] As Augustus had demolished the extravagant house of Vedius Pollio, replacing it with a portico for public recreation, the *Porticus Liuiae,* so Vespasian, publicizing a break with personal extravagance, replaced Nero's Domus Aurea with the Colosseum. As Tiberius had vowed temples to Concordia and the Dioscuri to celebrate harmony within the Domus Augusta and, in particular, brotherly unity, so Domitian's building programme featured monuments honouring members of the new imperial family. Domitian too marked a new era by holding *Ludi Saeculares* in 88 and reinvigorated Augustus' programme of moral

---

[37] Enn. 94-95 Sk. On the temple of Mars Ultor and this passage, see Newlands (1995) 87-90; Barchiesi (2002) 1-22.

[38] Darwall-Smith (1996). Vespasian's Temple of Peace had a greater affinity with Augustus' Porticus Liuiae than his Forum Augusti, since it was public space featuring a garden for strolling with works of art on display.

and cultural renewal, replacing as his inspiration Palatine Apollo with the virgin goddess Minerva.

The new cycle of civil war and the near destruction of the Capitoline temple left its mark on all three Flavian epics. Valerius' heroes encounter civil conflict at almost every stage of their journey. Statius' Thebes, poetically used by Ovid as a negative model for Rome,[39] provided the setting for 'conflict not simply civil but fratricidal.'[40] Analogies became sharper when the setting was not only Roman but historical. In his *Punica* Silius uses imagery and intertexts drawn from Lucan's Civil War to indicate that first Rome and then later Carthage is destined for defeat, inserting in the Roman ranks at Cannae warriors whose names and characteristics resonate with some of the main players in Rome's civil wars.

When Silius came to describe the aftermath of Rome's defeat at Cannae, this supremely intertextual poet recalled Horace's 7th and 16th *Epodes*. Although Horace and Silius speak from different perspectives within disparate genres, both contrive a poetic resolution to a crisis through interweaving, literally and symbolically, themes of Roman cult and Roman civil war.

Reacting to the crisis in relationships between Octavian, Antony and Sextus Pompeius in 39-38 BC, Horace argues in *Epode* 16 that whereas no foreign enemy has succeeded in destroying Rome, it will be the Romans themselves who destroy their culture from within:

> altera iam teritur bellis ciuilibus aetas
>   suis et ipsa Roma uiribus ruit. (1-2)
>
> Another generation is being worn down by civil strife and Rome is destroying herself.

Contrasting Rome's power to conquer foreign foes with her self-destructive civil wars, he urges his contemporaries to abandon their native gods and shrines to wild beasts in exchange for escape to the realm which Jupiter has prepared for a pious race, *piae genti*, where there are no wars. He describes these putative exiles as *melior pars*[41]

---

[39] Ovid *Met.* 3-4. See Hardie (1990); Feldherr (1997); Braund (2006).
[40] Sen. *Phoen.* 324-325.
[41] Hor. *Epod.* 16.15 and 37.

and men of virtue, *uos quibus est uirtus* (39), in contrast to those who remain in Rome, who are effeminate, *mollis,* and devoid of hope of a better future, *exspes*.[42]

The corresponding incident, which Silius describes, occurs at Canusium after the Roman defeat at Cannae. It is reported as historical by Livy and Valerius Maximus.[43] L. Caecilius Metellus, degenerate son of an illustrious father,[44] plots conspiracy with a group of Roman aristocrats to flee abroad, abandoning Italy to the victorious Carthaginians. Silius presents his intertextual link with Horace in a single word, *impia,* set in the same prominent *sedes*. If we compare Silius' line, *impia formido ac maior iactabat Erinys*,[45] with Horace's, *impia perdemus devoti sanguinis aetas*,[46] it becomes clear that the impious terror and madness which drives Metellus to desertion has the same roots, internal discord, as Horace's *impia aetas*.[47] Whereas Horace urges his Romans flee from *nefas* generated by their *impia aetas*, the Flavian epicist transfers the adjective, *impia,* to the cowardice of the exiles and their leader Metellus, whose evil plot proves his, and their, degeneracy from the virtue of their ancestors.[48] Simultaneously he combines this direct allusion to Horace's *impia aetas* with the madness of Tisiphone, *maior Erinys*,[49] who goads Silius' Saguntines to mass suicide, which was regarded by the Flavian epicists as an allegory for the self-destruction of civil war.[50] Finally, as violators of the Roman military oath of

---

[42] Hor. *Epod.* 16.37-38: *mollis et exspes/ inominata perpremat cubilia!*
[43] Liv. 22.53.5; Val. Max. 5.6.7.
[44] L. Caecilius Metellus (cos. 251, 247 BC) who triumphed after a significant victory at Panormus in the First Punic War and, as Pontifex Maximus, rescued the Palladium from a fire in the temple of Vesta (Ovid *Fast.* 6.437-454).
[45] Sil. *Pun.* 10.419.
[46] Hor. *Epod.* 16.9.
[47] Cf. Verg. *G.* 1.511: *saeuit toto Mars impius orbe*.
[48] Sil. *Pun.* 10.422-423: *degeneremque manum ad deformia .../ consulta*. The name Metellus has ill-omened literary resonances which begin with Horace's allusion to Pollio's history of the civil war, *motum ex Metello consule ciuicum* (Hor. *Carm*. 2.1.1-2). Rome's civil war was thought to originate in the political alliance of Caesar and Pompey during the consulship of Q. Metellus Celer in 60 BC. Cf. Vell. Pat. 2.44.1: *inita potentiae societas quae urbi orbique terrarum… exitiabilis fuit.*
[49] Sil. *Pun.* 2.2.595, 609, 625, 695. Silius' Erinys reappears to inspire self-destruction at the Capuan traitor Virrius' suicidal banquet: *accumbiturque toris epulaturque improba Erinys* (*Pun.* 13.291-293).
[50] Cf. Luc. 4.533-534, where Vulteius and his men are confident that their mass suicide will surpass all previous military *fides* and *pietas* (498-499).

loyalty, Metellus and his companions would suffer vengeance from another *maior Erinys*, who traditionally avenged perjury.[51]

In both poems escape from Roman reality is paramount. Metellus' splinter group of Roman nobles are voluntary exiles, who decide after their defeat at Cannae to flee from the deadliest foe in Horace's list of conquered enemies, *parentibus abominatus Hannibal* (16.8).[52] Horace's poetic 'wherever the wind blows', *quocumque per undas/ Notus uocabit aut proteruus Africus*,[53] corresponds to Silius' vague *trans aequor* (418). All seek a refuge where contact with Rome will be permanently severed. So great is Metellus' revulsion at the memory of Cannae that he and his conspirators desire to consign Rome herself to oblivion, seeking a refuge *alio in orbe* (423), where they will never hear of Rome again: *(nulla) patriae penetraret fama relictae*, (425). Here Silius betrays Metellus' emotion subtly by the word *patria*. Repressed *memoria* in the interest of painless *obliuio* has resonances with Lucan's post Pharsalian vision of Rome, where her *nomina* will be a legend[54] and her illustrious monuments in ruins like Troy.[55]

Historical epic, however, has no place for Horace's illusory escape route to Jupiter's Golden Age paradise, but Silius introduces an intersection with Roman cult in the sanctity of taking and breaking military oaths.[56] In this context Horace too alludes to the exiled Phocaeans, who swore and then rescinded an oath never to return to their country.[57] The adjectives which Silius uses to describe Metellus, *degener* and *deformis*, imply retrogression from the values of Rome's mid-republican nobility, wherein lies the contrast between Metellus, who proves unfaithful to the traditional values of his *gens,* and Rome's future leader, Scipio, whose actions are inspired by *Fides* and *Pietas*. Heralded by a dramatically spondaic line, Scipio, *flammata...mente* (426), confronts

---

[51] Luc. 1.572-576.
[52] Historiographic accounts in Livy (22.53.4-5) and Valerius Maximus (5.6.7).
[53] Hor. *Epod.* 16.22-23.
[54] Luc. 7.391-396.
[55] Luc. 9.973: *nullum sine nomine saxum*.
[56] *Fides* defined by Ennius as observing the sanctity of oath: *qui ius igitur iurandum uiolat, is Fidem uiolat* (Cic. *Off.* 3.104). Silius' stereotypical description of Hannibal: *fideique sinister/ is fuit* (*Pun.* 1.57-58).
[57] Hor. *Ep.* 16.17-18: *Phocaeorum/ uelut profugit execrata ciuitas*. Cf. Hdt. 1.165. Besieged by Persians 540 BC the Phocaeans prefer exile to surrender, but nevertheless break their oath by returning to Phocaea.

the conspirators. With sword drawn, he prescribes a potent oath of loyalty which invokes all that is sacred to Roman patriots: each member of the Capitoline triad, the Dei Indigetes, Rome's most ancient ktistic gods, and, as a sign of his outstanding *pietas,* the life of his father: *perque caput nullo leuius mihi numine patris* (437). The conspirators purge their guilt by swearing a new oath of military loyalty[58] and the *Furor* of civil dissent is extinguished within the Roman ranks.

Scipio's decisive action against Metellus' short-lived rebellion reflects two Flavian cultural attitudes: antipathy to internal division and the high value set on powerful leadership in the pursuit of Roman conquest and imperialism. Among the writers of the Flavian period the intersection of Roman cult with civil war has strong moral and philosophical overtones. To underline the perversity of civil war Statius describes the *nefas* of his Theban conflict with vocabulary associated with religious ritual, *instaurare* and *firmare*.[59] He expresses the antipathy of Oedipus' sons through the cultic ritual of their shared funeral pyre where the flame divides and the logs, even the remnants of their shattered bodies, symbolically recoil one from another.[60] The recurrent poetic motif that civil war equalled Rome's self-destruction[61] was allegorized by the Flavian writers in horrific scenes of mass suicide. At this period Ovid's entertaining exegeses of cultic justification for the Battle of Philippi were superseded by angst-filled Flavian imagery and Rome's pastoral ktistic fratricide eclipsed by the dark hatred of Statius' sons of Oedipus, which, for some contemporaries, hinted at the danger of jealous rivalry within the family of Vespasian.[62]

---

[58] *Pun.* 10.447-448: *dictataque iurant/ sacramenta deis et purgant pectora culpa.*
[59] Stat. *Theb.* 11.497-508. Cf. Virg. *Aen.*10.543-544, 2.689-693. On this see Bessone (2018).
[60] Stat. *Theb.* 12.429-48.
[61] Erinys, as well as Tisiphone, appears to drive citizens to kill themselves in Sil. *Pun.* 2.595, 609, 625, 695 and 13.291-293, where Virrius and his companions resort to voluntary suicide prompted by *despecta et violata Fides*.
[62] See McNelis (2007) 5-6.

Bibliography

Barchiesi, A. (1997), *The Poet and the Prince. Ovid and Augustan Discourse*, Berkeley/ Los Angeles/ London, p. 128.
Barchiesi, A. (2002), '*Martial Arts. Mars Ultor* in the *Forum Augustum*: a Verbal Monument with Vengeance', in G. Herbert-Brown (ed.), *Ovid's Fasti. Historical Readings at its Bimillennium*, Oxford.
Beard, M. (1988), 'A Complex of times: No more sheep on Romulus' birthday', *Proceedings of the Cambridge Philological Society* 33, 1-15.
Beard, M. (1995), 'Rereading Vestal Virginity', in R. Hawley, B. Levick (edd.), *Women in Antiquity. New Assessments*, London, 166-177.
Bessone, F. (2018), 'Signs of Discord. Statius' Style and the Traditions on Civil War', in L. Ginsberg, D. Krasne (edd.), *After 69CE: Writing Civil War in Flavian Rome*, Berlin/ Boston, 89-107.
Braund, S. (2006), 'A Tale of Two Cities: Statius, Thebes and Rome', *Phoenix* 60, 259-276.
Castagnoli, F. (1972), *Lavinium*, Rome.
Darwall-Smith, R.H. (1996), *Emperors and Architecture. Flavian Rome*, Brussels.
Erskine, A. (2001), *Troy between Greece and Rome*, Oxford.
Feeney, D. (1992), '*Si licet et fas est:* Ovid's *Fasti* and the problem of free speech under the Principate', in A. Powell (ed.), *Roman Poetry and Propaganda in the Age of Augustus*, Bristol, 1-25.
Feldherr, A. (1997), 'Metamorphosis and Sacrifice in Ovid's Theban narrative', *Materiali e discussioni per l'analisi dei testi classici* 38, 25-55.
Fraschetti, A. (1988), '*Cognata numina*: culti della citta e culti della casa del principe in epoca Augustea', *Studi Storici* 29, 941-965.
Fraschetti, A. (1990), *Il Principe e Roma*, Rome/ Bari.
Girard, R. (1977), *Violence and the Sacred*, transl. P. Gregory, Baltimore/ London.
Hardie, P.R. (1990), 'Ovid's Theban History: the first anti-Aeneid?', *Classical Quarterly* 40, 224-235.
Herbert-Brown, G. (1994), *Ovid and the Fasti. A Historical Study*, Oxford.

Holloway, R.R. (1994), *The Archaeology between Early Rome and Latium*, London.

Jal, P. (1963), *La Guerre Civile à Rome: étude littéraire et morale*, Paris.

Kellum, B. (1985), 'Sculptural Programs and Propaganda in Augustan Rome: the temple of Apollo on the Palatine,' in R. Winkes (ed.), *The Age of Augustus*, Louvain, 169-176.

Kellum, B. (1990), 'The City Adorned: Programmatic Display at the Aedes Concordiae Augustae', in K. Raaflaub, M. Toher (edd.), *Between Republic and Empire. Representations of Augustus and his Principate*, Berkeley, 276-307.

Koortbojian, M. (2013), *The Divinization of Caesar and Augustus. Precedents, Consequences, Implications*, Cambridge.

Labate, M., Rosati, G. (2013), *Tua, Caesar, aetas: un personaggio, un'epoca, un mito. Riflessioni preliminari*, Heidelberg.

Littlewood, R.J. (2006), *A Commentary on Ovid's* Fasti, *Book 6*, Oxford.

Littlewood, R.J. (2017), *A Commentary on Silius Italicus'* Punica *10*, Oxford.

Lott, J.B. (2004), *The Neighbourhoods of Augustan Rome*, Cambridge.

McNelis, C. (2007), *Statius'* Thebaid *and the Poetics of Civil War*, Cambridge.

Newlands, C.E. (1995), *Playing with Time. Ovid and the Fasti*, Ithaca.

Parker, H.N. (2004), 'Why were the Vestals Virgins?', *American Journal of Philology* 125, 565-601.

Pomeroy, A. (2008), '*Fides* in Silius Italicus' *Punica*', in F. Schaffenrath (ed.), *Silius Italicus: Akten der Innsbrucker Tagung vom 19-21 Juni 2008*, Frankfurt am Main, 59-76.

Robinson, M. (2011), *A Commentary on Ovid's* Fasti, *Book 2*, Oxford.

Roche, P. (2009), *Lucan. De bello ciuili, Book 1*, edited with a commentary, Oxford.

Stöckinger, M. (2013), 'Inalienable Possessions : the *di penates* in the Aeneid and in Augustan Culture', in M. Labate, G. Rosati (edd.), *Tua, Caesar, aetas: un personaggio, un'epoca, un mito: riflessioni preliminari*, Heidelberg.

Tarrant, R. (2012), *Virgil, Aeneid, Book 12*, Cambridge.

Weinstock, S. (1960) 'Two archaic Inscriptions from Latium,' *Journal of Roman studies* 50, 112-118.
Weinstock, S. (1971), *Divus Iulius*, Oxford.
Wiseman, T.P. (1995), *Remus. A Roman Myth*, Cambridge.
Zanker, P. (1988), *The Power of Images in the Age of Augustus*, transl. A. Shapiro, Ann Arbor.

Ovidian 'Learning' in *Heroides* 20 and 21 (Acontius and Cydippe)*

FRANCIS CAIRNS
The Florida State University

Heroides 20 and 21 are the *Epistles* exchanged by the lovers Acontius and Cydippe. The first extant version of their love-story is preserved in the *Aetia* (fr. 67-75 Pf.) of Callimachus, who says he found the tale in the Cean history of the local historian Xenomedes (*Aetia* fr. 75.53-5, 74-77 Pf.). E.J. Kenney summarised the story economically:

> Acontius, a beautiful boy from Ceos, fell in love with the equally beautiful Cydippe of Naxos on seeing her at a festival in Delos. He threw in the way of her nurse an apple on which he had written 'I swear by Artemis to marry Acontius.' The nurse picked it up and being unable to read, asked Cydippe to read the inscription, which she did, aloud. She kept the incident to herself and returned to Naxos and to the marriage which her father had already arranged for her. Meanwhile Acontius had also gone home, where he betook himself into the countryside to lament his situation and carve her name on the trees. In Naxos a day was three times arranged for Cydippe's wedding, but three times she mysteriously fell ill so that it could not take place. The fourth time her father went to Delphi, where Apollo told him of the oath and advised him to fulfil it. So Acontius and Cydippe were married and founded the distinguished clan of the Acontiadae.
>
> Kenney (1996) 15-16

In this paper I want to examine some elements of *Heroides* 20 and 21 which can be classified loosely as examples of Ovidian 'learning'.[1]

---

* This is a revised and lightly annotated version of a paper delivered on 26th September 2014 at *XIV AD Saeculum Augustum International Conference. The Age of Augustus*, Universidade de Lisboa, Faculdade de Letras. Translations of passages from the two *Heroides* to a large extent are, or derive from, those of Kenney (1996), with certain modifications. I have made my own decisions about Latin texts. I am grateful to Darja Šterbenc Erker and Kris Fletcher for advice given after the delivery of the paper; they are, of course, not responsible for its faults.

[1] In another paper on *Heroides* 20 and 21 presented on 1st February 2014 at the E. Togo Salmon Graduate Conference in Classical Studies, McMaster University I discussed aspects of the two *Epistles*' intertextual relations with earlier poetic texts. The contents of that presentation and of this paper will contribute to a comprehensive article on *Heroides* 20 and 21.

The first two involve areas of technical expertise. Hellenistic poets like Ovid were expected to know what they were talking about when they handled technical subjects, ranging from the most intellectual – astronomy, physics, philosophy, medicine, geography, botany, zoology and so forth – to the most banausic, for example the tools and skills of the farmer, the road-maker, or the carpenter. I shall argue for Ovid's competence first in an intellectual area, Roman law, and then in the everyday craft of sailing in the Aegean. Both these areas, I shall suggest, bring us close to Ovid's real-life experiences. I shall then explore some undervalued or unnoticed aspects of Ovid's *doctrina*; this will involve topics falling under the heading of '(book)-learning' as it is more narrowly understood by specialists in Hellenistic poetry, that is, meta-literary and programmatic uses of imagery, lexicography, textual criticism, and Homeric scholarship. Ovid is not usually credited with the same deep interest in these topics as characterises his Hellenistic Greek predecessors. But what emerges even from a cursory study of these two *Heroides* is that he was more assiduously 'learned' in the Hellenistic sense than his casual façade might suggest.

The present paper assumes the advances in the understanding and appreciation of Ovid's double *Heroides* made by E.J. Kenney, whose Commentary on *Epistles* 16-21 and article of 1999[2] established beyond doubt their Ovidian authorship, and whose articles of 1969 and 1970 on legal references in *Heroides* 20 and 21 and elsewhere in Ovid showed that of the three surviving Roman elegists he had the greatest interest in, and knowledge of, Roman civil and criminal law. The part played by legalisms in the two *Heroides*, especially in *Epistle* 20, is quite remarkable. *Epistle* 20 is packed with terms and concepts in which Ovid's original audiences would have perceived a legal or quasi-legal flavour – whether or not they were precise technicalities of Roman law. There is, of course, nothing surprising about a Roman poet introducing references to the law.[3] Many Roman poets, including Horace, Tibullus,

---

[2] Kenney (1996), (1999). The translations of *Her.* 20 and 21 offered or implied by Kenney (1996) are utilised freely in this paper, with adaptations where appropriate.

[3] Prop. 1.18, itself also based (perhaps at one remove) on Callimachus' Acontius and Cydippe episode, is cast generically as a defence speech, and this may have influenced *Her.* 20 and 21.

and Propertius, do so,[4] and they could expect their allusions to be grasped because every Roman citizen needed a modicum of legal knowledge in order to function competently as a citizen; Cicero even claims that Roman boys up to the time of his youth learned the Twelve Tables by heart in school.[5] Ovid was particularly prone to legalisms and quasi-legalisms for reasons discussed below.

Much of the legal material of *Heroides* 20 and 21 has long been known.[6] J. van Iddekinge's brief treatise of 1811 had already identified some of it; it was then discussed more systematically in the first decade of the twentieth century by M.M. Pokrowskij,[7] and finally Kenney, in his article of 1970, analysed most of it in detail. It perhaps goes without saying that Ovid's handling of legalisms is by no means straightforward or serious. Many of the legalistic claims which he puts into the mouth of Acontius in *Epistle* 20 are wittily irrelevant, or questionable, or actually contrary to Roman law; similarly Cydippe's attempts to play the lawyer in *Epistle* 21 are comically inadequate.[8] Ovid's wit, however, does not mean that his knowledge of and interest in a wide range of technical legal topics is superficial.

Legalisms detected by earlier scholarship in *Epistle* 20, where their density is greater, plus a few items added by myself, are as follows (some of the same legal material recurs in *Epistle* 21):

1. legal obligation created by *sponsio* in the *sponsalia* ceremony (20.27-29);
2. employment of a jurisconsult (20.30);
3. denials of due process through trial *in absentia* (20.79, 91);
4. the lack of a *patronus* (20.91);
5. *dominium, manus iniectio, uindicatio*, the formal claim *meus(a) est* used in transfers of quiritary ownership (*dominium*) and *manumissio*, and the analogous *nostra futura est* (20.145-150);

---

[4] Tibullus, who was a soldier by profession, employs few legalisms; for discussion of them cf. Gebhardt (2009) Index I: Verzeichnis der beschprochenen Textstellen s.v. Tibull. Propertius (for whose legalisms cf. ibid. s.v. Properz) introduces them much more freely, in part because he was intended for a legal career and received some legal instruction: cf. Cairns (2006) 27-28.

[5] Cf. Cic. *De Leg.* 2.59: *discebamus enim pueri XII ut carmen necessarium, quas iam nemo discit.* The status of this claim is uncertain: Cicero may be indulging in a myth of 'the good old days', i.e., either exaggerating the achievements of his own generation, or understating the later continuation of the practice.

[6] van Iddekinge (1811) 16, 25, 32-33, 57, 71, 74, 90, 96, 98.

[7] Pokrowskij (1907-1910). Pokrowskij's findings were reworked by Coletti (1962) 294-299.

6. *adulterium* (20.148);
7. *ius iurandum*, i.e. Cydippe's oath, repeatedly mentioned or referred to from line 1's *iurabis* on, along with its concomitants and consequences. *promittere* and the more formal *spondere* are sometimes substituted, and *ius* and *iura* occur frequently, as do *iniuria* and *periuria* and *perfida* and *adiuro* and *pango*; *fides*, *dolus* and *fraus* appear throughout, *foedus* occasionally. *teste*, *testificatur* and *testatur* stress that Cydippe's oath was witnessed by the goddess Diana (Artemis), and *noceo*, *poena*, and *fallere* are legal in context;
8. *pactum conuentum*.[9]

My more detailed remarks will be confined to *pactum conuentum*; this last legal area of *Epistle* 20 has not been sufficiently emphasised in past scholarship, and it brings us close to the personality and life of the poet Ovid. In 20.151-158 Acontius invokes 'pactum conuentum' when (in his own imagination) he is arguing against his rival for Cydippe's hand:

> nec mihi credideris; recitetur <u>formula pacti;</u>
>   neu falsam dicas esse, fac ipsa legat.
> alterius thalamo, tibi nos, tibi dicimus, exi;
>   quid facis hic? exi: non uacat iste torus.
> nam quod habes et tu <u>gemini uerba altera pacti,</u>   155
>   non erit idcirco par tua causa meae.
> <u>haec mihi se pepigit,</u> pater hanc tibi, primus ab illa;
>   sed propior certe quam pater ipsa sibi est.

> And don't take my word for it – let us have the *actual terms of the agreement* read out; and, so you don't say it is untrue, let her read it herself! Get out of someone else's marriage chamber, yes, you, it's you I'm talking to! What are you doing here? Out! That bed is not free! Although you too have *the text of another agreement identical with mine*, your case is not, as you will find, for that reason equal with mine. *She agreed to give herself to me*, her father her to you; he is first (but only) after her; but she is surely more closely related to herself than is her father.[10]

---

[8] I shall expand on these topics in the comprehensive article referred to in n. 1.

[9] A possible addition to this list, but only if the emendation proposed at *Her*. 20.144 by Hollis (1994) is correct, would be a joking reference there to Roman law provisions about rights of way.

[10] Cf. Kenney (1996) 204-205 on lines 151-158.

Pacti (151, 155) and *pepigit* (157) are unmistakable references to *pactum conuentum*,[11] which was an informal agreement between two parties. Such agreements were nevertheless legally enforceable because the praetor in his *edictum praetorium de pactis* had undertaken to enforce them:[12]

> Ait praetor: 'Pacta conuenta, quae neque dolo malo, neque aduersus leges plebis scita senatus consulta <decreta> edicta principum, neque quo fraus cui eorum fiat facta erunt, seruabo.'
>
> The praetor declares 'I shall protect *pacta conuenta* (i.e. agreements, mutual understandings) which were concluded neither by fraud, nor contrary to statutes, plebiscites, resolutions of the senate, imperial decrees, or edicts, nor with the intention to evade fraudulently one of those enactments.'
>
> *Digest* 2.14.7.7
> transl. Berger (1953) s.v. *pactum*, adapted

The praetor went on in his edict to declare that he would not uphold an agreement not based on good faith: *Dolo malo ait praetor pactum se non seruaturum*. The *Digest* then defines *dolus malus* as 'the product of cunning and deceit': *dolus malus fit calliditate et fallacia* (2.14.7.9).

These extracts from the praetorian edict show that Ovid was thinking about the entire legal context of *pactum conuentum* when composing *Heroides* 20 and 21, and that he had in mind the legal defences of *dolus malus* and *fraus* available to defendants brought into court for a breach of *pactum conuentum*. Acontius had already undercut his own case when earlier in *Epistle* 20 he had admitted his *fraus* and *dolus*:

> sit fraus huic facto nomen, dicarque dolosus,
>   si tamen est quod ames uelle tenere dolus.
>   31-32
>
> Let my deed be called 'fraud' and let me be called 'in bad faith', but only if it is 'bad faith' to want to possess what you love.

This concession, along with Acontius' admission of his own *calliditas* in lines 25 and 126 (in further references to the praetor's

---

[11] Pace Coletti (1962) 295 n.3 (unduly sceptical).
[12] Acontius had referred to the same concept earlier when he said that he was seeking the fulfilment of *pactam fidem, non crimina* (20.7).

edict) completely undermine his claim of *pactum conuentum*; and they show that Acontius' repeated legalistic assertions about oaths, promises and so forth have at the end of the day no legal merit. They also make clear Ovid's lively interest in the concept of *pactum conuentum*.

One reason why Ovid was so concerned about *pactum conuentum* was because of the importance of this legal institution in Ovid's career and everyday life. Ovid was destined by his father for the law and the senate, and he was given the *latus clauus* by Augustus.[13] His family was locally important but had no earlier senators, so he started his career in the vigintivirate, where he apparently served in two annual junior magistracies, both legal in nature; this iterated service was typical of men lacking a senatorial background. Ovid was first a *tresuir capitalis*,[14] one of the three judges in the criminal court which dealt summarily with offences committed by the lower orders in Rome; then he was a *decemuir stlitibus iudicandis*,[15] one of the magistrates who presided in the centumviral court. Ovid also served later as one of the *centumuiri*, and his name appeared in the *Album Iudicum*, the list from which judges in private cases were selected:

> nec male commissa est nobis fortuna reorum
>   lisque decem deciens inspicienda uiris.
> res quoque privatas statui sine crimine iudex,
>   deque mea fassa est pars quoque uicta fide.
>
> *Tristia* 2.1.93-96

> The fate of those on trial was well entrusted to me, as were lawsuits to be tried before the *decemuiri*. I also adjudicated private cases, and my judgements were not impugned: even the losers admitted my good faith.[16]

So, although Ovid abandoned his aspirations for a senatorial career after the vigintivirate, he remained a legal practitioner, which goes far to explain the high legal content of his poetry. He will have continued to

---

[13] Ov. *Tr.* 4.10.29.
[14] Cf. Ov. *Tr.* 4.10.33-34; Ovid describes himself ambivalently there as a 'tresuir', but he cannot have been a *monetalis*, since this office was reserved for men of senatorial ancestry. His role as a 'IIIuir capitalis' seems confirmed by *Tr.* 2.1.93.
[15] Cf. also Ov. *Fast.* 4.384.
[16] See Owen (1924) 139-141 ad loc., *Tr.* 2.541-5422 (Ovid's equestrian status) with Owen (1924) 278 ad loc., Bablitz (2007) 98-99.

act as a *iudex* as long as he was in Rome; and most of the cases which he decided will have been disputes about the performance or non-performance of informal agreements – *pacta conuenta*. That is why *pactum conuentum* is a major and live issue in *Epistle* 20.

Ovid's expertise in nautical matters can now be considered. For Acontius to encounter Cydippe on Delos, Cydippe had to sail to Delos from Naxos. In *Epistle* 21 Cydippe describes her journey:

> tunc mea difficili deducta est aequore nauis,
>   et fuit ad coeptas hora sinistra uias.
> quo pede processi? quo me pede limine moui?
>   picta citae tetigi quo pede texta ratis?   70
> bis tamen aduerso redierunt carbasa uento;
>   mentior, a demens! ille secundus erat!
> ille secundus erat qui me referebat euntem,
>   quique parum felix inpediebat iter.
> atque utinam constans contra mea uela fuisset;   75
>   sed stultum est uenti de leuitate queri.
> mota loci fama properabam uisere Delon
>   et facere ignaua puppe uidebar iter.
> quam saepe ut tardis feci conuicia remis,
>   questaque sum uento lintea parca dari!   80
> et iam transieram Myconon, iam Tenon et Andron,
>   inque meis oculis candida Delos erat;
> quam procul ut uidi, 'quid me fugis, insula,' dixi,
>   'laberis in magno numquid, ut ante, mari?'
>   *Heroides* 21.67-84

My ship was launched then on a troublesome sea, and it was an ill-omened hour to start a journey. With what step did I come forth! With what step did I leave the threshold? With what step did I board the swift painted ship? Twice, however, my sail-boat returned to port driven by the unfavourable wind. Ah, I am crazy, I lie – it was a favourable wind! It was a favourable wind that tried to bring me back as I went, and tried to hinder a journey that held little happiness for me. I wish it had blown consistently against my sails – but it is foolish to complain of the fickleness of a wind. Moved by the fame of the place I was in eager haste to visit Delos, and I thought I was travelling on a sluggish ship. How often I railed at the oars for being slow and complained that not enough canvas was being loosed to the wind! And now I had passed by Myconos, now Tenos and Andros, and white Delos was before my eyes. When I saw it from far off, 'Island, why are you eluding me?' I cried; 'surely you are not afloat in the great sea as you were before?'

Cydippe's account is intriguing in a number of ways. It occupies 18 lines, the same number as is allocated to the description of her stay on Delos which follows (21.85-102), and much of Cydippe's narrative is taken up with the checks which delayed her voyage; her vessel was twice driven back to port by adverse winds (71-74); she complains that it was slow with sluggish oars and (so she thought) an inadequate amount of sail (78-80). These comments are probably sly jokes about Cydippe's lack of expertise in sailing. Then at last Cydippe passes Myconos, and then Tenos and Andros, and finally she can see Delos, although Delos is still elusive (81-82).

Kenney did not think that Cydippe's account was credible in factual terms; he commented:

> From Naxos to Delos is barely 20 miles. A glance at the map will show that the direct voyage from Naxos to Delos does not take one past Andros and Tenos, and only by a stretch of language past Myconos. It seems that the ship bucketed around the Aegean for several days (cf. 83-4); but a head wind would have taken her S., not N.W. of her destination. Much ink has been spilled on the problem; the simplest solution is that O. liked the sound of the names and sacrificed geographical accuracy to poetic atmosphere.
>
> Kenney (1996) 226 on lines 81-82

More recently another scholar has tried to explain Cydippe's account by claiming that Ovid was composing something akin to a *technopaignion* in line 81: 'The direction of writing from left to right seems to correspond to the south to northern geographical location of the islands.'[17]

Both these approaches are inherently implausible. What could have motivated Ovid to give an account of the Naxos-Delos voyage which, if his modern commentators are to be believed, would have struck many of his contemporary Roman readers as inaccurate? After all, Delos had been under the effective control of Rome since 166 BC, when Rome entrusted its administration to Athens, and it was one of the main centres of Aegean trade and shipping for some hundred years thereafter; it was in decline in Ovid's day but was still a famous site. Some of Ovid's readers would have visited Delos or had friends who had been there; so they would have known about travel in the sea-lanes around Delos, and,

---

[17] Kyriakidis (2010) 9-10, 9.

if Ovid had given an unrealistic account of a voyage in those parts, this would not have enhanced his poetic reputation. I suggest instead that Cydippe's voyage is an accurate depiction of what travellers sailing to Delos from Naxos might have experienced in Ovid's day, and might still experience nowadays if travelling in a sail-boat.

A preliminary question about Ovid's account of Cydippe's voyage is whether he knew when the Delian festival, for which (in Ovid's imagination) Acontius and Cydippe came to the island, was celebrated. It is unlikely that he did: the two possible festivals (on these see further below) were held in the Delian months *Hieros* (February/ March) and *Lenaion* (January/ February), i.e. outside the normal Greek sailing season: and, if Ovid had envisaged her voyage as taking place in those months, he would surely have commented on its unusual timing.[18] He presumably assumed that Cydippe sailed in the summer/autumn months. A voyage from Naxos to Delos at that time would still have been problematic. Here are some extracts from a modern web-site offering travel advice for those sailing in the tourist season from Paros, Naxos's neighbour island, to Myconos, the larger island near Delos:

> Transportation between Paros and Mykonos is tricky ... As there is an international airport in Mykonos, it is wise not to wait for the last day to catch your flight, but to go back there one day earlier! ... Try to avoid old boats ... Do not rely on information that the weather will 'certainly' be good – even if it looks as if it might not change! ... Please!!! DO NOT rely on the last boat to take you to your destination. At least take the second before last to make sure you do not miss your flight! (We have seen it happen – often!) ... Beware: The weather can be very calm and beautiful – but ... They say that the Aegean Sea is the most dangerous in the world because it can change drastically within just minutes.
> www.paros-online.com/en/ferry-travel (accessed 13/08/2014)

The sailing conditions around Delos are not unique to that area; they are typical of the central Aegean in general. James Beresford has described the two main factors involved, the Etesian winds and the sea-currents:

> ... across the Aegean it is the etesians that govern the wind regime throughout the summer months. They blow from either the north or northeast in the central and northern regions of the summertime Aegean ... Graeco-Roman

---

[18] *Her.* 21.67-68 are too generalised and conventional to be construed as such a comment.

> vessels heading for the northern reaches of the Aegean would have had to undertake voyages which involved sailing directly into the face of the wind. The problems ... were compounded by the fact that the sea-currents, like the prevailing winds, also flow to the south. Although the speed of the Aegean's currents rarely exceeds 1/2 knot ..., strong etesian winds will increase their velocity, especially in the channels that separate the numerous islands from each other and the mainland, making straits like those of Euboea, Andros, Tenos and Mykonos even more difficult to negotiate for vessels attempting to make progress to the north during the summer sailing season.
>
> Beresford (2013) 80-81[19]

The upshot is that, for Cydippe's ship to have gone in a straight line from Naxos to Delos, it would have needed to sail (and row)[20] directly into the wind. This would have been impossible: ancient ships could certainly sail against the wind,[21] but at best they could sail no closer than 70 degrees to the wind.[22] That is the explanation of how Cydippe could have 'passed' Andros, Tenos and Myconos – not because Ovid 'liked the sound of the names' or was composing a species of *technopaignion*, but because ancient ships could not sail on a straight course from Naxos to Delos in summer/autumn. An ancient sailing vessel would have had to tack, probably several times, in a north-easterly or north-westerly direction before approaching Delos from the north-east or north-west. Cydippe's imagined route cannot be reconstructed with certainty, but since Syros is not mentioned, and since the straits to the west were dangerous,[23] Ovid may have been thinking of her vessel as taking the eastern route to Delos.

There is an interesting confirmation of Ovid's awareness of winds and currents in the Aegean at *Metamorphoses* 13.630. Virgil had described how the Trojans sailed from Thrace to Delos with the aid

---

[19] Beresford (2013) 81-82 added another factor which affects sailing in the Northern Aegean, namely the huge outflow of water from the Black Sea in the late spring and early summer which increased the south-flowing current; this will, however, have had a lesser effect in the central Aegean.

[20] No wonder Cydippe was complaining about sluggish oars!

[21] '...even when it came to sailing against the wind, the abilities of the brailed square sail have been consistently underrated and trials of replicated Graeco-Roman ships indicate that windward sailing was feasible using the sail technology of antiquity.' (Beresford [2013] 164, with evidence.)

[22] See Beresford (2013) 163-168.

[23] See the passage quoted above from Beresford (2013) 80-81.

of *Auster*, the South Wind (*Aeneid* 3.61, 70). This is, of course, an impossibility since the Trojans were sailing south, and Ovid in retelling the story corrected Virgil by wittily substituting 'utilibus ventis aestuque secundo' (with useful/ usable winds and a favouring current).[24] It should be no surprise, then, that Ovid has given us an accurate account of a voyage from Naxos to Delos: he could himself have experienced it, or heard about it from a friend, or read about it. The travelogue which follows at 21.95-102, the description of Delos through the medium of Cydippe's sightseeing there (21.65-102), also shows Ovid aiming at the technical accuracy which learned Hellenistic and Roman poets prized. The main attractions of Delos – the temples, porticos, and statues, the horn altar, and the tree that Leto held onto while giving birth – are ticked off one by one. The narrative of Cydippe's voyage and her stay and sightseeing on Delos, which is almost certainly longer than anything that might have corresponded to it in Callimachus' *Aetia*, gives *Epistle* 21 greater depth and verisimilitude; it also seems to reflect real-life experience.

The examples of Ovid's *doctrina* which follow belong to categories more commonly characterised as 'learning' by students of Hellenistic poetry, viz. programmatic declarations employing symbolic imagery, lexicography, textual criticism, and Homeric scholarship. While composing *Heroides* 20 and 21, with their background in one of Callimachus' *aetia*, Ovid seems to have been keenly aware of the celebrated and much imitated programmatic prologue of the entire *Aetia* (fr. 1 Pf.), and of other Callimachean literary programmes. Ovid alludes to three key concepts associated with them: avoidance of length, *doctrina* itself, and *ponos/ labor*. They have been discussed summarily by Alessandro Barchiesi,[25] and here too they can be handled briefly. In *Aetia* fr. 1.4 Pf. Callimachus indirectly rejected the notion of writing 'tens of thousands of lines'.[26] Ovid picks up this idea at various places in the two epistles: he makes both Acontius and Cydippe reject excessive length when writing their letters:

---

[24] See Casali (2007) 188-189.
[25] Barchiesi (1993) 356-357.
[26] In *Aetia* fr. 1.3 Pf. Callimachus linked his rejection of length with ἓν ἄεισμα διηνεκές (one continuous poem), but his Roman followers sometimes appear to ignore that qualification.

> longior infirmum ne lasset epistula corpus   20.241
>
> so that a longer letter may not tire your sick body
>
> iam satis invalidos calamo lassauimus artus
>   et manus officium longius aegra negat.   21.245-246
>
> Now I have tired my weak limbs sufficiently with writing, and my sick hand refuses to do its duty any longer.

Similarly Cydippe comments on her own thinness and physical weakness in a writing context, and thinness is a well known image for the stylistic self-restraint to which Callimachus, his predecessor Philetas, and their followers aspired:

> quam tibi nunc gracilem uix haec rescribere quamque
>   pallida uix cubito membra leuare putas?   21.15-16
>
> How wasted away do you think she is who can scarcely pen this answer to you, how sallow the limbs that she can scarcely raise on one arm?[27]

Cydippe's thinness and pallor also feature at 21.215-220.

Doctrina itself surfaces in remarks made by both Acontius and Cydippe about the 'learning' of Acontius' inscription upon the apple:

> *uerba* ferens doctis insidiosa notis   20.210
>
> bearing deceitful words in learned signs
>
> inque parum fausto *carmine* docta fui.   21.182
>
> I was 'learned' when I read an ill-omened verse

In both these passages *doctis/ docta* may also refer to Callimachus' ἐδίδαξεν (fr. 67.1).

Ponos/ labor appears in Cydippe's complaint about the *labor* that writing her letter to Acontius demands:

> inde meos digitos iterum repetita fatigat;
>   quantus sit nobis aspicis ipse labor.   21.27-28[28]

---

[27] Contrast, however, Kenney (1996) 217 on lines 15-16.
[28] It may or may not also be relevant that Acontius claims that both Diana and he himself are 'labouring' on Cydippe's behalf: *consulit ipsa tibi, neu sis periura, laborat,/ et saluam salua te cupit esse fide* (20.111-112); *non agitur de me; cura maiore laboro./ anxia sunt causa pectora nostra tua* (20.197-198).

Taken out again from there it fatigues my fingers; you can see for yourself what toil it cost me.

Next are some examples of Ovidian *doctrina* in the two Epistles with a more general background in the learned activities of the Hellenistic *grammatici*. Ovid and his contemporaries studied Greek poetry with Greek teachers, and they encountered not just the texts of Greek poets, but also the scholia to their works, along with the ancestors of the lexica which have survived from late antiquity. It is no surprise, then, that Ovid was aware of ancient lexical controversies about terms used by Callimachus in his Acontius and Cydippe *aetion*, and that Ovid reflects these controversies in *Heroides* 20 and 21. Two examples of this have received some attention in earlier scholarship, but I want to focus more sharply on them here: they are πολύκροτος (fr. 67.3 Pf.), and the name 'Acontius'.

Callimachus described Acontius as 'not ... πολύκροτος':

Αὐτὸς Ἔρως ἐδίδαξεν Ἀκόντιον, ὁππότε καλῇ
ἤθετο Κυδίππῃ παῖς ἐπὶ παρθενικῇ,
τέχνην – οὐ γὰρ ὅγ' ἔσκε πολύκροτος – ὄφρα λέγο..[
τοῦτο διὰ ζωῆς οὔνομα κουρίδιον.

fr. 67.1-4 Pf.

Eros himself *taught* Acontius, when the boy burned
  with *love* for the girl Cydippe,
his tricks – for he was not very *cunning* – in order that ...
  all through his life ... that lawful *name*.

transl. Harder (2012) 1.231

The meaning of πολύκροτος was disputed in antiquity: it was glossed either as 'cunning', or as 'noisy'/ 'talkative'.[29] In *Epistle* 20.21-32 there is a whole series of allusions to πολύκροτος and its Callimachean context;[30] Ovid for the most part accepts the meaning 'cunning', and it is always either the cunning of Acontius or the cunning of his teacher, Amor.

<u>deceptam</u> dicas nostra te <u>fraude</u> licebit,
  dum <u>fraudis</u> nostrae causa feratur *amor*.

---

[29] For πολύκροτος cf. Coletti (1962) 299-301, Cairns (2003), Harder (2012) 2.551 ad loc.
[30] For etymological and other aspects of this passage not covered here cf. Cairns (2002), (2003).

<u>fraus</u> mea quid petiit, nisi uti tibi iungerer uni?
    id me, quod quereris, conciliare potest.
<u>non</u> ego natura nec sum tam <u>callidus</u> usu;   25
    <u>sollertem</u> tu me, crede, puella, facis.
te mihi *<u>conpositis</u>*, siquid tamen egimus, a me
    astrinxit <u>*uerbis* ingeniosus</u> *Amor*.
<u>*dictatis*</u> ab eo feci sponsalia <u>*uerbis*</u>,
    consultoque fui iuris *Amore* <u>uafer</u>.   30
sit <u>fraus</u> huic facto <u>nomen, dicarque dolosus</u>,
    si tamen est, quod *ames*, uelle tenere <u>*dolus*</u>!
                                        20.21-32

You are welcome to say that you were <u>deceived</u> by my <u>fraudulence</u>, provided you accept that the reason for my <u>fraudulence</u> was *love*. What else did my <u>fraudulence</u> aim at except my union with you and only you? What you are complaining about ought to make me acceptable to you. I am not <u>cunning</u> by nature or through practice; it is you, girl, who make me <u>crafty</u>. If I played any part, it was in fact the clever *Love-god* who bound you to me with <u>the words that I wrote down</u>. It was with words <u>*dictated by him*</u> that I betrothed us, and I became <u>cunning</u> by using *Love* as my legal adviser. This action may be *named* <u>'fraudulence'</u>, and <u>I may be called 'cunning'</u>, if it is *guile* to want to possess what you *love*.

deceptam fraude (21), *fraudis* (22), *fraus* (23), *callidus* (25), *sollertem* (26), *ingeniosus* (28), *vafer* (30), *dolosus* (31) and *dolus* (32) – all these words and phrases by implication assign the sense 'cunning'[31] to the disputed πολύκροτος. In her Commentary on the *Aetia* Annette Harder opined that Callimachus had exploited both meanings, but that Ovid opted only for 'cunning'. Her remark about Callimachus is correct, but the repeated *uerbis* of lines 28 and 29 points to the alternative meaning 'talkative' and reveals that Ovid also knew the alternative explanation of πολύκροτος. Indeed Ovid's phrase *uerbis ingeniosus* (28) combines the two glosses, with *uerbis* (29) underscoring the point.[32] *Amor* is present three times in this passage (22, 28, 30) to echo Callimachus' Ἔρως (1), and *dicar* and *nomen* (31) correspond with Callimachus'

---

[31] Harder (2012) 2.550-551 on fr. 67.3 Pf.
[32] In line 27 Gω offer *arte*; Barchiesi (1993) 356 apparently accepts this reading and points out several possible implications. If it is correct, *arte* reflects τέχνην in *Aetia* fr. 67.3 Pf. *artes* in 20.47 (*si non proficient artes, ueniemus ad arma*) is another possible reference; see also below on 21.222.

οὔνομα (4); these terms of course function as 'etymological markers'.[33] There may be a further correspondence between ἐδίδαξεν (Callimachus 1) and *dictatis* (Ovid 29).

Ovid's Acontius keeps on alluding to πολύκροτος, glossing it (as noted) mainly as 'cunning':

    mille doli restant; cliuo sudamus in imo
       ardor inexpertum nil sinet esse meus.   20.41-42

A thousand tricks still remain; we are sweating at the bottom of the slope. My burning love does not permit anything to be left untried.

    insidiis esto capta puella meis   20.66

I grant that you were caught through my wiles

    teque mea laedi calliditate puto   20.126

I reckon that you are being damaged by my craftiness

But on one occasion Ovid again combines 'cunning' with '(written) talkative': in *uerba ferens doctis insidiosa notis* (bearing deceitful words in learned signs, 20.210) the two interpretations are compounded.

Further allusive interpretations of πολύκροτος come in *Epistle* 21, but Cydippe does not seem to know the 'talkative' gloss:

    ... insidias legi, magne poeta, tuas!   21.110

I read your deceit, great poet!

    quidue uir elusa uirgine laudis habes?   21.116

What kind of praise do you, a man, gain from tricking a girl?

    ... parum prudens capta puella dolis   21.122

An incautious girl caught by wiles

    ingenii uideas magna tropaea tui   21.214

to see the great trophies won by your cleverness

    'arte nec est', dices, 'ista petita mea'   21.222

You will say 'this is not the girl I wooed by my craft'

---

[33] For 'etymological markers' cf. Cairns (1996) 30-51 = Cairns (2007) 313-335; for *nomen* etc. Cairns (1996) 29-31 = Cairns (2007) 313-315.

Insidias (110), *elusa* (116), *dolis* (122), *ingenii* (214), and *arte* (222) all suggest 'cunning', with *arte* also looking specifically to Callimachus' τέχνην (fr. 67.3 Pf.);[34] and Cydippe implicitly contrasts her own *simplicitas* to Acontius' cunning ingenuity at 21.104: *visaque simplicitas est mea posse capi* (and my guilelessness looked like an easy catch). The fact that Cydippe's learning is not as extensive as that of Acontius is only one of a series of inadequacies on her part which differentiate her from the cleverer Acontius, and which allow Ovid to make jokes at her expense and to treat her in a patronising, albeit sympathetic, way.

Etymologies of the name Ἀκόντιος deriving it from ἀκόντιον (javelin) or from ἄκων (point) appear at two loci in Callimachus' *aetion*.[35] Ovid puts into Cydippe's mouth explicit remarks about the etymology of Acontius' name prefaced by the etymological marker *nomen*:[36]

> mirabar quare tibi *nomen Acontius* esset;
> quod <u>faciat longe uulnus, acumen</u> habes.
> certe ego conualui nondum de uulnere tali,
> ut <u>iaculo</u> scriptis eminus icta tuis.   21.209-212

> I wondered why your name was Acontius [i.e. javelin man]: you have a point such as deals a wound at a distance. I have assuredly not recovered from such a wound, I who was struck from afar by your writings as if by a javelin.[37]

There is also another (indirect) allusion to an etymology of Acontius' name at 21.229: *durius ut ferro iam sit tibi pectus, Aconti* (although your heart was now harder than iron, Acontius); here the etymon hinted at may be the standard ἀκόντιον/ἄκων; but it might alternatively be ἀκόνη, 'whetstone';[38] there may too be an even more indirect allusion to the common etymon at 20.231-232: *e quibus alterius mihi iam nocuere sagittae,/ alterius noceant ne tibi tela, caue!* The arrows of one of them have already wounded me; take care that the darts of the other do not wound you.

---

[34] See above n. 32.
[35] Cf. Harder (2012) 2.569 on fr. 69.1 Pf. and 2.571-572 on fr. 70.2 Pf.
[36] Cf. also Cairns (2003) 240 and nn. 5-7.
[37] Cf. Kenney (1996) 242 on lines 209-212.
[38] Cf. Cairns (2003) 240 and n. 6.

Two new proposals will now be made about this same type of verbal *doctrina* in the two *Heroides*. The first concerns a dream which, in *Epistle* 20, Acontius claims to have had:

> Haec tibi me <u>in somnis</u> iaculatrix scribere *Phoebe*;
> haec tibi me uigilem scribere iussit Amor;
>
> 20.229-230
>
> Archeress Diana told me in a dream to write these things to you, and Love told me to do so when I was awake.

No such dream occurs in the fragments of the Callimachean *aetion*; but nevertheless the Ovidian couplet is strangely reminiscent of the two mutilated lines of the *aetion* which introduce the Delphic oracle given to Cydippe's father:

> τέτρατον [ο]ὐκέτ' ἔμεινε πατὴρ ἐ....φ..ρ...[
> Φοῖβον· ὁ δ' <u>ἐννύχιον</u> τοῦτ' ἔπος ηὐδάσατο
>
> *Aetia* fr. 75.20-21 Pf.
>
> Her father did not wait for a fourth time ...
> *Phoebus*; and he spoke this word *at night*
>
> transl. Harder (2012) 1.237

The Callimachean word ἐννύχιον has been regarded as problematic by modern scholarship. Delphic oracles were not given at night, and Apollo's worshippers, unlike those of his son Asclepius, did not practice incubation. The alternative rendering 'obscure' is ruled out by the clarity of Apollo's instructions; so some commentators have wished to read ἐμμύχιον ('in his temple') instead.[39] At *Works and Days* 523 the MSS of Hesiod present either μυχίη or νυχίη, and at *Theogony* 991 the MSS offer νύχιον where Aristarchus preferred to read μύχιον; this more or less guarantees that there was a debate in antiquity about the two forms and their meanings. *In somnis*, in combination with the naming of Diana as *Phoebe*, suggests that Ovid was rendering ἐννύχιον here. Ovid's testimony does not seem to have been noticed by the commentators on Callimachus, but it confirms (at the very least) that the MS of Callimachus which Ovid consulted read ἐννύχιον. The gloss

---

[39] Cf. Harder (2012) 2.601-603 ad loc. for the evidence and bibliography.

probably also displays Ovid's knowledge of a debate over ἐννύχιον, and so constitutes another learned feature of this pair of elegies.[40]

The last, multi-faceted example of Ovidian *doctrina* in *Heroides* 20 and 21 is more elusive than the others: it is clear enough that learning is involved in it, but it is not clear what Ovid's aims are. He describes the sacrifice made by Cydippe's mother on Delos over four lines:

> protinus egressae superis, quibus insula grata est,
>   flaua salutatis tura merumque damus;
> dumque parens aras uotiuo sanguine tingit,
>   sectaque fumosis ingerit exta focis
>
> 21.91-94

> As soon as we came forth, we greet the gods to whom the island is sacred and offer them yellow incense and neat wine, and while my mother stains the altars with votive blood, and heaps the cut entrails upon the smoking fire-altars ...

Ovid must be alluding to Callimachus *Aetia* fr. 67.5-6 Pf., where in an apostrophe of Apollo the poet narrates that Acontius and Cydippe came to Delos from their respective homes:

> ἦ γάρ, ἄναξ, ὁ μὲν ἦλθεν Ἰουλίδος ἡ δ' ἀπὸ Νάξου,
>   Κύνθιε, τὴν Δήλῳ σὴν ἐπὶ βουφονίην
>
> For, lord of Cynthus, he came from Ioulis and she from Naxos to your ox-sacrifice on Delos.

There are, however, three differences between the Ovidian ritual and its Callimachean antecedent: first, Cydippe's mother's sacrifice is a private affair while the ox-sacrifice is a public event which draws participants from other islands; second, whereas Callimachus writes of an 'ox-sacrifice', the animal offered by Cydippe's mother is not identified; third, Callimachus specifies that the ox-sacrifice is made to Apollo, but Cydippe's mother makes her offering 'to the gods to whom the island is sacred', that is, not just to Apollo but also to his sister Diana and their mother Leto – the entire Delian triad. These differences are not casual or accidental: proof comes from an observation of Sergio Casali on a different passage of Ovid. When discussing Ovid's rewriting of the

---

[40] In Antonius Liberalis *Met.* 1 (a partial calque on the Acontius-Cydippe story) the heroine sails(!) νύχιος.

Virgilian account of the voyage of Aeneas and the Trojans from Thrace to Delos, Casali pointed out that Ovid 'corrected' Virgil on the question of sacrifice on Delos: whereas Virgil failed to make Aeneas sacrifice there to Apollo,[41] Ovid explicitly introduced such a sacrifice in his own version of Aeneas' visit to Delos.[42] The relevant Ovidian lines are:

> ture dato flammis uinoque in tura profuse
> caesarumque boum fibris de more crematis
> regia tecta petunt ...
>
> *Metamorphoses* 13.636-638
>
> When incense has been given to the flames, and wine has been poured over the incense, and the livers of the sacrificed bulls have been burned in the ritual manner, they make for the royal palace ...

Aeneas' sacrifice proceeds here in the same (standard Roman) fashion[43] as that of Cydippe's mother; and in *boum* (637) Ovid is perhaps alluding to Callimachus' βουφονίην. Moreover Ovid's Aeneas tours Delos and sees its sights in much the same way (although more briefly, *Metamorphoses* 13.634-635) as Cydippe and her mother do in *Heroides* 21. It looks, then, as though Ovid had a mental stereotype of a 'visit to Delos' which included a sight-seeing tour and a bull sacrifice. This could imply that the animal sacrificed by Cydippe's mother was a bull too, but it may instead highlight the absence of that information in the *Heroides* passage.

How, then, can the differences between the Delian sacrifices in the *Heroides* and the *Aetia* be explained? First, some facts about Delian festivals: there was a Delian month named *Bouphonion*, but there was no Delian festival called Βουφονία[44] – although there was a well-attested Βουφονία festival at Athens in honour of Zeus.[45] The main, indeed the only, Delian festival honouring Apollo in Callimachus' day and thereafter was the annual Ἀπολλωνία, held not in the month

---

[41] Anchises does sacrifice bulls, one each to Neptune and Apollo, on Delos after the oracle is given (*Aen.* 3.118-119); this is clearly another allusion to the Delian Ἀπολλωνία festival (on which see below).
[42] Casali (2007) 189-192.
[43] For the standard Roman sacrifice see Šterbenc Erker (2013) 107.
[44] Cf. Bruneau (1970) 65-66; hence the assertions of Coletti (1964) 302-303 about Delian rituals and about the accuracy of Ovid's account of them are now superseded.
[45] Cf. Harder (2012) 2.554-555 on fr. 67.6 Pf.

Bouphonion but in the month *Hieros*.[46] At the Ἀπολλωνία a bull was sacrificed; it was, it seems, usually provided by individual worshippers.[47] Callimachus was probably referring to the Delian Ἀπολλωνία, but Ovid either misunderstood (or chose to misunderstand) him as referring to a non-existent Βουφονία festival. In that case, by failing to mention that the sacrificial animal was an ox, Ovid was probably correcting Callimachus over the title of the festival, just as he corrected Virgil over Aeneas' visit to Delos: Ovid's implication will have been that Callimachus had confused the Delian Ἀπολλωνία with the Attic Βουφονία. Such a correction would show Ovid emulating and rivalling Callimachus in one of the very fields in which Callimachus specialised in the *Aetia* – the cults of Greek cities.

What, then, of Ovid's substitution of the entire Delian triad for Apollo alone as recipients of Cydippe's mother's offering? This may be another correction by Ovid: regular sacrifices to Apollo, Artemis and Leto on Delos in the Delian month of *Lenaion* are attested.[48] It is possible that Ovid knew of this institution, and felt that Callimachus should have selected it as the event which drew the lovers and their families to Delos, given the important role played by Artemis/ Diana in the development of the story of Acontius and Cydippe. A restoration in one of the inscriptions which testify to the sacrifices to the Delian triad in *Lenaion* (*ID* 119.A20) makes it mention lambs for sacrifice. This suggests an alternative motive for Ovid's silence about the victim offered by Cydippe's mother; he may have felt that a bull-offering was out of proportion to a private sacrifice. If Ovid was thinking along these lines, he obviously had information about Delos other than from his Callimachean model; Semus of Delos is an attractive possible source. Ovid is not likely to be drawing on contemporary Delian practice: Delos was ravaged by Mithridates in 88 BC, and by pirates in 69 BC, and was in a low condition throughout Ovid's lifetime. Few inscriptions dated to after 69 BC have been found on Delos, and only a handful (5 or 6 of the second century AD) record Delian religious rituals.[49] At all events

---

[46] Cf. Bruneau (1970) 65-93.
[47] Cf. Bruneau (1970) 65; this might speak for the notion that Cydippe's mother sacrificed a bull, but see below.
[48] Cf. Bruneau (1970) 91-93.
[49] Cf. Bruneau (1968) 695.

Ovid was clearly playing the *doctus poeta* in his bold correction(s) of Callimachus, and in his probable allusion to a more recondite Delian sacrifice.

Of the aspects of Ovid's learning in *Heroides* 20 and 21 explored in this paper his stress on legalisms, and on 'pactum conuentum' in particular, brings us close to his career, and the authenticity of Cydippe's voyage and the accuracy of Ovid's accounts of Delos may also reflect (perhaps indirectly) Ovid's own life experience. The generic, topical and conventional aspects of ancient poetry should never be downplayed. But it seems not only legitimate but also illuminating to seek to identify features of ancient poetry which can be linked directly with the poets as real individuals working within a historical context. Another aspiration of the present paper has been, as an antidote to lingering perceptions of Ovid as a shallow writer, to highlight elements of learning in the two *Epistles* which bring Ovid closer to the ideal of the Hellenistic *poeta doctus*. Ovid often plays the fool, but, if he is any kind of fool, he is a learned fool.

Bibliography

Bablitz, L. (2007), *Actors and Audience in the Roman Courtroom*, London/ New York.

Barchiesi, A. (1993), 'Future reflexive: two modes of allusion and Ovid's *Heroides*', *Harvard Studies in Classical Philology* 95, 333-365.

Beresford, J. (2013), *The Ancient Sailing Season*, Leiden/ Boston.

Berger, A. (1953), *Encyclopedic Dictionary of Roman Law. Transactions of the American Philosophical Society* 43, 333-809.

Bruneau, P. (1968), 'Contribution à l'histoire urbaine de Délos', *Bulletin de correspondance hellénique* 92, 633-709.

Bruneau, P. (1970), *Recherches sur les cultes de Délos à l'époque hellénistique et à l'époque impériale*, Paris.

Cairns, F. (1996), 'Ancient 'Etymology' and Tibullus: On the Classification of 'Etymologies' and on 'Etymological Markers'', *Proceedings of the Cambridge Philological Society* 42, 24-59 = Cairns (2007) 308-340.

Cairns, F. (2002), 'Acontius and his οὔνομα κουρίδιον: Callimachus *Aetia* fr. 67.1-4 Pf.', *The Classical Quarterly* 52, 471-477.
Cairns, F. (2003), 'The "Etymology" in Ovid *Heroides* 20.21-32', *Classical Journal* 98, 239-242.
Cairns, F. (2006) *Sextus Propertius. The Augustan Elegist*, Cambridge.
Cairns, F. (2007), *Papers on Roman Elegy (1969-2003)*, Bologna.
Casali, S. (2007), 'Correcting Aeneas's Voyage: Ovid's Commentary on *Aeneid* 3', *Transactions of the American Philological Association* 137, 181-210.
Coletti, M.L. (1962), 'Aconzio e Cidippe in Callimaco e in Ovidio' (Call. fr. 67 Pf. e Ovid. *Her.* 20.17ss.)', *Rivista di cultura classica e medioevale* 4, 294-303.
Gebhardt, U.C.J. (2009), *Sermo juris: Rechtssprache und Recht in der augusteischen Dichtung*, Leiden.
Harder, A. (2012), *Callimachus, Aetia. Introduction, Text, Translation, and Commentary*, 2 vol., Oxford.
Hollis, A. (1994), 'Rights of Way in Ovid (*Heroides* 20.146) and Plautus (*Curculio* 36)', *Classical Quarterly* 44, 545-549.
Kenney, E.J. (1969), 'Ovid and the law', *Yale Classical Studies* 21, 243-263.
Kenney, E.J. (1970), 'Love and legalism: Ovid, *Heroides* 20 and 21', *Arion* 9, 388-414.
Kenney, E.J. (1979), 'Two disputed passages in the *Heroides*', *Classical Quarterly* 29, 394-431.
Kenney, E.J. (1996), *Ovid Heroides 16-21*, Cambridge.
Kenney, E.J. (1999), '*Vt erat nouator*: Anomaly, Innovation and Genre in Ovid, *Heroides* 16-21', *Proceedings of the British Academy* 93, 399-414.
Kyriakides, S. (2010), '*Heroides* 20 and 21: motion and emotions', *Leeds International Classical Studies* 9, 1-13.
Owen, S.G. (1924), *P. Ovidi Nasonis Tristium Liber Secundus*, Oxford.
Pokrovskij, M.M. (1907-1910), 'Neue Beiträge zur Charakteristik Ovids', *Philologus* Supplementband 11, 351-404.
Šterbenc Erker, D. (2013), *Religiöse Rollen römischer Frauen in 'griechischen' Ritualen*, Stuttgart.
van Iddekinge, J. (1811), *Dissertatio Philologico-Juridica: De insigni in poeta Ovidio Romani juris peritia*, Amsterdam.

Ovid and the Evolution of the *sphragis* over the Course of the Augustan Principate

KRISTOPHER FLETCHER
Louisiana State University

A claim that the term 'Augustan' has the potential to be misleading because of how wide a range of time it covers will meet little resistance; there is a world of difference between the Rome of 27 BC and that of AD 14. But it is one of those wonderful coincidences of history that one of the greatest Roman writers should have a career that maps so neatly onto the reign of the first emperor. Ovid seems to have started publishing in the mid 20's, and kept at it until he passed away in AD 17; the slight time lag on either side of his career relative to Augustus' practically begs for a reading of Ovid's responses to Augustus.[1]

But this is not to be yet another general discussion of what Ovid thought of Augustus.[2] Instead, I will examine two passages from Ovid's poetry – one from earlier in his career and one closer to the end – in order to explore the ways in which they not so much comment upon Augustus and his regime as reflect the changing nature of Rome over the long tenure of his rule.[3] These two passages are *sphragides*, or 'poetic seals', the first one in *Amores* 3.15 and the second at the end of the *Metamorphoses*. While these passages come from different stages in Ovid's own life and poetic career, they can also be read as mirroring the shifting political ideologies over the course of Augustus' reign: the former offers a fractured, inward-looking view of Rome and an Italy that is still coming to grips with its own identity in the wake of the

---

[1] Cf. Galinsky (1996) 228: 'in a way, [Ovid] is the truest product of the Augustan age.' As Martelli (2013) 154 n. 24 observes, however, 'because Ovid does in fact outlive Augustus, he is just as easily characterised as the first of the Tiberians.' For the dating of Ovid's poems see Syme (1978).
[2] For the limited usefulness of terms such as 'Augustan' and 'anti-Augustan' see the seminal Kennedy (1992) along with the counter-arguments in Davis (2006) 9-22.
[3] For the evolution of Augustus' approaches and policies over the course of the principate, see, e.g. Salmon (1956) and Zanker (1988). For the idea that poetry evolved over the course of the principate see Galinksy (1996) 226-229, though he perhaps overstates the extent to which Ovid belonged to a wholly different generation than the other major Augustan poets.

Social and Civil wars, and the latter presents an externally directed view of Roman power.

Ovid offers unique material for such a discussion because of the overlap of his career with that of Augustus. He is also the Augustan poet with the longest career, having published over a longer span of time than his peers. But to show that Ovid's *Amores sphragis* reflects more general concerns from earlier in the principate, I will also examine other Augustan *sphragides*, the majority of which are closer in time to the *Amores* and display similar views of Rome and Italy, in part by identifying their authors with their home regions as well as – or even instead of – with Rome. A comparison with these other *sphragides* – by both Ovid and others – will show how different the *sphragis* in the *Metamorphoses* is in its treatment of Rome and the idea of place more generally.

For the purposes of my discussion I will define a *sphragis* as a poet's declaration of his identity by using or alluding to his name and/or referring to his place of origin, usually at the beginning or end of a poem or collection of poems, and often accompanied by a claim about the value and/or immortality of his poetry, which refers explicitly or implicitly to an intended audience,[4] and often with an epitaphic quality.[5] While this term can be used broadly to include a great number of passages scattered through various works, I focus my discussion primarily on statements widely accepted as *sphragides* 'that come at the beginning or end of works because of their more obviously self-conscious nature and because they often make the most sweeping claims. As Peirano has recently shown, the *sphragis* is paratextual and 'marks the outer edge of the book,' and I am interested in the ways in which these *sphragides* connect the poet's glory to places in the world outside the poems.[6]

---

[4] The most extensive discussions of the *'sphragis'* are Paratore (1959), who focuses on Ovid; Kranz (1961), who broadly traces the phenomenon from its origins through Ovid (108-124 covers the Roman material); and now Peirano (2014), who discusses some of the problems with using the term *sphragis*, not least the fact that such passages do not always include the author's name and so do not protect the work's authenticity in any meaningful way (225). But cf. Martelli (2013) 26-28 on the ways in which poets use 'signatures' as a way to guarantee authorial identity.

[5] Cf. Peirano (2014) 242: 'To sign and seal, then, is already to suggest the possibility of one's absence and thus ultimately of one's death.'

[6] Peirano (2014) 226. For more on Ovid's 'paratextual strategies', see Jansen (2012ª), (2012ᵇ), and (2014ᵇ).

In *Amores* 3.15, Ovid bids farewell to love poetry and declares that he will write in weightier genres.[7] This *sphragis* includes a boast about the quality of Ovid's poetry, which will allow it to survive (*superstes*, 20), and although Ovid does not name himself, he identifies himself by focusing on Paelignia; the bulk of the poem treats the connection between his hometown, Sulmo, and the elegies (Ovid, *Amores* 3.15.3-14):

>   quos ego composui, Paeligni ruris alumnus,
>   (nec me deliciae dedecuere meae)
>   si quid id est, usque a proauis uetus ordinis heres,   5
>   non modo militiae turbine factus eques.
>   Mantua Vergilio gaudet, Verona Catullo;
>   Paelignae dicar gloria gentis ego,
>   quam sua libertas ad honesta coegerat arma,
>   cum timuit socias anxia Roma manus.   10
>   atque aliquis spectans hospes Sulmonis aquosi
>   moenia, quae campi iugera pauca tenent,
>   'quae tantum' dicet 'potuistis ferre poetam,
>   quantulacumque estis, uos ego magna uoco.'

The poem as a whole emphasizes the way people are tied to the place in which they were born and which wins the glory from their success. As Mantua rejoices in Vergil and Verona in Catullus (7), so Ovid in turn hopes to be the pride of the Paeligni.[8] Framed this way, Ovid's success as a poet does not reflect at all on Rome, but on the region in which he was born. Ovid seems to view himself as Paelignian first, and Roman second. Ovid reinforces this idea as the poem continues, as he imagines a foreigner or outsider (*hospes*, 11) coming to Sulmo and marveling that such a small place could produce such a great poet. Ovid links his glory specifically with Sulmo, and his vision of fame involves someone traveling to his hometown. His glory is local, and not connected with Rome.

---

[7] It is impossible to know for sure when Ovid wrote this particular poem because of the editing he tells us he did to the *Amores*, but the original version would likely have had some sort of *sphragis*. For the dating of the *Amores* and the difficulties posed by the existence of a first edition see Martelli (2013) 34-67 and McKeown (1987) 74-89, who 'very tentatively' conjectures that Ovid published the second edition of the *Amores* between 12 and 7 BC (78).

[8] Cf. *Am.* 2.1.1-2: *Hoc quoque composui Paelignis natus aquosis/ ille ego nequitiae Naso poeta meae*.

Rome, however, appears in the poem, but only as an enemy; Ovid defines the Paeligni as opponents of Rome during the Social war, and as being on the 'right' side: they were fighting for *libertas* and their arms were *honesta* (9). Such criticism further distances Ovid's accomplishments from Rome. Ovid also alludes to the Social and presumably Civil wars in discussing his family (*Am.* 3.15.5-6), noting that he is an *eques* because his ancestors were, in contrast to those people that gained the rank as a result of recent military service in the wars. The insult is primarily classist, but also political in the sense that it critiques the effects that the wars have had. Overall, then, Ovid's *Amores sphragis* connects his poetic legacy not with Rome, but Sulmo, which he defines in opposition to Rome. The poem reflects the fractured Italy of the first two-thirds of the first century, a landscape that also affects poetry, since his inclusion of other poets' homelands implies that poetic glory generally redounds to the hometown, and not to Rome.[9]

The final lines of the *Metamorphoses* reveal a very different view of poetic glory and its relationship with Rome. After his prayer to the gods for Augustus' long life and then eventual deification, Ovid 'seals' his poem (*Metamorphoses* 15.871-879):

> iamque opus exegi, quod nec Iouis ira nec ignis
> nec poterit ferrum nec edax abolere uetustas.
> cum uolet, illa dies, quae nil nisi corporis huius
> ius habet, incerti spatium mihi finiat aeui;
> parte tamen meliore mei super alta perennis   875
> astra ferar, nomenque erit indelebile nostrum;
> quaque patet domitis Romana potentia terris,
> ore legar populi, perque omnia saecula fama,
> (siquid habent ueri uatum praesagia) uiuam.

Although there are many parallels between this and *Amores* 3.15, key differences between these passages are immediately obvious:[10] Ovid does not identify himself by referring to either his name or hometown,

---

[9] For an important reminder that few 'Roman' poets are from Rome and the need for Augustan poets to grapple with the changing meanings of the terms 'Rome' and 'Italy' see Johnson (2001).

[10] For some of the parallels between *Am.* 1.15, 3.15, and *Met.* 15.871-877 see Veremans (2006) 386.

and he does not refer to Rome or any of the landmarks in the city.[11] In fact, Ovid uses no place names whatsoever. Consequently, there is no longer any sign of the split between the homeland and Rome. Rather, Ovid focuses on the abstract concept of *Romana potentia*. Success is not defined in terms of a specific place – whether Rome or one's hometown – but as something that can happen anywhere. Roman power spreads through conquest (*domitis*, 877), and it opens the way for the spread of Ovid's poetry. Put this way, the *populus* of 878 encompasses a large, broadly defined group.[12]

There are multiple reasons for the differences between these two *sphragides*. If we believe that Ovid finished the *Metamorphoses* knowing that he was going to be relegated, or even revised the poem while in Tomis, then an obvious reason for this changing view of Rome from the *Amores* to the *Metamorphoses* is his geographical position outside of Rome.[13] Being away from the city made Ovid more aware of Rome's power and what 'Rome' could mean away from Italy. Some of the difference may also be due to Ovid's increased age. Ovid employs the metaphor of poetry as tomb and tombstone first employed by Horace (see below), and the focus on death in the *Metamorphoses sphragis* may reflect Ovid's awareness of his own aging. The latter *sphragis* may also reflect his increasing ambitions as he got older. To attempt an epic – especially one that ostensibly covered all time – offered greater potential fame than any amatory poetry.[14] The *Metamorphoses* is a grander, more ambitious poem than his earlier works, and it makes sense that its *sphragis* would be appropriate to its genre.[15] Similarly,

---

[11] Martelli (2013) 163-164 argues that Ovid suppresses his name here to inscribe himself in a 'virtual community of poets', including Ennius, Lucretius, and Homer.

[12] One parallel not discussed at length below is Horace *Odes* 1.1.29-36, esp. 36: *sublimi feriam sidera uertice*, a claim that Ovid surpasses by asserting that he will be borne *super alta perennis/ astra* (875-876). For other parallels beyond the ones discussed below see Bömer (1986) ad *Met*. 15.871-872.

[13] As Paratore (1959) 192 notes, references to the homeland take on new significance post-relegation. For the possibility that Ovid wrote the *Metamorphoses* thinking about exile, see Johnson (2008) 117-124.

[14] Paratore (1959) 192-193 sees this *sphragis* as an unhappy compromise between personal poetry and epic and suggests that it reflects the general weakening of Ovid's poetic ability. This argument seems untenable, as by almost any measure, the *Metamorphoses* is Ovid's most ambitious work.

[15] Veremans (2006) 383 notes that the tenderness of elegy is an appropriate leitmotif in *Amores* 3.15. And, as Wickkiser (1999) stresses, we must read this *sphragis* as part of its larger poem, not a self-contained and removable section.

as a poem about change, the *Metamorphoses* arguably requires a less concrete *sphragis*. As Pythagoras says at the beginning of the poem's final book (*Met.* 15.418-435), all things change and even famous cities fall, so the poem's subject matter itself may warn away from the connection between a poem's success and any one specific place.[16] Also, as the work of a more established poet, the *Metamorphoses* may not require the same kind of self-identification.

But this *sphragis* may also testify to the increasing chronological distance from the Social and Civil Wars.[17] The two poems may have been written as much as thirty years apart, one near the beginning and the other near the end of the Augustan principate, and reflect the political changes of the time. Support for this hypothesis comes from a comparison of these two *sphragides* with other Augustan *sphragides*, which makes clear how similar the *Amores* one is to its contemporaries and how unique the *Metamorphoses* one is. The *sphragides* that closely precede or are coeval with the *Amores* share the same connection with a local region, and exhibit similar tensions between Rome and other parts of Italy, from which the poets come. These contemporary *sphragides* likewise touch on the prospect of military campaigns led by Augustus, and his path to glory by those means, whereas the *Metamorphoses sphragis* reflects the results of such campaigns and the increasingly Roman nature of the world.

Propertius offers possibly the first Augustan *sphragis* in the final poem of the *Monobiblos*, which identifies the poet through his connection with various places and their role in recent conflicts (Propertius 1.22):[18]

---

[16] Veremans (2006) 384-386 argues that in this *sphragis* Ovid establishes a connection between Neopythagorean beliefs about the immortality of the soul and his belief in the immortality of his poetry.

[17] For the dangers of plotting any kind of simple chronology when discussing Ovid, see the excellent study of Martelli (2013), who nevertheless notes that, 'Ovid invites us to plot the construction and transformation of his authorial identity according to its interaction with (and subjection to) the transformation forces of state power, as he uses events that belong to the career of Augustus and other members of the imperial family in order to mark the chronological involutions to which revision subjects his works' (28).

[18] Heslin (2010) argues that we should date Propertius Book 1 to 33 BC, in which case it would clearly predate all of the other *sphragides* discussed here.

> Qualis et unde genus, qui sint mihi, Tulle, Penates,
>   quaeris pro nostra semper amicitia.
> si Perusina tibi patriae sunt nota sepulcra,
>   Italiae duris funera temporibus,
> cum Romana suos egit discordia ciues,   5
>   (sed mihi praecipue, puluis Etrusca, dolor:
> tu proiecta mei perpessa es membra propinqui,
>   tu nullo miseri contegis ossa solo):
> proxima suppositos contingens Vmbria campos
>   me genuit terris fertilis uberibus.   10

Propertius' use of the conventions of epitaph allows him to recall the traditional connection between elegy and mourning, and also to begin with a series of questions about his identity.[19] These questions, however, do not ask for Propertius' name, suggesting that it is of secondary importance.[20] Propertius instead identifies himself by naming his homeland.

The bulk of the poem reveals the tensions of the preceding half century. As Ovid does, Propertius defines his origins and homeland in terms of the Social and Civil Wars, filling the poem with proper nouns and adjectives (*Perusina, Romana, Etrusca, Vmbria*).[21] While there are ambiguities in the poem, these 'names fix the events politically, chronologically and geographically in the real world.'[22] This poem, however, does not set up the same kind of clear-cut opposition between Rome and a part of Italy as the *Amores sphragis* does, as it expresses the ambivalence of the war, both through the unidentified *patria* in line 3 and the reference to *suos...ciues* in line 5 – which seemingly includes the people fighting against Rome, thereby proleptically declaring them citizens or even asserting that they were citizens all along.[23] Like Ovid

---

[19] Nicholson (1999) 154-155, Peirano (2014) 234-237.
[20] Nicholson (1999) 155. Putnam (1976) 104 suggests that the inclusion of the anonymous *propinquus* represents a break from the 'egocentric' *sphragis* tradition.
[21] Galinsky (1996) 227 cites this poem as an example of Propertius' aversion to war and the general obsession with the war between Antony and Octavian in poetry of this era. DuQuesnay (1992) offers an explicitly pro-Octavian reading of 1.21 and 1.22 in response to earlier anti-Octavian readings. For additional discussion of the tensions in this poem between Rome and other parts of Italy, see Nethercut (1971) and Putnam (1976).
[22] Nicholson (1999) 159.
[23] On Propertius' 'conflicted hybridity' see Johnson (2001) 9-12. Cf. Pogorzelski (2009), who shows that Vergil proleptically presents the war between the Trojans and Latins in the second half of the *Aeneid* as a civil war. Roller (2001) 29-43 talks about the two ways of presenting one's opponents in a civil war, using either the 'assimilating' or 'alienating' viewpoint.

in his *Amores sphragis*, however, Propertius identifies himself with his homeland instead of Rome, and connects this identification with the earlier discord in Italy.[24]

Vergil, too, refers to his hometown at the beginning of the second half of the *Georgics*, when he declares that he must sing of something new (*Georgics* 3.8-16):

> temptanda uia est, qua me quoque possim
> tollere humo uictorque uirum uolitare per ora.
> primus ego in patriam mecum, modo uita supersit,   10
> Aonio rediens deducam uertice Musas;
> primus Idumaeas referam tibi, Mantua, palmas,
> et uiridi in campo templum de marmore ponam
> propter aquam, tardis ingens ubi flexibus errat
> Mincius et tenera praetexit harundine ripas.   15

This passage identifies the poet through his homeland and by alluding to Ennius' famous epitaph claims for itself the same kind of poetic immortality, which Vergil now links with Octavian.[25] Ovid's *Metamorphoses sphragis* also alludes to this Ennian passage, and uses a similar building metaphor, but the treatment of place here is more similar to the *Amores* passage. Vergil's *sphragis* shares the same connection between poetic glory and the place of one's birth as in *Amores* 3.15, and Vergil explains what it is that will make him famous: his bringing of Hesiod's Muses to the *patria* – a word whose meaning he complicates by the subsequent reference to the Mincius, a river from near Vergil's home region of Mantua. Vergil's poetic glory, as he conceives of it here, is his translation – literal and metaphorical – of Greek agricultural didactic to Mantua. Although Vergil will build a temple to Caesar, as with the *Amores* poem, there is the same local focus, with everything coming back to the place of the poet's birth.

In the final lines of the fourth book of the *Georgics*, Vergil returns to these claims and offers a *sphragis* for the work as a whole (*Georgics* 4.559-566):

---

[24] Cf. Propertius 4.1.63-64: *ut nostris tumefacta superbiat Vmbria libris/ Vmbria Romani patria Callimachi.*

[25] Ennius fr. 46 Courtney: *nemo me lacrimis decoret nec funera fletu / faxit. cur? uolito uiuos per ora uirum.*

>   haec super aruorum cultu pecorumque canebam
>   et super arboribus, Caesar dum magnus ad altum   560
>   fulminat Euphraten bello uictorque uolentis
>   per populos dat iura uiamque adfectat Olympo.
>   illo Vergilium me tempore dulcis alebat
>   Parthenope studiis florentem ignobilis oti,
>   carmina qui lusi pastorum audaxque iuuenta,   565
>   Tityre, te patulae cecini sub tegmine fagi.

Like the *Metamorphoses* passage, this *sphragis* comes at the end of a multi-book hexameter poem. It forms a pair with the passage from the beginning of Book 3, and there is a responsion between the two. While the first passage mentioned Vergil's region of origin, this one connects Vergil with another part of Italy, Naples, a place of which he seems to have been fond, and where he spent some amount of time (and where, according to the ancient biographical tradition, he was buried).[26] Caesar again looms large, and this time it is he who is *uictor* rather than Vergil. The most important difference between the two passages, however, is that the latter shows a dynamic Caesar, moving eastward on campaign and then eventually to Olympus. While Vergil stays at home and enjoys *otium*, Caesar is about the *negotium* of empire.[27]

Perhaps the most obvious model for Ovid's *Metamorphoses sphragis* is the final poem of Horace's original, three-book collection of *Odes*, but it, too, looks more like the *'Amores sphragis'* in its conception of Rome and the poet's personal ties (Horace, *Odes* 3.30):[28]

>   Exegi monumentum aere perennius
>   regalique situ pyramidum altius,
>   quod non imber edax, non Aquilo impotens
>   possit diruere aut innumerabilis
>   annorum series et fuga temporum.   5
>   non omnis moriar, multaque pars mei

---

[26] *Vita Donati* 36. For the connection between the language of autobiography and epitaph in this passage see Peirano (2014) 230.

[27] See Kyriakidis (2002) on this contrast, which he sees as an Epicurean criticism of the *uita actiua*. He also suggests that Vergil mentions Naples in part because of its associations with Epicureanism.

[28] Cf. Wickkiser (1999) 123 on the *sphragides* in *Odes* 3.30 and *Metamorphoses* 15, 'Horace and Ovid…are not responding to the same years of the Augustan period – [Ovid's] *sphragis* is written at least 25 years after the publication of Books 1-3 of the *Odes*.'

> uitabit Libitinam: usque ego postera
> crescam laude recens, dum Capitolium
> scandet cum tacita uirgine pontifex.
> dicar, qua uiolens obstrepit Aufidus   10
> et qua pauper aquae Daunus agrestium
> regnauit populorum, ex humili potens
> princeps Aeolium carmen ad Italos
> deduxisse modos. sume superbiam
> quaesitam meritis et mihi Delphica   15
> lauro cinge uolens, Melpomene, comam.

This is the *locus classicus* for the metaphor of poem as tombstone, and one of the boldest claims of the immortality granted a poet through his work.[29] The poem is Augustan in its use of *princeps* and its language of rewards reminiscent of the *Res gestae*.[30] The use of a building metaphor may also allude to the transition of Rome from brick to marble under Augustus' watch.[31] But despite its reference to the Capitoline, it presents success as something defined in terms of one's place of birth, and there are still traces of the Roman/ Italian division.[32]

Beyond the initial contrast with the monuments of kings and the pyramids, Horace limits himself to Italy and Greece, and is content with what he has brought to Italy.[33] While focusing on translation, he defines success in primarily Greek terms, such as the Delphic laurel, and Melpomene.[34] As he sees it, his claim to fame is the introduction

---

[29] See e.g. the discussion of Woodman (1974) 116-117 (with earlier bibliography) and Rubino (1985) 105. Peirano (2014) 233 argues that casting this as an epitaph enacts closure by alluding to the poet's death, and that the focus on what will survive inverts the usual life-death trajectory in epitaphs.

[30] Galinsky (1996) 354-355.

[31] Simpson (2002) argues that the constant building activity in the Augustan period influenced writers and that the building metaphor in *Odes* 3.30 reflects the Augustan building program (58).

[32] Vergil also refers to the Capitoline at *Aen.* 9.446-449 in his apostrophe of Nisus and Euryalus. Although not a *sphragis*, the passage shares traits with both Horace 3.30 and Ovid's *Metamorphoses sphragis*, and the reference to *imperium* foreshadows Ovid's reference to *potentia*. Vergil is referring to political power, but also to empire, broadly defined, echoing Jupiter's declaration of *imperium sine fine* (*Aen.* 1.278).

[33] Many scholars take the reference to the pyramids as a reflection of Egypt's contemporary importance. E.g., Gibson (1997) sees the pyramids as a possible allusion to Gallus' fate. Sullivan (2014), however, argues that the pyramids are an allusion to how scrolls were collected and arranged.

[34] See Putnam (1973) 5 for the paradoxical mix of Greek and Italic elements, which he also detects in *Odes* 1.1 (17). Cf. Galinsky (1996) 350-355.

of lyric poetry to Italy, a feat all the more impressive because Horace came from an undistinguished family and a region of Italy known for being poor. His success, then, is envisioned as being spoken of back home – which will happen as long as the city of Rome and its temples survive.[35] As with Vergil, there is a certain cultural imperialism here, but this domination is phrased as bringing things from outside the center back to the center, and even more particularly to the parts of Italy from which these poets come.[36] Both passages look inward, as did *Amores* 3.15.

Like the *Amores sphragis*, this poem exploits the contrast between the modesty of the poet's birthplace and the magnitude of the poet's glory.[37] The focus on the homeland also recalls the beginning of *Georgics* 3, as both mention rivers from the poets' home regions.[38] Likewise, as did Vergil's, so Horace's reputation rests upon a transfer of Greek poetry (and its meters) into Italian poetry; both stake their claims to immortality on their pioneering translations, very literally in their cases, as they both mention bringing Greek verse to Italy.[39] And this '*primus* language' implies a lack in these places that the poet remedies; they need such poets to bring back material to them.[40] There is no sign of such a lack at home at the end of the *Metamorphoses*, as Ovid looks outward.[41]

---

[35] Oliensis (1998) 102-153 argues that Horace is an 'imperial poet' in the sense that his progress from *impotentia* to *potentia* correlates to the progress from civil war to Augustan stability. Cf. Williams (1968) 368: 'The concept ... links Horace's *Odes* with the destiny of the Roman Empire itself – an appropriate concept for an Augustan poet, in view of the new relationship between poet and state.' Rubino (1985) 107-108 rightly observes that the poem presents Rome as an institution, of which Horace will become part.

[36] As Woodman (1974) 124 notes, one of the metaphors enacted by *deducere* – used by both Horace (*Odes* 3.30.14) and Vergil (*G.* 3.11) – is that of colonization. Cf. Galinsky (1996) 354-355, who notes that the term also has triumphal connotations, and that triumphs ended on the Capitoline.

[37] Paratore (1959) 186.

[38] For the Aufidus as a symbol of poetic power and inspiration in this poem, see Woodman (1974) 122-124. Putnam (1973) 9 notes that Horace also connects Daunia with civil war in *Odes* 2.1.33-36.

[39] Nisbet, Rudd (2004) *ad* 13-14 suggest that Horace uses *Italos* instead of *Latinos* 'to stress his own place of origin.'

[40] On what he calls '*primus* language', see Meban (2008). Cf. Hinds (1998) 52-63 on how the language of primacy often involves restating a previous author's claim to primacy.

[41] Paratore (1959) 179-180 notes that Propertius presents himself as an *inventor* (as at 4.1.64). Ovid, however, does not frame his contributions in such terms, as if he considers himself beyond that stage of Latin poetry's development.

Although *Odes* 3.30 is the most famous, Horace wrote numerous *sphragides*. The first is at the end of *Odes* 2, a poem that has received attention primarily because its third strophe (9-12) shows Horace undergoing a metamorphosis, and scholars have been sharply divided as to whether the scene is humorous or serious.[42] Regardless of how we read the third strophe, however, the catalogue of places to which the swan-poet will fly is similar to Ovid's *Metamorphoses sphragis* in looking outward (Horace *Odes* 2.20.13-20):[43]

> iam Daedaleo notior Icaro
> uisam gementis litora Bosphori
>   Syrtisque Gaetulas canorus   15
>   ales Hyperboreosque campos.
> me Colchus et qui dissimulat metum
> Marsae cohortis Dacus et ultimi
>   noscent Geloni, me peritus
>   discet Hiber Rhodanique potor.   20

Horace's view of success in this poem is not just that he will not entirely die (7-8, 21-24), but that his glory will spread to the corners of the world.[44] Unlike Ovid's claim, however, Horace's is not open-ended.[45] He names specific places, not all of which were part of the empire; Hyperborea, for instance, was in some sense not even real.[46] This claim complements that to come in 3.30; Horace will be spoken of

---

[42] Thévenaz (2002) 862 n. 4 offers a good bibliographic overview of the issue.
[43] Thévenaz (2002) 879 n. 40 notes that the end of *Metamorphoses* 15 combines *Odes* 2.20 and 3.30.
[44] Erasmo (2006) 375-376 compares this *sphragis* with that in *Georgics* 4, concluding that 'what was a contrast between poet and emperor in Vergil becomes a comparison in Horace,' suggesting further that Horace 'presents his odes as poetic *res gestae*' (377).
[45] See Oliensis (1998) 179-180 on the similarities and differences between the two, and on 2.20 being bounded both in space and time, starting in January and ending in December. Contra Kidd (1971) 6, who sees Horace as claiming that his fame will extend in place and time.
[46] Bonfante (1992) 38 observes that the Geloni were recently conquered by Augustus. Thévenaz (2002) 865 shows how the places mentioned are appropriate to the swan. Tatum (1973) 9 considers the places synonymous with danger, saying that they are barbaric and that some of the epithets are strange (23-24). Pascal (1980) 106-108, however, shows that *peritus* is not an inappropriate term, and notes the appearance of Spain in both *Odes* 2.20 and *Epistles* 1.20, connecting these appearances with the growing literary scene in Spain that would flourish in the next couple of generations. Cf. West (1998) 146, who also notes that the increased Romanization in Gaul and Spain vs. the east explains the adjectives, and also fits with *Epistles* 1.20.

back home, but his voice will also reach the ends of the known world.[47]

Whether we date *Epistles* 1 to 21 or 19, it is nearer in time to (at least the first edition of) the *Amores* than the *Metamorphoses*, and like the former includes an allusion to the Civil Wars (Horace *Epistles* 1.20.9-13):

> quodsi non odio peccantis desipit augur,
> carus eris Romae donec te deserat aetas;   10
> contrectatus ubi manibus sordescere uulgi
> coeperis, aut tineas pasces taciturnus inertis,
> aut fugies Vticam aut uinctus mitteris Ilerdam.

Oliensis considers this poem 'the first full-fledged envoi in the Western literary tradition' because it dramatizes the ultimate separation between author and text.[48] While this claim is true in a strict sense, the same gesture underlies all of these *sphragides*, which presuppose that the author will not be there with his text to speak for it; at some point, the text will have to speak for itself. This separation anxiety (as it were) explains why Horace and those following him use the language and formulae of epitaphs, which overlaps with that of autobiography. Thus this poem, like 2.20, includes a short autobiography (19-28). This consideration of what will happen to the text once it leaves the author's hands also explains the frequent reference to prophets in *sphragides*, as with Horace's reference to an *augur* here.

While in his address to his book (figured as a slave), Horace limits the areas of the world that will read his poem, he notes that he will reach readers others than those that he had in mind.[49] The references to Utica and Ilerda have been taken as representative of 'ignorant provinces',[50] in part because Horace specifically defines his poems' value in terms

---

[47] Johnson (1966) 275 considers 2.20 a foil to 3.30, with the latter being subtle and the former being over the top, but with both expressing the same general idea. Cf. Hornbeck (2013) 161, who considers 2.20 and 3.30 as expressing the same idea, with the latter being less hyperbolic, and suggests that 'The moderation of 4.40 confirms the hubris of 2.20' (166). For further comparison of 2.20 and 3.30 see Thévenaz (2002) 885-886.
[48] Oliensis (1995) 211.
[49] Harrison (1988) argues that this deflation fits the genre of the *Epistles*. Pearcy (1994) 461 suggests that Horace's bitterness comes from reaching the wrong readers.
[50] E.g. Harrison (1988) 474. Mayer (1994) ad loc. suggests that the book might run to North Africa because Greek dominated in the East. As noted above, however, Spain is not portrayed as ignorant in *Odes* 2.20.

of being in Rome (10), and then later ties himself to Rome, noting that *me primis urbis belli placuisse domique* (23).[51] While in 2.20 Horace speaks of fleeing the envy of the city (4-5), here he defines success in Rome as primary; it is only when the book is old that it will travel to the provinces.[52]

This passage presages the *sphragis* in Ovid's *Metamorphoses* by focusing on the book's travels to places at the edge of the empire.[53] But the references to these two cities recalls the *Amores sphragis*, as both were sites of notable encounters in the war between Caesar and the Republicans.[54] To go back to these places would be in some sense to revisit the Civil War by abandoning the safety of the city, where people value literature. The fact that these are provinces and sites of Civil War battles means that they are doubly markers of Roman conquest.[55] They are lands to which *Romana potentia* has spread – and in which it has been reconfirmed. This *sphragis*, looking both back and forward, encompasses aspects of Ovid's two *sphragides*.

Ovid echoes the connection between Rome and the *Aeneid* in another of his early *sphragides*, the final poem of the first book of *Amores* (Ovid, *Amores* 1.15.23-8):[56]

> carmina sublimis tunc sunt peritura Lucreti,
>   exitio terras cum dabit una dies.
> Tityrus et fruges Aeneiaque arma legentur,   25
>   Roma triumphati dum caput orbis erit.
> donec erunt ignes arcusque Cupidinis arma,
>   discentur numeri, culte Tibulle, tui.

---

[51] Harrison (1988) 475 sees in *belli* an allusion to Augustus.

[52] Harrison (1988) 476: 'Thus Horace in the poetic seal to his first book of epistles presents himself as a clay-footed mortal tied to the earth and the city, and this is to be seen as a kind of humorous antidote to his claims for poetic greatness and immortality in the *Odes*.' Cf. Bonfante (1992) 32-3. Oliensis (1995) 223 notes that this poem reverses *Odes* 3.30, focusing on what will die instead of on what will survive.

[53] Cf. Oliensis (1998) 177: 'the begrimed book is a popular success, its journey to the provinces a variation on the grand tour of the proud swan-poet of *Odes* 2.20.'

[54] For Utica's fame as the site of Cato's death, see Plin. *HN* 5.24: *Vtica ... Catonis morte nobilis*; Mela 1.34: *Vtica ... fato Cato insignis*. I thank Chris Caterine for these references and for fruitful discussion of Cato's connection with Utica.

[55] Barchiesi (2005) 403 notes that these are bloody battlefields in places that became Roman through conquest.

[56] For the various places scholars have located *Amores* 1.15 in the first edition, see Martelli (2013) 51 n. 46. For the verbal and structural echoes between 1.15 and 3.15 see Veremans (2006), who argues that they should be read as a diptych (384). Oliensis (2014), however, argues for reading 1.15 as part of its book, and as a diptych with 1.14.

In this catalogue of poets, Ovid connects poets with their subject matter, claiming that as long as those subject matters exist, so too will those poets. The poem's only reference to Rome comes in this catalogue, and this couplet distances Ovid from Rome in two ways. First, it is introduced because of its connection with the subject matter of Vergil's poems. Second, there is a hint that Rome might not forever be in this position, as Ovid sandwiches this description between claims about the world's existence and the endurance of love – both of which are implicitly more long-lasting.[57] But this couplet also reflects an inward notion of Roman power, with the center being the most important part. The fame of the quintessentially Roman poet Vergil depends upon Rome maintaining its position.

Unlike in the *Metamorphoses*, Ovid makes no link between the power of Rome and his own poetic success. On the contrary, after his catalogue, he claims (Ovid *Amores* 1.15.31-34):

> ergo cum silices, cum dens patientis aratri
>   depereant aeuo, carmina morte carent:
> cedant carminibus reges regumque triumphi,
>   cedat et auriferi ripa benigna Tagi.

While Vergil's success is tied to the continuing dominance of Rome, Ovid's own success transcends political power and material wealth – as well as time.

All of the above *'sphragides'* come from significantly earlier in the principate than the *Metamorphoses* and so it is unsurprising that many of them reflect the fractured nature of the Italy most of these poets grew up in and perhaps also the tenuous nature of Rome's existence. While there are significant differences in age between these poets – especially Ovid, who was much younger than the others – they all reflect similar concerns. By the time Ovid was writing the *Metamorphoses* during the bulk of the first decade of the first century

---

[57] Similarly, as McKeown (1989) 387-378 notes, this poem offers a defense of poetry by claiming that it brings immortality and by arguing against the Roman stance that service to the state is the best thing. In the latter regard, the poem can to some extent be read as un-Roman or anti-Roman.

of this era, however, Rome was in many ways a different place.[58] While it is possible to debate the extent to which Augustus' claims about peace and his responsibility for unity are true, certainly Italy was a more unified entity by this time, and there are fewer signs of tension between Rome itself and other parts of Italy.[59] Furthermore, as Richardson has shown, the Roman conception of their power as a territorial empire, with a distinction between Italy as a whole and everything else, is a development of the Augustan period, the culmination of the Social Wars as well as the conquests and colonies of Sulla, Pompey, and Julius Caesar.[60]

Thus, the *sphragis* to Ovid's *magnum opus* is unique among its literary ancestors – including those written earlier by the same author. Although strikingly short it is a more forceful and ambitious statement – as is appropriate to Ovid's most ambitious poem. Ovid's claim is also a product of its times in the sense that most of the hard work had already been done, in terms of the translation of Greek literary modes into Latin verse. While Horace and Vergil focus on that accomplishment, Ovid is able to turn his gaze to something bigger. This is a bold claim, but savvy in connecting the success of the empire with Ovid's own success; the two are mutually supportive enterprises, and essentially coterminous.[61] Whereas in his earlier poem Ovid had focused on his poetry's ability to change the reputation of Sulmo, in the *Metamorphoses* he links himself with Roman power in the broadest sense. This conception of empire fits with the one that Richardson argues developed under Augustus.

I do not mean to imply, however, that Ovid's views of his poetic immortality follow a simple linear trajectory, and that his later conception of the connection between place and poetic glory completely replaces his earlier one. Rather, this later view of Roman power complements his earlier ideas, which still persist. For instance, in another

---

[58] The general consensus is that Ovid wrote both the *Metamorphoses* and *Fasti* between AD 1 and 8. See Myers (1994) 63 n. 10 for a brief survey of bibliography on the matter. McKeown (1987) 78, however, examines Ovid's rate of composition over the course of his career and considers it unlikely that Ovid wrote both works in such a short period of time, and so likely started one or both earlier.

[59] E.g. Augustus, *Mon. Anc.* 25.2: *iurauit in mea uerba tota Italia sponte sua et me bel[li] quo uici ad Actium ducem depoposcit.*

[60] Richardson (2008).

[61] See Habinek (1998) 151-169 on the pivotal role Ovid's exile poetry plays in the construction of the Roman Empire. Cf. Wheeler (1999) 205: 'This claim to universal popularity is bold, but could it not also be that Ovid's work is itself an expression and example of *Romana potentia*?'

poem – *Tristia* 3.7, his address to his disciple and possible daughter-in-law Perilla – Ovid recalls Horace *Odes* 3.30 and the *Aeneid* 9 passage by focusing on the Roman center (*Tristia* 3.7.43-54):[62]

> singula ne referam, nil non mortale tenemus
>   pectoris exceptis ingeniique bonis.
> en ego, cum caream patria uobisque domoque,   45
>   raptaque sint, adimi quae potuere mihi,
> ingenio tamen ipse meo comitorque fruorque:
>   Caesar in hoc potuit iuris habere nihil.
> quilibet hanc saeuo uitam mihi finiat ense,
>   me tamen extincto fama superstes erit,   50
> dumque suis uictrix omnem de montibus orbem
>   prospiciet domitum Martia Roma, legar.
> tu quoque, quam studii maneat felicior usus,
>   effuge uenturos, qua potes, usque rogos!

The sentiment is much the same as at the end of the *Metamorphoses*, and the connection with Rome's military power is the same, as emphasized by the words: *uictrix*, *domitum*, and *Martia*. And while Ovid draws a sharp distinction between Caesar's power and his own poetic immortality in this poem, Ovid's poetic success depends upon the continued existence of Rome's outward-looking power.

That this shift in Ovid is not due just to the nature of the *Metamorphoses* is also clear from another poem, the *sphragis* to the fourth book of the *Tristia*. This poem – the longest Augustan *sphragis* – uses the language of epitaphs and identifies Ovid by providing his fullest autobiography,[63] including the year of his birth, and another statement that his family's rank predates the Civil Wars (7-8).[64] In this poem, Ovid establishes his origin from outside of the city, although now he defines his hometown not in opposition to Rome, but in terms of its physical distance from Rome – which has only increased now that he has been relegated (Ovid *Tristia* 4.10.1-4):

---

[62] For Perilla's identity and her status as a *scripta puella* see Ingleheart (2012).
[63] Fairweather (1987) 181, 186-188.
[64] In her discussion of this poem, Fairweather (1987) 193-195 argues for similarities between Ovid's autobiography and Augustus', noting, e.g., the significance of 43 to both of them, and raising the possibility that Ovid played up these similarities as part of his *apologia* and appeal to Augustus.

> Ille ego qui fuerim, tenerorum lusor amorum,
>   quem legis, ut noris, accipe posteritas.
> Sulmo mihi patria est, gelidis uberrimus undis,
>   milia qui nouies distat ab urbe decem.

Ovid then defines his young life in relation to the city: he goes there with his brother (15-6), and frames his initial success only in terms of the city, as his *Amores* were *totam cantata per urbem* (59). Everything to this point in the poem thus focuses on Rome as the center, but without any sense of the tension between it and other parts of Italy seen in earlier *sphragides*.

Ovid continues to tell the story of his family life and poetic career, including his relegation, before ending with an address to the Muse and his declaration of immortality based on the fame he enjoys while alive (Ovid *Tristia* 4.10.125-132):

> nam tulerint magnos cum saecula nostra poetas,   125
>   non fuit ingenio fama maligna meo,
> cumque ego praeponam multos mihi, non minor illis
>   dicor et in toto plurimus orbe legor.
> si quid habent igitur uatum praesagia ueri,
>   protinus ut moriar, non ero, terra, tuus.   130
> siue fauore tuli, siue hanc ego carmine famam,
>   iure tibi grates, candide lector, ago.

Amidst the now-familiar claims the contrast with how Ovid describes the beginning of his career is striking: no longer is he only sung through the whole city; he is read in the entire world (128).[65] There is no longer a connection between fame and city of origin. Rather, Ovid imagines himself transferred from the Ister to Helicon (119-120).[66] Ovid has achieved rare fame while still alive (121-122) and he transcends the city as he transcends the world (129-130) – just as he did at the end

---

[65] Ovid strikes some similar notes earlier in the *Amores*: in the *sphragis* to the first book, for instance, he expresses his desire to be sung in the whole world (1.15.7-8). As Vessey (1981) 617 observes, however, Ovid does not connect this desire to Rome. It is only in the *Metamorphoses* that he explicitly connects his poetry's spread through the world with Roman power.

[66] Martelli (2013) 169 compares Ovid's use of *abducis* (119) to Vergil's *deducam* (G. 3.11): '[Ovid's] is not therefore a triumph of Roman conquest over the prestige-conferring cultural goods of Hellenism, but one of inspiration and mental flight over the physical geography and juridical boundaries of empire.'

of the *Metamorphoses*.⁶⁷ Ovid ends the poem by thanking his reader (131-132) because he knows that his success depends upon his poems being read – which can happen anywhere.⁶⁸

The parallel between the two poems is strengthened by the echoes of the *Metamorphoses sphragis* at the end of *Tristia* 4.10. As Martelli notes, the verbs in the future tense in the *Metamorphoses sphragis* are turned into the present tense in 4.10 (e.g. *legar/ legor*), showing that Ovid's predictions have come true.⁶⁹ The echo in *Tr.* 4.10.129 of *Met.* 15.879 (*siquid habent ueri uatum praesagia*) makes the point explicit.⁷⁰ Both of these *sphragides* echo Augustan propaganda, and reflect both Ovid's wider view of the world and also the difference between the 20's BC when he began writing and the first two decades of the new millennium – and thus the difference between the beginning and end of the Augustan principate.⁷¹

None of this is to say that Ovid agreed with all of Augustus' policies, or that the end of the *Metamorphoses* indicates any kind of direct political support of the *princeps*. Regardless of their views of each other, however, by the end of Ovid's career, he and Augustus were engaged in different aspects of the same project: spreading and consolidating Roman power. And in this sense, Ovid is very much an 'Augustan' poet. But there is no such trace of that project in the *Amores*

---

⁶⁷ For Ovid's fame while still alive see *Pont.* 4.16, a *sphragis* that begins: *Inuide, quid laceras Nasonis carmina rapti?/ non solet ingeniis summa nocere dies,/ famaque post cineres maior uenit. et mihi nomen/ tum quoque, cum uiuis adnumerarer, erat* (1-4).

⁶⁸ As Fairweather (1987) 195 notes, one *lector* is Augustus, but he is not the only reader.

⁶⁹ Martelli (2013) 170. Ovid returns to the future tense, however, in *Tr.* 5.20, another *sphragis* of sorts, though that poem is dedicated to his wife, to whom Ovid claims, *dumque legar, mecum pariter tua fama legetur,/ nec potes in maestos omnis abire rogos* (5-6). Ovid had also used *legar* at *Tr.* 3.7.52 (above).

⁷⁰ Although according to Newman (1967) 106 the *Metamorphoses* shows the 'utter collapse of the *uates* ideal', Ovid's use of the term seems pointed in the context of making prophecies. In his discussion of the *Metamorphoses sphragis* (112-113) Newman asks who these *uates* are supposed to be as a way to show that Ovid did not understand how Vergil was using the term, but it is possible to read the *Tristia* 4.10 passage as meaning that Ovid and all of his sphragistic predecessors from Ennius on are the *uates*.

⁷¹ In *Mon. Anc.* 26-33, for instance, Augustus focuses on the extension of the Roman Empire and its influence. Cf. Wickkiser (1999), who sees a positive relationship between Ovid and Augustus in this *sphragis*, and suggests that Ovid alludes to and complements the Augustan building project. She does, however, note that Ovid's reference to *Romana potentia* implies that 'Ovid is not limited by Augustus' achievement. These comparisons between princeps and poet clearly weigh in Ovid's favor' (134).

sphragis,[72] and the difference between the two passages – and poems – suggests that the term 'Ovidian' can perhaps be as misleading and reductive as the term 'Augustan' is.[73]

Bibliography

Barchiesi, A. (2005), 'Centre and Periphery', in S. Harrison (ed.), *A Companion to Latin Literature*, Oxford, 394-405.

Bömer, F. (1986), *P. Ovidius Naso. Metamorphosen. Buch 14-15*, Heidelberg.

Bonfante, L. (1992), 'The Poet and the Swan: Horace *Odes* 2.20', *La parola del passato* 47, 25-45.

Davis, P.J. (2006), *Ovid & Augustus. A Political Reading of Ovid's Erotic Poems*, London.

DuQuesnay, I.M. Le M. (1992), '*In memoriam Galli*: Propertius 1.21', in T. Woodman, J. Powell (edd.), *Author and Audience in Latin Literature*, Cambridge, 52-83.

Erasmo, M. (2006), 'Birds of a Feather? Ennius and Horace, *Odes* 2.20', *Latomus* 65, 369-377.

Fairweather, J. (1987), 'Ovid's Autobiographical Poem, *Tristia* 4.10', *The Classical Quarterly* 37, 181-196.

Galinsky, K. (1996), *Augustan Culture. An Interpretative Introduction*, Princeton.

Gibson, B.J. (1997), 'Horace, *Carm*. 3.30.1-5', *Classical Quarterly* 47, 312-314.

Habinek, T.N. (1998), *The Politics of Latin Literature. Writing, Identity, and Empire in Ancient Rome*, Princeton.

Harrison, S.J. (1988), 'Deflating the *Odes*: Horace, *Epistles* 1.20', *Classical Quarterly* 38, 473-476.

---

[72] This is not to say, however, that there is nothing political about Ovid's love poetry. See Davis (2006) for one example of how we can read these poems as political (specifically anti-Augustan).

[73] I would like to thank my fellow panelists Sanjaya Thakur and Karen Acton and our moderator Cláudia Teixeira for their help before, during and after the panel. I would also like to thank Victoria Pagán, Cristiano Castelletti, and the anonymous reader for helpful questions, comments, and bibliographic suggestions.

Heslin, P. (2010), 'Virgil's *Georgics* and the Dating of Propertius' First Book', *Journal of Roman Studies* 100, 54-68.
Hinds, S. (1998), *Allusion and Intertext. Dynamics of Appropriation in Roman Poetry*, Cambridge.
Hornbeck, C. (2013), '*Caelum ipsum petimus*: Daedalus and Icarus in Horace's *Odes*', *Classical Journal* 109, 147-169.
Ingleheart, J. (2012), 'Ovid's *scripta puella*: Perilla as Poetic and Political Fiction in *Tristia* 3.7', *Classical Quarterly* 62, 227-241.
Jansen, L. (2012[a]), 'On the Edge of the Text: Preface and Readers in Ovid's *Amores*', *Helios* 39, 1-19.
Jansen, L. (2012[b]), 'Ovidian Paratexts: Editorial Postscript and Readers in *ex Ponto* 3.9', *Materiali e discussioni per l'analisi dei testi classici* 67, 81-110.
Jansen, L. (ed.) (2014[a]), *The Roman Paratext. Frame, Texts, Readers*, Cambridge.
Jansen, L. (2014[b]), 'Modern Covers and Paratextual Strategy in Ovidian Elegy', in L. Jansen ed., *The Roman Paratext. Frame, Texts, Readers*, Cambridge, 224-242.
Johnson, P.J. (2008), *Ovid Before Exile. Art and Punishment in the Metamorphoses*, Madison.
Johnson, W.R. (1966), 'The Boastful Bird: Notes on Horatian Modesty', *Classical Journal* 61, 272-275.
Johnson, W.R. (2001), 'Imaginary Romans: Vergil and the Illusion of National Identity', in S. Spence (ed.), *Poets and Critics Read Virgil*, New Haven, 3-16.
Kennedy, D.F. (1992), '"Augustan" and "Anti-Augustan": Reflections on Terms of Reference', in A. Powell (ed.), *Roman Poetry and Propaganda in the Age of Augustus*, London, 26-58.
Kidd, D. A. (1971), 'The Metamorphosis of Horace', *Journal of the Australasian Universities Language and Literature Association* 35, 5-16.
Kranz, W. (1961), 'Sphragis. Ichform und Namensiegel als Eingangs- und Schlußmotiv antiker Dichtung', *Rheinisches Museum* 104, 3-46, 97-124.
Kyriakidis, S. (2002), '*Georgics* 4.559-566: The Vergilian Sphragis', *Kleos* 7, 275-289.

Martelli, F.K.A. (2013), *Ovid's Revisions. The Editor as Author*, Cambridge.
Mayer, R. (1994), *Horace. Epistles Book 1*, Cambridge.
McKeown, J.C. (1987), *Ovid: Amores. Text, Prolegomena and Commentary in Four Volumes*, vol. 1: *Text and Prolegomena*, Liverpool.
McKeown, J.C. (1989), *Ovid: Amores. Text, Prolegomena and Commentary in Four Volumes*, vol. 2: *A Commentary on Book One*, Liverpool.
Meban, D. (2008), 'Temple Building, *Primus* Language, and the Proem to Virgil's Third *Georgic*', *Classical Philology* 103, 150-174.
Myers, K.S. (1994), *Ovid's Causes. Cosmogony and Aetiology in the* Metamorphoses, Ann Arbor.
Nethercut, W.R. (1971), 'The ΣΦΡΑΓΙΣ of the *Monobiblos*', *American Journal of Philology* 92, 464-472.
Newman, J.K. (1967), *The Concept of Vates in Augustan Poetry*, Brussels.
Nicholson, N. (1999), 'Bodies without Names, Names without Bodies: Propertius 1.21-22', *Classical Journal* 94, 143-161.
Nisbet, R.G.M., Rudd, N. (2004), *A Commentary on Horace: Odes Book 3*, Oxford.
Oliensis, E. (1995), 'Life After Publication: Horace, *Epistles* 1.20', *Arethusa* 28, 209-224.
Oliensis, E. (1998), *Horace and the Rhetoric of Authority*, Cambridge.
Oliensis, E. (2014), 'The Paratext of *Amores* 1: Gaming the System', in L. Jansen (ed.), *The Roman Paratext. Frame, Texts, Readers*, Cambridge, 206-223.
Paratore, E. (1959), 'L'evoluzione della 'sphragis' dalle prime alle ultime opere di Ovidio', *Atti del convegno internazionale Ovidiano (Sulmona, maggio 1955)*, Sulmo, 173-203.
Pascal, C.B. (1980), 'Another Look at the Swan Ode', *Latomus* 39, 98-108.
Pearcy, L.T. (1994), 'The Personification of the Text and Augustan Poetics in *Epistles* 1.20', *Classical World* 87, 457-464.
Peirano, I. (2014), ''Sealing' the Book: The *sphragis* as Paratext', in L. Jansen (ed.), *The Roman Paratext. Frame, Texts, Readers*, Cambridge, 224-242.

Pogorzelski, R.J. (2009), 'The 'Reassurance of Fratricide' in the *Aeneid*', *American Journal of Philology* 130, 261-289.
Putnam, M.C.J. (1973), 'Horace C. 3.30: The Lyricist as Hero', *Ramus* 2, 1-19.
Putnam, M.C.J. (1976), 'Propertius 1.22: A Poet's Self-Definition', *Quaderni urbinati di cultura classica* 23, 93-123.
Richardson, J. (2008), *The Language of Empire. Rome and the Idea of Empire from the Third Century BC to the Second Century AD*, Cambridge.
Richardson, L., Jr. (1977), *Propertius. Elegies 1-4*, Norman.
Roller, M.B. (2001), *Constructing Autocracy. Aristocrats and Emperors in Julio-Claudian Rome*, Princeton.
Rubino, C.A. (1985), 'Monuments and Pyramids: Death and the Poet in Horace, *Carmina* 3.30', *Classical and Modern Literature* 5, 99-111.
Salmon, E.T. (1956), 'The Evolution of Augustus' Principate', *Historia* 5, 456-478.
Simpson, C.J. (2002), '*Exegi monumentum*: Building Imagery and Metaphor in Horace, *Odes* 1-3', *Latomus* 61, 57-66.
Stewart, D.J. (1967), 'The Poet as Bird in Aristophanes and Horace', *Classical Journal* 62, 357-361.
Sullivan, M. B. (2014), 'On Horace's Pyramids (*C.* 3.30.1-2)', *Cambridge Classical Journal* 60, 100-108.
Syme, R. (1978), *History in Ovid*, Oxford.
Tatum, J. (1973), '*Nec usitata nec tenui ferar*', *American Journal of Philology* 94, 4-25.
Thévenaz, O. (2002), 'Le cygne de Venouse: Horace et la métamorphose de l'*Ode* 2.20', *Latomus* 61, 861-888.
Veremans, J. (2006), 'La sphragis dans les *Amours* d'Ovide: une approche stylistique et rhétorique', *Latomus* 65, 378-387.
Vessey, D.W.T. (1981), 'Elegy Eternal: Ovid, *Amores* 1.15', *Latomus* 40, 607-617.
West, D. (1998), *Horace, Odes 2. Vatis Amici*. Text, Translation and Commentary, Oxford.
Wheeler, S.M. (1999), *A Discourse of Wonders. Audience and Performance in Ovid's* Metamorphoses, Philadelphia.
Wikkiser, B. (1999), 'Famous Last Words: Putting Ovid's *sphragis* Back Into the *Metamorphoses*', *Materiali e discussioni per l'analisi dei testi classici* 42, 113-142.

Williams, G. (1968), *Tradition and Originality in Roman Poetry*, Oxford.

Woodman, T. (1974), '*Exegi monumentum*: Horace, *Odes* 3.30', in T. Woodman, D. West (edd.), *Quality and Pleasure in Latin Poetry*, Cambridge, 115-128.

Zanker, P. (1988), *The Power of Images in the Age of Augustus*. transl. A. Shapiro, Ann Arbor.

Virgil's *sulcus primigenius* of Augustan Rome

† CRISTIANO CASTELLETTI
University of Fribourg

Introduction

In Castelletti (2012ᵃ) I first discussed the possibility that Virgil embedded his *sphragis* at the beginning of the *Aeneid*, through a particular kind of *technopaignion*[1] (that I have called boustrophedon acrostic),[2] inspired by Aratus. Let us summarize the key points:

> ἘκΔιὸς ἀρχώμεσθα, τὸν οὐδέποτ' ἄνδρες ἐῶμεν
> ἄρρητον. Μεσταὶ δὲΔιὸς πᾶσαι μὲν ἀγυιαί,
> πᾶσαι δ' ἀνθρώπων ἀγοραί, μεστὴ δὲ θάλασσα
> καὶ λιμένες, πάντη δὲΔιὸς κεχρήμεθα πάντες.
> Τοῦ γὰρ καὶ γένος εἰμέν, ὁ δ' ἤπιος ἀνθρώποισι   5
> <u>δεξιὰ σημαίνει</u>, λαοὺς δ' ἐπὶ ἔργον ἐγείρει
> μιμνῄσκων βιότοιο, λέγει δ' ὅτε βῶλος <u>ἀρίστη</u>
> <u>βουσί</u> τε καὶ μακέλῃσι, λέγει δ' ὅτε δεξιαὶ ὧραι
> καὶ φυτὰ γυρῶσαι καὶ σπέρματα πάντα βαλέσθαι.
> Arat. *Phaen.* 1-9 Kidd (1997)

Let us begin with Zeus, whom we men never leave unspoken. Filled with Zeus are highways and all meeting places of people, filled are the sea and the harbours; in all circumstances we are all dependent on Zeus. For we are also his children, and he benignly gives helpful signs to men, and rouses people to work, reminding them of their livelihood, tells when the soil is best for oxen

---

[1] On the so-called *technopaignia* (acrostics, acronyms and other kind of letter-plays) see in particular Luz (2010), Kwapisz, Petrain, Szymanski (2013), Castelletti (2014), Castelletti (2015ᵃ) and Castelletti (2015ᵇ).
[2] Technically, acrostics are composed of the first letters of a sequence of verses and telestichs of the last ones. We call *acroteleuton* the combination of an acrostic and a telestich. Since the reading direction of this *technopaignion* follows a boustrophedon movement (which includes the first and the last letter of each line, and changes direction at each verse), and therefore is not a genuine *acroteleuton*, we will keep the simplified definition of boustrophedon acrostic, which allows immediate visualisation of this composition's pattern.

and mattocks, and tells when the seasons are right both for planting trees and for sowing every kind of seed.³

As pointed out by K. Volk,⁴ Aratus' *Phaenomena* describes the constellations as a sign system devised by Zeus for the benefit of human beings. Aratus figuratively depicts these signs as though they were 'letters in the sky', a veritable text inscribed in the physical world. The writing metaphor is pervasive in Aratus' poem and the *Phaenomena* thus presents an important early instance of the concept of the 'readability' of the world, which is also expressed by an extensive use of *technopaignia*, such as acrostics and other forms of letter play. In some passages of the poem, the signs function as keywords (signposts), as δεξιὰ σημαίνει, at the beginning of line 6, which seems to say: 'the right side/ the right indicates', that is, that we should start reading from the right. Indeed, it is at the right end of line 6 that we find the first letter of the acrostic. The last word of the following line (7) is ἀρίστη, which could be taken as a suggestion that the reader should proceed from right to left (a wordplay on ἀρίστη > ἀριστερά). The first word at the beginning of line 8 is βουσί. Therefore, it does not seem completely senseless to read δεξιὰ σημαίνει (and ἀριστερά) ... βουσί, as a message meaning 'the right (and then the left) point to the oxen', that is: an allusion to a boustrophedon movement. Indeed, if we follow the signs provided by the poet, and we consider the first and the last letters of the section included among the keywords (l. 6-8), starting from the end of line 6 (as suggested by δεξιὰ σημαίνει) the boustrophedon reading brings forth the sequence IΔMHI, that is ἰδμῇ (= ἰδμοσύνῃ, as attested by Hesychius)⁵ 'with wisdom, knowingly'.

The fact that the very first⁶ *technopaignion* composed by Aratus is a boustrophedon acrostic is highly significant. Indeed, the boustrophedon imitates the movement of the plough pulled by oxen, and Aratus precisely mentions agriculture in the passage under discussion (*Phaen.* 5-9).

---

³ The translations from Aratus' *Phaenomena* are by Kidd (1997); Vergil's *Aeneid*, by Ahl (2007); Suetonius' *Lives of the Caesars*, by Edwards (2000); Propertius', by Goold (1990) adapted; Festus' and Solinus' by Wiseman (2015). Unless otherwise stated, the other translations are my own.
⁴ See Volk (2012).
⁵ Hsch. I 217: ἰδμῇ ἰδμοσύνῃ. Cf. *LSJ*, s.v. ἰδμή, ἡ = ἰδμοσύνη (knowledge, skill).
⁶ Aratus composes a wordplay on his own name in the two first lines of the poem (ἐῶμεν/ ἄρρητον, 1-2, on which see Bing [1990], Bing [1993] and Katz [2008]), however, the programmatic and paradigmatic function of *technopaignia* is fully developed in the composition of lines 6-8.

Besides, ploughing is a fairly common metaphor for writing (verse) ever since the Greek archaic poets (see e.g. Pind. *Nem.* 6.32, 10.26) and this image also survives in Latin literature.[7] Indeed, the Latin verb *arare* means 'to plough', but is also used metaphorically for 'to write (poetry)': the image is the same, that of an object leaving a trace either on a field or on a writing surface.[8] Yet, it is precisely this idea of trace, of sign (σῆμα), that can be seen, identified, and also reproduced, that is at the origin of the process of writing.

The aim of this *technopaignion* is therefore programmatic: the sky, the visible world and its manifestations (*ta phainomena*), can be read, given that stars, just like letters, are considered to be στοιχεῖα (*elementa*), basic elements that have been placed where they belong by divine intervention.[9] The boustrophedon acrostic is the first paradigm provided by Aratus, to reach the ἰδμή (knowledge), required to read not only the poem, but the entire universe. And this is indeed what the word ἰδμή implies: knowledge derived from 'seeing' (the verb ἰδεῖν, 'to see', and οἶδα 'I know, because I have seen' share the same etymology).[10]

This Aratean *technopaignion* seems to have inspired several ancient authors,[11] the most significant of whom is Virgil:

---

[7] On the metaphorical use of ploughing for writing (verse) in Greek poetry, see e.g. Bing (1984). For a discussion on the survival of this analogy (also found in the 'indouinello ueronese') and the assimilation *stilus* = *uomer*, see Thraede (1965) 79-116.

[8] Cf. *ThlL* 2.627.43-6, s.v. aro II, quoting e.g. Mart. 4.86.11 *(libelle) inuersa pueris arande charta*. Virgil chose the *boustrophedon* primarily to pay tribute to one of his main literary models, Aratus. The tribute is all the more eloquent as it not only reproduces a technique already used by the Hellenistic poet, but also connects the verb *arare*, with the name Aratus.

[9] The equation star = letter is never made explicit in the *Phaenomena*. However, as Volk (2012) 212 correctly points out 'unlike Lucretius, who repeatedly likens the atoms of the physical world to the letters in his own poem (see e.g. Lucr. 1.823-827, 2.688-699, 2.1013-1022), Aratus makes no straightforward claim that the phenomena he describes behave in the manner of a script and does not employ language that unambiguously refers to writing. Nevertheless, there are numerous indications in both the *Phaenomena* itself and the history of its reception that point to the implicit idea of written signs.' Several examples of reception of the Aratean 'heavenly writing' are discussed in Castelletti (2015ª).

[10] Cf. Chantraine (1999), s.v. οἶδα.

[11] For a full discussion on the genuineness of the acrostic ἰδμῇ, see Castelletti (2012ª). It would be hardly a coincidence that in the famous passage of the *Theriaka* in which Nicander signs his poem with the acrostic ΝΙΚΑΝΔΡΟΣ (*Ther.* 345-53) the word that provides the second letter of the signature is ἰδμοσύνη (= ἰδμῇ), especially since this word does not otherwise occur in Nicander's work, and that it refers to Zeus, whose ἰδμοσύνη is praised.

> Arma uirumque cano, Troiae qui primus ab oriS
> Italiam fato profugus Lauiniaque ueniT
> Litora, multum ille et terris iactatus et altO
> Vi superum, saeuae memorem Iunonis ob iraM.
>
> Verg. Aen. 1.1-4 Geymonat (2008)
>
> Arms and the man I sing of Troy, who first from its seashores, Italy-bound, fate's refugee, arrived at Lavinia's coastlands. How he was battered about over land, over high deep seats by the powers above! Savage Juno's anger remembered him.

As I discussed in Castelletti (2012ª), the sequence A-S-T-I-L-O-M-V, which reads as a boustrophedon acrostic, should be understood as follows: '*A STILO M[aronis] V[ergili]*', that is 'from the stylus of Virgilius Maro', the poet's *sphragis*. The word *MARONIS* would be confirmed by *IRAM*, the last word in the fourth line, which, read in reverse (that is, in the direction of the acrostic), provides not only the M, but also *MAR*.

Firstly, this *technopaignion* seems to have a precise metapoetic function. Using the word *stilus* (an *instrumentum scriptorium* that can also be used as a weapon), Virgil not only signs his masterpiece but also indicates to which poetic genre it belongs, that is, epic. Indeed, Virgil (= Tityrus) used the *calamus* at the beginning of the *Eclogues* to celebrate the *Musa tenuis*, whereas in the *Aeneid* he will use the *stilus* to celebrate the *arma uirumque*.[12] In what follows, I would like to argue not only that this Virgilian *sphragis* has been noticed and imitated by other ancient authors, but that it conveys highly significant ideological messages, going far beyond the usual definition of *technopaignia*, as mere literary amusement.

The Propertian Answer

It is well know that a Virgilian contemporary fellow poet, Propertius, provides the first mention of the composition of the *Aeneid*. Indeed, in the last elegy of his second Book, where the poet composes his own *sphragis* (celebrating his beloved Cynthia and himself),[13] Propertius

---

[12] For an exhaustive discussion on these metapoetic allusions, see Castelletti (2012ª) 90-94.
[13] Cf. Prop. 2.34.85-94, with Fedeli (2005).

also expresses his *recusatio* towards an epic poem, arguing that Virgil is instead assuming the task of writing a poem in which he will celebrate Augustus' recent triumphs, as well as the origins of the Roman people.

> Me iuuet hesternis positum languere corollis,
>   quem tetigit iactu certus ad ossa deus;   60
> Actia Vergiliu<m> Custodis litora Phoebi,
>   Caesaris et fortis dicere posse ratis,
> Qui nunc Aeneae Troiani suscitat armA
>   Iactaque Lauinis moenia litoribuS.
> Cedite Romani scriptores, cedite, GraI!   65
>   Nescio quid maius nascitur IliadE.
>
> Prop. 2.34.59-66 Fedeli (2005)

> My pleasure is to loll amid the garlands of yesterday, for the god of unerring aim has pierced me to the bone: that of Virgil is to be able to sing the Actian shores over which Apollo watches, and the brave fleet of Caesar; even now he is stirring to life the arms of Trojan Aeneas and the walls he founded on Lavine shores. Give way, you Roman writers, give way you Greeks! Something greater than the Iliad is coming to birth.

In these famous lines, Propertius announces contents and topics of the Virgilian masterpiece, with several quotations *ad verbum* of the *Aeneid*'s prologue.[14] Scholars have devoted a number of comments to these lines, but there is something that to my knowledge has gone unnoticed.

The three first words of line 61, *Actia Vergiliu<m> Custodis*, spell the acronym A V C, which can also be found in *Arma Virumque Cano* (Verg. *Aen.* 1.1), echoing *Ab Vrbe Condita*, as pointed out by Froesch (1991). No one, at least to my knowledge, has noticed the other wordplays framing this crucial passage, namely the boustrophedon acrostics AQIS and ICNE, which can be read starting from the last letter of line 63 (A of *armA*), and ending with the last letter of line 65 (E of *IliadE*). Compared to the incipit of the *Aeneid*, the reading direction would be inverted (but this would not be a problem, considering the *variatio in*

---

[14] For a detailed commentary of this passage, including textual criticism (textual problems are completely irrelevant for our argumentations) see mainly Fedeli (2005) 987-994. A useful discussion can also be found in O'Rourke (2011).

imitando),[15] but it would be the same as for Aratean IΔMHI, discussed above.

Once again, all this could be just a coincidence, but AQIS and ICNE are very meaningful words. Before any analysis, we need to clarify that AQIS is to be understood as AQ(u)IS (= *aquis*, plural ablative of *aqua*),[16] and ICNE is to be understood as IGNE (= *igne*, singular ablative of *ignis*). The use of grapheme C for G is well attested in archaic Latin, as we can read in several inscriptions, for instance the one (boustrophedon) of the 'Black Stone', where we find *recei* (= *regei*).[17] As we will see, Propertius' intentional choice of composing archaising words would be completely justified by the context of these *technopaignia*.

Considering that AQ(u)IS and ICNE are two ablatives, which we could understand as 'from the waters', and 'from the fire', it is really tempting to see an allusion to the Odyssean and to the Iliadic parts of the *Aeneid* (Books 1-6: the voyage over the sea, and 7-12: the destructive fire of war). Besides, we notice that AQ(u)IS ends on *litoribus* and ICNE on *Iliade* (Aeneas survives the dangers of the sea, after escaping from the fire of Troy).

According to the second Book of the *Aeneid*, the flames of the Trojan fire respectfully give way to *pius Aeneas*.[18] Ovid draws on this aspect when describing the origin of the rituals performed during the *Parilia*, the festivities in honour of the Roman deity Pales (cf. Ov. *Fasti* 4.783-800). It is interesting to note that during the *Parilia*, which, according to Ovid's account, are closely related to the *dies natalis*

---

[15] For other interesting examples of *uariatio* in composing *technopaignia*, see Valerius Flaccus' and Statius' *sphragis*, discussed in Castelletti (2015a).

[16] Q for QU is attested by several Latin inscriptions, especially archaic; see for instance the Duenos inscription: *deiuos qoi med mitat. nei ted endo cosmis uirco sied* (CIL 1².4 = ILLRP 2). Moreover, consider also the abbreviations QIQE for *quinque* and QIR for *Quirina (tribus)*, cf. Cappelli (2012) 578. Lastly, see also Quint. *Inst.* 1.7.14 *fortasse enim sicut scribebant, etiam loquebantur* (referred to ancient times). In any case (as we shall see), Propertius' archaisms are inspired by the Virgilian ones (especially *mos qis ei*).

[17] The *Niger Lapis* inscriptions (on which see below p. 301-302) are in CIL 1².1 = ILLRP 3. In the Duenos inscription (see previous footnote) we read *uirco* (= *uirgo*), in CIL 1².60 *cratia* (= *gratia*). Consider also Diomedes (1.423 K.): *G noua est consonans, in cuius locum C solebat adponi, sicut hodieque cum Gaium notamus....scribimus C*. Other examples are discussed in Traina (1960) 11-12.

[18] Cf. Verg. *Aen.* 2.632-633.

Romae (21th April), the rituals are celebrated with fire and water,[19] a practice that could have been introduced by Aeneas himself.[20] A few lines later, Ovid points out that Romulus lights a fire on an altar, before tracing the *sulcus* of the walls with the plough.[21] The Propertian acrostics AQ(u)IS and ICNE could therefore also be alluding to this important aspect, once again closely related to the origins of Rome.

Certainly only the poet could tell us if all of this is accidental or deliberate, but it seems that these Propertian *technopaignia* all point to the same direction: the origins of Rome. By composing such an elaborate frame, in his *recusatio* to an epic poem, Propertius would praise (or challenge) his colleague Virgil, who has endeavoured to write a poem on the origins of the Roman people, alluding not only to its contents and purposes, but also to the sophisticated compositions embedded in it. In this witty poetic competition, Propertius would show himself as gifted as his colleague, and thus provide us (in his sphragistic elegy!), with an eyewitness confirmation of the intentionality of Virgil's boustrophedon *sphragis*.

This first class, contemporary reader, could help us better understand Virgil's complex *sphragis*.[22]

As we have just discussed, Propertius would have composed two words in boustrophedon acrostic, AQ(u)IS and ICNE. Virgil as well seems to have composed two boustrophedon acrostics in the incipit of the *Aeneid*. The first one (A *STILO M V*) is in the first 4 lines. The second is to be found few lines farther, in the invocation of the Muse:

> **M**usa, mihi causas memora, quo numine laes**O**
> **Q**uidue dolens regina deum tot uoluere casu**S**
> **I**nsignem pietate uirum, tot adire labore**S**
> **I**mpulerit. tantaene animis caelestibus ira**E**?
> Verg. *Aen.* 1.8-11 Geymonat (2008)

---

[19] Cf. Ov. *Fasti* 4.787-791.
[20] Cf. Ov. *Fasti* 4.799-800.
[21] Cf. Ov. *Fasti* 4.823-826.
[22] Another ancient witness of Virgil's boustrophedon acrostics is provided by a later text, the *Aenigmata* ascribed to Symphosius (a collection of one hundred riddles of three hexameters each, dating between the end of the 4th century and the beginning of the 6th century, where the answer to each riddle is contained in its *titulus*). In the first of the riddles (the *titulus* of which is STILUS/ GRAPHIUM) the author embedded the boustrophedon acrostic TAVROD, an archaizing form of ablative ending in -d (also found in the *Niger Lapis*' inscription) of the word *taurus* 'the ox': For a discussion of this *technopaignion*, see Castelletti, Siegenthaler (2016).

Muse, let the memories spill through me. What divine will was wounded, what deep hurt made the queen of the gods thrust a famously righteous man into so many spirals of chance to face so many labours? Anger so great: can it really reside in the spirits of heaven?

If we read lines 8-11 the same way we did for lines 1-4, the boustrophedon sequence spells *MOS QIS EI*. In his invocation to the Muse, the poet asks several questions (*q̱uo numine laeso, q̱uidve dolens regina deum.., tantaene animis caelestibus irae?*), to which we could also add the one written in boustrophedon acrostic (note the polyptoton of the interrogative adjective): *MOS Q(u)IS EI* that is *quis mos [est] ei?* (dative of possession) 'what is his/ her *mos*?'

Before deciding if this *technopaignion* is intentional, we first need to understand its possible meaning. It is well known that *mos* is a very significant word, and Virgil confers upon it special importance, as it occurs 44 times in the *Aeneid*.[23] An important topic for Virgilian Epic, *mos* is also one of the pillars of Augustan reforms and propaganda, especially in the form of *mos maiorum*, an expression evoking the joint nature of Roman civilian and political history. In the passage under examination, the *regina deum* is of course Juno, and the *insignem pietate virum* is Aeneas, who embodies and carries several aspects of the *mos* (*maiorum*), accordingly first and foremost by Jupiter's will, stating that Aeneas *moresque viris et moenia ponet* ('he'll give men civilized ways and fortified ramparts,' *Aen*. 1.264).[24]

In the seminal vision of Virgil's epic poem, the origins of Rome's greatness and security are firmly anchored in faithfulness to the *mores*, a concept that is articulated in a very famous line of Ennius: *moribus antiquis res stat romana uirisque* ('The Roman state stands on ancient customs and manhood,' *Annales* 156 Skutsch = 500 Vahlen). The first four words of this hexameter (*M̱oribus A̱ntiquis Ṟes Ṣtat*) spell the acronym *MARS*, as observed by Hendry (1994). It is of course difficult to prove the intentionality of this composition, but it is also legitimate to wonder (with Hendry) whether there would be a possible

---

[23] On the use of *mos* in Virgil and its ideological contextualization, see Tremoli, Bianco (1987).
[24] Describing the indigenous populations of Latium, king Evander says *quis neque mos neque cultus erat, nec iungere tauros ... norant* ('people devoid of all manners or culture, who hadn't a notion of how to yoke oxen,' *Aen*. 8.315-316).

connection between this acronym and the famous Virgilian acrostic MARS (inserted at the beginning of the description of the important indigenous cult of Janus), which originates from the word *mos*:[25]

> **M**os erat Hesperio in Latio, quem protinus urbes
> **A**lbanae coluere sacrum, nunc maxima rerum
> **R**oma colit, cum prima mouent in proelia Martem,
> **S**ive Getis inferre manu lacrimabile bellum
> Verg. Aen. 7.601-604 Geymonat (2008)
>
> Men had a custom in Latium's Hesperian days, which the later Alban cities adopted and hallowed. It now is the practice in mighty Rome's great empire, when men rouse Mars for a new set of battles: say, for example, they're planning to bring war's tears to the Getae (...).

If Virgil had intentionally drawn inspiration from the Ennian acronym MARS to compose his acrostic MARS, this would be an interesting example of intertextuality through *technopaignia*.[26] It is difficult to prove, as we said. At any rate, the Ennian parallel is interesting for several reasons. Indeed, it seems that Virgil himself embedded one or more acronyms in the incipit of the *Aeneid* (as we will discuss below). But what is most important, for the sake of the topic we are debating in these pages, is that Ennius himself has embedded his own sphragis in one of his works (we don't know which one), by means of an acrostic, as witnessed by Cicero (*Diu.* 111): *ea, quae ἀκροστιχίς dicitur, cum deinceps ex primis uersus litteris aliquid conectitur, ut in quibusdam Ennianis: Q. ENNIUS FECIT* ('what is termed 'acrostic' wherein the initial letters of each verse taken in order convey a meaning; as, for example, in some verses of Ennius: Q[uintus] Ennius wrote it.').

If we go back to *MOS Q(u)IS EI* in the *Aeneid*'s incipit, it is reasonable to argue that the anaphoric *ei* is deliberately left open to several identifications. Indeed, it could be referred to Juno,[27] or to Aeneas, but also to a literary model, such as Homer (the invocation to the Muse is

---

[25] On the genuineness of this acrostic (signalled to the reader through the key-words *prima mouent... Martem*), see Fowler (1983).
[26] For other examples of intertextual *technopaignia*, see Castelletti (2012ᵇ) and (2015ᵃ); see in particular the acrostic AIDOS in V. Fl. 3.430-434 drawing on Hom. *Il.* 5.787 = 8.228.
[27] In this case, *mos* could probably be interpreted as referring to a personal behaviour or psychological state; for examples with discussion, see Tremoli, Bianco (1987) 603.

openly recalling the Homeric model),[28] or Ennius. As we will see, to this identification we could add another one, bearing strong ideological meanings.

Maxime mathematicae operam dedit (vsd 15)

If we want to try to shed light on this rich and complex material, and answer the many questions it raises, we should keep in mind the context in which Virgil and his contemporary Augustan poets were writing. I will propose a reading of this elaborate Virgilian *sphragis*, stating once again that this can only be a working hypothesis that only the poet could definitively confirm.

In the first four lines of the *Aeneid*, Virgil 'signs' his poem, through the boustrophedon acrostic *a stilo M[aronis] V[ergili]*. As discussed above, ploughing has been a fairly common metaphor for writing (verse) ever since Greek archaic poets and this image also survives in Latin literature, where the Latin verb *arare* ('to plough'), is also used metaphorically for 'to write (poetry)'. The analogy between a *stilus* and a plough (and between the writing process and ploughing) was already known before Virgil, as testified, for example, by a fragment of Titus Quinctius Atta (died in Rome in 77 BC), quoted by Isidore of Seville (*Etym*. 6.9.2): *uertamus uomerem/ in cera mucroneque aremus osseo* ('let us turn the ploughshare in the wax, and plough with a point made of bone'). Therefore, associating the *stilus* to a boustrophedon movement, Virgil seems to hint at a very precise image: that of a *sulcus*, a trace left by a plough in the ground. Construed with an ablative of origin (*a stilo*), at the very beginning of a poem dedicated to the origins (of the *Vrbs*), the plough Virgil wanted to allude to would hardly be a generic one, but more likely the one used during a foundation ritual, to trace the *sulcus primigenius*.[29]

Concretely, of course, the trace of the *sulcus primigenius* is not boustrophedon. But the point is that in the Virgilian *technopaignion* the

---

[28] The first word (*Musa*) recalls the first line of the *Odyssey*, and the last one (*irae*), the first of the *Iliad*.

[29] On the rituals of Roman cities' foundations and their links with Rome's foundation, see Briquel (2000) and Carandini (2006ᵃ) 410-440. See also Carandini, Cappelli (2000) 275-277 and Castelletti (2015ᵇ) 223-224 for visual reconstructions.

boustrophedon is used to recall the image implied on the verb *arare*: that of a trace (a *sulcus*) left on the surface during the act of ploughing; concretely as well as metaphorically. Indeed, as we will see below, the image of ploughing is to be intended both as 'writing' (the poet uses his *stilus* to write and 'sign' his work) and as a trace left in the ground (during the ritual of foundation).

Bearing this last point on mind, we will be able to better understand the function of the two boustrophedon acrostics, as well as the whole meaning of this elaborate Virgilian *sphragis*.

As pointed out by Lansing,[30] Virgil uses 48 words to compose the first sentence of the *Aeneid* (spanning over lines 1-7), and this seems hardly a coincidence, given that 48 recalls the total number of books of the Homeric poems (24 *Iliad* + 24 *Odyssey*). Moreover, Virgil has probably drawn inspiration from Apollonius, who employs 24 words for his first sentence of the *Argonautica*. If we consider how much care and *labor limae* Virgil devoted to his poems, we should not be surprised if he really had counted his words. One could of course be skeptical about this, especially if considering the *scriptio continua*, which could make the division between the words less clear. However, there is a base unit that can be calculated with absolute precision: the letter. The question is therefore: did Virgil count his letters?

Before proceeding with any calculations, we should ask ourselves whether this operation would make any sense. The answer is rather logical. If what we have discussed so far is not just pure chance, that is, if Virgil really did compose these *technopaignia* deliberately, following the Aratean model, we might assume that he considered his letters as *stoicheia*, as *elementa*, single basic elements that can aggregate, such as stars in the sky, to compose more complex entities (words, or constellations). We know from the *Vitae Vergilianae* that Virgil was particularly interested in 'mathematica' (to be understood as astrological computations)[31] and his interest for numbers and numerology is fairly evident in all of his works.[32] We might then conclude that, if Virgil had really counted his letters, he would have done that in a highly

---

[30] Lansing (2008).
[31] Cf. *VSD* 15 *Inter cetera studia medicinae quoque ac maxime mathematicae operam dedit.*
[32] On Virgil's interest for numerology see Brugnoli, Scarcia (1987), Morgan, Thomas (2013), with bibliography, and Castelletti (2015ᵇ) 225-232.

significant passage. The incipit of the *Aeneid* is certainly a very good place for such an operation.

Let us then count the letters of the first 11 lines of the poem (Verg. *Aen.* 1.1-11 Geymonat [2008]):

Arma uirumque cano, Troiae qui primus ab oris	1	(37)
Italiam fato profugus Lauiniaque uenit	2	(34)
litora, multum ille et terris iactatus et alto	3	(38)
ui superum, saeuae memorem Iunonis ob iram,	4	(35) **[144]**
multa quoque et bello passus, dum conderet urbem	5	(40)
inferretque deos Latio; genus unde Latinum	6	(36)
Albanique patres atque altae moenia Romae.	7	(36) **[112]**
Musa, mihi causas memora, quo numine laeso	8	(34)
quidue dolens regina deum tot uoluere casus	9	(37)
insignem pietate uirum, tot adire labores	10	(35)
impulerit, tantaene animis caelestibus irae?	11	(38) **[144]** TOT **400 letters**

The total amount of letters in lines 1-4 is 144; in the following three lines, 112, whereas in the last four lines it is again 144. Grand total: 400 letters.[33] How should we read these numbers? If Virgil has really counted his letters, my interpretation is as follows.

Virgil composed a boustrophedon acrostic in the first four lines of the poem (which correspond to a total of 144 letters) and another boustrophedon acrostic in lines 8-11 (another 144 letters). 144 is precisely the square of 12, a very evocative number. Indeed, there are 12 Books of the *Aeneid*, but 12 is also a number that suits the ancient sexagesimal system of measurement.[34]

Considering that Virgil composed two boustrophedon acrostics, in lines 1-4 and 8-11, we might argue that the poet wanted to symbolically 'plough' twice, a square surface of 12 x 12. In the first surface (lines

---

[33] I have used Virgil's edition of Geymonat (2008) (the text of these lines is the same as Mynors [1969]). Concerning *Aen.* 1.1-11, the only difference with other editions (for instance Conte [2009]) concerns the *uexata quaestio* of *lauiniaque* vs *lauinaque* of line 2. Given that the question is still unsolved, because there are good reasons to support each reading, if the numerical observations discussed in these pages are correct, they would support the reading *lauiniaque* over *lauinaque*.

[34] For instance, l'*actus* is 120 Roman feet. Note also that *arma uirumque* are precisely 12 letters. If the numerology discussed here is correct, did it have any influence over other authors? I think for instance of the *Symposium duodecim sapientium*, in which the first cycle is composed by 12 hexameters, each of 6 words (with some exceptions) of 6 letters. On this work, see Friedrich (2002).

1-4), where the perspective is subjective and focused on the present (*arma uirumque cano*), the poet placed his name (*Maro Vergilius*). In the second (lines 8-11), in which he addresses the memory of the Muse, to make her recall what happened in the past (*Musa mihi causas memora*), he deliberates about the *mos* (*maiorum*).

If all this is not a mere coincidence, the composition would have profound ideological implications. Indeed, Virgil could have allusively reproduced in his text what Augustus was concretely building on the Palatine: the *Roma quadrata*.

Roma quadrata

What and where was the *Roma quadrata* mentioned in ancient sources, is still an unsolved and very debated question.[35] There is no room here to go through the entire debate again, but I would like to provide the ongoing discussions with some new elements of reflection.

The oldest preserved mention of *Roma quadrata* is by Ennius, quoted in Festus (pp. 310-312 Lindsay):

> Quadrata Roma in Palatio <locus> ante templum Apollinis dicitur, ubi reposita sunt, quae solent boni ominis gratia in urbe condenda adhiberi, quia saxo munitus (codd. minitus) est initio in speciem quadratam. Eius loci Ennius meminit cum ait: 'et †quis est erat† Romae regnare quadratae.'

> A place on the Palatine in front of the temple of Apollo is called 'square Rome'. It is where those things are stored which are customarily used for the sake of a good omen in founding a city. (It is so called) because it was originally built of stone in a square shape. Ennius refers to this place when he says 'And (...) to rule over square Rome.'

---

[35] The latest contribution on the topic is Wiseman (2015), who associates *Roma quadrata* with the equal plots shared out among Romulus' citizens, arguing that 'Romulus marked out from the hut the first square plot, 240 feet each way, based on a surveyor's cardo that could also be thought of as an astrologer's cardo defining the city's fated life; the plot was called *Roma quadrata*, a phrase later misused by historians as if it referred to the city walls.' Seminal works on *Roma quadrata* are Grandazzi (1993), Mastrocinque (1998), Coarelli (1999ª), Carandini (2000) 121-123, Krause (2001) 193-201, Krause (2002), Krause (2004) 46-48, Carandini (2006ᵇ) 162-165, Bruno (2010) 294-196, Coarelli (2012) 145-165, Carandini (2014) 16-25 and 321. See also Castelletti (2015ᵇ) 226-232.

What Ennius really did mean by *Roma quadrata* is very difficult to know. Other authors describe the location of *Roma quadrata*, and some also provide its dimensions, which can be very variable, and this has caused a number of problems of interpretation for both ancient and modern authors.

Some of the misunderstanding may be due to the fact that the fire of AD 64 has largely destroyed the republican and Augustan Palatine, and the hilltop was redeveloped as an imperial palace, the *domus Tiberiana*. What was probably a (square?) area once, was gradually identified as or mistaken for a place or a monument (and became a particular toponym), which may have been part of the palace. This could probably explain the differences of dimensions provided by ancient sources,[36] which seem to refer to (at least) two different entities: an area as big as the whole Palatine, and a smaller monument, located in the *area Apollinis*. At any rate, if we compare all the ancient testimonies, although authors offered different dimensions for it, *Roma quadrata* was naturally thought of as a square area (or single place/ object).[37]

For the purpose of this paper it is not necessary to know exactly what and where Romulus' *Roma quadrata* was, but what its symbolism was for Virgil and Augustus. In this respect, even if what is commonly considered to be the house of Augustus has been recently questioned,[38] modern scholars tend to agree on the fact that Augustus has built his residence on the Palatine, in order to establish a direct link with what was considered the area where Romulus founded the city. This project began already around 43 BC, when Octavian (who was actually born on the Palatine) bought the house of Hortensius,[39] located near to the hut from which Romulus was thought to have taken the auspices for the foundation (the *tugurium Faustuli*, or the *casa Romuli*, which is perhaps

---

[36] To this, we might add possible confusions originating from conversion into another language, as seems to be the case for the Greek text of Appian (*bas*. fr. 1a9), who refers to a perimeter of 4 x 4 stadia, probably converting a Roman dimension of 4 x 4 actus. On this topic, see Coarelli (1999ª) 207-208, Coarelli (2012) 147-148, Krause (2002) 99.

[37] Apart from Festus (quoted above), see Plut. *Rom*. 9.4 and Dion. Hal. 1.88.2.

[38] The identification as house of Augustus of the domus immediately west and south of Apollo's temple podium goes back to Carettoni's excavations of 1956. The house is still on display to the public as such, but its identification (accepted by the majority of the scholars) has been recently questioned, in particular by Claridge (2010) 142-143 and Wiseman (2012) and (2015).

[39] Cf. Suet. *Aug*. 72.1.

the same as the *curia Saliorum*).⁴⁰ From 36 BC Octavian/ Augustus bought other houses in the same area, and later also built the temple of Apollo.⁴¹ Therefore, regardless of the precise dimensions and location of the Romulean *Roma quadrata*, the majority of modern scholars agree on the highly symbolic meaning of this Augustan operation, aiming at recovering a *lieu de mémoire* (called *Roma quadrata*) related to the mythical founder of the city, within the building complex created by Augustus on the Palatine.⁴² Scholars also point out the relevance of the augural aspect of this place, fairly evident in every ancient account of the city's foundation, included the ones by Festus (see above) and by Solinus (quoting Varro):

> [17] nam, ut adfirmat Varro auctor diligentissimus, Romam condidit Romulus, Marte genitus et Rhea Siluia, uel ut nonnulli Marte et Ilia: dictaque primum est Roma quadrata, quod ad aequilibrium foret posita. [18] Ea incipit a silua quae est in area Apollinis, et ad supercilium scalarum Caci habet terminum, ubi tugurium fuit Faustuli. Ibi Romulus mansitauit, qui auspicato murorum fundamenta iecit duodeuiginti natus annos.
>
> Solinus 1.17-18 Mommsen

> For as Varro, a most careful author, asserts, Romulus the son of Mars and Rhea Silvia, or as some say Mars and Ilia, founded Rome. [18] It was first called 'square Rome' because it was placed at the balancing-point.⁴³ It begins from the grove, which is in the precinct of Apollo, and has its end at the brow of the stairs of Cacus, where the hut of Faustulus was. That was where Romulus stayed overnight. After taking the auspices he laid the foundations of the walls at the age of eighteen years.

If we admit that in Augustan age, *Roma quadrata* was thought to be a square surface (this would be entirely logical, if we think of the

---

⁴⁰ Cf. Coarelli (2012) 149-157, Wiseman (2015) 109.
⁴¹ Cf. Vell. Pat. 2.81.3 and Cass. Dio 49.15.5.
⁴² This aspect is clearly highlighted by Coarelli and Carandini, who agree on the interpretation of *Roma quadrata* 'ridotta' ('reduced') as a monument built by Augustus to connect his new complex (house and temple of Apollo) to the *templum* from which Romulus was thought to have taken the auspices for the foundation (the *tugurium Faustuli – casa Romuli*); see Coarelli (2012) 148-165, Carandini (2014) 16-25, 321.
⁴³ It is difficult to understand the exact meaning of *ad aequilibrium*. Carandini (2006ᵃ) 185 translates it 'a livello del monte', Coarelli (2012) 148 *liuellata* or *in piano*. Wiseman (2015) interprets it as a chronological allusion, based on astrology: 'Solinus' phrase *ad aequilibrium posita* probably represents a Varronian statement that Rome was founded under Libra, on the summit of the Palatine.'

Roman concern to find an ideal geometric model, which would be detectable and reproducible in all the colonies and cities founded by the Romans),[44] could it be possible to find traces of it in the architecture of the incipit of the *Aeneid*? Virgil might have done the following operations, maybe inspired by a Varronian taste for erudition.[45]

In lines 1-4 (of 12 x 12 letters) Virgil created his own (literary) *Roma quadrata*, sealing it with his signature, whereas in lines 8-11, the invocation of the Muse (also a square of 12 x 12 letters) he recalled the one of the (literary) founder: Homer/ Ennius.

Such a specular structure would precisely mirror what Augustus was building on the Palatine: his own ('artificial') *Roma quadrata*, next to the one thought to be of the founder (Romulus).[46] Moreover, Virgil seems to have embedded in his text hints alluding to Augustan ideology, exploiting numerology and epigraphic language. Indeed, we can infer that the symbology of the number 12 may allude not only to the number of books of the poem, but also to the number of birds (vultures) spotted by Romulus on the hill: the favourable augury that granted him the privilege to found (or to rule over) the city. But there are also 12 vultures that appeared to Augustus as he took the auspices in the Campus Martius for his first consulate (on 19th August 43 BC), an important analogy pointed out by Suetonius (*Aug.* 95) *primo autem consulatu et augurium capienti duodecim se uultures ut Romulo ostenderunt* ('in his first consulship, when he was taking the auspices, twelve vultures appeared to him, as they had to Romulus'). The importance of Augustus' recuperation of Romulus' symbolism is widely known, starting with his very same *cognomen* (*Augustus*), that Octavian accepted instead of the more straightforward (but also more problematic) *Romulus*.[47]

---

[44] On this respect, see Dion. Hal. 1.88.2, Varro *Ling.* 5.143, Cato *Orig.* fr. 18 Peter, 1.18 a Chassignet, Gell. 16.13.9. For a discussion, see Briquel (2000).

[45] Symbolic numerology can also be traced in some ancient authors referring the measurements of *Roma quadrata*. According to Coarelli (2012) 147-148 Appian would have adapted his measures to render them numerologically more meaningful; an erudite operation, inspired by neoplatonism, which is very frequent in Varro.

[46] This is Carandini's interpretation, agreed by Coarelli, according to whom *Roma quadrata* 'ridotta' ('reduced') refers to two different entities, sharing the same name and function, ideologically connected because they were emblematic places (related both with the first and with the new founder of the city).

[47] According to Cassius Dio (53.16.7-8) Octavian craved the *cognomen Romulus*, but this was discarded to avoid the feeling that he wanted to restore the *regnum*.

In this case too, Suetonius provides us with an emblematic passage (*Aug.* 7):

> Postea Gai Caesaris et deinde Augusti cognomen assumpsit, alterum testamento maioris auunculi, alterum Munati Planci sententia, cum quibusdam censentibus Romulum appellari oportere quasi et ipsum conditorem urbis, praeualuisset, ut Augustus potius uocaretur, non tantum nouo sed etiam ampliore cognomine, quod loca quoque religiosa et in quibus augurato quid consecratur augusta dicantur, ab **auctu** uel ab auium gestu gustuue, sicut etiam Ennius docet scribens:
> Augusto augurio postquam incluta condita Roma est [= Ann. 155 Skutsch = 502 Vahlen].
>
> Later on he took the surnames of Gaius Caesar and then of Augustus, the first in accordance with the will of his great-uncle, the second on the proposal of Munatius Plancus. Responding to the suggestion of others that Augustus ought to be called Romulus on the grounds that he too was, as it were, a founder of the city, Munatius argued successfully that he should rather take the name Augustus, a name not only new but also grander. For holy places, also, and places where something has been consecrated by augural rites are termed 'august', either from the term for an increase in dignity or from the phrase denoting the movements or feeding of birds, as Ennius too tells us when he writes:
> After renowned Rome was founded with august augury.

If we return to the incipit of the *Aeneid*, we can observe that, if the three first words *Arma Virumque Cano* (v. 1) spell out the same acronym as *Ab Vrbe Condita*, considering also the fourth word (*Troiae*),[48] the acronym would be *AVCT*, which is commonly used in Latin as abbreviation for *auctor* and *auctoritas*. The *auctor* of the *Aeneid* is of course Virgil, who uses precisely the same word to claim the paternity of the *sphragis* in the *Georgics* (*namque is certissimus auctor*, *G.* 1.432).[49] But *auctoritas* is also one of the pillars of Augustus' political program,[50] linked with the concepts of growth and prosperity,

---

[48] As observed above the model for an acronym inserted in the first four words of the line, is likely to be Ennius.
[49] On Virgil's syllabic acrostic *sphragis* MAVE PV (*G.* 1.429-33), see Somerville (2010) and Danielewicz (2013).
[50] Augustus himself mentions *auctoritas* in *Mon. Anc.* 34.3. It is indeed *auctoritas* that rendered him superior to the others, although he was formally equal by *potestas*. For a discussion on the nature of Augustus' power and the relationships between *imperium*, *potestas* and *auctoritas*, see Ridley (2003) 222-227.

as testified by the supposed etymological connection between *augeo* and *Augustus*. Through the name 'Augustus',[51] Octavian recalls his function of 'saver' of the Republic, putting forward his image of founder of a new era for the history of the community, of *auctor* of the *res publica*'s rebirth.[52]

It is indeed as a new Romulus that Augustus re-founds the city,[53] after the *nefas* of the civil wars. The restoration of the *mores* and the recovery of the *mos maiorum* are of primary importance in his political agenda.

We can now grasp the most significant aspect of the Virgilian architecture. Indeed, in his elaborate and perfectly balanced composition of the *Aeneid*'s incipit, Virgil connects at the same time himself (the new Homer, but also the new Ennius) to the founder of epic poetry,[54] and the new founder of Rome (Augustus) to the first founder of the *Vrbs* (Romulus).[55] The main aspect characterizing both Virgil's and Augustus' work is the innovation of the tradition.[56] In this regards, we can now better understand the question raised by the boustrophedon acrostic *mos q(u)is ei*. The anaphoric pronoun could indeed be referring to real historical persons, or mythical ones. The question in acrostic though

---

[51] On this aspect see Mazzarino (1966) 621-624, who links 'Augustus' to *augeo* and connects the epithet to the augural aspect; the scholar argues that *Augustus* expresses the power of growth of the *princeps*. The etymology though is still debated, and even among the ancients it was not easy to establish (the sources hesitate between *augur* and *augeo*). For a study on this etymology (ancient and modern), the choice and the implications of the *cognomen Augustus*, see Todisco (2007) who points out that it is from Augustus onward (until modern times) that the connection between *augustus* and *augeo* is made (the connection could therefore be a product of Augustus himself).

[52] This aspect is also evident in an edict of Augustus (referred by Suet. *Aug.* 28), in which the *fundamenta rei publicae* are to be laid, and the potential of *auctoritas* to be exploited. On the occasion and the date of this edict (likely an important public event for the community), see Todisco (2007) 454-455.

[53] The roles of *auctor/conditor* and *seruator* (mutually interconnected) are also established in the *Fasti Praenestini*; see Todisco (2007) 455.

[54] Did Virgil also consider Aratus as a founder (of *technopaignia* composition)?

[55] According to Servius, Virgil links Augustus to Romulus in *Aen.* 1.292 (*Remo cum fratre Quirino iura dabant): uera tamen hoc habet ratio, Quirinum Augustum esse, Remum uero pro Agrippa positum*. On the relationship between Quirinus/ Augustus and Agrippa/Remus, see Wiseman (1995) 144-150. On Octavian's use of the Romulean myth (a canny politician, Octavian, never completely identified with Romulus), see Kienast (1982) 93 n. 45 (with previous bibliography); Martin (1994) 406-408; Hurlet (2001) 156-157; Roddaz (2003) 400; Todisco (2007) 455-456.

[56] Scholars have extensively discussed innovation and tradition in Augustan culture, see e.g. Galinsky (1996).

is addressed to the Muse, whom the poet asks to recall the *causas* (in which it is not difficult to see an allusion to the *aitia* of Callimachus, who indeed has a dialogue with the Muses in his first two books). Therefore, in a specular manner with lines 1-4, where the first four words (*Arma uirumque cano Troiae*) are fundamental for the solution of the *technopaignia*, in lines 8-11 as well, the first four words (*Musa mihi causas memora*) suggest that the *aition* to which the *technopaignion* is referring to, could be Romulus' foundation ritual. The repetition of the concept of memory (explicit in the verb *memora*, and implicit in *Musa*, daughter of Mnemosyne) is significant. As previously argued, lines 8-11 would allude to Romulus' *Roma quadrata*, a *monumentum* whose memory has lasted for centuries, and which Augustus wanted to hand down to posterity.

From a structural point of view, the source of inspiration seems to be Ennius' line quoted above[57] in which the first four words (*Moribus Antiquis Res Stat*) spell out the acronym MARS. Besides, in Ennius as well as in Virgil (*Aen*. 1.1-4 and 8-11) the first four words span over the same metrical length.

Lastly, we should try to understand the meaning of *Aen*. 1.5-7 in this elaborate Virgilian composition. These lines describe the main steps leading from the foundation of Lavinium to Rome,[58] and key-words[59] such as 'dum conderet urbem' (v. 5) and 'altae moenia Romae' (v. 7), placed along the two 'symbolically ploughed areas' of 12 x 12 letters, mark out the Virgilian structure. Lines 5-7 are not 'ploughed' (they don't conceal any boustrophedon acrostic). Shall we interpret this as an allusion to the custom of lifting the plough (thus interrupting the tracing of the *sulcus*) where the founder wanted to locate the gates of the city?[60]

---

[57] *Moribus Antiquis Res Stat Romana uirisque* (*Annales* 156 Skutsch = 500 Vahlen).
[58] 'And he suffered profoundly in war to establish a city, settle his gods into Latium, making this land of the Latin's future home to the Elders of Alba and Rome's mighty ramparts.'
[59] We have already pointed out the relevance of keywords used to hint at the presence of *technopaignia*. These keywords are very useful clues to establish the genuineness of some compositions, but ancient poets did not always use them, or sometimes they are less evident. In the incipit of the *Aeneid*, where the poet needed to deal with several factors (included maybe the quantity of letters to use), the main clues are certainly the collocation of the passage (the very beginning of the poem) and the context, providing the appropriate background for the *technopaignia* discussed in these pages. Other more concrete signals are the *Wortstellung* and acronyms such as AVC(T).
[60] Cato *Orig*. fr. 18 Peter, 1.18 a Chassignet (= Serv. *in Aen*. 5.755).

Or would these three lines allude to the *mundus*, a hole or underground pit dug in the centre of the city that is being founded, where votive offerings are laid?[61] Note that in line 6, which is in the exact middle of the first 11 lines of the poem, there is an arrival point (*inferretque deos Latio*, the arrival of the Penates in Latium, closing the section devoted to Aeneas' mission) and a starting point (*genus unde Latinum*, from which start the subsequent events lead to the foundation of Rome). The *umbilicus Vrbis* (the *omphalos*) would therefore be exactly in the centre of the poem's incipit (lines 1-11), more precisely after the caesura between *Latio* and *genus* (line 6). Or lastly, the function of these three lines, recalling Rome's history backwards (from the mythical past to the historical present) is yet to separate (and at the same time to ideologically connect) the two *Roma quadrata* ('ridotta') embedded in lines 1-4 and 8-11 (maybe according to the proportions the real monuments had on the Palatine?). In any case, from a numerological point of view, these 3 lines can be added together with the 4 previous or with the following 4, to obtain the symbolic number 7 (as the Roman hills or kings).

It would be difficult and risky to put forward other hypotheses. At any rate (to conclude with numerological speculations), if the importance of the idea of *Roma quadrata* was firstly to preserve and to perpetrate the memory of an ancestral place, ideally reproduced in every foundation of a new colony, we might wonder how fortuitous it is that the grand total of the letters of *Aen.* 1.1-11 is 400. Indeed 400 square *actus* are precisely 200 *iugera*,[62] namely 1 *centuria*. If Virgil did really count his letters to build his (symbolic) architecture, we should not be surprised that the numerology at the very beginning of his poem on the origins of the Vrbs should allude to the method of centuriation.[63]

---

[61] Ovid locates the *mundus* on the Palatine (cf. *Fasti* 4.831-834), whereas for Plutarch (*Rom.* 11), who identifies it with the *umbilicus Vrbis*, it was on the Forum. On the identification of the *Mundus* with the *umbilicus*, see Coarelli (1983) 199-226; with the *Roma quadrata* 'ridotta', see Coarelli (2012) 151-155.

[62] It is useful to bear in mind that these units of measurement are linked with ploughing (and therefore the boustrophedon), as testified by Plin. *HN* 18.3.

[63] It is interesting to note that the quantity of letters of *Aen.* 1.12-22 is 398 (400, if we read *Samo et hic* with V¹, at line 16), and that of *Aen.* 1.23-33 is again 400 (for coherence, the edition is still Geymonat [2008]). The total number of letters used for the entire prologue of the *Aeneid* (1.1-33) is 400 + 398 (or 400) + 400 = 1198 (or 1200!). What does this mean? Shall we suppose that Virgil wanted to give a last *labor limae* in order to make ends meet, and reach a precise total of 1200

Conclusions

Virgil's scrupulousness in composing the incipit of his poem on Rome's origins, in which not only every single word has been selected with care, but maybe also every letter, is reverberated in a *sphragis* that can be considered as a (literary) act of foundation. As Augustus proposes himself as a new Romulus and founder of a new Rome, in which the recovery of the *mores* is a pillar of his ideological program, Virgil proposes himself as a new founder (of epic poetry), perhaps even building his own *Roma quadrata*, on the scale of (and near to) the one of the founder Homer/ Ennius. The recuperation of *memoria* (and the *mos* is part of it), is conveyed through architecture, concrete as well as literary. In this respect, the interpretation of the boustrophedon acrostic a *stilo M[aronis] V[ergili]* as a literary act of foundation, would be plausible even without the numerological speculations on the quantity of letters. Indeed, even considering only the *technopaignia* (acronyms and acrostics) of the first 11 lines, the messages would have been rather clear for the readers they were addressed to (first of all Augustus and his intelligentsia). The acronyms are well known and widely used,

---

(= 12×100) letters? Assuming that Virgil wanted to have 3 sections of 400 letters each, for an interesting total of 12×100, since boustrophedon acrostics are only in the first section (lines 1-11), the numerology could indeed allude to the centuriation system: lines 1-11 (*Roma quadrata*?) would contain the model to be reproduced, whereas the other two sections (lines 12-22 and 23-33) have the same dimensions (400 letters), but they have not been 'ploughed' yet. Note also that 1200 could refer to the fact that Rome would have lasted for 1200 years. Indeed, Varro regarded the twelve vultures as significant for the fate of Rome: his friend Vettius, an expert in augural lore, interpreted them as a sign that the gods were granting Romulus' city twelve centuries of existence; see Varro *Ant. hum.* fr. 18.4 Mirsch (Cens. *Die nat.* 17.15). Maybe all these numbers are pure chance, but as counterproof we can observe that after line 33 (which actually ends the prologue, with a clear allusion to a foundation: *tantae molis erat Romanam condere gentem*), not only there are no more semantic divisions in sections of 11 verses (as instead is the case in lines 1-33), but there is no longer a repetition of the same amount of letters (lines 34-44 = 405 letters; lines 45-55 = 401 letters, lines 56-66 = 426 letters). Another counterproof (always using Geymonat [2008]) is that in none of the other 11 books of the poem, the first 11 lines amount to a total of 400 letters (nor do they bear boustrophedon acrostics!): *Aen.* 2.1-11 = 393 letters; *Aen.* 3.1-11 = 414; *Aen.* 4.1-11 = 409; *Aen.* 5.1-11 = 424; *Aen.* 6.1-11 = 421; *Aen.* 7.1-11 = 402; *Aen.* 8.1-11 = 405; *Aen.* 9.1-11 = 382; *Aen.* 10.1-11 = 428; *Aen.* 11.1-11 = 412; *Aen.* 12.1-11 = 416. The same conclusions can be drawn on Lucretius (*DRN* 1.1-11 Martin = 404 letters), Ovid (*Met.* 1.1-11 Tarrant = 397), Lucan (1.1-11 Housman = 406), Valerius Flaccus (1.1-11 Ehlers = 409), Statius (*Theb.* 1.1-11 Klotz = 402), Silius Italicus (*Pun.* 1.1-11 Delz = 395). Lastly, we can also add Hom. *Il.* 1.1-11 Allen = 359 letters (363, including iota subscript and elision); Hom. *Od.* 1.1-11 von der Mühll = 396 (405); Arat. *Phaen.* 1.1-11 Martin = 388 (398), Ap. Rhod. *Arg.* 1.1-11 Vian = 392 (402).

from monumental inscriptions to numismatics, and fully exploited by Augustan propaganda. Note that if AVC is sometimes attested even for 'Augustus',[64] AV(G) was the common abbreviation for both 'Augustus' and 'augur'.[65] The priesthood of the augurs[66] (that the ancients believed it was created by Romulus) was in charge of deciphering and interpreting the signs provided by the deity, a function entirely similar to the one needed to understand the (Aratean) *technopaignia* (as the paradigmatic IΔMHI shows). This relationship between sky and earth, sign and interpretation, divine and human will, past and present, will be a constant not only throughout the *Aeneid*, but also during the building of the Augustan principate, the same years in which Virgil wrote his masterpiece. Virgil's *sphragis* seems therefore to condensate what Ennius states about the foundation of the Vrbs: *Augusto augurio postquam incluta condita Roma est* (*Ann.* 155 Skutsch = 502 Vahlen).

Even if *a stilo M V* does not sound particularly elegant (nor does *mos qis ei*),[67] the evocative power of the tool (a 'pen', a weapon, a plough)[68] and the morphology of the *technopaignion*, produce a remarkable expressive impact. The choice of boustrophedon script and archaizing words (the Virgilian *mos qis ei* and the Propertian *aqis* and *icne*), suggest that Virgil (and Propertius) may have taken inspiration from a monument that in Roman collective memory was related to the origins of Rome: the complex of the *Niger Lapis* and its *boustrophedon*

---

[64] See CIL 10.6640 (= ILS 3338), CIL 11.3310 (= ILS 533).
[65] This acronym could provide new evidence supporting Carandini's interpretation of *Roma quadrata*, endorsed by Coarelli (on which, see Coarelli [2012] 161). Both scholars link the original place of the *auspicatio* (that is the *tugurium Faustuli* – *casa Romuli*) with the one created by Augustus (and imitated by Virgil in *Aen.* 1.1-4), namely the *Roma quadrata* 'ridotta' – 'Auguratorium'.
[66] For Augustus' (and Caesar's) symbolic use of the augury, see e.g. Hurlet (2001) and Koortbojian (2013) 50-77.
[67] Even if stylistically not flawless, both formulations are nonetheless grammatically correct. For other occurrences of ablative of origin used in connection with the preposition *a*, without a verb (e.g. *dulces a fontibus undae* in Verg. *G.* 2.243), see *ThlL* 1.28.28-63, s.v. *a, ab*). The fact is that Virgil needed to make things work on several levels, starting with the poetical text, which needed to make sense, and had to respect the metrical rules. If he also had to count the letters, this would have made things even more difficult.
[68] It is useful to remind ourselves that in the *Georgics* Virgil exploited the metaphor of the plough (chariot) and ploughing as symbol of the *Saturnia regna*, the golden age, and therefore as a metaphor for the cosmic and political order (see Wilhelm [1982]). The plough is also one of the farmer's 'arma' (cf. *G.* 1.160-175, with Farrell [1991] 70-79).

inscriptions.[69] In any case, we don't even need to speculate on possible links with this controversial monument,[70] given that Virgil and his contemporaries knew well that the boustrophedon was a very archaic kind of writing,[71] and they certainly had at their disposal many more archaic texts that we have today. Therefore, we can better understand the morphology and the contents of the *technopaignia*[72] composed in the incipit of the *Aeneid* (and in the Propertian answer), as they refer to the origins of Rome.

An extraordinarily rich work, the *Aeneid* is also a poem on urban settlement and colonization, an *aition* explaining the presence of the

---

[69] On the complex of the *Niger Lapis*, its monuments and inscriptions, see Coarelli (1983) 161-188 and Coarelli (1999ᵇ) (the scholar identifies the monuments under the *Niger Lapis* as the *Volcanal*). The inscription is still nowadays very difficult to understand. At any rate, among the most intelligible words are *recei* (probably dative of *rex*) and *iouxmenta* (perhaps *iumenta*, 'yoked animals'), which are of course rather suggestive, if related to Romulus' ritual ploughing. Also note that Mastrocinque (1998) discusses the hypothesis that the Romulean *Roma quadrata* was actually in the Forum (maybe the Comitium itself), whereas the one on the Palatine was a product of Augustus, who wanted to recreate the topography of the Forum. This interpretation relies on the controversial passage of Plutarch (*Rom.* 11), the only ancient source locating Romulus' foundation pit in the Comitium.

[70] The inscription on the stone block under the *Niger Lapis* was probably no longer visible from around 80 BC, when the monuments were partially destroyed and covered by a new pavement. Varro would thus have had the time to see it. Dionysius of Halicarnassus (2.54.2) mentions that Romulus, after his victory over the Camerini, vowed a bronze chariot to Hephaestus, close to which he erected a statue of himself, bearing an inscription celebrating his deeds (in Greek characters). This inscription (likely in archaic Latin), is probably the same as the one Dionysius mentions in 3.1.2, describing the gravestone of Hostus Hostilius (who was buried in the most important area of the Forum). In both cases, it is possible that the monuments and the inscription are those of the *Niger Lapis* (see Coarelli [1983] 175-177 and Coarelli [1999ᵇ]). Even if the complex of the *Niger Lapis* was buried under the slabs of black marble by Sulla (though it has also been argued that Julius Caesar may have buried the site during his re-alignment of the Comitium), it is legitimate to argue that such an important inscription would have been copied and stored in archives (maybe by Varro himself), or that Augustan intellectuals might have accessed that significant place, linked with the origins of Rome. The *Niger Lapis* complex raised several (uncertain and ambiguous) interpretations among ancient sources: Romulus' grave (e.g. Varro, ap. Ps. Acro *ad Epod.* 16.13), that of Faustulus (Dionysius of Halicarnassus 1.87.2) or Hostus Hostilius (ibid. 3.1.2). Festus considered the site ominous, marking off a place of burial (the burial spot of Romulus, before he disappeared and made his burial impossible, or Hostus Hostilius, cf. *De verb. sign.* p. 184 Lindsay). For discussion and comments, see Coarelli (1983) 167-168, Coarelli (1999ᵇ) Wiseman (2015) 94-95.

[71] See e.g. Mar. Victorin. *gramm.* 6.55.25.

[72] It is useful to remind ourselves that the *libri sibyllini*, which Augustus transferred into Apollo's temple on the Palatine (the heart of his monument-house) after burning every other Greek and Latin book of prophecies (cf. Suet. *Aug.* 31.1; Serv. *in Aen* 6.72), were composed with *technopaignia*, as witnessed by Cic. *Diu.* 2.112.

Trojan Penates in Latium.[73] If the Virgilian *sphragis* at the beginning of the poem can ultimately be understood as a literary act of foundation, another such act may be seen at the end of the poem, creating a sort of ring composition. Indeed, the scene when Aeneas thrusts his sword in Turnus' body,[74] putting an end to the (civil) war and laying the foundation for the future creation of Rome, might ring to us as an echo of the first act of foundation. Both are performed through the iron (of the *stilus/ uomer*, and of Aeneas' sword), and the echo is reverberated in the significant words *ferrum*[75] ... *condit*.

Bibliography

Ahl, F. (2007), *Virgil, Aeneid*, Oxford.
Bing, P. (1984), 'Callimachus' cows. A riddling *recusatio*', *Zeitschrift für Papyrologie und Epigraphik* 59, 1-8.
Bing, P. (1990), 'A Pun on Aratus' Name in verse 2 of the *Phainomena*?', *Harvard Studies in Classical Philology* 93, 281-285.
Bing, P. (1993), 'Aratus and his Audiences', *Materiali e discussioni per l'analisi dei testi classici* 31, 99-109.
Briquel, D. (2000), 'La leggenda di Romolo e il rituale di fondazione delle città', in A. Carandini, R. Cappelli (edd.), *Roma. Romolo, Remo e la fondazione della città*, Milano, 39-44.
Brugnoli, G., Scarcia, R. (1987), s.v. 'Numerologia', in *Enciclopedia Vergiliana*, vol. 3, 788-793.

---

[73] On the ktistic aspect of Virgil's *Aeneid*, see Horsfall (1989), Thomas (2013) and Fletcher (2014). Among the several mentions of acts of foundation in the poem, see firstly the ones showing Etruscan-Roman customs (as the tracing of a *sulcus primigenius*): *pars optare locum tecto et concludere sulco* (1.425, Dido), *urbem designat aratro* (5.755, Aeneas in Sicily), *humili designat moenia fossa* (7.157, Aeneas at the mouth of the Tiber).
[74] Cf. Verg. *Aen.* 12.950-952. *hoc dicens ferrum aduerso sub pectore condit/ feruidus; ast illi soluuntur frigore membra/ uitaque cum gemitu fugit indignata sub umbras* ('and, as he speaks, he buries the steel in the heart that confronts him, boiling with rage. Cold shivers send Turnus' limbs into spasm. Life flutters off on a groan, under protest, down among shadows'). Note that in these three last lines of the poem, the first letters are H F V (acronym of *Hoc Fecit Vergilius*, echoing the Ennian acrostic *Q. Ennius fecit*?) and the last ones (from the bottom up) SAT (= *sat*?). Or *(Hoc Ferro) Vergilius Scripsit*?
[75] Note that Virgil uses the word *ferrum* for the plough in *G.* 1.50, 147 and 2.220.

Bruno, D. (2010), 'La fossa con ara romulea e la *Roma Quadrata* di Augusto', in A. Carandini (ed.), *La leggenda di Roma*, vol. 2: *Dal ratto delle donne al regno di Romolo e Tito Tazio*, Milano, 287-96.

Cappelli, A. (2012), *Dizionario di abbreviature latine ed italiane* (Seventh edition), Milano.

Carandini, A. (2000), 'Variazioni sul tema di Romolo: Riflessioni dopo La nascita di Roma (1998-1999)', in A. Carandini, R. Cappelli (edd.), *Roma. Romolo, Remo e la fondazione della città*, Milano, 95-150.

Carandini, A. (2006[a]), *La leggenda di Roma*, vol. 1: *Dalla nascita dei gemelli alla fondazione della città*, Milano.

Carandini, A. (2006[b]), *Remo e Romolo: Dai rioni dei Quiriti alla città dei Romani (775/750 – 700/675 a.C.)*, Torino.

Carandini, A. (2014), *La Roma di Augusto in 100 monumenti*, Torino.

Carandini, A., Cappelli, R. (2000), *Roma. Romolo, Remo e la fondazione della città*, Milano.

Castelletti, C. (2012[a]), 'Following Aratus' plow: Vergil's signature in the *Aeneid*', *Museum Helveticum* 69, 83-95.

Castelletti, C. (2012[b]), 'A 'Greek' Acrostic in Valerius Flaccus (3.430-4)', *Mnemosyne* 65, 319-323.

Castelletti, C. (2014), 'Aratus and the Aratean tradition in Valerius' Argonautica', in A. Augoustakis (ed.), *Flavian Poetry and its Greek Past*, Leiden/ Boston, 49-72.

Castelletti, C. (2015[a]), 'Nel solco di Arato: lasciare il segno scrivendo con le stelle. Esempi da Apollonio, Virgilio, Valerio Flacco e Stazio', in F. Guidetti (ed.), *Poesia delle stelle tra Antichità e Medioevo*, Pisa.

Castelletti, C. (2015[b]), 'Virgile, Properce, Auguste et la Roma quadrata. La sphragis comme acte de fondation', *Revue des études latines* 93, 213-236.

Castelletti, C., Siegenthaler, P. (2016), 'Virgilian echoes in the *Aenigmata Symposii*. Two unnoticed technopaignia', *Philologus* 160, 133-150.

Chantraine, P. (1999), *Dictionnaire étymologique de la langue grecque*, Paris.

Claridge, A. (2010²), *Rome. An Oxford Archaeological Guide*, Oxford.
Coarelli, F. (1983), *Il foro romano 1: periodo arcaico*, Roma.
Coarelli, F. (1999ª), 'Roma Quadrata', in M. Steinby (ed.), *Lexicon Topographicum Vrbis Romae*, 4, Roma, 207-209.
Coarelli, F. (1999ᵇ), 'Sepulchrum Romuli', in M. Steinby (ed.), *Lexicon Topographicum Vrbis Romae*, 4, Roma, 295-296.
Coarelli, F. (2012), *Palatium. Il Palatino dalle origini all'impero*, Roma.
Conte, G.B. (2009), *P. Vergilius Maro, Aeneis*, New York (repr. 2011).
Danielewicz, J. (2013), '*Vergil's certissima signa* reinterpreted: the Aratean lepte-acrostic in *Georgics* I', *Eos* 100, 287-295.
Edwards, C. (2000), *Suetonius. Lives of the Caesars*, Oxford.
Farrell, J. (1991), *Vergil's Georgics and the Traditions of Ancient Epic. The art of Allusion in Literary History*, New York/ Oxford.
Fedeli, P. (2005), *Properzio: Elegie, Libro 2. Introduzione, testo e commento*, Cambridge.
Fletcher, K.F.B. (2014), *Finding Italy. Travel, Colonization and Nation in Vergil's Aeneid*, Ann Arbor.
Fowler, D.P. (1983), 'An Acrostic in Vergil (*Aeneid* 7.601-604)?', *Classical Quarterly* 33, 298.
Friedrich, A. (2002), *Das Symposium der 'XII sapientes': Kommentar und Verfasserfrage*, Berlin/ New York.
Froesch, H. (1991), '*Arma Virumque Cano*. Beobachtungen zu den Eingangswörtern der Aeneis', *Anregung* 37, 309-312.
Galinsky, K. (1996), *Augustan Culture. An interpretative Introduction*, Princeton.
Geymonat, M. (2008²), *P. Vergili Maronis Opera*, Roma.
Goold, G.P. (1990), *Propertius, Elegies*, Cambridge (MA).
Grandazzi, A. (1993), 'La Roma quadrata: mythe ou réalité?', *Mélanges de l'École française de Rome* 105, 493-545.
Hendry, M. (1994), 'A Martial Acronym in Ennius?', *Liverpool Classical Monthly* 19, 108-109.
Horsfall, N. (1989), 'Aeneas the colonist', *Vergilius* 35, 8-27.
Hurlet, F. (2001), 'Les auspices d'Octavien/Auguste', *Cahiers du Centre Gustave-Glotz* 12, 155-180.

Katz, J.T. (2008), 'Vergil Translates Aratus: *Phaenomena* 1-2 and *Georgics* 1.1-2', *Materiali e discussioni per l'analisi dei testi classici* 60, 105-123.

Kidd, D. (1997), *Aratus, Phaenomena*, Cambridge/ New York.

Kienast, D. (1982), *Augustus. Prinzeps und Monarch*, Darmstadt.

Koortbojian, M. (2013), *The divinization of Caesar and Augustus. Precedents, Consequences, Implications*, Cambridge/ New York.

Krause, C. (2001), '*In conspectu prope totius urbis* (Cic. *dom.* 100). Il tempio della libertà e il quartiere alto del Palatino', *Eutopia* 1, 169-201.

Krause, C (2002), 'Il cardo del quartiere palatino e la *Roma quadrata* augustea', *Eutopia* 2.2, 99-113.

Krause, C. (2004), 'Die *Domus Tiberiana* – Vom Wohnquartier zum Kaiserpalast', in A. Hoffmann, U. Wulf (edd.), *Die Kaiserpaläste auf dem Palatin in Rom*, Mainz, 33-588.

Kwapisz, J., Petrain, D., Szymanski, M. (2013), *The Muse at Play, Riddles and Wordplay in Greek and Latin Poetry*, Berlin.

Lansing, R.H. (2008), 'Vergil's homage to Homer in Aeneid 1.1-7', *Vergilius* 54, 3-8.

Luz, C. (2010), *Technopaignia. Formspiele in der griechischen Dichtung*, Leiden/ Boston.

Martin, P. M. (1994), *L'idée de royauté à Rome 2: Haine de la royauté et séductions monarchiques (du IVe siècle av. J.-C. au principat augustéen)*, Clermont-Ferrand.

Martin, J. (1998), *Aratos, Phénomènes*, Paris.

Mastrocinque, A. (1998), '*Roma quadrata*', *Mélanges de l'Ecole française de Rome. Antiquité* 110, 681-697.

Mazzarino, S. (1966), 'Le alluvioni 54 a.C./23 a.C., il *cognomen Augustus*, e la data di Hor. *Carm.* 1.2', *Helikon* 6, 621-624.

Morgan, J.D., Thomas, R.F. (2013), s.v. 'Numerical patterns', in R.F. Thomas, J.M. Ziolkowski (edd.), *The Vergil Encyclopedia*, Malden, 918-920.

Mynors, R.A.B. (1969), *Vergili Maronis opera*, Oxford.

O'Rourke, D. (2011), 'The representation and misrepresentation of Virgilian poetry in Propertius 2.34', *American Journal of Philology* 132, 457-497.

Ridley, R.T. (2003), *The Emperor's Retrospect. Augustus'* Res Gestae *in Epigraphy, Historiography and Commentary*, Leuven.

Roddaz, J.-M. (2003), 'La métamorphose: d'Octavien à Auguste', in S. Franchet D'Espèrey, V. Fromentin, S. Gotteland, J-M. Roddaz (edd.), *Fondements et crises du pouvoir*, Bordeaux, 397-418.

Somerville, T. (2010), 'Note on a reversed acrostic in Vergil *Georgics* 1.429-33', *Classical Philology* 105, 202-209.

Thomas, R.F. (2013), s.v. 'foundation literature', in R.F. Thomas, J. M. Ziolkowski (edd.), *The Vergil Encyclopedia*, Malden, 500-502.

Thraede, K. (1965), *Studien zu Sprache und Stil des Prudentius*, Göttingen.

Todisco, E. (2007), 'Il nome *Augustus* e la 'fondazione' ideologica del principato', in P. Desideri, M. Moggi, M. Pani (edd.), *ANTIDORON. Studi in onore di Barbara Scardigli Forster*, Pisa, 441-462.

Traina, A. (1960), *L'alfabeto e la pronunzia del latino*, Bologna.

Tremoli, P., Bianco, G. (1987), s.v. 'mos', in *Enciclopedia Virgiliana*, vol. 3, Roma, 601-606.

Volk, K. (2012), 'Letters in the sky. Reading the signs in Aratus' *Phaenomena*', *American Journal of Philology* 133, 209-240.

Wilhelm, R.M. (1982), 'The Plough-Chariot: Symbol of Order in the *Georgics*', *Classical Journal* 77, 213-230.

Wiseman, T.P. (1995), *Remus. A Roman myth*, Cambridge.

Wiseman, T.P. (2012), '*Roma Quadrata*, archaic huts, the house of Augustus, and the orientation of Palatine Apollo', *Journal of Roman Archaeology* 25, 371-387.

Wiseman, T.P. (2015), 'Rome on the Balance: Varro and the Foundation Legend', in D.J. Butterfield (ed.), *Varro Varius. The Polymath of the Roman World*, Cambridge, 93-122.

Stories on Temples: Monumental Art, Characterization, and Hospitality in the *Aeneid*

SILVIO CURTIS
University of California, Los Angeles

'Histories, Vergil knows, are made by *men*,' writes Page DuBois in *History, Rhetorical Description, and the Epic* (emphasis in the original).[1] Yet her discussion of ekphrasis as historical memory in the *Aeneid* focuses not on the makers or sponsors of art but on Aeneas as a viewer of art, demonstrating Aeneas's linear development 'in choosing a Roman future over the Greek past.'[2] This paper will examine how the *Aeneid*'s descriptions of public historical monuments reflect on the monuments' sponsors: Dido, who built the temple of Juno in Carthage; Daedalus, who built the temple of Apollo at Cumae; and Latinus, who uses the temple in Laurentum as his palace. The ekphraseis show these characters displaying different social affiliations through their commemoration of the past. Dido's temple in Carthage and Latinus's in Laurentum contrast Dido's cosmopolitanism with Latinus's local affiliation, while Daedalus's temple at Cumae marks his isolation from the human realm and his affinity with the divine one.

Dido and the Temple at Carthage: *Aen.* 1.441-493

When Aeneas first learns from the disguised Venus that a storm has driven him to Carthaginian territory, he worries whether the Carthaginians have heard of him. He says that he came *Troia antiqua, si uestras forte per auris/ Troiae nomen iit* ('from ancient Troy, if by chance the name of Troy has passed through your ears,' 1.375-376),[3] and that he is *ignotus*, 'unknown' (1.384), in Africa. Dido's temple answers that uncertainty.

---

[1] DuBois (1982) 29.
[2] DuBois (1982) 30.
[3] All translations are my own.

The ruler of Carthage has placed her temple and its decorations in a political, public location: the center of her city (1.441). She has her throne at the center of the building (1.505), using it as the setting for her public role as queen. There *iura dabat legesque uiris, operumque laborem/ partibus aequabat iustis aut sorte trahebat* ('she was giving judgments and laws to men, and making the labor of the works equal with fair portions or assigning it by lot,' 1.507-508). The temple, as the geographical, religious, and political center of the city, can convey messages to the entire community. In this socially significant location, Dido has chosen to display a representation of a subject geographically distant from both Carthage and Tyre: the Trojan War.

The subject matter of the pictures has no literal connection to Carthage. Vergil provides an introductory summary of his account:

> ... uidet Iliacas ex ordine pugnas
> bellaque iam fama totam uulgata per orbem,
> Atridas Priamumque et saeuum ambobus Achillem.
> 1.456-468
>
> He sees the Ilian fights in order and the wars already spread by hearsay through the whole Circle, the Atreides and Priam and, savage to both, Achilles.

From this, the temple artwork appears to depict the Trojan War, focusing on the same events as the *Iliad*. In the descriptions of individual scenes, we find both Trojans and Greeks in abundance, as well as the Trojans' Ethiopian and Amazon allies. There is no literal reference to Carthage or even to Tyre.

There are, however, at least two scenes that suggest analogies with Carthage. The last picture described provides the most salient parallel. It shows Penthesilea leading the Amazons in battle. In the Carthaginian context, a picture of Penthesilea would bring Dido to mind. Michael C. J. Putnam shows how the transition from the ekphrasis back into the main narrative of the *Aeneid* blends the picture of Penthesilea with the literal presence of Dido.[4] But even apart from the narrative strategies analyzed by Putnam, the thematic similarity between Penthesilea and Dido as female generals connects them in the mind of a reader and

---

[4] Putnam (1998ª) 255-258.

suggests that the Carthaginians in the poem would also connect them. Female leaders are of course not common in classical epic, and Vergil explicitly calls attention to their unusual status both in Dido's case and Penthesilea's. He has Venus interrupt her introduction of Dido to remark, *dux femina facti* ('a woman is leader of the deed,' 1.364), a restatement of what she has already said that can only have exclamatory force. A similarly gendered comment closes the passage about Penthesilea: *audetque uiris concurrere uirgo* ('and, though a maiden, she dares to compete with men,' 1.493). Therefore, the depiction of Penthesilea on Dido's temple works as a depiction of Dido herself and the civic role she performs in that very building.

But Dido's portrait creates ominous implications which the depiction of the supplication of the women at the temple of Minerva in Troy reinforces:

> interea ad templum non aequae Palladis ibant
> crinibus Iliades passis peplumque ferebant
> suppliciter, tristes et tunsae pectora palmis;
> diua solo fixos oculos auersa tenebat.
>
> 1.479-482

> Meanwhile the Ilian women were going to unkind Pallas's temple, their hair undone, and they were carrying a robe in supplication, sad and beating their breasts with their palms; the goddess, turning away, was holding her eyes fixed on the ground.

This passage alludes to the Trojan supplication of Athena at *Iliad* 6.286-312. On Helenus's advice (*Il.* 6.77-101) Hector asks his mother to take the Trojan women to Athena's temple and pray for the death of Diomedes. They supplicate the goddess, bringing her a fine robe and promising animal sacrifices, but she remains hostile: ἀνένευε δὲ Παλλὰς Ἀθήνη ('but Pallas Athena nodded in denial,' *Il.* 6.311).

Dido's temple ostensibly commemorates the favor that Juno has promised to show Carthage: *sic nam fore bello/ egregiam et facilem uictu per saecula gentem* ('for so it would be a race outstanding in war and easy of livelihood through the ages,' 1.444-445). The queen intends her monument to honor a reciprocal relationship between a goddess and a city that worships her. But the monument shows Minerva/Athena, Juno/Hera's ally in the *Iliad*, abandoning a city that worships her. If Aeneas fails to consider how the temple decorations reflect on Juno, whom they are intended to honor,[5] he is not alone. Dido herself fails to notice all the implications of the art that she has commissioned.

Dido's dialogue with the Trojans following the ekphrasis explains why she cares about the recent history of Troy. When Ilioneus calls Carthage a 'barbarian territory' (*barbara ... patria*, 1.539-540), she reassures him, using her knowledge of the Trojans and of the Trojan War as her key counterargument. According to her, the Carthaginians' knowledge of the Trojan War marks them as part of civilized humanity, a cultural sphere whose universality she proclaims even as she associates it with the east:

> quis genus Aeneadum, quis Troiae nesciat urbem,
> uirtutesque uirosque aut tanta incendia belli?
> non obtunsa adeo gestamus pectora Poeni,
> nec tam auersus equos Tyria Sol iungit ab urbe.
>
> 1.565-566

> Who could be unaware of the race of the children of Aeneas, of the city of Troy, the manhood and the men or such great conflagrations of war? We Phoenicians do not have such numbed breasts, nor does the Sun yoke his horses so far out of sight of the Tyrian city.

The universality that Dido attributes to the Trojan War story accounts for its function on the temple walls at Carthage. Her speech to Ilioneus does not aim at differentiating Carthage from other cities. Instead, she wants to prove that Carthage is a civilized city by displaying her knowledge of the eastern Mediterranean. In fact, she goes on to offer the Trojans membership in her polity, emphasizing that their ethnicity poses no obstacle:

> uultis et his mecum pariter considere regnis?
> urbem quam statuo, uestra est; subducite nauis;
> Tros Tyriusque mihi nullo discrimine agetur.
>
> 1.572-574

> Do you in fact want to settle in these kingdoms with me equally? The city that I govern is yours; moor your ships; Trojan and Tyrian will be treated with no distinction for me.

---

[5] As Beck (2007), among others, recognizes.

We can infer that Dido intends the choice of theme to carry the same message about Carthaginian identity as she articulates to Ilioneus. It affiliates Carthage with an eastern Mediterranean sphere of intercity cultural exchange, downplaying any distinctions between Carthaginians or Phoenicians and other members of that sphere.

Dido's display of knowledge about Troy in support of her hospitality to the Trojans bears some similarity to the rhetoric of historical Greek states that claimed kinship with the Trojans to justify establishing friendly relations with Rome.[6] However, it is not the same rhetorical strategy, because Dido does not claim any kinship or other prior relationship to the Trojans. In fact, she first learned of Troy through showing hospitality to the Trojans' enemy, the Greek Teucer (1.619-626). She reports his judgment that Trojan ancestry would be an honor (1.626), but no such ancestral connection underlies her interest in Troy. Instead, she implies that everyone, regardless of ancestry, should value Trojan history.

Before moving on from our consideration of Dido, we should note another ekphrasis associated with her, much less developed than the description of the temple to Juno but contrasting notably with it in content. Dido welcomes Aeneas to Carthage with a banquet amid luxurious decorations, including tableware decorated with images from the history of her royal ancestors:

> at domus interior regali splendida luxu
> instruitur, mediisque parant conuiuia tectis:
> arte laboratae uestes ostroque superbo,
> ingens argentum mensis, caelataque in auro
> fortia facta patrum, series longissima rerum
> per tot ducta uiros antiqua ab origine gentis.
> 1.637-642

> But the inner house is prepared, splendid with regal pomp, and they ready the banquet in the middle of the building: cloths worked with craft and with proud purple, abundant silver on the tables, and, engraved in gold, the mighty deeds of the fathers, a long series of matters taken through so many men from the ancient beginning of the race.

---

[6] Erskine (2001) 162-197 discusses this phenomenon in detail.

The description makes it clear that, despite Dido's use of non-Phoenician imagery and her enthusiastic welcome to the Trojans, she also remains affiliated with a historical narrative about her own family. She displays this art less publicly than the temple decorations, in her *domus interior*, and as host of an aristocratic banquet rather than in her more overtly political tasks of day-to-day government. Furthermore, while Dido clearly takes responsibility for the content of the temple artwork by directing its construction, Vergil leaves ambiguous how much responsibility Dido takes for the content of the engravings. In fact, the juxtaposition with Aeneas's gift to her of treasure rescued from Troy, which comes only a few lines later (1.647-655), brings to mind the possibility that Dido still uses old tableware from Carthage that she stole back from Pygmalion, not anything manufactured on her instructions. Still, while Dido does not display her family history as prominently as the Trojan War images with their universalizing message, she does not hide it either. A Roman reader, aware of the Punic Wars, would notice the potential for tragic conflict between her ancestral affiliations and her cosmopolitan policy.

Daedalus and the Temple at Cumae: *Aen.* 6.14-33

In contrast to the elaborate narrative of Aeneas's arrival in Carthage, Daedalus's carvings get little introduction. After the death of Palinurus, Vergil gives us thirteen lines about Aeneas landing at Cumae and finding the temple, then announces, *Daedalus, ut fama est ...* ('Daedalus, as there is a story ...,' 6.14), disorienting the reader; Daedalus seems irrelevant to what has gone before. Vergil waits five more lines to clarify the connection by explaining that Daedalus made the temple that Aeneas is entering.

The abruptness of Daedalus's introduction into *Aen.* 6 results from the isolation of his temple. We learn about Dido before encountering her temple because she has surrounded it with a city-state. Daedalus, on the other hand, has built his temple in the wilderness. Aeneas reaches it without meeting another human being, so far as the poem tells us.

The temple decorations at Cumae, unlike the ones at Carthage, tell a story directly relevant to their context. They tell Daedalus's own story, that is, the story of how he came to Cumae. The carvings show two locations: Athens and Crete, maybe one of them on each door (*contra elata mari respondet Cnosia tellus* ['opposing, separated by the sea, the Cnosian soil balances it,' 6.23]). In Athens, they depict the Athenians killing Minos's son (6.20) and Minos forcing them to send youths to be offered to the Minotaur as atonement. (6.20-22). The Cretan scenes explain the Minotaur's origin by showing Pasiphae having sex with the bull (6.24-26), then continue to the Labyrinth (6.27), and, lastly, Daedalus helping Theseus through the Labyrinth (6.28-30), the offense because of which Daedalus has to flee Crete. Together, the scenes create a chain of cause and effect leading to Daedalus's exile in Italy.

The scenes of events on Crete highlight not only their effects on Daedalus but also his active role in them. One shows Pasiphae *supposta... furto* ('put under [the bull] by fraud,' 6.24) – that is, by using the cow suit that Daedalus made for her. It reminds us that without Daedalus, the Minotaur would not exist. Another scene shows the Labyrinth, which is Daedalus's work too. The chronologically last scene gives us not Daedalus's creations but *Daedalus ipse* ('Daedalus himself', 6.28), making him, not Theseus or Ariadne or the Minotaur, the protagonist.

Because Daedalus chooses to portray his own story, his images affect his characterization. To describe them, Vergil packs eleven lines with the vocabulary of transgression, suffering, and deception: *poenas* ('penalty', 6.20), *miserum* ('pitiable', 6.21), *crudelis* ('cruel', 6.24), *furto* ('fraud', 6.24), *nefandae* ('unspeakable', 6.26), *labor* ('toil', 6.27), *error* ('wandering', 6.27), *miseratus* ('pitying', 6.28), *dolos* ('trickery', 6.29), *ambages* ('riddles', 6.29), and *caeca* ('blind', 6.30). Daedalus's role in the story relates particularly closely to deception and its undoing. He brings the Minotaur into existence with his *furtum* (6.24), his *doli* and *ambages* render the Minotaur's victims helpless with *labor* and *error*, and he undoes that same trickery, bringing about the Minotaur's death, for Ariadne's benefit. Elsewhere, the *Aeneid* attributes special powers of truth and deception to prophets and deities, but not normally to mortals.

Daedalus shows the strongest similarity to the gods in his flight on artificial wings from Crete to Italy. He does not depict the flight on the temple, but commemorates it there by dedicating the wings to Apollo (6.18-19). He travels through the sky (6.15) among the constellations

(6.16), that is, in the realm of the deities. Vergil explicitly marks Daedalus's flight as an exploit outside the natural human realm by using the expressions *ausus se credere caelo* ('daring to entrust himself to the sky,' 6.15) and *insuetum per iter* ('by an unprecedented route,' 6.16). On the journey, Daedalus loses his son Icarus, and Vergil tells us that Daedalus tried to depict this scene on the temple as well, but could not bring himself to because of his grief (6.30-33).

If Daedalus had shown Icarus on the temple, he would have been the only relative of Daedalus on it. The only other characters mentioned are Androgeos, who bears only a tenuous and circumstantial connection to Daedalus through the consequences triggered by his death; the Athenians, who through the agency of Minos become victims of Daedalus's craft; and Pasiphae, Ariadne, and (extremely elliptically) Theseus, whom Daedalus makes a beneficiary of his uncanny powers. No permanent social or political institution binds any of these characters to Daedalus. Nor does Aeneas find relatives or fellow citizens of Daedalus at Cumae, but only a solitary priestess who calls the carvings irrelevant (6.37). In a poem that makes political and familial heritage two of its most emphatic and intertwined themes, Daedalus is an anomaly.

Charles Segal and Michael C. J. Putnam have both dealt with the relationship between Daedalus's characterization and Aeneas's.[7] Both recognize nuances in the comparison, but Putnam emphasizes the similarities and Segal emphasizes the differences. Like Aeneas and Dido, Daedalus is an exile who searches for a new home.[8] As with Aeneas, Daedalus's actions result in tragic deaths for which art cannot provide emotional closure – Icarus's death in Daedalus's escape from Crete and the victims of Aeneas's war in Italy, especially Turnus.[9] Putnam also calls attention to Aeneas's attempts to deceive Dido earlier in the *Aeneid*, drawing a parallel with Daedalus's deceptive capabilities.[10] However, Aeneas's deceptions in book 1 are not intentional, and his attempts at deception in book 4 do not succeed. Daedalus deceives

---

[7] Putnam (1987), Segal (1965).
[8] Segal (1965) discusses this parallel between Aeneas and Daedalus (644). Putnam (1987) notices some parallels between Aeneas, Daedalus and Dido (188 n. 22).
[9] Putnam (1987) 191-198.
[10] Putnam (1987) 186-197.

intentionally and successfully, which removes him more clearly from the human sphere of existence.

Daedalus's genealogical isolation from the rest of history offers another contrast with Aeneas and with Dido. In discussing the tragic character of historical memory in *Aeneid* 6, Segal writes:

> Yet here appears the major difference between Daedalus and Aeneas: Aeneas *does* leave the past behind. His is a glorious future. Daedalus has no future, only a past, the past commemorated on the golden doors. His line will not survive him.[11]

Though Aeneas gets some of his allies killed, like Pallas, and kills enemies who should have been allies, like Turnus, his heirs ultimately survive. Daedalus's son dies. It bears noticing that Daedalus's artwork does not extend very far backward in time either. He has a past, but it is only one generation long. Dido, on the other hand, has pictures of her ancestors, even if she does not display them prominently. The next decorated temple, the one in Laurentum in book 7, contrasts with Daedalus's even more strikingly.

Latinus and the Temple at Laurentum: *Aen.* 7.170-191

In book 7 of the *Aeneid*, the description of the temple-palace of Picus at Laurentum marks Latinus as a character with affiliations reaching far backward and forward in time, unlike Daedalus's, but limited to his own geographical area, unlike Dido's.[12] A flashback summary (7.45-106) tells us that Latinus descends from a line of local kings going back to Saturn (7.47-49) and reveres the spirit of his dead father Faunus (7.81-106). The continuation of his family line has become endangered, since he has only one daughter and no surviving sons (7.50-52).

As Bleisch observes, '[t]he ekphrasis of Picus's *regia* echoes the ekphrasis of Juno's temple in *Aeneid* 1 in both form and narrative function.'[13] Like Dido, Latinus has his throne in the middle of a temple (*solio medius consedit auito* ['he seated himself in the middle on his

---

[11] Segal (1965) 644.
[12] See Bleisch (2003) for a pioneering analysis of this passage in the context of ekphrasis.
[13] Bleisch (2003) 92.

ancestral throne,' 7.169]) with the temple prominently placed in the city ('urbe fuit summa' ['was at the top of the city,' 7.171]). But unlike the Carthaginian temple, which from the imperfect *condebat* ('was founding,' 1.447) seems to be still under construction, the temple in Laurentum already has a long tradition attached to it. At one time it belonged to Picus, Latinus's grandfather (7.171). It has become a setting for political and religious ceremony:

> hic sceptra accipere et primos attollere fascis
> regibus omen erat; hoc illis curia templum,
> hae sacris sedes epulis; hic ariete caeso
> perpetuis soliti patres considere mensis.
>
> 7.173-176

> It was an omen for the kings to take their scepters and raise their first fasces here; this temple was their assembly hall, this the seat for their holy meals; here, when a ram was slaughtered, the fathers used to sit down at continuous tables.

The temple at Laurentum, as a long-established ceremonial center, provides an effective place for representations of the past.

And in fact it contains them: *quin etiam ueterum effigies ex ordine auorum/ antiqua e cedro ... uestibulo astabant* ('and also, to be sure, representations of the old ancestors in order, made from ancient cedar, stood in the entrance,' 7.177-181). The statues not only remind the *Aeneid*'s characters and readers of the history of the Latins, but also construct Latin identity in a way that resonates with Augustus's revival of conservative Roman values. The simple wooden images 'stand as an implicit critique of the luxury of the new Rome' and they contrast with Aeneas's luxurious dress in Carthage,[14] the bronze temple where Dido puts her images of the Trojan War, and the golden tableware on which her own ancestors are portrayed. The inclusion of Sabinus, *uitisator curuam seruans sub imagine falcem* ('the grapesower keeping his curved sickle in portrayal,' 7.179), marks the Latins as agricultural.

---

[14] Following the interpretation of DuBois (1982) 30. Reed (2007) takes the opposite view (59), arguing that because cedar is imported it marks the Latins as Oriental. However, Vergil represents cedar as growing in Italian forests at *Aen.* 11.137. I believe that Vergil's mythological poetry ignores the real-world geographical distribution of the tree, and the relevant contrast in this passage is that between wood and more ostentatious materials such as bronze.

The many war trophies displayed among the statues (7.183-186) mark them as militaristic, reinforcing the frequent prophecies in the *Aeneid* of Rome's military strength.

Bleisch follows the lead of W.A. Camps[15] in identifying parallels between the fictional Latin temple and the real temple of Jupiter Optimus Maximus on the Capitoline Hill in Rome. Building on the insight, she identifies further correspondences with the Roman Regia and the temple of Apollo on the Palatine.[16] In fact, most of the fictional temple's similarities with the real temple to Jupiter also parallel the temple to Apollo: they are all tall buildings on high hills displaying military spoils and housing meetings of the senate. In Bleisch's analysis, the palace of Picus can reflect both real temples at the same time because 'Augustus seemingly conceived of the Palatine as taking over the functions of the old Capitoline.'[17] The ambiguity suggests that the original readers of the *Aeneid* would associate Picus's palace-temple not with a particular contemporary building but with a civic function, one that both the old temple to Jupiter and the new temple to Apollo had exemplified. Further, we can now see the temple in Carthage as a second fictional example of the same role.

Following the ekphrasis, Latinus's welcome to the Trojan messenger Ilioneus parallels Dido's welcome to Aeneas in book 1, but with pointed differences. Like Dido, Latinus has heard of the Trojans, and like Dido, he reassures them that he and his subjects obey the norms of hospitality. But unlike Dido, he draws no connection between those two facts. He explains the Latins' hospitality as a native tradition, calling them *Saturni gentem haud uinclo nec legibus aequam,/ sponte sua ueterisque dei se more tenentem* ('Saturn's race, kind not at all by compulsion or laws, guiding itself by its own will and the character of the old god,' 7.203-204). He mentions his knowledge of the Trojan War only as a brief aside at the beginning of his speech (7.195-196).

The rest of the dialogue with Ilioneus continues to demonstrate the difference between Latinus's reasons for welcoming the Trojans and Dido's. Despite Latinus's downplaying of the Trojans' fame in his

---

[15] Camps (1969), 56.
[16] Bleisch (2003) 95-98.
[17] Bleisch (2003) 97 n. 17.

welcome, Ilioneus clearly does not get the point. Even though Latinus has already said that he knows who the Trojans are, he replies with a pompous self-introduction more than twenty lines long, proclaiming their universal fame in terms like Dido's but embellished with even more rhetorical flourishes (7.217-238) before offering, rather condescendingly, an alliance and gifts of Trojan treasure (7.239-248). Yet as Latinus decides how to answer,

> ... nec purpura regem
> picta mouet nec sceptra mouent Priameia tantum
> quantum in conubio natae thalamoque moratur,
> et ueteris Fauni uoluit sub pectore sortem: ...
>
> 7.251-254

Neither the purple painting nor the Priamean scepters move the king as much as he delays over the marriage and bedchamber of his daughter, and he turns over deep in his chest the divination of old Faunus: ...

Then when he does answer, he offers Lavinia to Aeneas on the spot, explaining as follows:

> [monstra] generos externis adfore ab oris,
> hoc Latio restare canunt, qui sanguine nostrum
> nomen in astra ferant.
>
> 7.269-272

[portents] sing that sons-in-law will arrive from foreign shores and stop in this Latium, ones who with their blood will take our name among the stars.

Latinus shows interest in an alliance with Troy on the instructions of his deified ancestor and in order to ensure the continuation and future glory of his family. Just as Latinus rules surrounded by images of his ancestors, he cares about universal fame only insofar as it will belong to his descendants.

The overall picture of Latinus in *Aen.* 7 is that of a locally rooted king. But certain details, particularly the mentions of Saturn, complicate that picture by suggesting that geographical affiliations can change from generation to generation. Saturn's own affiliations are paradoxical: in H.S. Versnel's words, he 'unites the connotations of the arch-Roman and the prototypical foreigner.'[18] His presence as Latinus's biological grandfather (7.48-49) and the cultural ancestor of all the Latins (7.202-204), with his depiction in the ekphrasis (7.180), implicates Latinus and his subjects in the same geographical ambiguity. At the same time, Latinus remembers that Dardanus, founder of Troy, was originally a foreigner to Asia and a native of Italy:

> ... his ortus ut agris
> Dardanus Idaeas Phrygiae penetrarit ad urbes
> Threiciamque Samum, quae nunc Samothracia fertur.
> 7.206-208

> ... that Dardanus had penetrated to the Idan cities of Phrygia and Thracian Samos, which is now named Samothrace, after arising from these fields.

Ilioneus agrees: *hinc Dardanus ortus* ('Dardanus arose from here,' 7.240). A reader of the *Aeneid* would see Saturn and Dardanus as models for Aeneas, another cultural founder figure who must establish a locally affiliated lineage though himself a foreigner.[19] Aeneas himself, of course, is not there to learn the lesson.

Carthage Revisited

According to Putnam, 'because it [Dido's temple] stands as the initial example of the trope [ekphrasis] in the epic, it sets a pattern against which later uses will be measured.'[20] Yet the ekphraseis of public monuments show a pattern against which, in retrospect, the Carthaginian temple shows up as an exception. Latinus is a ruler, and the temple-palace in Laurentum portrays the history of his royal office. Daedalus is an exile, and his temple portrays how his personal story led to his exile. Dido, both a ruler and an exile, portrays neither her ancestors nor her own deeds.

---

[18] Versnel (1993) 139.
[19] Bleisch (2003) 103-104, also comments on Saturn as a model for Aeneas, though she sees the implications somewhat more pessimistically. Compare also her observation that the *regia* 'is the Trojans' initiation into what it means to be Italian,' Bleisch (2003) 94.
[20] Putnam (1998^b) 23.

Ralph Hexter has already remarked on how little Vergil's Dido shows signs of a distinctive ethnic identity, and in particular how she builds a temple to Juno rather than to a Punic deity such as Tannit, wondering, 'are the Punic peoples so lacking in their own history that they must adopt Rome's?'[21] He answers that Dido's characterization makes sense because, from a Roman imperialist perspective, anyone would want to be Roman: building a temple to a Roman goddess 'emblematizes Dido the outsider who wants entrée into Roman history and culture, even before the arrival of Aeneas.'[22] Hexter sees the contrast between the detailed description of the temple and the passing reference to the portrayal of Dido's ancestors on her tableware as part of the same phenomenon.[23]

Nicholas Horsfall has read Dido as an example of the anti-Punic stereotypes familiar to Romans from historiography.[24] However, as Hexter sees and as we have seen in this paper, the *Aeneid* shows Dido as a capable ruler and a hospitable host. Such a positive characterization contradicts Horsfall's reading. 'Violence, greed, duplicity, and hatred'[25] do not describe the Dido of book 1. Even the Dido of book 4 does not display greed or duplicity; in fact, she will accuse Aeneas of duplicity (4.366), arguably with justification. Ethnic stereotypes may underlie Venus and Jupiter's fears about Dido, but her behavior contradicts them. As her speech to Ilioneus shows, Dido fails to conform to stereotypes about foreigners precisely because she does not want to be a foreigner. This characterization, which portrays Dido positively without abandoning Roman ethnocentrism, stands out all the more clearly in contrast to the openly xenophobic portrayal of Cleopatra on the shield of Aeneas, which pointedly does not assimilate the Egyptian pantheon to the Roman one (8.698-700).

Although Dido does not want to be a foreigner, Hexter oversimplifies in saying that she wants to be Roman. She wants to be Trojan, or rather, she wants membership in a cultural sphere which gives the Trojans a central place. But the Trojans are not Romans yet. DuBois's analysis of Aeneas's reaction to Dido's temple makes clear that Troy

---

[21] Hexter (1992) 356.
[22] Hexter (1992) 356.
[23] Hexter (1992) 358-359.
[24] Horsfall (1990) 127-144.
[25] Horsfall (1990) 144.

forms part of Aeneas's eastern past, and his destiny requires him to break away from it.[26] Thus, though Aeneas participated in the Trojan War and Dido only knows of it by hearsay, their shared fascination with it serves to show how similarly Aeneas and Dido think at this point in the story.

A last note on Dido: though her relationship to the past stands out as unusual compared with Daedalus's and Latinus's, it does not seem to mark her as feminine or as Phoenician. We have seen that, far from marking her ethnicity, this aspect of Dido's characterization dissociates her from Roman stereotypes about Phoenicians. As for gender, while this paper has not definitively proved that it has no role in explaining her choice to portray the Trojan War, it has uncovered no evidence of such a role (though it does explain why, having chosen to display Trojan War scenes, she includes Penthesilea in her selection). As already mentioned, Dido's characterization in book 1 finds more of a foil than a parallel in Cleopatra, another foreign female ruler in the *Aeneid*. It seems more likely that Dido's attitude toward the past relates to her characterization as an individual and to the specific circumstances of Vergil's fictional Carthage.

Laurentum Revisited

Making a distinction between Trojans and Romans also helps sharpen our understanding of ethnic characterization in the Laurentine palace. Bleisch sees ambiguity in the passage's characterization of the Latins: 'The *regia* ekphrasis offers an interpretive crux: in one reading the Latins are reassuringly already Roman; in another reading, the Latins are the Italian resistance.'[27] But those readings do not contradict each other. The Latins threaten to resist Aeneas because they are already more Roman than he is.

In Picus's palace the local past of Italy prefigures Augustan Rome. The history of Troy as depicted by Dido does not. At this point, it is Aeneas's attachment to his Trojan past that threatens to impede Roman destiny. In the ekphrasis of the Carthaginian temple and throughout

---

[26] DuBois (1993) 32-35. The theme of breaking away from Troy is widely discussed in Vergilian scholarship, of course. One helpful treatment appears in Quint (1993) 53-65.
[27] Bleisch (2003) 89.

the first half of the *Aeneid* we have had ample evidence of Aeneas's attachment to his past. Here, we encounter a different past, an emphatically Roman one and one to which Aeneas remains an outsider. For many in the *Aeneid*'s original audience, this passage more than any other may have brought home the message that Aeneas, in joining a Roman ancestor, does need to leave his own past behind. The Trojans, not the Latins, would unsettle an imperialistic Roman reader of *Aen.* 7.

Conclusion

The ekphraseis associated with Carthage and Laurentum show how the characters that Aeneas meets parallel the development in his personality that DuBois identifies. In book 1, Dido, like Aeneas, clings to the Trojan-centered, eastern tradition that constitutes his past. In book 7, Latinus introduces the Roman tradition that, as he is coming to accept, will constitute his future. Daedalus does not correspond as exactly to Aeneas because he stands apart from all historical traditions. Even so, he has just reached Italy after a dangerous journey when he raises the temple, like Aeneas as he views the temple. Daedalus's story has already failed to continue into the future. Dido's Carthage, while it does have a glorious future ahead of it, will ultimately fail too.

It remains to investigate whether the *Aeneid* deliberately draws any connection between the characters' successful or unsuccessful futures and their attitudes to the past. In Dido's case, a consideration of Roman attitudes toward the North Africans of Vergil's own time, in the same way as Hexter's article and this paper take into account stereotypes about pre-Roman Carthage, might prove especially illuminating. The differentiation between Dido's and Latinus's attitudes to local identity in the *Aeneid* raises the question of how to interpret real Roman buildings like Augustus's temple to Apollo, which as described in Propertius 2.31 combined scenes from Roman history and Greek mythology. Comparison with Homer and other intertextual models could also provide insights about sponsors of art in Vergil, in the same way that comparison with Homer enriches Beck's discussion of Aeneas as a viewer of Dido's temple to Juno. Literary descriptions of art remain a rich source of evidence about ancient poetics and ancient society, and within that category, descriptions of publicly displayed historical art form an important subtype.

Bibliography

Beck, D. (2007), 'Ecphrasis, Interpretation, and Audience in *Aeneid* 1 and *Odyssey* 8', *American Journal of Philology* 128, 433-549.

Bleisch, P. (2003), 'The *Regia* of Picus: Ekphrasis, Italian Identity, and Artistic Definition in *Aeneid* 7.152-93', in P. Thibodeau, H. Haskell (edd.), *Being There Together. Essays in Honor of Michael C. J. Putnam on the Occasion of His Seventieth Birthday*, Afton, 88-109.

Camps, W.A. (1969), *An Introduction to Vergil's Aeneid*, London.

DuBois, P. (1982), *History, Rhetorical Description and the Epic. From Homer to Spenser*, Cambridge.

Erskine, A. (2001), *Troy between Greece and Rome. Local Tradition and Imperial Power*, Oxford.

Hexter, R. (1992), 'Sidonian Dido', in R. Hexter, D. Selden (edd.), *Innovations of Antiquity*, New York.

Horsfall, N. (1990), 'Dido in the Light of History', in S.J. Harrison (ed.), *Oxford Readings in Vergil's Aeneid*, Oxford.

Putnam, M.C.J. (1987), 'Daedalus, Virgil and the End of Art', *American Journal of Philology* 108, 173-198.

Putnam, M.C.J. (1998^a), 'Dido's Murals and Virgilian Ekphrasis', *Harvard Studies in Classical Philology* 98, 243-275.

Putnam, M.C.J. (1998^b), *Virgil's Epic Designs. Ekphrasis in the Aeneid*, New Haven.

Quint, D. (1993), *Epic and Empire: Politics and Generic Form from Virgil to Milton*, Princeton.

Reed, J.D. (2007), *Virgil's Gaze. Nation and Poetry in the Aeneid*, Princeton.

Segal, C.P. (1965), '*Aeternum per Saecula Nomen*: The Golden Bough and the Tragedy of History, Part 1', *Arion* 4, 615-657.

Versnel, H.S. (1993), *Inconsistencies in Greek and Roman Religion,* vol. 2: *Transition and Reversal in Myth and Ritual*, Leiden.

'Desacralization' and the Lowering of Vergilian Epic in Three Epigrams of Martial

ROBSON TADEU CESILA
Universidade de São Paulo

> se (...) un eroe mitico passa da un genere letterario di alta dignità (epos, tragedia, storiografia) ad un genere tenue come, ad esempio, la poesia elegiaca o il romanzo, in tale passaggio potrà subire una radicale metamorfosi: diverrà oggetto di parodia e dovrà addirittura adattarsi al rovesciamento delle sue caratteristiche e delle sue competenze.
>
> Paolo Fedeli (1989) 384

Among the texts analysed by Paolo Fedeli in a 1989 essay from which the excerpt above was taken, there are three hexameters from chapter 132 of the *Satyricon* of Petronius that clearly cite verses from Vergil's *Aeneid* and *Eclogues*. In the passage of the Petronian novel, the narrator Encolpius addresses his penis to criticize its impotence. However, it remains inert, indifferent to his rebukes:

> Illa solo fixos oculos auersa tenebat,
> nec magis incepto uultum sermone mouetur
> quam lentae salices lassoue papauera collo.[1]

Fedeli observes that the first two lines of the passage above are exactly identical to *Aen.* 6.469-470 and that the third is a result of a combination of *Aen.* 9.436 (*languescit moriens lassoue papauera collo*) and *Ecl.* 5.16 (*lenta salix quantum pallenti cedit oliuae*).[2] *Aeneid* 469-470 describe Dido's behavior when Aeneas encounters her in the Underworld. He tries to justify his departure from Carthage, a fact that had caused the Phoenician queen's suicide in book 4, but Dido's ghost remains silent and keeps her eyes fixed on the ground. Having

---

[1] Italian translation by Fedeli (1989) 394: 'quella col volto girato teneva gli occhi fissi al suolo, né si era mossa in volto da quando le ho rivolto la parola, più che un salice flessibile o un pupazzo dal collo molle.'
[2] Fedeli (1989) 394-395.

refused to reply to any of Aeneas' excuses, she turns away to attend her deceased husband Sychaeus.[3] The sequence of the Vergilian passage (6.471) compares Dido's silent and immobile behaviour to the rocks, a comparison which is not suitable to describe Encolpius' flaccid member. Therefore, in the third verse of *Satyricon*'s cited passage, Petronius increases the irony of his text by leaving the sequence of *Aen.* 6.469-470 and inserting a line that mixes *Aen.* 9.436 and *Ecl.* 5.16 (which respectively alludes to 'poppies with weary necks' and 'flexible willows'), drawing a comparison between the flaccid member and not the hardness of the rocks, but instead the flabbiness and looseness of the stalks of willows and poppies.

Fedeli concludes that Petronius' lines '... istituiscono implicitamente un parallelo fra l'ovvio mutismo del membro di Encolpio e il silenzio di Didone,'[4] exerting therefore a 'desacralizing' (*dissacratorio*) effect on the Vergilian passage, which is elevated, pathetic and serious and presents the sufferings of the two lovers in an unexpected, awkward and tense encounter. In other words, the serious context of the epic genre[5] is brought to the irreverent, ribald and obscene context of the Petronian novel. The *Aeneid* passage is thus lowered, or 'desacralized', and this effect can be attributed – as Fedeli himself suggests in the epigraph to this paper – to the transposition of elements (which may be characters, lines, words, situations, *topoi*, etc.) of a high, elevated genre – the epic – to a low, *tenuis* genre – the novel.[6] Moreover, such 'desacralization' ('dissacrazione') of Vergil's epic poem occurs not

---

[3] In turn, as Fedeli (1989) 396 observes, the Vergilian episode is an imitation of the encounter between Odysseus and Ajax in the Underworld, an event narrated in book 11 of the *Odyssey* (vv. 541 ff.). Odysseus invites the son of Telamon to put aside his anger, but Ajax, still resentful of the Ithacan hero because of the contest between them for the armor of Achilles, answers not a word and silently walks away.

[4] Fedeli (1989) 394.

[5] It is important to remember that even the love between Dido and Aeneas is part of the epic project of Vergil, since the Trojan hero abandons the queen of Carthage and leaves that city because his divine mission is to found a new Troy in Italian lands.

[6] In fact, our epigraph was taken from Fedeli's study, in the same essay from 1989, of the metamorphosis of the mythological hero Heracles through the different literary genres in the Augustan age: an heroic and aetiological character in the *Aeneid* (8.175-305), in the *Fasti* of Ovid (1.543-586) and in Livy 1.7.3-15, Heracles 'goes down' to the degrading part of the elegiac *exclusus* in Propertius' elegy 4.9, in which he is the lover 'che di fronte alla porta chiusa della donna amata pronuncia il suo paraclausíthyron' (Fedeli [1989] 388. For the complete study of such a metamorphosis of Heracles, see pages 383-393).

only when one reads the alluding text – Petronius' text – but also when the *Aeneid* passage (the text alluded to) is reread,

> ... perché implicitamente Petronio invita a rileggere anche il contesto del modello alla luce del nuovo contesto in cui esso viene inserito. Il lettore che, muovendo dal passo petroniano, ritornerà a quello virgiliano, stabilirà inevitabilmente un grottesco e irriverente parallelo fra Didone e il membro inerte di Encolpio. Si può esser certi, d'altronde, che proprio per ottenere questo effetto Petronio ha citato quei versi virgiliani.[7]

We can detect the same lowering effect, with elements brought from higher genres to the so-called lower genres, in Martial's poetry. Along with elegiac poetry and the novel, the epigram is one more example of the *tenuis* genre mentioned by Fedeli in our epigraph. We will demonstrate below how the 'lowering' or 'desacralization' effect on Vergil's *Aeneid* occurs in three epigrams that allude to it. It will obviously be a small sample of the phenomenon, which is so rich in the epigrammatist's corpus, where texts of other authors of elevated genres experience the same 'desacralizing' effect. And the lowering of the Vergilian epic could be exemplified by many others epigrams of Martial apart from the three used below.

Consider first the poem 3.78, in which Martial attacks a man named Paulinus, who would have urinated from a moving ship[8]:

> Minxisti currente semel, Pauline, carina.
> Meiere uis iterum? Iam Palinurus eris.

The pentameter brings the threat: if that ill-mannered man urinates again from the ship, he will become a *Palinurus*. The humor at the end of the epigram obviously depends upon the perception and interpre-

---

[7] Fedeli (1989) 395. Another passage from the *Satyricon* in which *Aeneid* is desacralized is the episode of the widow of Ephesus, where Petronius cites verses from book 4 of the epic poem and draws a parallel between the figure of Dido and the widow who is the main character of the story. The ideal of the *uniuira* ('the woman who had only one husband during her life') present in Dido (recall that she commits suicide also because of her remorse for not remaining faithful to the memory of her deceased husband) is 'lowered' by the parallel with the widow of Ephesus. This woman's attitude is to order her new lover to nail to the cross the corpse of her deceased husband, so that she can prevent the punishment and the loss of the new lover, the soldier who was guarding the crucified. We are grateful to Professor Paulo Sérgio de Vasconcellos (State University of Campinas) for this remark.

[8] The text of Martial is always from Shackleton Bailey's edition (1993).

tation of the intertext that is represented by that proper noun. In the *Aeneid*, Palinurus is the helmsman of Aeneas' ship and he is first mentioned in book 3: in vv. 202 ff. he is steering the ship of the Trojan hero during a terrible storm and is able to take the ship to the Strophades Islands at the end of the tempest. In the same book, in vv. 509 ff., Palinurus appears again, but this time he is looking at the stars and concludes that it is time to restart the voyage towards Italy. A little later, in vv. 562 ff., the helmsman is back in the narrative, now skilfully steering the rudder of Aeneas' ship in order to avoid Charybdis.

But it is in book 5 that Palinurus' misfortune is presented by Vergil and that is why it is the book to which Martial's epigram alludes more directly. After his appearance at the beginning of the book (vv. 12 ff.), where the helmsman tries to control the ship during a storm that hits Aeneas' fleet just after the departure from Carthage, Palinurus will appear again at the end of the book (vv. 799 ff.). Here, he is the victim demanded by the sea-god Neptune in exchange for a safe journey for Aeneas and all his other companions. But let us allow Vergil himself to narrate the fate of the helmsman (*Aen.* 5.835-871):[9]

> iamque fere mediam coeli Nox umida metam   835
> contigerat, placida laxarant membra quiete
> sub remis fusi per dura sedilia nautae,
> cum leuis aetheriis delapsus Somnus ab astris,
> aëra dimouit tenebrosum et dispulit umbras,
> te, Palinure, petens, tibi somnia tristia portans   840
> insonti; puppique deus consedit in alta
> Phorbanti similis funditque has ore loquelas:
> 'Iaside Palinure, ferunt ipsa aequora classem,
> aequatae spirant aurae, datur hora quieti.
> pone caput fessosque oculos furare labori.   845
> ipse ego paulisper pro te tua munera inibo.'
> cui uix attollens Palinurus lumina fatur:
> 'mene salis placidi uultum fluctusque quietos
> ignorare iubes? mene huic confidere monstro?
> Aenean credam (quid enim?) fallacibus auris   850
> et caeli totiens deceptus fraude sereni?'
> talia dicta dabat, clauumque adfixus et haerens
> nusquam amittebat oculosque sub astra tenebat.

---

[9] The text of Vergil is always from Mynors' edition (1969).

> ecce deus ramum Lethaeo rore madentem
> uique soporatum Stygia super utraque quassat   855
> tempora, cunctantique natantia lumina soluit.
> uix primos inopina quies laxauerat artus,
> et super incumbens cum puppis parte reuulsa
> cumque gubernaclo liquidas proiecit in undas
> praecipitem ac socios nequiquam saepe uocantem;   860
> ipse uolans tenuis se sustulit ales in auras.
> currit iter tutum non setius aequore classis
> promissisque patris Neptuni interrita fertur.
> iamque adeo scopulos Sirenum aduecta subibat,
> difficilis quondam multorumque ossibus albos   865
> (tum rauca adsiduo longe sale saxa sonabant),
> cum pater amisso fluitantem errare magistro
> sensit, et ipse ratem nocturnis rexit in undis
> multa gemens casuque animum concussus amici:
> 'o nimium caelo et pelago confise sereno,   870
> nudus in ignota, Palinure, iacebis harena.'

Palinurus, overcome by Sleep, who had taken the shape of Phorbas[10] and argued that the calm of the waves granted by Neptune had made the helmsman's attention unnecessary, falls into the sea together with a part of the stern and the rudder, which has broken off.[11] It is no use crying for his companions' help, since they are sound asleep. Even Aeneas only realizes the accident when the ships are already approaching the Sirens' rocks; accordingly, the hero can only lament his companion's death.

More details of Palinurus' sad fate will be provided in book 6, where the character is brought back to the light, but now as a ghost wandering through the infernal regions (6.295-383).[12] Aeneas, who had gone down to the Underworld with the Sibyl, in order to meet his father Anchises, catches sight of the old boatman Charon in his endless work of ferrying the souls of the dead across the Styx, taking them to Hades' kingdom on the opposite bank (6.295-316). But only the souls of the deceased who were given a proper burial can be ferried on the old man's boat, as

---

[10] Perhaps the character mentioned in the *Iliad* (14.490-492) as the father of the Trojan warrior Ilioneus, who is killed by the Greek Peneleos in the Homeric passage (cf. Williams [2002] 203).

[11] As R. Williams (2002) 199 notes, this accident looks like the one suffered by Phrontis, Menelaus' helmsman (see *Od.* 3.278-285).

[12] This intertext between Martial 3.78 and *Aen.* 6.337 ff. was indicated by Citroni (1987) 399.

the Sibyl explains to Aeneas (6.317-330). Among the unburied dead is Palinurus,[13] who replies to the Trojan hero's questions concerning the circumstances of the accident (6.347-362):

> ille autem: 'neque te Phoebi cortina fefellit,
> dux Anchisiade, nec me deus aequore mersit.
> namque gubernaclum multa ui forte reuulsum,
> cui datus haerebam custos cursusque regebam,   350
> praecipitans traxi mecum. maria aspera iuro
> non ullum pro me tantum cepisse timorem,
> quam tua ne spoliata armis, excussa magistro,
> deficeret tantis nauis surgentibus undis.
> tris Notus hibernas immensa per aequora noctes   355
> uexit me uiolentus aqua; uix lumine quarto
> prospexi Italiam summa sublimis ab unda.
> paulatim adnabam terrae; iam tuta tenebam,
> ni gens crudelis madida cum ueste grauatum
> prensantemque uncis manibus capita aspera montis   360
> ferro inuasisset praedamque ignara putasset.
> nunc me fluctus habet uersantque in litore uenti.

Thus Aeneas learns that Palinurus, having fallen into the sea and having become a plaything of the waves, had been thrown into barbarian lands, attacked and killed by their inhabitants.[14] In the verses that follow the passage above, Palinurus asks the Trojan hero to bury his body, which is still on the beach, or to allow him to board Charon's boat with the two living people (Aeneas and the Sibyl, 6.363-371). The priestess denies Palinurus' request, but calms him by predicting that his body will be buried by those who will find it on the beach

---

[13] The encounter between Aeneas and Palinurus in the Underworld is modelled on the encounter between Odysseus and Elpenor in the same place (*Od.* 9.51-83). Both Palinurus and Elpenor tell the circumstances of their deaths and beg the heroes for a burial. However there are important differences between the two characters, since Elpenor was not the helmsman of Odysseus and his death was not in the sea: after getting drunk, he fell from a roof of Circe's palace (see Williams [2002] 198).

[14] As pointed out by Williams (2002) xxv-xxviii, there are many inconsistencies between the story of Palinurus' death narrated in 5.835-871 and that one which the helmsman's ghost himself tells to Aeneas in 6.337-362. See two examples: 1) in book 5, the god Sleep pushes Palinurus overboard, but in book 6 the helmsman denies any divine intervention in his death; 2) in book 5, the sea is calm and so the rudder breaking and the helmsman's fall and death look like supernatural facts caused by divine powers; however, in book 6 Palinurus says that the sea was rough and this had been the cause of the accident.

and that the burial place will bear the helmsman's name (6.372-383).[15]

Returning to the epigram, we can understand the threat under which Paulinus acts if he perpetrates the rude act of urinating from the ship again: he will have the same fate as Palinurus, i.e., falling into the sea. This final point can be interpreted in two different ways that are not mutually exclusive and are both based on the reading of the intertexts with Vergil's *Aeneid*. The first of these interpretations is the following: if Paulinus urinates again from the ship, he will fall down into the sea because it is dangerous to do it from a moving ship (*currente ... carina*); such an act can shift one's focus and can cause an accident. So Palinurus' example should be a warning to Paulinus since the helmsman had fallen into the waves because of sleep and a moment of distraction when he was looking at the stars (see above *Aen.* 5.852-561).

According to the second interpretation, which we favour, the pentameter sounds like an effective threat on the part of the *persona loquens*: if Paulinus childishly urinates from the ship again, the *persona* himself or the other crew members will be in charge of punishing him by pushing him into the sea. Therefore, Paulinus will have the same fate as Palinurus, who was metaphorically pushed by the god Sleep (see above *Aen.* 5.858-861).

Regardless of which interpretation is to be favoured (if only one is to be preferred), there is also another element that cooperates with the epigram's final point. We are referring to the pun on the helmsman's name, which is based on a false etymology of which Martial makes conscious and skilful use. That pun depends on the segmentation of the word *Palinurus* into the Greek words πάλιν, *pálin*, adverb, 'again') and οὐρεῖν (*oureîn*, verb, 'to urinate').[16] Therefore, the pentameter would be read as follows: if Paulinus urinates (*oureîn*) again (*pálin*), he will be a *Palinurus* (*pálin oureîn*). In short, if the person attacked by Martial urinates again from the ship, he will be a Palinurus not only because he will have the same fate of the Aeneas' helmsman (falling into the

---

[15] The Capo di Palinuro, on the coast of the region known today as Campania, in southern Italy. Therefore, the story of Palinurus in the *Aeneid* is aetiological, since it explains the origin of the name of that place (Austin [1986] 136).

[16] This pun is pointed out by Izaac (1930) 108 n. 1, Pimentel (2000) 158 n. 170, Richard (1931) 450 n. 605, Watson (2003) 326 and many others. According to Sullivan (1991) 246, the correct etymology derives the name from οὖρος (*oûros*, 'watcher').

sea), but also because the word *Palinurus* means, according to the 'etymology' hinted at, 'the one who urinates again'.

The effects produced by the intertexts with the *Aeneid* in the epigram in question are appropriated by Martial to produce the final point of his epigram. Naming the person attacked Paulinus is not a random choice; on the contrary, such a choice is due to the sonorous similarity with the name of Aeneas' helmsman (*Palinurus* and *Paulinus* share the syllables *pa-*, *li-* and *nu-*). The Vergilian character and his terrible fate are removed from the high and extremely pathetic context of *Aeneid* book 5 (narrating the death of the helmsman) and 6 (the encounter with Aeneas in the Underworld) and they are taken to the playful and low environment of Martial's epigram, in which they are adapted to a 'desacralizing' scene where a person childishly urinates from a ship. The parallel established between the author of this act – Paulinus – and the steersman Palinurus ends up lowering the latter to the degrading condition of the man attacked by the epigrammatist. Apart from the sonorous similarity between the proper names, such a process of degrading the Vergilian character is reinforced by the repetition of the impolite verb *meiere* ('to piss') at the beginning of both the hexameter and the pentameter.

Consider now a pair of epigrams – 2.83 and 3.85 – that relate autotextually to each other, and, intertextually, to *Aeneid* 6.[17] These poems are both based on the theme of adultery (*adulterium*) – this is understood in its Latin sense of 'sexual intercourse between a married woman and a man other than her husband'[18] – and on the punishments that the cheated husband was allowed to inflict on his wife and her lover, according to the Roman legal and moral code. In both epigrams these punishments correspond to the mutilation of the nose and ears, but the husband was also allowed to mutilate other parts of the lover's body (such as the penis itself), to whip him or even to sodomize him.[19]

In 2.83, Martial mocks a husband who got his revenge on his wife's lover in a very ineffective way:

---

[17] These intertexts were pointed out by Citroni (1987) 399.
[18] Hornblower, Spawforth (1999) 15 s.v.
[19] See also Williams (2004) 253.

> Foedasti miserum, marite, moechum,
> et se, qui fuerant prius, requirunt
> trunci naribus auribusque uultus.
> Credis te satis esse uindicatum?
> Erras: iste potest et irrumare.

It is not enough, according the poet, to cut the lover's nose and ears off as revenge, because the main organ used in the illicit acts, the *mentula*, stays intact. This way the adulterer can still commit adultery again by receiving oral sex (*irrumare*) from the unfaithful wife.[20]

The intertext of this epigram is with *Aeneid* 6 (vv. 494-547), in which Aeneas, just after the encounter with Dido's ghost, starts wandering in the region of the Underworld where illustrious warriors dwell, and he ends up meeting, among them, the ghost of Deiphobus, Priam's son and the husband of the beautiful Helen after Paris' death. According to the Vergilian version told in this passage, when the Greeks finally managed to invade the city, Menelaus and Odysseus, aided by Helen herself, surprised Deiphobus asleep and inflicted some of the punishments that were reserved for the lovers of married women upon him: mutilation of the nose, ears and hands (6.494-512):

> Atque hic Priamiden laniatum corpore toto
> Deiphobum uidet et lacerum crudeliter ora,   495
> ora manusque ambas, populataque tempora raptis
> auribus et truncas inhonesto uulnere naris.
> uix adeo agnouit pauitantem ac dira tegentem
> supplicia, et notis compellat uocibus ultro:
> 'Deiphobe armipotens, genus alto a sanguine Teucri,   500
> quis tam crudelis optauit sumere poenas?
> cui tantum de te licuit? mihi fama suprema
> nocte tulit fessum uasta te caede Pelasgum
> procubuisse super confusae stragis aceruum.
> tunc egomet tumulum Rhoeteo in litore inanem   505
> constitui et magna manis ter uoce uocaui.
> nomen et arma locum seruant; te, amice, nequiui
> conspicere et patria decedens ponere terra.'
> ad quae Priamides: 'nihil o tibi, amice, relictum;
> omnia Deiphobo soluisti et funeris umbris.   510
> sed me fata mea et scelus exitiale Lacaenae
> his mersere malis; illa haec monimenta reliquit.

---

[20] In fact, *irrumare* is not the only option left for the lover, because he would still be able to have vaginal intercourse (*futuere*).

Deiphobus, for taking Helen – Menelaus' spouse – as his wife, commits the same crime already committed by Paris and also becomes an *adulter*. Thus, he receives the punishments that were inflicted on those convicted of such a crime at the time of the *Aeneid*'s composition.[21] As is customary in the Underworld, Deiphobus' ghost still possesses the injuries and mutilations which he had received at the moment of his death. He is so disfigured that even Aeneas, who had known him, finds it difficult to recognize him.

The context of mutilation as punishment of a married woman's lover was brought from the Vergilian passage by Martial (although Deiphobus is not mentioned in the epigram as he will be in 3.85). However, the allusion to the passage of the *Aeneid* is more evident in line 3, where *trunci naribus auribusque uultus* refers to *Deiphobum ... lacerum .../ ... populataque tempora raptis/ auribus, et truncas inhonesto uulnere nares* from lines 495-497 of Vergil. We can observe the reuse of Vergilian vocabulary by the epigrammatist: the adjective *truncus* in the plural (in the *Aeneid* passage, this is in the accusative case, qualifying *nares*; in Martial's verse, in the nominative, qualifying *uultus*), the noun *naris* used in the plural (in the *Aeneid*, it is accusative, complementary to *lacerum*; in the epigram it is ablative, complementary to *trunci*) and the noun *auris*, in the same case and number, ablative plural, *auribus* (in Vergil's passage, the complement of *populata*; in Martial's, of *trunci*).

By alluding to the passage in *Aeneid* 6, both in its content (the use of Vergil's version of Deiphobus' punishment by the mutilation of nose and ears) and in the form (the reuse of words from 495-497 of the passage of Vergil), Martial transfers the serious and sad context of the encounter – in the Underworld, between Aeneas and the disfigured ghost of the Trojan prince Deiphobus – to the debauched and obscene setting of the epigram 2.83, in which those same punishments that had been inflicted on the epic character – the cause of his great pain and suffering – are now satirized as useless because the adulterer of the epigram still has the option of practising oral sex on the unfaithful

---

[21] Homer, as noted by Austin (1986) 171, does not mention this version, according to which Deiphobus would have become the new husband of Helen after Paris' death and would have been disfigured and killed by Menelaus.

wife. The words *moechus*[22] and *irrumare*, which belong to the obscene vocabulary,[23] obviously contribute to the process of 'desacralizing' the elements brought from the Vergilian epic text.

Epigram 3.85 is a variation on the same theme, but now Deiphobus is explicitly cited:

> Quis tibi persuasit naris abscidere moecho?
>   non hac peccatum est parte, marite, tibi.
> Stulte, quid egisti? nihil hic tua perdidit uxor,
>   cum sit salua tui mentula Deiphobi.

Here the lover's nose is also mutilated by the husband as a form of punishment.[24] In Vergil's text, the nose was one of the body parts of which Menelaus deprived Deiphobus. But it is the direct mention of this character in line 4 that leaves no doubt that Martial is alluding to the Vergilian passages about the death of Deiphobus.[25] The epigrammatist playfully hints that it is no use cutting off the adulterer's nose, as Menelaus did to Deiphobus, since the penis of his wife's *Deiphobus* remains intact.

The conclusions about the intertextual effects produced by the allusions to the *Aeneid* in 3.85, as was expected, are the same as those for 2.83. By transferring Deiphobus' sad mutilation story from book 6 of Vergil's epic poem to the playful and obscene scenery (see the terms *moechus* and *mentula*)[26] of this epigram, Martial causes the lowering of the epic elements and 'desacralizes' them in order to produce the malicious humour that closes the poem. From the three epigrams analysed (just a small sample of the phenomenon, as stated), it can be seen that, even though Martial frequently draws a distinction between epigrammatic poetry and the so-called 'higher' genres,[27] he collects

---

[22] The word is borrowed from Greek and equivalent to the Latin word *adulter* (Williams [2004] 254). Note also the alliteration of the [m] in *MiseruM, Marite, MoechuM*.
[23] For *moechus* and *irrumare*, see Adams (1982), respectively 142 and 125-130.
[24] Observe the syntactic effects in the first line, in which *naris* is 'separated' from *moecho* in order to represent inside the verse the act of separating/cutting off the nose of the adulterer. This effect is reinforced by the fact that the word which separates the two terms is *abscidere*, meaning 'to separate', 'to cut off'.
[25] The epigram in question can even help in identifying and proving the intertexts in 3.83, where the character is not cited by name.
[26] About *mentula* as an obscene word, see Adams (1982) 9-12.
[27] See Martial *Apoph*. 1 and 185, 4.14 and 49, 5.30, 8.3, 9.50, 10.4, 35.1-9 and 64 and 12.94.

from the latter many raw materials that can be creatively incorporated and manipulated into epigrams in order to create the most various meanings. Therefore, the 'desacralization' or lowering of the Vergilian epic is only one of the many textual effects that are possible. In fact, such 'desacralization' is only a textual effect, a form of creatively manipulating the elements borrowed from the Vergilian text; it does not represent any type of devaluation of Vergil's poetry, an author whom the epigrammatist – and many at his time – considered the greatest figure of Latin literature, as evidenced by the epithets that Martial uses when mentioning him: *magnus* (see 4.14.14, 11.48.1, 12.67.5), *cothurnatus* (5.5.8, 7.63.5), *sacer* (8.55.3), *aeternus* (11.52.18), *facundus* (14.185) and *summus* (12.3.1).

Bibliography

Adams, J.N. (1982), *The Latin Sexual Vocabulary*, London.
Austin, R.G. (1986[r]), *P. Vergili Maronis Aeneidos Liber Sextus*, with a commentary, Oxford.
Bailey, D.R.S. (1993), *Martial. Epigrams*, edited and translated, Cambridge (MA).
Cesila, R.T. (2004), *Metapoesia nos epigramas de Marcial: tradução e análise*, MA thesis, Campinas.
Cesila, R.T. (2008), *O palimpsesto epigramático de Marcial: intertextualidade e geração de sentidos na obra do poeta de Bílbilis*, PhD thesis, Campinas.
Citroni, M. (1987), 'Marziale', in F. della Corte (org.). *Enciclopedia Virgiliana*, vol. 3, Roma, 396-400.
Fedeli, P. (1989), 'Le intersezioni dei generi e dei modelli', in G. Cavallo, P. Fedeli, A. Giardina (edd.), *Lo Spazio letterario di Roma Antica*, vol. 1: *La Produzione del Testo*, Roma, 375-397.
Hornblower, S., Spawforth, A., edd. (1999[3]), *The Oxford Classical Dictionary*, Oxford.
Izaac, H.J. (1930), *Martial. Épigrammes*, texte établi et traduit, vol. 1, Paris.
Mynors, R.A.B. (1969), *P. Vergili Maronis Opera*, Oxford.

Pimentel, C.S. (2000), *Marcial. Epigramas*, vol. 1, tradução de Delfim Ferreira Leão (*Livro dos Espectáculos*), José Luís Brandão (livros I e II) e Paulo Sérgio Ferreira (livro III), introdução e notas de Cristina Pimentel, Lisboa.

Richard, P. (1931), *Les Épigrammes de Martial*, texte établi, traduit et annoté, vol. 1, Paris.

Sullivan, J.P. (1991), *Martial: the Unexpected Classic*, Cambridge.

Torrão, J.M.N. (2004), 'Autores de referência na obra de Marcial', *Humanitas* 56, 137-159.

Vasconcellos, P.S. (2001), *Efeitos Intertextuais na* Eneida *de Virgílio*, São Paulo.

Vasconcellos, P.S. et al., org. (2008), *Eneida brasileira: tradução poética da epopéia de Públio Virgílio Maro*, Campinas.

Watson, L., Watson, P. (2003), *Martial. Select Epigrams*, Cambridge.

Williams, C. (2004), *Martial. Epigrams, Book Two*, edited with introduction, translation, and commentary, Oxford.

Williams, R.D. (2002), *Aeneid V*, edited with a commentary, London.

A Gadibus ad ostium Albis fluminis. Considerations on the Symbolic Image of Gades in the *Res gestae*

PAMINA FERNÁNDEZ CAMACHO
Universidad de Cádiz

The text known as the *Res gestae diui Augusti* is a gift, not only for scholars who study the age of Augustus, but for all scholars of antiquity who study the influence of ideological issues on the way the world is conceived and depicted. What better example of an ideologically conditioned geographical text could there be than the chronicle in which the *princeps* himself gives a propagandistic summary of his own doings, including his conquests?[1] As a text, the *Res gestae* encompasses the entire world, and re-imagines its very geography in the way most convenient for the newly established power. This includes the geography of the Far West, whose various descriptions and related legends had been influenced by political issues at least since the extant testimonies from fifth century Athens.[2] As might be expected, the ruler who made the polemical decision to renounce his family legacy of pursuing expansion beyond the shores of the Ocean would continue this tradition, giving a political orientation to the western geographical data that appear in his work.

There is, in particular, one paragraph of the *Res gestae* that may prove very interesting for those who study the different representations of the Far Western landscape of the Roman world. It is Paragraph 26, where the limits of Roman expansion under the *princeps* are listed:

> Omnium prouinciarum populi Romani, quibus finitimae fuerunt gentes quae non parerent imperio nostro, fines auxi. Gallias et Hispanias prouincias, item

---

[1] In this paper we follow the scholarly convention of considering Augustus the 'author' of the work. As Scheid (2007) xxvi-xxviii pertinently observes, the *Res gestae* was probably composed by his secretaries in the final years of his life, though under his own direction and depending on his approval.

[2] Fernández Camacho (2013ᵇ) 9-30, Antonelli (1997) 135-168.

> Germaniam qua includit Oceanus a Gadibus ad ostium Albis fluminis pacaui. Alpes a regione ea, quae proxima est Hadriano mari, ad Tuscum pacificaui, nulli genti bello per iniuriam inlato. Classis mea per Oceanum ab ostio Rheni ad solis orientis regionem usque ad fines Cimbrorum nauigauit, quo neque terra neque mari quisquam Romanus ante id tempus adit, Cimbrique et Charydes et Semnones et eiusdem tractus alii Germanorum populi per legatos amicitiam meam et populi Romani petierunt. Meo iussu et auspicio ducti sunt duo exercitus eodem fere tempore in Aethiopiam et in Arabiam, quae appellatur Eudaemon, maximaeque hostium gentis utriusque copiae caesae sunt in acie et complura oppida capta. In Aethiopiam usque ad oppidum Nabata peruentum est, cui proxima est Meroe. In Arabiam usque in fines Sabaeorum processit exercitus ad oppidum Mariba.

The western border is represented here by a significant expression: *qua includit Oceanus a Gadibus ad ostium Albis fluminis*. It is interesting for several reasons. The first observation that can be made is that the mention of a city is not at all frequent in the text. According to Nicolet, the *Res gestae* contains 55 geographical names, of which only six belong to cities.[3] Of those six, two, Actium and Ariminum (present-day Rimini) occur, respectively, on account of the great victory achieved there in 31 BC, and on account of various services and public works sponsored by the emperor, and therefore belong firmly to the field of concrete reality. Nabata, Meroe and Mariba, on the other hand, appear in the context of boundaries, where names of rivers and tribes are much more frequent, and they share at least two features: a semi-legendary status in the ears of the listeners, and the fact that they are not part of the Roman empire and can only be woven into the chronicle through various artifices of conquest, such as mentioning expeditions of dubious success and proximity to other places already mentioned.[4] These names effectively weave an illusion of distance and exoticism into the text, the same distance and exoticism traditionally connected with the edges of the world represented by Arabia and Ethiopia, both fabulous countries in the Greek and Roman imagination.[5] Gades is mentioned with a similar intent, with one important difference: unlike Meroe, Nabata or Mariba, it was part of the Roman empire and very

---

[3] Nicolet (1988) 34-35.
[4] Vanotti provides a summarized account of the history of these expeditions in Vanotti (1987) 234-249.
[5] Romm (1994).

much a real and well-known city in the Augustan era, located in a two-island archipelago near the southwestern coast of Baetica.[6]

The ambiguous status of this city, caught between the legendary geography of the edges of the world and the real geography of the empire, is not a new occurrence, but rather the result of a long literary history tying *Gadeira,* or Gades, to the Far West of Greek and Roman myth, either directly or via other toponyms such as Tartessos or Erytheia, which gradually came to be identified with it. There is no evidence that Hesiod was thinking of either Gades or the Strait of Gibraltar when he composed his *Theogony,* where Erytheia already occurs as a place near the river Ocean, realm of the three-headed monster Geryon before he was killed by Herakles.[7] But by around 600 BC, when Stesichorus composed his *Geryoneia,* Erytheia had already become connected to Tartessos, a name given to a river which cannot be identified with any pre-existing Greek mythical reality.[8] A century later, Pindar mentioned Gadeira for the first time in his fourth Nemean Ode, where he speaks of Γαδείρων τὸ (...) ζόφον, 'the dark twilight of Gadeira', referring to the western end of the world, which cannot be reached by mortal man.[9] The dark and sinister overtones attributed by Hesiod to the Ocean, home to the monsters of myth and deities related to night and darkness, were thus transferred to a real toponym for the first time in literature. Also, in a fragment attributed to Pindar by Strabo, Gadeira is equated to the Strait of Gibraltar, called πύλας Γαδειρίδας, or Gates of Gadeira, the end of the known world.[10]

It was only a matter of time before a set of circumstances brought together the mythical Erytheia and the real – but mythologized – Gadeira. The context has been identified as fifth-century Athens and the work of Pherecydes the genealogist.[11] According to Strabo, this Pherecydes identified the island where the city of Gadeira was located as

---

[6] The most informative contemporary source is Strab. 3.5.3-10.
[7] Hes. *Theog.* 287-292: τρικέφαλον Γηρυονῆα (...)/ τὸν μὲν ἄρ' ἐξενάριξε βίη Ἡρακληείη/ βουσὶ παρ' εἰλιπόδεσσι περιρρύτῳ εἰν Ἐρυθείῃ.
[8] Stesich. Fr. 7 *SLG* (= Strab. 3.2.11): σχεδὸν ἀντιπέρας κλεινᾶς Ἐρυθείας Ταρτησσοῦ ποταμοῦ παρὰ παγὰς ἀπείρονας ἀργυρορίζους ἐν κευθμῶνι πέτρας.
[9] Pind. *Nem.* 4.69-70.
[10] Strab. 3.5.5.
[11] Fernández Camacho (2013ᵇ), cf. supra; Antonelli (1997), cf. supra.

Erytheia, where Herakles killed the monster Geryon.[12] The motivation behind such an identification – here we agree with Antonelli – seems to be mainly ideological in nature. Athens was at the height of its maritime expansion, taking over Greek markets in the west. The role of the hero Herakles as defender of civilization against the barbarians and explorer of distant lands, being the first conqueror of Asia Minor and the first explorer to reach the western end of the world, was highlighted and exploited by the Athenians, who now saw themselves as fulfilling the same role.[13] Gradually, the enemies of the hero became identified with the enemies and rivals of the Greek world: the Trojans were the mythical predecessors of the Persian empire which now occupied their land; Busiris, a 'new mythological character' who became popular in this period,[14] was a caricature of the xenophobic kings of Egypt; the twins Alebion and Dercynes, substituted by a dragon or a tyrant by the name of Tauriscus in other sources, represented the ferocity of the Ligurians who threatened Greek Massalia.[15] It was in this context that Geryon was made to rule the island of Gadeira, at the time occupied by an influential Phoenician merchant city and the head of a trading alliance known as the 'Circle of the Strait',[16] whose salted fish exports were well known among the Athenian populace as τάριχος γαδειρικόν.[17] Elsewhere we have argued that this Geryon, king of Erytheia, had in fact become a negative substitute for the colony's own god, the Phoenician Melqart, whose name translates as 'king of the city'.[18] The city of Gadeira was therefore 'mythologized' into the scenario of the Tenth Labour of Herakles, the cattle raid, and its god into the villain of the story. The Pillars of Herakles, which would become the most popular way of referring to what Pindar used to call 'gates of Gadeira', would stand for a long time as a half-mythical, half-geographical proof

---

[12] Strab. 3.5.4.
[13] Hall (1991). Cf. Eur. *Heracl.*, Hdt. 9.27, Isoc. 4.57-60, 5.34, 5.112, 12.194.
[14] Livingstone (2001) 87.
[15] Cf. Mela 2.71, Tzetz. *Chil.* 2.340 ff., Apollod. *Bibl.* 2.5.10, Hyg. *Poet. astr.* 2.6.3, Amm. Marc. 15.9.6, 15.10.9.
[16] The term was coined by Tarradell (1960), (1968). On its present-day implications, cf. Domínguez Pérez (2011).
[17] Eup. *Testimonia Hispaniae Antiqua* 2.A 47b (= Steph. Byz, s.v. Γάδειρα), Antiph. *Testimonia Hispaniae Antiqua* 2.A 47c (= Ath. 118d), cf. García-Bellido (1942) 3.
[18] Fernández Camacho (2013ᵇ) 19.

of the Greeks' symbolic claim over the area. In various texts, written in different periods, we find evidence of a long cultural debate over who came first and to whom did the Pillars 'belong'.[19]

By the fourth century BC, however, the whole idea of Athenian dominion of the seas had soured considerably. The city-state had been defeated in the Peloponnesian War, and its most ambitious naval venture, the Sicilian invasion, had met disaster. There were still attempts, with the second Delic-Attic league, to restore the city's former glory, but they would ultimately end in failure. This was the time for two renowned Athenian intellectuals to set their own ideas in writing in an attempt to influence the policy of their contemporaries, providing us with invaluable information about the ideological trappings of Athenian power. The first of these intellectuals was the rhetorician Isocrates, who in several of his speeches displayed the whole Athenian ideological arsenal of the past century in an attempt to recreate the former influence of his city. After losing faith in Athens, he re-forged it all into a new ideology of power at the service of the strong man of the time, Philip of Macedon, who was better able to make Isocrates' dreams of Greek unity against the barbarians come true. Throughout this process, Herakles retained his importance as a symbol, since the Athenians were considered his spiritual heirs, the avengers and protectors of his children, while Philip claimed him as his direct ancestor.[20]

The second author was Plato, who had a different view of things, especially regarding rule over the seas, which Athenians regarded as their due. Plato believed that Athens' growing interest in maritime affairs had been instrumental in its corruption and downfall.[21] His *Menexenus* includes a parody of the popular tropes used by Isocrates in the *Panegyricus* and *Panathenaicus*.[22] More interestingly, the *Timaeus* and the *Critias* constitute a full-scale subversion of those tropes. In Plato's telling, the ancient – and virtuous – Athens of mythical times had adopted the same role in the Atlantis myth as in the Persian wars: it united and led the resistance against a tyrannical empire. This was the cornerstone of Athens' claim to have led the Greeks since the battle of

---

[19] Cf. for example Strab. 3.5.5-6, Clearch. Fr. 67 Wehrli (= Zenob. 5.48).
[20] Isoc. 12.59-60, 5.112.
[21] Pl. *Leg.* 706 b-d.
[22] Pissavino (1981) 217, Loraux (1981) 268-270.

Salamis. However, in Plato, the tyrannical empire turned out to be more similar to the real Athens than to its enemy: it ruled over the seas and launched an attack to expand its influence, whereas the ancient, mythical Athens had had a limited amount of land and did not even possess a harbour or a fleet (Vidal-Naquet [1981]). Furthermore, the empire of Atlantis was located in the Far West, though traditionally all threats of annexation had come from the east. True to its literary role, Gadeira is, once again, the only real place connected to this imaginary empire, ruled by descendants of Poseidon, as Geryon was in Greek myth.[23] The Platonic fiction's greatest acknowledgement of the ideological depiction of the Far West in contemporary Athens is the mention of the first king's twin, whose name, unlike those of his nine brothers, is given in two different languages. *Eumelos*, or 'rich in herds' (the main attribute of Geryon in myth) is the 'Greek translation' (Ἑλληνιστὶ) of an original name in the 'native language' (τὸ δ' ἐπιχώριον): *Gadeiros.* This prince ruled over the 'Gadiric region' (τῆς Γαδειρικῆς... χώρας). The propaganda has been subverted; the mythical construct turned against those who created it.

The Hellenistic period was the golden age of scientific geography, which would gradually set aside the tenets of mythical geography and replace them with new ways to measure and describe the known world. Though Greek scientific geography was not, in fact, as scientific, in a modern sense, as has been assumed by some, and both myth and extra-geographical considerations still underlay many of the new formulations,[24] it is true that the work of these geographers changed the landscape of the west in many ways.

On the exploratory front, Pytheas' expedition to the northern ocean enlarged that part of the globe by many degrees; as for the south, the main point of debate was the shape and size of the African continent and the possibility of circumnavigating it. The adventures of Eudoxus of Cyzicus under the Ptolemies connected the name of Gadeira to

---

[23] Pl. *Criti.* 113e-114b: λῆξιν δὲ ἄκρας τῆς νήσου πρὸς Ἡρακλείων στηλῶν εἰληχότι ἐπὶ τὸ τῆς Γαδειρικῆς νῦν χώρας κατ' ἐκεῖνον τὸν τόπον ὀνομαζομένης, Ἑλληνιστὶ μὲν Εὔμηλον, τὸ δ' ἐπιχώριον Γάδειρον, ὅπερ τ' ἦν ἐπίκλην ταύτῃ ὄνομ' ἄ<ν> παράσχοι.

[24] A case in point, as Pietro Janni points out, would be how the Parallel of Rhodes, established as a universal point of reference in measuring latitude, is made to cross the most important places in the area, whether actually aligned or not. Cf. Janni (1984) 65-73, Prontera (1989) 175-177.

an expedition which would attempt this feat, and so would, later, the Alexander biographers, who attributed similar plans to the late king of Macedon.[25]

But Gadeira itself would be affected by the greatest change of all, which was primarily a change in mindset. It was at this time that the landscape of the Strait underwent a process of rationalization. Until now, the island-city of Gadeira had been the focal point of geographical reference in the area: it had been considered the end of the world and of Europe, as the landmark of the Strait. The mythical landscape had been assimilated to it, identified with it. But the Strait, for this new geography, was not in Gadeira anymore. Gadeira could not claim to be the limit of anything, as it lay at the centre of a bay, miles away from the Strait proper.[26] There were capes that ran further to the west, such as the Sacred Cape, tagged on by Artemidorus at the end of the old itineraries, which had previously ended at the Phoenician city, the distance between the two landmarks still remaining, centuries later, as *quidquid a Gadibus procurrit*[27]. Gadeira had effectively been debunked from its old role as the symbolic landmark of the Far West, and it had become nothing more, nothing less than a real place.

There is evidence of the confusion and debate caused by these changes in several contemporary and later sources, offering us a glimpse of what will no doubt have been a much larger issue. In the *Periplous* of Scylax, contradictory information is given about the Pillars being in the Strait *and* the Pillars being in Gadeira, even going as far as to venture a strange compromise: one of the Pillars is described as set in the Strait, the other in Gadeira.[28] Several texts mention two islands consecrated to Herakles and Hera and located in the Strait, which are no more than an unintended doublet of the two islands consecrated to those gods that used to be interchangeable with the Strait itself: the

---

[25] Strab. 2.4.1 (on Pytheas), 2.3.4-5 (on Eudoxus). The plans of Alexander are mentioned in Curt. 10.1.17-18, Diod. Sic. 18.4.4, Arr. *Anab.* 7.1.2, Plut. *Vit. Alex.* 68. An in-depth study of this historical information is provided by Nenci (1958ª) 215-257.

[26] Strab. 3.5.6: τὰ δὲ Γάδειρα οὐκ ἐν τοιούτοις ἵδρυται τόποις ὥστε ἀποδηλοῦν ἐσχατιάν, ἀλλ᾽ ἐν μέσῃ πως κεῖται μεγάλῃ παραλίᾳ κολπώδει.

[27] Plin. *HN* 2.242, Mart. Cap. 6.611: 'Verum Artemidorus dimensioni praedictae adiicit quidquid a Gadibus procurrit.'

[28] Peretti (1979) 167.

islands of Gadeira.[29] Most revealing of all, Strabo's account of the geographical debate about the true location of the Pillars identified two main sides to the argument: those who still identified the symbolic landmark with Gadeira and/or its temple, and those who thought that the Pillars were in the Strait, better suited as an important landmark. Not surprisingly, the first were mainly the locals, and the second were the Greek geographers.[30]

This was largely the state of things when Augustus came to power. Gadeira, or Gades as the Romans called it, had been displaced by the geographers from the position of privilege it used to enjoy in mythical geography. It retained some of its former attributions as the point of departure for legendary destinations, rooted in the reputation of the Phoenicians as seafarers and informants about the unknown regions that lay beyond. There were also a number of paradoxographical and mythical characterizations attributed to it by Greek and Roman authors, albeit mostly in a rationalized way.[31] Many of them were limited to the area of the temple of Melqart, the last refuge of the outer world.

It is in this context that the *Res gestae* mentions Gades as the landmark of the west once again: not the Strait, not the Sacred Cape, and not the real Western limit of Roman expansion, which was Great Britain, where Augustus's adoptive father Caesar had landed in 55 BC. In a very interesting paper, Zecchini has studied the repercussions of this landing in Great Britain, which was seen as a conquest of the furthermost land encountered by the Romans, a land beyond the *oikoumene* itself, but which was not then followed by any attempt to establish a permanent presence in the island, much less conquer it.[32] To paraphrase the man himself, Julius Caesar went, saw, and that was all he needed to grant himself a conquest, a symbolic one at least. The impact of that visit can be gauged by the mark it left in the literature of the time: even a poet as little concerned with either politics or Caesar

---

[29] Strab. 3.5.3, Avien. *Ora* 352-361, Scymn. 139-146. This theory of the doublet is formulated in Cataudella (1989-1990) 315-337.

[30] Strab. 3.5.5: καὶ Δικαίαρχος δὲ καὶ Ἐρατοσθένης καὶ Πολύβιος καὶ οἱ πλεῖστοι τῶν Ἑλλήνων περὶ τὸν πορθμὸν ἀποφαίνουσι τὰς Στήλας. οἱ δὲ Ἴβηρες καὶ Λίβυες ἐν Γαδείροις εἶναί φασιν· οὐδὲν γὰρ ἐοικέναι στήλαις τὰ περὶ τὸν πορθμόν.

[31] Fernández Camacho (2013ᵃ).

[32] Zecchini (1987) 253-266.

as Catullus echoes the feeling of nationalistic pride evoked by the British affair.[33]

This venture, however, posed a problem for Caesar's successor, especially as all the major decisions about war and peace came to rest on him alone. Contrary to the ideology that understood Rome as a power in continuous geographical expansion, Augustus gradually found that he had to compromise on many fronts in order to stabilize the empire. It was a time of relative consolidation and even some uncomfortable retreats, such as the Varus fiasco in Germania, the death of Gaius Caesar in the middle of his eastern campaign and the diplomatic manoeuvres in Armenia and Parthia (described rather flatteringly in §27 of the *Res gestae*), leading to the discontinuation – and active discouragement – of further interest in Britain or any other land not already subject to the Romans by the time of the *princeps*' old age and death[34]. Zecchini analyses the literature of the time to find a number of examples of the ideological struggle over this subject throughout Augustus's reign, all of them set against the backdrop of the 'legacy of Caesar': that is, the sometimes inconvenient notion that Julius Caesar was the model that Augustus, as his heir, had to emulate and surpass. In the work of the poets and historians of the Augustan era, Zecchini identifies an 'early period', starting when Octavian claimed the Caesarean inheritance and culminating in the years between 27 and 24 BC (the time when Augustus was fighting the Spanish campaign, and therefore, according to the geographical data of the day, facing Britain, which stood on the opposite shore of the Ocean). In this period there are quotations, to be found in Vergil's *Georgics* (29 BC) and in Horace's *Epodes* and *Odes* (38-23 BC), that mention Britain as a land beyond the Ocean which would soon be fully conquered by Augustus.[35] The second period would begin after Augustus' return from Spain

---

[33] Catull. 11.9-12. Cf. also App. *B Civ.* 4.8.34, Diod. Sic. 5.21.2, Suet. *Iul.* 25.2, Plut. *Vit. Caes.* 23.3.

[34] Examples of this discouragement are Cassius Dio's and Tacitus' account of the public reading of the testament of Augustus in *Roman History* 56.33.5-6 and *Ann.* 1.11.4, respectively, where he articulates this policy as a piece of advice for his sucessor. Tacitus also mentions the same story in another of his works, the *Agricola,* making specific mention of Britannia as the land whose conquest was supposed to have been neglected by Tiberius (*Agr.* 13.2).

[35] Verg. *G.* 3.25, Hor. *Epod.* 7.7, *Carm.* 1.35, 3.5, perhaps 1.21, too. There is also Propertius' elegy 27 of his second book (written before 23 BC, cf. Camps [1977]), where he seems to echo some kind of rumour about expeditions against the Parthians and Britons, though it could merely be a literary trope.

and his claim that he had returned *a Britannia insula totum orbem terrarum tam bello quam amicitiis Romano imperio pacis abundantia subditum*.³⁶ Leaving aside the debate on the extent of falsehood in this statement,³⁷ the rather roundabout phrasing *tam bello quam amicitiis* is very reminiscent of the *Res gestae*'s enumeration of diplomatic relations with foreign chieftains and kings as an elaborate substitute for conquests that never took place, including the mention of the British chieftains Dumnobellaunus and Tincomarus in §32, right behind the equally problematic kings of Parthia.³⁸ From that time onwards, the Augustan writers would 'change their tune' on Britain, which would only be mentioned as an exotic land which had nothing to do with the limits of the empire (Prop. 4.3), or – and this is what interests us here – it would be replaced as limit by other landmarks such as the Vergilian *extremi Morini* (*Aen.* 8.727), a Gaulish tribe, or, in a more mythological register, *beluosus qui remotis/ obstrepit Oceanus Britannis* (Hor. *Carm.* 4.14.47-48) and the even more old-fashioned *hesperio (Solis) cubili* (4.15.16).³⁹

This was not mere wordplay or careless rhetoric. Rome could not retreat from a place that had previously been 'conquered' by the *diuus Iulius*, and Augustus, as his son and heir, would have felt this problem with particular acuteness. If we also take into consideration the importance of dominion over the west as the only feat by which Rome could outdo the model of all conquerors, Alexander the Great, whom Augustus had studiously tried to emulate and surpass on a personal level,⁴⁰ it becomes apparent that Britain must have been a sore spot in Augustus' foreign policy. On the other hand, Rome could not afford to become involved with an entirely new province, inhabited by countless tribes and cut off by the sea from the rest of the empire. After the *princeps* returned from Spain without having re-conquered Britain,

---

³⁶ Liv. fr. 65 Jal (= Ap. *In canticum canticorum* 12.53).

³⁷ Zecchini (1987) 264 n. 32.

³⁸ On these two chieftains and their historical relationship with Rome and Augustus, cf. Cooley's commentary on § 32 of the *Res gestae* (Cooley [2009]).

³⁹ Zecchini mentions the exception of Ovid, who would once more set the discordant note in Augustan propaganda by exalting the British exploits of Caesar in the *Metamorphoses*, an implicit comparison that Augustus would not have appreciated (Zecchini [1987] 265-266).

⁴⁰ Nenci (1958ᵇ) 258-308. On this subject, cf. also Gagé (1940) 425-438, Seston (1968) 1-13, Vanotti (1987), cf. supra.

several measures were undertaken: mentions of Britain were indirectly, if not directly, discouraged in the literature of the time, except to present them as too remote or not worth the trouble,[41] expeditions were sponsored to sail to the north of Europe, effectively redirecting public attention to other legendary limits such as the fabled 'Caspian Strait',[42] and, last but not least, the literature of the time would rescue the symbolic importance of the ancient landmarks: the setting of the Sun, the Ocean, and, once again, Gades, all of which would obscure what lay beyond them with the ancient shine of their fame.

A general move to 'shrink' the world back to outdated parameters, as Bianchetti has shown in her studies of ancient geography, is an ideological operation that started long before the time of Augustus and dates back at least to the first well-known pro-Roman geographer, Polybius of Megalopolis. In his fragmentary geographical volume, this author attacks Pytheas and rejects the credibility of the accounts of his expedition to the northern ocean, which had provided a basis for the Hellenistic geographers' enlargement of the world. According to Bianchetti, 'La polemica dello storico nei confronti di Pitea, il cui viaggio a Thule è giudicato impossibile, assume l'aspetto di una revendicazione della superiorità delle imprese romane, in particolare quelle di Scipione Emiliano, rispetto a tutte le altre.'[43] In this way, Polybius could bring back the *oikoumene* to a size better suited to Roman interests. His criticism of this particular point is parroted by Strabo, who wrote during the reign of Augustus and had a similar interest in embellishing certain geographical data to show Rome in a more glorious light.[44]

---

[41] Strab. 4.5.3. Strabo, one of the most faithful parrots of the new regime's ideology, in that paragraph presents us with a contemporary version of the classic fable about the fox who could not reach the grapes. He minimizes Caesar's expedition, and then proceeds to offer an account, similar (again) to the one in *Res gestae* 32, about the ties of friendship between Augustus and important chieftains, finishing with calculations which prove that conquering the island would actually be counterproductive for Rome and its economy.

[42] Hence the mention, in the same paragraph, of the fact that a fleet sent by Augustus had explored the north of Europe *ad solis orientis regionem usque ad fines Cimbrorum nauigauit, quo neque terra neque mari quisquam romanus ante id tempus adit* (*Res gestae* 26). Tacitus (*Germ.* 34) later notes that the leader of that expedition was Drusus and that his success was dubious at best (cf. Dion [1973] 463-485), though Vanotti is rather of the opinion that Augustus was referring to the later and much less ambitious expedition of Tiberius (Vanotti [1987], cf. supra)

[43] Bianchetti (1997) 80.

[44] Cf. n. 24.

The negative move of 'trimming' unnecessary areas, as we have already seen in the case of Horace's *Odes,* is balanced by the positive move of exalting ancient landmarks of mythical Far Western geography. The Ocean, for example, would play a preeminent role in early imperial ideology, to the extreme of becoming a cosmic enemy whose conquest Caligula celebrated with a lavish triumphal ceremony.[45] Revealingly enough, this triumph was, once more, a cover-up for the emperor's failed invasion of Great Britain. As for Gades, all the elements we have analysed, namely its links to the Ocean and the end of the *oikoumene*, literary fame, importance as a setting for the old myths, plus its contemporary status as a fully Romanized city, birthplace of the first foreign consul and the first foreign general to receive triumphal honours, who was also the builder of one of the Roman theatres and personal friend of the emperor, all contributed to loading it with ideological connotations that were both of venerable age and of modern significance.[46] It is in this context that, we believe, Gades is highlighted among the borders of the empire in the *Res gestae*, in connection with both the Ocean (natural limit of the inhabited world once again), and the recent German expedition *ad solis orientis regionem usque ad finem Cimbrorum*. Mentioning Gades as the western border of the empire meant that Rome had conquered a symbolic – if not real – end of the world and made it Roman. Contemporary and later descriptions of Gades highlight the influence, the level of civilization and the prosperity of the city as well as its mythical and paradoxographical traits, in brutal contrast to the dismissal of Britain as poor, remote and uncivilized, unable to provide the empire with any practical benefits.[47] The value and significance of this city in a text such as Augustus' *Res gestae* is therefore double: that of highlighting what is said (that the empire reaches to the Ocean) and hiding what is *not* said, namely that Augustus has abandoned any claim to what lies beyond it, along with the western legacy of Julius Caesar. It also reinforces the positive

---

[45] Suet. *Calig.* 46-47.
[46] As discussed in Cruz Andreotti (1994). The first foreign consul was Cornelius Balbus the Elder, friend and supporter of Caesar, while the general who achieved a triumph and built the Roman theatre was his nephew, Cornelius Balbus the Younger, friend and supporter of Augustus. Cf. Rodríguez Neila (1973).
[47] The comparison between Strab. 3.5.3 and Strab. 4.5.3 is quite illuminating.

comparison between the Roman emperor and the Macedonian king, since the name *Gades* occurs very prominently in the tradition of the Alexander historians known as Alexander's 'western plans', which involved a western expedition with Gadeira as destination, but which was thwarted by the conqueror's early death.[48]

This significance can also be supported by other indications that come not only from the data transmitted by geographers such as Strabo or historians such as Livy (who mentions Gades as point of departure of Hannibal's expedition against Rome and later as a city that established an early *foedus* with Rome, which was later ratified and its original conditions improved by the Roman Senate),[49] but also by the Augustan poets themselves. Already in Book 2 of his *Odes*, Horace mentions Gades twice as a distant place (*Carm.* 2.2: *remotis Gadibus*, and 2.6: *Septimi, Gadis aditure mecum...*, reminiscent of Catull. 11: *Furi et Aureli, comites Catulli...*, where Britain, not Gades, was the farthest place that those faithful friends would go), and there was a rumour at the time involving a man from Gades who had come to meet the historian Livy *ab ultimo terrarum orbe*, later transmitted by Pliny the Younger in one of his *Letters*.[50] However, the main revival of interest in the old Heraclean myths located in that particular place happened in connection with Augustus and two of his political manoeuvres: the revival of the cults at the *Ara Maxima*, an ancient shrine which commemorated Hercules and his defeat of Cacus after his return from Spain (in 29 BC), and the *princeps*' own triumphant return from his Spanish campaign, just at the time when he decided to put an end to the British affair.[51] The ancient Erytheia became, once again, an interesting place in the history of conquest of the furthermost limits.

It was in the reign of Claudius, after the conquest of Britain finally became a fact, that the euphoria of transgressing the limits of the

---

[48] Cf. n. 24.
[49] Liv. 21.21, 28.23-37, 32.2.
[50] Plin. *Ep.* 2.3.
[51] Prop. 4.9, Hor. *Carm.* 3.14, Verg. *Aen.* 8.201-204. Outside poetry, both Dionysius of Halicarnassus and Diodorus Siculus show an inordinate amount of interest and detail in that particular episode as well, which connects both Augustus and his triumphal Spanish campaign and the renewal, in 29 BC, of the ceremonies at the *Ara Maxima,* which commemorated the hero's detour via Rome and his killing of Cacus, and which the *princeps* had used to celebrate his triumph, cf. *Ant. Rom.* 1.39-44, Diod. Sic. 4.17-9.

oikoumene came to be reflected in literature again. Flavius Josephus gives the following words to Herod Agrippa, when he describes the crushing power of Rome:

> μᾶλλον δὲ καὶ ταύτης ἐζήτησάν τι πλέον· οὐ γὰρ ἐξήρκεσεν αὐτοῖς ὅλος Εὐφράτης ὑπὸ τὴν ἀνατολὴν οὐδὲ τῶν προσαρκτίων ὁ Ἴστρος ἥ τε μεσημβρινὴ μέχρι τῶν ἀοικήτων ἐρευνηθεῖσα Λιβύη <u>καὶ Γάδειρα πρὸς ἑσπέραν, ἀλλ' ὑπὲρ Ὠκεανὸν ἑτέραν ἐζήτησαν οἰκουμένην καὶ μέχρι τῶν ἀνιστορήτων πρότερον Βρεττανῶν διήνεγκαν τὰ ὅπλα.</u>
>
> Joseph. *B.J.* 2.363

This is part of a longer speech which Nicolet (following Friedländer) has considered to be copied from a source in Augustan rhetoric, perhaps even the *breuiarium totius imperii* mentioned by Suetonius as having being read to the senate together with the *Res gestae* itself and the last dispositions of Augustus.[52] That original source would have mentioned Gades as the western limit of the empire, only to be altered after the conquest of Britain made it necessary to add the sentence that follows. Whether this – tempting – guess is accurate or not, this 'double take' is certainly symbolic of the change in mentality that had taken place so recently. Rhetoric would still remember the Γαδείρων τὸ ζόφον, but now, for the moment at least, it had been left behind.

Bibliography

Antonelli, L. (1997), *I greci oltre Gibilterra*, Rome.
Bianchetti, S. (1997), 'Conoscenze geografiche e rappresentazioni dell'ecumene nell'antichità greco-romana', in C. Tugnoli (ed.), *I contorni della terra e del mare. La geografia tra rappresentazione e invenzione della realtà*, Bologna, 51-92.
Camps, W.A. (1977r), *Propertius. Elegies, Book 1*, Cambridge.
Cataudella, M.R. (1989-1990), 'Quante erano le colonne di Ercole', *Annali della Facoltà di Lettere e Filosofia dell'Università di Macerata* 22-23, 315-337.
Cooley, A.E. (2009), *Res gestae diui Augusti: Text, Translation and Commentary*, Cambridge.

---

[52] Nicolet (1988) 252-257. Cf. Suet. *Aug.* 101.

Cruz Andreotti, G. (1994), 'La visión de Gades en Estrabón. Elaboración de un paradigma geográfico', *Dialogues d'histoire ancienne* 20, 57-85.

Dion, R. (1973), 'La géographie d'Homère, inspiratrice de grands desseins impériaux', *Bulletin de l'Association Guillaume Budé*, 463-485.

Domínguez Pérez, J.C. (2011), *Gadir y el Círculo del Estrecho revisados. Propuestas de la arqueología desde un enfoque social*, Cadiz.

Fernández Camacho, P. (2013[a]), 'La fuente del Heracleo de Gades en la ciencia antigua', *Cuadernos de Filología Clásica: Estudios Griegos e Indoeuropeos* 23, 277-293.

Fernández Camacho, P. (2013[b]), '*Gadeira*, el décimo trabajo de Heracles y la política de Atenas', *Euphrosyne* 41, 9-30.

Friedländer, P. (1969), *Plato: An Introduction*, vol. 1, transl. H. Meyerhoff, Princeton/ New York.

Gagé, J. (1940), 'Hercule-Melqart, Alexandre et les Romains à Gadès', *Revue d'Études Anciennes* 42, 425-438.

García-Bellido, A. (1942), 'La industria pesquera y conservera española de la Antigüedad', *Investigación y Progreso* 1, 1-8.

Hall, E. (1991), *Inventing the Barbarian. Greek Self-Definition Through Tragedy*, Oxford.

Janni, P. (1984), *La mappa e il periplo. Cartografia antica e spazio odologico*, Macerata.

Livingstone, N. (2001), *A Commentary on Isocrates' Busiris*, Leiden.

Loraux, N. (1981), *L'invention d'Athènes: histoire de l'oraison funèbre dans la cité classique*, Paris.

Mangas, J. – Plácido, D. (1999), *Testimonia Hispaniae Antiqua*, vol. 2 B, *La Península Ibérica prerromana: de Éforo a Eustacio*, Madrid.

Nenci, G. (1958[a]), 'Realtà e leggenda dei disegni occidentali di Alessandro', *Introduzione alle guerre persiane e altri saggi di storia antica*, Pisa, 215-257.

Nenci, G. (1958[b]), '*L'imitatio Alexandri* nelle *Res gestae diui Augusti*', *Introduzione alle guerre persiane e altri saggi di storia antica*, Pisa, 258-308.

Nicolet, C. (1988), *L'inventaire du monde. Géographie et politique aux origines de l'empire romain*, Paris.

Peretti, A. (1979), *Il periplo di Scilace. Studio sul primo portolano del Mediterraneo*, Pisa.

Pissavino, P. (1981), 'Il Menesseno platonico e la critica all'Atene immaginaria', *Il pensiero politico* 14, 189-213.

Prontera, F. (1989), 'Géographie et mythes dans l'isolario des Grecs', in M. Pelletier (ed.), *Géographie du monde au Moyen Âge et à la Renaissance*, Paris, 169-179.

Rodríguez Neila, J.F. (1973), *Los Balbos de Cádiz. Dos españoles en la Roma de César y Augusto*, Sevilla.

Romm, J.S. (1994), *The Edges of Earth in Ancient Thought. Geography, Exploration, and Fiction*, Princeton.

Seston, W. (1968), 'Gadès et l'Empire Romain', *Cuadernos de Historia* 2, 1-13.

Scheid, J. (2007), *Res gestae diui Augusti. Hauts faits du divin Auguste*, Paris.

Tarradell, M. (1960), *Marruecos púnico*, Tetouan.

Tarradell, M. (1968), 'Economía de la colonización fenicia', in M. Tarradell (ed.), *Los fenicios*, Barcelona, 279-314.

Vanotti, G. (1987), 'Prospettive ecumeniche e limiti reali nella definizione dei confini augustei', in M. Sordi (ed.), *Il confine nel mondo classico*, Milan, 234-249.

Vidal-Naquet, P. (1981), 'Athènes et l'Atlantide: Structure et signification d'un mythe platonicien', *Le Chasseur Noir. Formes de pensée et formes de societé dans le monde grec*, Paris, 335-360.

Zecchini, G. (1987), 'La Britannia da Cesare a Claudio', in M. Sordi (ed.), *Il confine nel mondo classico*, Milan, 250-271.

The Obituary of Augustus in Tacitus, *Annals* 1.9-10

VICTORIA EMMA PAGÁN
University of Florida

Every student of Roman studies who eventually arrives at the magnificent subject of Augustus has been confronted by the awful truth, that the contemporary historical sources for the period, the historians who lived during the reign of Augustus and who recorded events first hand, are gone. In the words of Sir Ronald Syme:

> The written history of the time has vanished utterly, no political speech survives, no pamphlet, no memoirs. Compared with what went before and what came after, the Age of Augustus acquires the paradoxical dignity of an obscure and highly controversial period. Recourse must be had to official documents – with due caution; to the Augustan poets – again with due caution. And silence itself will be revealing.[1]

Emilio Gabba some thirty years later reminds us to consult what we can of Nicolaus of Damascus' biography of Augustus composed between 25-20 BC; Dionysius of Halicarnassus' *Roman Antiquities* written in the middle of Augustus' reign; and the later Greek writers Philo of Alexandria at work under the later Julio-Claudians; Plutarch, roughly contemporary with Tacitus; and Aelius Aristides whose speeches help us understand the ideologies of the historians Appian and Cassius Dio, both of whom transmit continuous, albeit much later, narratives of the period. There is much to be gleaned.

On the Latin side, however, we are left with three sources of limited use. Livy should be ideal; he was a contemporary of Augustus, but his books devoted to the period survive only in epitome. Velleius Paterculus belonged to the next generation and wrote a history under the emperor Tiberius; however, his overt encomium undermines his authority as a reliable source. The imperial biographer Suetonius preserves some quotations of Augustus' letters and memoirs and is clearly drawing

---

[1] Syme (1950) 4.

on contemporary sources like Nicolaus of Damascus. Yet Suetonius wrote more than one hundred years later in the age of Hadrian, in the era of the five good emperors, 'the period in the history of the world during which the condition of the human race was the most happy and prosperous,' in the words of Edward Gibbon. Suetonius was a writer of a different time, with a different purpose. Professor Gabba surveys all of these sources, both Greek and Latin, and ends his essay on the ancient historians' attitudes toward the reign of Augustus with Tacitus:

> Tacitus is the last, almost impotent protagonist of an approach which applied to the historical interpretation of Augustus and the Empire the unattainable political ideal of a centre of power *susceptible to influence from below*.[2]

I should like to rescue Tacitus from last place and demonstrate his potency as a source for understanding the era of Augustus.[3] Tacitus' fullest treatment of Augustus comes at the beginning of the *Annals*, Book 1.9-10. The passage is often referred to as the *Totengericht*, or judgement of the dead, a more accurate German term than the English 'obituary,' although both will be used here. A close reading of these two paragraphs will show that the Augustan center of power *was* susceptible to influence, though not from below, not from individuals: opposition had been obliterated. Nor was the Augustan center of power susceptible to influence even from corporate bodies like the Senate, the praetorian guard, or the armies. Rather, Augustus was susceptible to the changing circumstances in which he found himself, to the vicissitudes of fortune that assail from all directions; and he was subject to the choices he made at any given moment in response to his circumstances. Neither the Augustan institution nor attitudes toward it were static entities but the result of dynamic processes. If we lend ourselves to the ironies of the passage, then we begin to see the importance of change over time and to recognize that centers of power *are* susceptible – that they are created and maintained by their vulnerabilities as much as by the exercise of sheer force or domination. Such an argument risks exonerating Augustus from responsibility for his outright wrongdoings;

---

[2] Emphasis mine. Gabba (1984) 85.
[3] Wiseman in this volume begins from the same critical juncture and attempts to retrieve Augustus' life and times through his contemporaries; he traces the ideology of the *populus Romanus* from the age of Cicero to the *Res gestae*.

yet Tacitus provides more than enough material to temper even the most sanguine reading.

The *Totengericht* has not been ignored; on the contrary, scholars have analyzed its sources, its metahistorical commentary, and its position within Tacitus' historical agenda. Their findings underpin any critical interpretation of the passage. *Quellenforschung* dominated early studies. The *Res gestae diui Augusti* is the catalogue of Augustus' achievements he intended to be inscribed on bronze tablets and erected in front of his mausoleum upon his death. Augustus' masterpiece of self-fashioning could not have been ignored by Tacitus, whether, as Haverfield argued a century ago, as a point of departure 'for a bitter condemnation of the first acts of the first emperor,' or, as Lord argued, as the source of favorable elements in the obituary.[4] The more recent analysis by Velaza reveals far less uniformity in Tacitus' use of the *Res gestae*. Some items from the inscription are treated positively, some negatively, and some are unparalleled.[5] According to Koestermann, Tacitus must have studied the *Res gestae* carefully with the intention of distancing his account from Augustus' overt aggrandizement which our historian regards with suspicion, and my approach is sympathetic to this type of reading.[6] No doubt the language of the obituary echoes phrases in the *Res gestae*, such that it is reasonable to assume that Tacitus was familiar with this widely disseminated document.

Against this official document we can compare the funeral oration for Augustus delivered by Tiberius as recorded in the historian Dio, some one hundred years after Tacitus (56.35-41). Schwartz first proposed that Tacitus and Dio had a common, lost source, but the notion was rejected by Klingner, Syme, Koestermann, and Briessmann.[7] Although the theory was resuscitated by Tränkle, Manuwald insists that the differences between Tacitus and Dio are so profound as to rule out the possibility of a common source.[8] According to Flach if a common source

---

[4] Haverfield (1912) 199, Lord (1927). Urban (1979) demonstrates Tacitus' engagement with the inscription in several passages in the *Annals*, not just 1.9-10.

[5] Velaza (1993) 350.

[6] Koestermann (1961) 343-344.

[7] Schwartz (1899) 1716, Klingner (1986) 531, Syme (1958) 273, Koestermann (1961) 349, Briessmann (1963) 100. For Mehl (1981) 63 it is unlikely that Dio used Tacitus exclusively or at least as the main source.

ever existed, Dio must have modified it in favor of Augustus, whereas according to Manuwald Tacitus would have modified the original.[9]

Instead of examining the obituary vis-à-vis other authors, Willrich examines the obituary within the context of Tacitus' own writing. The beginning of the *Histories* can help us understand Tacitus' depiction of Augustus; Galba's adoption of Piso is analogous to Augustus' adoption of Tiberius.[10] We might detect here what Woodman has called 'substantive imitation,' whereby the details of a poorly documented event in the reign of Tiberius are substantiated by imitating a better documented event from the long year 69.[11] Nor is it so difficult then to imagine the poorly documented events in the reign of Tiberius colored by the contemporary events of Tacitus' own lifetime. The *Histories* narrate the adoption of Piso; the *Annals* take as their starting point the adoption of Tiberius. Both suggest the troubled and troubling accession of Hadrian.[12] For on August 9, 117, Hadrian was in Syria when he received a letter stating that Trajan had adopted him. On August 11, Trajan died at Selinus with rumors of poison in the air. The adoption was abrupt; the signatures uncustomary. Such clouds cast shadows across Tacitus' desk.[13]

Hence the second point of contention raised by the *Totengericht*: does the passage reflect the attitudes that were current when Augustus died in the year 14, or are we reading the opinion of Tacitus writing under the clouds of 117? Only Shotter and Tränkle have attempted to argue that Tacitus faithfully reports the diverse viewpoints registered in the year

---

[8] Tränkle (1969), Manuwald (1973), cf. Velaza (1993). Guia (1983) argues that Dio's praise of Augustus and his final assessment indicate an almost unconditional evaluation of Augustus that engages themes, experiences, and political reflections of the Severan senator and his age.
[9] Flach (1973) 129, Manuwald (1973) 371.
[10] Willrich (1927) 54-58; see also Koestermann (1961) 344 n. 43.
[11] Woodman (1979) 152.
[12] Syme's thesis, stated most explicitly at (1958) 481: 'The early chapters of Book 1 [of the *Annals*] depict political behavior, pitilessly – the fraudulent protestations of loyal subjects, discreetly modulated between mourning and rejoicing, and the eager rush to voluntary enslavement. State ceremonial, public professions, and secret conflicts – the whole thing may seem to hint and foreshadow the accession of Hadrian.'
[13] On the death of Trajan, see *Scriptores Historiae Augustae, Hadr.* 4; Charlesworth (1927) 56 suggests a different point of reference from within Tacitus' own lifetime: 'his own bitter experience and the tradition he had before him so worked upon his mind that he was prepared to find in the early Principate the tyranny to which Domitian had eventually transformed it. It is this prejudice which causes him to give the extraordinary caricature of Augustus' life and achievements which stands at the beginning of his *Annals*.'

14. Lenchantin, Pippidi, Von Fritz, Witte, and Ceauşescu believe that the passage reveals Tacitus' hostility toward the principate in general;[14] Willrich, Klingner, Miller, and Velaza discern in the obituary Tacitus' disappointment in Trajan's principate in particular.[15] Borgo argues that the passage reflects hostility toward Tiberius specifically.[16] No doubt *inuentio* is a key ingredient of ancient history writing, and Tacitus exercises it at every turn;[17] the context of production – those cloudy days will have influenced the historian's conception and execution of the brief account of the reign of Augustus.

The most recent scholars to consider Augustus in the *Annals* approach from opposite directions: O'Gorman considers the refusal to write about Augustus, Devillers the promise. For O'Gorman, 'authorial refusal is ... aligned with imperial refusal.' When Tacitus elects to begin with the reign of Tiberius and not of Augustus (a fact which bothered Syme over the course of his career), Tacitus is engaging in a *recusatio* with political implications.[18] Devillers examined the *Totengericht* in light of Tacitus' promise to write the history of Augustus at *Annals* 3.24.3: *sed aliorum exitus, simul cetera illius aetatis memorabo, si effectis, in quae <te>tendi, plures ad curas uitam produxero*. Devillers argues that the obituary, apparently constructed on an axis of approval and disapproval, is better regarded as demonstrating relevant and irrelevant categories for the writing of history,[19] that is, the items in paragraph nine do not matter as much as the items in paragraph ten, and these distinctions would have guided Tacitus in his construction of the promised history.

A century of scholarship has enriched our understanding of Tacitean historiography, its sources, ideology, and methodology. Yet the *Totengericht* also portrays the principate of Augustus not as a static entity but as a dynamic, ever-changing process. *Annals* 1.9-10 is framed in

---

[14] Shotter (1967); Tränkle (1969); Lenchantin (1938) 344-345; Pippidi (1965) 20; von Fritz (1957); Witte (1963) 157; Ceauşescu (1974) 194; Velaza (1993) 354.
[15] Willrich (1927) 78; Klingner (1986) 536; Miller (1969) 103; Velaza (1993) 338, 354.
[16] Borgo (1986).
[17] Tacitus' hand is most evident in the description of Augustus as *machinator doli*, an allusion to Epeos, the architect of the Trojan horse at *Aen.* 2.264: *doli fabricator*, detected by Miller (1969) 105 and explored in further detail by Putnam (1989).
[18] O'Gorman (1995) 102.
[19] Devillers (2009) 321.

diametrically opposed categories of praise and blame (*extollebatur arguebaturue*, 1.9.3) inherited from the rhetorical tradition of epideictic oratory that sought to demonstrate or deny the value of a person or thing, and this dichotomy has been reinscribed in the modern pro- and anti-Augustan debates. To surmount this impasse, W.R. Johnson seeks

> if it is possible (and it may not be possible), ... not a composite picture of the whole man, a summation of his character and his achievement, but a detailed analysis of how he kept changing and why he kept changing.[20]

It is my contention that in addition to the overt summations of Augustus' character and his achievement whether good or bad in *Annals* 1.9-10 Tacitus expresses an awareness, if not a detailed analysis, of how Augustus kept changing and why he kept changing. Johnson reminds us that 'All of us assume a stability for the regime and a constancy of attitude towards the regime that did not exist.'[21] Therefore to retrieve as much information about Augustus as possible from the *Totengericht* we should assume instability of regime and inconstancy of attitude. In what follows I shall attempt to unearth two types of instabilities: the contingencies that signal the instability of fortune, and the ironies that signal the instability of language. Tacitus may not replace Syme's utterly vanished written history of the time, but he is surely of more use than Gabba's last, almost impotent protagonist.

Contingency: the instability of fortune

According to Gabba, Tacitus applied to the interpretation of Augustus the unattainable political ideal of a center of power susceptible to influence from below. But if Augustus was not susceptible to individuals or corporate bodies, then he was susceptible to chance, as demonstrated in the first two sentences of the obituary:

> (1) Multus hinc ipso de Augusto sermo, plerisque uana mirantibus: quod idem dies accepti quondam imperii princeps et uitae supremus, quod Nolae in domo et cubiculo, in quo pater eius Octauius, uitam finiuisset. (2) numerus etiam consulatuum celebrabatur, quo Valerium Coruum et C. Marium simul

---

[20] Johnson (1973) 176.
[21] Johnson (1973) 172.

> aequauerat, continuata per septem et triginta annos tribunicia potestas, nomen imperatoris semel atque uicies partum aliaque honorum mutiplicata aut noua.

Tacitus dismisses these vapid observations of the majority, who are overly impressed with nothing more than luck. The perspicacious reader (and who among us would not want to be worthy of Tacitus' admiration?) will rid herself altogether of this ridiculous tendency to attribute any meaningful causation to mere fortune. Yet, as Jonas Grethlein contends in his study of fifth-century Greek literature,[22] there is a place in history for contingency, that which is possible but not necessary. Semantically related to chance, luck, fortune, or even fate, contingency is a frame for action in its own right. Things that *can* happen do not *have to* happen, creating tension between expectation – what can and usually does happen – and experience – when expectations are thwarted.

One modern example will suffice: one does not expect airplanes to be flown into skyscrapers, although they certainly can be, and, contrary to expectation, they certainly were, and the experience of Americans has been radically and permanently changed by that which was always possible but not necessary. Furthermore, we might consider George W. Bush's responses to the contingencies of September 11 over time: first we see the president, receiving news in a Sarasota elementary school twenty minutes after the attack; then we hear his address to the nation later that evening; then two years later he invades Iraq. Bush was not in control of the events on September 11, but he was in control of his responses which changed over time and to which he was subject once he made his decisions. No doubt September 11 is a sensational example that hardly compares with the feeble contingencies Tacitus registers in the first two sentences (although Tacitus is far too capable a historian to transmit *quisquiliae* without some purpose). One does not expect a man to die in the same room as his father, and on a significant anniversary, although one certainly can, and, contrary to expectation, Augustus did. One does not expect one man's number of consulships to equal the consulships of two other statesmen, but they did. Although these anecdotes can and should be discounted for their content, nevertheless they alert us to the presence of contingency,

---

[22] Grethlein (2010).

which should not be discounted, because then we would lose sight of how contingency is managed. Grethlein describes three strategies for managing contingency, which are evident in our passage: regularity, continuity, and development.[23]

Nobody likes to be fortune's fool, and although Augustus was susceptible to fortune he was not slave to it. He was able to gain a purchase on the future, even though civil war and triumvirate had thwarted the Roman's previous expectations of themselves, their society, and their way of life. Puppets of chance, yet the Romans' identity was stabilized by three commemorative strategies. First, recurrent and recognizable patterns of behavior occurring at regular intervals (daily, monthly, annually, or the hundred year *saeculum*) provide guidance for the here and now, against the vagaries of the future. In sentence 9.2, while the numerology of the number of consulships is negligible, their regularity is a powerful way to assert stability in the face of uncertainty.

M. Valerius Corvus was consul four times in 348, 346, 343, and 335 BC, and reputedly twice more in 300 and 299 (suffect); C. Marius was consul seven times between 107 and 86 BC. Thus the two examples span about four hundred years of consular history such that Augustus' consulships appear to extend the pattern. The highly irregular (perhaps even extravagant) number of consulships is naturalized when seen as merely the addition of two historical exempla. From time to time, there have been men who have held the consulship repeatedly; Augustus' thirteen consulships extends and thereby regularizes the pattern.

Grethlein's second strategy is tradition; by linking the past to the present to the future, tradition establishes continuity that helps create and maintain stable identity. After discarding the empty observations of the *plerique* in sentences 9.1-2, Tacitus next records the favorable opinions of wise men: *at apud prudentes uita eius uarie extollebatur* (9.3). Yet even among the *prudentes*, the strategies for managing contingency are evident. In sentence 9.5, the continuity of the republic is asserted, albeit under a new name: *non regno tamen neque dictatura, sed principis nomine constitutam rem publicam*. Kingship and dictatorship are rejected so that the Republic can remain. Verbal repetition signals the continuity: in the very first sentence of the *Annals*, Tacitus states

---

[23] Grethlein (2010) 9.

that Augustus, with the name of *princeps* (*principis nomine*) took under his command everything exhausted by civil war.

Third, development is perhaps the most powerful strategy for neutralizing the force of contingency, for development is itself a patently dynamic process of change over time; however, its sheer momentum operates against the unpredictability of chance and reveals that identity is the result of a process and not the victim of circumstance. At the end of sentence 9.5 (the last words of praise for the reign of Augustus before Tacitus launches into the criticism of 10.1), development seizes chance in its tracks. The results are an empire with legions, provinces, fleets working in unity, law among citizens, deference among allies, Rome refurbished and resplendent. Change there was; however, the developments of empire are transparent and therefore all the more reassuring. Thus continuity, regularity, and development manage the outcomes of what are otherwise uncontrollable forces. By firmly insisting that no right thinking person would fall for the balderdash of the *plerique*, Tacitus simultaneously calls attention to the very force of contingency he seeks to disarm.

In fact, Tacitus acknowledges the potency of contingency on Augustus' ability to secure a successor at *Annals* 3.24.2: *ut ualida diuo Augusto in rem publicam fortuna, ita domi improspera fuit* ('as sturdy as the fortune of Augustus was in matters of state, so unfavorable was it within his own home'). Tacitus goes on to list the infamous infidelities of the Julias. Yet in the *Totengericht,* fault rests with a different woman, *postremo Liuia* (10.5), Livia allegedy responsible for the deaths of Gaius, Lucius, and Agrippa Postumus,[24] even Marcellus, if we believe Dio (53.33.4). With only a daughter (whom he banished) and a string of untimely funerals, it would seem Augustus was obliged to make the choice according to chance: Tiberius or none.

Irony: the instability of language

The accession of Tiberius was the result of a choice made at a given time; indeed the principate of Augustus was not a static artifact but a dynamic, ever-changing process. Even the *prudentes* of 9.3 who

---

[24] Woodman (2004) 8 n. 32.

praised Augustus recognized this much at least when the *res publica* is described as one 'in which at that time there had been no place for law' (*in qua nullus tunc legibus locus*). The adverb *tunc* implies a specific point of time in the past. Tacitus returns to this lawless period of time in Book 3 in greater detail: once Pompey lost the battle of Pharsalus, civil wars continued for twenty years *non mos, non ius* (3.28.1). Augustus' actions are thus historically situated within a specific period of time.

Similarly, in the next sentence, Augustus had made many concessions to Antonius 'while avenging himself on the killers of his father' (*dum interfectores patris ulcisceretur*, 9.4); the proviso clause suggests that Augustus' actions toward Antonius would have been different were he *not* avenging his father.[25] Brutus and Cassius were defeated at Philippi in 42, but not before the triumvirs perpetrated the proscriptions that resulted in the execution of Cicero (against the wishes of Augustus, if we believe Plutarch, who records the three day debate).[26]

The next sentence begins with an explicit temporal conjunction, *postquam*: 'after [Lepidus] had aged from apathy, and [Antonius] had been sunk by his lusts' (9.4). Such temporal markers, *tunc*, *dum*, and *postquam* indicate the passing of time and the changing circumstances under which Augustus was constrained to make decisions. His ascent did not take place under static conditions but within individual temporal contexts.

Pharsalus, Philippi, Actium: each battle had its own unique causes and effects. Yet Tacitus whitewashes these differences by referring not to Octavian but to Augustus, the name that was not assumed until the year 27, that is, until after Actium. Tacitus begins the obituary with the name Augustus: *multus hinc ipso de Augusto sermo* (9.1). Augustus is the antecedent of the pronoun *eius* in sentence 3, his life comes under scrutiny by the *prudentes*. Tacitus does not distinguish between

---

[25] This is the translation of Woodman (2004) 7. For *dum* in a temporal sense, see Furneaux (1896) 194, although generally *dum* = *dummodo*, 'provided that,' as per Koestermann (1963) 97. For Goodyear (1972) 157, *dum* approximates the *ut* of a purpose clause that would convey 'the apologetic argument of *pietas erga parentem* more effectively than a temporal sense.'

[26] Plu. *Cic.* 46.3: ἐγίγνοντο δ'αἱ σύνοδοι μόνοις ἀπόρρητοι περὶ πόλιν Βονωνίαν ἐφ'ἡμέρας τρεῖς, καὶ συνῄεσαν εἰς τόπον τινὰ πρόσω τῶν στρατοπέδων ποταμῷ περιρρεόμενον. λέγεται δὲ τὰς πρώτας ἡμέρας διαγωνισάμενος ὑπὲρ τοῦ Κικέρωνος ὁ Καῖσαρ ἐνδοῦναι τῇ τρίτῃ καὶ προέσθαι τὸν ἄνδρα, τὰ δὲ τῆς ἀντιδόσεως οὕτως εἶχεν. On the other hand, Suet. *Aug.* 27.1 reports that although reluctant at first, once they were begun Augustus carried out the proscriptions more fiercely than his colleagues (*sed inceptam utroque acerbius exercuit*).

Octavian and Augustus: not in paragraph 9, and in fact nowhere in the *Annals*. Such monolithic nomenclature militates against the perception of change indicated by the temporal adverbs. Tacitus thus creates a problem in his grammar, whereby he describes a static entity, *Augustus*, in terms that call attention to his dynamic rise to power. Irony thus arises from the perceived difference between what is said (*tunc*, *dum*, *postquam*) and what is not said (*Octauianus*).[27]

A second irony pulls the reader into its undertow, for although the essential quality of change over time is perceptible, it does not appear to have affected the outcome, that 'there had been no other remedy for his disaffected fatherland than that it be ruled by one man' (*non aliud ... remedium*, 9.4). Tacitus presents the principate as a foregone conclusion, as if everyone should have known what was to come. Or, if the remedy should come as a surprise to some, the historian at least in hindsight knows full well this singular outcome, and confident in this knowledge he can pity those who may stumble in the darkness of their ignorance. Kingly rule (*regno*) and dictatorship (*dictatura*) were not options in Roman ideology and both are easily dismissed as impossible, rendering the choice meaningless.[28] Tacitus' formulation of sentences 3-5 allows us to apprehend the dynamic rise of Augustus as perceived by the *prudentes* and their foregone conclusion, *non aliud remedium*, of a new form of government called the principate. Yet implicit in this statement is the denial of agency or self-determination in the process. When the *prudentes* acknowledge there was no other remedy, they are in the same breath conceding power. By lending ourselves to ironies such as these, we can begin to detect some of the instabilities in attitudes toward the regime.

A third irony comes to light when we probe the semantics of *prudentes*. In addition to *Annals* 1.9.3, the lexicographers Gerber and Greef cite four substantive uses of the adjective *prudens*, in which the word means 'einsichtsvoll, verständig' (insightful, intelligent).[29] Yet earlier uses are not straightforward. In the *Agricola*, Tacitus speaks

---
[27] O'Gorman (2000) 11. Haynes (2012) 287 is especially sensitive to the ways Tacitus' 'determinedly difficult language creates an oxymoron.'
[28] Barthes (1972) 153 calls these kinds of meaningless choices *ninisme*, 'neither-norism'; cf. the remarks of Haynes (2012) 286-288 on Tacitus' ability to recreate 'the nothing', *le néant*.
[29] Gerber, Greef (1962) 1231-1232.

not of intelligent men but men only pretending to be intelligent (*specie prudentium*, 25.3). In the *Dialogus*, the wise and the common folk have the same level of understanding: *idque non doctus modo et prudens auditor sed etiam populus intellegit* ('and this not only the learned and wise listener but even the common crowd understands,' 32.2); in the next sentence the precepts of the wise are ignored (*praecepta prudentium*, 32.3). In the *Histories*, 'the advice of the wise and the rumor of the commoners are heard with equal measure' (*consilia prudentium et uolgi rumor iuxta audiuntur*, 3.58.3). These uses betray an ambivalence about a quality which can be pretended, ignored, and equated with the qualities of the common crowd. The intelligence of the *prudentes* is undermined.

Of course some of the *prudentes* also blame Augustus (*arguebaturue*, 9.3). Are the instabilities of contingency and irony still at work in paragraph 10? If anything they are brought into high relief:

> (1) Dicebatur contra: pietatem erga parentem et tempora rei publicae obtentui sumpta; ceterum cupidine dominandi concitos per largitionem ueteranos, paratum ab adulescente priuato exercitum, corruptas consulis legiones, simulatam Pompeianarum gratiam partium. (2) mox ubi decreto patrum fasces et ius praetoris inuaserit, caesis Hirtio et Pansa, siue hostis illos, seu Pansam uenenum uulneri adfusum, sui milites Hirtium et machinator doli Caesar abstulerat, utriusque copias occupauisse; extortum inuito senatu consulatum, armaque, quae in Antonium acceperit, contra rem publicam uersa; proscriptionem ciuium, diuisiones agrorum ne ipsis quidem, qui fecere, laudatas. (3) sane Cassii et Brutorum exitus paternis inimicitiis datos, quamquam fas sit priuata odia publicis utilitatibus remittere, sed Pompeium imagine pacis, sed Lepidum specie amicitiae deceptos; post Antonium, Tarentino Brundisinoque foedere et nuptiis sororis inlectum, subdolae adfinitatis poenas morte exsoluisse. (4) pacem sine dubio post haec, uerum cruentam: Lollianas Varianasque clades, interfectos Romae Varrones Egnatios Iullos.

From the outset it would seem the purpose of §10 is to re-write §9. These detractors reject outright the very same motive of filial piety posited by the supporters. They also reject historical contingency, *tempora rei publicae*, as nothing more than a pretense; no regularity, continuity, or development will be found here. However, some inconsistencies are observable. Attention to temporal phrases reveals an awareness of the very change over time denied above: *adulescente* calls attention to the youthful Octavian, whose deeds become more violent with the passing of time, marked by the temporal adverb and conjunction *mox ubi* ('subsequently when', 10.2). The thirteen consulships, presented as a simple math problem in sentence 9.2, become a single crime extorted from an unwilling senate in 10.2; however the *arma ciuilia* of sentence 9.3 are given more context in 10.2: *armaque, quae in Antonium acceperit, contra rem publicam uersa* ('arms which he had been given to deal with Antonius [were] turned against the state,' 10.2). The purpose of the *arma* changed over time: intended for Antonius, the *arma* eventually served a different cause. Perhaps the most telltale are the proscription of citizens and land confiscations; these were merely hinted in paragraph 9.3 as the concessions Augustus made to Antonius while avenging himself on his father's killers. Now these vile acts were 'not praised even by those who did them' (*ne ipsis quidem, qui fecere, laudatas,* 10.2) indicating unstable attitudes among contemporaries. The relationship with Antonius was under continual revision, *post Antonium*: 'subsequently Antonius, enticed by the Tarentine and Brundisian treaties and by a wedding to his sister, had paid the penalty of a guileful relationship with his death' (10.3). The culmination is peace, but bloodstained: *pacem sine dubio post haec, uerum cruentam* (10.4). At the crux of this chiastic *sententia* is a temporal prepositional phrase, *post haec*, signaling that this bloodstained peace came about after a series of events, each of which could have ended differently. The rhetorically controlled *sententia* obscures the historically uncertain realities; *tempora rei publicae* exerted more influence over the course of events than detractors would care to admit.

Conclusion

The *Totengericht* has generated two sets of scholarly responses that derive from the same problem, namely the temporal distance between the events that occurred in the age of Augustus, and the later narration of the events. In terms of *Quellenforschung*, we have either the contemporary *Res gestae*, written by Augustus himself, or we have the funeral oration of Tiberius, recorded in Dio. In terms of *inuentio*, either we are reading the contemporary attitudes of the year 14 that would have been recorded according to the principles of probability and necessity, or we are reading the concerns on Tacitus' mind in 117 that would have been recorded according to the principles of metahistorical analysis. Either way the obituary retains its dualities of praise and blame. But attention to the forces of contingency and irony push the passage beyond the problems of *Quellenforschung* and metahistory and beyond the traditional pro- and anti-Augustan interpretations.

Tacitus twice denies contingency its force. First, he discards the observations of the *plerique*, then he refuses *tempora rei publicae* as a credible motive for Augustus' actions. Yet the rhetorical trope would appear to backfire, for Tacitus' repeated disavowal of the role of chance in historical causation only draws attention to its power all the more, and this is because nothing ever happens in a historical vacuum; everything is situated in time. Supporters point to the ways Augustus managed his exigencies. He regularized magistracies, continued the republic, developed the empire. The accession of Tiberius was a choice not so much dictated as subject to chance itself. Yet detractors cannot speak against Augustus' deeds without situating them temporally.

Then there are the ironies: the dynamics of Octavian's rise to power described under monolithic nomenclature; the inevitability of the Augustan remedy for the ailing republic, when at the time the outcomes were not self-evident; the slippery semantics of the word *prudentes*. Ironies riddle the opinions of the detractors as well: time leaves its stamp on paragraph 10. If not even those who perpetrated the atrocities of the triumvirs could agree on the morality of their acts, then how can one assume stability in attitudes toward Augustus and how can one assume stability in his reactions toward these shifting attitudes?

Such a reading of *Annals* 1.9-10 reminds us that while Augustus kept changing throughout his life (even if *adulescente* is as close as Tacitus will come to the name Octavian), the composition of his subjects – the men he worked for and against, the men who worked for and against him – kept changing as well, as evidenced most explicitly in that memorable line just three paragraphs into the *Annals*: 'Young men were born after Actium, even several of the elders born during the civil wars: was there anyone left who had seen the republic?' (*quotus quisque reliquus, qui rem publicam uidisset?*, 1.3.7). Although Shotter and Tränkle fail to convince that the *Totengericht* records opinions from the year AD 14, nevertheless they remind us that those opinions surely existed, that they were not consistent among all of Augustus' ever-changing subjects, and that they were not persistent over time. Indeed, Tacitus' own attitude toward Augustus was not static. Ceaușescu has traced the image of Augustus across the Tacitean corpus, as it degenerates from neutral in the *Dialogus*, to unenthusiastic in the *Histories*, to contemptuous in the *Annals*.[30] Had Tacitus fulfilled his promise at *Annals* 3.24.3 to write a history of Augustus, no doubt his attitude would have changed yet again.

We may assume that the changing realities were as apprehended and misapprehended by Augustus' lost contemporaries as they were by the later generations accessible to us. Of course to reach those lost contemporaries we would have to turn to Syme's 'official documents – with due caution; to the Augustan poets – again with due caution,' but these are like insects caught in amber: perfectly preserved specimens, in perfect isolation. When reckoning the achievement of the man who was able to stabilize the Roman world after the enormous upheaval of decades of civil war, it is easy to see that Augustus did so not entirely by wielding a blunt instrument, but by carefully crafting a public image and by manipulating pre-existing institutions to his advantage: that much is surely evident in the obituary. But Augustus was also responding to the contingencies of specific pressures at any given time, to which he might have reacted differently. We cannot know whether the outcome would have been the same, but we can acknowledge that the consolidation of power under the name of princeps was the product of a series of dynamic negotiations in response to the forces of contingency that beset from all directions, not just below.

Bibliography

Barthes, R. (1972), *Mythologies,* selected and translated from the French by Annette Lavers, New York.

Borgo, A. (1986), 'Augusto e l'istituzione del principato. Osservazioni a Tacito, Ann. 1, 1-10', *Vichiana: Rassegna di studi classici* 15, 74-97.

Briessmann, A. (1963), Review of C. Questa, *Studi sulla fonti degli Annales di Tacito*, Roma 1960, *Gymnasium* 70, 99-102.

---

[30] Ceaușescu (1974); Pippidi (1965) 20 sees an 'aversion to the Augustan regime' in every sentence of the *Annals* from 1.4 to 4.33.

Ceauşescu, P. (1974), 'L'image d'Auguste chez Tacite', *Klio* 56, 183-198.
Charlesworth, M. (1927), 'Livia and Tanaquil', *Classical Review* 41, 55-57.
Devillers, O. (2009), '*Sed aliorum exitus, simul cetera illius aetatis, memorabo* (*Ann*. III, 24, 2). Le règne d'Auguste et le projet historiographique de Tacite', in F. Hurlet, B. Mineo (edd.), *Le Principat d'Auguste: Réalités et représentations du pouvoir Autour de la Res Publica Restituta*, Rennes, 309-324.
Flach, D. (1973), *Tacitus in der Tradition der antiken Geschichtschreibung*, Göttingen.
Furneaux, H. (1896²), *The Annals of Tacitus*, vol. 1: *Books I-VI*, Oxford.
Gabba, E. (1984), 'The Historians and Augustus', in F. Millar, E. Segal (edd.), *Caesar Augustus. Seven Aspects*, Oxford, 61-88.
Gerber, A., Greef, A. (edd.) (1962, reprint), *Lexicon Taciteum*, 2 vols., Hildesheim.
Goodyear, F.R.D. (1972), *The Annals of Tacitus, Books 1-6*, vol. 1: *Annals 1.1-54*, Cambridge.
Grethlein, J. (2010), *The Greeks and their Past. Poetry, Oratory and History in the Fifth Century BCE*, Cambridge.
Guia, M.A. (1983), 'Augusto nel libro 56 della storia romana di Cassio Dione', *Athenaeum* 61, 439-456.
Haverfield, F. (1912), 'Four Notes on Tacitus', *Journal of Roman Studies* 2, 195-200.
Haynes, H. (2012), 'Tacitus' History and Mine', in V.E. Pagán (ed.), *A Companion to Tacitus*, Malden (MA), 282-304.
Johnson, W.R. (1973), 'The Emotions of Patriotism: Propertius 4.6', *California Studies in Classical Antiquity* 6, 151-180.
Klingner, F. (1986), 'Tacitus über Augustus und Tiberius: Interpretationen zum Eingang der *Annalen*', in V. Pöschl (ed.), *Tacitus*, Darmstadt, 513-556.
Koestermann, E. (1961), 'Der Eingang der *Annalen* des Tacitus', *Historia* 10, 330-355.
Koestermann, E. (1963), *Cornelius Tacitus Annalen*, Band I: Buch 1-3, Heidelberg.
Lenchantin de Gubernatis, M. (1938), 'Augusto e Tacito', *Rivista di filologia e di istruzione classica* 16, 337-345.
Lord, L.E. (1927), 'Note on Tacitus' Summary of the Reign of Augustus', *Classical Review* 41, 121-122.

Manuwald, B. (1973), 'Cassius Dio und das 'Totengericht' über Augustus bei Tacitus', *Hermes* 101, 352-374.
Mehl, A. (1981), 'Bemerkungen zu Dios und Tacitus' Arbeitsweise und zur Quellenlage im 'Totengericht' über Augustus', *Gymnasium* 88, 54-64.
Miller, N. (1969), 'Style and Content in Tacitus', in T. Dorey (ed.), *Tacitus*, London, 99-116.
O'Gorman, E. (1995), 'On not writing about Augustus: Tacitus' *Annals* Book 1', *Materiali e discussioni per l'analisi dei testo classici* 35, 91-114.
O'Gorman, E. (2000), *Irony and Misreading in the Annals of Tacitus*, Cambridge.
Pippidi, D.M. (1965), *Autour de Tibère*, Rome.
Putnam, M. (1989), 'Virgil and Tacitus, *Ann*. 1.10', *Classical Quarterly* 39, 563-564.
Schwartz, E. (1899), 'Cassius Dio', in Pauly-Wissowa, *Realencyclopädie der classischen Altertumswissenschaft*, vol. 3, 1684-1722.
Shotter, D. (1967), 'The Debate on Augustus (Tacitus, *Annals* 1 9-10)', *Mnemosyne* 20, 171-174.
Syme, R. (1950), *A Roman Post-Mortem: An Inquest on the Fall of the Roman Republic*, Sydney.
Syme, R. (1958), *Tacitus*, 2 vols., Oxford.
Tränkle, H. (1969), 'Augustus bei Tacitus, Cassius Dio, und dem älteren Plinius', *Wiener Studien* 82, 108-130.
Urban, R. (1979), 'Tacitus und die *Res gestae diui Augusti*: Die Auseinandersetzung des Historikers mit der offiziellen Darstellung', *Gymnasium* 86, 59-74.
Velaza, J. (1993), 'Tácito y Augusto (*Ann*. I 9-10)', *Emerita* 61, 335-356.
von Fritz, K. (1957), 'Tacitus, Agricola, Domitian, and the Problem of the Principate', *Classical Philology* 52, 73-97.
Willrich, H. (1927), 'Augustus bei Tacitus', *Hermes* 62, 54-78.
Witte, B. (1963), *Tacitus über Augustus*, Dissertation, Münster.
Woodman, A.J. (1979), 'Self-imitation and the substance of history: Tacitus, *Annals* 1.61-5 and *Histories* 2.70, 5.14-15', in D. West, A.J. Woodman (edd.), *Creative Imitation and Latin Literature*, Cambridge, 143-155.
Woodman, A.J. (2004), *Tacitus. The Annals*, Indianapolis.

Plutarch's Augustus

SUSAN JACOBS
Columbia University

Plutarch of Chaeronea, whose dates are roughly AD 45-120, is perhaps best known for his series of *Parallel Lives*, which include 22 of the original 23 sets of paired accounts of the careers of Roman and Greek statesmen of the past. The period of Roman history covered in the *Lives* extends through Mark Antony's final defeat at Alexandria in 30 BC, which marked the point when Augustus assumed sole control of Rome's empire. Plutarch dealt with the life and career of Augustus in his series of *Lives* dedicated to the Caesars (the *Life of Augustus* is listed as no. 26 in the Lamprias catalogue), which included *Lives* of eight emperors beginning with Augustus and ending with Vitellius.[1] From this series, only the *Lives* of *Galba* and *Otho* have survived. As a result, we do not have a succinct portrait of Augustus from Plutarch. Instead, we must piece together a portrait from Plutarch's references to Augustus in three contexts: in treatises of the *Moralia*; in Augustus' appearances as Octavian in the *Parallel Lives* of Romans of the late Republic;[2] and finally, in Plutarch's authorial comments in the *Lives* that mention Augustus' later conduct as Emperor.

This paper examines the portrait of Augustus that emerges from Plutarch's writings. As we will see, not only does Plutarch present Augustus as a blend of strengths and weaknesses as a political leader, but he molds his account of events in Augustus' career to illustrate the principles of statesmanship articulated in his treatises in the *Moralia*. In these treatises, incidents involving Augustus exemplify specific precepts more than 20 times.[3] After a brief summary of the key precepts

---

[1] See Jones (1971) 72-80 and Georgiadou (1988) and (2014) on the *Lives of the Caesars*.
[2] Augustus appears three times in *Lives* associated with earlier periods: at *Numa* 20.2, he is named as another ruler under whom the gates of Janus were closed; at *Pericles* 1.1 Augustus' comment about misdirected affection is used as a lead-in to a discussion of misdirected love of learning; and *Romulus* 17.3 cites Augustus' comment that he 'loved treachery but hated a traitor.'
[3] These incidents can be found at *Moralia* 68b, 207a-208a, 319e-320a, 322b, 508a-b, 784d and 814d-e.

of political action in the *Moralia*, this paper addresses how Plutarch uses Augustus to depict these principles in action in *Cicero*, *Brutus* and *Antony*. Ultimately, Augustus emerges as a positive role model in some areas of leadership and a deterrent model in others. By modifying historical accounts, Plutarch shapes his narrative of specific episodes to highlight the parallels to the political challenges faced by the educated elite of his own day, transforming Augustus into a meaningful role model for men pursuing political and military careers under the empire.

Augustus in the *Moralia*

Several treatises of the *Moralia* focus primarily on the proper conduct of men active in political life.[4] *Philosophers and Men in Power* (776a-779c) and *To an Uneducated Ruler* (779d-782f) emphasize the duty of the ruler to administer justice and to assure the safety and well-being of those under his care – actions that win ready obedience from the ruled.[5] In two other treatises, *Political Precepts* (798a-825f) and *Old Men in Politics* (783a-797f), Plutarch articulates principles of statesmanship for men performing administrative and diplomatic functions in the cities of the Greek East. In these works, Plutarch adopts a pragmatic perspective in defining the skills and judgment needed to be effective in the political roles open to the elite in his own day. The wide-ranging advice in these treatises was supplemented by narrower treatments of specific challenges in *On Compliancy* (528c-536d), *On Inoffensive Self-Praise* (539a-547f), *How to Tell a Flatterer from a Friend* (48e-74e) and *How to Profit from Enemies* (86b-92e).

Political Precepts provided the broadest range of practical advice for the political arena.[6] In addition to a discussion of the criteria for choosing a political career and the importance of a reputation for moral virtue, the treatise includes insights into how to manage political relations with various groups – including the people, colleagues, friends, rivals and imperial representatives. The principles for managing these

---

[4] See Pelling (2014) for a summary of Plutarch's political philosophy and key treatises.
[5] Passages on the ruler's duty are found at 776d and 780d-781c. See Roskam (2002) 175-189 and (2009) 132-138.
[6] On advice in *Political Precepts*, see de Blois (2004) 57-58, Beck (2004) 108-109 and Teodorsson (2008) 341-342.

relationships are illustrated in the *Parallel Lives*, where Plutarch's heroes demonstrate the judgment and techniques needed to meet a variety of challenges, such as how to gain trust by practicing virtue, how to engage constructively with the people and how to handle enemies.[7] Plutarch also explains how to engage Roman authority to benefit one's city, citing Areius' relationship with Augustus as an example of how to manage such relations (814d-816a). The principles that center on relations with a mentor (805f-806f), persuading the people (799b-800f) and managing partnerships and rivalries (807a-811a) are especially relevant for Augustus' early career, extending from his return to Rome after Julius Caesar's murder until Antony's death.

In *Old Men in Politics*, Plutarch focuses on the constructive role of older, experienced statesmen in managing public affairs, including their influence in acting as mentors and moderating the ambition and rashness of younger men.[8] In this treatise, Augustus is grouped with Pericles, Agesilaus and Cato the Elder as an old man who greatly benefitted his state in old age (784d-f). However, Augustus is also associated with disreputable conduct early in his career before becoming a model of excellent leadership later.[9] Indeed, the evolution of young men driven by ambition into older men seasoned by experience is highlighted in Plutarch's comment that 'all agree that Augustus' political acts toward the end of his life became by no small measure more kingly and more useful to the people' (784d).[10]

Augustus also appears as a role model for current leaders in Plutarch's treatise *Sayings of Kings and Commanders* (172a-208a), which was addressed to Trajan.[11] This collection contains 15 entries for Augustus (206f-208a) in areas where he largely exemplifies positive

---

[7] The topics covered include moral character and reputation (800b-801b), arts of persuasion (801c-804c), relations with the *demos* (799b-780f, 818a-824a), managing friendships (807a-809a), managing enmities and rivalries (809b-811a), sharing power with others (811b-803d), diplomacy with the overlord (813d-816a) and cooperating with colleagues (816a-817f).

[8] Key passages are found at 790d-791a and 795a-796d.

[9] *On Delays in Divine Vengeance* (548a-568a) discusses men who come to power using lawless means or despite outrageous conduct, but use their power to benefit their states (551d-552d), pointing to Cimon as a great nature who would not have benefitted his state had he been banished for incest as a youth, as Alcibiades was for his shocking behavior in the marketplace (552b). In the *Lives*, Caesar also engages in questionable practices to acquire power, but then uses it to good effect (*Dion-Brut Comp.* 2.2-3).

[10] All citations are based on the Loeb volumes, and translations are modified versions of Loeb.

[11] See Beck (2002) and Stadter (2014) 9-20.

conduct, including in managing anger, winning over one's subjects and exercising clemency.[12] Of these entries, three are also found in other treatises of the *Moralia* and three in the *Lives*. For instance, his success in gaining popularity by paying Caesar's bequests (207a) is mentioned in *Cicero* 53, *Antony* 16 and *Brutus* 22.[13]

The most extensive treatment of Augustus in the *Moralia* is in *On the Fortune of the Romans* (316b-326c). Here, Augustus is quoted praying that the gods bestow his own fortune on his grandson (319d), and Plutarch asserts that Fortune imposed Augustus on Cicero and Mark Antony in order that they might, through their own deeds and victories, raise Augustus to become the leading citizen (319e):

> It was for Augustus that Cicero governed, Lepidus was a general, Pansa was victorious, Hirtius fell and Antony acted outrageously. For I count as a part of Augustus' fortune even Cleopatra, on whom, as on a reef, so great a commander was wrecked and crushed so that Augustus might rule alone.
>
> 319f

In the *Parallel Lives*, the theme of Fortune at work in transitioning the Roman Republic into a monarchy is woven into the *Lives* of *Julius Caesar*, *Pompey* and *Cato Minor*[14] and remains an underpinning of Augustus' rise to power as reflected in *Cicero*, *Brutus* and *Antony*, to which we now turn.

Life of Cicero

Although Augustus plays a secondary role in the *Lives* of late-Republican leaders and cannot be excluded from the historical account,

---

[12] Passages cover how to manage anger (207c-f); win the support of subjects (207a-c, 207e, 208a); exercise clemency (207b, 207e-f); and deal with traitors and wrongdoers (207a, 208b). See Ash (2008) for a discussion of anecdotes and Plutarch's use of direct speech to underscore the relations between ruler and ruled.

[13] The other overlaps with the *Lives* and *Moralia* included incidents where Augustus says he loves treachery but hates a traitor (207a, also in *Rom.* 17.2); enters Alexandria with Areius (207b; also *Ant.* 80.2-3 and *Pol. Prec.* 814d); prays that his grandson is granted his own good fortune (207e; *Fortune of the Romans* 319d); and comments that he was an old man to whom old men listened when he was young (207e; also *Old Men in Politics* 784d).

[14] At *Phocion* 3.3, Plutarch describes Cato Minor as fighting a battle against Fortune, who ultimately overthrew the Republic through other men.

Plutarch's characterization of him is not perfunctory.[15] Instead, Augustus plays two critical roles in conveying the lessons for statesmen in these *Lives*. On the one hand, he is a foil who helps highlight the key character traits and judgments that determined the political successes and failures of the central heroes. On the other hand, he illustrates the vulnerabilities of young men on the road to power and the challenges of forging alliances and thwarting rivals.

In *Cicero*, Augustus (Octavian) enters the narrative in Chapter 43 when he arrives from Apollonia to assume his inheritance. When Antony refuses to hand over the money needed to pay Caesar's bequests, Augustus' step-father, Philip, and brother-in-law, Marcellus, come 'with the youth' (μετὰ τοῦ νεανίσκου) to make a pact with Cicero (*Cic.* 44.1). Augustus is presented at this stage as a stripling (τὸ μειράκιον) in need of a mentor, who is passive in the negotiations with Cicero and submits to him (ὑπῄει αὐτὸν) to the extent of calling him father (45.2). The motives and the consequences of this alliance are important to Plutarch's characterization of both Cicero and Augustus in the *Life*. While Augustus expected to benefit from Cicero's political influence and eloquence, Cicero sought greater security (ἀσφάλειαν) based on Augustus' wealth and army (44.1). Plutarch names three additional motives for the alliance on Cicero's part: 1) Cicero's dream that Octavian was marked by Jupiter to end the civil wars; 2) his hatred of Antony; and 3) his natural craving for honor (44.5-45.1). This dream, as noted by Moles,[16] was originally attributed to Catullus, but is employed here as a positive vision of the ultimate benefits that would flow to Rome at the end of a struggle during which Octavian would conduct himself as a 'ruthless opportunist'. To some extent, the dream implies some kind of divine oversight of Octavian's conduct and gives his actions divine sanction.

However, while the expectations of both men were realized in the immediate aftermath of the alliance – with Augustus acquiring the insignia of a praetor and Cicero succeeding in having Antony driven

---

[15] Wardman (1974) 175 describes Augustus and Antony as 'cardboard figures on the edge of the narrative' in *Brutus*, while Ash (2008) 558 suggests that Augustus, as Octavian, appears in the *Lives* because the action requires it. This paper argues that Plutarch's portrayal of Octavian is carefully crafted and purposeful.

[16] Moles (1988) 195.

from the city – later events lent credence to Brutus' criticism, cited by Plutarch, that 'it was clear that in flattering (θεραπεύων) Augustus on account of fear of Antony, Cicero was not bringing about liberty for his country, but wooing a master for himself (δεσπότην φιλάνθρωπον αὑτῷ μνώμενος)' (*Cic.* 45.2).[17] Although portrayed as passive in the beginning, Augustus subsequently is shown actively managing the alliance with Cicero to his own advantage. Having acquired the authority of a pro- praetor through Cicero's influence, Augustus again turns to Cicero when he becomes alarmed at the senate's attempts to call away his troops after Mutina: Augustus begs Cicero to obtain the consulship for both of them, promising to defer to Cicero in political matters and describing himself as 'a stripling who sought only name and fortune' (τὸ μειράκιον ... ὀνόματος καὶ δόξης γλιχόμενον) (45.5). However, after later becoming consul, Augustus 'dismissed' Cicero (Κικέρωνα μὲν εἴασε χαίρειν) and divided power with Antony and Lepidus (46.2). Plutarch underscores the political calculation behind Augustus' actions, by inserting the comment that Cicero 'was led on and cheated, an old man by a young man' (ἐπαρθεὶς ὑπὸ νέου γέρων καὶ φενακισθείς, 46.1) and citing Augustus' own admission that he, 'in an emergency' (ἐν δέοντι), had used Cicero's love of power to induce him to sue for the consulship (45.6). The dynamics of this 'alliance' echo those of Caesar with Pompey, who lent support to Caesar when he was building his power, only to be overthrown when Caesar had attained it (*Pompey* 46.2).

Plutarch's characterization of Augustus as shifting his alliances in order to advance his power provides an essential backdrop to a central lesson for older statesmen: namely, that mentoring an ambitious young man can be perilous, since the protégé may hide his true ambitions and turn against his mentor when his political advancement is threatened. Plutarch uses the relations between Cicero and Augustus to provide a new perspective on guiding the young, a topic raised both in *Old Men in Politics* (795e) and *Political Precepts* (805f-6b), where it is the duty

---

[17] Cic. *Ad Brutum* 1.17.6 (Brutus to Atticus). The error on Cicero's part is reiterated in the *synkrisis*, where Plutarch cites Laelius' criticism of Cicero for supporting Augustus' bid for the consulship, 'which was contrary to the law since he was still a beardless youth,' and again quotes Brutus (*Ad Brutum* 1.17.2; Brutus to Atticus) accusing Cicero of 'having reared up a tyranny greater and more severe than that which he himself had overthrown' (*Dem-Cic Comp.* 4.4).

of the older man to act as a mentor and of the young man to honor his mentor throughout his career. Cicero's experience alerts older statesmen to the hidden agendas of the young, while placing Augustus' conduct in a questionable light. The inclusion of the warnings of Brutus – both in the *Life* and in the *synkrisis* (*Dem-Cic Comp.* 4.4) – underscores Plutarch's desire to amplify this lesson. As we will see, Plutarch modifies this characterization of Augustus' early career in *Brutus* and *Antony* in order to emphasize different lessons for statesmen.[18]

Similarly, across these *Lives*, different degrees of blame are attached to Augustus' complicity in the proscriptions that lead to Cicero's death. In *Cicero*, Plutarch does not excuse Augustus, but he softens the opprobrium by reporting that Augustus had struggled for two days to save Cicero before giving in (*Cic.* 46.5). Furthermore, Plutarch closes the *Life* describing how Augustus in later years spoke highly of Cicero to his grandson – calling him 'a learned man and a lover of his country' (49.5) – and, after Antony's death, appointed Cicero's son as his colleague in office (49.6).[19] By inserting these extra details from Augustus' later career, Plutarch lends support to the possibility that Augustus' abandonment of Cicero was an act of political necessity that masked his true nature.

Life of Brutus

In *Brutus*, Plutarch designs his account of Augustus' alliance with Cicero to serve a different purpose: namely, to showcase the effects of Brutus' commitment to liberty and hatred of despotism, as well as his foresight about the threat Augustus posed to Rome, in general, and to Cicero, in particular. After recounting Augustus' arrival from Apollonia and his alliance with Cicero in Chapter 22 – where the alliance is motivated by Cicero's hatred of Antony – Plutarch quotes two of

---

[18] Pelling (2002ª) 2-4 suggests that the changes in characterization between *Cicero*, *Brutus* and *Pompey* reflect Plutarch's becoming better informed about Roman history after he had written *Demosthenes-Cicero*. Pelling (1988) 34-36 discusses how Plutarch's presentation of key events is molded to suit the themes of each *Life*, a common trait found in comparisons across all the *Lives*.

[19] Pelling (2002ᵇ) 368-369 discusses the role of the 'modifying vignette' which recalls the drama of incidents in the *Life* and introduces a further resolution. Such anecdotes serve to refine the characterizations of both the central heroes and the key protagonists.

Brutus' criticisms: that Cicero had formed an alliance with one would-be despot because of his hatred for another and that he had asked that Octavian be established as tyrant as a reward for driving Antony from the tyranny (*Brut.* 22.4-6). Both comments categorize Augustus as one of 'the tyrants' Brutus was fighting against (28.4).

Plutarch's portrait of Augustus in *Brutus* reinforces this perception to some extent: Augustus wins favor with the people and Caesar's soldiers by distributing money (*Brut.* 22.3) and acquires the consulship by using the threat of force to compel the Romans to elect him in spite of his youth (27.3) – details that had not been included in, and even contradict to some extent, the account given in *Cicero*. Moreover, as his first act as consul, Augustus forces through an indictment of Brutus and Cassius for killing the first magistrate of the city without a trial, and, in their absence, the jurors are compelled to condemn them (27.4). With regard to the proscriptions, Plutarch simply reports that Augustus, Antony and Lepidus proscribed 200 men, including Cicero, and makes no attempt to lessen the blame that should attach to Augustus (27.6). The tyrannical flavor embedded in Augustus' conduct, which was absent from *Cicero*, helps sharpen the portrait of Brutus as an honorable man fighting tyranny.

In *Brutus*, Plutarch summarizes the incidents culminating in Augustus' consulship without mentioning Cicero (*Brut.* 27.1-5). Instead, Augustus is shown independently maneuvering for power and becoming an object of fear to the Romans, while he himself began to fear Brutus as a rival. It is the desire to thwart Brutus that induces Augustus to initiate the reconciliation with Antony (27.2-3). In a letter to Atticus quoted by Plutarch in Chapter 29, Brutus even implies that Augustus is the senior partner in the alliance with Antony, writing that 'the penalty Mark Antony was paying for his folly was deserved, since ... he had given himself to Octavian as an appendage' (29.10).[20] Moreover, Brutus continued, if Antony were not defeated at Philippi, he would

---

[20] Earlier, at *Brutus* 18.3-6 and 20.1-3, Plutarch had given two reasons for Brutus' objection to murdering Antony: first, it would be unjust because Antony was not abusing power like Caesar, and, secondly, because he believed that the goodness in Antony would induce him to join Brutus' side after Caesar was dead. Here (*Brutus* 29.10), Brutus' criticism of Antony traces back to this expectation that Antony would make the 'right choice' after Caesar's murder and not choose Octavian's side. In *Antony*, Plutarch describes Antony as the appendage of Cleopatra (προσθήκη τῆς γυναικὸς, *Ant.* 62.1).

later be defeated by Augustus (29.11). By comparison to the portrait in *Cicero*, where Augustus, as a political newcomer, makes calculated use of the influence and ambition of an older mentor and then comes under the influence of Antony, in *Brutus* he is an adept operator considered an equal partner – if not leading partner – in his alliance with Antony. To further the characterization of Brutus as a principled man fighting for liberty, Augustus is painted with the same tyrannical qualities that Brutus had associated with Julius Caesar (e.g. 7.7, 10.4-6, 35.4-6). At Philippi (*Brut.* 38.3), both Augustus and Antony are portrayed as men seeking 'to conquer and rule' and to this end willing to engage in acts of cruelty and injustice (46.2-3). Plutarch explains the course of events as guided by divine forces (ὁ θεός) wishing to remove the only man (i.e. Brutus) standing in the way of the man who was able to rule (i.e. Augustus), now that Rome required a monarchy (47.7).[21] This comment highlights a central lesson for statesmen in *Brutus*: namely, that the power of virtue is severely limited in a corrupt political environment. In such a state, men like Augustus and Antony, who are fighting for tyranny and power rather than liberty and honor, are eventually victorious.

At the end of *Brutus*, Plutarch softens the characterization of Augustus as a would-be tyrant. Augustus is shown in Chapters 52 and 53 reconciling with Messalla – Brutus' close comrade – and kindly receiving Strato, the man who had assisted Brutus in committing suicide (*Brut.* 52.7-8; 53.1-3). Plutarch brings the ultimate outcome into view by reporting that both Strato and Messalla were avid supporters of Augustus at Actium. Plutarch further emphasizes the differences between Augustus and Antony by including the exchange of praise by Messalla and Augustus at a later date:

> And it is said that Messalla himself, after he had been praised by Augustus because at Philippi he had been most hostile to him for the sake of Brutus, but at Actium had offered himself most zealously, responded, 'As for me, let me say, O Caesar, I have always been part of the side that was better and more just.'
>
> *Brutus* 53.3

---

[21] Plutarch attributes Brutus' failure to learn of the defeat of Augustus' fleet – which would have prompted him to delay the second battle – to chance (47.5) and divine forces (47.7). Earlier, Octavian had barely escaped when his camp was taken, having left because of his friend's dream (41.7).

The more tolerant side of Augustus is further displayed in the *synkrisis*, which closes with a vignette of Augustus expressing respect for Brutus, when he allows Brutus' statue to remain standing in Mediolanum and praises the city's magistrates for being true to their friends even in adversity (*Dion-Brut Comp*. 5.1-4).[22] Like the positive scenes at the end of *Cicero*, this anecdote helps balance the negative impression created by Augustus' conduct during his alliance with Antony.

Plutarch also uses the *synkrisis* to *Dion-Brutus* to clarify other aspects of Augustus' character. Plutarch emphasizes the benefits that flowed to Augustus as the heir of Caesar, whose fame, even after his death, supported his friends and whose name immediately raised the one who used it 'from a helpless boy to the first of the Romans' (ἐκ παιδὸς ἀμηχάνου πρῶτον εὐθὺς εἶναι Ῥωμαίων) and was worn by him 'as a charm' (ὡς ἀλεξιφάρμακον) against the power and hatred of Antony (*Dion-Brutus Comp*. 4.4). Moreover, Plutarch further distances Augustus from being labeled 'a tyrant' by introducing a contrast between Julius Caesar and Dionysius as 'tyrants' that could be applied to Augustus as well:

> For Dionysius did not deny that he was a tyrant, and he filled Sicily full of countless evils; whereas the rule of Caesar, although it provided no few problems to its opponents while it was being established, to those who were overpowered and accepted it, it was a tyranny in name and appearance only and initiated no deed that was either savage or tyrannical. Instead, he seemed to be given by a divine force as a most gentle physician to problems that required a monarchy.
>
> *Dion-Brutus Comp*. 2.2-3

Based on the positive incidents reported from Augustus' actions as Emperor, the same assessment could be made about Augustus as well. Thus, while Brutus' opposition to both Julius Caesar and Augustus was nobly motivated, the men he had accused of aiming at tyranny were, in fact, necessary remedies for the degenerate times in Rome.

---

[22] Again, the incident is reminiscent of the story of Julius Caesar (*Caes*. 57.6-7, *Cic*. 40.4) after Pharsalus ordering that the statues of Pompey that had been thrown down be set up again, an action that prompted Cicero to comment that in setting up Pompey's statues Caesar firmly fixed his own (*Caes*. 57.6-7). In *Caesar*, the action is reported as a positive reflection of Caesar's magnanimity.

Life of Antony

In *Antony*, the portraits of Augustus found in *Cicero* and *Brutus* are integrated into a fuller picture of the maturation of Augustus from the young Octavian entering the political arena to the leader, 14 years later, who held Cleopatra as a prisoner and directed affairs as the sole ruler of the Roman empire. This *Life* illustrates the point that, in the hands of a good monarch, supreme power can be used to benefit all citizens, while, in the hands of a self-serving ruler, such authority damages the state. Although Augustus and Antony are partners early in the *Life*, over the course of the narrative the two men emerge as opposites in how they use monarchical power after they have acquired it.

In *Antony*, Augustus first appears in Chapter 11, accompanying Julius Caesar when he is met by Antony on his way back from Spain. Antony's reactions to Augustus help characterize both men. Plutarch reports in Chapter 16 that, after Caesar's death, Augustus greeted Antony as his father's friend, while Antony 'looked down on him as a stripling' (ὥσπερ μειρακίου καταφρονῶν, *Ant.* 16.1-2). As in other *Lives*, Plutarch cites Antony as a primary force behind Augustus' alliance with Cicero, but expands the list of grievances: Antony not only refuses to give the funds to pay Caesar's bequests, but he also repeatedly insults Augustus and opposes his bid for the tribuneship (16.2). After the alliance with Cicero, Augustus gains the support of the senate, as well as the goodwill of the people and the backing of Caesar's soldiers (16.3). This success turns Antony's initial contempt into fear (16.3) and gives Augustus the upper hand throughout the remainder of their association.

As in *Cicero*, Antony's conduct is influenced by a dream in which Augustus appears as a man destined to defeat his opponents: in this case, Antony dreams that his right hand is struck with a thunderbolt (*Ant.* 16.4).[23] In *Antony*, this dream precipitates a second break with Augustus, which culminates in Antony being voted a public enemy by the senate and then defeated at Mutina, while Augustus obtains the authority of a pro-praetor and then acquires a large army after the deaths of Hirtius and Pansa (17.1). Plutarch's account in *Antony* does

---

[23] No other author mentions this dream (Pelling [1988] 159).

not emphasize the role of Cicero in propelling Augustus' rapid rise. Instead, the focus shifts to Augustus' rejection of Cicero after Mutina, which Plutarch attributes to the fact that Augustus 'saw that Cicero clung to liberty' (τῆς ἐλευθερίας ὁρῶν περιεχόμενον, 19.1).

In *Antony*, as in *Cicero* and *Brutus*, it is Augustus who initiates the reconciliation leading to the formation of the 2nd triumvirate, but Plutarch here explicitly attributes the alliance to an attempt to quash liberty in Rome (19.1). Plutarch portrays Augustus as fully participating in dividing up the empire 'as an ancestral inheritance' (ὥσπερ οὐσίαν πατρῴαν, 19.1) and in proscribing his enemies:

> Each demanded the right to kill his enemies and to save his friends. But in the end, because of their anger towards the men they hated, they abandoned both the honor due their kinsmen and the goodwill due their friends, and [Augustus] gave up Cicero to Antony. Nothing, in my opinion, could be more savage or cruel than this exchange. For by giving murders in exchange for murders, they equally killed the men they gave up with the men they took, and they were more unjust towards their friends, whom they slew without hating them.
> *Ant.* 19.2-3

Although this condemnation of the proscriptions casts equal blame on Augustus and Antony – making no mention, for instance, of Augustus' efforts to save Cicero as reported in *Cicero* (46.5) – Plutarch places most of the responsibility for the 'odiousness' of the rule of the triumvirate on Antony, as a man who was older than Augustus and more influential than Lepidus (20.3). Nevertheless, Augustus is shown demanding to share the wealth Antony was appropriating (21.4).

In the events reported through Philippi, Augustus is presented as a much stronger and self-reliant political rival than he appears to be at this stage in *Cicero* or *Brutus*. This more forceful characterization in *Antony* provides a basis for Plutarch to portray the evolution of Augustus into a good monarch after Philippi, when the geographical separation of Augustus and Antony allows a clearer differentiation between the moral character and political priorities of the two men. Between Philippi (*Ant.* 20) and Actium (61-68.3), the deterioration in Antony's performance as a leader and general under the influence of Cleopatra's flattery – which is at the heart of the lessons of *Antony* – is reinforced by comparison to Augustus' more laudable conduct in the

West. Initially, Augustus is described as 'wearing himself out in civil strife and wars,' battling Fulvia and Lucius Antonius (24.1, 30.1), while Antony enjoyed peace and leisure with Cleopatra (24.1). The contrast between Augustus and Antony is further accentuated by the differences between Octavia and Cleopatra.[24] Octavia, subsequent to her marriage to Antony (31.2), performs a central role in characterizing – almost re-characterizing – Augustus as a good monarch who values traditional Roman virtue and excellence in others.[25] Augustus is described as 'exceedingly fond' (ἔστεργε δ' ὑπερφυῶς) (31.1) of his sister and reconciles with Antony through her influence.[26] The significance of these details to Plutarch's intended lessons is suggested by their absence in other ancient accounts.[27] The elaboration of Octavia's virtue and constructive influence casts Cleopatra's flattery and destructive impact into sharper relief (56.2, 57.2, 59.3-4).

At Actium, Augustus is portrayed as competent and prepared, in contrast to Antony. Augustus' fleet was 'thoroughly fitted out' (ἐξηρτυμένον) with ships that were easily steered, swift and fully manned, while Antony's ships had inadequate crews and sailed poorly (*Ant.* 62.1-2). Although Augustus was initially 'out-generaled' (καταστρατηγηθεὶς) when Antony induced him to withdraw by positioning his ships as if ready for battle, during the battle of Actium Augustus executed an effective strategy in surrounding Antony's ships with several of his own smaller vessels and engaging them in battle (65.5-66.2). After Actium, Augustus settles affairs with Athens and distributes supplies (68.4-5), but refuses all requests from Antony to settle matters outside the field of battle (72.1, 73.1).

The final ten chapters of the *Life* (*Ant.* 78-87), following the death of Antony, provide the longest continuous depiction in Plutarch's corpus

---

[24] Pelling (1988) 13-14 discusses Octavia as a foil who represents Roman values and duty, and later (215) notes the distinction between Octavia drawing the men toward peace and Cleopatra leading them to war.
[25] Octavia is described as a 'wonder of a woman' (χρῆμα θαυμαστόν, 31.1), widely respected for her moral character. In contrast, Antony's characteristic self-indulgence is reinforced and expanded by Cleopatra.
[26] Augustus follows Octavia's advice when she appeals to him to reconcile with Antony at Brundisium (*Ant.* 35.1-2) and acquiesces to Octavia's refusal to move out of Antony's house (54.1). Augustus does not move against Antony until public opinion recoils from Antony's rejection of Octavia and his desire to be buried in Egypt with Cleopatra.
[27] Pelling (2002ᵇ) 114 n. 64 notes that other ancient accounts make far less of Octavia's role.

of Augustus exercising sole authority.[28] It is here that Plutarch distances Augustus from his more reprehensible conduct before Philippi and clearly reveals his desire to present the Emperor Augustus as a positive model for rulers. Augustus is depicted exercising generosity, moderation and fairness in his relations with the conquered. The incidents chosen to characterize Augustus after Actium manifest the same qualities of character as the stories about his conduct as emperor in the other *Lives*.[29] He is not vindictive, but even weeps at the news of Antony's death and expresses regret that his efforts to reconcile were not reciprocated (78.2).[30] Having entered Alexandria in company with Areius, he spares the city, as well as the philosopher Philostratus (*Ant.* 80.1-3), and he is gracious in granting burial rights first to Antony (82.1) and then later to Cleopatra and her maids (86.4). Apart from Antony's oldest son, Antyllus, Augustus spares the children of Antony and Cleopatra (87.1), and he kills Caesarian only after Cleopatra's death, supported by the advice of the philosopher, Areius (81.2). In all of these areas, Augustus exemplifies the justice, generosity, clemency, restraint of anger and mildness towards the defeated that constitute the essential attributes of Plutarch's ideal statesman in the *Moralia*. Thus, the final chapters of *Antony*, as in *Cicero* and *Brutus*, serve the function of 'rehabilitating' Augustus' image, which earlier in the *Life* was cast in doubt by his complicity in reprehensible conduct in partnership with Antony.

Adapting the Historical Record

Since Plutarch had a variety of historical accounts from which to choose when he created his own version of events between the murder of Caesar and the suicide of Antony, his choice of details to include or exclude and his embellishments clarify the specific lessons in

---

[28] Pelling (2002b) 106 emphasizes the focus on Cleopatra in the final chapters rather than Octavian's conduct.

[29] As discussed above, in *Cicero*, Augustus praises Cicero to his grandson and also names Cicero's son as his co-consul and in *Brutus* he is generous to Brutus' close allies Messalla and Strato after Philippi and is lenient with the people in Gaul who have kept Brutus' statues in place.

[30] Augustus' reaction parallels Julius Caesar's shedding tears when he received Pompey's seal ring (*Pomp.* 80.5, *Caes.* 48.2). Pelling (1988) 309 notes that such scenes are *de rigeur* as a reaction to the defeat of a great enemy.

statesmanship each *Life* was designed to convey.[31] Thus, the different portraits of Augustus as a relative political novice in *Cicero*, a would-be tyrant in *Brutus* and a shrewd political rival in *Antony* can all be traced to particular historical accounts, which provide a plausible backdrop for Augustus' actions in each *Life*. For instance, in *Cicero*, the portrait of Augustus immediately following Caesar's murder reflects the man Cicero describes in his *Philippics* and letters, while in *Brutus* Augustus is painted as the 'would-be tyrant' Brutus described in his letters. By modifying the motives attributed to Augustus in each *Life*, Plutarch reinforces the perceptions and judgments driving the behavior of the central heroes and sharpens his portrait of their characters and critical choices as statesmen.

However, all of the depictions of Augustus as a young statesman have negative undertones, though varying in degree, and all are balanced by positive vignettes about Augustus' laudable conduct later as Emperor. This dichotomy in Augustus' persona is a central component of accounts of his career in other sources, in which his questionable conduct as a young statesman is variously explained as part of a strategy to acquire power for its own sake or as actions that were unavoidable if Augustus were to achieve his lofty goal of punishing his father's assassins. Tacitus, for instance, presents the two alternative points of view in his summary of Augustus' funeral:

> Among men of intelligence, however, his career was praised or arraigned from varying points of view. According to some, 'Filial duty and the needs of a country, which at the time had no room for law, had driven him to the weapons of civil strife – weapons which could neither be forged nor wielded with clean hands.' ... On the other side it was argued that 'filial duty and the critical position of the state had been used merely as a cloak: come to facts, and it was from the lust of dominion that he excited the veterans by his bounties ... and affected a leaning to the Pompeian side. Then, after usurping by senatorial decree the symbols and powers of the praetorship, ... he had wrung a consulate from the unwilling senate and turned against the commonwealth the arms he had received for quelling Antony.'
>
> Tac. *Annals* 1.9-10

---

[31] Pelling (2011) 12-13 comments that the various viewpoints of similar events as recorded in different *Lives* convey 'an important historical insight, that good history is complicated and multi-vocal, admitting conflicting perspectives and requiring engagement with viewpoints that may eventually be incompatible.'

Plutarch's characterization of Augustus draws on both of these viewpoints. In *Antony*, in particular, Augustus is complicit and willing in the reprehensible actions before Philippi, but after the empire is divided, Augustus is portrayed as a good monarch committed to traditional Roman values.[32] This juxtaposition of Augustus' conduct during the civil wars and his conduct as emperor echoes the assessment of Dio Cassius (56.43-5) that Augustus' blameworthy conduct had been dictated by circumstances and that he should be judged based on his conduct after he became the victor.

Conclusion

Plutarch's portrait of Augustus in each of the three *Lives* examined in this paper illustrates political themes that recur throughout the *Parallel Lives*. First, in *Cicero* and *Brutus*, Augustus (as Octavian) helps illustrate the limits of the power of virtue and commitment to liberty – in and of themselves – to secure the best outcomes in corrupt political environments. Cicero's expectation that he could guide Octavian to preserve the Republic was shattered when Octavian responded to the political realities by reconciling with Antony. Brutus' virtue and foresight, in turn, did not prevent his defeat at Philippi at the hands of the man he had saved from being murdered with Julius Caesar (*Brut.* 17.3-6).

Secondly, the portrait of Augustus in *Antony* underscores Plutarch's view that a statesman must 'do what the situation requires' on the road to power, but then must exercise that power, once acquired, to the common benefit of all. These principles are clearly stated in *Political Precepts*, where Plutarch directs the statesman first 'to accommodate the desires of the people as he finds them' (τοῖς ὑποκειμένοις ἤθεσιν εὐάρμοστον εἶναι) until he has built his reputation and confidence in his leadership (799c). After he has acquired power and public trust, he is then expected to lead the people towards what is better (πρὸς τὸ βέλτιον ὑπάγοντα, 800b). On this basis, a praiseworthy statesman may be forced by circumstances to engage in bribery, violence and

---

[32] See Millar (1984), Yavetz (1984; 1990), Eder (1990), Galinsky (2005), Gruen (2005) and Galinsky (2012) for a modern perspective on the dynamics of the late Republic and the impact of Augustus' personality and policies on the principate.

deceit as he rises to prominence, but these actions are exonerated, to some degree, when he exercises power in the common interest. This paradigm is illustrated in Plutarch's treatment of Augustus in the *Lives*, where the problematic portrayals of Augustus as a statesman on the rise are balanced with snapshots of his praiseworthy conduct later as Emperor.

This depiction of Augustus echoes Plutarch's depiction of Julius Caesar's career in the *Lives*, where Caesar's early conduct also suggested that he would become a self-serving tyrant, but once in power he acted as 'a most gentle physician' and good monarch (*Caes.* 28.4-5, 57.1, *Dion-Brut Comp.* 2.2-3).[33] Plutarch's Augustus also echoes Caesar in other respects. Augustus, as a young statesman, uses the influence of an established figure (Cicero) to propel him rapidly into a position of power, just as Julius Caesar used Pompey. Both men were viewed as would-be tyrants by Brutus, whose assumption was proven to be wrong in both cases. Indeed, for both Julius Caesar and Augustus, Plutarch reports anecdotes of their respect for defeated opponents, with each man shown weeping at the news of an enemy's death (*Ant.* 78.2, *Pomp.* 80.5, *Caes.* 48.2) and later allowing his enemy's statues to stand (*Dion-Brut Comp.* 5, *Caes.* 57.6). Finally, in the conflict between Augustus and Antony at Actium, Plutarch introduces the parallel to Caesar and Pompey at Pharsalus (*Ant.* 62.3). Through these correspondences, Plutarch enables Augustus, at some level, to repeat, and then complete, Caesar's efforts to transform Rome into a monarchy. Ultimately, in the *Moralia* and *Lives*, Augustus' actions as emperor predominate: as an older man, his behavior puts him in league with Pericles, Agesilaus and Cato the Elder as a leader whom the men of Plutarch's day should emulate.

---

[33] A similar pattern is also found in the account of Otho's career: his early career, as described in *Galba*, is blameworthy, but his conduct as the ruler in *Otho* is praiseworthy (if flawed).

Bibliography

Ash, R. (2008), 'Standing in the Shadows: Plutarch and the Emperors in the *Lives* and *Moralia*', in A.G. Nikolaidis (ed.), *The Unity of Plutarch's Work*, Berlin, 557-575.
Beck, M. (2002), 'Plutarch to Trajan: the Dedicatory Letter and the Apophthegmata Collection', in P.A. Stadter, L. van der Stockt (edd.), *Sage and Emperor*, Leuven, 163-173.
Beck, M. (2004), 'Plutarch on the Statesman's Independence of Action', in L. de Blois et al. (edd.), *The Statesman in Plutarch's Works*, I, Leiden, 105-114.
Beck, M. (ed.) (2014), *A Companion to Plutarch*, Chichester.
Bowersock, G.W. (1965), *Augustus and the Greek World*, Oxford.
de Blois, L. (2004), 'Classical and Contemporary Statesmen in Plutarch's *Praecepta*', in L. de Blois et al. (edd.), *The Statesman in Plutarch's Works*, vol. 1, Leiden, 57-66.
de Blois, L., Bons, J., Kessels, T., Schenkeveld, D., edd. (2004), *The Statesman in Plutarch's Works*, vol. 1, Leiden.
Eder, W. (1990), 'Augustus and the Power of Tradition: The Augustan Principate as Binding Link between Republic and Empire', in K.A. Raaflaub, M. Toher (edd.), *Between Republic and Empire*, Berkeley, 71-122.
Eder, W. (2005), 'Augustus and the Power of Tradition', in K. Galinsky (ed.), *Age of Augustus*, Cambridge, 13-32.
Galinsky, K. (ed.) (2005), *Age of Augustus*, Cambridge.
Galinsky, K. (2012), *Augustus. Introduction to the Life of an Emperor*, Cambridge.
Georgiadou, A. (1988), 'The *Lives of the Caesars* and Plutarch's Other Lives', *Illinois Classical Studies* 13, 349-356.
Georgiadou, A. (2014), 'The Lives of the Caesars', in M. Beck (ed.), *A Companion to Plutarch*, Chichester, 251-266.
Gruen, E.S. (2005), 'Augustus and the Making of the Principate', in K. Galinsky (ed.), *Age of Augustus*, Cambridge, 33-51.
Jones, C.P. (1971), *Plutarch and Rome*, Oxford.
Millar, F. (1984), 'State and Subject: The Impact of Monarchy', in F. Millar, E. Segal (edd.), *Caesar Augustus. Seven Aspects*, Oxford, 37-60.

Millar, F., Segal, E. (edd.) (1984), *Caesar Augustus. Seven Aspects*, Oxford.
Moles, J.L. (1988), *Plutarch. The Life of Cicero*, Eastbourne.
Nikolaidis, A.G. (ed.) (2008), *The Unity of Plutarch's Work*, Berlin.
Pelling, C. (1988), *Plutarch. 'Life of Antony'*, Cambridge.
Pelling, C. (2002ª), 'Plutarch's Method of Work in the Roman Lives', in C. Pelling (ed.), *Plutarch and History. Eighteen Studies*, Swansea, 1-44.
Pelling, C. (2002ᵇ), 'Plutarch's Adaptation of his Source Material', in C. Pelling (ed.), *Plutarch and History. Eighteen Studies*, Swansea, 91-115.
Pelling, C. (2002ᶜ), 'Is death the end? Closure in Plutarch's Lives', in C. Pelling (ed.), *Plutarch and History. Eighteen Studies*, Swansea, 365-386.
Pelling, C. (2004), 'Do Plutarch's Politicians Never Learn?', in L. de Blois et. al. (edd.), *The Statesman in Plutarch's Works*, vol. 1, Leiden, 87-104.
Pelling, C. (2011), *Plutarch. Caesar*, Oxford.
Pelling, C. (2014), 'Political Philosophy', in Beck (ed.), *A Companion to Plutarch*, Chichester, 149-162.
Pelling, C., ed. (2002), *Plutarch and History*, Swansea.
Raaflaub, K.A., M. Toher (edd.) (1990), *Between Republic and Empire*, Berkeley.
Roskam, G. (2002), 'A Παιδεία for the Ruler', in P.A. Stadter, L. van der Stockt (edd.), *Sage and Emperor*, Leuven, 175-189.
Roskam, G. (2009), *Plutarch's* Maxime cum principibus philosopho esse disserendum, Leuven.
Stadter, P.A. (2014), 'Plutarch and Rome', in M. Beck (ed.), *A Companion to Plutarch*, Chichester, 13-31.
Stadter, P.A., van der Stockt, L., edd. (2002), *Sage and Emperor*, Leuven.
Syme, R. (1939), *The Roman Revolution*, Oxford.
Teodorsson, S.-T. (2008), 'The Education of Rulers in Theory (*Mor.*) and Practice (*Vitae*)', in A.G. Nikolaidis (ed.), *The Unity of Plutarch's Work*, Berlin, 339-350.
Wardman, A.E. (1974), *Plutarch's Lives*, London.

Yavetz, Z. (1984), 'The *Res Gestae* and Augustus' Public Image', in F. Millar, E. Segal (edd.), *Caesar Augustus: Seven Aspects*, Oxford, 1-36.

Yavetz, Z. (1990), 'The Personality of Augustus: Reflections on Syme's *Roman Revolution*', in K.A. Raaflaub, M. Toher (edd.), *Between Republic and Empire*, Berkeley, 21-41.

Hellenistic Poetry in the Augustan Age: the Metapoetic Prose of Parthenius of Nicaea

RAFAEL GALLÉ CEJUDO*
University of Cadiz

In writing the title of this chapter, we are aware that the attentive reader might accuse us of committing a double *contradictio in terminis*, since on the one hand it refers to Hellenistic poetry in the Augustan Age, in other words the height of the Imperial era, the chronological period immediately following the Hellenic period; and on the other, it refers to the possible metapoetic values of a work in prose: the Ἐρωτικὰ Παθήματα of Parthenius of Nicaea.

However, in our defence we will argue that readers will also be aware that besides being the author of this brief treatise, Parthenius was also one of the most reputed poets of the end of the Alexandrian period, and furthermore, one whose literary activity mainly took place within a Roman context, placing him in a privileged position astride these two golden ages of poetry, the Hellenistic and the Augustan. As for the apparent contradiction presented by a metapoetic examination of a work in prose, the keys to interpretation are offered by Parthenius himself in the letter-prologue preceding the collection of short stories that comprise the *Erotika Pathemata*. As is well known, this work consists of 36 love stories, most of which have a tragic and grisly end, which Parthenius extracted and compiled with the apparent purpose of creating a storehouse from which to draw material for future poetic compositions. It is, therefore, at least on paper (and disregarding from the outset any type of non-literal interpretation of this epistolary preface), a work born from verse and destined for verse, a work with a poetic vocation but attired in prose.

---

* We thank the DGICYT (the Spanish Directorate-General for Scientific and Technical Research) for supporting the project 'Las migraciones poéticas entre la prosa y el verso: el papel referencial de la elegía helenística' (FFI2017-85015-P).

Thus, Parthenius' *Erotika Pathemata* presents itself as an ideal work for a study of the concept of μεταποίησις in its broadest sense: on the one hand, the ancient meaning of μεταποίησις as an exercise consisting in transferring the idea contained in a poetic text to a work in prose; and on the other, the modern rhetorical and stylistic sense in poetry that refers to the study and analysis of poetic phenomena. In these lines, however, we will only consider this second meaning, having reserved the first for an extensive study that is almost completed and will soon see the light of day.

As already stated, the roots of this brief treatise (Parthenius' *Erotika Pathemata*) can be traced back to the dawn of the Hellenistic period, thus allowing the possibility of analysing – with the sedate perspective offered by a distance of two or three centuries – the implicit metapoetic premises that illuminate poetic works of the Alexandrian Age; and, at the same time, with sufficient chronological proximity to assess its reception in the great Latin poetry of the Augustan Age. To this end, we will adopt a two-pronged approach by conducting: 1) an analysis of the preceptive and programmatic indications (and even the literary pose) of the letter-prologue to the *Erotika Pathemata*; and 2) an analysis, by way of example, of one of the chapters in the work, for which purpose we have chosen a well-known episode, chapter 33 'On Assaon', which recounts the story of Niobe's ill-fated family.

As regards the letter-prologue, it will be best to read it in its entirety before exploring it in detail:

> Παρθένιος Κορνηλίῳ Γάλλῳ χαίρειν
> Μάλιστά σοι δοκῶν ἁρμόττειν, Κορνήλιε Γάλλε, τὴν ἄθροισιν τῶν ἐρωτικῶν παθημάτων, ἀναλεξάμενος ὡς ὅτι μάλιστα ἐν βραχυτάτοις ἀπέσταλκα. τὰ γὰρ παρά τισι τῶν ποιητῶν κείμενα, τούτων μὴ αὐτοτελῶς λελεγμένων, κατανοήσεις ἐκ τῶνδε τὰ πλεῖστα. αὐτῷ τέ σοι παρέσται εἰς ἔπη καὶ ἐλεγείας ἀνάγειν τὰ μάλιστα ἐξ αὐτῶν ἁρμόδια. διὰ τὸ μὴ παρεῖναι τὸ περιττὸν αὐτοῖς, ὃ δὴ σὺ μετέρχῃ, χεῖρον περὶ αὐτῶν ἐνενοήθης· οἱονεὶ γὰρ ὑπομνηματίων τρόπον αὐτὰ συνελεξάμεθα, καί σοι νυνὶ τὴν χρῆσιν ὁμοίαν, ὡς ἔοικε, παρέξεται.
>
> 3 κείμενα τούτων, μὴ αὐτοτελῶς λελεγμένα Lehrs; 5 <μηδὲ> διὰ Lehrs; 6 <μὴ> χεῖρον Sakolowski; ἐννοηθῇς Lehrs

> Parthenius to Cornelius Gallus, greetings.
> Since it seems to me, Cornelius Gallus, that you would be the most suitable recipient, I am sending you this anthology of passionate loves that I have

prepared in the shortest possible form. These stories can be found in the works of several poets, although they are not written there separately, and you will already know most of them from these texts. And now it is you who will be able to exalt them in hexametric or elegiac verse depending on which they are best suited to. And as they do not exhibit that exquisiteness which is always your aim, you will form a worse opinion of them; in truth, I have compiled them as if they were simply some notes and, as is customary, they will now perform that same function for you.

Although this is such a rich text that it requires a detailed and separate analysis of each of the phrases and terms contained therein (indeed, no few studies have been entirely devoted to this famous passage from Hellenistic literature), for the question that occupies us I propose that we focus our attention on the sentence

αὐτῷ τέ σοι παρέσται εἰς ἔπη καὶ ἐλεγείας ἀνάγειν τὰ μάλιστα ἐξ αὐτῶν ἁρμόδια

And now it is you who will be able to exalt them in hexametric or elegiac verse depending on which they are best suited to.

This is without doubt one of the fundamental sentences in the passage, since the measured choice of words and the precise syntactic order introduce some of the key elements related to the compositional process. First, the clearly emphatic use of the phrase αὐτῷ τέ σοι παρέσται can be neither accidental nor inconsequential.[1] Therefore, rather than indicating a possible poetic reciprocity (the traditional interpretation), in the sense that just like the poets from whom the stories were originally taken, Gallus too will be able to return them to the poetic form,[2] the use of such an emphatic construction might rather suggest the Latin poet's exclusive pertinence and supreme suitability: Gallus is the most appropriate person, he now has the material available, he already

---

[1] Despite the reluctance of Zangoiannis (1900) 460, who proposed replacing it with οὕτω δέ σοι.
[2] For example Lightfoot (1999) 369, who has also suggested that the use of the pronoun might imply the work of rendering into verse compared with the schematic presentation of Parthenius' passages, and even that most of the sources were poetic.

knows the stories,[3] and it is now his responsibility alone to give poetic stature (exalt/ ἀνάγειν) to the texts. Indeed, rather than being employed with a semantic value that approaches forms such as ἀποκαθίστημι ('restore'), in this passage ἀνάγω is clearly embedded, as rightly indicated by Zimmermann, in the theoretical and literary framework of the opposition between poetry and prose and the degradation that occurs to the original poetic language when transformed into prose discourse. This idea – which may have its roots in the teachings of the Stoics – that in the origins of language, primordial poetic expression lost its adornment, was stripped of metre and was thus transformed into prose discourse, is conceived as a 'descent' from the ornamental and sublime carriage of poetry, a debasement to the ground and a humiliated passage on foot. The antonymic terminology of ἀνάγειν is recurrent in the main passages that address the question from a meta-literary perspective:

> **κατέβη** ἀπὸ τῶν μέτρων ὥσπερ ὀχημάτων ἡ ἱστορία καὶ **τῷ πεζῷ**...
> Plut. *De Pyth. or.* 24

History descended from verse as if from a carriage and by means of pedestrian diction...

> **ὁ πεζὸς** λόγος, ὅ γε κατεσκευασμένος, μίμημα τοῦ ποιητικοῦ ἐστι. (...) εἶτα οἱ ὕστερον ἀφαιροῦντες ἀεί τι τῶν τοιούτων εἰς τὸ νῦν εἶδος **κατήγαγον** ὡς ἂν ἀπὸ ὕψους τινός· καθάπερ ἄν τις καὶ τὴν κωμῳδίαν φαίη λαβεῖν τὴν σύστασιν ἀπὸ τῆς τραγῳδίας καὶ τοῦ κατ' αὐτὴν ὕψους **καταβιβασθεῖσαν** εἰς τὸ λογοειδές (...) καὶ αὐτὸ δὲ **τὸ πεζὸν** λεχθῆναι τὸν ἄνευ τοῦ μέτρου λόγον ἐμφαίνει τὸν ἀπὸ ὕψους τινὸς **καταβάντα** καὶ ὀχήματος εἰς τοὔδαφος.
> Strabo 1.2.6

---

[3] Cf. our comment Gallé Cejudo (forthcoming) with regard to τὰ πλεῖστα in the preceding sentence. There we discuss a previously unexplored possibility that is far removed from the preconceived utilitarian function traditionally attributed to Parthenius' prologue, and which might find support in the formulas that comprise the dedicatory genre. This interpretation revolves around the idea that the passages are taken from a stock repertoire (they can be found in any author) and that although they are not conveyed in their complete form (or separately), this is not a problem because Gallus (who is an educated man and the one who knows this material best) 'already recognises most of those that have been sent to him.' This much less conventional interpretation is, however, more in line with dedicatory and epistolary humility formulas such as 'I am sure that you know it, but even so I will still send it' (the epistolary topic of sender's *mea mediocritas*) and is also in the same line, although here with an inversion of the formula, as the preface to Plutarch's *Mulierum uirtutes* (*Mor.* 234d).

> Prose – at least the well-crafted kind – is an imitation of poetic language (...) Later, subsequent authors made prose descend as if from a certain sublimity. Likewise, it could also be said that comedy originated in tragedy, and that it was also made to descend from its corresponding sublimity to the spoken language (...) And the very fact that the word devoid of metre receives the name of 'pedestrian' reveals that it has descended from a certain sublimity, as from a carriage to the ground.

Nevertheless, this passage might admit of a different interpretation, as an example of irony, framed (inevitably) within the context of the humility formulas typical of literary prologues, exactly the same semantic level as in the following sentence in which Parthenius laments that his compositions do not come up to Cornelius Gallus' habitual literary standards. It should be borne in mind that in the previously cited passage from Strabo's *Geography* (1.2.6), the author states that prose, at least the best-crafted or most complex kind, is an imitation of poetic language (ὁ πεζὸς λόγος, ὅ γε κατεσκευασμένος, μίμημα τοῦ ποιητικοῦ ἐστι). Parthenius, conscious and convinced of the literary quality of his work, would be speaking ironically about the possibility that Gallus could improve it, returning it to the lofty and sublime carriage of poetry.

It is also significant that the options Parthenius offers Gallus should be the hexameter or the elegiac distich (εἰς ἔπη καὶ ἐλεγείας). This limited selection of metre might reflect poetic tastes or inclinations in the historical and literary context of Augustan Rome (romance literature, mythological or legendary content and a preference for the hexameter and the elegiac distich), or alternatively, it may indicate a precise generic identification between form and content, supported by the fact that the metric passages cited *plenis uerbis* in Parthenius' work correspond exclusively to hexametric or elegiac forms (cf. Parth. 11 *Byblis*, 14 *Antaeus*, 21 *Pisidice* and 34 *Corythus*). However, although both metric combinations do offer the poet relative literary variety from the point of view of content (epyllia, encomia, epicedia, catalogues and narratives, etc.), the truth is that Parthenius is in some way restricting the Latin poet's creativity. Hence, this choice of metre should perhaps be understood as expressing a generic value, in the sense that Gallus can adapt the passages to the poetic form that he deems most appropriate. Nevertheless, it remains a further example of Parthenius' condescension or the literary challenge he poses to the Latin poet, especially when we consider that as a poet, the Nicaean was characterised by the wide range of metric forms he employed: ἐλεγειοποιὸς καὶ μέτρων διαφόρων ποιητής.[4]

Finally, the last part of the sentence (τὰ μάλιστα ἐξ αὐτῶν ἁρμόδια) is also open to two possible interpretations, the much more restrictive of which is the one that has traditionally received wider acceptance. This relates to the circumscribing idea that either not all the passages are useful or appropriate for Gallus, or that only the most appropriate motifs or stories from among those selected – and thus not all of them – can be adapted to epic verse or elegiac couplets. However, this interpretation contradicts, or at least considerably limits, the initial statement in the letter-prologue which affirms the specific suitability of Cornelius Gallus as the recipient of the collection (μάλιστά σοι... ἁρμόττειν).[5] This apparent aporia can be resolved by means of a non-restrictive interpretation of the partitive (ἐξ αὐτῶν) and ruling out any kind of synecdoche (*pars pro toto*) for ἁρμόδια. In other words, it is not that Gallus can use 'the most appropriate of the motifs', but that the Roman poet may use all the material, adapting it as required (τὰ μάλιστα ἁρμόδια), to the hexameter or the distich; he can, therefore, use all the passages in the *Erotika Pathemata* according to how best they are suited to one or the other metre. Regardless of which interpretation is accepted, what this passage does imply is a dual reasoning: on the one hand, that not all the material in the *Erotika Pathemata* comes from compositions in epic or elegiac verse, because this would mean that the work of writing in metre or creating a new poetic adaptation had already been done; and on the other, that Parthenius does not consider the process of rendering anew in verse or 're-poeticisation', 'desprosification' (ἀνα – or rather ἀντι- μεταποίησις), to be a simple task but one rather that requires the dedication of an experienced poet, one capable of restoring – returning once again to the words of Plutarch (*De Pyth. or.* 24 = *Mor.* 406e) – bare language (τοῦ λόγου συναπολυομένου) with simple, modest adornment (τὸ ἀφελὲς καὶ λιτὸν

---

[4] Cf. *Suda* s.v. Παρθένιος (π 664).
[5] It might even be sustain the rejected interpretation that in line 1, μάλιστα may be referring to ἁρμόττειν in the sense of 'particularly adaptable'; cf. in this respect our thoughts in Gallé Cejudo (forthcoming).

ἐν κόσμῳ) to its original impressive and refined nature (τὸ σοβαρὸν καὶ περίεργον). Applied to the various disciplines, this would be to retrace the path by which history began to distinguish truth from fiction (τοῦ μυθώδους ἀπεκρίθη τὸ ἀληθές), philosophy to substitute the amazing with the clear and didactic (τὸ σαφὲς καὶ διδασκαλικὸν ἀσπασαμένη μᾶλλον ἢ τὸ ἐκπλῆττον), and the oracles were rendered comprehensible and plausible (τὸ συνετὸν καὶ πιθανόν) by stripping them of epic verse, strange terms, circumlocutions and obscurity (ἀφελὼν δὲ τῶν χρησμῶν ἔπη καὶ γλώσσας καὶ πε καὶ ἀσάφειαν).

Thus, having shed light on some of the programmatic keys that Parthenius introduces in the letter-prologue, we can now move on to a brief study of a chapter that illustrates the author's stance towards poetry. As indicated earlier, this section will concern chapter 33 'Assaon', a well-known story which recounts the ἐρωτικὸν πάθημα of Niobe's family.

> Περὶ Ἀσσάονος
> Ἱστορεῖ Ξάνθος Λυδιακοῖς καὶ Νεάνθης β΄ καὶ Σιμίας ὁ Ῥόδιος.
> Διαφόρως δὲ καὶ τοῖς πολλοῖς ἱστορεῖται καὶ τὰ Νιόβης· οὐ γὰρ Ταντάλου φασὶν αὐτὴν γενέσθαι, ἀλλ' Ἀσσάονος μὲν θυγατέρα, Φιλόττου δὲ γυναῖκα· εἰς ἔριν δὲ ἀφικομένην Λητοῖ περὶ καλλιτεκνίας ὑποσχεῖν τίσιν τοιάνδε. τὸν μὲν Φίλοττον ἐν κυνηγίᾳ διαφθαρῆναι, τὸν δὲ Ἀσσάονα τῆς θυγατρὸς πόθῳ σχόμενον αὐτὴν αὑτῷ γήμασθαι. μὴ ἐνδιδούσης δὲ τῆς Νιόβης, τοὺς παῖδας αὐτῆς εἰς εὐωχίαν καλέσαντα καταπρῆσαι. καὶ τὴν μὲν διὰ ταύτην τὴν συμφορὰν ἀπὸ πέτρας ὑψηλοτάτης αὐτὴν ῥῖψαι, ἔννοιαν δὲ λαβόντα τῶν σφετέρων ἁμαρτημάτων διαχρήσασθαι τὸν Ἀσσάονα ἑαυτόν.
>   Parth. 33 (Calderón Dorda [1988])

> On Assaon
> This story is related by Xanthus in his *Lydiaca*, Neanthes in book 2, and Simmias of Rhodes.
> Many others also narrate a different version of the story of Niobe, in which it is said that she was not the daughter of Tantalus, but of Assaon, and the wife of Philottus, and that for having disputed with Leto about the beauty of their children, her punishment was as follows: Philottus perished while hunting and Assaon, consumed with love for his daughter, desired her to become his wife. But when Niobe refused, he invited her children to a banquet, and burnt them all to death. As a result of this tragedy, she flung herself from a high rock; in turn, Assaon, once he realised his crime, took his own life.

As is made perfectly clear from the first sentence of the chapter, in *Erotika Pathemata* 33 Parthenius offers a completely different version from that which for many other authors is the myth of Niobe: διαφόρως δὲ καὶ τοῖς πολλοῖς ἱστορεῖται καὶ τὰ Νιόβης.[6]

Indeed, from its first mention in *Iliad* 24.602 ff., the story of Niobe has seen multiple variants with regard to its main mythemes: the number of children varies considerably from one source to another; the husband's name is variously given as Amphion, Zethus, Alalcomenos and Philottus; the father's name also varies from Tantalus to Pelops to Assaon to Asonides.[7] Furthermore, there are substantial differences with regard to the way in which Niobe's children die, whether pierced to death with arrows loosed by Leto's children or burnt to death by their grandfather in a fire at the palace or during a banquet. Finally, the circumstances of Niobe's death also vary from one source to another, ranging from being turned into stone, to metamorphosis into ice, to suicide. The only unchanging element in all the preserved versions of this story is the account of Niobe's ὕβρις, bragging that her children are more beautiful (or more numerous) than Leto's and thus bringing upon herself the goddess' consequent punishment, although here again, there are discrepancies regarding the punishment. According to some sources, the goddess instructs her children to kill Niobe's, while in others, Leto brings about the accidental death of Niobe's husband and arouses the incestuous desires of her father who, when faced with Niobe's refusal to accede to his sexual demands, decides to burn his grandchildren to death in revenge. All the above-mentioned variants, and above all the two lines of general development of the story, would have come from two more widespread versions: the Theban version already mentioned and the Lydian tradition (in which even the name of the heroine is not Niobe, but Elymen or Elymene). Everything indicates

---

[6] It is not necessary to remove the first καί in the sentence, as proposed by Meineke and accepted by some editors, and even less the second. The first restricts the differences to those between the present version and a more widespread version, if πολλοῖς is understood as an associative dative (in the same sense as, for example, E. *Med.* 579 πολλὰ πολλοῖς εἰμι διάφορος), and the second adds the story of Niobe to the other chapters in Parthenius' anthology, in which – as was postulated in the letter-prologue – what is sought is thematic originality. It is not necessary, therefore, to link this second καί to the final paragraph of chapter 32 (Anthippe), in which the aetiology of the name of Epirus is explained as a minority version transmitted only by some (φασὶ δέ τινες), or to Chapter 28 (Clite) which is also introduced by the formula διαφόρως ἱστορεῖται.

[7] The Homeric scholium to *Iliad* 24. 617a does not confirm the paternity of Asonides, but neither does it deny it.

that the version given by Parthenius in the *Erotika Pathemata*, although not the original, would have been relatively heavily influenced by the Asian variant.

It is therefore necessary to analyse the literary and contextual elements of this story in order to shed light on the question. In this respect, the manchette in the Heidelberg Codex indicates that this same story had already been recounted by the historians Neanthes of Cyzicus and Xanthus of Lydia,[8] and by the poet Simmias of Rhodes (*CA* fr. 5):

Fig. 1: *Codex Palatinus Heidelbergensis* 398, f. 187 v.° (*in marg. sup.*):
Ἱστορεῖ Ξάνθος Λυδιακοῖς καὶ Νεάνθης β' καὶ Σιμίας ὁ Ῥόδιος.

The mention of this poetic version by Simmias hints at a process of rendering this or another Hellenistic poetic source into prose (μεταποίησις), since although the mythological episode of Niobe had appeared previously in other, much earlier poetic works, the annotations and commentaries suggest that these were all based on the Theban version.[9] Although no fragment of the version by Simmias remains, the testimonies of the scholia to Homer and Euripides confirm that much of Parthenius' narrative follows the version of the historian Xanthus, one of the authors cited by the manchette. Thus, the scholia to Euripides' *Phoenicians* relate that according to the version by the Lydian, Philottus is killed by a bear during a hunt (ἐν κυνηγεσίῳ, an annotation which follows another giving the number of children, namely ten males and ten females according to Xanthus):

> Ξάνθος δὲ ὁ Λυδὸς δέκα καὶ δέκα ἐκ Φιλόττου τοῦ Ἀσσυρίου, ὃς ᾤκει ἐν Σιπύλῳ, ὃς ἀνῃρέθη ἐν κυνηγεσίῳ ὑπὸ ἄρκτου.
>
> *Schol. E. Ph.* 159

meanwhile, the Homeric scholia to the *Iliad* 24. 617a recounts the incestuous demands made upon Niobe by her father (here called Asonides), her refusal and his murder of his grandchildren in a fire:[10]

---

[8] Cf. for Neanthes *FGrH* 84 fr. 6 and for Xanthus *FGrH* 765 fr. 20a.
[9] Cf. Euphor. *CA* frg. 102 and even the *Niobe* of Aeschylus (*TGrF* p. 50 and 228).
[10] As previously mentioned, the annotation in the scholia is not conclusive as regards Asonides' paternity, but the similarity with the version by Parthenius practically confirms the relationship.

ὁ δὲ Λυδὸς (*i.e.* Xanthus [*FGrH* 765] fr. 20b) φησὶν ὅτι Ἀσσωνίδης ἐρασθεὶς αὐτῆς καὶ μὴ πεισθείσης ἐπ' ἄριστον τοὺς παῖδας καλέσας ἐνέπρησεν. ἡ δὲ φυγοῦσα ηὔξατο λιθωθῆναι. b(BE3E4)T τινὲς δὲ εἰς κρύσταλλον αὐτὴν μεταβεβλῆσθαί φασιν.

Schol. Hom. Il. 24.617a (= Eustath. 1368.7)

However, this same Homeric scholia also states that in Xanthus' version, Niobe is turned into stone (λιθωθῆναι), and that according to other sources, she metamorphoses into ice (εἰς κρύσταλλον), but no mention is made of a suicide by dashing herself from a high rock. Thus, as in many other chapters in the *Erotika Pathemata*, Parthenius has opted to seek another source, either one that merges the version of incest with that of suicide, or one that enables him to incorporate the suicide into Xanthus' version, in order to thus rationalise the myth.[11] While it is true that this new source was not necessarily the poetic text by Simmias (or even the possible prose version by Neanthes), neither can Parthenius' use of it for his version be completely ruled out.

All of this leads us to the conclusion that according to the commentaries and documents preserved, the process of μεταποίησις, the prose rendering of the story of Niobe proposed by Parthenius, has involved at least two fundamental actions from a compositional point of view: on the one hand, the anthologist has opted for a very minoritarian version, perhaps influenced by the increasing ascendency of the Asian version, diametrically opposed, except in the ethical dimension of ὕβρις, to the Hellenic version (the Theban saga) that had been transmitted by the Homeric paradigm; and on the other hand, Parthenius has rationalised all the episodes of death in the story, that of the husband while hunting, of the children burnt to death by an incestuous grandfather, of Niobe herself by committing suicide rather than being metamorphosed (neither into stone nor ice) and that of Assaon, who also takes his own life, overcome by remorse. This kind of gruesome but ἀνθρώπινον – human – end, in which divinity plays no part, endows the story with considerable poignancy due to its proximity to the human sphere. Parthenius also introduces an incestuous note that guarantees the

---

[11] For Billault (2008) 19 Parthenius, an authority on the lesser-known versions of the myth, makes use of them to bear witness to this narrative proliferation by means of the juxtaposition inherent to mythological literature.

resence of the frenzied erotic element, a passionate love (a ἐρωτικὸν πάθημα) within the framework of a well-known myth, but which lacks, as Ovid's *Metamorphoses* plainly show, a clearly amatory element.

Bibliography

Bethe, E. (1903), 'Die Quellenangaben zu Parthenios und Antoninus Liberalis', *Hermes* 38, 608-617.
Billault, A. (2008), 'La littérature dans les *Erotika Pathémata* de Parthénios', in A. Zucker (ed.). *Littérature et érotisme dans les Passions d'amour de Parthénios de Nicée*, Grenoble, 13-26.
Calderón Dorda, E. (1988), *Partenio de Nicea. Sufrimientos de amor y fragmentos*, Madrid.
Francese, Ch. (1995), *Parthenius of Nicaea and Roman Love Stories*, Ann Arbor.
Francese, Ch. (2001), *Parthenius of Nicaea and Roman Poetry*, Bern/ Frankfurt a. M.
Gallé Cejudo, R.J. (forthcoming), 'Ποίησις καταλογάδην *versus* ἔμμετρος ποίησις: la prosificación como recurso metaliterario', in R.J. Gallé Cejudo, M. Sánchez Ortiz de Landaluce, T. Silva Sánchez (edd.), *Studia Hellenistica Gaditana II. Migraciones temáticas entre la prosa y verso en la Literatura Helenística e Imperial*, Bari.
Jacoby, F. (1876-1959), *Die Fragmente der griechischen Historiker*, Leiden.
Lightfoot, J.L. (1999), *Parthenius of Nicaea. Extant Works edited with Introduction and Commentary*, Oxford.
Mayer G'Schrey, R. (1898), *Pathenius Nicaeensis quale in fabularum amatoriarum breuiario dicendi genus secutus sit. Diss.*, Heidelberg.
Melero Bellido, A. (1981), *Partenio de Nicea. Sufrimientos de amor*, Madrid.
Montes Cala, J.G. (2010), 'Poesía en verso o en prosa: los antecedentes clásicos de una polémica literaria', in J. M.ª Maestre Maestre et al. (edd.). *Humanismo y pervivencia del mundo clásico*, Alcañiz/ Madrid, 2023-2060.
Nauck, A. (1964), *Tragicorum Graecorum Fragmenta. Supplementum... adiecit B. Snell*, Hildesheim (repr. Leipzig 1889^2).

Powell, J.U. (1925), *Collectanea Alexandrina: reliquiae minores poetarum Graecorum aetatis Ptolemaicae, 323-146 aC.: epicorum, elegiacorum, lyricorum, ethicorum*, Oxford.

Sellheim, C.A.R. (1930), *De Parthenii et Antonini fontium indiculorum auctoribus. Diss.*, Halle an der Saale.

Zangoiánnis, D.K. (1900), 'Κριτικαὶ παρατηρήσεις εἰς Παρθένιον Περὶ ἐρωτικῶν παθημάτων', *Ἀθηνᾶ* 12, 459-475.

Zimmermann, F. (1934), 'Parthenios' Brief an Gallus', *Hermes* 69, 179-189.

Zucker, A., ed. (2008), *Littérature et érotisme dans les Passions d'amour de Parthénios de Nicée*, Grenoble.

Conon's Account of Caunus and Byblis (Cono 2): Structure and Innovation

NEREIDA VILLAGRA*
Centro de Estudos Clássicos da Faculdade de Letras da Universidade de Lisboa

1. Conon's work has come down only through Photius' summary.[1] The author is never mentioned in our sources and the only information we have about this set of narratives is what is told by the Byzantine patriarch, which is very little: the title of the work, Διηγήσεις, *Narratives*,[2] that it was dedicated to Archelaus Philopator, who is identified with Philopatris, the king of Cappadocia between 36 BC and AD 17,[3] and, in the epilogue, Photius refers briefly to the style, describing the work as 'Attic in style, graceful and charming in his constructions and words, having a certain terseness and avoiding the commonplace' (translation Brown, 2002).

The collection, in its preserved form, is composed of 50 independent narratives on different subjects, mainly mythical, which show no thematic unity. Thus, the organisational criteria of this material is difficult to assess. We are also in obscurity regarding issues such as the readership of the *Diegeseis* or its main objective.[4] The proximity between Conon's text and the *Erotica Pathemata* of Parthenius of

---

* This paper was written with the support of the post-doctoral scholarship awarded by the Fundação para a Ciência e a Tecnologia – Portugal (SFRH/BPD/90803/2012).
[1] There is a recent edition of the text with translation and commentary by Brown (2002). On Conon see also Meliado (2015) 1084-1086; Henrichs (1987) 244 f.; Hoefer (1890); Martini (1922); Ressel (1996-1997); Blakely (2011).
[2] Brown (2002) 6-8 points out that there are no precedents of the term being used to designate brief prose narratives. Besides the Callimachean summaries, it is also attested as a title and for two works attributed to Plutarch. Cf. Cameron (2004) 71-76, who underlines that the term is a rhetorical category for 'unadorned narrative' (75), but it would also designate a 'brief mythological tale' (76). It seems to have been the original or at least what Photius would have read as its title. On titles vd. also Del Mastro (2014).
[3] The manuscripts say Philopator, which is agreed to be a mistake for Philopatris. Vd. Brown (2002) 2-3, who quotes extensive bibliography on the history of Cappadocia.
[4] Ibáñez Chacón (2007) 41-65 analyses Photius' appreciations of Conon in the context of the summaries of similar works contained in codices 186-190 and concludes that the nature of this work is closer to paradoxography than is generally accepted.

Nicaea has often been stressed.⁵ Indeed, besides the fact that these authors belong to the same period – if the identification of Archelaus is correct – their works are both assembled stories, arranged in chapters independent from each other, both have a similar length and both are dedicated to a specific person.⁶ These formal similarities speak in favour of the idea that Photius' summaries are close to the original text. However, there is an important difference between Parthenius' and Conon's texts: whereas the first work has a clear thematic rationale – it is a collection of miserable love stories – Conon's criteria for the selection of narratives were not thematic,⁷ if Photius' summary reflects the original structure and contents. Another work that can be compared to the *Diegeseis* is the Μεταμορφώσεων Συναγωγή of Antoninus Liberalis.⁸ This also has a similar structure of concise narratives of mythical material organised in independent chapters. But Antoninus' work again has a thematic criterion for the selection of the stories: the fact that they explain a metamorphosis.⁹

Regarding the state of the text, some chapters of Photius' summary are more concise than others and the patriarch himself comments on his intention to summarise the stories in a briefer way after the third narrative, but approximately the final 15 texts are longer.¹⁰ We are not sure whether this variation in length is due to a difference in the original or the longer summaries are closer to the original text. An Oxyrhynchus papyrus (52.3648) edited in 1984 preserves part of a text that partially

---

⁵ Henrichs (1987) 245 n. 12; Brown (2002) 8, 10; Lightfoot (1999) 227-229. On Parthenius vd. Lightfoot (1999), who edits the fragments and the mythographic work; Calderón Dorda (1998); Cuartero (1981); Sanz Morales (2002) 79-89.

⁶ Lightfoot warns that it is not possible to assume that Parthenius' book was personally adressed to Gallus, and this would apply as well to Conon if the information on Archelaus comes from an epistolary preface, since epistolary prefaces were more honorific than utilitarian in their time (Lightfoot [1999] 223-224).

⁷ For a comparison of the two texts see Lightfoot (1999) 227-230; see also Henrichs (1987) 245; Pellizer (1993) 294; Cameron (2004) 9-12; Higbie (2007) 249; Meliado (2015) 1085-1086.

⁸ It might be also interesting to compare Libanius' Διηγήματα (Westermann [1843] 350-389) for, besides the coincidence of the titles, these accounts offer an array of subject-matter similar to Conon's summary. In the case of Libanius, the variety of subjects is explained by the nature of the work, a set of rhetorical exercises with a pedagogical aim.

⁹ On Antoninus Liberalis vd. Papathomopoulos (1968), Calderón Dorda, Ozaeta Gálvez (1989), Celoria (1992), Sanz Morales (2002) 131-137.

¹⁰ Conon 3: οὕτω μὲν καὶ ἡ τρίτη διήγησις. Ἀλλὰ τί μοι δεῖ μικροῦ μεταγράφειν ταύτας, δέον πολλῷ κεφαλαιωδέστερον ἐπελθεῖν. 'This is the third tale. But is it necessary that I transcribe them in detail? I shall approach in a more general way' (translation Brown).

matches narratives 46 and 47.[11] The comparison of these fragments with Photius' summaries does not allow any conclusion because, in one case, both texts are very similar but, in the other, there is a bigger distortion. On the other hand, we cannot be certain that the papyrus contains the original work of Conon, for it could also be a summary. Conon's most recent editor argued that, if we take into account Photius' testimonies about his own working method, we can consider the longer summaries 'a reliable guide of the contents of the *Diegeseis*.'[12] When the papyrus is compared to Photius' text, it is apparent that despite the differences in the wording, the patriarch's account follows quite the same order of episodes as the papyrus. As mentioned above, we do not know whether the papyrus fragments contain Conon's original work. We could be comparing two summaries – or some other type of rearrangement of the original. However, the fact that both texts present the same episode sequence must be significant. Also, in the introduction to the *Bibliotheke*, Photius declares that he will give less attention to common works.[13] So, it can be inferred that he gives more attention to the rare ones. Since he describes the *Diegeseis* as ἀνακεχωρητόκος τοῖς πολλοῖς, 'distant from the commonplace', he should have reproduced its contents extensively, if he was consistent. Therefore, I will work under the hypothesis that, in the longer summaries, the general structure of the plot, i. e, the episode sequence, goes back to the original. Also, in the case of the chapter we are analysing, Photius' declaration is a good argument in favour of the idea that this narrative is close to the original. Indeed, when he says, after the third chapter, that from there on he will offer shorter summaries (see n. 10), we can assume that at least in the first three accounts he is transcribing the original in a quite complete way.

2. In this paper, I study the episode structure of the account of Caunus' and Byblis' incestuous love. It must have been a very popular story in Hellenistic and later times since several versions have been

---

[11] Harder (1984) 5-12, Luppe (1986) 121-122, Brown (2002) 317-320.
[12] Brown (2002) 35-39. Lightfoot is more cautious (Lightfoot [1999] 228-229). Hägg (1973) analyses Photius' methodology and concludes that in some codices he relies on the original texts to summarise them.
[13] 'Ἡμῖν δὲ καὶ ὅσον ἐπιπολάζει τῶν ἀνεγνωσμένων καὶ οὐδὲ τὰς σὰς διὰ τὸ πρόχειρον ἴσως διαπέφευγε μελέτας, οὐδὲ τούτοις τὴν ἐπὶ τοῖς ἄλλοις ὁμοίαν ἐθέμεθα φροντίδα, ἀλλὰ κατὰ τὸ ἑκούσιον τὸ ἀκριβὲς αὐτῶν ὑπερώφθη.'

preserved. This nicely allows a wider comparison with contemporary treatments of the same story, both in mythography and in other genres, and with earlier and later versions, which are also mythographical and poetical. Besides Conon's account, two prose versions are preserved: Parthenius' – who quotes some verses of Nicaenetus' and his own poetic version – and Antoninus Liberalis'. The manchette in Parthenius' manuscript informs us that the myth was also to be found in Aristocritus and Apollonius Rhodius. The manchette in Antoninus' text quotes Nicander as an authority.[14] Other poetical versions are Ovid's,[15] which is the longest treatment of the myth, and the one by Nonnus of Panopolis.[16] And we have still other references to the myth in the scholia to Theocritus, Stephanus Byzantinus and Diogenianus.[17]

In all versions, the erotic-incestuous theme, the aetiology of a water source and the foundation of a city which will bear Caunus' name appear over and over again.[18] I will focus my discussion on how these three elements are used and combined to build the plot. Narratology has traditionally made a distinction between fabula, the events in chronological order, the story, the group of events, and the text, the 'verbal representation of the story'.[19] In my analysis, I will isolate the events and try to show that the order in which they are put in the text has an impact on the fabula. That is to say, the text itself creates the *reality* of the events and this choice can inform us about the work itself.[20]

---

[14] Jacoby (1950) Aristocritus 493 F1; A.R. Fr. 5 (Powell); Nicaenet. Fr. 1 (Powell); Nicaenet. F1 (Powell). On the manchettes in Parthenius vd. Lightfoot (1999) 247-256, who quotes Hercher (1852) and Bethe (1903) for different views in the discussion of the reliability of the manchettes; vd. also Papathomopoulos (1968) 159 f. (also the first to apply the term manchette to the titular scholia of the Heidelbergensis codex) and Sellheim (1930).

[15] Ovid also refers to this myth in *AA*. 1.283-284.

[16] Cono 2; Parth. 11; Ov. *Met.* 9.450-665; Ant. Lib. *Met.* 30; Nonn. *D.* 13.548-561; Nic. *Fr.* F46 G-S.

[17] Sch. Theocr. *Id.* 7.115c; Diogenian. 5.71; St. Byz. s.v. Καῦνος. For discussions of this myth vd. Rohde (1974⁵) 99 f. n. 2, Bömer (1977) 411-416, Irving (1990) 300, Lightfoot (1999) 433-436, Chuvin (1991) 139-140, Brown (2002) 59-60.

[18] Conon's interest in aetiological and love myths is stressed already by Henrichs, who considers him an inheritor of Hellenistic models (1987) 245; also Meliado (2015) 1085: 'The subjects treated (…) closely connected to themes already widely exploited by previous poets and prose writers, above all in the Hellenistic period.'

[19] De Jong, Nünlist, Bowie (2004) XVIII.

[20] For further reading concerning theory on plot and story vd. Culler (1996) 93-102. Lightfoot (1999) 433 classifies the myth in the folk story-types of tears becoming a fountain or river (D.457.18.1 and 18.2) and brother-sister incest (T415.1 and 415.2) according to Stith Thompson index.

On the other hand, if we take into account that the literary genre or purpose of the text provides a frame for the poetical construction of the story, the assessment of how Conon's version is built can shed light on the nature of the *Diegeseis*.

3. Conon's account, after a genealogical and ethnographical introduction, explains that the siblings felt a passionate love for each other. Then it refers first Byblis' destiny and secondly Caunus':

> Δεύτερον τὰ περὶ Βυβλίδος, ὡς παῖς ἦν Μιλήτῳ,† ἔχουσα ἐξ αὐτῆς ἀδελφὸν Καῦνον. Ὤικουν δὲ Μίλητον τῆς Ἀσίας, ἣν ὕστερον μὲν Ἴωνες καὶ οἱ ἀπ' Ἀθηνῶν μετὰ Νηλέως ὁρμηθέντες ᾤκησαν, τότε δ' ἐνέμοντο Κᾶρες, ἔθνος μέγα, κωμηδὸν οἰκοῦντες. Καύνῳ δ' ἔρως ἐγείρεται ἀμήχανος τῆς ἀδελφῆς Βυβλίδος· ὡς δ' ἀπετύγχανε πολλὰ κινήσας, ἔξεισι τῆς γῆς ἐκείνης. Καὶ ἀφανισθέντος μυρίῳ ἄχει κατεχομένη ἡ Βυβλὶς ἐκλείπει καὶ αὐτὴ τὴν πατρῴαν οἰκίαν, καὶ πολλὴν ἐρημίαν πλανηθεῖσα, καὶ πρὸς τοὺς ἀτελεῖς ἱμέρους ἀπαγορεύουσα, βρόχον τὴν ζώνην τινὸς καρύας καθάψασα ἑαυτὴν ἀνήρτησεν. Ἔνθα δὴ κλαιούσης αὐτῆς ἐρρύη τὰ δάκρυα καὶ κρήνην ἀνῆκε, Βυβλίδα τοῖς ἐπιχωρίοις ὄνομα· Καῦνος δὲ πλανώμενος εἰς Λυκίαν φθάνει, καὶ τούτῳ Προνόη (Ναῒς δ' ἦν αὕτη) ἀναδῦσα τοῦ ποταμοῦ τά τε συνενεχθέντα τῇ Βυβλίδι λέγει, ὡς ἐχρήσατο Ἔρωτι δικαστῇ, καὶ πείθει αὐτὸν αὐτῇ ἐπὶ τῷ τῆς χώρας λαβεῖν τὴν βασιλείαν, (καὶ γὰρ εἰς αὐτὴν ἀνῆπτο) συνοικῆσαι. Ὁ δὲ Καῦνος ἐκ τῆς Προνόης τίκτει Αἰγιαλόν, ὃς καὶ παραλαβὼν τὴν βασιλείαν, ἐπεὶ ὁ πατὴρ ἐτελεύτησεν, ἤθροισέ τε τὸν λαὸν σποράδην οἰκοῦντα καὶ πόλιν ἔκτισεν ἐπὶ τῷ ποταμῷ μεγάλην καὶ εὐδαίμονα, Καῦνον ἀπὸ τοῦ πατρὸς ἐπονομάσας.

> The second is about Byblis, that she was the daughter of Miletus... having a brother Caunus from her. They lived at Miletus in Asia, which Ionians and those who set out from Athens with Neleus later colonized, but which the Carians inhabited at that time, a populous race that lived in villages. There arose in Caunus an impossible love for his sister Byblis, and when he had tried many things without success, he left the country. After he disappeared Byblis was utterly disconsolate, and she too left her father's house, wandering through a great wilderness, and despairing of her unsatisfied passions, she fastened her belt as a noose to a walnut tree and hanged herself. There, as she wept the tears poured down and created a spring, known to the local inhabitants as Byblis. Caunus reached Lycia in the course of his wanderings, and Pronoe (she was a Naiad) rose from the river to tell him what had happened to Byblis – how she had made Eros her judge – and persuaded him to live with her on the condition that he receive the rulership of the country (for it appertained to her). Caunus fathered by Pronoe a son Aegialus, who also succeeded to the throne when his father died, assembled the people that

lived in scattered groups, and founded a large and wealthy city by the river, naming it Caunus after his father.

Text and Translation by Brown (2002).

Let us first contextualise the text both in the *Diegeseis* and in its literary environment. The account is the second summary, preceded by the one on Midas and the Brigians and followed by the one on Locrus, Alcinous' brother. The first text on Midas is a combination of the different traditions on this character in a single narrative. The story runs in a way that leads to the rationalistic explanations of the settlement of the Phrygians, the same peoples as the Brigians whose name was altered, and of the belief that Midas had donkey ears – a belief which evolved from a misunderstanding of the metaphorical way to refer to the fact that he was very well informed.

The third summary, on Locrus, tells how he emigrated to Italy and acceded to power by marrying the daughter of Latinus, how he was then killed by Heracles by accident and how he gave his name to the city. The story is again composed of different episodes which lead to the explanation of Locrus' toponym: after being killed, Locrus appeared in his tomb to the inhabitants and ordered them to call the city after him.

The subject-matters of these three first accounts are, thus, very different. However, aetiological elements, foundation narratives and explanations of city names are to be found in the three of them and this seems to be their purpose: the sequence of episodes brings the reader to the explanation of an element of the present, the name of a population, the origin of an expression and of a belief, the foundation of a city, the name of a fountain or the name of a city.

Regarding the subject-matter, the tale of Byblis and Caunus is the first love story in the collection. We do not find another narrative of an erotic topic until the eighth chapter, on Canobus. Love as the main theme – and erotic episodes inserted into narratives with a non-erotic narrative line – are found in many chapters spread through the whole compilation and it is not possible to establish a specific part of the *Diegeseis* dedicated to love myths. The love stories in the collection are rather macabre and normally have a tragic ending,[21] similar to what

---

[21] But other times, the erotic element or episode is simply the previous step for an eponymous hero's birth. A study on the love theme in Conon can be found in Mignogna (2000) 315-355.

we find in Parthenius. Thus, the treatment of the love theme nicely fits with its literary context: stories of pathetic love became very popular in Hellenistic times through erotic elegy and this tendency continued into Roman times.[22] As Calderón Dorda pointed out,[23] Hellenistic erotic elegy expressed emotional conflicts in a mythical dimension and used the love stories themselves as αἴτιον: as proof of the poets' point stressing a conception of love as a pathos, as we find also in Parthenius. On the other hand, the narrative on Byblis and Caunus is also a story of incest, a topic which appears in two other narratives in the *Diegeseis*, narrative 9 on Semiramis, and 28 on Tennes and Hemithea. The story-type of incestuous relations appears already in Greek tragedy and receives increasing attention and new treatments in Hellenistic literature.[24] In our text, the incest is not consummated; it is only an incestuous passion. However, this feeling is enough to cause the escape of the brother and the death of the sister. Conversely, the other two stories of incest in Conon have a 'happy ending'. Semiramis consummates the incest with her son and the story is used to explain the origin of the Median and Persian custom of incestuous marriages. The story on Tennes and Hemithea also deals with a passion between a brother and sister. The father is against it but they succeed in escaping and uniting. The island where they arrive, Tenedos, receives its name from the brother. Conon adds an episode which explains the origin of the expression 'axe of Tennes', which bears no relation to the incestuous love story. Thus, the narrative on Caunus and Byblis contrasts with these two in the fact that it portrays an incestuous passion not consummated and with a tragic resolution – Byblis' death. However, it also has a positive consequence: the foundation of the city of Caunus.

It is worth stressing that the narratives on erotic myths in Conon mostly include a foundational narrative or have an aetiological finality – in fact, only two accounts on a love subject do not also have any aetiology or foundation myth. Besides the already mentioned narratives on Semiramis and Tennes, the erotic myths are the following:

---

[22] On the literary context vd. Brown (2002) 16-22; on the topic of love in Hellenistic literature vd. Calderón Dorda (1997) 1-16; Cairns (1979) 21-24. On Greek literature in the Imperial age vd. Whitmarsh (2001).

[23] Calderón Dorda (1997) 3.

[24] On the incest, especially on Parthenius' originality in its treatment, vd. Francese (2001) 132-143.

Account 8 articulates the unhappy love of Theonoe for Canobus with the account of his death by a viper. He was then buried in one of the Nile's mouths, which subsequently bears his name.

Narrative 10 explains the name Pallene of the Thracian Chersonesus as derived from Pallene, Sithon's daughter who helped Cleitus to win her in a suitors' contest.

Narrative 16 tells the passion of Promachus for Leucocomas, both Cretan. Leucocomas constantly rejected him and Promachus finally offered a prize to another young man. Then, Leucocomas committed suicide out of jealousy.

Narrative 17 combines the episode of Heracles' killing Syleus, his hospitality relations with Syleus' brother Dicaeus, his love for Syleus' daughter and marriage to her, her death and Heracles' sorrow. This is adduced as the reason for the fact that the inhabitants of Thessaly, instead of a tomb for the girl, built a shrine for Heracles.

In account 21 Iasion attempts to rape an apparition of Demeter and consequently dies. His brother Dardanus, full of sorrow, leaves Samothrace and ends up founding Dardania.

The 23rd story is of Oenone, again a long summary. It explains how Oenone, the first wife of Paris, out of jealousy for Helen, used her own son to create a conflict between Paris and Helen. The outcome, however, was that he killed his son. Oenone promised not to help him, so he died from the wound he had received from Philoctetes. At the last moment she changed her mind and tried to help him but it was too late. She killed the messenger who pronounced her guilty of Paris' death and then commited suicide.

The account on Narcissus (24) includes the episode of Aminias, a boy rejected by Narcissus who committed suicide with the sword Narcissus had sent to him, and begged the god to take revenge on his behalf. This led to Narcissus' love for himself and his death. His name was given to the flower that appeared for the first time on the spot where he shed his blood.

Narrative 31 is on Procne's unfortunate marriage to Tereus, who rapes and mutilates her sister Philomena. The sisters plan to kill him but the three of them undergo a metamorphosis which is used to explain why hoopoes chase nightingales and swallows.[25]

---

[25] On Procne see Ibáñez Chacón (2013) 95-119.

In account 40 Conon offers a rationalised version of Perseus' rescue of Andromeda which explains the origin of the myth on the sea monster Cetus and of the conversion of men into stone. At the end the text adds that Perseus and Andromeda went to Greece and that Argos was settled under his rule. This provides an aetiology of the monster Cetus, the petrification of the men and also an explanation for how Perseus became the king of the Argolid.

As we see, only narratives 16 (Promachus and Leucocomas) and 23 (Oenone) do not include an aetiology in a wider sense, including under this term any element that is used to explain the present – thus, metamorphosis, explanations of the origin of an element of nature, foundation myths and eponymy.[26] In fact, aetiology and foundation narratives have a recurrent presence in the *Diegeseis*[27] and it has been stressed that this is the feature which provides homogeneity to the work.[28] Again, this characteristic is not exclusive of our text. We find aetiological myths already in Hesiod, in Euripides and in the fragmentary mythographers from the sixth and fifth centuries.[29] It was developed as a mark of erudition in Alexandrine literature and it continued in the literary fashion of Hellenistic and Imperial times.[30] Indeed, the expansion of the Greeks over new territories that increased with Alexander, and their contact with different cultures fed the interest in myths that explained the origin of different realities – geographical formations, rituals, traditions, cities or their names. On the other hand, the appearance and development of a librarian culture with centres that

---

[26] For a definition of aetiology, vd. Delattre (2009) 285-310, who defines it as a logical and narrative mechanism between two elements in the discourse, with eponymy being one of the possible relations that aetiology establishes (Delattre [2009] 297-298). Valverde Sánchez (1989) 21-52 considers that aetiology in a wide sense can be identified with different types of narratives on the causes of the present day (25), but he envisages foundation literature as a specific genre (or subgenre), on the frontier of historiography and epics, which has its roots in Ionian prose and the logographers and is again incorporated into poetry by Alexandrine and Hellenistic poets (26).

[27] This suggests a comparison to Callimachus' *Aitia*. Despite the stylistic differences, Conon's text, if Photius' summary reflects the original structure, would follow the Callimachean principle of the *poikilia*: a variety of subjects with no thematic unity, but only an aetiological explanation. On this see Henrichs (1987) 245.

[28] Brown (2002) 12 n. 55.

[29] On foundation myths and aetiology in early mythographers vd. also Fowler (2013) xi-xxi.

[30] On motifs and themes in Parthenius contextualised in the Hellenistic literature vd. Lightfoot (1999) 240-245.

held a large number of books allowed for erudite investigations of local subjects. To mention some examples, Callimachus composed a work only on aetiologies, the *Aitia*. Apollonius Rhodius also used it at length in his *Argonautica*,[31] and several poems on the foundations of cities are attributed to him.[32] Eratosthenes' *Catasterisms* is also a collection of a special kind of *aition* myth. Ovid, greatly influenced by Hellenistic Greek literature, often includes *aitia* and foundation myths in his *Metamorphoses* and the origins of Roman holidays and associated traditions are explained in his *Fasti*. The mythographers Parthenius and Antoninus Liberalis also include aetiologies, metamorphoses, foundations of cities or eponym myths. Thus, the fact that Conon's account of Byblis and Caunus combines the erotic with the aetiological and the foundational is not surprising at all, given the literary context of the Imperial Hellenic world. However, as I will try to show, it also presents some specificities.

4.1. If we turn to the plot of Conon's narrative 2 on and focus on its structure, the following episodes can be isolated:

0. Introduction; origin of Bybles and Camus, ethnographical informaton about Miletus.	Δεύτερον τὰ περὶ Βυβλίδος, ὡς παῖς ἦν Μιλήτῳ, ἔχουσα ἐξ αὐτῆς ἀδελφὸν Καῦνον. Ὤικουν δὲ Μίλητον τῆς Ἀσίας, ἣν ὕστερον μὲν Ἴωνες καὶ οἱ ἀπ' Ἀθηνῶν μετὰ Νηλέως ὁρμηθέντες ᾤκησαν, τότε δ' ἐνέμοντο Κᾶρες, ἔθνος μέγα, κωμηδὸν οἰκοῦντες.
1. Love of Caunus.	Καύνῳ δ' ἔρως ἐγείρεται ἀμήχανος τῆς ἀδελφῆς Βυβλίδος·
2. Failed attempt of seduction.	ὡς δ' ἀπετύγχανε πολλὰ κινήσας,
3. Departure of Caunus.	ἔξεισι τῆς γῆς ἐκείνης.
4. Byblis' sadness, departure and pursuit of her brother.	Καὶ ἀφανισθέντος μυρίῳ ἄχει κατεχομένη ἡ Βυβλὶς ἐκλείπει καὶ αὐτὴ τὴν πατρῴαν οἰκίαν, καὶ πολλὴν ἐρημίαν πλανηθεῖσα,

---

[31] On the *aition* in Apollonius vd. Valverde Sánchez (1989).
[32] On the *ktisis* poems attributed to Apollonius vd. Sistakou (2011) 311-340.

5. Byblis' love.	καὶ πρὸς τοὺς ἀτελεῖς ἱμέρους ἀπαγορεύουσα,
6. Byblis' death (suicide by hanging; implicitly caused by Caunus' departure and her unfulfilled feelings).	βρόχον τὴν ζώνην τινὸς καρύας καθάψασα ἑαυτὴν ἀνήρτησεν.
7. *Aition* of the name of the fountain.	Ἔνθα δὴ κλαιούσης αὐτῆς ἐρρύη τὰ δάκρυα καὶ κρήνην ἀνῆκε, Βυβλίδα τοῖς ἐπιχωρίοις ὄνομα·
8. Arrival of Caunus.	Καῦνος δὲ πλανώμενος εἰς Λυκίαν φθάνει
9. Pronoe tells Caunus that Byblis has died.	καὶ τούτῳ Προνόη (Ναῒς δ᾽ ἦν αὕτη) ἀναδῦσα τοῦ ποταμοῦ τά τε συνενεχθέντα τῇ Βυβλίδι λέγει, ὡς ἐχρήσατο Ἔρωτι δικαστῇ,
10. Pronoe persuades him to marry her.	καὶ πείθει αὐτὸν αὐτῇ ἐπὶ τῷ τῆς χώρας λαβεῖν τὴν βασιλείαν, (καὶ γὰρ εἰς αὐτὴν ἀνῆπτο) συνοικῆσαι.
11. Marriage with Pronoe, birth of Aegialus.	Ὁ δὲ Καῦνος ἐκ τῆς Προνόης τίκτει Αἰγιαλόν,
12. Aegialus inherits the kingdom.	ὃς καὶ παραλαβὼν τὴν βασιλείαν, ἐπεὶ ὁ πατὴρ ἐτελεύτησεν
13. Foundation of Caunus.	ἤθροισέ τε τὸν λαὸν σποράδην οἰκοῦντα καὶ πόλιν ἔκτισεν ἐπὶ τῷ ποταμῷ μεγάλην καὶ εὐδαίμονα,
14. *Aition* on the toponym Caunus (eponymy).	Καῦνον ἀπὸ τοῦ πατρὸς ἐπονομάσας.

I would like to highlight some elements: 1) We do not know that Byblis is also in love with Caunus until we read why she commits suicide: καὶ πρὸς τοὺς ἀτελεῖς ἱμέρους ἀπαγορεύουσα, βρόχον τὴν ζώνην τινὸς καρύας καθάψασα ἑαυτὴν ἀνήρτησεν. 2) An *aition* of the name of a fountain closes the narrative on Byblis. 3) Pronoe needs to persuade Caunus to unite with her. The fact that she tells him that Byblis has died can be seen as one of the ways of persuading him. Inheriting the kingdom would be a second argument of persuasion.

Pronoe is a common nymph's name, but she is not attested elsewhere as being related to Caunus. 4) Pronoe's episode has been interpreted as a narrative related to a specific type of foundation myth where a hero unites with a minor local divinity, such as a nymph.[33] It is a narrative mechanism to start a genealogy independently from the former inhabitants of the land, as the nymph does not belong to the civilised world, but rather to wild nature.[34] 5) Caunus does not found the city that bears his name, but his son Aegialus does. Conon's version on the foundation of Caunus is unique. It is generally accepted that Aegialus appears in Parthenius' account of Lyrcus as the former king of Caunus,[35] which is an emendation to the text which transmits Ἀβιάλον. As the manchette of the narrative on Lyrcus quotes Apollonius Rhodius' poem on Caunus, also quoted in the manchette of Parthenius' account on Byblis, Brown and Lightfoot point out that, therefore, it is quite probable that Conon depends on Apollonius Rhodius for this account.[36]

4.2. Parthenius' chapter on this myth can be divided into two parts, each one being dedicated to a different version. In the first one, after a prose introduction, some verses of Nicaenetus are quoted.[37] The second part gives the version which was the most popular according to Parthenius. He quotes again some verses, this time of his own creation. In both cases, the prose introduction and the quoted verses are different from a literary point of view: whereas the prose part can be regarded as mythographical, Nicaenetus' fragment belongs to the hexametric poem titled *Lyrcus*, and Parthenius' own fragment is from one of his elegiac poems.[38] Parthenius' prose can be seen as a paraphrase of the poems he quotes but, since the quoted poems are lost, we cannot be sure of the nature of the relation between the prose and the poetic quotation. I should emphasize that not all the information in the verses is included in the prose, nor do the verses contain all the elements mentioned

---

[33] Calame (1988) 159.
[34] Lightfoot (1999) 434 and n. 149.
[35] Parth. 1.
[36] Lightfoot (1999) 371 and n. 2, Brown (2002) 59.
[37] This does not correspond with the sources quoted on the manchette, which are Aristocritus and Apollonius.
[38] On Nicaenetus' text see Durbec (2009).

in the prose. In the first case, Nicaenetus' fragment starts with the departure exile and foundation of a city by the father of the siblings and their birth. Thus, these are the antecedents of the episode Parthenius is focusing on.[39] The poem includes a reference of the metamorphosis of Byblis which is not mentioned in the prose. In the second version, the prose section gives much more information than the verses, which only relate how Byblis died. Thus, the verses are totally embedded in Parthenius' prose.[40] Therefore, for our current purpose – analysing the plot – I think that in both cases the prose introduction and the quoted verses should be taken as narrative units, even though they belong to different genres and have clear stylistic differences. Also, since Nicaenetus' and Parthenius' poems are fragmentary, we cannot study the episode sequence of their narratives.

The *enjeux* of literary genres and the different versions in Parthenius are stylistic resources of an erudite literary text, which contrasts with the state of Conon's work. From a literary point of view, it is clear that there is a big qualitative difference – also with Ovid, Nonnus and even Antoninus. However, since the focus of this paper is on the plot of Conon's version, I will compare only the order of events to Parthenius' plots – and to the other authors' plots.

With regard to the episode sequence in the first version, Parthenius paraphrases Nicaenetus, explaining that Caunus fell in love with his sister and, as he was unable to control his desires, he left his house and founded a city, in which he established the Ionians that had been dispersed. Then he quotes Nicaenetus' poem, which starts with a reference to the hero Miletus and his foundation of the Oecousian city, his union to Tragasia who gave birth to the siblings.[41] The poem continues, referring to Caunus' passion for Byblis, his escape, that he was the first Ionian to found a city, and that Byblis became an owl

---

[39] Vd. Biraud, Voisin, Zucker (2008) 136: 'Cette seconde version n'est pas seulement une mise en vers de l'argument: elle offre un catalogue des procédés épiques.'

[40] Biraud, Voisin, Zucker (2008) 137 considers the fact that the same subject-matter is presented in different ways, has the purpose of setting an example of literary composition: 'un récit y est en perpétuelle métamorphose grâce à des variantes successives qui affectent à la fois le fond et la forme.' On quotations in ancient texts vd. Darbo-Peschanski (2004ª) 9-21, and (2004ᵇ) 9-21.

[41] As I am focusing on Parthenius, I have printed here Lightfoot's text. However, it has been rightly – from my point of view – argued that the *lacunae* and the *cruces* are unnecessary in Nicaenetus' text. Vd. Giangrande (1982) 81-82, White (1982) 185-192.

and cried out about the absence of her brother. Therefore, the structure of episodes in the plot of this account would be (I use the numbers assigned to the events in Conon's account):

1. Caunus' love.	Parthenius' authorial voice: Νικαίνετος μὲν γάρ φησι τὸν Καῦνον ἐρασθέντα τῆς ἀδελφῆς,
	Quotation of Nicaenetus (v. 4): ... Βυβλίδα. τῆς ἤτοι ἀέκων ἠράσσατο Καῦνος
3. Departure of Caunus.	Parthenius: ὡς οὐκ ἔληγε τοῦ πάθους, ἀπολιπεῖν τὴν οἰκίαν
	Quotation of Nicaenetus (v. 5-6): βῆ δὲ †φερενδιος† φεύγων ὀφιώδεα † Κύπρον†, καὶ †κάπρος ὑλιγενὲς † καὶ †Κάρια† ἱρὰ λοετρά.
	Parthenius: καὶ ὁδεύσαντα πόρρω τῆς οἰκείας χώρας πόλιν τε κτίσαι καὶ τοὺς ἀπεσκεδασμένους τότε Ἴωνας ἐνοικίσαι.
13. Foundation of the city.	Quotation of Nicaenetus (v. 8): ἔνθ' ἤτοι πτολίεθρον ἐδείματο πρῶτος Ἰώνων.
6. Metamorphosis of Byblis.	Quotation of Nicaenetus (v. 9-10): αὐτὴ δὲ γνωτὴ ὀλολυγόνος οἶτον ἔχουσα Βυβλὶς ἀποπρὸ πυλῶν Καύνου ὠδύρατο νόστον.

As we see, Parthenius repeats in prose only the fact that it was Caunus who fell in love with Byblis and that he founded a city where he united the Ionians. The plot here would end with Byblis' transformation, which is equivalent to her death in narrative terms.[42] The motif that

---

[42] On metamorphosis vd. Irving (1990) especially 300 on Byblis. On the metamorphosis of Byblis vd. Buxton (2009) 199-202.

Byblis was transformed into a nightingale is referenced in a typically allusive poetic way. The fact that she mourned the absence of her brother could be suggesting that Byblis also felt passionate love for her brother. Therefore, one wonders whether Nicaenetus' poem could have been Conon's source, or could have triggered Conon's variant of the mutual love. However, all the other details are completely different. On the other side, Parthenius, who had much better access to the poem than we do, is clearly interpreting from this poem that it was Caunus who felt a passion for the sister (Νικαίνετος μὲν γάρ φησι τὸν Καῦνον ἐρασθέντα τῆς ἀδελφῆς) and he is making contrast between the two versions.[43]

In the second version, it is referred in prose that Byblis is the one who falls in love with Caunus and she declares her love to him. The boy rejects her, escapes and ends up founding the city which will bear his name. Finally, Byblis commits suicide by hanging herself. Parthenius then quotes some of his own verses on how Byblis dies. He adds a final note in prose explaining that, according to some, a fountain was formed from Byblis' tears which is named after her. Thus, the episodic structure of this narrative would be as follows:

5. Love of Byblis.	οἱ δὲ πλείους τὴν Βυβλίδα φασὶν ἐρασθεῖσαν τοῦ Καύνου
2*. Failed attempt of seduction (by Byblis).	λόγους αὐτῷ προσφέρειν καὶ δεῖσθαι μὴ περιιδεῖν αὐτὴν εἰς πᾶν κακὸν προελθοῦσαν·
3. Departure of Caunus.	ἀποστυγήσαντα δὲ οὕτως τὸν Καῦνον περαιωθῆναι εἰς τὴν τότε ὑπὸ Λελέγων κατεχομένην γῆν,
13. Foundation of Caunus (by Caunus).	ἔνθα κρήνη Ἐχενηΐς, πόλιν τε κτίσαι
14. *Aition* of the name of the city.	τὴν ἀπ' αὐτοῦ κληθεῖσαν Καῦνον.
	Prose version: τὴν δὲ ἄρα ὑπὸ τοῦ πάθους μὴ ἀνιεμένην, πρὸς δὲ καὶ δοκοῦσαν αἰτίαν γεγονέναι Καύνῳ τῆς ἀπαλλαγῆς, ἀναψαμένην ἀπό τινος δρυὸς τὴν μίτραν ἐνθεῖναι τὸν τράχηλον.

---

[43] Cf. sch. Theocr. *Id.* 7.115c infra.

6. Death of Byblis (suicide by hanging, because she thinks she is the reason for Caunus' departure).	Parthenius' own poem quoted: λέγεται δὲ καὶ παρ' ἡμῖν οὕτως· ἡ δ' ὅτε δή <ῥ'> ὀλοοῖο κασιγνήτου νόον ἔγνω, κλαῖεν ἀηδονίδων θαμινώτερον, αἵ τ' ἐνὶ βήσσης Σιθονίῳ κούρῳ πέρι μυρίον αἰάζουσιν. καί ῥα κατὰ στυφελοῖο σαρωνίδος αὐτίκα μίτρην
6. *Aition* of the name of the fountain.	ἁψαμένη δειρὴν ἐνεθήκατο· ταὶ δ' ἐπ' ἐκείνῃ βεύδεα παρθενικαὶ Μιλησίδες ἐρρήξαντο. φασὶ δέ τινες καὶ ἀπὸ τῶν δακρύων κρήνην ῥυῆναι ἀίδιον τὴν καλουμένην Βυβλίδα.

Francese pointed out that Parthenius' treatment of the incest theme focuses on 'the desire as an erotic pathology'.[44] The scholar concluded that this was an innovation of the Nicaean author. One of his arguments is that the former treatments of the myth of Byblis and Caunus (from which only indirect fragments have been transmitted) would have presented the incest in a non-erotic way, describing it as a crime or a trangression and subordinating the narrative to local historical interests. Francese did not include Conon in his study of this tradition. As we will see, Ovid also develops the sentimental part of the incest, with a focus on Byblis' psychology. The fact that Parthenius' and Ovid's versions focus on the erotic aspect of the story shows that they both belong to the same literary tradition, closely connected to the erotic elegy. Conon's construction of the story, on the other side, puts him in relation to a different literary genre or fashion, one more connected to foundation literature.

4.3. Antoninus Liberalis' version starts with the story of Miletus, the Cretan founder of the city which bears his name and tells how he fathers Caunus and Byblis – similarly to what we read in the quoted verses of Nicaenetus but he develops the antecedents in a very different way. I will skip this part and focus on the narrative on the siblings, who are twins in this version. Immediately after mentioning the birth

---

[44] Francese (2001) 138.

of Caunus, Antoninus explains that the city in Caria bears its name because of him. Then, he tells that Byblis had many suitors but she did not want to get married because she was in love with her brother. When she could not control her passion any more, she tried to jump from a rock but the nymphs saved her and turned her into a Hamadryad nymph.[45] The waterfall that exists in that rock was called after her. The structure of this passage of Antoninus' text runs as follows (Papathomopoulos 1968):

14. *Aition* on the name of the city Caunus.	καὶ ἐγένοντο δίδυμοι παῖδας αὐτῇ Καῦνος [καὶ Βυβλίς], ἀφ' οὗ πόλις ἐστὶν ἔτι νῦν ἐν Καρίᾳ Καῦνος,
– Rejection of suitors.	ταύτης ἐγένοντο πλεῖστοι μνηστῆρες ἐπιχώριοι καὶ κατὰ κλέος ἐκ τῶν πέριξ πόλεων.
5. Love of Byblis for Caunus.	ἡ δὲ τῶν μὲν λόγον ἐποιεῖτο βραχύν, αὐτὴν δὲ ἄφατος ἔρως ἐξέμηνε τοῦ Καύνου.
6. Attempt to commit suicide (to hide her passion) and metamorphosis of Byblis into a nymph.	καὶ τὸ πάθος ἄχρι μὴν ἐδύνατο κρύπτειν ἐλελήθει τοὺς γονεῖς· ἐπεὶ δὲ καθ' ἡμέραν εἴχετο χαλεπωτέρῳ δαίμονι, νυκτὸς ἔγνω καταβαλεῖν ἐκ τῆς πέτρας ἑαυτήν. καὶ ἡ μὲν εἰς τὸ πλησίον ὄρος παρελθοῦσα ῥίπτειν ἑαυτὴν ἐπεχείρησε, νύμφαι δὲ κατέσχον οἰκτείρασαι καὶ πολὺν ὕπνον ἐνέβαλον καὶ αὐτὴν ἤλλαξαν ἀπ' ἀνθρώπου εἰς δαίμονα καὶ ὠνόμασαν ἁμαδρυάδα νύμφην Βυβλίδα καὶ ἐποιήσαντο συνδίαιτον ἑταιρίδα.
7. *Aition* of the name of the waterfall.	καλεῖται δὲ καὶ τὸ ῥέον ἐκ τῆς πέτρας ἐκείνης ἄχρι νῦν παρὰ τοῖς ἐπιχωρίοις Δάκρυον Βυβλίδος.

It is worth stressing that in this version, the foundation of Caunus is not explained as a consequence of the brother's escape, nor is Byblis' death caused by Caunus' departure, but instead by her attempt to hide her own feelings. As for Byblis' destiny as a Hamadryad nymph, these

---
[45] On this type of nymph see Larson (2001) 33, 73-74, 203-204.

type of nymphs were seen by the Greeks as tree spirits. Therefore, this detail can be seen as narratively equivalent to the hanging from an oak in Parthenius' second version, or the hanging from a nut-tree in Conon.

4.4. Ovid's version in the *Metamorphoses* puts its focus on Byblis' inner struggle, developing it in a masterful way.[46] If we stick to the plot structure, the account starts with Byblis' and Caunus' birth as twins, it then refers to Byblis' passion, which gradually grows until she decides to send a letter to Caunus. He receives the letter in a very negative way. She suffers. He leaves Miletus and founds a city. Then she goes after him but falls upon the ground, exhausted, and turns into a water-source. Thus, it follows the same episodic structure as Parthenius' second account and it shares with it the detail of Byblis' confession to Caunus, though developed in a typically Ovidian way – through a letter. I follow Tarrant's text (2004):

5. Byblis' love.	(455-510) 455-456: Byblis Apollinei correpta cupidine fratris: [non soror ut fratrem, nec qua debebat, amabat.]
2* Failed attempt of seduction (Byblis).	(511-573, 630-603) 511-514: Si tamen ipse mei captus prior esset amore, forsitan illius possem indulgere furori. Ergo ego, quae fueram non reiectura petentem, ipsa petam! Poterisne loqui? poterisne fateri? 521-522: et meditata manu componit uerba trementi; dextra tenet ferrum, uacuam tenet altera ceram.
– Canus' rejection.	(574-579) 574-576: Attonitus subita iuuenis Maeandrius ira proicit acceptas lecta sibi parte tabellas uixque manus retinens trepidantis ab ore ministri.

---

[46] For a commentary on Ovid's version vd. Bömer (1977) 411-468.

4. Byblis' sorrow.	(580-633) 580-582: ille fugit pauidus, dominaeque ferocia Cauni dicta refert. palles audita, Bybli, repulsa, et pauet obsessum glaciali frigore corpus.
8. Caunus' departure.	633: mox ubi finis abest, patriam fugit ille nefasque,
13. Foundation of a city.	634: inque peregrina ponit noua moenia terra.
4. Byblis' sadness and search for Caunus.	(635-649) 638-640: Iamque palam est demens inconcessaeque fatetur spem Veneris, siquidem patriam inuisosque Penates deserit et profugi sequitur uestigia fratris.
6. Metamorphosis of Byblis.	(650-663) 655-656: muta iacet uiridesque suis tenet unguibus herbas Byblis, et umectat lacrimarum gramina riuo. 663-664: sic lacrimis consumpta suis Phoebeia Byblis uertitur in fontem,
7. *Aition* of the fountain's name.	664-665: ... qui nunc quoque uallibus illis nomen habet dominae nigraque sub ilice manat.

The way Ovid refers to Caunus' foundation is very brief and vague, and he does not mention the city's name. His account ends again with Byblis' metamorphosis, this time into a water-source. In the *Ars Amatoria* Ovid mentions Byblis briefly noting that she fell in love with her brother and committed suicide by hanging herself.[47]

---

[47] *Ars* 1.283-284: 'Byblida quid referam, uetito quae fratris amore/ Arsit et est laqueo fortiter ulta nefas?'

4.5. Nonnus of Panopolis gives a very particular account in which Caunus is Miletus' brother and chief of the Carians (548-549). The myth is inserted in the description of Dionysus' army and Nonnus places this fact in a time prior to the love story. Therefore, the fact that Caunus is the ruler of the Carians is not connected with the incest narrative.

1. Caunus' love.	(550-558) οὔ πω γὰρ δυσέρωτα δολοπλόκον ἔπλεκε μολπὴν γνωτῆς οἶστρον ἔχων ἀδαήμονος, οὐδὲ καὶ αὐτὴν ἀντιτύπου φιλότητος ὁμοζήλων ἐπὶ λέκτρων Ζηνὶ συναπτομένην ἐμελίζετο σύγγονον Ἥρην Λάτμιον ἀμφὶ βόαυλον ἀκοιμήτοιο νομῆος, ὀλβίζων ὑπ' ἔρωτι μεμηλότα γείτονι πέτρῃ νυμφίον Ἐνδυμίωνα ποθοβλήτοιο Σελήνης· ἀλλ' ἔτι Βυβλὶς ἔην φιλοπάρθενος, ἀλλ' ἔτι θήρην Καῦνος ὁμογνήτων ἐδιδάσκετο νῆις ἐρώτων·
3. Departure of Caunus.	(559) οὔ πω δ', ἁβροκόμοιο κασιγνήτοιο φυγόντος,
6. Metamorphosis of Byblis.	(560-561) δάκρυσιν ὀμβρηθεῖσα δέμας μορφώσατο κούρη, καὶ ῥόον ὑδατόεντα γοήμονος ἔβλυε πηγῆς.

Some motives in Nonnus remind elements of the Ovidian version: the example of Hera and Zeus as siblings and a couple – a fact mentioned by Byblis in Ovid – and the description of her metamorphosis. Despite the allusive style, it is clear that Caunus is in love with Byblis and that her metamorphosis is caused by his departure. Verse 557, ἀλλ' ἔτι Βυβλὶς ἔην φιλοπάρθενος, might refer to a passion in Byblis too. This would suggest a possible connection to the Cononian version, where the passion is mutual. Nevertheless, even if Nonnus was following a version of a mutual love, this would not be conclusive to establish a relation of dependence of Conon's text.

4.6. The short notes of Stephanus Byzantinus and Diogenianus follow that same pattern found in the second narrative of Parthenius, Antoninus or Ovid in a very schematic way:

> St. Byz.:
> <Καῦνος,> πόλις Καρίας, ἀπὸ Καύνου, οὗ ἡ ἀδελφὴ Βυβλὶς ἐρασθεῖσα φεύγοντος ἐκείνου [ἀπήγξατο].

> Diogenian. 5.:
> <Καύνιος ἔρως:> ἐπὶ τῶν μὴ κατορθουμένων ἐπιθυμιῶν. Καύνου γὰρ ἐρασθεῖσα ἡ ἀδελφὴ καὶ μὴ τυχοῦσα τοῦ ἔρωτος, ἀνεῖλεν ἑαυτήν.

The word order of Stephanus' note can be interpreted as meaning both that the city was named after Caunus and that it was founded by him. Diogenianus' note is interesting as it relates the myth to an expression already attested in the fourth century.[48] He does not mention the foundation of the city, neither does the scholion to Theocritus. This last text refers to the version in which the brother is the one in love. However, the way he refers to Byblis' reaction can be interpreted either as parallel to Parthenius' first text – where she deplores the absence of her brother – or as a possible parallel to Conon's version. The scholion leaves open the reason of Byblis' suffering:

> Sch. Theocr. *Id.* 7.115c:
> ἧς ἐρασθεὶς ὁ Καῦνος ἀπέλιπε Μίλητον. ἐκείνη δὲ μὴ φέρουσα ἀπήγξατο. ταύτης ἡ κρήνη ὁμώνυμος.

5. This comparison highlights some particular elements in Conon's narrative. First, it is the only version, as we noted above, where the passion between Caunus and Byblis is explicitly mutual. The motif of the passion in Conon is, thus, duplicated. The reciprocity of the feeling, however, is not stated at the beginning of the account, but is discovered when Byblis commits suicide. Also Nicaenetus, Nonnus and the scholion to Theocritus might suggest that the love was mutual, though this would not prove a direct relation with Conon's text.

Secondly, Byblis' death happens in the middle of Conon's account, but in all the other texts it is always this episode that gives closure

---

[48] Arist. *Rh.* 1402b3. Vd. Lightfoot (1999) 433; Mignogna (2000) 319.

to the narrative – either her death or metamorphosis or the *aition* of the water-source and its name. After Byblis' death, Conon shifts the space to Lycia, where Caunus has arrived, and he inserts Pronoe's episode, which is unparalleled.

Conon's account is the only version which refers to the foundation of Caunus at the conclusion of the narrative: it is the final consequence of the miserable passion of the siblings. This is an original feature in clear contrast to all other versions. In Conon, Caunus' fear of his own feelings leads to his departure, which leads to the death of Byblis and her death, in turn, allows the union of Caunus with Pronoe, the birth of Aegialus and the foundation of the city which will bear Caunus' name. This whole chain of events must be significant: it allows one to emphasise the foundational and eponymous aspects of the story. The fact that no other source mentions the episodes of the arrival in Lycia and the union to Pronoe, not even Parthenius who probably consulted Apollonius Rhodius, suggests that the combination of this episode with the one on Byblis' death might be an innovation of Conon. He is not merely transcribing a popular account, but is rather reshaping it and dedicating more space to the foundation narrative, perhaps in order to adapt it to the interests of his audience.

Pronoe's intervention, explaining that Byblis has died allows Conon to justify why Caunus, who was so desperately in love with his sister that he had to leave his land, finally unites with Pronoe. This suggests that Conon is building a single account combining different episodes in a cause-consequence chain which ultimately leads to the foundation of the city and the *aition* of its name. Thus, the episodes which were isolated in the previous part of this paper do not correspond to an abstract ideal fabula, but the fabula, the actual version of when and why things happened is created by the way the facts are placed in the text. Sometimes temporal or causal relations are explicit, but at other times they are only suggested by the succession of events put in a paratactic way.

If we interpret the Pronoe's episode according to Calame's description of the myth type in which a nymph's and a hero's union starts or restarts a genealogy (vd. supra), Conon's story would be depicting Caunus as the first to civilise that land. One wonders therefore if behind this version might lie a claim to the Ionian character of the city, since

Parthenius and the poem he quotes refer to the Ionian nature of Caunus and to the fact that he united the dispersed Ionians. The detail on dispersion is also mentioned in Conon's text. However, Conon is explicit in placing the story in the times when Miletus was not yet Ionian but Carian.[49] Thus, he would be stressing its Carian origin. This can be connected with Conon's general tendency to include the myths of Asia Minor.[50]

It can be useful to add here some data about Archelaus, to whom the work is dedicated. Coins minted in his time show that he held the title of Κτίστης, which indicates that his ascension was considered a sort of refoundation of the reign or dynasty.[51] Also, there is an Archelaus, mentioned by Diogenes Laertius for having authored a work on the territories conquered by Alexandrer[52] who has been identified with Archelaus Philopatris.[53] If this identification is correct, the stress on the foundational purpose of Conon's narrative would have a deeper meaning. It has been suggested that the purpose of the *Diegeseis* could be to provide Archelaus with material for his work, in a similar way to Parthenius with Gallus, but this hypothesis has lately been abandoned, as both introductions have a rhetorical character and the dedications are made in honorific terms.[54] It is important to add that Dion Chrysostomus mentions a rhetor called Conon who has traditionally been considered a different author.[55] Some scholars, though, identify him with the mythographer and suggest that Conon might have been a Greek rhetor in charge of the education of the members of the royal family at Archelaus' court.[56] If this is correct and Conon's audience was actually Archelaus' court, as Brown proposed ([2002] 12), the clear interest in the

---

[49] On the connection with Caria vd. the Blakely (2011) commentary on this chapter of Conon.
[50] Vd. Brown (2002) 9. Lightfoot stresses concerning Parthenius that his interest in exotic and local myths has an erudite and literary goal, rather than a political purpose, which might be the case also for Conon (1999) 232-233.
[51] Brown (2002) 3 n. 13, quotes the following sources: Dittenberger (1803) 358. Cf. Simonetta (1977), Leschhorn (1984) 293-300, Sullivan (1990) 398.
[52] D.L. 2.17: Γεγόνασι δὲ καὶ ἄλλοι τρεῖς Ἀρχέλαοι· ὁ χωρογράφος τῆς ὑπὸ Ἀλεξάνδρου πατηθείσης γῆς, ὁ τὰ Ἰδιοφυῆ ποιήσας, ἄλλος τεχνογράφος ῥήτωρ.
[53] Jacoby (1957) 26 T1-2.
[54] Henrichs (1987) 244. On the introductory letters vd. Ruppert (1911), Zimmermann (1934), Lightfoot (1999) 222-224.
[55] D. Chrys. 18.12.
[56] Brown (2002) 4-5, Ibáñez Chacón (2007) 61-62.

foundational side of the tradition of Byblis and Caunus, as well as the fact that aetiological and foundation are persistent elements in the entire collection, seem very suitable for such an audience.

Bibliography

Bethe, E. (1903), 'Die Quellenangaben zu Parthenius und Antoninus Liberalis', *Hermes* 38, 608-617.
Biraud, M., Voisin, D., Zucker, A. (edd.) (2008), *Parthénios de Nicée. Passions d'amour*, Grenoble.
Blakely, S. (2011), 'Conon (26)', in I. Worthington (ed.) *Brill's New Jacoby*, online reference: BNJ- contributors, 5th February 2016, http://referenceworks.brillonline.com/entries/brill-s-new-jacoby/conon-26-a26.
Bömer, F.P. (1977), *P. Ovidius Naso:* Metamorphosen. *Kommentar 4. Buch VIII-IX*, Heidelberg.
Brown, M.K. (2002), *The Narratives of Conon. Text, Translation and Commentary of the Diegeseis*, München/ Leipzig.
Buxton, R. (2009), *Forms of Astonishment. Greek Myths of Metamorphosis*, Oxford.
Cairns, F. (1979), *Tibullus. A Hellenistic Poet at Rome*, Cambridge.
Calame, C. (1988), *Métamorphoses du mythe en Grèce antique*, Genève.
Calderón Dorda, E. (1997), 'Los tópicos eróticos en la literatura helenística', *Emerita* 65, 1-16.
Calderón Dorda, E. (1998), *Sufrimientos de amor y fragmentos*, Madrid.
Calderón Dorda, E., Ozaeta Gálvez, M.A. (1989), *Antonino Liberal. Metamorfosis*. Introducción de Esteban Calderón Dorda, traducción y notas de Mª Antonia Ozaeta Gálvez, Madrid.
Cameron, A. (2004), *Greek Mythography in the Roman World*, Oxford/ New York.
Celoria, F. (1992), *The Metamorphoses of Antoninus Liberalis. A Translation With Commentary*, London/ New York.
Chuvin, P. (1991), *Mythologie et géographie dionysiaques. Recherches sur l'œuvre de Nonnus de Panopolis*, Clermont-Ferrand.
Cuartero, F. (1982), *Parteni de Nicea, Dissorts d'amor. Text revisat i traduccio de Francesc J. Cuartero*, Barcelona.

Culler, J. (1996), 'Fabula and Sjuzhet in the Analysis of Narrative: Some American Discussions', in S. Onega, J.A. García Landa (edd.) *Narratology: an Introduction*, London/ New York, 93-102. Reprinted from the original in *Poetics Today* 1 (1980), 27-37.

Darbo-Peschanski C. (2004[b]), 'La citation et les fragments: les Fragmente der griechischen Historiker de Felix Jacoby', in C. Darbo-Peschanski (ed.), *La citation dans l'Antiquité*, Grenoble, 291-300.

Darbo-Peschanski, C. (2004[a]), 'Les citations grecques et romaines', in C. Darbo-Peschanski (ed.), *La citation dans l'Antiquité*, Grenoble, 9-21.

De Jong, I., Nünlist, R., Bowie, A.M. (edd.) (2004), *Narrators, Narratees, and Narratives in Ancient Greek Literature*, Leiden.

Del Canto Nieto, J.R. (2003), *Antonino Liberal. Metamorfosis*, Madrid.

Del Mastro, G. (2014), *Titoli e annotazioni bibliologiche nei papiri greci di Ercolano*, Napoli.

Delattre, C. (2009), 'Aitiologia: mythe et procédure étiologique', *Metis* 7, 285-310.

Dittenberger, W. (1903), *Orientis Graeci Inscriptiones Selectae. Supplementum Sylloges Inscriptionum Graecarum*, vol. I, Leipzig.

Durbec, Y. (2009), 'Nicainetos de Samos: un poète hellénistique', *Appunti Romani di Filologia* 11, 21-24.

Egan, R.B. (1971), *The Diegeseis of Conon. A Commentary with an English Translation*. Diss., Los Angeles.

Fowler, R.L. (2000), *Early Greek Mythography*, vol. 1: *Texts*, Oxford/ New York. Fowler, R.L. (2013), *Early Greek Mythography*, vol. 2: *Commentary*, Oxford/ New York.

Francese, C. (2001), *Parthenius of Nicaea and Roman Poetry*, Frankfurt am Main.

Giangrande, G. (1982), 'A textual problem in Nicaenetus', *Corolla Londinensia* 2, 81-82.

Gibson, C.A. (2013), 'True or false? Greek myth and mythography in the Progymnasmata', in S.M. Trzaskoma, R.S. Smith (edd.), *Writing Myth. Mythography in the Ancient World*, Leuven, 289-308.

Hägg, T. (1973), 'Photius at Work. Evidence from the Bibliotheca', *Greek, Roman and Byzantine Studies* 14, 213-222.

Harder, M.A. (1984), 'Conon, Diegeseis?', *The Oxyrhynchus Papyri* 52, London, 5-12.

Henrichs, A. (1987). 'Three approaches to Greek mythography', in J. Bremmer (ed.), *Interpretations of Greek Mythology*, 242-277.
Hercher, R. (1852), '*Symbolae Criticae ad Arriani libellum de Venatione*', *Philologus* 7, 448-465.
Higbie, C. (2007), 'Hellenistic mythographers' in R.D. Woodard et al. (edd.), *The Cambridge Companion to Greek Mythology*, Buffalo, 237-254.
Hoefer, U. (1890), *Conon. Text und Quellenuntersuchung*, Greifswald.
Ibáñez Chacón, Á. (2007), 'El mitógrafo Conón en la Biblioteca de Focio', *Erytheia* 28, 41-65.
Ibáñez Chacón, Á. (2013), 'Conón *Narr.* 31: Procne', *Maia* 65, 95-119.
Irving, P.M.C.F. (1990), *Metamorphosis in Greek Myths*, Oxford.
Jacoby, F. (1950), *Die Fragmente der griechischer Historiker. Dritter Teil: Geschichte von Städten und Völkern* (*Horographie und Ethnographie*), B Nr. 297-607, Leiden.
Jacoby, F. (1957), *Die Fragmente der griechischen Historiker. Erster Teil: Genealogie und Mythographie. A. Vorrede. Text. Addenda. Konkordanz*, Leiden.
Larson, J.L. (2001), *Greek Nymphs. Myth, Cult, Lore*, Oxford. Leschhorn, W. (1984), *Gründer der Stadt*, Stuttgart.
Lightfoot, J.L. (1999), *Parthenius of Nicaea. The Poetical Fragments and the 'Erotica Pathemata'*, Oxford.
Luppe, W. (1986), 'Review of H.M. Cockle (ed.), *The Oxyrhynchus Papyri, 52*', *Classical Review* 36, 121-122.
Martini, E. (1922), 'Conon (9)', *Realencyclopädie der classischen Altertumswissenschaft* 11.2, cols. 1335-1338.
Meliado, C. (2015), 'Mythography', in F. Montanari, S. Matthaios, A. Rengakos (edd.), *Brill's Companion to Ancient Scholarship*, Leiden, 1057-1089.
Mignogna, E. (2000), 'Conone, *Narrazione*', in A. Stramaglia (ed.), *Eros. Antiche trame greche d'amore*, Bari, 315-351.
Papathomopoulos, M. (1968), *Antoninus Liberalis. Les Métamorphoses*, Paris.
Pellizer, E. (1993), 'La mitografía', in G. Cambiano et al. (edd.), *Lo spazio letterario della Grecia antica*, vol. 1: *La produzione e la circolazione del testo*, tomo II: *L'ellenismo*, Roma, 283-303.

Ressel, M. (1996-1997), *Conone, Narrazioni. Introduzione, edizione critica, traduzione e commento*. Diss., Trieste.

Rohde, E. (1974⁵), *Der griechische Roman und seine Vorläufer*, Darmstadt.

Ruppert, J. (1911), *Quaestiones ad historiam dedicationis librorum pertinentes*. Diss., Leipzig.

Sanz Morales, M. (2002), *Mitógrafos griegos: Eratóstenes, Partenio, Antonino Liberal, Paléfato, Heráclito, Anónimo Vaticano*, Madrid.

Sellheim, C.A.R. (1930), *De Parthenii et Antonini fontium indiculorum auctoribus*. Diss., Halle an der Saale.

Simonetta, B. (1977), *The Coins of Cappadocian Kings*, Freiburg.

Sistakou, E. (2011), 'In Search of Apollonius' Ktisis Poems', in T. Papaghelis, A. Rengakos, *Brill's Companion to Apollonius Rhodius*, 2nd revised ed., Leiden.

Sullivan, R.D. (1990), *Near Eastern Royalty and Rome. 100-30 BC*, Toronto.

Tarrant, R.J. (2004), *P. Ovidi Nasonis Metamorphoses*, Oxford.

Thompson, S. (1955-8), *Motif-index of folk-literature: A classification of narrative elements in folktales, ballads, myths, fables, mediaeval romances, exempla, fabliaux, jest-books, and local legends. Revised and enlarged edition*, 6 vols. Bloomington (Ind.).

Valverde Sánchez, M. (1989), *El aition en las Argonáuticas de Apolonio de Rodas*, Murcia.

Westermann, A. (1843), *Mythographi Graeci*, Brunswick.

White, H. (1982), 'Parthenius and the story of Byblis', *Corolla Londinensia* 2, 185-192.

Whitmarsh, T. (2001), *Greek Literature and the Roman Empire. The Politics of Imitation*, Oxford.

Zimmermann, F. (1934), 'Parthenius' Brief an Gallus', *Hermes* 69, 179-189.